The Synod of Dordt (1618–1619) and the Canons: Historical Perspectives

REFORMED HISTORICAL-THEOLOGICAL STUDIES
General Editors
Joel R. Beeke and Jay T. Collier

BOOKS IN SERIES:

The Christology of John Owen
Richard W. Daniels

The Covenant Theology of Caspar Olevianus
Lyle D. Bierma

John Diodati's Doctrine of Holy Scripture
Andrea Ferrari

Caspar Olevian and the Substance of the Covenant
R. Scott Clark

Introduction to Reformed Scholasticism
Willem J. van Asselt et al.

The Spiritual Brotherhood
Paul R. Schaefer Jr.

Teaching Predestination
David H. Kranendonk

The Marrow Controversy and Seceder Tradition
William VanDoodewaard

Unity and Continuity in Covenantal Thought
Andrew A. Woolsey

The Theology of the French Reformed Churches
Martin I. Klauber, ed.

Doctrine in Development
Heber Carlos de Campos Jr.

The Theology of the Huguenot Refuge
Martin I. Klauber, ed.

The Claims of Truth
Carl R. Trueman

Providence, Freedom, and the Will in Early Modern Reformed Theology
Richard A. Muller

Arminius and the Reformed Tradition
J. V. Fesko

The Roots of Reformed Moral Theology
Bruce P. Baugus

The Theology of Early French Protestantism
Martin I. Klauber, ed.

Predestination in Early Modern Reformed Theology
Richard A. Muller

Understanding the Divine in Early Modern Reformed Theology
Richard A. Muller

The Synod of Dordt (1618–1619) and the Canons: Historical Perspectives
Donald Sinnema

The Synod of Dordt (1618–1619) and the Canons: Historical Perspectives

Donald Sinnema

Edited by Erik A. de Boer

Reformation Heritage Books
Grand Rapids, Michigan

The Synod of Dordt (1618–1619) and the Canons
© 2025 by Donald Sinnema

All rights reserved. No part of this book may be used or reproduced in any manner whatsoever without written permission except in the case of brief quotations embodied in critical articles and reviews. Direct your requests to the publisher at the following addresses:

Reformation Heritage Books
3070 29th St. SE
Grand Rapids, MI 49512
616-977-0889
orders@heritagebooks.org
www.heritagebooks.org

Printed in the United States of America
25 26 27 28 29 30/10 9 8 7 6 5 4 3 2 1

Library of Congress Cataloging-in-Publication Data

Names: Sinnema, Donald W., 1947- author | Boer, Erik Alexander de editor
Title: The Synod of Dordt (1618-1619) and the Canons : historical perspectives / Donald Sinnema ; edited by Erik A. de Boer.
Description: Grand Rapids, Michigan : Reformation Heritage Books, [2025] | Series: Reformed historical-theological studies | Includes bibliographical references and index.
Identifiers: LCCN 2025007963 (print) | LCCN 2025007964 (ebook) | ISBN 9798886861785 paperback | ISBN 9798886861792 epub
Subjects: LCSH: Synod of Dort (1618-1619 : Dordrecht, Netherlands) | Synod of Dort (1618-1619 : Dordrecht, Netherlands). Canones Synodi Dordrechtanae
Classification: LCC BX9478 .S56 2025 (print) | LCC BX9478 (ebook) | DDC 238/.42—dc23/eng/20250416
LC record available at https://lccn.loc.gov/2025007963
LC ebook record available at https://lccn.loc.gov/2025007964

Contents

Abbreviations vii
Preface – *Erik A. de Boer* ix

1. The Synod of Dordt (1618–1619): An Overview 1
2. Procedural Wrangling in the Remonstrant Case at Dordt ... 29
3. The Belgic Confession at the Synod of Dordt 51
4. The Heidelberg Catechism at the Synod of Dordt 81
5. The Doctrine of Election at the Synod of Dordt 109
6. Disagreements and Doctrinal Dissension among Delegates at the Synod of Dordt 137
7. Church–State Entanglements at the Synod of Dordt 167
8. The Missing Correspondence between the States General and Its State Delegates at the Synod 215
9. Reformed Scholasticism and the Synod of Dordt 247
10. The Church Order of Dordt in Historical Perspective 289
11. Calvin and the Canons of Dordt 315
12. Calvin as Viewed by the Remonstrants at Dordt 337
13. The Drafting of the Canons of Dordt 363
14. The Canons of Dordt: Historical Context and Theology ... 383
15. The Canons of Dordt: From Judgment on Arminianism to Confessional Standard 391

16. Distortions of the Canons: The Tilenus Abbreviation,
    the Five Points of Calvinism, and TULIP 415

Appendix 1: Overview of Synod of Dordt Sessions 439
Appendix 2: Editions of the Canons of Dordt (1619–2019) 463
Appendix 3: Bibliography of Sinnema Writings.............. 491
Name Index... 499
Subject Index.. 505

Abbreviations

Acta	*Acta Synodi Nationalis, in nomine Domini nostri Jesu Christi, Autoritate Illustr. et Praepotentum DD. Ordinum Generalium Foederati Belgii Provinciarum, Dordrechti habitae anno MDCXVIII et MDCXIX.* Leiden: Elzevir, 1620.
Acta et Scripta	*Acta et Scripta Synodalia Dordracena Ministrorum Remonstrantium in Foederato Belgio.* Harderwijk, 1620.
ADSND	Sinnema, Donald, Christian Moser, Erik A. de Boer, and Herman J. Selderhuis, eds. *Acta et Documenta Synodi Nationalis Dordrechtanae (1618–1619)* (Göttingen: Vandenhoeck and Ruprecht, 2015–).
Balcanqual	Walter Balcanqual letters, in John Hales, *Golden Remains.* London, 1673.
BC	Belgic Confession
Breitinger	J. J. Breitinger journal, in Zentralbibliothek Zürich, MS B235
CD	Canons of Dordt
CO	Calvin, John. *Opera quae supersunt omnia.* Edited by Baum, Cunitz, and Reuss. 59 vols. Brunswick: Schwetschke, 1863–1900.
Comm.	Commentary
DCO	Dordt Church Order

Five Articles	The five points of the Remonstrant position in the 1610 Remonstrance
Hales	John Hales letters, in John Hales, *Golden Remains*. London, 1673.
HC	Heidelberg Catechism
Hesse	Heppe, Heinrich, ed. "Historia Synodi Nationalis Dordracenae sive Literae delegatorum Hassiacorum de iis quae in Synodo Dordracena acta sunt ad Landgravium Mauritium missae." *Zeitschrift* für die *historische Theologie* 23 (1853): 226–327.
HStAM	Hessisches Staatsarchiv Marburg
MS/MSS	manuscript/manuscripts
NA, S.G.	Nationaal Archief, The Hague, Archief Staten-Generaal
OSA	Utrechts Archief, Oud Synodaal Archief
Praestantium	*Praestantium ac Eruditorum Virorum Epistolae Ecclesiasticae et Theologicae*. Amsterdam, 1660.
rej./rejs.	rejection/rejections in the Rejection of Errors sections in the Canons of Dordt
RSG	Smit, J. G., and J. Roelevink, eds. *Resolutiën der Staten-Generaal, Nieuwe Reeks 1610–1670*. Vols. 3 and 4. 's-Gravenhage: Martinus Nijhoff, 1975–1981.
sess.	session
Sibelius	Journal of Caspar Sibelius. "Annotationes ad Synodum Dordracenam." Regionaal Archief, Dordrecht, 150, MS 1113.
Tronchin	Archives Tronchin. Musée Historique de la Réformation, Geneva.
Ward	Samuel Ward Papers. Sidney Sussex College, Cambridge.
Zurich	Zentralbibliothek Zürich

Preface

Erik A. de Boer, editor

This is the title that I, as a colleague and a friend, would have chosen for this book: *The Essential Sinnema: The Collected Articles of Donald Sinnema on the Synod of Dordt (1618–1619)*. I truly believe that here the reader will find the most important studies Don has written on that very important council of the Reformed churches, the national synod as it was held in Dordrecht for six months from late 1618 to mid-1619.

The national Synod of Dordrecht of 1618–1619 was a landmark in the history of the Reformed churches. This assembly was more than its official name "national" expresses. It was the highest-level gathering of all Reformed churches in Europe that was possible at the time. The provinces of the Netherlands were well represented, but the Church of England and Scotland also sent their delegates. The French Reformed churches had appointed four theologians (although the king did not permit them to leave the country). From the German territories, the Palatinate and Hesse sent representatives, as did Nassau-Wetteravia and the cities of Bremen and Emden (on behalf of the churches of East Frisia). In addition, the Swiss Cantons (Zurich, Bern, Schaffhausen, Basel) and Geneva were represented. The "national synod" of Dordt was, for the most important part of its agenda, a pan-European council of Reformed churches.

Donald Sinnema is a professor and a scholar who has devoted much of his attention and time to the study of the national Synod of Dordt in the Netherlands. Don is also a husband, a father, a friend, and an impersonator of Johannes Bogerman, president of the synod. It is safe to say that no one knows more about the Synod of Dordt than Don Sinnema. But he shares his knowledge with the rest of us, which brings us to the present volume.

When you read this preface, you have in your hands the *opera minora* of Dr. Donald Sinnema on the national Synod of Dordt. A good number of these articles have been published earlier but have been revised for this book and republished with permission; some articles are brand-new. We only speak of his "minor writings" because his major writings include his doctoral dissertation, as well as the ongoing editing of all the proceedings and documents of the Synod of Dordt. So far in this series, three impressive volumes have appeared, with seven more in the making. The title of the series is, in scholarly Latin, *Acta et Documenta Synodi Nationalis Dordrechtanae (1618–1619)*, abbreviated in this volume as *ADSND*—that is, "The Acts and Documents of the National Synod of Dordt." This ambitious program of research and publication was first conceived in 2008, and the first steps were undertaken in 2010, a decade before the 400th anniversary of the synod. At that time, Don wrote up a prospectus for the project and assembled an initial inventory of Dordt documents, some of which he has retrieved from archives throughout Europe.

Don Sinnema's 75th birthday in 2022 seemed a good occasion to begin compiling the many studies he wrote over the years on various aspects of the synod.

A few words may suffice to paint a picture of the man behind the impressive book series and collected articles.

Don Sinnema's roots lie—where else?—in the Low Countries. In 1892, his maternal great-grandparents, Garrit and Hendrika Willemsen, emigrated from Nijverdal in the province of Overijssel to Paterson, New Jersey. Garrit labored as a weaver but saw no future in this line of work. One of their seven children, Willem (who would become Don's grandfather), was five years old at the time in which they emigrated. They were part of a larger emigration of people from Nijverdal.[1] The

---

1. Donald Sinnema, "From Nijverdal to Nieuw Nijverdal: The Immigration of Nijverdallers as Pioneers to Southern Alberta," April 2021, self-published, Academia.edu.

family moved to the prairies of southern Alberta, Canada, in early 1905, homesteading at Leavings (now Granum), and became members of the very first Christian Reformed Church in Canada.[2] Don has documented the history of this Dutch settlement and church with a meticulous historical approach that is typical for him.[3]

Donald Wilfred Sinnema, son of Cornelis Sinnema and Hilda Willemsen, was born in Lethbridge, Alberta, on 14 January 1947. Don grew up in that first Dutch settlement on a farm near Granum.

He pursued undergraduate studies and received his bachelor's degree at Dordt College (now Dordt University), in Sioux Center, Iowa (1969). There he met and married Lois Gerritsma on 23 July 1971. They had three children. She died of cancer in 2006.

Don also studied for a year in Heidelberg, Germany, and Amsterdam (1973–1974). Don's interest in the Synod of Dordt began when, in 1974, he came upon the first Latin edition of the *Acta* of Dordt (1620) at a used book shop in Amsterdam. The volume had a tattered spine, and he happily acquired it for only one hundred guilders. In Heidelberg, he studied German and examined multiple volumes from the early Reformed tradition. This was followed by a master's degree in philosophical theology at the Institute for Christian Studies in Toronto (1975). He then worked as a research-writer for the Biblical Studies Project of the Curriculum Development Centre in Toronto (1975–1977).

Don completed his academic education with a PhD in Historical Theology at the University of St. Michael's College – University of Toronto (1985). The title of his dissertation is "The Issue of Reprobation at the Synod of Dort (1618–19) in Light of the History of this Doctrine." The dissertation has remained a standard work and will soon be published in revised form.

Don served as professor of theology at Trinity Christian College in Palos Heights, Illinois, from 1987 to 2012. He developed many theology courses, with his primary field being church history. As a

---

2. Donald Sinnema, *Pioneer Church Life: The Beginnings of the First Christian Reformed Church in Canada (1903–1911)* (Nobleford, Alberta: Rocky Coulee Press, 2005).

3. See Donald Sinnema, ed., *The First Dutch Settlement in Alberta: Letters from the Pioneers Years, 1903–14* (Calgary: University of Calgary Press, 2005).

theology professor, he sought to teach the biblical message of a full-orbed gospel that views Christ as Lord of every area of life.

After his retirement, he moved to Michigan, settling—where else?—in the city of Holland, together with his wife, Carla Mulder Brouwer, whom he married in 2012.

This volume is dedicated to Don Sinnema on his birthday, which happens to have symbolic significance for his field of study. "You asked about my birthday. Actually, I just turned 75 on the 14th of January, the same day that the 1610 Remonstrance was presented to the States of Holland and West Friesland, and the same day that the cited Remonstrants were expelled from the Synod of Dordt in 1619."

Print of Synod of Dordt, 1619; printmaker unknown
Rijksmuseum Amsterdam, no. RP-P-OB-77.282

> Table by fireplace: synod officers
> Table in center: cited Remonstrants
> Benches upper left: state delegates
> Benches right: foreign delegates
> Benches for French delegates, vacant
> Benches lower left: Dutch delegates
> Dutch Theologians on top bench
> Benches at rear: Dutch delegates

Kloveniersdoelen, where the synod was held

CHAPTER 1

The Synod of Dordt (1618–1619): An Overview

The Synod of Dordt was the most significant synod of the Dutch Reformed tradition. Within the whole Reformed tradition, it ranks with the Westminster Assembly (1643–1653) in significance. And it was one of the most important events in the seventeenth-century Netherlands, with great consequences for politics, the church, and the culture of the Dutch Republic.

Occasion for the Synod
The Synod of Dordt was convened in the Dutch city of Dordrecht. The synod's primary goal was to settle the Arminian controversy that had agitated the Netherlands for over twenty years. This controversy centered on the doctrines of grace, specifically concerning predestination and related points. The foundational issue concerned the relationship between God's sovereignty in bringing about salvation and human responsibility in salvation.

The controversy began with the teaching of Jacobus Arminius (1560–1609) in the 1590s, when he was pastor at the church of Amsterdam. The controversy became more heated after he became a professor of theology at Leiden University in 1603. At that time, there were only two universities in the Netherlands—one in Leiden, and one in Franeker in Friesland. At Leiden, there were only three professors in the faculty of theology, so Arminius was teaching most of the future ministers in the country.[1]

It was also at Leiden University where Arminius clashed with his colleague Franciscus Gomarus. Arminius taught that predestination was based on God's foreknowledge of whether a person would choose or not choose to have faith. On the other hand, Gomarus taught that predestination was simply a sovereign decision of God's will to select certain people for salvation, without considering a person as sinful.

After Arminius died in 1609, his followers drew up a document that summarized his views in Five Articles. The document is known as the *Remonstrance of 1610*. The Five Articles were at the heart of the controversy, as it escalated all the way to the Synod of Dordt. In brief, these articles stated the following:

1. God predestined sinners based on His foreknowledge of their faith or unbelief.

2. Christ died for all people, but only believers are saved.

3. Fallen man does not have saving faith by his own free will, unless he is regenerated by Christ.

4. God's grace is made available to humans, but one can choose to accept or resist grace.

5. It is uncertain whether believers can fall from a state of grace. By 1611, Arminians affirmed that believers can fall from grace.[2]

Because of the *Remonstrance of 1610* with these Five Articles, the Arminians became known as Remonstrants.

---

1. On Arminius, see Carl Bangs, *Arminius: A Study in the Dutch Reformation* (Nashville: Abingdon, 1971); Keith D. Stanglin and Thomas H. McCall, *Jacob Arminius: Theologian of Grace* (Oxford: Oxford University Press, 2012).

2. The *Remonstrance* is printed in G. J. Hoenderdaal, "Remonstrantie en Contraremonstrantie," *Nederlands Archief voor Kerkgeschiedenis* 51, no. 1 (1970): 49–92. An English translation of the *Remonstrance of 1610* is found in Peter Y. De Jong, ed., *Crisis in the Reformed Churches: Essays in Commemoration of the Great Synod of Dort, 1618–1619* (Grand Rapids: Reformed Fellowship, 1968), 207–9.

The Synod of Dordt (1618–1619): An Overview

In the spring of 1611, the States of Holland and West Friesland organized a conference of six Remonstrants and six Contra-Remonstrants in The Hague to seek a resolution of the conflict. This Hague conference failed to achieve unity.

Throughout the 1610s, the controversy became very heated and spread from the university to the churches to broader Dutch society, so much so that even the fishmongers in the Leiden market were arguing over predestination. Church and state were very much interwoven in the Dutch Republic, so the theological controversy became entangled with political issues and even threatened the country with civil war. Johan van Oldenbarnevelt (the leading politician in the province of Holland) supported the Remonstrant cause. On the other side, the army commander, Prince Maurice (of the House of Orange), supported the Contra-Remonstrant or orthodox Reformed cause.[3]

During the course of the controversy, there were occasional calls to hold a national synod to deal with the issue. No national synod had been held since the Synod of The Hague in 1586. Convening a national synod was the prerogative of the Dutch government—specifically, the States General in The Hague—and this political assembly kept delaying. After a decade of strife in the church and the state, the States General finally decided that a national synod should be held to settle the controversy.

After King James I of England urged the States General in 1617 to convene a national synod to deal with the religious strife for the sake of the nation's peace and unity, it made the first serious deliberations to do just that.[4] However, not all of the seven Dutch provinces agreed. Four provinces—Gelderland, Zeeland, Friesland, and Groningen—pressed to hold a national synod, but the provinces of Holland, Utrecht, and Overijssel (which had significant Remonstrant populations) objected.

---

3. On Oldenbarnevelt, see Jan den Tex, *Oldenbarnevelt*, vol. 2, *1606–1619* (Cambridge: Cambridge University Press, 1973), chs. 10, 12. For the political situation, see Jonathan I. Israel, *The Dutch Republic: Its Rise, Greatness, and Fall 1477–1806*, Oxford History of Early Modern Europe (Oxford: Clarendon, 1998), chs. 19–20.

4. Eric Platt, *Britain and the Bestandstwisten: The Causes, Course and Consequences of British Involvement in the Dutch Religious and Political Disputes of the Early Seventeenth Century*, Reformed Historical Theology 28 (Göttingen: Vandenhoeck and Ruprecht, 2015), ch. 4.

Nevertheless, the four-province majority proceeded to take steps to hold a national synod, including the adoption, in November 1617, of Articles to Convene a national synod. These articles spelled out the conditions under which the national synod was to take place—including its time, its place, its agenda, its voting procedures, the composition of its delegates, the invitation of foreign theologians, the preparation by provincial synods, and the condition that doctrinal matters must be determined on the basis of Scripture alone and not of human writings.[5]

Finally, in the summer and fall of 1618, under political pressure, the provinces of Overijssel, Utrecht, and, later, Holland were pressured to agree to the convening of the national synod.

In a sense, the outcome of the Remonstrant case was determined already in the political arena, when, in the summer of 1618, Prince Maurice disbanded the local militia (*waardgelders*) in various Dutch cities and arrested Oldenbarnevelt for treason in August. He replaced local pro-Remonstrant political officials in Holland and Utrecht with officials who supported the Contra-Remonstrant cause. In spite of the political intrigue, the synod was determined to give the Remonstrants a fair hearing.

Since the States General was basically in charge of the synod, it also sent its own state delegates to the synod to act on its behalf. The States General paid for most of the costs of the synod for a whole six and a half months (well over 120,000 guilders), including the expenses of the foreign delegates. The various Dutch provinces were expected to pay the expenses of the Dutch delegates from their provinces.

Location and Facilities

The synod was hosted by the oldest city in Holland—Dordrecht—on an island at the junction of major rivers. It was the city where, in 1572, the Dutch Republic was founded under the leadership of William of Orange. Dordrecht was a prominent center of international commerce during the Dutch Golden Age. It was to this city of Dordrecht that the synodical delegates arrived by boat.[6]

---

5. The Articles to Convene the national synod are printed in *ADSND*, 2/1:46–48, 741–45.

6. On Dordrecht as the host city, see Fred van Lieburg, *Synodestad: Dordrecht 1618–1619* (Amsterdam: Prometheus, 2019).

The synod itself met in the Kloveniersdoelen, the grand meeting hall for the local musketeers' guild. There the *klovers*, or guns of the guards, were stored. The Kloveniersdoelen was renovated for the synod by the city carpenter. Special benches were installed on the second floor of the building for over one hundred delegates.

Official public ceremonies, at the beginning and at the end of the synod, were held in the magnificent eleventh-century Grote Kerk.

After the synod was over, the stately Kloveniers meeting hall eventually fell into disrepair. It was torn down two hundred years later to make way for a prison. Now on this site is a modern building of the court of justice. On the side of the building is a little picture of the synod and a commemorative sign.

Participants at the Synod

This was a *national* synod of the Dutch Reformed churches, but the synod had an *international* character, as is evident from the list of participants.[7]

There were eleven Dutch delegations at the synod. Nine of these delegations were sent from the nine Dutch provincial and particular synods. Most of these provincial synods sent four ministers and two elder delegates. Almost all were Contra-Remonstrants, since the Remonstrants were in the minority in the country. The Walloon (or French Reformed) churches in the Netherlands also sent a delegation. Since Remonstrants were prominent in the province of Utrecht, the delegation from this province was a split delegation—half Remonstrant and half Contra-Remonstrant. As a result, there were two minister delegates and one elder delegate at the synod who were Remonstrants. (They participated in the Pro-Acta sessions, but the two Remonstrant ministers were pressured to join the cited Remonstrants when the Remonstrant case came up on the agenda in early December.)

There was a separate delegation of five theologians from the Dutch universities and academies (illustrious schools)—Johannes Polyander from Leiden, Sibrandus Lubbertus from Franeker, Franciscus Gomarus from Groningen, Antonius Thysius from Harderwijk,

---

7. See Fred van Lieburg, "The Participants at the Synod of Dordt," in *ADSND*, 1:lxiii–cvii.

and Antonius Walaeus from Middelburg. So there was a total of fifty-eight Dutch delegates.

In addition to the Dutch delegates, the States General invited a number of leading Reformed theologians from other countries to help deal with the Arminian controversy. There were twenty-six foreign delegates from eight territories with Reformed churches—Great Britain, the Palatinate, Hesse, four Swiss cantons, Nassau-Wetteravia, Geneva, Bremen, and Emden. The foreign theologians were given full voting rights, along with the Dutch delegates.

There was even an Anglican bishop in attendance—the honorable George Carleton—as head of the British delegation. To show him proper honor, a canopy was built over the British benches.

Theologians from the Reformed (Huguenot) churches in France were also invited, and two of them were on their way, but the Catholic king of France, Louis XIII, refused to let them attend. To show deference to the French, the synod left their seats open, next to the British.

The Elector of Brandenburg was also invited to send two theologians to the synod. They did not attend, however, due to illness and Lutheran opposition.

There were also eighteen state delegates at the synod, representing the States General. Their role was to give direction on procedural matters and to ensure that the synod dealt only with ecclesiastical matters and did not impinge on political affairs. They did not enter into the theological issues.[8]

The final group of participants at the Synod of Dordt were not actual delegates. Thirteen Remonstrant leaders were summoned to appear before the synod to have their views examined. The synod wanted to judge whether any of the Remonstrant views, especially their Five Articles, deviated from the accepted doctrine of the Dutch Reformed churches. Leiden theologian Simon Episcopius was their spokesman.

In its early sessions, the synod sent these Remonstrant leaders letters of citation requiring them to appear within fourteen days. They were called "to state, explain, and defend" their views of the five Remonstrant articles, and they were also supposed to submit any

---

8. On the state delegates, see Johanna Roelevink, "Introduction to the Acts and the Instructions of the Delegates of the States General," in *ADSND*, 1:liii–lxi.

doubts they had about the Belgic Confession and the Heidelberg Catechism.[9] When they were present in the synod, the cited Remonstrants were seated around a table in the middle of the hall.

The officers of the synod were seated at a table in the front by the fireplace—the president, two secretaries, and two assessors (vice presidents).

The seating arrangement in the hall honored the rank of the delegations. To the right of the officers were the state delegates and their secretary—Daniel Heinsius, the history professor and librarian at Leiden University. Farther on the right were the five Dutch theologians. To the left were all of the foreign delegates—the British first, and then the other foreign theologians by rank. The Dutch delegates sat on the right side in front of the five Dutch theologians, and in the benches in the back. The Dutch delegations were seated according to the rank of their provinces in the States General.

For sessions open to the public, spectators could stand behind the fence or sit up in the two balconies at the back of the hall. Some of the best places were taken by women and girls, who came to take in the spectacle.

For the sake of the foreign delegates, the synod was conducted in the Latin language, since that was the only language everyone knew. Latin was the language of the university, where ministers were trained, whether at Leiden University, the Geneva Academy, Heidelberg University, or the Frisian university at Franeker.

It may be noted that during the course of the lengthy synod, four delegates died and three went home sick.

Procedures of the Synod

First of all, voting at the synod was by delegation, not by individual delegate. On any issue, advice was presented by all nineteen delegations, following the order of their rank—first the foreign delegations by order of their international status in relation to the Dutch Republic, the British first—and then the Dutch delegations, according to their provincial seating order in the States General. It was usually expected

---

9. Letters of citation were sent to the Remonstrants by both the synod and the state delegates; see *ADSND*, 1:15–16; and *Acta*, 1:20.

that the advice of the delegations be written, and each was read in the synod. Based on the advice of all nineteen delegations, the synod officers then drew up a common synodical decision. Revisions of this were made by the full synod, and then the president called for final approval by a majority of the delegations.[10]

Sometimes, for special tasks, committees were appointed by the synod—for example, to draft the Canons, to report to the States General, to deal with the Kampen case, to deal with the Hoorn case, to draft a new form of subscription for ministers, and to prepare an authoritative text of the Belgic Confession in Dutch, French, and Latin.

On doctrinal matters, the only standard that was allowed to determine truth was the Bible, and not any human writings. This was spelled out in the government Articles to Convene the synod.

Phases of the Synod
The Synod of Dordt met for six and a half months from 13 November 1618 to 29 May 1619—in a total of 180 half-day sessions. The proceedings of the synod consisted of four phases:

(1) The Pro-Acta sessions lasted about three weeks, before the cited Remonstrants arrived.

(2) When they arrived in early December, the synod was largely entangled in procedural bickering with the Remonstrants for five long weeks, until President Bogerman expelled them from the synod in mid-January.

(3) After the Remonstrant expulsion, for almost four months the synod examined Remonstrant writings and prepared its response. Based on advice from each of the nineteen delegations, the synod issued its judgment, the Canons of Dordt.

(4) In the Post-Acta sessions, after the foreign theologians returned home, the Dutch delegates focused on other matters pertaining to the Dutch churches, especially the church order.

---

10. On the procedures of the synod, see H. Kaajan, *De Pro-Acta der Dordtsche Synode in 1618* (Rotterdam: T. De Vries, 1914), 42–59.

The Synod of Dordt (1618–1619): An Overview

The following is an overview of each of these four phases.

Phase One: The Pro-Acta Sessions (13 November–6 December 1618)
From 13 November to 6 December, the synod was occupied with opening formalities and various non-doctrinal matters.

After opening ceremonies at the Grote Kerk, the officers of the synod were selected—Johannes Bogerman as president; Festus Hommius and Sebastianus Dammannus as secretaries; and Jacobus Rolandus and Hermannus Faukelius as assessors, or vice presidents.

Then the credentials of the various Dutch delegations were read. The credentials of the foreign theologians had been presented to the States General.

Since the primary reason for holding the synod was to deal with the Remonstrant controversy, on 16 November it was decided to summon a group of thirteen Remonstrant leaders to appear before the synod. While waiting for them to arrive, the synod addressed five non-doctrinal matters that were of significance for the Dutch churches:

1. First, there was a great need for a new Dutch Bible translation, based on the original Hebrew and Greek. A new translation was authorized by the synod, just a few years after the English King James Version (1611). Several criteria were adopted for the new translation, including the following: that translators were to stick to the text and manner of speaking of the original languages, as much as clarity of the Dutch language would permit; that they should preface each book with a succinct summary; that they should add brief notes about obscure passages; that in addressing God, the Dutch term *Ghy* (You) should be used; that the name JEHOVA should be translated by the term HEERE in capital letters; that the accepted division of chapters and verses should be observed; and that it would be useful to add aids, such as maps, chronologies, genealogies, and an index at the end of the Bible. It was also decided to translate the apocryphal books from the Greek, but to print them at the end of the Bible in a different font, with a title and preface indicating that these are human writings. The synod also approved a list of translators and reviewers (*revisores*) for

both the Old and New Testaments.[11] It was not until 1637, nineteen years later, that the translation work was completed. The Dutch government financed this *Staten-vertaling* (States Bible).

2. The synod discussed the topic of catechizing. Several guidelines were adopted for Heidelberg Catechism preaching, which was sorely neglected in some places. All ministers were earnestly instructed to hold Sunday afternoon catechism services, even if only their own families attended. And magistrates should be asked to prohibit manual labor and other desecrations of the Sabbath that prevent people from attending the services.[12]

The synod also discussed and made a decision on the best ways of teaching the Heidelberg Catechism in three spheres: the Christian home, school, and church.[13] The synod asserted that the duty of parents is to instruct their children in the basics of the Christian religion, involve them in family prayers, take them to catechism services, review the sermons, and have them memorize related Scripture passages.

Schools where youth are instructed in the fundamentals of Christian doctrine need to be established in the cities and in every village. Teachers are to be members of a Reformed church; they must subscribe to the Catechism and the Belgic Confession and be well trained in catechism teaching. The duty of teachers is to teach students to memorize and understand the rudiments of the Catechism, and they must take their students to the catechism services. Three forms of catechism are to be used in the schools: (1) A simple catechism for beginners, with the Apostles' Creed, the Decalogue, the Lord's Prayer, the sacraments, and church discipline; (2) A compendium of the Heidelberg Catechism for intermediate students; and (3) the Heidelberg Catechism for advanced students.

The duty of ministers in the church is to preach catechism sermons that are brief and adapted to the level of youth. They must also visit the schools to see that teachers are not neglecting proper catechism teaching. For adults and older youth who are not well instructed, ministers

---

11. On the new translation, see *ADSND*, 1:16–24; and Kaajan, *Pro-Acta*, 60–152.
12. *ADSND*, 1:24–25.
13. On the manner of catechizing, see *ADSND*, 1:25–30; 2/2:76–130; and Kaajan, *Pro-Acta*, 153–220.

should hold weekly meetings in homes, or in the consistory room, to explain the main doctrines of the Christian religion and review the catechism sermons. Those who desire to join the church should meet to be carefully instructed for three or four weeks before the Lord's Supper.

3. The synod also dealt with an issue from the Dutch colonies in the East Indies about whether slave children who were part of Christian families should be baptized. There was agreement that older children should be instructed in the basics of the Christian faith and profess their faith before being baptized. As for young children, there was disagreement at the synod—some argued for baptism, following the example of Abraham, who circumcised his whole household; others argued against their baptism because baptism is a sign of the covenant, and non-Christians and their children are not part of the covenant. The synod, by majority, decided that slave children (of non-Christian parents) who were taken into Christian families should not be baptized until they reached the age of discretion.[14]

4. The synod adopted some regulations for the training of students preparing for the ministry in Dutch Reformed churches. The synod focused on five issues: May students preach in public worship services? May they perform baptisms? Should they attend consistory and classis meetings? May they read Scripture in public worship? And should the synod make binding decisions on these matters, or only offer advice? The synod agreed that non-ordained persons should not administer the sacraments. As for preaching or exhorting, the synod left this to the discretion of the classes. They also left the matter of attending consistory and classis meetings, as well as the question of the public reading of Scripture, to the discretion of the local churches. On whether the synod should make binding decisions, the synod decided not to do so, but only to give advice.[15]

---

14. On the issue of baptism of slave children, see *ADSND*, 1:30–31; 2/2:131–67; and Kaajan, *Pro-Acta*, 221–59.

15. On the deliberations about theological training, see *ADSND*, 1:30–32; 2/2:168–97; and Kaajan, *Pro-Acta*, 260–303.

5. Since there was concern that the printing of Remonstrant ideas was not being well regulated, the synod delegations also presented their advice on the matter of abuses in the printing trade. Due to the arrival of the cited Remonstrants, no decision was made on this issue, but soon after, on 22 December, the States General issued an edict forbidding unauthorized publications about the synod. At its conclusion, the synod sent a request to the States General to take stronger measures.[16]

Phase Two: Procedural Bickering with the Remonstrants (6 December 1618–14 January 1619)

When the thirteen summoned Remonstrant leaders arrived at the synod, they and the synod argued for more than a month about procedural matters. The Remonstrants first appeared on 6 December, and President Bogerman expelled them five weeks later on 14 January—before the synod even got to the real theological issues.[17]

The Remonstrants were led by Leiden theologian Simon Episcopius. The day after they arrived, Episcopius delivered a long speech to explain the motives and background of the Remonstrant position.[18] After his speech, Bogerman told him he did not have permission to speak. He also asked Episcopius for a copy of his speech, but he said he had no other copy. Then the synod found out he did have another rough copy, so Bogerman accused him of lying. He strongly denied lying and contended that he said he had no other copy "neatly enough written out."

The fundamental cause of the procedural bickering was the fact that the two sides identified the central issue in the controversy differently. For the synod, the main issue was Remonstrant doctrinal deviation in their view of predestination. The Remonstrants said that God, from eternity, predestines or chooses people based on the faith

---

16. On printing abuses, see *ADSND*, 1:33–34; 2/2:198–226; and Kaajan, *Pro-Acta*, 304–35.

17. For more detail on the debates between the synod and the Remonstrants over procedure, see Donald Sinnema, "Procedural Wrangling in the Remonstrant Case at the Synod of Dordt (1618–1619)," in *More than Luther: The Reformation and the Rise of Pluralism in Europe,* ed. Karla Boersma and Herman J. Selderhuis (Göttingen: Vandenhoeck and Ruprecht, 2019), 289–306. Reprinted in this volume; see chapter 2.

18. For Episcopius's speech, see the *Acta*, 1:341–51.

The Synod of Dordt (1618–1619): An Overview 13

that He foresees a person will choose to have in history. In that view, the decision belongs to the person, not to God. For the Remonstrants, the main issue centered on extreme views of reprobation advocated by certain Reformed theologians.

For the synod, the crux of the issue was whether the church has the right to *judge* doctrinal views that deviate from its confessional standards. They claimed the right and the obligation to guard the church against false teaching. The synod wanted to examine and judge questionable Remonstrant teachings about predestination and related points. The Remonstrants wanted full freedom to refute Contra-Remonstrant views of reprobation, but since they were not delegates, they did not get to set the agenda. So they tried, every chance they could, to push the issue of reprobation into the discussion.

Already, when the Remonstrants first arrived, they raised the issue of the synod's authority. They wanted this to be a conference where both sides would discuss the issues as equal parties. There already was such a conference of equals in 1611—the Hague Conference—but it did not bring any resolution.

On 11 December, the Remonstrants presented a formal protest that they could not recognize the synod as their lawful judge, because, they said, the synod's members were the opposing party in the conflict, and because many of the Dutch delegates had participated in schisms.[19]

On 13 and 17 December, the Remonstrants agreed to submit brief *Statements* (*Sententiae*) of their views of the Five Articles.[20] However, this raised more debate, since these statements criticized Contra-Remonstrant views more than they presented their own views.

Then President Bogerman demanded that the Remonstrants produce their doubts and observations on the Belgic Confession and the Heidelberg Catechism, but this also caused problems. They wanted their Five Articles to be treated first. On 21 December, the Remonstrants submitted their *Observations* (*Considerationes*) on the Belgic Confession, which they offered as suggestions for revision, not as

---

19. *ADSND*, 2/2:350–54.
20. The Remonstrant *Sententiae* are printed in the *Acta*, 1:113–14, 116–22. Translation in De Jong, *Crisis*, 221–29.

objections to the doctrine of the Confession. They were reprimanded for not submitting observations on the Heidelberg Catechism and for submitting their observations jointly rather than individually. Finally, on 27 December, they submitted their *Observations* on the Catechism, also as suggestions for revision.[21]

For weeks, there were arguments about every possible procedural matter; for example:

- Could the Remonstrants only discuss their view of election, or could they also treat reprobation?
- Should they positively state their views, or could they negatively refute opposing views?
- May they refute only Dutch Contra-Remonstrants, or may they also refute foreign theologians?
- Is reprobation to be treated before or after election?
- Should they present their views orally or in writing?
- Should they answer questions orally or in writing?
- Should they answer questions before or after presenting their own explanations?
- Should they answer questions individually or jointly as a group?
- How much freedom should the Remonstrants have to present their views and refute others?
- Is such freedom a matter of conscience or only a matter of procedure?

In these debates, both sides did make some concessions, but in the end, they could not agree on procedure. In late December, when Bogerman tried to orally examine the Remonstrants with questions that he posed to them individually, they refused to answer. The proceedings were at an impasse.

At the end of December, the state delegates at the synod sent a delegation to the States General in The Hague to report on the

---

21. For the Remonstrant observations on the Belgic Confession and on the Heidelberg Catechism, see *Acta et Scripta*, 1:83–99, 102–33.

The Synod of Dordt (1618–1619): An Overview   15

Remonstrants' obstinacy and to receive direction. On 1 January, the States General issued a resolution that approved the actions of the synod and ordered the Remonstrants to submit. If they would not cooperate, the States General said that the synod should examine their opinions from their writings, outside of their presence.[22]

In early January, to facilitate the examination of Remonstrant views in their Five Articles, President Bogerman dictated the *Articuli* on Article I. This was a summary of Remonstrant views from their writings, with references to passages where these views were expressed.[23]

On 11 January, the synod recalled the Remonstrants, and Bogerman tried to examine them one last time. He asked a question from a prepared list, but again they refused to answer.

Then Episcopius made a concession. If the freedom to explain, defend, and refute as much as they thought necessary were granted to them, they were ready to receive the list of questions and answer in writing. But Bogerman refused to hand over the list.

By majority, the synod then decided to examine the Remonstrants from their writings, as the States General had authorized. The state delegates gave them until Monday, 14 January, to submit. On Saturday, the state delegates met privately with the Remonstrants for a final attempt to get them to cooperate. But it was in vain.

On Monday, 14 January, Bogerman called in the Remonstrants and asked them to state categorically—yes or no—whether they would obey the States General and the synod. Episcopius replied by submitting a long document, the *Declaratio*, explaining their view of Article I. In the preface, he stated that the Remonstrants could not in good conscience obey the synod's decrees.[24]

At that point, President Bogerman lost patience and angrily expelled the Remonstrants from the synod in a passionate speech. He rehearsed the synod's dealings with the Remonstrants and accused them of great obstinacy, deceit, and lies. Finally, he expelled them with these words: "In the name of the state delegates and the synod, you are dismissed! Get out [*Exite*]!" As they were leaving, one

---

22. The States General 1 January resolution is printed in *ADSND*, 2/2:641–44.
23. The *Articuli* on Art. I is printed in *ADSND*, 2/2:781–91.
24. The Remonstrant *Declaratio* on Art. I is printed in *Acta et Scripta*, 2:3–46.

of the Remonstrants was heard to utter, "Out from this assembly of the wicked!"

While Bogerman's manner of expelling the Remonstrants was less than tactful, he did not expel them simply in a fit of anger. The States General, and the Dutch and foreign delegations, had all advised their dismissal.

Phase Three: Preparing a Response to the Remonstrants (15 January–9 May 1619)

After the Remonstrants were expelled, the Synod of Dordt spent more than three months carefully examining their views *from their writings* and preparing its *judgment* on the Remonstrant case—popularly known as the Canons of Dordt. The process of drafting the Canons was very careful and elaborate.[25]

First, the synod decided on a new procedure for its deliberations. In morning sessions, each of the delegations was to meet privately to examine and form its judgment on the Five Remonstrant Articles. In afternoon public sessions, a number of Dutch and foreign theologians would present speeches that responded to the main Remonstrant arguments in their writings.[26]

From 17 January to 27 February, many of the theologians gave speeches on various aspects of the Five Articles—Sybrandus Lubbertus, Franciscus Gomarus, George Carleton, Paul Tossanus, Antonius Thysius, Johannes Polyander, Antonius Walaeus, John Davenant, Samuel Ward, Rudolphus Goclenius, and Abraham Scultetus all spoke on Article I, concerning election, and Heinrich Alting spoke on reprobation. Walter Balcanqual and Georg Cruciger addressed Article II, on Christ's death and the extent of redemption. Paul Stein, Sebastian Beck, and Johann Alsted spoke on Article IV, concerning conversion and how it occurs. Because it was recognized since the Hague Conference of 1611 that Article III was not a matter of controversy,

---

25. On the process of drafting the Canons, see Donald Sinnema, "The Drafting of the Canons of Dordt: A Preliminary Survey of Early Drafts and Related Documents," in *Revisiting the Synod of Dordt (1618–1619)*, ed. Aza Goudriaan and Fred van Lieburg (Leiden: Brill, 2011), 291–311. An abbreviated version of this article is printed in this volume; see chapter 13.

26. *ADSND*, 1:114–15.

The Synod of Dordt (1618–1619): An Overview 17

Article III was usually combined with Article IV in discussions of these issues. Article V, on perseverance, was addressed by Wolfgang Mayer, Gomarus, Polyander, Théodore Tronchin, and Jean Diodati. In addition, Matthias Martinius and Heinrich Isselburg each gave speeches to counter Conrad Vorstius; and Ludwig Crocius spoke on justification contra Petrus Bertius.

On these issues, there were usually good discussions. But sometimes the discussions got a little heated between some of the delegates. Professor Gomarus got into such a dispute with Martinius of Bremen over the role of Christ in election that he actually challenged him to a duel; he had to be restrained lest they come to blows. And on the issue of whether God is the physical cause of conversion, there was a major dispute between the Bremen theologians Martinius and Ludwig Crocius, on the one hand, and Lubbertus, Gomarus, and Heidelberg theologian Abraham Scultetus, on the other.[27]

On 10 January, President Bogerman had dictated to the synod the *Articuli* on Article I, which he, with the help of the other officers, had drawn up to summarize the views of the Remonstrants, together with references to their writings where these views were presented. Now, on 16 January, he dictated the *Articuli* on Article II; on 8 February, he dictated the *Articuli* on Article III/IV; and on 25 February, he dictated the *Articuli* on Article V. These summaries of Remonstrant views made it easier for the synod delegations to draw up their judgments of the Five Articles.[28]

Meanwhile, the Remonstrants had to remain in another room in the Kloveniersdoelen, and they continued to submit long written explanations and defenses of their Five Articles. They wrote these documents to fulfill the obligation in their citation letters to "state, explain, and defend as much as they consider necessary" their views of the Five Articles. Already in December, they had submitted their *Statements* (*Sententiae*) on the Five Articles. On the day they were expelled from the synod, Episcopius submitted their *Explanation* (*Declaratio*) on Article I. Now, under pressure from the state delegates,

---

27. See my article, "Disagreements and Doctrinal Dissension among Delegates at the Synod of Dordt." Reprinted in this volume; see chapter 6.
28. For the *Articuli*, see *ADSND*, 2/2:781–800.

on 7 February they submitted their *Defensio* of Article I and their *Declaratio* on Article II. On 15 February, they submitted their *Declarationes* on Articles III/IV and V. On 25 February, they submitted their *Defensio* on Article II, and finally, on 19 March, they submitted their *Defensiones* on Articles IV and V. The synod patiently read most of these documents.

After the Remonstrants were expelled, the nineteen Dutch and foreign delegations worked separately, examining each of the Five Remonstrant Articles from their writings and forming their judgments (*iudicia*) on these Articles. From 6 to 21 March, all of these *iudicia*—eighty-three of them—on each of the Five Articles were read in the synod and discussed in closed session. The delegations were expected not only to offer a judgment on the Remonstrant views but also to present the orthodox Reformed understanding of each issue.

In addition to the *iudicia*, a statement on the Five Articles sent by the elderly Heidelberg theologian David Pareus was read in the synod. A similar *Confessio* on the Five Articles was sent by Pierre du Moulin, one of the French delegates who was prevented from attending the synod by King Louis XIII. Du Moulin's statement was read after the Canons had already been approved.[29]

When all the *iudicia* had been read in the synod, President Bogerman commented on how much harmony there was in all of them. Then it was time to draw up a single judgment of the synod on the Remonstrant case, based on the *iudicia* of the nineteen delegations. Bogerman gave advice on the form of the Canons—that they must be presented simply and that they must not be scholastic but ecclesiastical in character. Bishop Carleton also offered suggestions and agreed that they should be written in a popular, rather than scholastic, style.[30]

On 21 March, President Bogerman announced that he had taken it upon himself, as the president of the synod, to draw up the synod's judgment on Remonstrant Articles I and II, in the first two chapters of the Canons. It had taken Bogerman four drafts to come up with a version of the first chapter that he dictated to the synod the next day.

---

29. See *ADSND*, 1:131–32, 147; printed in *Acta*, 1:202–31, 287–97.
30. See Klaas Dijk, *De Strijd over Infra- en Supralapsarisme in de Gereformeerde Kerken van Nederland* (Kampen: Kok, 1912), Bijlage C, xviii–xix.

But then, there was a bit of a stir, especially from some of the British and South Holland delegates. They thought he was trying to draw up the Canons all by himself and then merely seek the synod's approval. In the debate that followed, Bogerman complied when the state delegates proposed that a drafting committee of nine do the work of drawing up the Canons.[31]

Along with the two vice presidents, Rolandus and Faukelius, and Bogerman as president, the drafting committee was made up of three foreign theologians—Bishop Carleton from Britain, Abraham Scultetus from Heidelberg, and Jean Diodati from Geneva—and three Dutch theologians—Johannes Polyander, Antonius Walaeus, and Jacobus Trigland.

For the next three weeks, the synod did not meet in regular session, but the drafting committee worked diligently to draw up the Canons. The committee started with Bogerman's dictated draft and kept revising until they reached the final version. The first committee draft was dictated to the delegations on 29 March and 5 April, and the nineteen delegations had the opportunity to offer suggestions for improvement. Then the drafting committee revised this draft and dictated it again to the delegations for more suggestions. They went back and forth like this, for a second and third committee draft, as well as the final draft. In all, there were eight drafts of the first chapter alone.

The Canons were written up in five chapters (with Chapters III and IV combined, because Article III was not a matter of controversy) as a response to the Remonstrant Five Articles on predestination and related points. Since that was the specific focus, the Canons were not intended to present a comprehensive summary of all Reformed theology.

Like the *iudicia*, each chapter of the Canons had two parts—a negative and a positive section. The Rejection of Errors section was primary, because the whole reason for the Canons was to bring a judgment on Remonstrant errors. But it was thought advisable to add a positive section for each chapter, so that the churches would understand the orthodox Reformed teaching about these five points under dispute.

---

31. See Balcanqual, 2:139–40.

This whole process took three weeks, and then the synod again met in full session to make some final changes. These changes centered on Chapter II of the Canons, rejections 2 and 6, which had to do with the hypothetical or absolute necessity of a likeness of our nature in Christ, a matter to which the British objected. At long last, on 23 April, every delegate approved and signed each chapter of the Canons. Later, the synod approved a Conclusion to the Canons, dealing with the issues of false accusations against the Reformed position and hard sayings uttered by some Reformed theologians. Also approved was a Preface to the Canons.[32]

Here, a few words about the character of the Canons are appropriate:

First, the Canons are thoroughly based on the Bible, as understood at the synod. Every member of the synod had to swear an oath that all deliberations on doctrine would be based on Scripture alone and not on any human writing—not even the Belgic Confession or the Heidelberg Catechism. So the Canons are full of biblical references.

The leading Reformed theologians of Europe were present at Dordrecht and working on the Canons, so the Canons are no sham condemnation of Remonstrant views. They were carefully crafted by the most scholarly theologians of the day.

The Canons are one of the best statements ever written about the relationship of God's sovereignty in salvation and human responsibility. The Canons present in very careful terms the delicate balance between God's sovereign work of grace in salvation and human responsibility to respond in faith and obedience, with the priority given to God's grace.

The Canons, first of all, emphasize that salvation is totally by God's grace, from beginning to end, and not by human deeds or choices. God took the initiative in saving sinful humans, already deciding back in eternity to graciously elect or choose his own for eternal life—long before they were even born or did any human deed.

Yet, the Canons fully recognize that, even though salvation is totally God's work, humans must respond in faith and obedience.

---

32. A critical edition of the Canons of Dordt is published in J. N. Bakhuizen van den Brink, ed., *De Nederlandse Belijdenisgeschriften in Authentieke Teksten* (Amsterdam: Ton Bolland, 1976), 225–80.

The Synod of Dordt (1618–1619): An Overview 21

It's not as if God comes halfway to offer grace, and then it is our responsibility to reach out and accept the grace—that is the Arminian view. Rather, salvation is totally by God's grace. God's grace works to change sinful hearts and enables them to respond in faith. In fact, at the very moment in which God changes human hearts, they are able to respond, through the Holy Spirit's work in them. So believing is a human action and responsibility, but at the same time, it is totally a gift of God.

It is also worth emphasizing how pastoral the Canons are. If a person is struggling with doubts about their election and salvation, the Canons guide them to look at their life for the fruits of election, such as faith, sorrow for sin, and a hunger for righteousness; to look to God's promises about salvation; and to look for the testimony of the Holy Spirit, which assures them that they are children of God. Then they can be sure that nothing can separate them from God. The Canons also give comfort to believing parents who lose a child in infancy. At the same time, the Canons also challenge false security, laxity, and indifference.

After the Canons were adopted, the synod drew up a Sentence, deposing the fifteen cited Remonstrants from their offices in the ministry.

By order of the States General, the synod then reviewed the Belgic Confession and the Heidelberg Catechism. All of the delegates affirmed that the *doctrine* contained in the Confession and the Catechism fully agrees with God's Word.[33]

During this phase of the synod, four other discipline cases were also handled by the synod. First was the Kampen case of four Remonstrant ministers from the city of Kampen.[34] Second was the Geysteranus case of two brothers, Petrus and Johannes, who were Remonstrant ministers suspected of various heterodox teachings.[35] Third was the case of Johannes Maccovius, the Franeker University theologian who

---

33. See the articles in this volume on the Belgic Confession and the Heidelberg Catechism (chapters 3 and 4, respectively).

34. On the Kampen case, see Erik A. de Boer, "*De Causa Ecclesiae Campensis* or: How Four Local Ministers Ended up on the National Agenda," in *More than Luther*, 307–20.

35. On the Geysteranus case, see the *Acta*, 1:279–83.

was accused of extreme statements (such as claiming that God is the author of sin) and of using excessively scholastic categories in dealing with theology. Maccovius was given a serious reprimand to avoid such excessive scholasticism.[36] Fourth was the case of Conrad Vorstius, who was accused of a variety of heterodox errors, which were condemned by the synod.[37]

Finally, on 6 May, with great ceremony, the members of the synod solemnly processed from the meeting hall to the Grote Kerk of Dordrecht. Following two coaches full of ladies, the state delegates led the way, followed by the synod members, two by two.

When all the delegates, along with a large number of spectators, were seated in the church, President Bogerman mounted a podium in front of the choir where the synod members were seated and offered a prayer in the Latin tongue for about a half hour. He thanked God profusely for the harmonious outcome of this venerable synod. Then the two secretaries, Hommius and Dammannus, ascended the podium and took turns reading aloud each chapter of the Canons until their voices were hoarse, publicly proclaiming this document to the whole world. Secretary Dammannus then read the names of every delegate who had signed the Canons. Each man doffed his hat as his name was called.

A few days later, the foreign theologians were dismissed with generous words of thanks for their willingness to come and help the Dutch deal with the crisis in the Netherlands.[38]

Then followed a magnificent banquet. The whole synod was plentifully treated with meat and drink. Their ears were entertained with agreeable stringed music, and women sang from behind the curtains.[39]

The state delegates presented each of the foreign theologians with a costly gold medallion bearing a picture of the synod. (The Dutch delegates later received a silver medallion.) Then the foreign theologians

---

36. On the Maccovius case, see Willem van Asselt, "On the Maccovius Affair," in *Revisiting the Synod of Dordt*, 217–41.

37. On the Vorstius case, see Dolf te Velde, "Collateral Damage? The Condemnation of Conrad Vorstius by the Synod of Dordt," in *More than Luther*, 321–37.

38. See *ADSND*, 1:154–55; Balcanqual, 2:165–66.

39. *Historisch Verhael van't ghene sich toeghedraeghen heeft binnen Dordrecht, in de Jaeren 1618 ende 1619* ([Amsterdam], 1623), 215v.

left for home, several of them stopping in The Hague on the way. There, on 13 May, some of them witnessed the beheading of Oldenbarnevelt, who was convicted of treason.

Phase Four: The Post-Acta Sessions (13–29 May 1619)
After the foreign theologians were dismissed, the Dutch delegates stayed for another three weeks to deal with matters of concern to the Dutch churches. The language of the synod then switched from Latin to Dutch, and the sessions were closed to the public. The matters addressed in this phase included the following:[40]

1. The synod read and approved in substance the most recent Church Order of 1586, from the Synod of The Hague. Then, based on gravamina (overtures) from the provincial synods, eight articles were revised—articles 4 and 5 (the calling of ministers), 9 (admitting priests to the ministry), 44 (church visitors), 55 (approval of books), 58 (forms for baptism), 67 (observance of holy days), and 69 (Psalm-singing and permitted hymns); and six new articles were added—articles 8 (persons with exceptional gifts for ministry), 28 (the duty of Christian magistrates), 42 (voting rights, for churches with more than one minister), 48 (correspondence between provincial synods), 49 (synodical deputies), and 59 (baptism of adults). The result was the Church Order of Dordt, with eighty-six articles.[41] The synod decided to petition the States General for approval of this church order, so that it might have the authority of public law. On 25 May, the synod gave definitive approval to this church order, and it was signed by the officers three days later. Although the Dordt Church Order was not uniformly

---

40. On the Post-Acta sessions, see *ADSND*, 1:156–86; and H. H. Kuyper, *De Post-Acta of Nahandelingen van de Nationale Synode van Dordrecht in 1618 en 1619 gehouden* (Amsterdam: Höveker & Wormser, 1899).
41. The Church Order of Dordt was first published in *Kercken-ordeninge, gestelt inden Nationalen Synode der Ghereformeerde Kercken, te samen beroepen ende gehouden by laste vande Hooghmo. Heeren Staten Generael van de Vereenighde Nederlanden, binnen Dordrecht, inden Iare 1618 ende 1619* (Utrecht: Salomon de Roy, 1620). An English translation is in *The Doctrinal Standards, Liturgy, and Church Order of the Netherlands Reformed Congregations* (Sioux Center, Iowa: Netherlands Reformed Book & Publication Committee, 1991), 179–89.

approved by all the Dutch provinces, it remained the prototype of Dutch Reformed church polity for centuries.

2. The right of patronage, the long-standing right of Dutch nobles and large landowners to appoint ministers, was debated. The state delegates indicated that it would not be possible to do away with this right, but abuses could be corrected. So, the synod drew up nine articles to correct patronage abuses, for recommendation to the States General.[42]

3. A policy for the calling of new ministers was adopted, consisting of election by a consistory in consultation with the local magistrate, a classical examination of doctrine and life, approbation by the local magistrate and by the local congregation, and public installation. A similar policy was adopted for the calling of ministers to a new congregation.

4. Decisions were made on eighteen gravamina forwarded by the provincial synods to the national synod. These included decisions on: church visitors; synodical deputies; correspondence between provincial synods; persons with exceptional gifts for the ministry; voting rights for churches with more than one minister; forms of subscription; observance of religious holidays; Psalm-singing and permitted biblical hymns; papal and Mennonite baptisms; baptism before marriage; correspondence with foreign churches; a uniform marriage ordinance; church discipline; baptism outside of worship services; admitting priests to ministry; university reform; a general school ordinance; marriage with those outside the Reformed church; desecration of the Sabbath; and churches under the cross.[43]

---

42. On this issue, see Sjaak Verwijs, "The Synod of Dordt and the *Ius Patronatus*," in *A Landmark in Turbulent Times: The Meaning and Relevance of the Synod of Dordt (1618–1619)*, ed. Henk van den Belt, Klaas-Willem de Jong, and Willem van Vlastuin (Göttingen: Vandenhoeck & Ruprecht, 2022), 277–89.

43. A nineteenth gravamen was presented to the synod from the North Holland and Zeeland synods concerning the need for missions to the East Indies and other lands, but the only decision was a request to the States General to encourage such missions and undertake means to spread the gospel to these lands. See Kuyper, *Post-Acta*, 150, 184, 267, 437, 443.

5. Ten articles on university reform were drawn up, with a request that provinces that had a university or an illustrious school observe these articles. One key article insisted that a professor of theology should be called only with the approval of the provincial synod or its deputies. Another article required that all professors subscribe to the Belgic Confession and the Heidelberg Catechism.

6. Six regulations for Sunday observance were approved to deal with differences concerning this issue in the Zeeland churches. A key distinction was made between ceremonial elements (which have been abolished) and moral elements (which are still valid) in the fourth commandment.

7. A new form of subscription was adopted for ministers, by which they were required to affirm that the doctrine contained in the Belgic Confession, the Heidelberg Catechism, and the Canons of Dordt fully agreed with the Word of God.[44] A similar form of subscription was adopted for rectors and teachers in the schools and for sick visitors. Another form of subscription for theology professors, regents, and vice-regents of the theological colleges was also approved.

8. A Dutch translation of the Canons of Dordt was read and approved.

9. In the Kampen case of four Remonstrant ministers, it was decided to depose two of the ministers, Voscuyl and Schotlerus.

10. The *text* of the Belgic Confession in Dutch and French was reviewed, and some revisions of the text were made in order to prepare a uniform text of the Confession. Special attention was paid to article 22, which related to the controversy over Johann Piscator's denial of the imputation of Christ's active obedience.

11. In the Hoorn case, relating to the appeals of three Hoorn ministers, the Synod of Dordt considered the judgment of the North Holland synod against them well founded but advised this synod to try to

---

44. On the history of the form of subscription, see Donald Sinnema, "The Origin of the Form of Subscription in the Dutch Reformed Tradition," *Calvin Theological Journal* 42, no. 2 (Nov. 2007): 256–82.

reconcile with Wellsingius. Wallesius and Rodingenus, who withdrew their appeals, were referred back to the North Holland synod.[45]

12. A form for adult baptism was approved, along with questions to be asked of the adults.

13. A short beginner's catechism and a mid-level catechism for more advanced students were approved, but these were then set aside in favor of the *ABC Boekje* already in use, as well as the *Kort Begrip*, the compendium of the Heidelberg Catechism that was drafted in 1608 by Hermannus Faukelius for use in Middelburg.

14. A delegation was appointed to go to the States General to thank it and to request that it confirm the synod's decisions. They were also to present to the States General a list of seventeen requests (*Libellus Supplex*). These requests included: approve and implement the synod's acts; approve an Act of Approbation of the Belgic Confession and the Heidelberg Catechism; approve the Dordt Church Order; approve and pay for the new Dutch Bible translation; establish regulations for school reform; recommend university reform to the provinces; establish a general school order for lower schools; establish a uniform marriage ordinance; establish printing regulations; encourage missions in foreign lands; support ministers for persecuted churches under the cross; replace priests with Reformed ministers; establish order against wandering priests; forbid Sabbath-breaking; abolish shameful recreations and cursing; remove abuses of oaths; and encourage provinces to properly support ministers.

15. A committee was appointed to examine a condensed version of the synod's Acta (*Acta Contracta*).

16. Classis Dordrecht was appointed as the synodical classis for the next national synod, which was expected to be held in three years. It was also decided to invite the Dutch churches scattered in England and Germany.

---

45. On the Hoorn case, see Kuyper, *Post-Acta*, 203–4, 225–27, 236–42, 257–59, 271–72.

17. A review of the liturgical forms was referred to the committee dealing with the *Acta Contracta*.

On 29 May, after six and a half months, the Synod of Dordt finally ended, again with a procession to the Grote Kerk, where local minister Balthazar Lydius preached a sermon and led a prayer of thanksgiving. Then all delegates returned to the synod meeting hall, where the state delegates thanked the synod, and President Bogerman thanked the state delegates and each provincial delegation.

Aftermath

On 2 July, the States General approved an Act of Approbation of the Canons of Dordt. The Canons were accepted by the Dutch Reformed churches throughout the Netherlands and began to function as one of the "Three Forms of Unity" to which all ministers were required to subscribe. The Church Order of Dordt was officially accepted only in the provinces of Gelderland, Utrecht, and Overijssel, but the main elements of church polity in the Dordt Church Order were generally followed in the Dutch Reformed churches.

Remonstrant ministers who refused to sign the form of subscription agreeing with the Canons were issued an "Act of Cessation" (*Acte van Stilstand*), a promise not to serve in the ministry and not to propagate their views. Those who refused were banished. The Dutch provincial synods deposed about two hundred Remonstrant ministers from ministry in the Dutch Reformed churches, and over eighty were banished from the country by the States General. However, a few years later, after the death of Prince Maurice in 1625, they were allowed to return. Under the leadership of Johannes Uytenbogaert, the Remonstrants, in the fall of 1619 (after an initial meeting in March), went on to establish their own separate church, the Remonstrant Brotherhood.

After the Synod of Dordt concluded, the official documents of the synod were gathered together and bound in seventeen folio volumes. These were kept in a large trunk, which was secured with eight locks. Each of the seven provinces and the States General were given keys. Once every three years, representatives from these eight bodies came to The Hague to open the trunk and check the state of the archives. Four hundred years later, the seventeen folio volumes are housed in the

Utrechts Archief.[46] Other Synod of Dordt documents are scattered in about twenty-five European archives. An international team of scholars is in the process of publishing, for the first time in four hundred years, all the documents of the synod.

---

46. See J. P. van Dooren, *Kisten en Kasten: 350 Jaar Kerkelijke Archiefdienst* (Den Haag: Persbureau Nederlands Hervormde Kerk, 1976).

CHAPTER 2

Procedural Wrangling in the Remonstrant Case at Dordt[1]

The Synod of Dordt, which met for six and a half months from mid-November 1618 to the end of May 1619, was convened primarily to settle the Arminian controversy that had agitated the Netherlands for about twenty years. The synod also considered other discipline cases and made decisions on a variety of other ecclesiastical matters.[2]

Although it was a national synod of the Dutch Reformed churches, it had a broad international character, since twenty-six Reformed theologians from eight foreign territories participated as full members

---

1. This article, slightly revised, is reprinted from *More than Luther: The Reformation and the Rise of Pluralism in Europe*, ed. Karla Boersma and Herman J. Selderhuis (Göttingen: Vandenhoeck and Ruprecht, 2019), 289–306.

2. The deliberations of the synod are reported in: *ADSND*, vol. 1; the letters of observer John Hales in his *Golden Remains* (London, 1673), 2:1–190; and the letters of the Hesse delegates, published in Heinrich Heppe, ed., "Historia Synodi Nationalis Dordracenae sive Literae delegatorum Hassiacorum de iis quae in Synodo Dordracena acta sunt ad Landgravium Mauritium missae," *Zeitschrift für die historische Theologie* 23 (1853): 226–327. Remonstrant reports of the synod are published in: [Bernardus Dwinglo], *Historisch Verhael van't ghene sich toeghedraeghen heeft binnen Dordrecht, in de Jaeren 1618 ende 1619* ([Amsterdam], 1623); [Caspar Barlaeus], "Epistolica Narratio eorum quae in Synodo Dordracena gesta sunt," in *Praestantium ac Eruditorum Virorum Epistolae Ecclesiasticae et Theologicae*, ed. C. Hartsoeker and P. van Limborch (Amsterdam, 1684), 513–27; and Geeraert Brandt, *Historie der Reformatie en andere Kerkelijke Geschiedenissen in en omtrent de Nederlanden* (Rotterdam: Barent Bos, 1704), vol. 3. Documents from the period of procedural debates are in vol. 2/2 of *ADSND* (Göttingen: Vandenhoeck and Ruprecht, 2018). Remonstrant documents submitted to the synod are published in *Acta et Scripta*.

of the synod. There were ten Dutch delegations, representing the provincial and particular synods, as well as five professors of theology from the various Dutch universities and academies. In addition, the Dutch government (the States General), which convened the synod, sent eighteen state delegates to supervise the proceedings and advise the synod, especially on matters of procedure.[3]

The Arminian, or Remonstrant, case was technically a case of doctrinal discipline, as the synod sought to examine and make a judgment about views of the Remonstrants concerning predestination and related points that were considered to deviate from the accepted doctrine of the Dutch Reformed churches.

In a sense, the outcome of the Remonstrant case was determined already in the political arena, when Prince Maurice of Orange, in the summer of 1618, disbanded the local militia in various Dutch cities and then replaced pro-Remonstrant political officials who supported the Advocate Oldenbarnevelt with officials who supported the Contra-Remonstrant, or orthodox Reformed, cause.[4]

Since the Contra-Remonstrants were dominant in the Dutch churches, the provincial synods sent to the Synod of Dordt only those sympathetic to the Contra-Remonstrant cause, except for Utrecht, which sent three Contra-Remonstrant and three Remonstrant delegates. In its early sessions, the synod summoned thirteen leading Remonstrants to have their views examined and judged. They chose Leiden theologian Simon Episcopius as their spokesman. When the Remonstrant case came up on the agenda, the two Utrecht Remonstrant ministers were pressured to join the cited Remonstrants.[5]

The general proceedings of the synod consisted of four phases: (1) In the Pro-Acta sessions, before the arrival of the Remonstrants, the synod spent three weeks discussing several non-doctrinal matters, including a new Dutch Bible translation, the manner of catechizing, and theological training. (2) During the five weeks after the Remonstrants arrived on 6 December 1618, until they were expelled from the synod on 14 January 1619, the Synod of Dordt was largely entangled

---

3. *ADSND*, 1:lxiii–cvii.

4. Jonathan I. Israel, *The Dutch Republic: Its Rise, Greatness, and Fall 1477–1806* (Oxford: Clarendon, 1998), 443–56.

5. *ADSND*, 1:36, 39–41; *Historisch Verhael*, 29r–31r.

in procedural debates with them. (3) After their expulsion, the synod took over three months to examine and prepare a judgment on the Remonstrant case—in the form of the Canons of Dordt. The synod also reviewed and approved the doctrine of the Belgic Confession and the Heidelberg Catechism and handled other discipline cases relating to four Remonstrant ministers of Kampen, the Geysteranus brothers, Johannes Maccovius, and Conrad Vorstius. (4) After this work was completed in early May and the foreign theologians returned home, in the Post-Acta sessions, the Dutch delegates discussed various matters of specific relevance to the Dutch churches, including a revised church order.

This article examines the course of the procedural debates in the second phase of the synod and casts light on the factors that led to the Remonstrant expulsion from the synod.

The Procedural Issues

A fundamental cause of the procedural debates lay in the fact that the two sides differently identified the central issue in the doctrinal controversy. For the Contra-Remonstrants, the issue was Remonstrant doctrinal deviation in their view of predestination and related points, especially in their view that God predestined people on the condition of foreseen faith. For the Remonstrants, the issue centered on extreme views of reprobation taught by certain Contra-Remonstrants and other Reformed theologians. Because the Remonstrants were not represented at the synod but were summoned before the synod to have their views judged, they were in a disadvantageous position. The synod, along with the state delegates, determined the agenda. In these circumstances, the Remonstrants made every attempt to have the reprobation issue placed on the agenda. They wanted to be assured that they would have full freedom to refute Contra-Remonstrant views of reprobation and that the synod would examine and declare its judgment on such views. This gave rise to much of the procedural contention.

When the Remonstrants arrived on 6 December, the first procedural issue to arise concerned the authority of the Synod of Dordt. Could the synod legitimately act as the judge of Remonstrant views? The Remonstrants pressed this point, because, as they saw it, the synod was composed of Contra-Remonstrants who were the adversarial party in the controversy, and they considered it manifestly unjust for one party in the dispute to act as the judge. Should not the synod function rather as a conference between equally represented parties and thereby seek an accommodated settlement of the dispute? For the synod, however, the crux of this issue was whether the church has the right to judge doctrinal views that deviate from the confessional standards of orthodoxy, in a case of ecclesiastical discipline.

After the authority question, the main procedural issues revolved around how the synod was to deal with the actual doctrinal questions in the controversy. Of these procedural issues, the most important were whether the Remonstrants would be allowed to refute Contra-Remonstrant views and whether they would be allowed to treat reprobation freely. This issue surfaced repeatedly in various forms.

Involved in many of these procedural debates were conflicting interpretations of the citation letters that summoned the Remonstrants. On 16 November, the synod and the state delegates each sent a letter citing thirteen leading Remonstrants to appear before the synod within fourteen days.[6] Both letters called for these Remonstrants to "state, explain, and, as much as they shall consider necessary, defend" their views of the Five Articles of the 1610 Remonstrance and asked them to submit any observations or doubts they had about the Heidelberg Catechism and the Belgic Confession. It is noteworthy that the citation letters of the state delegates mentioned the intention only to examine Remonstrant views, not to judge them. For this reason, the Remonstrants appealed more to this letter than to that of the synod. The letter from the synod specifically mentioned that the Remonstrant views would be examined and judged.

The Remonstrants repeatedly appealed to these letters as the basic documents that spelled out their obligations to the synod. These citation letters, however, lacked precision and did not address all possible procedural points that might arise. So, it was possible for the Remonstrants to interpret them differently than the synod on specific procedural points.

---

6. The letters of citation are in *ADSND*, 2/2:62–66.

Five categories of such procedural issues that surfaced throughout the debates with the Remonstrants may be identified: (1) Do the citation letters allow the Remonstants only to present their own views, or do they also allow the Remonstrants to refute opposing views? Does the reference to "defending" also include refuting? May the Remonstrants express their views not only in positive form but also in negative form? If also the latter, is refuting allowed only after or also during the presentation of their own views? May they refute only the Dutch Contra-Remonstrants, or may they also refute foreign theologians who hold the same views? (2) Do the citation letters allow the Remonstrants to deal not only with election but also with reprobation? Is the synod obligated to examine reprobation as well? Is reprobation to be treated before or after election? (3) How much freedom should the Remonstrants have to present their views and refute others? Specifically, does the phrase "as much as they shall consider necessary" refer only to defending, or does it also refer to stating and explaining? Who is to decide how much is necessary, the Remonstrants or the synod? Is their freedom unlimited, or must it be regulated by the synod in order to prevent deliberate abuse? Is this issue of freedom a matter of conscience, or is it only a matter of procedure and order? (4) Are the Remonstrant observations on the Catechism and the Confession to be submitted together with their views of the Five Articles, or are they to be submitted only after the Articles have been completely dealt with by the synod? Are the observations to be presented jointly or individually? Must the Remonstrants submit in writing not only their observations but also their views of the Five Articles, or may the Articles be discussed orally? (5) Must the examination of Remonstrant views be conducted only by way of questions, or may it also be conducted by way of a free presentation of their views? Which should come first, the questioning or the presenting of their views? Must the questions be answered orally or in writing? Must they be answered individually, or may the Remonstrants answer jointly as a body?

These were the main issues that entangled the synod in its five weeks of debates with the Remonstrants. Although both sides made some concessions, in the end they were unable to reach agreement on procedure.

Episcopius's Speech

On 7 December, Simon Episcopius delivered a long oration before the synod to clarify the motives and background of the Remonstrant position.[7] He asserted that they tried to publicly oppose detestable private beliefs about predestination that had given occasion to slanders against the Reformed churches. After the speech, President Bogerman asked Episcopius to hand in a copy of the speech, but Episcopius said that he had "no other copy" (according to many in the synod), or that he had "no other copy that was neatly enough written out [*satis nitide descriptum*]" (according to the Remonstrants). When it was discovered that Episcopius also had a rough draft of the speech, Bogerman accused him of lying for saying that he had no other copy. Episcopius bitterly denied the accusation.[8]

The Question of the Synod's Authority

When the Remonstrants first entered the synod on 6 December, the issue of its authority was already raised. When Episcopius stated that the Remonstrants were ready to have a conference (*collatio*) on the points in dispute, they were firmly reminded that the synod did not intend to hold a conference between equal parties; rather, they were summoned so that they might state, explain, and defend their view and await the synod's judgment.[9]

On 10 December, President Bogerman wanted to turn to the main issue of the synod, and he asked whether the Remonstrants were ready to state, explain, and defend their views on the Five Articles in writing.[10] But the Remonstrants wished to first read a paper that made two main points: First, the Remonstrants could not recognize the synod as their lawful judge, because most of its members were their confessed enemies, and because some of them were guilty of schisms. Second, they demanded that twelve conditions be met before they could recognize the synod. Their basic demands included the following: that both parties be equally represented; that the issues be judged by Scripture,

---

7. *ADSND*, 2/2:267–83.
8. *ADSND*, 1:38, 41–42, 50, 54–55; 2/2:284–86; *Historisch Verhael*, 28r, 31r–v, 49r, 52r–53v; Hales, 2:36–37, 49.
9. *ADSND*, 1:34–35; Hales, 2:29–30; *Historisch Verhael*, 12v–13r.
10. *ADSND*, 1:42; Hales, 2:36; *Historisch Verhael*, 31v.

not by the Confession or the Catechism; that a revision of these two confessions be considered; and that the synod seek accommodation, not decision. In other words, what the Remonstrants wanted was a conference between equal parties.[11]

This sparked a lengthy debate about the lawful jurisdiction of the synod. The conditions demanded by the Remonstrants were rejected, and they received a reprimand from the synod.[12] The state delegates also commanded them in a resolution to submit and proceed to the main issue without evasion.[13]

On 11 December, Episcopius presented a formal protest against the synod's reprimand and categorically rejected the authority of the synod as a legitimate judge of the controversy. However, the protest also stated that the Remonstrants were ready to proceed to the doctrinal matter, according to their conditions.[14]

The same day, the Remonstrants submitted a response to the state delegates' resolution directed against them. They promised obedience to political authority in all things not in conflict with their consciences and stated that they were ready to comply if certain conditions were met, much like the earlier twelve. Of note here is that the Remonstrants interpreted the reference to defending (in the citation letters) in a broad sense that included the refutation of opposing views.[15]

On 12 December, the synod considered the Remonstrant protest and, with the unanimous advice of the foreign delegates, declared it groundless.[16] The synod could not be denied its function as judge, because the practice of the church had always expected the faithful to oppose new opinions.[17] In the afternoon session, after much heated debate about whether they would submit, the Remonstrants presented a brief reply that expressed their willingness to cooperate according to the stipulations of the citation letters while reserving their judgment

---

11. *ADSND*, 1:42–43; 2/2:308–33.
12. *ADSND*, 1:43–48.
13. *ADSND*, 2/2:333–34.
14. *ADSND*, 1:48–49; 2/2:350–54; *Historisch Verhael*, 46v.
15. *ADSND*, 2/2:335–36.
16. *ADSND*, 2/2:359–417. The advice of the Dutch delegations was not read in the synod.
17. *ADSND*, 1:51–53.

against the synod as a lawful judge.[18] This was a slight capitulation on their part.

Bogerman then required that, on the next day, the Remonstrants present in writing their own views on Article I, concerning predestination, without refuting opposing views. Episcopius replied that the Remonstrants had always interpreted the citation letters to mean that the Five Articles would be treated in an oral conference and that only their observations on the Confession and the Catechism were to be presented in writing. This drew a rejoinder from the state delegates that the intention of the States General was to have the synod examine the written views of the Remonstrants, not to have an oral conference between two parties. When the Remonstrants complained that such a denial of their freedom to discuss orally and refute their opponents was too narrow an interpretation of the citation letters, they were assured that, after presenting their views in writing, they would be heard orally and that the matter of refuting would be considered after their views were treated. Finally, after much debate, the Remonstrants yielded and promised to present their views on Article I in writing the next day.[19]

The Remonstrant *Sententiae* on the Five Articles

The following day, 13 December, the Remonstrants submitted their *Sententia* on Article I in the form of ten theses.[20] Formally, at least, the Remonstrants offered the *Sententia* as the "statement" of their view, thus fulfilling the first of the three requirements—to state, explain, and defend—spelled out in the citation letters. In the theses, they took advantage of the occasion to focus especially on reprobation and to reject the Contra-Remonstrant position.

---

18. *ADSND*, 1:54–57; 2/2:356–57.
19. *ADSND*, 1:56–57; *Historisch Verhael*, 55r–v.
20. *ADSND*, 1:57; *Acta*, 1:113–14; *Acta et Scripta*, 1:71–73. A translation of the *Sententiae* is in Peter Y. De Jong, ed., *Crisis in the Reformed Churches: Essays in Commemoration of the Great Synod of Dort, 1618–1619* (Grand Rapids: Reformed Fellowship, 1968), 221–29.

The synod immediately complained that the *Sententia* stated what they did not believe and rejected the views of others more than it stated their own view.[21]

In the next session, the synod required the Remonstrants to submit their views on the other four Articles in dispute before beginning an examination of the issues, since the Five Articles were mutually connected. Bogerman added two admonitions: First, the Remonstrants must affirmatively present their own views rather than negatively oppose the views of others. If they wished to add a refutation of opposing views afterward, they might do so. Second, they must keep to the topic of election rather than odiously criticize the topic of reprobation. This topic could be treated afterward, as much as might be considered necessary.[22]

On 17 December, the Remonstrants submitted their *Sententiae* on Articles II–V. Like the Article I theses, these theses were both affirmative and negative in form. The Remonstrants appended to these *Sententiae* a number of reasons for expressing their views negatively and for treating the doctrine of reprobation. They listed fifteen reasons in defense of their right to negatively reject contrary doctrine, as well as seven reasons for treating not only election but also reprobation.[23]

It is apparent that the Remonstrants assumed Bogerman's admonitions to be more stringent than they actually were. Although the tone of the admonitions indicated a toughening of Bogerman's position, the admonitions were not a strict prohibition of refutation and of all treatment of reprobation. Bogerman had said that both would be permitted "afterward." But the Remonstrants only heard a prohibition of both.

In the conclusion to the *Sententiae*, the Remonstrants asserted that what distressed them most were the teachings of many Contra-Remonstrants on reprobation. These doctrines were injurious to God's honor and harmful to piety, and they had caused no small disturbances in the churches ever since the Reformation. The synod must publicly reject such doctrines.

---

21. *ADSND*, 1:57; *Historisch Verhael*, 57r; *ADSND*, 2/2:418–19.
22. *ADSND*, 1:58; *Historisch Verhael*, 57r–v.
23. *Acta*, 1:116–22; *Acta et Scripta*, 1:73–83; *ADSND*, 2/2:591–97.

Remonstrant Observations on the Confession and the Catechism

At the same session (17 December), Bogerman required each of the Remonstrants individually to produce their observations on the Belgic Confession and the Heidelberg Catechism. This sparked a new debate. The Remonstrants argued that the citation letters required that such observations be presented only after the Five Articles had been treated. In the end, the Remonstrants were given four days to present their observations.[24]

Meanwhile, during the 20 December session, Bogerman raised the issue of how the Remonstrants interpreted their citation letters. The synod decided that the phrase "as much as they shall judge necessary" in the citation letters referred only to the term "defend," not to "state" and "explain." Thus, the Remonstrants were to explain their views, not as much as they, but as much as the synod, would judge necessary. The Remonstrants bitterly regarded this interpretation as an attempt to restrain them from exercising their right to refute.[25]

On 21 December, the Remonstrants submitted their *Observations* (*Considerationes*) on the Belgic Confession, signed by all. In a preface, they insisted that they called into doubt no doctrine commonly accepted by the Reformed churches but only offered observations on matters of order and ways of speaking. Their intention was simply to present suggestions for confessional revision, not objections to the Confession that might be judged by the synod.[26] The Remonstrants were expected to have objections, especially to the Confession's article 16, which focused on election. But their brief observations dealt mainly with the interpretation of this article.

After the observations were submitted, the synod then reprimanded the Remonstrants for not presenting their observations on the Catechism at the same time and for presenting their observations on the Confession jointly rather than individually.[27] The state delegates also issued a resolution that the Remonstrants had not fulfilled the requirements regarding the Confession and the Catechism, and

---

24. *ADSND*, 1:60–61; *Historisch Verhael*, 62r–65v.
25. *ADSND*, 1:64; *Historisch Verhael*, 67v–68r.
26. *Acta et Scripta*, 1:83–102.
27. *Historisch Verhael*, 76v–77v.

they gave them until 27 December to submit their observations on the Catechism.[28]

After the Christmas adjournment, on 27 December the Remonstrants submitted their *Observations* on the Heidelberg Catechism. The main set of observations was jointly signed by Episcopius and seven other Remonstrants. Four others submitted individual observations. They were offered in the same spirit as the observations on the Confession, as suggestions for improvement in the review and revision of the Catechism.[29]

The Synod's 27 December Decision and the Remonstrant Reply

During the same session, President Bogerman informed the Remonstrants of the synod's decision that the liberty expressed in the citation letters' phrase "as far as you shall judge necessary" extended only to defending, and not to stating and explaining, their views. Bogerman asserted that it was the duty of the synod to examine Remonstrant views, not the views of others—which could possibly happen later— and therefore the Remonstrants should stick to their own view.[30] Episcopius answered that it was important to their consciences to refute the opposing view:

> We are not so much troubled with election, but the shoe pinches us above all in respect to that doctrine of reprobation which says God by an absolute and unconditioned decree reprobated the majority of mankind to eternal destruction.... This vexes us. Therefore, we must refute it.[31]

During the ensuing debate, Bogerman assured the Remonstrants that they would be allowed to refute opposing views after first presenting their own and that the synod would deal with reprobation, as much as it thought necessary, after election.[32] This indicates a slight softening in Bogerman's attitude, in contrast with the stern tone of his earlier admonitions. But his position remained basically the same:

---

28. *ADSND*, 1:66–67; 2/2:501–3.
29. *Acta et Scripta*, 1:102–33.
30. *ADSND*, 1:69–70; *Historisch Verhael*, 95v–96v.
31. Barlaeus, "Epistolica Narratio," 521.
32. Hesse, 264; Hales, 2:56; *Historisch Verhael*, 97v.

refuting and reprobation could be done later. These assurances did not satisfy the Remonstrants. They wanted full freedom to refute and treat reprobation.

At one point in the debate, the Remonstrant Philippus Pijnacker made the comment that, since the turmoil in the church arose from the issue of reprobation, it ought to be treated "in the first place." When Bogerman called this preposterous, Pijnacker tried to clarify his ambiguous comment by explaining that, by "first," he meant "especially" or "primarily."[33] Despite the explanation, the synod was left with the impression that the Remonstrants wanted reprobation discussed first.

Little progress was made because each side viewed the issue differently. The Remonstrants considered it a matter of conscience whether they would have the freedom to treat reprobation as much as they thought necessary. For Bogerman, the issue was simply a matter of order, whether reprobation would be treated before or after election.

The synod was left somewhat bewildered by the Remonstrant unwillingness to accept Bogerman's assurances about refuting and reprobation. Finally, to make its position clear to them, and to accommodate them as much as possible, the synod issued a decision, which declared that the synod decided to examine the Remonstrant view not only of election but also of reprobation, as much as it considered sufficient. As for the order, this was the prerogative of the synod to decide.[34]

This decision basically formalized Bogerman's earlier assurance regarding reprobation. But it did not mention refuting, and so it did not appear to grant to the Remonstrants any such freedom. It simply declared the synod's intention to examine the Remonstrant view of reprobation. To the Remonstrants, this was no concession; it even looked like a step back from Bogerman's assurances about refuting. What they wanted was the freedom to refute the Contra-Remonstrant view of reprobation. Besides, they thought that they, not the synod, should decide on the extent of such freedom.

The next morning (28 December), the Remonstrants submitted a long letter in response to the synod's decision. They felt that the decision restricted the freedom promised to them in the citation letters,

---

33. *Historisch Verhael*, 98r; Barlaeus, "Epistolica Narratio," 521.
34. *ADSND*, 1:70–71; 2/2:597–98; *Historisch Verhael*, 98v.

and so they reiterated their basic request that they be allowed, not only to state, explain, and defend their view of election as well as reprobation (here they did not want to argue about the order), but also to oppose the contrary view, in the manner that they should judge necessary. It was not sufficient that the synod allowed the Remonstrants to discuss their own view of reprobation as much as the synod itself thought necessary. This restriction deprived them of the freedom to fully defend their view and to oppose the contrary view.[35]

The Synod's Explanation of Its Decision

Now that the basic Remonstrant documents required by the citation letters had been submitted, it was thought necessary that the synod should orally examine the Remonstrants to get a fuller explanation of their views than was presented in their *Sententiae*, which were considered too negative and much too sketchy. This examination was to take the form of questions posed to the Remonstrants individually, so that each of them might give account of his own views. On this basis, it was hoped that the synod could make a better informed judgment.

Thus, on 28 December, Bogerman began to ask each Remonstrant the following question: "Do you still hold as your own view the Articles presented to the Hague Conference,[36] and especially the First Article?" This procedure of examination sparked a new set of debates about the validity of asking questions and the necessity of answering individually. The Remonstrants refused to answer this first question, most pleading that they could not proceed in good conscience without the freedom they requested.[37] At this point, the proceedings were locked in an impasse. The Remonstrants rejected the synod's decision and refused to answer questions without a guarantee of the freedom they sought.

In a closed session on 28 December, the synod then deliberated on how to proceed and whether some way of accommodation might be found. Though opinions varied—some thought the synod had already been too favorable to the Remonstrants, others thought they should

---

35. *ADSND*, 1:75–76; 2/2:600–607; *Acta et Scripta*, 1:134–39.
36. I.e., the Five Articles of the 1610 Remonstrance presented to the 1611 Hague Conference.
37. *Historisch Verhael*, 102r–104v; *ADSND*, 1:72–74; Hales, 2:59–61.

be granted all that they demanded, and others suggested a middle course[38]—the synod decided the next day to follow the third option: to supplement the decision by a further explanation, which declared that the synod had promised the Remonstrants that not only election but also reprobation would be treated immediately afterward, as much as the synod judged sufficient. Such freedom to treat reprobation had already been allowed by the synod's decision. But the decision had not mentioned that refuting would be allowed. The explanation conceded to the Remonstrants the freedom to refute—at least the views of Dutch Contra-Remonstrants, but not other Reformed theologians.[39] It is clear that the explanation softened the decision somewhat.

In the same session, the eight foreign delegations gave their advice about the equity of the synod's decision. All these delegations advised that the synod's decision was fair and ought to be obeyed and that election must be treated before reprobation. They repeatedly mentioned reasons for discussing election first.[40] These foreign recommendations are revealing, however, in their differing degrees of willingness to accommodate the Remonstrants. The English, Bremen, and Nassau-Wetteravia delegations were the most moderate. The most hostile advice was from the Palatine and Genevan delegations.

The Remonstrant 29 December Conditions

In the evening session of 29 December, the Remonstrants submitted a written reply to the synod's decision and explanation.[41] They asserted that they would fully explain and defend their view in writing—election first, and then reprobation—and refute the contrary view of the Contra-Remonstrants and of those they considered orthodox. Like the synod's explanation, this Remonstrant reply displayed a willingness to move a small step closer to the synod. Besides assuring the synod that the Remonstrants would treat election before reprobation, it made two concessions: (1) They were now willing to answer questions, though preferably in writing and only after presenting an explanation and defense of their own views; (2) Concerning the extent

---

38. Hales, 2:64.
39. *ADSND*, 1:77–79; 2/2:607–10.
40. *ADSND*, 1:80; 2/2:612–40.
41. *ADSND*, 2/2:610–11; *Acta et Scripta*, 1:143.

of their freedom, they promised not to misuse it and were willing to let the state delegates set reasonable time limits on their presentations.

Though somewhat conciliatory, this reply was by no means an unconditional submission to the synod's decision. The synod was not sensitive to the concessions that were made. It viewed the Remonstrant reply merely as a continuing refusal to submit except on their own conditions, rather than as a move toward accommodation in the procedural issue.

The various delegations then gave their advice on the Remonstrant reply. Most of the foreign and Dutch delegations expressed their weariness with the Remonstrant actions and advised that, if they would not submit, they should be dismissed from the synod and be judged from their writings.[42]

The Remonstrants were then asked to answer by a simple yes or no whether they would submit to the synod's decision. They answered that they adhered to their written reply.

The States General Resolution of 1 January

Since no progress could be made, the state delegates sent a delegation to the States General in The Hague to report on the obstinacy of the Remonstrants and to receive its direction.[43]

Meanwhile, the Remonstrants drew up a paper in which they argued that for the opposing party to prescribe to them their manner of defending truth and fighting error was not simply a matter of procedure but a matter of conscience.[44]

The delegation returned from The Hague with a resolution from the States General, dated 1 January 1619. It approved the decisions of the synod and the state delegates and commanded the Remonstrants to submit to them, or else face ecclesiastical and political censures. Should they continue in the same disobedience, the States General resolved that their opinions should be examined from their writings.[45]

At this point, on 3 January Bogerman again tried to examine the Remonstrants individually by asking them questions. The common

---

42. *Historisch Verhael*, 115v–116r; Barlaeus, "Epistolica Narratio," 523.
43. *ADSND*, 1:83; *Historisch Verhael*, 116v.
44. *ADSND*, 2/2:644–50; *Acta et Scripta*, 1:144–49.
45. *ADSND*, 1:84–87; 2/2:641–44.

Remonstrant reply was that they could not in conscience follow any procedure other than that indicated by their 29 December conditions.[46] Again the proceedings were locked in an impasse.

Bogerman's Questions and *Articuli* on the Remonstrant View
Caught in a deadlock with the Remonstrants, who refused to answer questions and submit unconditionally, the synod saw only one alternative: to begin implementing the States General's 1 January resolution to examine the Remonstrants from their writings, if they would not cooperate. So, in the evening of 3 January, Bogerman called together a committee of sixteen leading Dutch and foreign delegates, as well as six state delegates, for a private meeting to discuss how to implement the government's resolution.

This committee thought it advisable that the president, assessors, and secretaries extract the Remonstrant view from their writings, especially those written in their common name, and draw it up in a number of theses, with specific page references to sources. When approved by the synod, the theses would be read to the Remonstrants, and if they thought their view was not well understood, they could add a fuller explanation; but if they would remain silent, this would be taken as tacit approval.[47]

On 4 January, the procedure suggested the night before was proposed to the synod. Bogerman also proposed that, first, some questions be drawn up from their writings in order to better determine their view—he added that he had some already prepared—and that from these the theses could be formed. The synod approved this procedure.[48]

In the sessions of 5 and 7 January, Bogerman dictated to the synod the questions that he had prepared on Article I on the Remonstrant view of election.[49] They were examined by the Dutch professors, changed in some details, and approved by the synod.[50]

On 8 January, Bogerman dictated to the synod the *Theses* on Article I that he, with the help of the assessors and secretaries, had drawn

---
46. *ADSND*, 1:87–92; *Historisch Verhael*, 119, 122v; Hales, 2:68–69.
47. Hesse, 272; Hales, 2:70.
48. Hesse, 272; *ADSND*, 1:95–96.
49. *ADSND*, 1:96–97; 2/2:705–16.
50. *Historisch Verhael*, 129v.

up from the Remonstrant writings.⁵¹ Then, on 10 January, the various delegations began presenting their advice on the *Theses*. The majority agreed that the *Theses* fairly represented the Remonstrant view, but many advised certain changes or additions.⁵² In the evening session, Bogerman dictated some revisions to the Article I *Theses*, based on the suggestions offered by the delegations.⁵³ The final version was titled *Articuli* pertaining to a fuller explanation of the Remonstrant view.⁵⁴ The synod then decided to recall the Remonstrants and ask them whether the *Articuli* represented their view. But it was judged neither necessary nor advisable to give the Remonstrants a copy of the *Articuli*.⁵⁵ This denial to the Remonstrants of the synod's summary of their view can well be seen as very inconsiderate, even given their uncooperative attitude.

Opportunities for Compromise

The Remonstrants were recalled to the Friday morning session (11 January), after an absence of eight days. Bogerman wanted to try to examine them one more time. If the Remonstrants thought that the questions did not offer the opportunity for a full explanation of their view, he told them, they would be free to explain their position more fully afterward.⁵⁶

Then Bogerman began to pose a question to the Remonstrants from a prepared list.⁵⁷ Episcopius again refused to answer, and he replied instead by reading a paper that repeated their 29 December conditions. If the synod would allow them the freedom to explain and defend their views as much as they considered necessary, and to refute opposing views, then they were ready to answer a thousand questions

---

51. *ADSND*, 1:97; 2/2:717–23.
52. *ADSND*, 2/2:733–78.
53. *ADSND*, 2/2:779–81.
54. *ADSND*, 1:98; 2/2:781–91. The full title is "Articuli pertinentes ad Pleniorem Explicationem Sententiae Remonstrantium, circa Primum Hagiensem Articulum, Formati ex ipsorum Scriptis Editis, Declarationibus Authenticis, et Exhibitis Thesibus."
55. *ADSND*, 1:98–99.
56. *Historisch Verhael*, 131v.
57. *Historisch Verhael*, 132r; *ADSND*, 1:100.

either in writing or orally. Without this freedom, they saw no reason to answer questions.[58]

At this point, the debate about the extent of the freedom allowed to the Remonstrants flared up again. Now the specific issue was whether the Remonstrants should answer the questions before or after presenting their own explanations. The Remonstrants, who feared that their explanations would be confined within the limits of the questions, insisted that right order required their explanation first. Bogerman insisted that they first answer the questions, after which they might add a fuller explanation of what they thought was still lacking.[59]

Then Episcopius made a concession. The Remonstrants, he said, would not fight over a matter of order. If the freedom to explain, defend, and refute as much as they thought necessary were granted to them, they were ready to receive the list of questions immediately and answer in writing. They would incorporate their answers in their explanations, or add them, if the synod desired, and submit them together with their explanations.[60] The concession here was a willingness to go halfway and present their written answers together with, rather than after, their explanations.

Episcopius then asked for the list of questions, and many members of the synod indicated that they should be given. But Bogerman, supported by the state delegate Gregorius, refused, saying that it was not customary judicial procedure to hand written questions to cited persons. Bogerman then resumed the questioning, but the Remonstrants refused to answer.[61] The most promising opportunity thus far for a compromise solution to the procedural issue was now lost.

In the Friday evening session, the various delegations gave their advice on whether it was time to examine the Remonstrants from their writings outside of their presence. Many of the foreign delegations thought that the Remonstrants that morning seemed to move closer to the synod, and so most advised that the list of questions be given to them to be answered in writing. On the other hand, the Dutch

---

58. *ADSND*, 1:100; 2/2:729–31; *Acta et Scripta*, 1:153–54.
59. *Historisch Verhael*, 132r–135v; *ADSND*, 1:100–105; Barlaeus, "Epistolica Narratio," 525; Hesse, 275–76.
60. *Historisch Verhael*, 135v.
61. *Historisch Verhael*, 135v–136r; Barlaeus, "Epistolica Narratio," 525.

delegations advised that the Remonstrants be censured and that their views be examined from their writings, as the 1 January resolution of the States General had authorized.[62]

Since most of the delegates were Dutch, the synod decided by majority no longer to question the Remonstrants, but rather to examine their view of the Five Articles from their writings.[63] This decision was echoed by a resolution of the state delegates, which declared that the resolution of the States General was to be put into effect. However, until the following Monday they would still have the option to submit.[64]

On Saturday, 12 January, the state delegates summoned the Remonstrants privately to exhort them to reconsider their position and submit. After a heated debate, the Remonstrants repeated in writing the offer that Episcopius had made the day before—they were willing to add to their requested conditions that they were ready to answer questions on the Five Articles in writing and present them together with their explanations within a reasonable time. The state delegates said they could answer in writing or orally but made a slight concession that their answers could be presented together with their explanations. Now both sides were nearly on the same ground on the procedural question, but their mutual mistrust prevented any further accommodation or agreement. The state delegates gave them until Monday to reconsider.[65]

The Remonstrants Expelled

On Monday, 14 January, the state delegates reported to the synod on their meeting with the Remonstrants. They stated that their efforts had been in vain, since the Remonstrants still clung to their 29 December conditions. Nevertheless, they advised that the Remonstrants should be called in and commanded for the last time to submit.[66]

The assessors, secretaries, and foreign delegates were then asked to give their advice. They unanimously declared that no more

---

62. *ADSND*, 2/2:812–31; *Historisch Verhael*, 137; Hesse, 277.
63. *ADSND*, 1:106–7; *Historisch Verhael*, 137r.
64. *ADSND*, 1:107; 2/2:666–67.
65. *Historisch Verhael*, 138v–139v; *ADSND*, 1:485–88; Hesse, 278–79.
66. *ADSND*, 1:109–10.

freedom could be granted to the Remonstrants and that they should be dismissed.[67]

Without asking the Dutch delegates for advice, President Bogerman called in the Remonstrants and asked them to state categorically whether they would obey the States General and the synod or not.[68] Episcopius replied by submitting a long document that contained their *Explanation*, or *Declaratio*, on Article I, as well as a refutation of Contra-Remonstrant opinions on this Article buttressed with quotations from their writings.[69] Only the preface to this document was read. It affirmed that the Remonstrants could not in good conscience obey the synod's decrees. But it also asserted that the Remonstrants would not contend about procedure, provided the other conditions they asked for were met.[70]

Then, after asking the Remonstrants if they persisted in their position and being assured that they did, Bogerman expelled them from the synod in a passionate speech. He rehearsed the synod's dealings with the Remonstrants and accused them of great obstinacy, deceit, and lies. Finally, Bogerman exclaimed with great indignation, "Therefore, in the name of the state delegates and of the synod, you are dismissed. Get out [*Exite*]!"[71]

Bogerman's manner of dismissing the Remonstrants was certainly inexcusable, and it was offensive even to some members of the synod.[72] But the expulsion itself cannot be regarded as a decision made in a fit of anger. The synod had for some time considered it an option that the Remonstrants be examined and judged from their writings apart from their presence. The States General, in its 1 January resolution, had made the basic decision that the Remonstrants were to be judged from their writings if they would not submit. This government decision was merely put into effect by the 11 January decision of the synod and the resolution of the state delegates. The foreign delegations also advised dismissal on the day it occurred. Since the Remonstrants

---

67. *ADSND*, 1:110–11; *Historisch Verhael*, 139v–140r; Hales, 2:74–75.
68. *ADSND*, 1:111–12.
69. *Acta et Scripta*, 2:3–46.
70. *Acta et Scripta*, 1:156–57.
71. *ADSND*, 1:112–13; *Historisch Verhael*, 142r–143r; Hales, 2:76–77.
72. Hales, 2:78, 127.

remained unwilling to submit unconditionally, even though they had offered some concessions, their expulsion was almost inevitable, considering the atmosphere charged with mistrust and misunderstanding.

In the end, few procedural issues actually separated the two sides. After concessions on both sides, the only remaining differences were the following: (1) No agreement could be made on who would determine the extent of Remonstrant freedom: the synod or the Remonstrants. The synod wanted to retain the authority to set limits on such freedom in order to prevent Remonstrant abuse of it. The Remonstrants, on the other hand, feared that their freedom to defend and refute would be restricted if the synod set limits. Although they promised moderation and said that the state delegates could determine time limits, this did not satisfy the synod. (2) There was no agreement on whether the Remonstrants would be free to refute "orthodox" foreign theologians. The Remonstrants viewed the turmoil in the Dutch churches as caused by the foreign influence of men like Theodore Beza and Johann Piscator, and they wanted their extreme views checked. The synod and the foreign delegates, however, saw criticism of foreign theologians as an infringement upon the jurisdiction of foreign churches and countries over their own theologians.

The decisive factor that kept the two sides from further accommodation on procedure was their mutual mistrust and suspicion, which led to misunderstandings on both sides. Even when concessions were made, these were sometimes not recognized as such, or the motives were considered suspect. In this atmosphere, agreement was impossible.

Aftermath of the Expulsion

After the expulsion of the Remonstrants, the synod proceeded to examine their views from their writings. Since the state delegates required that they remain in Dordrecht, the Remonstrants continued to submit lengthy explanations and defenses of each of their Five Articles, most of which the synod read.[73] Meanwhile, a number of the theologians gave speeches on various aspects of the theological issues. In March, the nineteen Dutch and foreign delegations drew up

---

73. *Acta et Scripta*, 2:47–370; 3:1–349.

and presented their judgments (*iudicia*) on each of the Five Articles,[74] and, from these, a committee of the synod drafted a single judgment of the Remonstrant position.[75] Finally, after several drafts, on which the various delegations had the opportunity to suggest amendments, the synod approved the final version of the Canons of Dordt on 23 April.[76] In its "Rejection of Errors" sections, the Canons rejected the basic Remonstrant views on predestination and related points, and, in positive sections, they also spelled out the orthodox Reformed position. On 24 April, the synod issued a personal Sentence of the cited Remonstrants that deposed them from their ecclesiastical offices.[77]

---

74. *Acta*, 2:1–252; 3:1–292.

75. For the drafting process, see Donald Sinnema, "The Drafting of the Canons of Dordt: A Preliminary Survey of Early Drafts and Related Documents," in *Revisiting the Synod of Dordt (1618–1619)*, ed. Aza Goudriaan and Fred van Lieburg (Leiden: Brill, 2011), 291–311. An abbreviated version of this article is printed in this volume; see chapter 13.

76. A critical edition of the Canons is printed in J. N. Bakhuizen van den Brink, ed., *De Nederlandse Belijdenisgeschriften in Authentieke Teksten* (Amsterdam: Ton Bolland, 1976), 225–78.

77. *Acta*, 1:275–77.

CHAPTER 3

The Belgic Confession at the Synod of Dordt

Background: The Belgic Confession as a Confessional Standard and Early Editions

The Belgic Confession (BC) was the first doctrinal statement to function as a confessional standard in the early Dutch Reformed churches. It was written by Guido de Brès in 1561 with the purpose of instructing and comforting Reformed believers who were suffering under persecution and to convince Catholic authorities to tolerate the Reformed religion, since its adherents were not seditious rebels, like some Anabaptists, but law-abiding citizens loyal to the true gospel of Christ.

From the beginning, the BC was accepted by the Reformed churches of the Low Countries. De Brès wrote on behalf of the persecuted believers there, as is evident from the title of the original French edition, which states that it was made "with common consent" by believers dispersed throughout the Low Countries.[1]

Very early, the BC began to function as a confessional standard in these churches. At first, it served as a confessional witness to unity among the dispersed Reformed churches. A copy of the BC was simply

---

1. On the origin of the BC as a confessional standard and the development of forms of subscription, see Donald Sinnema, "The Origin of the Form of Subscription in the Dutch Reformed Tradition," *Calvin Theological Journal* 42 (2007): 256–82. On the background of the BC, see Nicolaas H. Gootjes, *The Belgic Confession: Its History and Sources* (Grand Rapids: Baker Academic, 2007), and Lyle Bierma and Donald Sinnema, "The Three Forms of Unity," in *The Oxford Handbook of Reformed Theology*, ed. Michael Allen and Scott R. Swain (Oxford: Oxford University Press, 2020), 236–41.

signed as an expression of this unity. Already in 1563, at the provincial synod of Armentieres (likely held at Antwerp), ministers, elders, and deacons were expected to "sign the Confession of faith agreed on among us." This implies that the BC was in some form adopted earlier.

The first national Synod of Emden (1571) decided that ministers should subscribe a copy of the BC as a sign of doctrinal unity. Within the next few years, this requirement began to be implemented among the churches within the Netherlands, and it was slowly extended to elders, deacons, and schoolteachers.

By the 1580s, the BC began to function not only as a witness to the unity of Dutch Reformed churches but also as a standard of orthodoxy in doctrine, as tensions arose within the churches between the strong Calvinist party and various Libertines. In the church order adopted by the national Synod of The Hague (1586), ministers and professors of theology were required to subscribe to the BC under threat of deposition if they refused.

Since simply signing a copy of the BC could be done according to one's own interpretation, forms of subscription were developed and required as a means of subscribing in order to specify what signing the BC meant. The first such form was developed by Classis Walcheren in Zeeland in 1574. After 1608, forms of subscription became more common in classes and provincial synods, as they attempted to preserve purity of doctrine in the context of the Arminian controversy.

The early history of the printings of the BC exhibits a significant diversity among its editions, with two main textual traditions. Already in 1561, the original de Brès text was published in French at Lyon as well as at Rouen. In 1562, it was reprinted in two editions. A Dutch translation of the original French appeared in Emden already in 1562, and this was reprinted several times: in [n.p.] 1563, [Emden] 1564, [Delft] 1566, Dordrecht 1578, Antwerp 1580, and [n.p.] 1613.[2]

---

2. On the history of the editions of the BC before Dordt, see W. Heijting, *De Catechismi en Confessies in de Nederlandse Reformatie tot 1585* (Nieuwkoop: De Graaf, 1989), 220–31; J. N. Bakhuizen van den Brink, ed., *De Nederlandse Belijdenisgeschriften in Authentieke Teksten* (Amsterdam: Ton Bolland, 1976), 11–27; F. Los, *Tekst en Toelichting van de Geloofsbelijdenis der Nederlandsche Hervormde Kerk* (Utrecht: Kemink, 1929), 1–77; Gootjes, *Belgic Confession*, 14–28, 161–77; and Lambregt van Langeraad, *Guido*

In May 1566, the French version of the BC was revised at the Synod of Antwerp. According to Gootjes's analysis, this was a significant revision that corrected numerous misprints, smoothed out Latinized sentence structures, abbreviated some parts of the text, made additions to others, and made some substantial corrections. On the whole, this revision improved the formulation of the text and provided greater clarity, with few substantial changes.[3]

This revision was published in [Geneva] 1566 and Anvers 1566. In 1580, an official manuscript copy from the Geneva edition was made for the Walloon churches, and it was used by ministers of these churches to subscribe to the BC from 1580 to 1668.

A new Dutch translation of the revised 1566 text, prepared by Arent Cornelisz, was published in Dordrecht in 1583. This translation was reprinted in Dordrecht 1591, Dordrecht 1593, Leiden 1607, Leiden 1609, Delft 1609, Delft 1610, and Delft 1613. Hermannus Faukelius, a minister of Middelburg, along with a Zeeland committee, edited what was called the *"Formulierenboek,"* published in Middelburg in 1611. This volume included two copies of the 1566 revised text of the BC in French (from the Walloon manuscript) and in Dutch (a somewhat revised version of the 1583 edition) on facing pages.[4]

In 1615, Antonius Thysius, a theologian at Harderwijk, published his *Leere ende Order*, which included copies of the Dutch text of both the original de Brès (from the 1563 edition) and the 1566 revision (from the 1583 edition) textual traditions.[5] In 1616, the *Historien der Vromer Martelaren* appeared at Dordrecht; under the year 1561, it included the Dutch translation of the original de Brès text of the BC.

The first Latin translation of the BC was included in the *Harmonia Confessionum Fidei*, assembled by Jean-Francois Salvart and

---

de Bray: zijn Leven en Werken (Zierikzee: Ochtman, 1884), 153–55. Van Langeraad lists several other editions that are not confirmed.

3. On the 1566 revision, see Gootjes, *Belgic Confession*, 97–99, 117–31.

4. *Belydenisse des Gheloofs der Kercken Iesu Christi inde Nederlanden nae de suyverheyt des Evangelij Ghereformeert* (Middelburg: Richard Schilders, 1611). For this 1611 edition, see H. H. Kuyper, *De Post-Acta of Nahandelingen van de Nationale Synode van Dordrecht in 1618 en 1619 Gehouden* (Amsterdam: Höveker & Wormser, [1899]), 350–52.

5. Antonius Thysius, *Leere ende Order der Nederlansche soo Duytsche als Walsche Ghereformeerder Kercken* (Amsterdam, 1615).

published in Geneva in 1581.[6] This translation followed the revised 1566 text. The *Harmonia* intended to show the harmony of Protestant confessions, including the BC, by listing together the articles of eleven confessions arranged topically under nineteen sections of doctrine.

The *Corpus et Syntagma Confessionum* (Geneva, 1612),[7] edited by Gaspar Laurentius, again offered a collection of Protestant confessions, with the intent to show their agreement with patristic doctrine, but this time each confession was published as a whole. The Latin translation of the BC is the same as that of the *Harmonia*.

A month before the opening of the Synod of Dordt, Festus Hommius published the *Specimen Controversiarum Belgicarum* (Leiden, 1618),[8] which presented a Latin translation of the 1566 version of the BC that was based on the *Harmonia* or *Syntagma* but revised in various places by Hommius. Within brackets, he included variant readings from the original version of the BC. Most articles are followed by quotations from Remonstrant sources to demonstrate that they deviated in many doctrines from the BC. For example, after article 16, on predestination, he listed quotations from Isaacus Welsingius, Jacobus Arminius, Simon Episcopius, the Hague Conference Remonstrants, Johannes Arnoldi Corvinus, Nicolaas Grevinchoven, and Adolphus Venator, which emphasized that God decreed to save believers based on foreseen faith. This work was intended for use at the synod, especially to introduce the foreign theologians to Remonstrant errors. Shortly after the synod opened, a Dutch translation of the *Specimen*, by Johannes à Lodensteyn, appeared under the title *Monster vande Nederlantsche Verschillen* (Leiden, 1618). Its translation of the BC was

---

6. *Harmonia Confessionum Fidei, Orthodoxarum et Reformatarum Ecclesiarum, quae in praecipuis quibusque Europae regnis, nationibus et provinciis, sacram Evangelii doctrinam pure profitentur* (Geneva, 1581). See Gootjes, *Belgic Confession*, 174–75.

7. *Corpus et Syntagma Confessionum Fidei, quae in diversis regnis et nationibus ecclesiarum nomine fuerunt authenticè editae in celeberrimis conventibus exhibitae publicaque auctoritate comprobatae* (Geneva, 1612). See Bakhuizen van den Brink, *Nederlandse Belijdenisgeschriften*, 25.

8. Festus Hommius, *Specimen Controversiarum Belgicarum, seu Confessio Ecclesiarum Reformatarum in Belgio, cuius singulis articulis subiuncti sunt articuli discrepantes, in quibus nonnulli ecclesiarum Belgicarum doctores hodie a recepta doctrina dissentire videntur* (Leiden, 1618).

based largely on the 1583 Dutch edition, with variants from the Dutch text of 1563 in brackets.⁹

The Remonstrant *Considerationes* on the Confession

For years before the Synod of Dordt, the Arminians had called for a revision (*revisie*) of the BC. Back in 1597, the States of Holland, led by Oldenbarnevelt, called on the States General to convene a national synod for the purpose of revising the BC. It was not until March 1606 that the States General agreed to call a national synod by approving an Act of Consent, which included a clause for the revision of the BC and the Heidelberg Catechism (HC).[10] A year later, a large majority of ministers at the Preparatory Convention, which gathered to make plans for a national synod, rejected the revision clause as the main purpose for a national synod, although a review could be a possible function of a synod.[11] Arminius, in his *Declaration of Sentiments* of 1608, supported the revision clause and provided a detailed argument for the need of a national synod to revise the BC and the HC. Arminius's main point was that confessions are fallible human writings, and so they should be regularly examined by the rule of Scripture to determine whether anything needs amendment.[12] After Arminius died, his followers drew up the 1610 Remonstrance, which also argued for a revision of the BC, since confessional writings must always be examined by God's Word to see if anything can be corrected or improved.[13] At the Hague Conference of 1611, the opponents of the Remonstrants argued against the need for a revision of the BC in their Counter-Remonstrance. While acknowledging that confessions, as human writings, do not have the same authority as Scripture, they insisted

---

9. On the *Specimen* and *Monster*, see Kuyper, *Post-Acta*, 345, 350; Gootjes, *Belgic Confession*, 139–42; and Bakhuizen van den Brink, *Nederlandse Belijdenisgeschriften*, 25–26.

10. On the political context of these discussions about revision, see Jan den Tex, *Oldenbarnevelt* (Cambridge: Cambridge University Press, 1973), 2:442–63.

11. D. J. de Groot, "De Conventus Praeparatorius van Mei 1607," *Nederlandsch Archief voor Kerkgeschiedenis* 27 (1934): 148–60.

12. Jacobus Arminius, "Declaration of Sentiments," in his *Works* (London, 1825), 1:637–66.

13. G. J. Hoenderdaal, "Remonstrantie en Contraremonstrantie," *Nederlands Archief voor Kerkgeschiedenis* 51, no. 1 (1970): 66–72.

that it was highly necessary, for the unity of the church concerning the right understanding of God's Word, that there be common forms of unity in doctrine, which all ministers should sign.[14]

When the Remonstrant leaders were summoned to appear before the Synod of Dordt to have their views examined, they were required to present in writing their views, not only on the controversial Five Articles, but also on the BC and the HC. Their letters of citation, sent out on 16 November 1618, specified the following:

> At the same time, they should also submit in writing to this synod all their Observations [*Considerationes*], if they have any, about the doctrine contained in the Confession and Catechism of these churches, and reasons for these observations, in order that the synod, having heard and considered everything, may more maturely be able to judge particular points in the fear of the Lord.[15]

In December, after the cited Remonstrants submitted their brief *Sententiae* on the Five Articles, President Bogerman demanded that they submit their observations on the BC and the HC. These they submitted on 21 December, signed by all.[16] In a preface, they insisted that they called into doubt no doctrine commonly accepted by the Reformed churches but only presented observations to be weighed carefully (*Considerationes perpendendas*) on matters of "phraseology, order or such ways of speaking [*vel phrasin spectent, vel ordinem, vel tales loquendi modos*] that can be taken in a worse manner, so that they appear to hinder piety." They suggested that these observations might be taken into account when the synod considered a review and revision of the BC.[17] All their observations were in question form, so that the Remonstrants avoided presenting their own opinion on matters where they had objections. It is evident that the Remonstrant intention was to present suggestions for confessional revision, not to present objections to the BC that might be judged by the synod.

This document began with general observations, consisting of thirteen questions. Then followed special observations, which included

---

14. Hoenderdaal, "Remonstrantie," 80–83.
15. *ADSND*, 1:15.
16. Printed in *Acta et Scripta*, 1:83–99.
17. *Acta et Scripta*, 1:83–86.

124 questions on thirty-one of the thirty-seven articles of the BC. Many of the observations are relatively insignificant. Some deal with the proper formulation of an article. Several focus on important doctrines, such as providence (art. 13), the imputation of Christ's merits (art. 22), and the difference between the Old and New Testaments (art. 25). And several touch on debated issues between the Remonstrants and the Reformed, such as human depravity (art. 14), election (art. 16), and the role of government in the church (art. 36).[18]

A good example of the Remonstrant approach was their observations on article 16, concerning the doctrine of election. The Remonstrants were expected to have objections especially to this article, but they offered only two observations, which dealt mainly with the interpretation of the article:

> 1. Since those words, "in liberating and saving those whom he, in his eternal counsel, has elected by his gracious goodness in Jesus Christ our Lord," can be and are taken in different ways—either so that particular persons as such are understood, or so that particular persons indeed are understood but clothed with faith [*fide circumscriptae*]—we ask in which sense ought the Confession be understood, and does not the latter sense agree more with the Confession?
>
> 2. Does the title agree with the content of the article? The title speaks of Election; the article itself speaks of its execution.[19]

Without stating an outright objection, the first question points to the Remonstrant view, with the suggestion that article 16 should be understood in the sense of the election of *believers*. This simply followed Arminius's interpretation of this article,[20] and it reflects the basic Remonstrant view that election is based on faith foreseen by God.

After the Remonstrant *Observations* were submitted, the synod did not spend time discussing their content. President Bogerman reprimanded the Remonstrants for not submitting their observations on the HC at the same time and for presenting their observations on the BC jointly, rather than individually. He also asked if these observations

---

18. See more extensive analysis in Gootjes, *Belgic Confession*, 142–48.
19. *Acta et Scripta*, 1:92–93.
20. Arminius, "Declaration of Sentiments," 1:590.

were the same as those that the Remonstrants had handed in to the States of Holland in 1608. Their answer was that these observations were the same but that some points had been altered and some new points added.[21]

Although the Remonstrant *Observations* on the BC were not discussed in the synod, their suggestions were taken into account during the Post-Acta sessions, when a committee worked on preparing a uniform text of the BC.

How an Examination of the Belgic Confession was Placed on the Synod's Agenda

The Synod of Dordt assumed that the BC (and the HC) had confessional status in the Reformed churches of the Netherlands. Thus the synod did not consider itself obligated to officially adopt the BC or the HC. The adoption of a confessional standard was not part of the synod's mandate from the States General (the Articles to Convene).[22] And it was not found in the letters inviting the delegates to the synod.

The Remonstrants had long contended that, since the BC and the HC are fallible human documents, it is the task of every national synod to examine whether they conformed to God's Word and, if necessary, to revise them. Most delegates of the Synod of Dordt rejected this notion for fear of creating uncertainty in the churches by having the confessions repeatedly subject to examination and revision. Besides, most delegates were convinced that the confessions, though human, were in accord with Scripture and therefore needed no such periodic examination. With this mood prevailing, the synod clearly was not inclined to add an examination (and possible revision) of the confessions to its agenda.

Nevertheless, the matter of examining the confessions was unexpectedly placed on the agenda late in the proceedings of the synod after the Canons had been drafted and approved. This was initiated not by the synod itself but by the States General, which made the following resolution on 27 April 1619:

---

21. *ADSND*, 1:65–67.
22. *Acta*, 1:15–18.

Concerning the Netherlands [Belgic] Confession and Catechism, the same shall be read in the whole synod, and after the reading, the foreign and Dutch theologians shall be asked whether they have also observed anything in doctrinal matters [*Doctrinalibus*] that conflicts with God's Word, or with the unity of the Reformed churches.[23]

It is clear that this was a call for an examination of the BC and the HC only on doctrinal matters, not on the specific wording of the text.

Why did the States General unexpectedly bring up this matter? Its intention was not to have the confessions revised, but rather to confirm the authority of the confessions, in face of Remonstrant criticisms of them, by a broad public affirmation of their doctrinal orthodoxy by both Dutch and foreign delegates at the synod. This is evident in a statement by Martinus Gregorii, spokesman for the state delegates, in which he informed the synod concerning the States General resolution that "they [the States General] indeed do not have doubts about the truth of such [the BC and the HC], but nevertheless great weight would be added to them, if they would be confirmed by the unanimous approval of all [*communibus omnium calculis confirmetur*]."[24] Also, by soliciting the approval of the foreign theologians and an affirmation of the agreement of the BC and the HC with the confessions of other Reformed churches, it appears that the States General sought a broad doctrinal consensus to strengthen a bond of unity between the Netherlands and other Reformed territories, especially against Rome.[25]

Thereafter, the synod's actions regarding the BC mainly consisted of two phases: (1) an examination of whether the doctrinal content of the BC was in accord with Scripture and other Reformed confessions; and (2) the preparation of a uniform text of the BC in French, Dutch, and Latin.

---

23. States General resolution, 27 April 1619; in The Hague, Nationaal Archief, Archives States General, 1.01.02, nr. 3178; cited in Kuyper, *Post-Acta*, 323.

24. Theodore Heyngius, "Acta Synodi Nationalis breviter conscripta"; MS of his journal at the Bibliotheek der Rijksuniversiteit Utrecht, MS 457, 150; cited in Kuyper, *Post-Acta*, 324.

25. Abraham Kuyper, *Revisie der Revisie-Legende* (Amsterdam: J. H. Kruyt, 1879), 125.

Examination of Doctrinal Content

SESSION 144, 29 April 1619, afternoon

Martinus Gregorii, on behalf of the state delegates, informed the synod of the States General resolution. According to the *Acta Authentica*, he stated that it was the will of the States General

> that the Confession of Faith of the Dutch Reformed churches, according to the custom followed in national synods, be reread and examined with the foreign theologians present, and that individual members of the synod, both foreign and provincial, freely declare if they observe anything in that Confession, in respect to dogmas and the substance of doctrine [*dogmata et substantiam doctrinae*], which seems to them does not agree with the truth revealed in God's Word or the confessions of other Reformed churches. Whatever has regard to method or phraseology [*methodum aut phraseologiam*] and whatever pertains to the polity and order [*regimen atque ordinem*] of the church, that is to be examined more thoroughly afterwards only by the provincial members.[26]

Concerning these directives from the States General, it is to be noted that: (a) Only the doctrinal content (*dogmata et substantiam doctrinae*) was to be examined, in order to determine whether it agreed with Scripture and with other Reformed confessions. (b) Precise textual matters (*methodum aut phrasiologiam*) were not to be dealt with at this time; instead, they were to be taken up later by the Dutch delegates alone in the Post-Acta sessions. (c) Likewise, points in the BC concerning church polity were not to be considered. Obviously, this matter was to be omitted to avoid confrontation with the English delegates who supported the episcopal system of the Church of England rather than the presbyterial perspective of the BC.

President Bogerman added that the whole BC would be read but that articles 30–32 (regarding church government) were to be left out of the discussion. He also advised the delegates not to attend to the text (*latinitate aut phraseologia*), but only to the doctrinal content.[27]

---

26. *ADSND*, 1:147–48. The *Acta Authentica* are the official acts of the Synod of Dordt; the Latin and Dutch *Acta*, published in 1620 and 1621, are a somewhat revised version.

27. Kuyper, *Post-Acta*, 325–26.

Before the BC was read, the question arose regarding which edition was to be considered authentic, since its editions frequently differed. The synod decided that the Latin *Syntagma* edition of 1612 should be read and examined.[28] The *Syntagma* edition of the BC was a Latin translation of the 1566 revised text.

Why was this *Syntagma* edition chosen for the reading and examination of the BC? It was in Latin, the language of the synod for as long as the foreign delegates were present. It was the best known international edition.[29] It contained a collection of Reformed confessions, and it was printed in Geneva. Because the *Syntagma* was published in 1612, it was likely more readily available to delegates at the synod. As a one-volume collection of thirteen Protestant confessions, the *Syntagma* was a handy source for comparing the BC with other Reformed confessions. In the *Syntagma*, the confessions were printed as a whole, whereas, in the earlier *Harmonia Confessionum* (1581), the articles of the various confessions were arranged together by topic, making it less convenient to use. These very practical reasons sufficiently explain the choice. There is no evidence to suggest a deliberate decision in favor of the *Syntagma* because it contained the 1566 revised version of the BC. The primary sources indicate no discussion on this point. The original de Brès version was simply not available in a Latin translation. Even though Hommius's Latin edition in his *Specimen* of 1618 included in brackets phrases of the de Brès version that were dropped in 1566, it would not have been appropriate to use the *Specimen*, since it was a private edition, and this work lay under some suspicion due to criticism, especially from the Remonstrants.

At this point, it may be asked, how aware was the synod of the difference between the editions that followed the de Brès version and those that followed the 1566 revision? The synod was clearly aware of discrepancies among the various editions in the various languages. The lack of a uniform text was long regarded as a problem. Although

---

28. Balcanqual, 2:160; Heyngius, "Acta," 149; Gisbertus Voetius, *Politicae Ecclesiasticae Pars Tertia & Ultima* (Amsterdam, 1676), 4:60. Cf. Kuyper, *Post-Acta*, 326. The details in Voetius's *Politica Ecclesiastica* are based on his recollection and on his journal, a firsthand account that is now lost.

29. Heyngius, "Acta," 149: "*utpote orbi Christiano notissimum*"; cited in Kuyper, *Post-Acta*, 326.

the original de Brès version had been forgotten in some quarters in the later sixteenth century (for example, the 1581 *Harmonia Confessionum* assumed that the BC first appeared in 1566), it may also be assumed that most delegates were aware of a difference between the de Brès version and the revision. There are a couple lines of evidence: (a) Antonius Thysius, in his *Leere ende Order* (1615), reproduced side by side the Dutch translations of 1563 and of 1583 (the latter based on the 1566 revision). This work was certainly known at the synod, and Thysius himself was a prominent delegate and a member of the committee to prepare a uniform text. (b) Hommius, in his *Specimen* (1618), included a Latin edition largely based on the *Harmonia* or the *Syntagma*, but additional phrases found in the de Brès version are included in brackets. In his forward, Hommius specifically referred to differences between earlier and later editions: "I have compared the Confession with the oldest French and Dutch editions, and if anything in the later editions was found to be omitted which appeared in the earlier editions, I here and there added those words in brackets, inserted to mark the distinction, for the sake of those who do not have the leisure to compare those diverse editions."[30] These words also indicate that Hommius's very intention was to remind the synod of differences between the two textual traditions. The *Specimen* was well known at the synod, since it was composed specifically for the synod's use, and copies of it had been sent to the foreign delegates. Hommius was also a leading delegate and a member of the committee to prepare a uniform text.

But, even assuming an awareness of the existence of the two versions, it cannot be determined how aware the delegates were of the precise differences between the two. Nevertheless, it is safe to assume that most delegates saw a difference only in wording, not in doctrinal content. For example, the Amsterdam delegate Heyngius reported (concerning session 155) that the synod appointed a committee to prepare a uniform text because the BC "is printed in some words diverse, although the same in substance."[31] The same sentiment had

---

30. Hommius, *Specimen*, "Ad Lectorem."
31. Heyngius, "Acta," 198; cited in Kuyper, *Post-Acta*, 338.

The Belgic Confession at the Synod of Dordt 63

been expressed at the South Holland Synod of 1606 and by Thysius in his *Leere ende Order* (1615).[32]

The BC (*Syntagma* ed.) was read in this session (except for arts. 30–32), and the various delegations were asked to examine the BC carefully and declare the next morning whether they found anything in the doctrine of the BC that did not agree with God's Word and that, therefore, must necessarily be changed.[33]

SESSION 145, 30 April, morning
The English delegates, the first to speak, declared that they had diligently examined the BC and that they had found nothing in it, regarding doctrine, which did not agree with the Word of God, even considering the Remonstrant *Observations* that they had examined. They said that they did observe some more minute points but that these could easily be amended in a new corrected edition prepared from compared copies.[34]

The previous evening, the British delegation had decided that Bishop Carleton, the head of their delegation, should also declare, in a temperate manner, their objections to the presbyterial system of church government found in articles 30–32—although debate on this was forbidden. In the morning session, Carleton did so and defended the episcopal system of the Church of England as the true apostolic form. He particularly objected to the idea that Christ instituted an equality among ministers:

> Therein he professed and declared our utter dissent in that point, and further shewed that by our Saviour a paritie of ministers was never instituted, that Christ ordained twelve Apostles and seventy disciples; that the authoritie of the twelve was above the other; that the Church preserved this order left by our Saviour. And therefore when the extraordinary authoritie of the Apostles ceased, yet their ordinarie authoritie continued in bishops, who succeeded them, who were by the Apostles themselves left in the government of the Church to ordaine ministers, and to see that they who were so ordained should preach no other doctrine; that in an inferiour

---

32. Kuyper, *Post-Acta*, 336; Thysius, *Leere ende Order*, Voorreden.
33. *ADSND*, 1:148.
34. *ADSND*, 1:148; Balcanqual, 2:161.

degree the ministers, that were governed by bishops, succeeded the 70 disciples; that this order hath bin maintained in the Church from the time of the Apostles. And herein he appealed to the judgement of Antiquity, or of any learned man now living, if any could speak to the contrary.[35]

This speech drew no response from the synod. Other English delegates, including John Davenant and Thomas Goad, also expressed approval of the BC, with the exception of articles 30–32. Samuel Ward and Davenant pointed out the omission of some words in article 22 of the BC in the Latin *Syntagma* edition—"and so many holy works that he has done for us"—and they advised that these be retained.[36]

SESSION 146, 30 April, afternoon
In turn, the other delegations—the foreign, and then the Dutch—expressed their judgments concerning the doctrinal content of the BC.

In their judgments, all remaining delegations declared that no doctrine contained in the BC conflicted with the truth expressed in Scripture and that all its doctrines agreed with this same truth and with the confessions of other Reformed churches. The foreign theologians strongly urged the Dutch to resolutely persevere in this orthodox confession of faith.[37]

The Hesse, Swiss, and Nassau delegations also requested that, on account of the variety of editions, some exact copy should be made and confirmed by the authority of the States General. The Basel delegates expressed the same concern as the British for retaining the omitted words in article 22.[38]

---

35. This summary of Carleton's speech is found in *A Ioynt Attestation, avowing that the Discipline of the Church of England was not impeached by the Synode of Dort* (London: M. Flesher, 1626), 10–11. This *Attestation* was written by the members of the British delegation in response to Richard Montagu's *Appello Caesarem* (London, 1625), which alleged that the Synod of Dordt condemned even the discipline of the Church of England. A similar report of Carleton's speech is found in the British delegation's weekly report to King James I. Printed in John Davenant, *An Exposition of the Epistle of Paul to the Colossians* (London: Hamilton, Adams and Co., 1831), xxvii. See also Balcanqual, 2:161; Voetius, *Politica Ecclesiastica*, 4:60; Kuyper, *Post-Acta*, 327.
36. Voetius, *Politica Ecclesiastica*, 4:60–61. Cf. Kuyper, *Post-Acta*, 328.
37. *ADSND*, 1:149.
38. Balcanqual, 161.

When it was the Genevan delegation's turn to speak, they submitted some written observations, which expressed approval of the BC, but added suggestions for amendments to ten articles that they said would remove even the mildest blemishes in the text.[39] At the same time, they asked that "that blot [*macula*] be wiped away, by which Genevans were marked today [*hodie*], as if the Confession was printed in bad faith [*mala fide*], and that this blame not fall on the republic."[40]

To what does this reference to a "blot" refer? It is most natural to view this as a reference to the criticism of Geneva for the omission of the words "and so many holy works that he has done for us" from article 22 of the BC in the 1612 *Syntagma*, which had been printed in Geneva. In particular, the mention of "today" supports this interpretation, because the omitted words had only been pointed out earlier that same day. This omission was a point of contention, because it allowed room for the controversial views of the German Reformed theologian Johann Piscator, who denied the imputation of Christ's active obedience to the law throughout His life as part of His redemptive work for human salvation.[41] Thus, the Genevan remark may be regarded as a response to the English or Basel delegates who, on that day, had just pointed out this omission in the *Syntagma* edition and had apparently

---

39. The "Suffragium Genevensium de Confessione Belgica" is printed in Nicolas Fornerod, ed., *Registres de la Compagnie des Pasteurs de Genève*, Tome XIV, *1618–1619* (Geneva: Droz, 2012), 458–61. The amendment suggestions relate to articles 1, 2, 8, 9, 13, 14, 16, 19, 35, and 36.

40. Sibelius, 112r; cited in Kuyper, *Post-Acta*, 329.

41. Piscator taught that justification was based only on the imputation of Christ's passive obedience in his suffering and death on the cross. On Piscator's denial of the imputation of Christ's active obedience, see Heber Carlos de Campos Jr., *Doctrine in Development: Johannes Piscator and Debates over Christ's Active Obedience* (Grand Rapids: Reformation Heritage Books, 2017), especially 26–27. Actually, the *Syntagma* of 1612 (p. 174) simply reprinted the Latin text of article 22 from the 1581 *Harmonia Confessionum* (p. 185), which was also printed in Geneva. The unexplained omission of these words in the *Harmonia* edition cannot have been related to Piscator's view, since his denial of the imputation of Christ's active obedience had not yet become public in 1581 (see Campos, *Doctrine*, 20). Nevertheless, the omission of the same words in the *Syntagma* of 1612 did allow room for Piscator's view, which by then had been debated for some twenty-five years; apparently, this is what raised the issue of the "blot" at Dordt.

blamed Geneva for it. The "blot" was not intended as a reference to the revised edition printed at Geneva in 1566.[42]

The Dutch delegations also requested the state delegates, in the name of the Dutch churches, to intercede with the States General, that it might be pleased to guard and establish (*tueri et stabilire*) the BC's orthodox doctrine, protected by its authority, in the Dutch churches.[43]

In its judgment, the Walloon delegation mentioned that the French National Synod of Vitré of 1583 had approved (*approbatam*) the BC.[44] They also pointed out that their Walloon churches had an "*exemplar exactissimum*" of the BC, which they were prepared to show, if need be.[45] It is almost certain that this "most exact copy" refers to the 1580 Walloon manuscript edition, which had been copied from the 1566 revised Geneva edition.

After the various delegations had given their judgments, President Bogerman concluded that the BC was approved by the venerable synod by unanimous consent (*unanimi consensus*). He also promised that an authentic text would be established in later sessions, one that would be determined from the oldest copies (*ex vetustissimis exemplaribus*) in cases where there were different readings.[46] With this, the first phase of the synod's actions ended.

Regarding this first phase, the following conclusions may be drawn:

1. Only the doctrine, not the text, of the BC was examined and approved by the various delegations.

2. Many at the synod expressed the need for a uniform text, and it was expected that such would be prepared in the Post-Acta sessions.

3. Although all delegations expressed approval of the doctrine contained in the BC, this approval did not include articles

---

42. Leonard Verduin argued that the "blot" referred to the blame put on Geneva for printing the revised text of the BC in 1566 (*Acts of Synod 1983* of the Christian Reformed Church, 399), but there is no evidence in the sources for this interpretation.
43. *ADSND*, 1:149.
44. *ADSND*, 1:149.
45. Sibelius, "Annotationes," 112v; cited by Kuyper, *Post-Acta*, 329.
46. Sibelius, "Annotationes," 112v; cf. Kuyper, *Post-Acta*, 330.

30–32 on church government. These articles were specifically omitted from the examination. Besides, the English delegation expressed clear disapproval of them.

4. After all nineteen delegations had declared their approval, Bogerman drew the conclusion that the BC was approved by the synod by unanimous consent. At this point, no official formula or statement of approval was drawn up.

5. What is the nature of the "approval" by the various delegations? It was simply a declaration that the doctrinal content of the BC (excluding articles 30–32) was in agreement with Scripture and other Reformed confessions. As a result, no doctrinal revision of the BC was necessary. This is not the same as an official *adoption* of the BC by the synod as a confessional standard of the Dutch churches. It was simply a *reaffirmation* of the doctrinal purity and orthodoxy of the BC. The unanimous and international character of that reaffirmation gave it the weight the States General sought.

6. All events relating to this first stage—from the unexpected placing of the matter on the agenda to Bogerman's conclusion about unanimous approval—happened in three sessions, between late Monday afternoon, 29 April, and Tuesday afternoon, 30 April—a period of no more than twenty-six hours. Since the delegations had to be ready to declare their judgments by 9 a.m. on Tuesday, they had no more than one evening to examine the BC in light of the Scriptures and other Reformed confessions. This was a hasty examination at best.

SESSION 153, 6 May, morning
In the ceremonious public session held in the Grote Kerk in Dordrecht, the Canons of Dordt were officially promulgated to the world. During this ceremony, after the Canons were read, Bogerman publicly declared that the doctrine in the BC and the HC had been read and examined in the synod and unanimously approved (*consentientibus*

omnium…approbatam) as orthodox and in agreement with the Word of God.⁴⁷

Although the term *approbatam* is used, this cannot be interpreted as an official adoption of the BC. In this ceremony, Bogerman simply made a public announcement, declaring the same conclusion—concerning the unanimous approval of the doctrine by all delegations—that he had stated at the end of session 146.

On 7 May, the States General received a report from the state delegates (dated 2 May), that the BC and the HC had been approved (*geapprobeert*), after a proper review and reading (*behoorlycke revisie ende lecture*), "with an agreement and harmony heard not without great fruit by all sincere friends of the true Reformed churches, and the common good of our Fatherland."⁴⁸

Preparation of a Uniform Text

The task of preparing a uniform text of the BC was taken up by the Dutch delegates in the first of the Post-Acta sessions (session 155), after the foreign theologians had departed. This matter was placed on the agenda because the state delegates had so directed in session 144, but also because it had been specifically requested by some of the delegations in their earlier judgments (in sessions 145 and 146). The need for a uniform text was a common concern.

Session 155, 13 May, morning

According to the *Acta Authentica*, the synod decided that Latin, French, and Dutch copies of the BC were to be compared—since a certain variety in some words was found in all editions—so that, from all the editions, one version might be formed in the three languages. Thereafter, this version would be considered the authentic one (*pro authentico*). In this comparison, special attention was to be paid to the copy that, until then, was considered authentic in the Walloon

---

47. *ADSND*, 1:155. Balcanqual, 2:166, also mentions full approval, but he uses the term *comprobatas*.

48. State delegates report to the States General, 2 May, received 7 May; in The Hague, Nationaal Archief, Archives States General, 1.01.02, nr. 3178; cited in Kuyper, *Post-Acta*, 332.

churches.[49] According to Heyngius's account of this session, the synod mandated its committee to compare the "oldest and principal copies… leaving the oldest copy (*oudste exemplaer*), as much as possible, in its entirety, and from that, doing the necessary modifications."[50]

For this task, a five-man committee—including Antonius Thysius, Hermannus Faukelius, Festus Hommius, Daniel Colonius, and Godefridus Udemans—was chosen.[51] The first three had been involved in preparing previous editions of the BC, and Colonius, a Walloon, was obviously chosen to work on the French edition.

Note that, in preparing a uniform text, the committee was to compare all editions in the three languages, that is, editions of both the original de Brès and the 1566 revision textual traditions. Preference was to be given to the oldest and most important editions. But the committee was to pay attention especially (*imprimis attendendum esse*) to the copy considered authentic by the Walloon churches, that is, the "*exemplar exactissimum*" that the Walloon delegation mentioned in session 146; in other words, the 1580 Walloon manuscript. Thus, this manuscript of the 1566 revision textual tradition was to serve as the most important source on which to base the comparison.

Heyngius's reference to using the "*oudste exemplaer*" as the basis for comparison would seem to refer to the original de Brès edition of 1561, but this does not square with the *Acta Authentica*, which mentions a preference for the 1580 Walloon manuscript. The reading of the *Acta Authentica*, as the more official document, must be preferred. Nevertheless, Heyngius is probably correct in describing the recommended procedure as that of making changes on one preferred edition. If this is true, it can be said that the 1580 Walloon manuscript was to serve as the basis for comparison.

Why was the 1580 Walloon manuscript given such a fundamental role? The primary sources on the synod do not indicate details of any discussion on this point, but it is not difficult to surmise the reasons. This manuscript was to be given special attention because:

---

49. *ADSND*, 1:156.
50. Heyngius, "Acta," 198; cited in Kuyper, *Post-Acta*, 338.
51. *ADSND*, 1:156.

1. By long usage, it served as the official edition for the Walloon churches, an important segment of the Reformed churches in the Netherlands; it had been subscribed by office-bearers in their synods since 1580. Thus, the *Acta Authentica* speaks of it as the copy considered "authentic" in the Walloon churches. The Dutch-speaking churches, on the other hand, did not consistently use a single edition for official use. That is why they especially felt the need for a uniform edition. Therefore, the 1580 Walloon manuscript was the only text that enjoyed longstanding official ecclesiastical recognition in the Netherlands.

2. Besides, in session 146, the Walloon delegation had specifically offered this "most exact" manuscript to the synod for its usage. By "*exactissimum*," they apparently meant that it was free from the copyist errors that plagued the printed editions. Such an exact copy would certainly have been considered an important source for the preparation of a uniform text.

For these immediate practical reasons, the 1580 Walloon manuscript was given a primary role. Here one sees no deliberate choice of the Walloon manuscript because it represented the 1566 revision textual tradition. The issue, whether to follow the original de Brès version or the revision text, was apparently not raised. Just as with the choice of the *Syntagma* edition earlier, very practical reasons are sufficient to explain the role given to the Walloon manuscript. The fact that both editions represented the revision text was a largely fortuitous matter. Since the revision textual tradition was dominant in both the French- and Dutch-speaking churches in the Netherlands from about 1583, it was natural for the synod to follow in this textual tradition without giving the issue much thought. Again, the synod most likely regarded the difference between the de Brès and revision texts as simply a difference in words, not in doctrinal substance.

It is interesting that no special role was given to the *Syntagma* edition in preparing the uniform text, even though it had earlier served as the basis for examining the doctrinal content of the BC. This is a strong indication that the two phases of the synod's actions with respect to the BC must be regarded as quite distinct. The *Syntagma* may also have been regarded as somewhat problematic for textual purposes, because it was a fairly free translation, as was evident by the omission of some words in article 22, for example.

The *Acta Authentica* (session 155) mentions that, when the uniform text was prepared, it would henceforth be considered as "authentic" (*pro authentica sit habendum*). What does "authentic" mean here? Did the synod want to prepare an authentic edition that faithfully reproduced the original BC, whether that be the 1561 or the 1566 edition? Or did the synod mean by "authentic" that it wanted a uniform text that would thereafter be regarded as having official ecclesiastical status? In this latter sense, authentic would simply mean official, or authorized. Judging from the texts that were finally approved by the synod, it must be concluded that "authentic" was meant in the second sense. The synod's uniform texts in French and Dutch did not exactly reproduce either the original 1561 or the 1566 edition.

SESSION 168, 21 May, afternoon
President Bogerman indicated that he wanted to end the synod soon and have the work on the text of the BC finalized by committee after the synod. This drew immediate objections from many delegates, especially from Franciscus Gomarus, who argued that the matter of changes in the BC should not be committed to a few but must be approved by the whole synod.[52]

There was a key issue at stake here: Who would decide concerning the words in article 22, which were missing in the *Harmonia* and *Syntagma* editions? Most delegates wanted the words restored, so as to exclude the questionable position of Johann Piscator, who denied the imputation of Christ's active obedience. Other delegates, including the Palatine and Hesse delegations, as well as President Bogerman, were sympathetic to Piscator's view and favored the omission of the words in article 22.[53]

---

52. Voetius, *Politica Ecclesiastica*, 4:54–55; cited in Kuyper, *Post-Acta*, 338.
53. Kuyper, *Post-Acta*, 339.

SESSION 171, 23 May, morning
After ten days of work, the committee was ready to present its uniform text in Dutch and French versions. The Latin version was not yet prepared. In this session, a reading of the Dutch and French versions was begun—article by article, through article 21—and reasons for improvements were given. Udemans read the Dutch version, and Colonius read the French.[54]

SESSION 172, 23 May, afternoon
It was decided to pass over article 22 for the time being and continue reading the later articles. When this was finished, the delegates were instructed that, if they thought anything was omitted that needed attention in this review, they should point out such matters.[55]

Then President Bogerman noted that three written statements on the BC had been left by the Genevan, Palatine, and Hesse delegations before they departed. These were read. The Genevan observations had been noted earlier in session 146, but now some of their suggestions for the improvement of ten articles were taken up in the revision of the text of the BC.[56]

The Palatine statement, submitted on 12 May, contained several points of advice, including that the BC and the HC should be confirmed by a solemn decree and that all ministers should be required to subscribe to them, or at least to approve the synodical decree. As for the omitted words from article 22, the Palatines asked the Dutch delegates not to cause strife due to the different views but to follow the example of other churches and be content with general phraseology (*generali phraseologia*) and biblical explanations such as Romans 5:18 and Philippians 2:8.[57]

Likewise, the Hesse statement expressed fear that dissension would arise among the Dutch delegates about the imputation of Christ's obedience for our righteousness, the issue raised by Piscator.

---

54. *ADSND*, 1:170.
55. *ADSND*, 1:171; Heyngius, "Acta," 214.
56. *ADSND*, 1:171. See Fornerod, *Registres*, 458–61, for analysis of the changes made due to the Genevan suggestions.
57. The Palatine statement is printed in Kuyper, *Post-Acta*, 514–15. Submitted by Abraham Scultetus, Paul Tossanus, and Heinrich Alting.

They thought that the dissension only concerned phrases and manners of speaking rather than doctrine and that it did not affect the foundation of salvation. Therefore, they asked the Dutch delegates to tolerate some difference of opinion on the matter and to teach with Scripture that Christ's obedience is imputed to us for righteousness, with the understanding of obedience in the sense of Philippians 2:8, where Christ is said to be obedient to the Father unto death, even death on the cross.[58]

In the discussion that followed on the issue of article 22, President Bogerman proposed, as a solution, a more general expression, "the obedience of Christ," in place of the omitted words "and so many holy works that he has done for us"; and he suggested that both differing views could take shelter under such a formulation. His proposal reflected the Palatine advice, but it received a strong reaction from the other Dutch delegates. Gelderland minister Eilardus van Mehen pointed out that the Palatine theologians only intended to prevent a specific condemnation of Piscator's opinion, but they could otherwise well tolerate that the text remain as it was. Finally, it was decided that the delegations would present their advice on the matter the next morning.[59]

SESSION 173, 24 May, morning
All the Dutch delegates submitted their advice on Bogerman's suggested change to article 22 and rejected it. The South Holland delegation, for example, listed nine reasons, composed by elder Johannes Latius, for rejecting Bogerman's proposal, including the following:

a. Since all changes in such writings are dangerous and scandalous and therefore ought not to be proposed without very urgent necessity.

b. Since now the synod is not dealing with making any change in the Confession but only with making a fixed and authentic copy by comparison of diverse copies. [This emphasizes

---

58. The Hesse statement is printed in Kuyper, *Post-Acta*, 515–16. Submitted by Georgius Cruciger, Paulus Steinius, Daniel Angelocrator, and Rudophus Goclenius.

59. Voetius, *Politica Ecclesiastica*, 4:56–57; cited in Kuyper, *Post-Acta*, 341.

the limited nature of the second phase of the synod's actions regarding the BC.]

c. Since our Confession was unanimously confirmed by the foreign theologians, although mention was expressly made that this article reads very differently in our original confession than was read in the Latin version.[60]

The issue was then brought to a vote regarding whether the BC should remain unchanged on this point. All but two delegates, Bogerman and Lubbertus, voted for an unchanged article 22. However, at the request of some delegates, in the same article, after "and so many holy works that he has done for us," the words "and in our place" were added, for the sake of greater clarity, in order to avoid a Socinian interpretation that took "for us" in the sense of "for our good."[61]

Then, after several small amendments to the text, the double copy of the BC as corrected (*exemplar utrumque ita correctum*), in both the Dutch and French languages, was approved (*approbatum*), and it was declared that only this version was to be considered authentic (*pro authenticis*) in the future. The copy was signed by the members of the committee. It was also declared that this version was to be accurately printed as soon as possible.[62]

The *exemplar utrumque ita correctum* specifically refers to a copy of the 1611 Middelburg edition of the BC,[63] which the committee had used as the basis for its comparison. This edition was edited by Hermannus Faukelius and was based on "the best copies from the year 1566," so it represented the 1566 textual tradition. On this copy, which included the Dutch (from the 1583 edition, a translation of the 1566 French edition) and the French (from the 1580 Walloon manuscript, which copied the 1566 edition) versions on facing pages, the committee apparently wrote in its textual corrections, and it was this copy that was approved. Unfortunately, it has been lost.[64]

---

60. Voetius, *Politica Ecclesisatica*, 4:55–57; cited in Kuyper, *Post-Acta*, 342.
61. *ADSND*, 1:171; Voetius, *Politica Ecclesiastica*, 4:55; Kuyper, *Post-Acta*, 344.
62. *ADSND*, 1:171–72.
63. *Belydenisse des Gheloofs der Kercken Iesu Christi inde Nederlanden* (Middelburg, 1611).
64. Kuyper, *Post-Acta*, 353. On the 1611 Middelburg edition, see Bakhuizen van

What was the nature of the synod's "approval" of the uniform Dutch and French texts? This was an official approval of the Dutch and French texts by a formal act of the synod. Yet this was only an official approval of a *uniform text* in these languages. No more than the preparation of a uniform text was on the agenda in this second phase, and no more was approved. This was not an official approval of the *doctrine* of the BC; the approval of the doctrine had occurred in the first phase. Neither can this official approval of the text be regarded as an *official adoption* of the BC as a doctrinal standard. The synod assumed such adoption, and at this point it was simply concerned with preparing and approving a uniform text so that there would no longer be confusion in the churches about which edition of the BC must be considered the officially approved edition.

With the official approval of the full text, the text of articles 30–32 on church government also received approval. No discussion on this issue in the second phase is recorded. After the English delegates had departed with the rest of the foreign theologians, it was safe for the Dutch delegates to quietly assume approval of the doctrinal content of these articles and to officially approve their text.

The committee had not finished the Latin version of the BC, since a whole new translation was needed. The synod gave Hommius the task of preparing a new translation, and it mandated the committee for the revision of the Acta Contracta to examine and approve it when completed.[65] This new Latin translation appeared in the published *Acta* in 1620, inserted at the end of session 146, leaving the mistaken impression that this text had then been approved by the synod. Yet, even though it did not receive the official approval of the synod in session, it did receive the synod's approval later by way of the committee acting on the synod's behalf. So the Latin text can also be regarded as an official text, though perhaps of secondary value.

From his careful study of the Dutch and French versions approved by Dordt, H. H. Kuyper concluded:

---

den Brink, *Nederlandse Belijdenisgeschriften*, 21; J. Borsius, "Hermannus Faukelius, zijn Leven, Karakter en Letterkundige Verdiensten," *Archief voor Kerkelijke Geschiedenis* 15 (1844): 225.

65. Kuyper, *Post-Acta*, 282.

a. As the basis for its comparison, the committee actually used a copy of the 1611 Middelburg Dutch and French edition, rather than the 1580 Walloon manuscript, because it was readily accessible, it contained both French and Dutch texts on facing pages, and it was almost identical to the Walloon text.

b. For comparison with this edition, the committee also made use of the 1561 French, 1566 French, 1563 Dutch, 1583 Dutch, 1612 Latin (*Syntagma*) editions, and Hommius's 1619 *Specimen*, each of which was the source of some textual changes. The committee also incorporated several suggestions from the Remonstrant *Considerationes* on the BC, which the synod had earlier demanded from them.[66]

c. Almost all textual changes made by Dordt were derived from earlier editions or translations or served to bring the French and Dutch texts into agreement. The few changes initiated by Dordt itself were improvements in the text or phraseology, not in the doctrinal content of the BC; even changes of a more essential nature served to provide a purer formulation of a doctrine rather than to change the doctrine.

d. The synod did not approve marginal Scripture references or titles above the articles.[67]

From his analysis of the BC, Nicolaas Gootjes listed five categories of changes that were made for the official Dordt edition of the BC:

a. Changes that were the result of objections made by the Remonstrants in their *Considerationes*.

b. Changes that brought the text of the BC closer to a statement from the Bible.

---

66. Kuyper took note of the influence of Remonstrant suggestions for the revision of articles 1, 2, 8, 13, 14, 18, 25, 30, and 35.

67. Kuyper, *Post-Acta*, 353, 355–90.

c. Several corrections in the text, some of which were mistakes found in previous editions.

d. In several cases, additions were made to the text of the BC. For example, "and in our place" and "of our sins" were added to article 22.

e. Textual references were omitted in the editions published at the order of the synod.[68]

SESSION 179, 28 May, afternoon
In this session, an Act of Approbation of the BC and the HC was read and approved. It was drawn up as an official response to the States General's resolution that the BC and the HC should be examined. This Act contained a summary of the first phase of the synod's actions and ended with a request that the States General maintain, propagate, confirm, and protect the doctrine taught in the BC and the HC:

> Therefore the foreign theologians and especially the deputies of the Dutch churches very subserviently and also very humbly request and implore the High and Mighty Lords of the States General of the United Netherlands, as true foster-parents [*Voedsterheeren*] of these churches, that their High Mightinesses be pleased to maintain, propagate, confirm, and protect [*handthaven, voortplanten, bevestighen, ende beschermen*] this orthodox Doctrine contained in the aforesaid Confession and Catechism by their authority more and more in their lands, and not tolerate that any violation or adulterating of this Doctrine be done, nor that any other doctrine be taught or promoted in the public churches of their lands.[69]

This Act of Approbation was submitted to the States General by a delegation of synodical officials on 30 May.

This delegation also submitted to the States General, on the same day, a report of the synod that summarized all of its actions. This included an account of the approval of the doctrine of the BC, as well as an account of the preparation of the uniform text:

---

68. Gootjes, *Belgic Confession*, 153–57. Cf. the analysis of Los, *Tekst*, 56.
69. Act of Approbation; printed in Kuyper, *Post-Acta*, 483; cf. 290.

Your High Mightinesses through your delegates let the synod know that it was your good intention that the synod should examine the Netherlands Confession and the Heidelberg Catechism, and judge whether anything in these writings concerning the doctrine contained in them would be found to be in conflict with God's holy Word; and, after an investigation, it was unanimously judged and explained, as your High Mightinesses and your Excellency shall be able to see in the act [of approbation] made about it, which we present to your High Mightinesses with this report....

Finally and last, copies of the Netherlands Confession (since they vary a lot) were collated, and (following what was resolved in the presence of the foreign delegates) from the diverse copies a Dutch and French copy was chosen, which should be considered as authentic [*autentycq*]. From this, a good copy will be communicated to your High Mightinesses as soon as possible, and the Latin copy will also be compared with the aforementioned copies.[70]

There was no request to the States General concerning the text of the BC.

The Form of Subscription

In session 159, during the Post-Acta sessions after the foreign theologians returned home, the Dutch delegates at the synod decided on 15 May to draft a new form of subscription, by which ministers were required to subscribe to the BC, the HC, and the Canons of Dordt as a testimony to their unity in orthodox doctrine. Such a form of subscription was intended to prevent the evasion of some who subscribed to confessions according to their own interpretation of what subscribing meant. On 17 May, the new form of subscription for ministers was approved. By signing it, a minister affirmed that all the articles and

---

70. "Sommier van t' rapport," in The Hague, Nationaal Archief, Archives States General, 1.01.02, nr. 3178; printed in Kuyper, *Post-Acta*, 477–78. Dordt's version of the Belgic Confession was published in Dutch as *Belydenisse des Gheloofs der Ghereformeerde Kercken in Nederlant* (Dordrecht: Fransoys Borsaler, 1619), and in French as *Confession de Foy des Eglises Reformées du Pays-Bas* (Dordrecht: Nicolas Vincent & Francoys Borsaler, 1619). Sometime after the synod, an Arabic translation of the Belgic Confession was prepared in manuscript, along with the Heidelberg Catechism, Liturgical Forms, and Church Order of Dordt. See Nabil Matar, "The Synod of Dort in Arabic: Bodleian MS Marsh 268," *The Seventeenth Century* 39 (2024), 719–30, who incorrectly dates the manuscript May 1619.

points of doctrine in these confessional documents "fully agree with the Word of God" and promised to diligently teach this doctrine and reject all errors that conflicted with it. If required by a church assembly, the minister must also be ready to give a further explanation of his sentiments on any article.[71]

On 25 May, a similar form of subscription was approved for professors of theology, and a shorter form was approved for schoolteachers. Whether elders must also subscribe to such a form was left to the discretion of the classes and provincial synods.

Some Conclusions

1. The Synod of Dordt did not officially adopt the BC as a confessional standard. It assumed such adoption when it began, and it continued to assume this during its actions regarding the BC, which consisted mainly of:

   a. A brief examination and reaffirmation of the doctrinal purity of the BC, and

   b. The preparation and official approval of a uniform text of the BC in French, Dutch, (and Latin).

The significance of these actions should not be overestimated. The most important events in the history of the ecclesiastical adoption of the BC occurred prior to the Synod of Dordt. The synod's actions should be seen as but one important step at the end of a nearly sixty-year process.

2. The issue of whether to follow the de Brès version or the 1566 revision was not debated or decided at Dordt. This matter was decided long before Dordt, in favor of the revision—whether by deliberate choice or by the weight of actual usage. Dordt simply followed the textual tradition that had been accepted since the 1580s.

3. The extensive influence of the Dutch government evident at Dordt must certainly be recognized, but this does not minimize the synod's actions. Although the States General had the BC placed on the synod's agenda, the synod made its own judgments on this matter.

---

71. *ADSND*, 1:158, 160, 167–68, 173–74. On the drafting of forms of subscription by the synod, see Sinnema, "Origin of the Form of Subscription," 271–76.

Johannes Bogerman, the president of the synod

CHAPTER 4

The Heidelberg Catechism at the Synod of Dordt

Very soon after the time it was written, the Heidelberg Catechism (HC) was in use among the Dutch-speaking Reformed churches. In 1563, the year the HC was composed at Heidelberg in the Palatinate, not one but two Dutch translations of the HC were prepared for Dutch congregations in exile—one an anonymous translation published in Emden, the other by Petrus Dathenus for his Dutch-exile congregation at Frankenthal in the Palatinate. In the Netherlands itself, the first evidence of teaching the HC appeared in Amsterdam, in 1566 by Peter Gabriel, before Reformed churches were formally established in the northern provinces. That same year, the earliest Dutch edition to be published in the Netherlands appeared at Delft. The popularity of the HC in the emerging Dutch Reformed churches is clear in that, by 1585, no fewer than sixty-one Dutch editions were published.[1]

As early as 1566, the practice of regular catechism preaching was instituted by Dathenus in his Dutch-refugee church at Frankenthal; this practice rapidly spread to the Low Countries. Gradually, synods sought to legislate a practice of regular Sunday afternoon catechism services in all Dutch Reformed churches. This concern was evident already in the Synod of Emden (1571). Finally, afternoon catechism

---

1. W. Heijting, *De Catechismi en Confessies in de Nederlandse Reformatie tot 1585* (Nieuwkoop: De Graff, 1989), 232–77.

services teaching the HC became fixed in the church order of the national Synod of The Hague in 1586.[2]

As early as 1568, the articles of Wesel[3] sought to give the HC confessional authority in the Dutch Reformed churches. The Wesel proposal expected ministers to express oral agreement with the doctrine in the French Confession, the Belgic Confession (BC), and the HC. However, for the next two decades, Dutch Reformed synods required subscription only to the BC, and not to the HC. But once the custom was established of using the HC in Sunday catechism services in most Dutch churches, it was but a small step to require that ministers subscribe to the HC along with the BC. This first happened in 1593 at the North Holland Synod of Alkmaar and at the South Holland Synod of Briel. By 1608, the earliest form of subscription for ministers required adherence to the doctrine contained in both the BC and the HC. Soon, both were considered "forms of unity" in the Dutch Reformed churches.[4]

Given the importance of the HC in the Dutch Reformed churches, it is no surprise that the HC, and its use in the churches, came up for discussion at the national Synod of Dordt (1618–1619), even though the synod was convened first of all to resolve the Arminian controversy. This article will discuss the six ways the HC came up on the agenda of Dordt: (1) in the regulation of afternoon catechism services; (2) in discussion of catechism instruction; (3) in the Remonstrant (Arminian) *Observations* on the HC; (4) in the Palatine delegates' response to the Remonstrant *Observations*; (5) in an examination and formal approval of the HC; and (6) in the composition of forms of subscription.

---

2. Donald Sinnema, "The Second Sunday Service in the Early Dutch Reformed Tradition," *Calvin Theological Journal* 32 (1997): 298–333.

3. Recent scholarship has shown that the so-called Convent of Wesel was not an actual assembly but a proposal by Petrus Dathenus for organizing the emerging Dutch Reformed churches. See Jesse Spohnholz, *The Convent of Wesel: The Event that Never Was and the Invention of Tradition* (Cambridge: Cambridge University Press, 2017).

4. Donald Sinnema, "The Origin of the Form of Subscription in the Dutch Reformed Tradition," *Calvin Theological Journal* 42 (2007): 256–82. On the reception of the HC in the Netherlands, see Willem van 't Spijker, ed., *The Church's Book of Comfort* (Grand Rapids: Reformation Heritage Books, 2009), 163–86.

Catechism Services

The first thing to recognize is that, in the Dutch churches before the Synod of Dordt, there were no separate catechism classes. Apart from some short-term instruction for those preparing to take the Lord's Supper, the only regular catechism instruction done in the churches occurred in the Sunday afternoon catechism services.

The matter of catechism services came to the synod in two gravamina (overtures). The provincial synod of Friesland requested Dordt to consider Sunday afternoon teaching of the HC in all churches and villages, since such teaching was neglected in many places. The second gravamen, from the synod of Overijssel, requested that the synod promote catechism teaching in rural areas and devise a good manner of catechizing.[5]

In its Pro-Acta sessions, before the arrival of the Remonstrants at the synod, Dordt took up the issue of catechism services on 27 November 1618, in session 14. President Bogerman first posed the questions: Shouldn't the HC be taught every Lord's Day in the afternoons? And how can this be attained? The discussion that followed revealed the sad state of catechism preaching, especially in the country villages—due to the negligence of pastors, pastors serving two churches, and the lack of Sunday observance. After many delegates offered suggestions for remedies, the synod came to a decision on catechism preaching.

The decision first reaffirmed article 61 of the last national synod, the Synod of The Hague (1586): "The pastors in all places shall ordinarily in the afternoon service briefly explain the summary of Christian doctrine contained in the Catechism presently accepted in the Dutch churches, in order that it can be completed in this way every year by following the divisions introduced in the Catechism for that purpose." The decision charged all pastors, under pain of ecclesiastical censure, to always preach sermons on the Catechism on Sunday afternoons. These afternoon services must not be neglected due to low attendance, even if pastors should preach to no one except their own families. Government authorities need to be asked to enact strict legislation prohibiting all everyday labor, and especially games, drinking parties, and other

---

5. Sinnema, "Second Sunday Service," 319. On the introduction of catechism preaching in the Dutch churches, see Van 't Spijker, *Church's Book*, 187–90, 199–202.

violations of the Sabbath. Combinations where a pastor served two churches should be abandoned; otherwise, the pastor should hold catechism services in each church on alternating Sundays. Church visitors should ensure that pastors were faithful in this responsibility, and if any who professed the Reformed faith refused to attend these afternoon services, they were worthy of ecclesiastical censure.[6]

Though the decision had been made, at this point the foreign theologians were asked to share their customs regarding catechism services. The British said their government imposed a fine on those absent from Sunday services. The Palatine delegates said the clergy first admonished absentees and then sought the magistrates' help. Ritzius Lucas, a member of the Emden delegation, commented that it was more necessary to teach the Catechism than to preach on a text from Scripture.[7]

In the Post-Acta sessions, when the synod revised the church order, no change was made to the article on catechism preaching. Instead, article 61 of the previous church order of The Hague was simply reaffirmed, following the decision of session 14.

Catechetical Instruction

The issue of the best way to do catechism instruction appeared on the agenda of Dordt by way of two gravamina from provincial synods. The South Holland Synod of Delft (1618) asked:

> Since a great ignorance of religion shows itself almost everywhere, the national synod is asked to prescribe some manner of catechizing adults as well as youth, by which to counter this misfortune.[8]

Likewise, the Zeeland Synod of Zierikzee (1618) proposed:

> We shall pursue with the national synod that a simple and particular manner of catechizing be introduced in all churches of our Union, not only to bring young children to a knowledge of salvation, but

---

6. *ADSND*, 1:24–25.
7. Hales, 2:5; *Historisch Verhael van't ghene sich toeghedraeghen heeft binnen Dordrecht, in de Jaeren 1618 ende 1619, tusschen de Nationale Synode der Contra-Remonstranten, ende hare geassocieerde ter eender, ende de Geciteerde Kercken-Dienaeren Remonstranten, ter ander zijden* (Amsterdam, 1623), 11r; Sinnema, "Second Sunday Service," 321–22.
8. H. H. Kuyper, *Post-Acta of Nahadelingen van de Nationale Synode van Dordrecht in 1618 en 1619 Gehouden* (Amsterdam: Höveker and Wormser, 1899), 425.

also many adults who are completely ignorant of the first fundamentals of the faith, as is already done with great success in some churches of Zeeland.[9]

After treating the issue of catechism services, the Synod of Dordt moved on to discuss the manner of catechizing on 27, 28, and 30 November, in sessions 14, 15, and 17. The content of the HC was to be discussed later, at the end of the synod. Since churches complained, and since it was evident by experience that catechism services did not sufficiently instruct ignorant youth in the first fundamentals of the faith at their mental level, or remove the ignorance of uneducated common people, the synod was asked at the end of session 14 to give serious thought to the most suitable means, besides catechism services, to instruct youth as well as adults in the Christian religion.[10]

The next morning (session 15), President Bogerman introduced the issue by giving a speech on the necessity and usefulness of catechizing. As described by synod observer John Hales,

> The Praeses first spake many things learnedly of the necessity of catechizing, that it was the basis and ground of religion, and the sole way of tranfusing the principles of Christianity into men; that it was very ancient, practiced by the Patriarchs, by the Apostles, by Origen, and approved by the consent of the Fathers; that from the neglect of this came the ignorance of the common sort, and that multitude of sects amongst them, of Papists, Anabaptists, Libertines, etc., whereas if an uniform course of teaching them their first principles had been taken up, there would not have been so many differences; that there was now greater necessity than ever of reviving this custom, because of the Jesuits who mightily labour in this kind, as appeared by some of their acts lately in Frisia, etc.[11]

Then both foreign and Dutch delegations presented their advice—some written, some orally—on the best means by which to catechize. Those who presented their advice orally were asked to put it in writing, so that, from all the advice, the synod's officers could draft the synod's decision on this matter.[12]

---

9. Kuyper, *Post-Acta*, 440.
10. *ADSND*, 1:25.
11. Hales, 2:9–10.
12. *ADSND*, 1:26.

Twenty-one documents were presented to the synod with advice on catechizing—seventeen from the delegations then present, two from the split Utrecht delegation, and two from individuals (Gomarus and Smoutius).[13] In these documents, the various delegations offered specific advice on how best to catechize. Several recurrent themes ran through these documents. A common theme was that there should be three kinds of catechizing: at home by parents, at school by teachers, and at church by the minister. Since catechism should be taught at the level of the student, two or three different kinds of catechism books were recommended: the youngest children should be taught the five main documents of the faith—the Apostles' Creed, the Decalogue, the Lord's Prayer, the institution of baptism and of the Lord's Supper; the middle group should use an abbreviated form of the HC with questions marked with asterisks, or the *Kort Begrip* of Middelburg, or a new booklet such as that; and the older students should use the whole HC.

For catechizing in the church, these documents frequently mentioned Sunday afternoon catechism services, where the minister explains a portion of the HC and also examines the children's knowledge. Three of the delegations recommended that teachers take their students to the catechism service. Some advised that parents should also be present at catechism services. Many recommended separate instruction, or at least examination, of those wishing to partake of the Lord's Supper.

Many of the documents advised that a minister and an elder visit the schools to check how well the students were catechized. And several documents also recommended that the local magistrate should check for the neglect of catechizing, pay teachers a sufficient wage, or take measures to stop the desecration of the Sabbath.

Two of the documents offered unique advice. The Utrecht Remonstrants asserted that the HC was too long and difficult for the young

---

13. The advice of the seven foreign delegations and of the Dutch delegations is printed in the *ADSND*, 2/2:76–127; the advice of the Dutch delegates is printed in Hendrik Kaajan, *De Pro-Acta der Dordtsche Synode in 1618* (Rotterdam, 1914), 336–51; Kaajan provides a summary of the advice of each of the delegations, 174–98. Sinnema, "Second Sunday Service," 322–25, also gives a summary. The Nassau-Wetteravian delegation had not yet arrived. The advice of the Frisian delegation is missing.

to understand, and they recommended that an easier catechism was needed, with answers to the questions consisting only of Scripture texts, not the words of men. And catechism preaching should begin with a Scripture text, as was the custom in some Reformed churches. The Walloon delegation explained that they used the French catechism (Calvin's Genevan Catechism), and they asked the synod not to replace this.[14]

When the various delegations finished giving their advice, President Bogerman indicated that he, together with the vice presidents and the secretaries, would compare all this written advice and from it draw up one form of catechizing, which would be presented to the synod to be approved or altered to its liking.[15]

In session 17, President Bogerman read to the synod the draft of a synodical decision on catechizing that he and the other officers had drawn up from the advice of the delegations.[16]

This decision provided policies for both youth and adults. For youth, there was to be a threefold manner of catechizing: in the home by parents, in the school by teachers, and in the church by ministers, elders, sermon readers, or visitors of the sick. Christian magistrates were to promote this work to ensure that each faithfully did their duty.

First, the duty of parents was to instruct their children in the basics of Christianity at their level, urge them to godliness, engage them in family prayers, and take them to church services. They should review catechetical sermons with them, read and explain Scripture passages, and assign some passages to be memorized. If parents are negligent in this task, they were to be admonished by the minister and, if necessary, by censure of the consistory.

Second, schools, where youth may be instructed in the fundamentals of Christian doctrine, should be established everywhere, and the state should provide adequate salaries to teachers, especially so that children of the poor may have free instruction. Teachers must be members of the Reformed church, be well trained in catechetical instruction, subscribe to the BC and the HC, and promise to diligently

---

14. *ADSND*, 2/2:117–19, 124–27.
15. Hales, 2:11.
16. *ADSND*, 1:26–30. Cf. Van 't Spijker, *Church's Book*, 211–13.

instruct their students in the fundamentals of Christianity according to the HC. They were to teach their students two days a week to memorize and understand the rudiments of the HC. For this purpose, three forms of the catechism were to be used: The first, for young children, shall contain the Apostles' Creed, the Decalogue, the Lord's Prayer, and the institution of the sacraments and of church discipline, along with simple questions and important passages of Scripture. The second form of catechism, for more advanced children, shall be a compendium of the HC, following the example of the Palatinate, where they used certain catechism questions identified with asterisks, or that of Middelburg, which used the *Kort Begrip* (Compendium). The third form, for older youth, shall be the whole HC, except for the Walloon churches, which could continue to use the Geneva Catechism. The magistrates should ban all papal catechisms from the schools. Teachers should see to it that students memorize these forms of catechism and properly understand the doctrine, by explaining it at their level and by examining whether they grasp the meaning. On Sundays, teachers should also take their students to the catechism services. To check on the teachers, the minister should visit the schools regularly; they should admonish any teacher found negligent, and if such teachers did not comply, the magistrate should replace them.

Third, the duty of ministers in the church was to preach on the HC in such a manner that their sermons were brief and adapted to the level of the youth and the adults. It also would be helpful to review these sermons.

Next, adults, especially those who have little or no schooling, should be better instructed in the basics of the Christian religion, since experience teaches that ordinary catechism services were not sufficient for many people. The minister, and an elder, should gather together such adults as may desire to learn in a weekly meeting, held in a home or the consistory room, to discuss with them the main points of the Christian religion at their level and review catechism sermons with them.

For those who desired to join the church, there should be separate catechism instruction for three or four weeks before the celebration of the Lord's Supper.

After the decision on catechizing was read, the issue (raised by the Utrecht Remonstrants) of reading a Scripture text before the catechism sermon resurfaced, since it was not mentioned in the decision. The custom in most places was not to take a text of Scripture, but a portion of the HC, as the text of the catechism sermon. The Remonstrants long complained that this elevated the HC above Scripture. In this discussion, the delegates of Gelderland proposed that it would be fit for ministers, before their catechetical sermons, to read not only the words of the HC but also some text of Scripture on which the doctrine of the HC was grounded. To this, President Bogerman answered that the custom of reading only the text of the HC was long established and that it could not conveniently be recalled.[17]

After further discussion, the synodical decision on catechizing was approved.

Several days later (session 20), the three Remonstrant delegates from Utrecht submitted a written protest to some points in the synod's decision on catechizing, including the requirement that teachers should bring their students to catechism services. They also raised again the issue of reading Scripture as the text for catechism sermons;[18] they requested that, at least, this should be left to the discretion of the pastors and the local churches. Bogerman replied that it was not the intention of the synod to take away this practice where it was in use but only to prohibit it where this was not done.[19]

A committee of three theology professors (Gomarus, Polyander, and Thysius) and three ministers (Faukelius, Lydius, and Udemans) was appointed to draw up drafts of the two proposed shorter catechisms, and they were instructed to stick as much as possible to the words of the HC.[20]

In one of the closing sessions of the synod (session 177), this committee presented its two shorter catechisms to the synod. The acts of

---

17. Hales, 2:15–16; Sinnema, "Second Sunday Service," 326.
18. The Utrecht Remonstrants had raised an objection to preaching on the Catechism, rather than on a passage of Scripture, already in session 9; [C. Barlaeus], "Epistolica Narratio eorum quae in Synodo Dordracena gesta sunt," in *Praestantium ac Eruditorum Virorum Epistolae Ecclesiasticae et Theologicae* (Amsterdam, 1684), 514.
19. *ADSND*, 2/2:128–30; Hales, 2:25; Sinnema, "Second Sunday Service," 327.
20. *ADSND*, 1:30.

the synod state that the simplest one was read and approved on the condition that some things be added from the HC; and regarding the mid-level catechism, which was not read due to its length, it was decided that either this catechism or the one already in use by the Middelburg church could be used.[21] In reality, the two newly drafted catechisms were quietly set aside, so that they would not be seen as new catechisms or detract from the HC. For younger children, it was decided to use the *ABC Boekje*, already in use in the Dutch schools, augmented by some questions from the simplest proposed catechism; and in place of the new mid-level catechism, the synod recommended the use of the *Kort Begrip*, the compendium of the HC that had been drafted in 1608 by Hermannus Faukelius (now one of Synod of Dordt's vice presidents) at the request of the Middelburg consistory.[22] Neither could be regarded as new catechisms.

The Remonstrant Observations on the Heidelberg Catechism

For well over a decade, Arminius and the Remonstrants had expressed concerns about the need to revise the BC and the HC, without offering outright criticism of these confessional standards, which might have put into question their loyalty to the Reformed faith. Their opponents suspected that they secretly harbored errors contradicting the Reformed confessions that they refused to express openly.

While there was yet no uniform form of subscription in the Dutch Reformed churches, the forms of subscription already in use in the provinces of Zeeland, Gelderland, Groningen, and Drenthe all specified that if any minister had any objections (*bedenken*) to the doctrine of the BC or the HC, they must submit such objections to the classis or synod for examination and judgment.[23] Thus, in the context of doctrinal controversy, the Contra-Remonstrants tried again and again to get the Remonstrants to produce any objections or observations they had, in order to bring them under discipline for their perceived doctrinal errors.

---

21. *ADSND*, 1:177.
22. Theodore Heyngius's journal, "Acta Synodi Nationalis breviter conscripta," in the Bibliotheek der Rijksuniversiteit, Utrecht, MS 457, 225; Kuyper, *Post-Acta*, 272–78; Kaajan, *Pro-Acta*, 211–13; Van 't Spijker, *Church's Book*, 161–63, 213–15.
23. Sinnema, "Origin of the Form," 268–71.

When the Remonstrant leaders were summoned to appear before the Synod of Dordt to have their views examined and adjudicated, their citation letters stated that they were summoned so that they might explain and defend their views of the Five Articles of the Remonstrants, which were then in controversy, but that "at the same time, they may also submit in writing to this synod all their *Observationes* [*Considerationes*], if they have any, about the doctrine contained in the Belgic Confession and Heidelberg Catechism of these churches, and the reasons for these observations, in order that the synod, having heard and considered everything, may more maturely be able to judge particular points in the fear of the Lord."[24]

After the Remonstrants appeared at the synod in early December 1618, there were six weeks of procedural squabbles between them and the synod about how to treat the issues in controversy. These squabbles also included the Remonstrant observations on the confessions. After the Remonstrants submitted their brief statements of their views on the Five Articles, President Bogerman, on 17 December, demanded that they submit their objections to the BC and the HC in the same session or the next day. The Remonstrants expressed surprise that their observations should be required so soon, since their letters of citation seemed to indicate that the controversy on the Five Articles should be resolved first before proceeding to their observations on the confessions. Bogerman replied that the synod ought to have the whole matter before it at once. He rejected their appeal, but he did allow them to withdraw to the antechamber to confer about the matter. When they returned, they declared they were resolved to finish defending the Five Articles before submitting their observations. This occasioned a lot of acrimony, until the secretary of the state delegates, Daniel Heinsius, pounded on the table and shouted that the state delegates commanded them to obey. Then Bogerman told the Remonstrants that they must answer individually, and he asked them one by one whether they were ready to present any observations. When it was revealed that they were not ready, after much debate the state delegates gave them first three, then four days to submit their observations, and they were to do so individually, not jointly, since they were summoned before the

---

24. *ADSND*, 1:15.

synod individually, not as a body. The Remonstrants promised that they would do their best to get their observations ready and that they would offer them individually, but that if any of them were of the same opinion, they would join with one another. To this the synod agreed.[25]

On 21 December, a rumor spread around Dordrecht that something extraordinary, long kept secret, was about to break out at the synod. For the first time, five or six women appeared as spectators, and thereafter, many women were present in public sessions. In this session, the Remonstrants submitted their *Observations* on the BC, signed by all of them, after which only the preface was read.[26] In this preface, the Remonstrants declared that they presented these as observations to be weighed carefully, which could serve to clarify the meaning of the BC and the HC. In these observations, they asserted that they called into doubt no dogma commonly accepted by the Reformed churches. These observations just related to "phraseology, order, or ways of speaking" that could be interpreted in a way that seemed to be a hindrance to godliness. So they only offered observations, without determining anything, except on points where they had already given their opinion in earlier writings. And they only presented these observations in order that they might be of service to the synod when it would begin a serious review and revision of the BC and the HC.[27]

The Remonstrant document began with general observations on both the BC and the HC. These observations were all posed in question form (which, again, would be worthy of consideration when the synod undertook a revision), with such questions as: Should these writings contain anything else than what is to be believed, hoped, and done for salvation? Are the main documents (*capita*) of religion plainly and precisely enough contained in the HC and the BC? Is everything treated in proper order in these writings? Can such writings rightly be called "secondary norms of faith [*norma secundaria fidei*]" (as Gomarus had asserted at the 1607 preparatory assembly)? Does the HC bear such authority that it is appropriate for pastors to read and explain it as the text for preaching, and for the people to listen with their heads

---

25. *ADSND*, 1:60–61; *Historisch Verhael*, 62r–65r; Hales, 2:51–53.
26. *Historisch Verhael*, 69r; *ADSND*, 1:65.
27. *Acta et Scripta*, 1:85–86.

uncovered (as if it were a Scripture reading)? Must the passages in the margin of these writings be regarded as part of the HC and the BC? Doesn't a perfect form of the HC require that it explicitly treat the authority, perfection, and perspicuity of Scripture in matters necessary to salvation?[28]

President Bogerman then asked the synod's opinion on the fact that the Remonstrants had not submitted their observations on the HC and that they had presented their observations on the BC jointly, not individually. Some thought they should be given more time to draw up their observations on the HC; but most thought they had not complied with the orders of the synod and deserved a reprimand. So the Remonstrants were called in, and Bogerman told them that they had transgressed the orders of the state delegates and the synod by not submitting their observations on the HC and by presenting their observations on the BC jointly. Episcopius replied that they did not have sufficient time to prepare their observations on the HC and that it seemed strange for the synod to insist that their remarks be presented individually, since they did not offer them as conclusions, but only as observations that might deserve some attention.[29]

Then a resolution of the state delegates was read, declaring that the Remonstrants had failed to comply with their commands by not presenting their observations on the BC and the HC at the same time and by not doing so individually, as they promised. Therefore, each one was to submit their observations on the HC without fail on 27 December, right after the Christmas break.[30]

Finally, on 27 December, the Remonstrants submitted their *Observations* on the HC. The larger document was signed by seven of the Remonstrants—Episcopius, Poppius, Corvinus, Dwinglo, Pijnacker, Sapma, and Neranus. Four others presented individual observations—Niellius, Goswinius, Matthisius, and Frederici. Three (Leo, Vezekius, and Rijckewaert) said that they had no remarks. Hollinger said that he had no particular remarks but that the larger document deserved

---

28. *Acta et Scripta*, 1:86–87.
29. *Historisch Verhael*, 76v–77r; John Hales to Dudley Carleton, 22 December 1618, in *Letters from and to Sir Dudley Carleton, Knt. during his Embassy in Holland from January 1615/16 to December 1620* (London, 1775), 322–24.
30. *ADSND*, 1:66–67.

attention; so, he was required to subscribe to that document. Bogerman then asked whether they had any other remarks; they said no.[31]

As in their observations on the BC, the Remonstrant observations on the HC were all posed in question form, rather than stated in direct assertion.[32] This approach protected them from being accused of teaching errors that contradicted the BC and the HC as confessional standards, to which office-bearers were supposed to subscribe. Besides, they presented them merely as suggestions worthy to be considered when the synod would undertake a revision of these documents.

In addition to their general observations on the HC, the Remonstrants offered particular observations on 74 of the HC's 129 questions, sometimes several observations on one question. Most often, the observations were rather superficial—questions like: Can't this be better stated? Is the order incorrect here? Isn't this answer incomplete? Does the Scripture text appropriately support the answer? Some observations, however, suggested a more substantive critique of the HC, although the Remonstrants denied that they deviated from basic Reformed doctrine. Here is a sampling of their observations:

In their general observations on the HC, the Remonstrants first asked whether the HC's manner of instruction is appropriate for instructing youth at their level, both with respect to the content, which is very heavy and difficult, and with respect to its manner of explaining things, since it does not appear to be well adapted to the level of children and the uneducated nor easily understood and retained by them.[33]

Three individual Remonstrants—Frederici, Goswinius, and Matthisius—also offered several general observations on the HC. Frederici asked: Shouldn't the HC consist, as much as possible, of the very words of Scripture? For catechism sermons, is it proper to first read from the HC, with the congregation's heads uncovered, without reading a text of Scripture? Doesn't this honor belong only to the Word of God? Since the common folk might regard the HC as the Word of God and as a canonical book, shouldn't some measure be taken to avoid this error, so that all may understand that the HC is just

---

31. *Historisch Verhael*, 81v, 89v–95v.
32. *Acta et Scripta*, 1:102–33.
33. *Acta et Scripta*, 1:102–3.

a human writing? Are ministers of the Word bound only to the catholic doctrine and substance of the HC's doctrine, or also to its words, phraseology, and circumstances? Are all the questions and answers of the HC necessary for salvation?[34] Goswinius asked: Can it properly be said that the HC is a "little Bible," by which all doctrine and sermons can be examined?[35] Matthisius asked: Isn't the HC incomplete, since it does not explicitly address the authority, perfection, and perspicuity of Scripture, nor the nature and attributes of God?[36]

On the HC's famous question 1, the Remonstrants asked several questions: Shouldn't the purpose (or end) of the HC be extended—not just for consolation in life and in death but also for instruction in the truth and for doing good (2 Tim. 3)? Are the words of answer 1, which express the assurance of consolation, aptly enough joined to the previous consolation, as if the assurance follows only as a consequence of the consolation, since the Holy Spirit is the efficient cause of all consolation? Does the phrase "all things must work together for my salvation" suggest that our sins do not hinder our salvation? Shouldn't these words be somehow restricted? Doesn't answer 1 end with the wrong order, when assurance of eternal life precedes willingness to live for Christ?[37]

In question 2, in place of the words "how great my sin and misery are," wouldn't it be more complete to say: how much by sin I have fallen from my created condition?[38]

Isn't the answer to question 3 incomplete, when it asserts that you come to know your misery from the law of God? Wouldn't it be better to add that we know our misery by examining our conscience and our abilities to fulfill the law?[39]

Sometimes, in their observations, the Remonstrants used the HC against their Reformed opponents. For example, in question 6, do the words that God created people in order to live with him in eternal blessedness refer to the whole human race? If so, how does this agree

---

34. *Acta et Scripta*, 1:132–33.
35. *Acta et Scripta*, 1:124.
36. *Acta et Scripta*, 1:127.
37. *Acta et Scripta*, 1:103.
38. *Acta et Scripta*, 1:103.
39. *Acta et Scripta*, 1:104.

with Reformed theologians who teach that God created the majority of the human race for destruction? And when question 9 asserts that Adam sinned, being tempted by the Devil, doesn't this contradict those who say that God, in a secret way, impels humans to sin?[40]

Sometimes, in their observations, the Remonstrants interpreted the HC as a confirmation of their own theology of the Five Articles, or they suggested changes that would be more in line with their own theology.

So, regarding question 20, which asks whether all are saved through Christ as all were lost through Adam, shouldn't a distinction be expressed here between the obtaining (*impetratio*) of salvation, which pertains to the whole human race, and the application (*applicatio*) of salvation, which pertains only to those who truly believe?[41]

In question 21, on faith, is the essence of faith rightly expressed, since a distinction ought to be made between justifying faith, which God requires of all to whom the gospel is proclaimed, and its special application, which happens when we believe? Also, doesn't it follow from the answer—that we are given eternal life by Christ's merit alone—that Christ is not only the instrument for the execution of the decree of election but also a cause of election to salvation?[42]

When question 37 says that Christ bore God's wrath against the sin of the whole human race, can't it be concluded that Christ gave satisfaction for the sins of the whole human race, and not just for the elect?[43]

Finally, in question 65, since the proclamation of the gospel is the means by which the Holy Spirit works faith in us, is it possible that faith is caused by an irresistible power in us?[44]

The Palatine Response to the Remonstrant Observations

When the Remonstrants submitted their observations on the HC on 27 December, Abraham Scultetus spoke up on behalf of the Palatine delegation. They wanted a copy of these observations, since they related

---

40. *Acta et Scripta*, 1:104, 105.
41. *Acta et Scripta*, 1:108.
42. *Acta et Scripta*, 1:108.
43. *Acta et Scripta*, 1:111.
44. *Acta et Scripta*, 1:114.

to their own HC, and since the Palatine elector had commanded his delegates to see that nothing was done to the prejudice of the churches of the Palatinate and to ensure that no changes would be made to their HC. They wanted a copy so they could examine and respond to these observations and then submit this to the synod's judgment.[45]

On 10 January and 4 February, the Palatine delegates reported that they were still preparing their response to the Remonstrant observations. When finished, they expected to send them to Heidelberg for approval by the church and university there and then present them to the synod.[46]

The response by the Palatine theologians was eighty-four pages long in manuscript.[47] It responded to each of the observations presented in the larger Remonstrant document and to some of the observations of the four individuals. It is likely that the Palatine response was prepared by Heinrich Alting, since this response was later published in 1646 as part of his lectures on the HC.[48]

Here is a sampling of the Palatine responses, related to the Remonstrant observations mentioned above.

Regarding the general observation about the HC's appropriateness for youth, the Palatine response was that it was so prepared that youth may find the milk of the elements of Christianity in it, and adults solid food in it. Its manner of explanation is very appropriate. In many editions, more difficult questions are distinguished from easier ones by asterisks. Also, the whole HC has been reduced to an epitome.[49]

As for using the very words of Scripture, the HC uses words and phrases of Scripture throughout. It is not necessary that the Catechism consist only of Scripture, because it ought to declare briefly and

---

45. *ADSND*, 1:69; *Historisch Verhael*, 95v; Hales, 2:55.

46. Hesse: 274; *ADSND*, 1:123.

47. Printed in *ADSND*, 2/2:503–90. The original Palatine document is in OSA, vol. C, 41r–82v. This document is not written in the hand of any of the Palatine delegates.

48. Heinrich Alting, *Scriptorum Theologicorum Heidelbergensium Tomus Tertius, continens Explicationem Catecheseos Palatinae* (Amsterdam, 1646), 6–400. Alting integrated the observations of the Remonstrants (whom he here calls *Novatores*) and the Palatine responses, sometimes revised and expanded, into his lectures on the HC, which he delivered at Heidelberg between 1619 and 1622, after returning from Dordrecht.

49. *ADSND*, 2/2:505.

popularly the chief points of religion from the Bible and according to the analogy of faith; it also ought to block the corruptions of heretics, who hide under the more general phraseology of Scripture.[50]

Concerning the reading of a Scripture text before a catechism sermon, the HC is a brief explanation of the main points of religion drawn from Scripture and approved by the church. So why not allow the HC to be read to the people in public assemblies? Whether or not the sermon is prefaced with a text of Scripture makes little difference. In the Palatinate, an appropriate Scripture text is read first.[51]

As for calling the HC a "little Bible," whoever said this escapes our notice, the Palatine theologians asserted. Instead, for them, the "little Bible" was the five main documents (*capita*) of the Christian religion—the Apostles' Creed, the Decalogue, the Lord's Prayer, and the institution of the Supper and of baptism; by these five documents all doctrine and sermons ought to be examined. The HC is a brief explanation of these documents drawn from Scripture. And when was it ever said that the HC is the Word of God or a canonical book?[52]

As to whether the HC is necessary for salvation, the main documents of religion contained in the HC are necessary for salvation. And ministers are indeed bound to these main documents as a norm for interpretation, but not to the explanations, except as to a form of ecclesiastical consensus that is necessary for preserving the purity of doctrine.[53]

Regarding the issue of whether the characteristics of Scripture and the attributes of the divine nature are lacking in the HC, this is not the case, since each of these topics is treated in a number of questions, even if only briefly.[54]

Moving on to the particular Remonstrant observations on question 1, the Palatine delegates asserted that the highest end of catechetical instruction is consolation in life and in death; the subordinate ends or purposes are instruction of the truth and of doing good. As to whether the phrase "All things must work together for my

---

50. *ADSND*, 2/2:506.
51. *ADSND*, 2/2:506.
52. *ADSND*, 2/2:507.
53. *ADSND*, 2/2:508.
54. *ADSND*, 2/2:509.

salvation" includes sin, they replied that these words are from Romans 8:28 and that they relate to the calamities and afflictions of Christians in this life. When commentators refer to sin in this context, they mean the following: these things, by accident, by God's gracious condoning, work together for the salvation of believers and make them more eager to seek God's mercy and more resolute to observe His ways. Those who see in this a license to sin never taste this lively consolation.[55]

The answer about the law, in question 3, is indeed complete; examining the conscience suitably follows in question 5. Not everything needs to be said in one place.[56]

On the Remonstrant suggestion to add the distinction between obtaining and applying salvation in question 20, the Palatine theologians replied that the distinction was unnecessary and superfluous, since nowhere in Scripture does it say that Christ obtained salvation for the whole human race. Besides, this phrase is ambiguous—for Christ can be said to have obtained salvation either by the breadth of His merit (which extends to the whole human race) or by the efficacy of His merit (which extends only to believers).[57]

From the words of question 21, the Palatine delegates said, it does not follow that Christ or His merit is a cause of election. God's mercy alone is the highest cause of all the benefits we receive, and from that alone flows our election. The merit of Christ is a subordinate cause, not of election but of the benefits mentioned in this question.[58]

When question 37 says that Christ sustained God's wrath against the sin of the whole human race, it is not speaking about the end and the fruit of Christ's death, as if Christ made satisfaction for not only the elect but also the reprobate; rather, it is speaking of the efficient and material cause of Christ's suffering—that He sustained God's wrath, which was caused by the sin of the whole human race. That Christ did not sustain God's wrath for unbelievers, nor make satisfaction for them, is evident in the fact that God's wrath remains for them to bear in eternity.[59]

---

55. *ADSND*, 2/2:509, 511.
56. *ADSND*, 2/2:516.
57. *ADSND*, 2/2:528.
58. *ADSND*, 2/2:540.
59. *ADSND*, 2/2:550.

As to whether faith, in question 65, is caused by an irresistible power, the Palatine delegates asserted that the power of implanting faith in us is by the efficacy of the Holy Spirit as the principal agent. The Holy Spirit, by His divine power, removes the resistibility that is in us; otherwise, no one would be converted.[60]

As it turned out, the synod never did specifically consider the Remonstrant observations on the HC nor the response of the Palatine theologians. Other issues were just too pressing.

Examination and Approval of the Heidelberg Catechism

After the synod finished drafting the Canons, the States General, on 27 April, approved the actions of the synod and then asked the synod to review the doctrine of the BC and the HC for anything that was not consistent with Scripture.[61] Hence, on 29 and 30 April, the synod read the BC, and both foreign and Dutch delegations declared that it contained no doctrine inconsistent with Scripture; the phraseology and the articles on church order were not up for discussion.

Then, on the morning of 1 May (session 147), state delegate Martinus Gregorii reported on the States General's intention to also have the HC reviewed and examined, and they wanted everyone to freely declare whether they thought there was anything in the HC inconsistent with the Word of God.[62] So, in this session, secretary Dammanus publicly read all the questions and answers of the HC; which Latin edition of the HC was used is not known. Every delegation was asked to declare their view of the doctrine contained in the HC, not the method or the phraseology. The delegations had until 4 p.m. that afternoon to prepare their judgments on this.[63]

That afternoon, the synod met in closed session (session 148) to hear the advice of the various delegations and to make its own judgment. President Bogerman first commented that Arminius and Uytenbogaert had twelve years earlier espoused a different interpretation of Christ's descent to hell than that found in article 44 of the HC,

---

60. *ADSND*, 2/2:565.
61. *RSG*, 4:108–9.
62. *ADSND*, 1:150. Gregorii's statement on the need to review the Catechism is found in the Acta Contracta, *ADSND*, 1:448–49.
63. *ADSND*, 1:150; Balcanqual, 2:162.

by appealing to the confessions of other Reformed churches. Already then, the answer to them was that the explanation of the HC's article 44, that Christ suffered the torments of hell on the cross, was the officially accepted interpretation of the Dutch churches, but this was not meant to do injustice to the interpretations of other churches.[64]

In their judgment, the British theologians praised the HC, saying that neither their churches, nor the French, had such an excellent catechism. The men who drafted it were singularly moved by the Spirit of God. In various other matters, some theologians exceeded them, but in drafting this Catechism, they had surpassed themselves.[65] In connection with question 103 on keeping the Sabbath holy, the British took notice of the serious offense given by the city of Dordrecht in neglecting the Lord's Day, and they asked the synod to request the magistrate not to allow open shops and markets on Sundays. However, on the matter of Christ's descent to hell, the British defended the right of their churches to interpret this differently, although they admitted that the Heidelberg interpretation was according to the analogy of faith. The Bremen delegates had the same reservation.[66]

The Palatine theologians then gave a short overview of the history of the HC. Which delegate presented the overview—Abraham Scultetus, Paul Tossanus, or Heinrich Alting—is not clear. But according to the journal of Caspar Sibelius (a minister delegate from Overijssel), they asserted that "three years before the Belgic Confession was presented [1566],[67] the Catechism was prepared by the work of Ursinus, Zanchi, Boquinus, and others, under the care of Frederick III

---

64. Sibelius, 112v; Kuyper, *Post-Acta*, 330.

65. Kuyper, *Post-Acta*, 330; Jacobus Trigland, *Kerckelycke Geschiedenissen* (Leiden, 1650), 1145.

66. Kuyper, *Post-Acta*, 330–31; Balcanqual, 2:162; Heyngius, "Acta," 150.

67. The reference to the BC being presented is the presentation of the BC to Emperor Maximilian at the 1566 Diet of Augsburg. While modern scholarship doubts that this actually occurred, at the time of the Synod of Dordt this was commonly believed; Nicolaas H. Gootjes, *The Belgic Confession: Its History and Sources* (Grand Rapids: Baker Academic, 2007), 96–97. For example, in *Belydenisse des Gheloofs der Kercken Iesu Christi inde Nederlanden* (Middelburg: Richard Schilders, 1611), "Tot den Leser"; and Antonius Thysius, *Leere ende Order der Nederlansche, so Duytsche als Walsche Ghereformeerder Kercken* (Amsterdam, 1615), (**) 3, A.

of pious memory."[68] This happens to be one of the very earliest documentary sources to actually mention names of the authors of the HC. But is the report reliable? The quote clearly suggests that the HC was a team project. Ursinus's primary role is well established. Olevianus is not mentioned, but he may be included in "others." As for Boquinus, the possibility of his input in the HC is credible, since he joined the Heidelberg theology faculty in 1557 and was there when the HC was drafted. Zanchi, however, is the challenge. Zanchi was still in Strasbourg in 1562–1563, when the HC was written, in the midst of the predestination controversy with the Lutheran Marbach, and he joined the Heidelberg theology faculty only in 1568, five years after the HC was written. But Zanchi had a close relationship with the Heidelberg theology faculty; in 1561, he visited Heidelberg in the midst of his controversy, and the Heidelberg theologians gave their judgment on that controversy in favor of Zanchi.[69]

---

68. Sibelius, "Annotationes," 112v: "Triennio ante exhibitam confessionem Belgicam, fuit concinnatus catechismus, opera Ursini, Zanchii, Boquini et aliorum cura Friderici III p. m." Heyngius, "Acta," 150, does not mention names, only that the HC was written with great care "a celeberrimis theologis." Theodore Tronchin's journal, in Tronchin, vol. 16, 160r, also does not mention names. Unfortunately, the Palatine delegate who addressed the Synod of Dordt (Scultetus, Tossanus, or Alting) is not mentioned in any of the sources. Scultetus (1566–1624) had first come to Heidelberg in 1590 as a student; he became court chaplain to Frederick IV in 1595 and became a professor of Old Testament at Heidelberg in 1618. Tossanus (1572–1634) studied at Heidelberg and Geneva and became a minister in Heidelberg, but his father, Daniel, had been chaplain to Elector Frederick III from 1573 to 1576 and later became professor of New Testament in Heidelberg. In 1605, Alting (1583–1644) became a tutor to Frederick V, whom he also catechized (cf. his *Catechetischer Unterricht des Pflazgrafen Friedrich V*, taught in 1606–1607), and then became professor of dogmatics at Heidelberg in 1613; his father, Menso, had been a student at Heidelberg in 1565 and was a friend of Olevianus. Alting has thus far been considered the earliest to actually name the authors of the HC, in a work of 1646 (his *Scriptorum*, 3:5; cf. Lyle D. Bierma, *An Introduction to the Heidelberg Catechism: Sources, History, and Theology*, with Charles D. Gunnoe Jr., Karin Y. Maag, and Paul W. Fields [Grand Rapids: Baker Academic, 2005], 59–60). Any of the three theologians would have been in a good position to know about and report on the history of the HC at the synod. At any rate, Sibelius can now be considered the second earliest report to actually name the authors of the HC. The earliest is Joannes Gerobulus, *Waerachtich Verhael van de Staet der Ghereformeerde Kercke…binnen Utrecht* (Utrecht, 1613), 34, which mentions only Ursinus.

69. Heinrich Alting, *Historia Ecclesiae Palatinae*, in Ludwig Mieg, *Monumenta*

Returning to the Palatine delegates' overview of the history of the HC, they said that the HC was attacked at various times by Lutherans, especially Heshusius, but that it was never proven untrue; even Frederick III himself had taken up the defense of the HC at the Diet of Augsburg in 1566. They also explained that the Remonstrant observations, which they had seen and examined, got the Remonstrants themselves into trouble with the HC, since it appeared that the HC was not in conflict with Scripture but with Socinus.[70]

From the judgments of the various delegations, the synod's decision was drawn: "It was declared, unanimously by all the foreign as well as Dutch theologians, that the doctrine contained in the Palatine Catechism wholly agrees with the Word of God, and it does not contain anything inconsistent with it, which needs to be changed or corrected." Probably because a major complaint in the Remonstrant observations was that the HC was not well suited to the level of youth and the uneducated, the synod also added: "This Catechism is a completely accurate compendium of orthodox Christian doctrine, adapted with singular wisdom not only to the level of tender youth, but also for the proper instruction of adults; and therefore this Catechism can be taught with great edification in the Dutch churches, and by all means ought to be retained."[71] The whole examination of the doctrine of the HC was completed within the two sessions of one day.

Later, the Remonstrants complained that a review of such importance was conducted behind closed doors and was done hastily, with hardly four hours spent deliberating on the HC. They also complained that the synod did not even consider the Remonstrant observations on the HC in its review.[72]

Although, in its Post-Acta sessions, the synod revised the text of the BC, it did not do so with the HC, since that was considered the

---

pietatis et literaria virorum (Frankfurt, 1701), 188; Jürgen Moltmann, *Prädestination und Perseveranz* (Neukirchen: Neukirchener Verlag, 1961), 97–100.

70. Sibelius, 112v; Heyngius, "Acta," 150; Kuyper, *Post-Acta*, 331.

71. *ADSND*, 1:150.

72. *Grouwel der Verwoestinghe staende in de heylighe plaetse; dat is, Claer ende warachtich Verhael vande voornaemste Mis-handelinghen, Onbillijcke Procedueren ende Nulliteyten des Nationalen Synodi ghehouden binnen Dordrecht inde Jaren 1618 ende 1619* (Enkhuysen, 1622), 2:37–39.

prerogative of the Palatine churches. So, while Dordt approved the doctrine of the HC, it did not produce an official text of it. Hence the most authentic Dutch text of the HC is the one that had earlier been authorized by the Zeeland provincial synod, the edition published in the 1611 *Formulierenboek*, printed at Middelburg by Richard Schilders.[73]

Toward the end of the synod, in session 177, the synod decided to prepare a document (*libellus supplex*) that would request the States General to confirm the synod's actions and follow up on some of them. This was presented to the States General on 30 May, the day after the synod ended. One item requested was that the States General confirm and defend the doctrine presented in the BC, the HC, and the Canons.[74] Attached to this request document was an act of approbation of the BC and the HC that the synod had approved a couple of days earlier (28 May). This act summarized the synod's actions in approving the BC and the HC and concluded with this request to the States General:

> [The synod] very subserviently and also very humbly requests and implores…that their High Mightinesses be pleased to maintain, propagate, confirm and protect this orthodox doctrine contained in the aforesaid Confession and Catechism by their authority more and more in their lands, and not tolerate that any violation or adulterating of this doctrine be done, nor that any other doctrine be taught or promoted in the public churches of their lands.[75]

---

73. J. N. Bakhuizen van den Brink, ed., *De Nederlandse Belijdenisgeschriften in Authentieke Teksten* (Amsterdam: Ton Bolland, 1976), 40, 149. In this edition, the title page for the catechism is *Catechismus ofte Onderwijsinghe in de Christelicke Leere, alsoo die in de Kercken ende Scholen der Keurvorstelicken Paltz ende der Nederlanden gheleert wort* (Middelburg: Richard Schilders, 1611).

74. Kuyper, *Post-Acta*, 362–63.

75. Kuyper, *Post-Acta*, 482–84. Sometime after the synod, an Arabic translation of the Heidelberg Catechism was prepared in manuscript, along with the Belgic Confession, Liturgical Forms, and Church Order of Dordt. See Nabil Matar, "The Synod of Dort in Arabic: Bodleian MS Marsh 268," *The Seventeenth Century* 39 (2024), 719–30, who incorrectly dates the manuscript May 1619.

Approval of Forms of Subscription

Early in the Dutch Reformation, only a copy of the BC was signed by ministers. In 1593, one sees the expectation that the HC be signed along with the BC. Then, as the Arminian controversy developed, both the BC and the HC became used as standards of orthodoxy. The Arminian perspective was that Scripture alone was the rule of faith and that the confessions should not be used as standards of doctrinal purity. Some Arminians signed the confessions according to their own sense of how they should be understood, so a simple signing of a copy of the BC and the HC was not a guarantee of one's orthodoxy. Hence, a more precise means of determining orthodoxy was needed; in this context, forms of subscription became prevalent in the Dutch churches. Beginning in 1608, Classis Alkmaar developed a form of subscription whereby ministers signified that both the BC and the HC agreed with the Word of God; soon, such forms of subscription were developed by various provincial synods, but there was no standard form.[76]

The Synod of Dordt first considered forms of subscription in its Post-Acta sessions, after the Arminian issue was resolved with the drafting of the Canons. In article 53 of its Dordt Church Order, the synod simply confirmed an article from the 1586 church order of The Hague declaring that ministers and theology professors must sign the BC, under threat of suspension. Then, on 14 May, the synod addressed several gravamina, including one from the South Holland Synod of Delft:

> Because the Remonstrants with their own hand sign the formulas of our unity, that is, the BC and Catechism, and yet interpret these in the wrong way, the national Synod is asked how this mischief can be counteracted, and that it see fit to read the form of subscription prepared at the Delft Synod and consider whether this form may protect the churches enough from the quibbling and reservations of all who are evasive.[77]

---

76. Sinnema, "Origin of the Form," 256–71.
77. Sinnema, "Origin of the Form," 271.

After some discussion, the next day the synod decided to draft a new form of subscription that required all ministers to subscribe, not only to the BC and the HC, but also to the Canons of Dordt:

> It was decided that a carefully prepared form of subscription shall be drawn up, by which ministers of the church shall subscribe to the Confession, the Catechism, and the synodical *Explanation* concerning the Five Articles of the Remonstrants, so that they may clearly bear witness to their orthodox views and to prevent the wrongful evasions of some about subscription.[78]

A committee was appointed to draft the new form of subscription for ministers, and, on 17 May, their draft was ready. After some changes, it was approved. In this new form, ministers declared that "all the articles and points of doctrine contained in this BC and HC of the Reformed churches of the Netherlands, together with the *Explanation* of some points of the aforesaid doctrine [the Canons] made by the national Synod of Dordrecht, 1619, do fully agree with the Word of God." They also promised to diligently teach this doctrine and oppose all errors in conflict with it. If they had any objections to this doctrine, they promised not to teach them, but rather to reveal them to church authorities for their judgment and be willing to give a further explanation if required, under the penalty of suspension if they refused.[79]

In the same session, the synod decided to extend such subscription to professors of theology, regents, rectors, and schoolteachers. A week later, separate forms of subscription, with wording that was similar to the form for ministers, were approved for professors of theology and regents, and for rectors and schoolteachers. For professors in other university departments, the synod recommended that they subscribe to the BC and the HC, but it prepared no form of subscription for them. As for subscription by elders and deacons, the synod left this to the discretion of local classes and provincial synods.[80]

---

78. Sinnema, "Origin of the Form," 272.
79. Sinnema, "Origin of the Form," 273–74.
80. Sinnema, "Origin of the Form," 274–76.

Conclusion

If one were to summarize the relationship of the synod to the HC in one sentence, it would be this: The Synod of Dordt officially confirmed and strengthened the authority of the HC in its two primary roles within the Dutch Reformed churches—as the principal pedagogical tool to provide instruction in the basic elements of the Reformed faith, and as a confessional standard to ensure orthodox Reformed teaching in the churches. Dordt did not adopt the HC for the first time, change it, or introduce any new role for it. It confirmed the doctrine of the HC and strengthened it by standardizing and regularizing roles and practices that were already in place in these churches—catechetical instruction in the home, school, and church; Sunday afternoon catechism services; pre-confession catechism classes; and its role as a confessional standard, alongside the BC and the Canons of Dordt, by the use of forms of subscription to be signed by ministers, teachers, and theologians.

IVDICIVM
SYNODI
NATIONALIS,
REFORMATARVM
ECCLESIARVM BELGICARVM,
habitæ
DORDRECHTI,
Anno 1618. & 1619.

Cui etiam interfuerunt plurimi insignes Theologi Reformatarum Ecclesiarum Magnæ Britanniæ, Palatinatus Electoralis, Hassiæ, Helvetiæ, Correspondentiæ VVedderavicæ, Genevensis, Bremensis, & Emdanæ,

DE
QUINQUE DOCTRINAE
Capitibus *in Ecclesiis Belgicis Controversis*.

Promulgatum VI. May, cIɔ. Iɔc. xix.

Cum Privilegio.

The first printing of the Canons of Dordt (Dordrecht 1619)

CHAPTER 5

The Doctrine of Election at the Synod of Dordt[1]

The doctrine of election as promulgated by the Synod of Dordt is rather well known; it is presented in Chapter I of the Canons of Dordt, which are still used as a confessional standard in Reformed churches of Dutch heritage. I will approach this topic by focusing on the process by which the synod examined the Remonstrant views on election, which were at the center of the controversy in the Dutch churches at that time, and then on how the synod formulated its own response or judgment of these views, a process ending in the drafting of the Canons.[2]

At the time of the Arminian, or Remonstrant, controversy, the confessional basis for the doctrine of election in the Dutch Reformed churches was quite minimal. The main statement was article 16 of the Belgic Confession:

> [God is] merciful in drawing and saving from this perdition those whom he, in his eternal and unchangeable counsel, has elected in Jesus Christ our Lord by his pure goodness, without any consideration of

---

1. This article, slightly revised, is reprinted from Frank van der Pol, ed., *The Doctrine of Election in Reformed Perspective: Historical and Theological Investigations of the Synod of Dordt 1618–1619* (Göttingen: Vandenhoeck and Ruprecht, 2019), 115–35.
2. In this article, I do not focus on the related issue of reprobation, a topic that I examined in Donald Sinnema, "The Issue of Reprobation at the Synod of Dort (1618-19) in Light of the History of this Doctrine" (PhD diss., University of St. Michael's College, Toronto, 1985). Translations in this article are mine.

their works. He is just in leaving the others in their fall and ruin into which they plunged themselves.³

The Heidelberg Catechism, in answer 54, merely describes the church as "a community elected to eternal life."

Although Calvin, Beza, Bullinger, and others in the Reformed tradition had written quite extensively about election, with varying emphases, the confessional statements of the Dutch Reformed churches left a number of issues relating to election undefined.

Arminius

The Arminian controversy that led to the Synod of Dordt began with the views of Jacobus Arminius on predestination. While he presented his views in various writings, the clearest expression of his position was in his *Verclaringhe* of 1608. Here he identified a fourfold order of decrees in predestination (here abbreviated):

(1) To save sinful man, God decreed to appoint His Son as Mediator.

(2) He decreed to save in Christ, for Christ's sake, and through Christ those who believe and persevere but to leave in sin and damn unbelievers.

(3) He decreed to administer the means necessary for repentance and faith.

(4) He decreed to save and damn particular persons, based on His foreknowledge of who, by grace, would believe and persevere and who would not.⁴

Arminius also described faith as a necessary condition foreseen by God in those to be elected. This did not mean election was conditional upon human merit, since faith is a gift of God's grace.⁵

---

3. J. N. Bakhuizen van den Brink, ed., *De Nederlandse Belijdenisgeschriften in Authentieke Teksten* (Amsterdam: Ton Bolland. 1976), 97–99.

4. G. J. Hoenderdaal, ed., *Verclaring van Jacobus Arminius* (Lochem: De Tijdstroom, 1960), 104–6; Arminius, *Works* (Grand Rapids: Baker, 1986), 1:589–90.

5. Jacobus Arminius, *Apologia adversus Articulos XXXI*, in his *Opera Theologica*

The Remonstrance of 1610

The basis of the debates that led to the Synod of Dordt was the Remonstrance of 1610, a summary of Arminius's key ideas in Five Articles, formulated by Arminius's followers after his death in 1609. Article I states:

> That God, by an eternal unchangeable decree, has in Jesus Christ his Son decreed, before the foundation of the world was laid, to save out of the fallen sinful human race those in Christ, for the sake of Christ, and through Christ, who by the grace of the Holy Spirit shall believe in this his Son Jesus and persevere in the same faith and obedience of faith by the same grace to the end; and on the other hand, to leave the impenitent and unbelievers in sin and under wrath, and to condemn them as alienated from Christ, according to the word of the holy Gospel in John 3:36: "Whoever believes in the Son has eternal life, and whoever is disobedient to the Son shall not see life, but the wrath of God remains on him," and also other passages of the Scriptures.[6]

The Hague Conference (1611)

In an attempt to settle the controversy over predestination and related ideas centering on the Five Remonstrant Articles, the States of Holland and West-Friesland arranged for a conference between six Remonstrant leaders and six Contra-Remonstrant leaders in The Hague in 1611. While this conference more clearly defined the issues, no agreement was reached between the two sides.[7]

It is important to recognize that several Remonstrant writings after the 1610 Remonstrance more clearly defined, developed, or drew out implications of the Remonstrant doctrine of election, in ways that went beyond statements of Arminius and the Remonstrance. Hence,

---

(Leiden: G. Basson, 1629), 138–40; Arminius, *Disputationes...Publicae et Privatae* (Leiden: T. Basson, 1610), 155; Arminius, *Works*, 1:681–86; 2:228.

6. G. J. Hoenderdaal, "Remonstrantie en Contraremonstrantie," *Nederlands Archief voor Kerkgeschiedenis* 51, no. 1 (1970): 74.

7. On the 1611 Hague conference, see P. Wijminga, *Festus Hommius* (Leiden: Donner, 1899), 104–22; H. Rogge, *Johannes Wtenbogaert en zijn Tijd* (Amsterdam: Y. Rogge, 1874–1876), 2:70–102; and William A. den Boer, "Nederlandse Gereformeerde Theologie op Weg naar de Synode van Dordrecht 1618-1619: De Haagsche Conferentie van 1611" (Doctoraalscriptie, Theologische Universiteit Apeldoorn, 2003).

for example, the idea that Article I of the Remonstrance described the *whole* decree of election was first presented in Remonstrant writings at the Hague Conference,[8] and the multiple distinctions within election between general and particular election, indefinite and definite election, incomplete and complete election, non-peremptory and peremptory election, revocable and irrevocable election, were first developed in later writings by Nicolaas Grevinchoven, Caspar Barlaeus, and the Gelderland Remonstrants.[9]

In the next seven years, the controversy only escalated as the debates heated and as many polemical writings were produced on both sides. Key figures for the Remonstrants included Johannes Uytenbogaert, Simon Episcopius, Nicolaas Grevinchoven, Johannes Arnoldi Corvinus, and Caspar Barlaeus, and for the Contra-Remonstrants, William Ames,[10] Franciscus Gomarus, Festus Hommius, and Petrus Plancius.

The Synod of Dordt (1618–1619)

To settle the religious controversy that agitated the Dutch churches and stirred up unrest in broader Dutch society, the States General finally convened the Synod of Dordt in 1618. Thirteen Remonstrant leaders were summoned before the synod, so that it might examine the disputed Remonstrant views. Before they arrived, the synod dealt with several other ecclesiastical matters in the so-called "Pro-Acta" sessions. After the Remonstrants arrived on 6 December 1618, there were five weeks of what may best be called procedural wrangling between the synod and the cited Remonstrants over how best to deal with the theological issues. During this period, the acrimony over procedure made discussion of the actual theological issues impossible. The

---

8. *Schriftelicke Conferentie, gehouden in s'Gravenhaghe inden Iare 1611, tusschen sommighe Kercken-dienaren, aengaende de Godlicke Praedestinatie metten aencleven van dien* (The Hague: H. Jacobsz., 1612), 57.

9. E.g., Nicolaas Grevinchoven, *Dissertatio Theologica de Duabus Quaestionibus hoc Tempore Controversis, quarum Prima est de Reconciliatione per Mortem Christi Impetrata Omnibus ac Singulis Hominibus; Altera, de Electione ex Fide Praevisa* (Rotterdam: M. Sebastiani, 1615), 105, 136–37.

10. For William Ames's polemical writings against the Remonstrants prior to the Synod of Dordt, see Takayuki Yagi, *A Gift from England: William Ames and His Polemical Discourse against Dutch Arminianism* (Göttingen: Vandenhoeck and Ruprecht, 2020).

Remonstrants wanted a conference between equal parties; the synod wanted a disciplinary procedure that would examine and judge the Remonstrant views. The Remonstrants wanted the discussion to focus on what they considered extreme Reformed views of reprobation; the synod wanted the discussion to focus on the Remonstrant view of election based on foreseen faith. While some procedural compromises were made, the Remonstrants did not fully cooperate with the questioning and procedures of the synod; this acrimonious period of procedural wrangling ended with the expulsion of the Remonstrants from the synod on 14 January 1619.[11]

Summary of Remonstrant Views by the Dutch Professors

During this procedural period, however, steps were taken behind the scenes to draw up a summary of Remonstrant views on the Five Articles based on their writings. This was done by the five Dutch professors of theology at the synod (Johannes Polyander, Sibrandus Lubbertus, Franciscus Gomarus, Antonius Walaeus, and Antonius Thysius) and was submitted to the president of the synod on 8 December 1618.[12] This document was not considered in this phase of the synod, but it was likely used as a resource when the *Articuli* on Remonstrant views were later prepared.

The professors' summary of the Remonstrant views on Article I consisted of eight points (including references to sources), which are presented here in abbreviated form:

(1) God decreed to save those in Christ who will believe and persevere; there is no other predestination to salvation.

---

11. For details, see Sinnema, "Issue of Reprobation," ch. 4; and Donald Sinnema, "Procedural Wrangling in the Remonstrant Case at the Synod of Dordt (1618–1619)," in *More than Luther: The Reformation and the Rise of Pluralism in Europe*, ed. Karla Boersma and Herman J. Selderhuis (Göttingen: Vandenhoeck and Ruprecht, 2019), 289–306. Reprinted in this volume; see chapter 2.

12. "Sententia Theologorum Remonstrantium de Quinque Articulis, quos in Collatione Hagiensi Defendere atque in Ecclesias Belgii Reformatas Introducere Conati Fuerunt. Collecta ex Scriptis Ipsorum a Quinque Sacrae Theologiae Professoribus Orthodoxis Belgis ad Synodum Nationalem Dordrechtanam Missis"; printed in *ADSND*, 2/2:289–91.

(2) In the general words of Article I, they understand also individual persons.

(3) Faith and perseverance are prior to election, since God, in electing, considered people as believing.

(4) In electing, God considered faith not as a cause giving rise to election but as an antecedent condition.

(5) Though they exclude from election a regard for works, yet they mention that, in electing, God considered faith and the obedience of faith.

(6) They reject that God's decree concerning the end and the means are one and the same.

(7) They deny that calling is a means of executing the predestination of individuals.

(8) They say that the cause for which God considered one people rather than another worthy of the gospel was only His good pleasure; nevertheless, they also say that God considered them worthy by a gracious valuing of them, by which He judges them suitable through a natural knowledge of His law and a better use of common grace.

The Remonstrant *Sententia* on Article I

In the citation letters by which they were summoned before the synod, the cited Remonstrants were asked to "state, explain and defend [*proponant, explicent et defendant*]" their own views of the Five Articles.[13] As a result, they presented three sets of documents on each of the Five Articles—a *Statement*, an *Explanation*, and a *Defense*.

On 13 December 1618, the cited Remonstrants submitted the *Statement* (*Sententia*) of their views on the First Article of the Remonstrance.[14] Of the ten theses of the *Sententia*, seven dealt with election; these are formulated partly in negative form, rejecting

---

13. *ADSND*, 1:15, 201.
14. "Sententia Remonstrantium, quam in conscientia sua Verbo Dei consentaneam esse arbitrati sunt hactenus, & etiamnum arbitrantur, circa Primum de Praedestinationis Decreto Articulum," in *Acta*, 1:113–14.

Contra-Remonstant views, and partly in positive form, expressing their own opinions. Especially rejected is (a) the supralapsarian position, (b) the view that the decree of salvation is a decree of the end absolutely intended, with means that inevitably lead the elect to their destined end, (c) that God has ordained the fall, and (d) that Christ as mediator is solely the executor of election (theses 1–3). Affirmed is the idea that Christ is not merely the executor of election but also the foundation (*fundamentum*) of the decree of election. Also affirmed is that God has ordained that Christ should be a propitiation for the sins of the whole world and that, by virtue of this decree, He has determined to justify and to save those who believe in Him and to provide the means necessary and sufficient for faith (theses 3 and 5). Especially pertinent is thesis 7:

> The election of particular persons is peremptory [*peremtoria*], out of consideration of faith in Jesus Christ and of perseverance…as a condition prerequisite for electing.[15]

Regarding children, the Remonstrants affirmed that all believers' children who die in infancy before they have committed any actual sin are sanctified in Christ and are not among the reprobate (theses 9 and 10).

The *Articuli* on Article I

With the synod and the Remonstrants deadlocked on procedure, the synod thought that the only alternative was to examine the Remonstrant views from their writings, following the 1 January 1619 resolution of the States General to examine the Remonstrants from their writings if they did not cooperate. To facilitate this procedure, on 8 January President Johannes Bogerman dictated to the synod a number of *Theses* on Article I, which were drawn up by him and the synod secretaries and assessors from Remonstrant writings. In drawing up these *Theses*, it is likely that the officers used, besides their own knowledge of the writings, the summary of Remonstrant views submitted by the five Dutch professors.

The various delegations then gave their advice on the *Theses*, concerning whether they faithfully presented Remonstrant views. On 10

---

15. *Acta*, 1:114.

January, Bogerman dictated a revised version of the *Theses* (now called *Articuli*) based on the advice received.[16]

In its final version, the *Articuli* contained twelve articles in which the synod officers tried to summarize the Remonstrant view of election.[17] In brief, the twelve points were as follows:

1. God made a four-part decree to save sinners: first, out of love for His creatures and to show mercy, He decreed to send His Son into the world to obtain redemption; second, He decreed to save those who repent and believe in Christ by a true persevering faith (in the Hague Conference, they said that this is the whole decree of predestination to salvation); third, He decreed the means necessary for repentance and faith; and fourth, He decreed to save individual believers.

2. Election to salvation is of many kinds: indefinite or definite, general (to save believers) or particular (to save individual believers), the latter being either incomplete, non-peremptory, and revocable, or complete, peremptory, and irrevocable.

3. The election of individual persons is based on their foreseen faith, obedience of faith, and repentance, as the condition of the new covenant required by God and fulfilled by man, which, as a favored worthiness by which one who is elected is regarded as more worthy than one who is not, moves God to elect.

4. Faith, repentance, obedience, and perseverance are not fruits or effects of election but antecedents to it.

5. The decree of election is not absolute, nor is God's good pleasure the only cause for which He elects this person rather than that one.

---

16. Sinnema, "Issue of Reprobation," 250–53. The advice of the delegations is printed in *ADSND*, 2/2:733–78.

17. "Articuli pertinentes ad Pleniorem Explicationem Sententiae Remonstrantium, circa I Hagiensem Articulum, Formati ex ipsorum Scriptis Editis, Declarationibus Authenticis, et Exhibitis Thesibus"; printed in *ADSND*, 2/2:781–87.

6. The decree of election to faith is prior to the decree of election to glory.

7. Just as Christ is the foundation and the meritorious cause of salvation, He is also the foundation and the meritorious cause of election to glory.

8. Faith is the cause of justification and of election, and yet it remains a gift of God.

9. Incomplete and non-peremptory election can be interrupted, and such elect persons can become reprobate and die.

10. No one in this life is peremptorily elect until he dies in faith, so there is no certain awareness of election in this life.

11. Election in the Old Testament is different than election in the New Testament.

12. We are uncertain whether there is an election of those unbelievers who have not heard the gospel but who are corrected by common grace or have some faith in God without a knowledge of Christ.

The Remonstrant sources on which Bogerman and the other synod officers based these points in the *Articuli* included the following:

- Jacobus Arminius, *Articuli Nonnulli Diligenti Examine Perpendi, eo quod inter ipsos Reformatae Religionis Professores de iis aliqua incidit Controversia*, appended to his *Epistola ad Hippolytum* (Delft, 1613), 21.

- Article I of the 1610 Remonstrance.

- Writings of the Hague Conference (1611): *Schriftelicke Conferentie, gehouden in s'Gravenhaghe inden Iare 1611, tusschen sommighe Kercken-dienaren, aengaende de Godlicke Praedestinatie metten aencleven van dien* (The Hague, 1612; 2nd ed., 1617), 35, 82, 89, 93, 94, 96, 109, 413; Henricus Brandius, trans., *Collatio Scripto habita Hagae-comitis anno ab incarnato Domino 1611, inter quosdam Ecclesiastas de divina Praedestinatione, & eius appendicibus* (Zierikzee, 1615) [Latin translation of *Schriftelicke Conferentie* by Contra-Remonstrant Henricus Brandius], 42, 109, 110, 127, 492.

- "Declaratio super sex articulis Collationis Delphensis" [Remonstrant response to the six articles of the 1613 Delft Conference, which was submitted to the South Holland synod of Delft in 1618].[18]

- Johannes Arnoldi Corvinus, *Defensio Sententiae D. Iacobi Arminii de Praedestinatione, Gratia Dei, Libero Hominis Arbitrio, &c.* (Leiden, 1613) [against Daniel Tilenus], 28, 52, 53, 56, 57, 265.

- Nicolaas Grevinchoven, *Dissertatio Theologica de Duabus Quaestionibus hoc Tempore Controversis, quarum Prima est de Reconciliatione per Mortem Christi Impetrata Omnibus ac Singulis Hominibus; Altera, de Electione ex Fide Praevisa* (Rotterdam, 1615) [against William Ames], 29, 108, 111, 116, 117, 132, 133, 136, 137, 138, 140, 191.

- [Caspar Barlaeus], *Epistola Ecclesiastarum, quos in Belgio Remonstrantes vocant, ad Exterarum Ecclesiarum Reformatos Doctores, Pastores, Theologos, qua Sententiam suam de Praedestinatione & annexis ei capitibus exponunt*, 2nd ed. (Leiden, 1617) [against the Classis Walcheren letter to foreign theologians], 34, 35, 36, 46, 49.

- "Status Quaestionis super Quinque Articulis" [Gelderland Remonstrant points of agreement and disagreement with the Contra-Remonstrants of the Gelderland synod of Arnhem in 1618].[19]

- Simon Episcopius, *Collegium Disputationum Theologicarum in Academia Leydensi privatim institutarum* (Leiden, 1618) [published by Festus Hommius], 35, 38, 39, 40, 41, 42, 45, 64, 65.

- *Sententia Remonstrantium* on Article I [theses submitted to the synod on 13 December 1618], theses 1, 2, and 7.

---

18. Printed in *ADSND*, 2/2:668–83.
19. Printed in *ADSND*, 2/2:684–89.

The Doctrine of Election at the Synod of Dordt

The Remonstrant *Declaratio* on Article I

The Remonstrants presented their *Explanation* (*Declaratio*) of Article I on 14 January, the day they were expelled from the synod. In thirty-two pages, they presented a more detailed explanation of Article I than in the theses of their *Sententia*. Episcopius was the author. Copies of the *Declaratio* were made by each delegation.

The *Declaratio* consists of three sections. The first focused on the concepts of election and reprobation. A basic distinction is made between God's *general* decree, by which He decided by His free choice to save believers and reprobate unbelievers, and His *special* decree, by which He decided to save certain individuals considered by God as believers destined to eternal life and to condemn others considered as unbelievers. The cause of the general decree is God's pure will; the special decree presupposes a consideration and regard for faith and unbelief. In this decree, faith and perseverance are conditions performed by humans, but they are not merits. The object of peremptory election to eternal life is all who believe (by the help of grace) and persevere in faith. And Christ is the foundation of the decree of election.[20]

The second section focused on the order of divine decrees in election. Here the Remonstrants identified seven decrees. This was an expanded version of the four decrees identified by Arminius. They added three decrees prior in order to his four: (1) God's decree to create man; (2) the decree to establish the law; (3) when Adam transgressed the law, God decreed to deliver miserable humans; (4) the decree to appoint a mediator to atone for sinners; (5) the decree to save all who would believe and persevere in faith; (6) the decree to provide the necessary means for faith; and (7) the decree to save individuals who would believe and persevere in faith.[21] This section also analyzed the supralapsarian and infralapsarian (here called *supralapsarii* and *sublapsarii*) positions on the order of decrees, positions that the Remonstrants rejected.[22]

In the third section of the *Declaratio*, the Remonstrants considered the issue of the election and reprobation of infants. They contended

---

20. "Declaratio Sententiae Remonstrantium circa Primum de Praedestinationis Decreto Articulum," in *Acta et Scripta*, 2:3–10.
21. *Acta et Scripta*, 2:10–11.
22. *Acta et Scripta*, 2:11–18.

that Contra-Remonstrants were accustomed to include among the reprobate not only children of unbelievers but also certain children of believers who die in infancy.[23]

Appended to the *Declaratio* was a *Syllabus Testimoniarum*, twenty-nine pages of quotations from writings of Reformed theologians, to demonstrate that these theologians indeed taught the ideas that the Remonstrants rejected in their *Sententia*. Many of these quotations focused on reprobation, since it was reprobation that the Remonstrants considered most offensive. Nevertheless, they also objected to certain Reformed statements on election, such as: "God decreed to elect some and reprobate others, before He decreed to create them"; "According to His good pleasure, God decreed to elect some to eternal life and reprobate others"; "Christ as mediator is not the foundation of the decree of election, but only the executor of this decree"; "The cause why some are called effectively, are justified, persevere in faith, and are glorified, is that they were elected absolutely to eternal life"; and "By His absolute decree, God destined to give Christ the mediator only to the elect."[24]

Speeches on Article I

Soon after the Remonstrants were expelled from the synod, various Dutch and foreign theologians presented public speeches on the Five Articles, while the various delegations worked to formulate their judgments on these Articles. Eleven speeches were presented on the topic of election between 17 and 28 January 1619.[25]

Sibrandus Lubbertus examined whether Scripture supports the idea that God's decree to save believers is the whole decree of predestination. Franciscus Gomarus explained the terms *eligere*, *electio*, and *electi* and proved that the subject of election is not persevering believers. Bishop George Carleton and Paul Tossanus briefly addressed several biblical passages relating to election. Antonius Thysius also examined the question of whether the decree to save believers is the whole decree of predestination, as well as the question of whether faith is the prerequisite condition for election. Johannes Polyander focused

---

23. *Acta et Scripta*, 2:21–24.
24. *Acta et Scripta*, 2:25–26, 28, 34, 35, 37.
25. *ADSND*, 1:116, 119, 120, 121. These speeches are preserved in OSA, vol. K. Lubbertus's speech is missing.

on several biblical passages, especially those concerning names written in the Book of Life. Antonius Walaeus focused mostly on Romans 9. John Davenant considered whether divine election is singular or of many kinds. Samuel Ward examined Remonstrant arguments that tried to prove that the decree to save believers is election to salvation because Christ is its foundation. The philosopher Rudolph Goclenius used principles of logic to refute a Remonstrant syllogism drawn from the execution of predestination. Finally, Abraham Scultetus focused on the awareness of election and its certainty.

The Remonstrant *Defensio* on Article I

On 7 February, the Remonstrants submitted a lengthy 385-page *Defense* of their views on Article I to the state delegates. Episcopius was the main author. Although parts of this *Defensio* were read to the synod between 18 and 23 February,[26] it was not discussed, and its impact on synod deliberations seems to have been minimal.

The *Defensio* opened by defining the state of the controversy and then examined in detail the main passages used by the Contra-Remonstrants to support their view of election and reprobation. Included among the election passages were two expositions of Romans 9, a shorter one by Episcopius and a lengthy one by Adrianus Borrius. The document ended with a detailed discussion of reprobation by Carolus Niellius.[27]

The *Iudicia* on Article I

During this time, the nineteen delegations prepared their own judgments (*iudicia*) on each of the Five Remonstrant Articles. Based on these, a single synodical judgment was to be drawn up. Since the Dutch professors Lubbertus and Gomarus each wrote their own judgments, there were actually twenty-one *iudicia* on Article I. These *iudicia* were read in the synod from 6 to 12 March.[28]

The great majority of these *iudicia* focused on refuting the following points in the Remonstrant position:

---

26. *ADSND*, 1:124, 127, 129.
27. *Acta et Scripta*, 2:47–278.
28. *ADSND*, 1:132–35.

- God's decree to save those who believe (that is, Article I) is the whole decree of predestination to salvation.[29]

- There are multiple forms of election: general and particular, the latter being either incomplete, non-peremptory, and revocable, or complete, peremptory, and irrevocable. Article I of the Remonstrance describes the general election of believers in general, as distinct from the particular election of individual persons.[30]

- The cause of the general decree is God's good pleasure, by which He decided from many possible conditions to select faith as the condition for salvation.[31]

- The cause or basis of the election of particular persons is God's foreknowledge of their faith and perseverance in faith.[32]

- Faith and perseverance in faith are prerequisite conditions for election, not fruits of election.[33]

- Non-peremptory (incomplete, until one's death) election is changeable; during one's life, an elect person can lose faith and become reprobate.[34]

- Since such election is changeable, there is no certainty of election in this life.[35]

Several *iudicia* also focused on the issue of the predestination of infants:

- There is no election or reprobation of infants who die, since they are too young to have faith.[36]

---

29. *Acta*, 2:6, 15, 24, 26, 35, 38, 41, 54, 63; 3:3, 14, 20, 25, 36, 47, 54, 63, 70, 85.
30. *Acta*, 2:7, 16, 28, 39, 42, 54, 64; 3:4, 15, 20–21, 37, 47, 57, 63, 71, 85.
31. *Acta*, 2:10, 17, 25, 39, 43, 53, 54; 3:5, 44, 47, 57, 63.
32. *Acta*, 2:6, 17, 25, 35, 39, 43, 53, 54; 3:5, 15, 21, 29, 34, 47, 56, 71, 80, 86.
33. *Acta*, 2:6–7, 17, 24, 35, 39, 44, 56, 64; 3:15, 22, 34, 38, 48, 58, 64, 71, 80, 86.
34. *Acta*, 2:7, 18, 30, 39, 43, 53, 56, 71; 3:6, 16, 22, 39, 48, 65, 73, 79, 85.
35. *Acta*, 2:9, 18, 32, 39, 44, 54, 57, 72; 3:7, 17, 22, 30, 33, 39, 48, 59, 66, 74, 82, 86.
36. *Acta*, 2:10; 3:10, 19, 23, 49, 69.

The Hesse and Frisian *iudicia* pointed out that there was a difference between Article I of the Remonstrance and later explanations of it. Both stated that Article I, in itself, is not unbiblical (though its ambiguity may hide errors), while the fuller explanations are unbiblical. Both also pointed out a contradiction in the Remonstrant position: When Remonstrants (at the Hague Conference) claimed that God's will to save believers is the *whole* decree of predestination to salvation, this contradicted Arminius's and their own view of four decrees of predestination, including the particular decree; the decree to save believers is just the second of the four decrees.[37]

For the *iudicia*, a key source for identifying Remonstrant errors was Bogerman's *Articuli*, which attempted to summarize the Remonstrant view of election. While the delegations drew upon the *Articuli* to varying degrees,[38] they did not slavishly follow Bogerman's list. It is apparent that the delegations also made use of the Remonstrants' own writings, at least to some extent. Where the *iudicia* cite the sources of heterodox opinions, these are sometimes drawn from the *Articuli*, but the references often appear to be based on an actual study of the documents.

The twenty-one *iudicia* also expressed the orthodox biblical view of election. The great majority of them emphasized the following points:

- A definition of election that focuses on particular persons and that includes a decree regarding both the end (salvation) and the means to the end.[39]

- The cause of election is merely God's good pleasure to save some and not others.[40]

- All but three of the *iudicia* expressed an infralapsarian viewpoint: God elected from the fallen human race.[41] Only

---

37. *Acta*, 2:24–26; 3:54–56; cf. North Holland, 3:26.
38. North Holland specifically mentions using the *Articuli*, along with various Remonstrant writings (*Acta*, 3:36).
39. *Acta*, 2:3, 16, 29, 35, 38, 41, 46, 54, 60; 3:11, 21, 22, 27, 33, 36, 42, 47, 56, 62, 70, 79, 85.
40. *Acta*, 2:3, 17, 35, 39, 43, 47, 60; 3:5, 15, 22, 28, 34, 38, 44, 47, 57, 63, 72, 80, 86.
41. *Acta*, 2:3, 16, 29, 38, 41, 46, 54, 60; 3:3, 11, 27, 36, 42, 43, 47, 56, 62, 70, 79, 80, 85.

Gomarus expressed his well-known supralapsarian position (in a weak form): God elected "from the whole human race (ex universo genere humano)."[42] The South Holland delegation also stated that election was from the whole human race, but they emphasized that it was not necessary to define whether the object of predestination is humanity considered by God as fallen or as not-yet-fallen, since, "in electing, he considered all people to be in an equal condition (in pari statu)," so that one was not viewed as more worthy than another.[43] The Swiss delegates spoke of God electing particular people "who would be delivered (liberandos) by Christ from the common misery," rather than of God electing from the common misery.[44]

- God predestined both the end and the means to the end, both to glory and to grace, at the same time.[45]

- Faith and perseverance in faith are fruits or effects of election, not conditions for election.[46]

- The decree of election is unchangeable and irrevocable, so none of the elect can become reprobate.[47]

- Almost all *iudicia* emphasized that, in this life, believers can have certainty or assurance of their election. As for the source of assurance, more than half stated that this certainty derives from the fruits or effects of election that believers see in themselves,[48] or, as some described it, climbing from the effects to the cause (Gelderland called this becoming certain of one's election a posteriori, and Nassau-Wetteravia called

---

42. *Acta*, 3:21.
43. *Acta*, 3:33, 34–35. Thus, the South Holland delegates thought that the differences over the object of predestination could be reconciled.
44. *Acta*, 2:35; see footnote 70.
45. *Acta*, 2:8, 29, 37, 39, 42; 3:11, 15, 21, 33, 56, 70, 83.
46. *Acta*, 2:5, 17, 27, 35, 39, 44, 56, 68; 3:15, 22, 28, 34, 39, 48, 58, 64, 71, 82, 86.
47. *Acta*, 2:5, 18, 30, 37, 39, 43, 49, 56, 71; 3:6, 12, 22, 27, 34, 39, 42, 48, 57, 65, 73, 79, 86.
48. *Acta*, 2:9, 19, 32, 44, 51, 61; 3:7, 13, 60, 75–76, 86.

The Doctrine of Election at the Synod of Dordt 125

this the analytical method[49]). Related to this, Hesse and Gelderland presented a form of the *syllogismus practicus*.[50] But several delegations (British, Hesse, Nassau-Wetteravia, Geneva, three Dutch professors, Gomarus, North Holland, Groningen, and Walloon) added that a certainty of election also comes from the internal testimony of the Holy Spirit in the heart of believers.[51] The British, Emden, and Gomarus also mentioned relying on biblical promises to believers.[52]

About half of the *iudicia* also addressed the issue of the election of infants who die in infancy:

- There is an election and reprobation of infants who die. Due to the promise of the covenant, such infants of believers are elect, or are reckoned to be elect.[53]

The *iudicia* rejected the Remonstrant position that Christ is the foundation (*fundamentum*) of election in the sense that He is the meriting cause (*causa meritoria*) of election.[54] But the various delegations themselves expressed some difference of opinion about what it means to be "elected in Christ" (Eph. 1:4). Does it mean that Christ is the *fundamentum* of election, or is He the *fundamentum* only of salvation? The British and Gelderland affirmed that He is the head and foundation of the elect. Only Drenthe specifically said that Christ as God-man, head, and mediator is the foundation of election.[55] Similarly, Gelderland asserted that, with the Father, the Son was the cause, source, and author of election; Bremen said that the decree of election was made in Christ as mediator and redeemer.[56] On the other hand, Emden and Gelderland asserted that Christ as mediator is the foundation of salvation.[57] In a similar vein, Hesse, Nassau-Wetteravia, Emden, and

---

49. *Acta*, 3:30; 2:44.
50. *Acta*, 2:32; 3:30.
51. *Acta*, 2:9, 32, 39, 50; 3:7, 23, 39, 75, 86.
52. *Acta*, 2:9, 72; 3:23.
53. *Acta*, 2:10, 37, 58; 3:10, 19, 23, 36, 49, 69.
54. *Acta*, 2:31, 68; 3:16.
55. *Acta*, 2:4; 3:28, 80–81.
56. *Acta*, 3:27; 2:55.
57. *Acta*, 2:67; 3:28.

Zeeland stated that Christ as mediator is the first ordained means to execute election, the foundation of other means; the Swiss described Him as the foundation of election as executed.[58] Emden even asserted that Christ as mediator is not the cause but an effect of election. God did not elect us because Christ died for us; Christ died for us because God elected us in Him. Emden admitted that people were elected in Christ before the foundation of the world, but they were not in Christ before the foundation of the world, since being in Christ happens only in time, when one is ingrafted in Christ through faith.[59]

The Palatine *iudicium* had a special section on the way to teach predestination popularly. The suggested order begins with the fall, moves to the promised Son as Savior from sin who is offered in the preached Word, then proceeds to faith as an unmerited gift of God that is given to whom He wishes, and finally rises from the horizon of time to election from eternity.[60] It is striking that this is the same way that Chapter I of the Canons begins. The beginning of Lubbertus's *iudicium* is somewhat similar.[61]

Drafts of the Canons

After all nineteen *iudicia* on the Five Remonstrant Articles were read in the synod, it was time to draft the synod's own judgment on the Five Articles—that is, the Canons. President Bogerman announced that he had prepared a draft of the Canons on Articles I and II. These he dictated to the synod for its input. But some delegates, especially from the foreign delegations, objected vigorously to this procedure of the synod basically confirming Bogerman's version of the Canons. So a drafting committee of nine persons was appointed, including three foreign theologians (Bishop George Carleton, Abraham Scultetus, and Jean Diodati), three Dutch theologians (Johannes Polyander, Antonius Walaeus, and Jacobus Trigland), along with President Bogerman and the assessors Hermannus Faukelius and Jacobus Rolandus. The synod did not formally meet for three weeks, from the last week of March to mid-April 1619, while this committee worked at preparing

---

58. *Acta*, 2:25, 39, 42, 60–61; 3:43; 2:35.
59. *Acta*, 2:65, 68.
60. *Acta*, 2:22.
61. *Acta*, 3:11.

The Doctrine of Election at the Synod of Dordt

the Canons, with input from all the delegations. The committee used Bogerman's dictated draft to prepare its own first draft of Chapter I. Then each of the nineteen delegations had the opportunity to present suggestions for amendments to this draft. The committee used these amendment suggestions to prepare its second committee draft. This process went back and forth three times, including a third committee draft, before the synod approved the final version of the Canons.[62]

Bogerman had, in fact, prepared three earlier drafts of Chapter I of the Canons before dictating his fourth draft to the synod. Hence, with the three committee drafts, there are a total of seven preliminary drafts of Chapter I of the Canons.[63]

A survey of the various drafts of the Canons is very illuminating.[64] This reveals that all of the positive articles of Chapter I of the Canons, except for one (art. 17), are based on Bogerman's dictated draft of this chapter. In fact, the basic articles of the final Canons, except for article 17, are all there already in Bogerman's third draft. The drafting committee, which included Bogerman himself, did not start over; rather, the committee simply took over Bogerman's draft, with all his articles, and modified it. Though they revised the formulations of his articles somewhat, they retained the basic topics. The only major structural changes they made were to split Bogerman's article 12 into two articles (later arts. 12 and 13) and, more significantly, in their second committee draft, to add a new article (art. 17) on the salvation of children of believers who die in infancy.

---

62. For more on the drafting process, see Donald Sinnema, "The Drafting of the Canons of Dordt: A Preliminary Survey of Early Drafts and Related Documents," in *Revisiting the Synod of Dordt (1618–1619)*, ed. Aza Goudriaan and Fred van Lieburg (Leiden: Brill, 2011), 291–311. An abbreviated version of this article is printed in this volume; see chapter 13.

63. Most of these drafts have been preserved, along with a variety of amendment suggestions from the various delegations and several drafting committee documents. Some one hundred of these drafting documents will be published in volume three of the new critical edition of Dordt documents: *ADSND*. No copies of the second and third committee drafts are extant, but I have been able to reconstruct these two drafts from the available documents.

64. See the appendix below on drafts of Chapter I of the Canons.

I will use Chapter I, article 7, which presents the definition of election, to illustrate the drafting process. Here is this article in Bogerman's very first draft:

> Election to salvation is God's eternal, free, and unchangeable decree by which, by His sheer and gratuitous good pleasure, before the foundation of the world, out of the entire human race fallen by its own fault into sin and ruin, He elected in Jesus Christ, from eternity, a definite multitude of people to eternal life, according to His good pleasure, by sheer and gratuitous grace, and decreed to effectively call them within time into the fellowship of His Son through His Word and Spirit, that is, to grant them faith, to justify, to sanctify, and, finally, after powerfully preserving them in the fellowship of His Son, to glorify them, for the demonstration of His mercy and the praise of His glorious grace.[65]

After revising this article three times, Bogerman dictated his fourth draft to the synod. In this draft, the definition of election in article 7 reads:

> Election to salvation is God's unchangeable decree by which, from eternity or before the foundation of the world, out of the entire human race fallen by its own fault from its original innocence into sin and ruin, according to the very free good pleasure of His will and by sheer and gratuitous grace, He elected to salvation in Jesus Christ particular ones, who were neither better nor more deserving than the others but lay in the common misery, and decreed to give them to His Son to be saved and to call and draw them effectively into His fellowship through His Word and Spirit, that is, to grant them true faith in Him, to justify, to sanctify, and, finally, after powerfully preserving them in the fellowship of His Son, to glorify them, for

---

65. OSA, vol. 5, 723: *Electio ad salutem est decretum Dei aeternum, liber[?] et immutabile, quo ex mero et gratuito beneplacito ante iacta mundi fundamenta, ex universo genere humano in peccatum et exitium sua culpa prolapso, certam multitudinem hominum, [ipso?] ab aeterno [et?] secundum beneplacitum, ex mera et gratuita gratia, ad vitam aeternam in Iesu Christo elegit, eosdem decrevit in tempore ad Filii sui communionem per Verbum et Spiritum efficaciter vocare, seu fide donare, iustificare, sanctificare, et in communione Filii potenter custoditos tandem glorificare, ad demonstrationem suae misericordiae et laudem gloriosae suae gratiae.*

the demonstration of His mercy and the praise of the riches of His glorious grace.[66]

In its first committee draft, the drafting committee largely accepted Bogerman's formulation of article 7, but it made several revisions:

> Election to salvation is God's unchangeable decree by which, before the foundation of the world, out of the entire human race fallen by its own fault from its original innocence into sin and ruin, according to the very free good pleasure of His will, by sheer grace, He elected definite particular people, who were neither better nor more deserving than the others but lay in the common misery, to salvation in Jesus Christ, whom He appointed from eternity to be the mediator and head of all those elected and the foundation of their salvation, and He decreed to give them to His Son to be saved and to call and draw them effectively into His fellowship through His Word and Spirit, that is, to grant them true faith in Him, to justify, to sanctify, and, finally, after powerfully preserving them in the fellowship of His Son, to glorify them, for the demonstration of His mercy and the praise of the riches of His glorious grace.[67]

---

66. OSA, vol. 5, 744: *Est autem electio ad salutem immutabile Dei decretum, quo ab aeterno sive ante iacta mundi fundamenta, ex universo genere humano ex primaeva integritate in peccatum et exitium sua culpa prolapso, secundum liberrimum voluntatis suae beneplacitum et ex mera gratuitaque gratia, quosdam aliis nec meliores nec digniores sed in communi miseria iacentes, in Iesu Christo ad salutem elegit, eosque Filio suo servandos dare et ad eius communionem per Verbum et Spiritum suum efficaciter vocare et trahere, seu vera in ipsum fide donare, iustificare, sanctificare, ac potenter in Filii sui communione custoditos tandem glorificare decrevit, ad demonstrationem suae misericordiae et laudem divitiarum gloriosae suae gratiae.*

67. Tronchin, vol. 18, 55r–v: *Est autem electio ad salutem immutabile Dei decretum, quo ante iacta mundi fundamenta, ex universo genere humano ex primaeva integritate in peccatum et exitium sua culpa prolapso, secundum liberrimum voluntatis suae beneplacitum, ex mera gratia, certos quosdam homines, aliis nec meliores nec digniores sed in communi miseria iacentes, in Iesu Christo, quem ab aeterno mediatorem et omnium electorum caput salutisque fundamentum constituit, ad salutem elegit, eosque Filio suo servandos dare et ad eius communionem per Verbum et Spiritum suum efficaciter vocare et trahere, seu vera in ipsum fide donare, iustificare, sanctificare, et potenter in Filii sui communione custoditos tandem glorificare decrevit, ad demonstrationem suae misericordiae et laudem divitiarum gloriosae suae gratiae.*

Final Version of the Canons

After two more drafts, the synod unanimously approved and subscribed the final version of the Canons on 23 April 1619.

Chapter I of the Canons begins with the fallen state of humanity and proceeds to God's gracious offer of the gospel. To explain why some respond in faith and others do not, this chapter then rises to the eternal decree of election and reprobation in article 6. This pattern, moving from time back to eternity, follows the pattern presented in the Palatine *iudicium*.

In its final form, the definition of election in article 7 of the Canons reads:

> Election is God's unchangeable purpose by which, before the foundation of the world, out of the entire human race fallen by its own fault from its original innocence into sin and ruin, according to the very free good pleasure of His will, by sheer grace, He elected in Christ (whom He also appointed from eternity to be the mediator and head of all those elected and the foundation of their salvation) to salvation a definite multitude of particular people who were neither better nor more deserving than the others but lay with them in the common misery; and so He decreed to give them to Him to be saved and to call and draw them effectively into His fellowship through His Word and Spirit, that is, to grant them true faith in Him, to justify, to sanctify, and, finally, after powerfully preserving them in the fellowship of His Son, to glorify them, for the demonstration of His mercy and the praise of the riches of His glorious grace.

If one compares the Latin of the final version of the Canons with Bogerman's dictated draft, it is evident that most of article 7 is taken from Bogerman's draft (highlighted in italics).

> *Est autem electio immutabile Dei* propositum, *quo ante iacta mundi fundamenta ex universo genere humano, ex primaeva integritate in peccatum et exitium sua culpa prolapso, secundum liberrimum voluntatis suae beneplacitum, ex mera gratia,* certam quorundam hominum multitudinem *aliis nec melior*um, *nec dignior*um, *sed in communi miseria* cum aliis *iacent*ium, *ad salutem elegit in Christo,* quem etiam ab aeterno mediatorem et omnium electorum caput salutisque fundamentum constituit, atque ita *eos ipsi salvandos dare et ad eius communionem per Verbum et Spiritum suum efficaciter vocare et trahere, seu vera in ipsum fide donare, iustificare, sanctificare* et *potenter in Filii sui communione*

custoditos tandem glorificare decrevit, ad demonstrationem suae misericordiae et laudem divitiarum gloriosae suae gratiae.[68]

It is interesting to see how changes were made in the drafting process of article 7. First, *propositum* was substituted for *decretum* in the final version of the Canons, probably to avoid violating the laws of logic, whereby, in a definition, a term is not to be defined by the same term.[69] In this case, earlier drafts defined election as God's "decree" by which…He "decreed."

Second, changes were made to how humans are identified as the object of election. From the very first Bogerman draft, they are elected "out of the entire human race fallen… [*ex universo genere humano…prolapso*]," reflecting the infralapsarian viewpoint. Throughout the drafting process, there was no change on this point.[70] But there are significant changes in how the elect are described. The dictated Bogerman draft simply states that God elected "particular ones [*quosdam*]."[71] The first committee draft changes this to "definite particular people [*certos quosdam homines*]," a move to further emphasize that a definite number of particular people are elected.[72] In its suggestions on the first commit-

---

68. Bakhuizen van den Brink, *Nederlandse Belijdenisgeschriften*, 232. An original signed copy of the Canons is found in OSA, vol. R.

69. In their suggestions for amendments to the second committee draft of article 7 (OSA, vol. 5, 143, 215), the Hesse and Bremen delegations had both suggested that the terms *elegit* and *decrevit* should be changed, lest the synod violate the laws of logic, which prohibit defining a term by the same term. These changes were not made in the third committee draft. But in the final version of article 7, the term *decretum* instead was changed.

70. In its suggestions to the first committee draft (Zurich Zentralbibliothek, MS A111, 383–84), the Swiss delegation cautioned the synod against defining points that many ecclesiastical confessions prudently declined to define, that is, matters about which there is freedom to think somewhat differently. Thus, the Swiss asserted that, in election, humans are to be considered "according to their condition and all together in all times, namely, as not yet created, as to be created, as created, as to be fallen, as fallen" (*secundum rationem ipsorum et omnium temporum universam, videlicet nondum conditos, condendos, conditos, lapsuros, lapsos*). Hence, they suggested that it would be safer to say that people were elected from the common misery whether considered as fallen in it (*prolapsus*) or as to be going to fall in it (*prolapsurus*), since, for God, there is no past or future, but everything is always present to Him. The drafting committee, however, did not change the infralapsarian formulation of article 7.

71. OSA, vol. 5, 744; Tronchin, vol. 18, 49v.

72. Tronchin, vol. 18, 55r.

tee draft, the Swiss delegation emphasized that the elect are a definite but innumerable multitude, on the basis on Romans 5:15 and Revelation 7:9; their main concern was to counter the frequent Remonstrant criticism that the Reformed position advocated that God predestined by far the greatest part of humanity to eternal death.[73] So the second committee draft changed the phrase to "a definite multitude of people [*certam hominum multitudinem*]."[74] Responding to this draft, the Overijssel delegation suggested that the phrase did not clearly enough emphasize the election of individual people.[75] For the same reason, the Zeeland delegation suggested "a definite multitude of individual persons [*certam singulorum personarum multitudinem*]."[76] To address this, the third committee draft changed the phrase to "a definite multitude of particular people [*certam quorundam hominum multitudinem*]."[77] This remained the same in the final version of the Canons.

Third, changes were made concerning how "in Christ" (Eph. 1:4) is related to election. The dictated Bogerman draft states that God "elected to salvation in Jesus Christ… [*in Iesu Christo ad salutem elegit…*]."[78] This leaves it rather ambiguous whether salvation was in Christ or whether election was in Christ. The first committee draft adds phrases describing Christ as mediator, head, and foundation: "in Jesus Christ, whom He appointed from eternity to be the mediator and head of all those elected and the foundation of their salvation, He elected to salvation… [*in Iesu Christo, quem ab aeterno mediatorem et omnium electorum caput salutisque fundamentum constituit, ad salutem elegit…*]."[79] Note that the insertion of these phrases separates "in Christ" from election and seems to emphasize that only salvation was in Christ, not election. Then, on the advice of Genevan delegate Théodore Tronchin, the second committee draft changed this to: "to salvation in Jesus Christ He elected, whom He also appointed… [*ad*

---

73. Zurich Zentralbibliothek, MS A111, 384–85.
74. OSA, vol. 5, 171; Sibelius, 95v.
75. OSA, vol. 5, 207.
76. OSA, vol. 5, 135.
77. Sibelius, 95v.
78. OSA, vol. 5, 744; Tronchin, vol. 18, 49v.
79. Tronchin, vol. 18, 55r.

salutem in Iesu Christo elegit, quem etiam…constituit]."[80] This formulation more clearly reconnected Christ to election and remained the same in the third committee draft. But in the final version of the Canons, this formulation was again changed, this time to: "to salvation He elected in Christ, whom He also appointed from eternity to be the mediator and head of all those elected and the foundation of their salvation [*ad salutem elegit in Christo, quem etiam…constituit*]."[81] The final wording makes it clear that it is election that is in Christ, and not just salvation, an emphasis that reflects Ephesians 1:4. The addition of "also [*etiam*]" clarifies that Christ played a role both in election and in salvation.

It is evident that, in its rejection of errors section, the Canons rejected the basic tenets of the Remonstrant position on election, especially the notion that, from eternity, God elected persons on the basis of His foreknowledge of their persevering faith. To remove confusion in the churches caused by the controversy and to establish them in the truth, the Canons also spelled out the orthodox Reformed view of election in its positive articles.[82] With input from leading Reformed theologians from throughout Europe, the Canons were the product of the best Reformed thought of the day. However, while they were very carefully framed, the Canons were written as a popular document with a pastoral and scriptural tone for use in the churches, and they did not attempt to define the issues with scholastic precision.[83] Moreover, due to some differences among members of the synod, both Dutch and foreign, the final Canons that were unanimously adopted by all members of the synod left some issues rather undefined. For example, while the basic formulation of the Canons is infralapsarian, they are framed

---

80. OSA, vol. 5, 161; Sibelius, 95v.

81. Bakhuizen van den Brink, *Nederlandse Belijdenisgeschriften*, 232.

82. Donald Sinnema, "The Canons of Dordt: From Judgment on Arminianism to Confessional Standard," in *Revisiting the Synod of Dordt (1618–1619)*, ed. Aza Goudriaan and Fred van Lieburg, Brill's Series in Church History 49 (Leiden: Brill, 2011), 331. A revised version of this article is printed in this volume; see chapter 15.

83. On the Canons as a popular rather than scholastic document, see Donald Sinnema, "Reformed Scholasticism and the Synod of Dort (1618–19)," in *John Calvin's Institutes: His Opus Magnum*, ed. B. van der Walt (Potchefstroom: Potchefstroom University for Christian Higher Education, 1986), 495–98, and W. Robert Godfrey, "Popular and Catholic: The *Modus Docendi* of the Canons of Dordt," in *Revisiting the Synod of Dordt*, 243–57.

in such a way that does not specifically define the object of election and that does not exclude the supralapsarian viewpoint.[84] What it means to be elected in Christ is not specifically explained. The precise sources of the assurance of election are not identified in detail. And avoided is any statement on the election or reprobation of dying children of unbelievers. As a committee-written document that tried to accommodate a moderate range of opinion among the orthodox Reformed, the Canons show some degree of latitude in its formulations.

---

84. Franciscus Gomarus was able to sign the Canons because he was able to interpret the popularly framed infralapsarian formulations of the Canons within his own supralapsarian perspective. On the infralapsarian–supralapsarian issue at Dordt, see Klaas Dijk, *De Strijd over Infra- en Supralapsarisme in de Gereformeerde Kerken van Nederland* (Kampen: Kok, 1912), ch. 3; and J. V. Fesko, "Lapsarian Diversity at the Synod of Dort," in *Drawn into Controversie: Reformed Theological Diversity and Debates within Seventeenth-Century British Puritanism*, ed. Michael A. G. Haykin and Mark Jones (Göttingen: Vandenhoeck and Ruprecht, 2011), 99–123.

Drafts of Chapter One of the Canons of Dordt

Bogerman				Committee			Final Canons	
1st	2nd	3rd	4th	1st	2nd	3rd	Final	Topic
1	1	1	1	1	1	1	1	God's right to condemn all people
	2	2	2	2	2	2	2	God's love manifested in His Son
		3	3	3	3	3	3	Preaching of the gospel
			4	4	4	4	4	Twofold response to the gospel
			5	5	5	5	5	Sources of unbelief and faith
2	{split} 6	6	6	6	6	6	6	God's eternal decree
3	3	7	7	7	7	7	7	Definition of election
4	4	8	8	8	8	8	8	A single decree of election
	5	9	9 {split} 10	9	9 {combined}	9	9	Election not based on foreseen faith
	6	10	10	11	10	10	10	Election based on God's good pleasure
	7	11	11	12	11	11	11	Election unchangeable
	8	12	12 {split} 13	12	12	12	12	Assurance of election
			14	13	13	13	13	Fruit of this assurance
	9	13	13	15	14	14	14	Teaching election properly
	10	14	14	16	15	15	15	Definition of reprobation
	11	15	15	17	16	16	16	Responses to the teaching of reprobation
				17	17	17	17	Salvation of infants of believers
	12	16	*	18	18	18	18	Proper attitude to election and reprobation

Rejection of Errors

				1	1	1	1	Decree to save believers is the whole decree
				2	2	2	2	Election of many kinds
				3	3	3	3	God's good pleasure not cause of electing individuals
				4	4	4	4	Faith a prerequisite condition
				5	5	5	5	Peremptory election based on foreseen faith
				6	**			
				7	6	6	6	Election is changeable
				8	7	7	7	No assurance of election
				9	8	8	8	God's will not cause of passing by in election
				10	9	9	9	God's good pleasure not cause of sending gospel

Note:
(1) Numbers indicate article numbers for each draft.
(2) All articles in the same row, whatever the number, address the same topic, but the exact formulations may change from draft to draft.

* Epilogue   ** Deleted

Franciscus Gomarus, theological delegate from Groningen

CHAPTER 6

Disagreements and Doctrinal Dissension among Delegates at the Synod of Dordt[1]

The main reason the Synod of Dordt was convened was to settle the Arminian controversy that had agitated the Netherlands for about twenty years. In responding to this controversy, the fifty-eight Dutch delegates at Dordt, assisted by twenty-six foreign theologians from eight foreign lands, showed unusual unanimity. The synod's answer to the Arminians, or Remonstrants, was the Canons of Dordt, which were approved and signed by every one of the Dutch and foreign delegates.[2] The Canons were based on position papers (*iudicia*) submitted by all nineteen delegations (eleven Dutch and eight foreign) on each of the Five Articles of the Remonstrants that were at the heart of the controversy. After each of these *iudicia* was read in the synod, the president, Johannes Bogerman, commented on how much harmony there was among all these statements presented by the various delegations.[3] The delegates of Dordt were united by the fundamentals of Reformed

---

1. This article is an expanded version of "Doctrinal Dissension among Delegates at the Synod of Dordt (1618–1619)," in *A Landmark in Turbulent Times: The Meaning and Relevance of the Synod of Dordt (1618–1619)*, ed. Henk van den Belt, Klaas-Willem de Jong, and Willem van Vlastuin (Göttingen: Vandenhoeck and Ruprecht, 2022), 173–91.

2. *ADSND*, 1:144, sess. 135 and 136.

3. *ADSND*, 1:140; Balcanqual, 2:139. John Hales was the chaplain of British ambassador Dudley Carleton; he reported to Carleton, who was in The Hague, on the synod's deliberations until early February 1619, when most sessions were closed to spectators like himself. Then British delegate Walter Balcanqual continued to send reports to Carleton.

doctrine, and they remained unified against their common opponents who challenged certain basic Reformed teachings.

Nevertheless, beneath the broad unity that the delegates of Dordt expressed against the Remonstrant threat, the delegates among themselves sometimes presented differing views on a wide variety of specific issues. At times, these differences erupted into open, and even bitter, dissension among some of the delegates on the floor of the synod.

Though it is a matter of degree, one can distinguish between disagreements expressed by delegates on certain issues, and open dissension in which the differences became personal and acrimonious.

The first hint of impending dissension arose amid discussion of the very first issue addressed by the synod, a new Dutch Bible translation. On 24 November, the question was posed whether the Hebrew name "Jehova" should be left untranslated or be rendered by "Heere" (Lord). President Bogerman preferred "Heere," but Matthias Martinius of Bremen pointed out that "Jehova" sometimes had a peculiar meaning not expressed by "Heere." Others agreed. Reporting on the session, John Hales noted that "great disputation would have arisen about this point," but the president cut off the discussion. The synod then opted for the capitalized "HEERE," and when the term had a peculiar meaning, it was to be marked with an asterisk, with "Jehova" in the margin.[4]

In what follows, I will first present lists of some of the disagreements that were expressed by delegates at the synod, on procedural as well as doctrinal issues, without elaborating, and then focus on four major doctrinal issues concerning which there was open dissension: (1) the debate over the role of Christ in election; (2) the *causa physica* debate; (3) the supralapsarian debate; and (4) the debate over the extent of the atonement.

Procedural and Doctrinal Disagreements

At the synod, the delegates expressed differences of opinion on a variety of procedural matters, of which I will just list some prime examples:

---

4. Hales, 2:7–8; *ADSND*, 1:22; H. Kaajan, *De Pro-Acta der Dordtsche Synode* (Rotterdam: T. De Vries, 1914), 120–21.

- Regarding whether to give the Remonstrants the list of questions by which President Bogerman was questioning them, most foreign delegations, except Geneva and Emden, advised that they be given the list, while most Dutch delegates opposed this.[5]

- The manner in which President Bogerman expelled the Remonstrants was considered too passionate and harsh, especially by some of the foreign delegates, although, that morning, they all supported the dismissal.[6]

- Regarding whether the Remonstrant ministers of Kampen should be suspended from office, all agreed except the Bremen delegates, who wanted a milder course of action; on this issue, Franciscus Gomarus clashed with Matthias Martinius.[7]

- Regarding the issue of whether to have sessions closed or open to the public for the reading of the *iudicia*, President Bogerman was opposed by the British delegation.[8]

- Whether to have President Bogerman draft the Canons or to appoint a committee to draft the Canons was a matter of contention between Bogerman, supported by the Palatine delegates (especially Abraham Scultetus) and most of the Dutch delegates (especially Sibrandus Lubbertus), and the British and South Holland delegates (especially Johannes Latius).[9]

- Regarding the question of whether, in the Conclusion of the Canons, to explicitly reject hard sayings (*phrases duriores*) of certain Reformed theologians or only false accusations

---

5. *ADSND*, 2/2:812–26; Hesse: 276–77; [Bernardus Dwinglo], *Historisch Verhael van't ghene sich toeghedraeghen heeft, binnen Dordrecht, in de Jaeren 1618 ende 1619* ([Amsterdam], 1623), 137r.
6. Balcanqual, 2:73–74; Hales, 2:78–79.
7. Balcanqual, 2:109.
8. Balcanqual, 2:121–23; Heppe, "Historia," 298–99.
9. Balcanqual to Secretary Naunton (26 March/5 April 1619), in *Praestantium ac Eruditorum Virorum Epistolae Ecclesiasticae et Theologicae* (Amsterdam: Henricus Wetstenius, 1684), 565; translation in James Arminius, *Works* (London, 1825), 1:501; Balcanqual, 2:140–41, 146–47.

of the Remonstrants, the Bremen, Hesse, and British delegates wanted certain hard sayings rejected, while the Dutch and other foreign delegates wanted to reject only false accusations.[10]

- Regarding the issue of whether foreign delegates should consent to the personal Sentence against the Remonstrants, all foreign delegates refused to do so except the Genevan and Emden delegations.[11]
- Whether to tolerate those who refuse to sign the Canons, but promise not to speak against them, was cause of a dispute among the Dutch delegates.[12]
- Regarding the issue of how to handle the Johannes Maccovius case, there was passionate debate involving the Genevan theologians, and also between Lubbertus and Festus Hommius.[13]

There were moments when these procedural differences escalated to some level of dissension. This can be seen especially in the debate regarding whether to appoint a drafting committee and in the case of the Kampen suspensions.

At the synod, there was also a significant variety of doctrinal issues concerning which the delegates expressed disagreements. Again, I simply present a list of some key examples:

- Regarding the issue of whether Catechism sermons should be based on a text of Scripture or only on questions and answers of the Catechism, the Utrecht Remonstrant delegation, along with the Gelderland and Drenthe delegates, advocated for the former position, while President Bogerman and the other Dutch delegations promoted the latter.[14]

---

10. Donald Sinnema, "The Issue of Reprobation at the Synod of Dort (1618–19) in Light of the History of this Doctrine," (PhD diss., University of St. Michael's College, Toronto, 1985), 419–30.
11. Balcanqual, 2:145–46, 154–55.
12. Balcanqual, 2:155; Heppe, "Historia," 310.
13. Balcanqual, 2:158.
14. Kaajan, *Pro-Acta*, 167, 185, 193–205.

- Regarding whether unordained students should be allowed to preach in public worship, the members of the synod were split, but Franciscus Gomarus and Antonius Thysius were especially opposed to this.[15]

- Regarding the question of whether slave children taken into Christian families should be baptized, the delegations from Britain, Hesse, Bremen, Zeeland, and Friesland, as well as the Dutch professors, argued for baptism, while the other delegations opposed this.[16]

- The nineteen delegations at Dordt held three positions on the nature of reprobation and six distinct positions on the causes of reprobation.[17]

- The delegations proposed different sources of assurance of salvation—from the effects of election that believers see in themselves (sometimes using the *syllogismus practicus*), to the internal testimony of the Holy Spirit, to relying on biblical promises.[18]

- The British delegates did not want to explicitly reject the view that some true believers can fall from grace and salvation.[19]

- The British objected to the statement in the Sentence of the Remonstrants that the doctrine of the Canons had the consent of "the Reformed" churches.[20]

- In the synod's review of the Belgic Confession, President Bogerman excluded articles 30–32 on church government in

---

15. Kaajan, *Pro-Acta*, 279–91.
16. Kaajan, *Pro-Acta*, 226–48. For analysis, see Rudolph M. Britz, "'n Vraag 'door de Christelijke predikanten uit Oost-Indië overgezonden.' Die Dordtse Sinode (1618-1619), die sending en die doop van kinders uit nie-Christelike ouers," *In die Skriflig* 53, no. 3 (2019): a2464, https://doi.org/10.4102/ids.v53i3.2464.
17. Sinnema, "Issue of Reprobation," 378–82.
18. *Acta*, 2:9, 19, 32, 39, 44, 50, 51, 61, 72; 3:7, 13, 23, 30, 39, 60, 75–76, 86.
19. Jay T. Collier, *Debating Perseverance: The Augustinian Heritage in Post-Reformation England* (New York: Oxford University Press, 2018), 83–88.
20. Balcanqual, 2:156; *Synodalia Hollandica*, Centrale Bibliotheek Rotterdam, Bibliotheek der Remonstrantsch-Gereformeerde Gemeente te Rotterdam, MS 58, 14/24 April.

order to avoid criticism of the English episcopal system; yet Bishop Carleton responded with a critique of the presbyterian system.[21]

- When the doctrine of the Heidelberg Catechism was reviewed, the British and Bremen delegates insisted on a different interpretation of the descent of Christ into hell than that which is found in question 44 of the Catechism.[22]

- Whether the Preface to the Canons should identify the pope as the Antichrist was a point to which the British objected.[23]

- The British complained about the neglect of Sabbath observance in Dordrecht and asked the synod to appeal to the magistrate to prevent shops from opening on Sunday; the synod later approved some articles on Sabbath observance as a provisional compromise to settle the Sabbath controversy in Zeeland.[24]

- In the revision of the text of article 22 of the Belgic Confession, the Palatine and Hesse delegates, along with President Bogerman and Lubbertus, wanted a formulation that would tolerate Johann Piscator's denial of the imputation of Christ's active obedience, over against the rest of the Dutch delegates, especially those of South Holland.[25]

These are just points of doctrinal *disagreement* concerning which there was no evident *dissension*. These lists are by no means complete.

---

21. Willem Nijenhuis, "The Controversy between Presbyterianism and Episcopalianism surrounding and during the Synod of Dordrecht 1618–1619," in *Ecclesia Reformata: Studies on the Reformation* (Leiden: Brill, 1972), 215–20; Balcanqual, 2:160–61; John Davenant, *An Exposition of the Epistle of Paul to the Colossians* (London: Hamilton, Adams & Co, 1831), xxvi–xxvii.

22. H. H. Kuyper, *De Post-Acta of Nahandelingen van de Nationale Synode van Dordrecht in 1618 en 1619 gehouden* (Amsterdam: Höveker & Wormser, 1899), 330–31; Balcanqual, 2:162.

23. Balcanqual, 2:157.

24. Balcanqual, 2:162; Kuyper, *Post-Acta*, 184–86, 190–93.

25. Nicolaas H. Gootjes, *The Belgic Confession: Its History and Sources* (Grand Rapids: Baker Academic, 2007), 151–52; Kuyper, *Post-Acta*, 339–44.

The Debate over the Role of Christ in Election

A week after the cited Remonstrants were expelled from the synod, while several theologians were giving speeches on election, a debate arose on 22 January 1619 about the meaning of Ephesians 1:4—"He elected us in Christ"—and the role of Christ in election. The issue was: In what sense is Christ said to be the foundation (*fundamentum*) of election?[26] Is God the Father alone the author of election, while Christ is only the "executor" of election who carries out the decree of election? Or is Christ the foundation of election, in that He is not only the executor of election but also the author of election?

In this session, delegates advocated various interpretations: Christ is the foundation of election because He was the "first of the elect," or because He is the "foundation of the elect," or because He is the "foundation of the benefits" that believers receive. Franciscus Gomarus contended for the first of these positions. When Matthias Martinius of Bremen spoke, he said that he had a scruple concerning the manner of Christ being the foundation of election and that he thought Christ was not only the executor of election but also the author of it. As John Hales reported the incident, as soon as Martinius finished speaking, Gomarus stood up and told the synod, "*Ego hanc rem in me recipio* [I take this to be against me]." Gomarus "therewithall casts his glove, and challenges Martinius with this proverb, '*Ecce Rhodum, ecce saltum*,'[27] and requires the synod to grant them a duel, adding that he knew Martinius could say nothing in refutation of that doctrine." Martinius easily handled this affront. President Bogerman soon pacified the situation, and the session concluded with prayer. However, "immediatly after prayers, he [Gomarus] renewed his challenge and required combat with Martinius again, but they parted for that night without blowes."[28]

---

26. *ADSND*, 1:119.

27. The proverb is explained by Erasmus in his *Adagiorum Chiliades* (Basel: Froben, 1541), 696–97. Literally, it means "Behold Rhodes; behold the leap." Erasmus explains that it was first uttered in response to a young man who claimed he had once performed an incredible jump in athletic games on the island of Rhodes. Someone challenged him to prove that claim, with the words, "*Hic Rhodus; hic saltus*," that is, "Here is your Rhodes; let's see that leap." I thank Joseph Tipton for this reference.

28. Hales, 2:87. Since session 65 was a closed session, it is doubtful that Hales was present. He probably heard about the incident from a British delegate.

Other reports of the incident vary in the details. In his journal, the Swiss delegate J. J. Breitinger states that Gomarus and Martinius were admonished to treat the matter with calmer spirits, since a "vehement contention [*contentio vehemens*]" had arisen between them about the meaning of "elected in Christ." Martinius asserted that even though Christ is not the meritorious cause of election (the Remonstrant view), He is the meritorious cause of electability (*eligibilitatis*).[29] An anonymous journal asserts that Martinius opposed some things Gomarus had said, and "thence they got a little heated and challenged each other to a duel [*sese invicem ad certamen provocavare*]."[30] The Overijssel delegate Caspar Sibelius reported that Martinius stated that we are elected in Christ as the foundation, with respect to both election to grace as well as election to glory. Christ was first elected, and we were elected as members in Him. When Martinius wished to prove this, Gomarus said that it could be proved by no syllogism.[31]

While duels of honor were usually fought by sword, Gomarus's challenge to Martinius appears to concern a verbal duel; in particular, a personal disputation in the presence of the synod. Geeraert Brandt's account of the incident interprets the duel in this sense,[32] as does Gomarus's biographer Van Itterzon.[33] Gomarus's added comment that "he knew Martinius could say nothing in refutation of that doctrine" points in this direction, and the proverb uttered by Gomarus can be best interpreted as "Here is your chance. Let's see you prove your position" in a disputation.[34]

---

29. Breitinger, 84v.
30. *Synodalia Hollandica*, 12/22 January.
31. Sibelius, 57r. Cf. Theodore Tronchin journal, vol. 16, 68r.
32. Geeraert Brandt, *Historie der Reformatie en andre Kerkelyke Geschiedenissen in en ontrent de Nederlanden* (Rotterdam: Barent Bos, 1704), 3:409: "Gomarus daegt Martinius ten disputen."
33. Gerrit Pieter van Itterzon, *Franciscus Gomarus* ('s-Gravenhage: Martinus Nijhoff, 1929), 231: "dit duel met woorden."
34. In 1524, Luther challenged Andreas Karlstadt to a theological duel (Ronald J. Sider, ed., *Karlstadt's Battle with Luther: Documents in a Liberal-Radical Debate* [Philadelphia: Fortress, 1978], 47–48). Amid a predestination controversy in Zurich in 1559, Theodor Bibliander allegedly challenged Peter Martyr Vermigli to a duel with a halberd (Joachim Staedtke, "Der Zürcher Prädestinationsstreit von 1560," *Zwingliana* 9 [1953]: 544–45). Cf. Donald Weinstein, "Fighting or Flyting? Verbal Duelling in Mid-Sixteenth-Century Italy," in *Crime, Society and the Law in Renaissance Italy*, ed.

Martinius was suspected of sympathizing with the Remonstrants on several points. To bring him to conformity, the next morning (23 January), British delegate Bishop George Carleton took upon himself "a kind of episcopal authority" and arranged a private meeting at his own lodging with one theologian from each of the foreign delegations. This was what he called a "little synod." He stressed the need for mutual consent and proposed that the foreign delegations cooperate in preparing their materials for the synod in order to avoid the scandal of conflicting views. In this meeting, Martinius would not change his views, but he promised moderation, so that there would be no dissension in the synod due to his opinions.[35]

Three days later, after a speech by British theologian John Davenant on election, the session was closed to spectators, for fear that some diversity of opinion might arise and give occasion to dissension. Some other theologians spoke on election, including Samuel Ward and Rudolphus Goclenius. Then Martinius again raised his concern about the sense in which Christ is said to be the foundation of election, and he requested that the matter be resolved by the synod. This time, Gomarus held his peace.[36]

The issue of Christ's role in election did not come up again until the *iudicia* of the nineteen delegations were read in early March. In their *iudicia* on Article I of the Remonstrance, the various delegations spoke with some diversity on the role of Christ in election: Christ is the head and foundation of the elect (British, Gelderland); as God-man, head, and mediator, Christ is the foundation of election (Drenthe); the Son, with the Father, is the cause, source, and author of election (Gelderland); the decree of election was made in Christ as

---

Trevor Dean and K. J. P. Lowe (Cambridge: Cambridge University Press, 1994), 204–20; François Billacois, *The Duel: Its Rise and Fall in Early Modern France*, ed. and trans. Trista Selous (New Haven: Yale University Press, 1990). John Hales had preached a sermon against duels earlier in The Hague; Hales, 1:63–89. A decade after the synod, William Ames, the theological advisor to President Bogerman, wrote a chapter on duels in his *De Conscientia* (Amsterdam: Ioannes Ianssonius, 1631), 329–30. Here he condemned duels as nothing but a devilish invention to tempt God.

35. George Carleton to Dudley Carleton, in Anthony Milton, ed., *The British Delegation and the Synod of Dort (1618–1619)* (Woodbridge, England: Boydell Press, 2005), 198–99; Hales, 2:87–88.

36. Hales, 2:91; *ADSND*, 1:120.

mediator and redeemer (Bremen); He is the foundation of election as executed (Swiss); Christ as mediator is the foundation of salvation (Emden, Gelderland); as mediator, He is the first ordained means to execute election (Hesse, Nassau-Wetteravia, Emden, Zeeland); Christ as mediator is not the cause but an effect of election (Emden).[37] But there is no report of further dissension on the matter.

When the Canons were being drafted, formulations of the issue also varied in different drafts. The draft dictated by President Bogerman somewhat ambiguously seemed to connect "in Christ" to salvation. The first committee draft separated "in Christ" from election by adding that Christ is the mediator, head, and foundation of salvation and seemed to imply that only salvation was in Christ. The second committee draft more clearly reconnected "in Christ" to election. But the formulation of the final version of the Canons deliberately connected "in Christ" to election, and not just to salvation, while adding that Christ was "also" appointed the mediator and head of the elect and the foundation of their salvation. Though it is not explicitly stated, the implication is that Christ is both the foundation of election and the foundation of salvation.[38]

The *Causa Physica* Debate

In discussions that led to the drafting of the Canons, a debate flared up among various members of the synod about the use of the scholastic category *causa physica* in theology. It was based on the scholastic distinction between physical and moral action.

On 12 February, in deliberations on Article III/IV concerning how God brings about human conversion, Matthias Martinius of Bremen posed the issue in this way: "Does God act physically (*physice*) in man's conversion? Are the exhortations, promises, and threats of the

---

37. Donald Sinnema, "The Doctrine of Election at the Synod of Dordt (1618–1619)," in *The Doctrine of Election in Reformed Perspective*, ed. Frank van der Pol (Göttingen: Vandenhoeck and Ruprecht, 2018), 127. See above, chapter 5.

38. Sinnema, "Doctrine of Election," 132. The original Latin reads: "...*ad salutem elegit in Christo, quem etiam ab aeterno Mediatorem et omnium electorum Caput salutisque fundamentum constituit.*"

gospel a moral action?"³⁹ His answer was that God is the physical cause of conversion.

The next day, the Franeker theologian Sibrandus Lubbertus responded and took exception to some of what Martinius had said the day before, especially the assertion that God is the physical cause of conversion. He provided some reasons against this idea and asked Martinius to address the reasons. Martinius responded, and their exchange sounded to Walter Balcanqual like mere philosophical speculation. In the course of this debate, Martinius appealed to Marburg philosopher Rudolphus Goclenius, who was present as a Hesse delegate. Goclenius pointed out that Themistius, Averroes, Alexander of Aphrodisias, and many others shared Martinius's opinion, and he asserted that this opinion was true in philosophy, but he would not prescribe it in theology. Lubbertus then confronted Goclenius also. After many words, the president cut them off.⁴⁰

When the synod returned to a discussion of Article III/IV on 19 February,⁴¹ it was Gomarus's turn to speak, but Lubbertus asked if he could first add a few things to what he had said in the earlier session. This speech simply renewed the strife between him and Martinius. Lubbertus mentioned two things: First, he said that he had been to Goclenius's lodging to confer with him about whether God might be called the *causa physica* of human actions, and he noted certain statements of Goclenius that tended to the negative. Goclenius confirmed that he had said this. Second, although Martinius had cited a passage from the respected Heidelberg theologian David Pareus for the affirmative, Lubbertus read many passages from Pareus that tended to the contrary. He appealed to the Palatine delegates who were colleagues of Pareus to speak what they knew of Pareus's mind about the matter.⁴²

---

39. Breitinger, 89r. Similarly, William Ames, the theological advisor of President Bogerman, had used the physical–moral distinction in describing the manner of conversion in his *Rescriptio scholastica et brevis* (Amsterdam, 1615), ch. 7. Likewise, he described the physical–moral distinction in his *Coronis ad Collationem Hagiensem* (Leiden, 1618), 170, and applied it to the efficacy of God's grace.

40. Balcanqual, 2:104–5; cf. Tronchin, vol. 16, 92r.

41. The day before, there was a confrontation between Gomarus and Martinius about the suspension of Remonstrant ministers in the Kampen case; Balcanqual, 2:109.

42. Balcanqual, 2:110; Breitinger, 89r; Tronchin, vol. 16, 96r–97v.

In what looked like it had been prearranged, Heidelberg theologian Abraham Scultetus then gave a written speech full of bitter words, according to Balcanqual. Scultetus copiously discussed Pareus's opinion and severely reproached (*graviter perstringit*) the Bremen delegates, without mentioning their names. He said that he did know that Pareus held a view contrary to what had been falsely attributed to him at the synod and that he could not endure to hear his dearest colleague be so abused as he had been by some of the delegates. Moreover, he was grieved that some in the synod would trouble sound theology by bringing in scholastic nonsense (*tricas scholasticas*), such as the idea that God is the physical cause of conversion (contra Martinius). Against Ludwig Crocius, Martinius's Bremen colleague, he said it was hard to believe that the present controversies could not be defined without the monstrous new terms *voluntas determinabilis*, *determinans*, and *determinativa* (used by Crocius), since, in the Scriptures, there are very many clear ways of speaking. He also said he was grieved in his soul that the metaphysics of the Jesuits was being taught in Reformed schools, under the pretext of which youth were little by little given to drink papal poison. And he never thought that orthodox theologians would find anything lacking in Calvin, as if he had not fully treated the teaching of man's conversion by free choice. Scultetus also said that God would surely punish this contempt of the simplicity of Scripture and that he would advise youth to avoid such teachers.[43]

Martinius answered with modesty that he would read Pareus's own words, which he did. And he wondered why Lubbertus brought these things up in public, since, out of his love for peace, he had sent his colleague Crocius to Lubbertus that very day with a lengthy explanation of the sense in which he had stated that God is the physical cause of conversion; Lubbertus had sent him word that he was fully satisfied with the explanation, so he thought the matter was peacefully settled.[44] Breitinger notes that Martinius loudly and extensively complained

---

43. Breitinger, 89r; Balcanqual, 2:111; *Synodalia Hollandica*, 9/19 February. The official *Acta Authentica* of the synod for 19 February simply states that, between the Dutch professors and the Bremen theologians, a discussion was held about various questions relating to Article III/IV and about the use of philosophy and philosophical terms in theological controversies; *ADSND*, 1:128.

44. Balcanqual, 2:111.

about the injuries that Lubbertus and Scultetus had inflicted upon him and his colleagues. Martinius also threatened that, if a place was not given in the synod to the legitimate justification of their view, they would not fail to address the situation in writing. President Bogerman then warned him to act with a calm and tranquil spirit.[45]

Finally, Gomarus was given his turn to speak, and he directed himself against the Bremen theologians in a passionate speech. He noted that Martinius, in response to Scultetus, had said he was sorry that he who had been a professor of theology for twenty-five years should be so treated for using a scholastic term. Gomarus told the synod that he himself had been a professor for not only twenty-five but thirty-five years. Next, he took on Crocius and warned the synod to take heed of these men who brought in these monstrosities of terms, the barbarisms of the schools of the Jesuits, namely, *determinare* and *non determinare voluntatem*. When he ended, President Bogerman gave many thanks to the most renowned doctor Gomarus for his learned and accurate speech.[46]

Then Bishop Carleton spoke up, asserting that synodical discussion was intended for edification, not for anyone to show zeal for strife. This made Gomarus furious; he reminded Bogerman that, here in the synod, matters were to be conducted not by authority but by reasons. Bogerman replied that the most renowned doctor Gomarus had said nothing against persons but only against their opinions and that, therefore, he said nothing worthy of reprehension.

Next in turn to speak was the Dutch theologian Antonius Thysius, who tried to soften the irritated feelings. He discreetly told the synod that he was sorry Martinius was so agitated about a speech that he himself said was true. As Thysius was speaking, Gomarus and Lubbertus, who sat next to him, pulled him by the sleeve, and in the hearing of all, chided him for saying so. Afterward, Thysius very modestly asked Martinius to give him satisfaction concerning one or two doubtful statements he had made. Thanking him for his courtesy, Martinius fully did so.[47]

---

45. Breitinger, 89r.
46. Balcanqual, 2:111–12.
47. Balcanqual, 2:112–13; Breitinger, 89r.

At the same time, Bogerman publicly read from a paper a list of all the harsh statements Martinius had made.[48]

At last, the session ended, one that was not free from "acrimony and agitation of spirits," according to Breitinger. It left Martinius angered, and he remained absent from the synod for several sessions.[49]

By 23 February, the Bremen delegates were so offended that they were ready to leave for home and to publish a narration of the harsh treatment they had received at the synod. They also brought their complaints to the state delegates, who were expected to deal with Gomarus.[50] On 22 and 23 February, the state delegates invited President Bogerman to meet with them to discuss how to restore unity.[51]

Balcanqual observed that "all the *Exteri* take to heart…that strangers should be used so disgracefully for using two school terms, which are both very common." To help quell the crisis, some of the foreign theologians requested the British delegation to try to reconcile the opposing parties. Already in the evening of 23 February, the British took steps to reconcile the Bremen delegates with Scultetus. The same day, Balcanqual wrote ambassador Dudley Carleton, suggesting that he offer counsel to President Bogerman in order to bring water to the fire.[52]

On 25 February, the ambassador wrote to Bogerman that he was anxious that some persons of hot-blooded temperament were causing a disturbance, and he urged Bogerman to introduce some moderation into the proceedings and restrain those of a more violent nature. He asserted that it should not have been necessary to publicly chastise one delegate (Martinius) so fiercely for borrowing words from the schools. If he and his whole delegation would withdraw from the synod, this would severely tarnish the synod, since the whole Christian world was watching, and there was nothing that would be more prejudicial to it than their disagreements and contentions.[53]

---

48. Balcanqual, 2:113.
49. Breitinger, 89v.
50. Balcanqual, 2:114.
51. *ADSND*, 1:493–94.
52. Balcanqual, 2:114.
53. Milton, *British Delegation*, 204–5; cf. 206, 207.

Carleton's advice had good effect. After receiving the letter, Bogerman entreated all members of the synod on 28 February to abstain from all bitterness and show meekness and brotherly kindness in synodical discussions. Having heard the ambassador's advice, Gomarus and Lubbertus tempered their speech.[54]

By 1 March, a private reconciliation was reached between the Bremen theologians and Scultetus, Gomarus, and Lubbertus, through the efforts of President Bogerman and the state delegates. The Bremen delegates were content with a private settlement, and the other three said they were sorry for what they had done. No more is heard of this debate.[55]

The Debate over Supralapsarianism

Franciscus Gomarus was the only delegate at Dordt who openly professed to hold the supralapsarian position of Theodore Beza and William Perkins—that God predestined persons to eternal life or death without considering them as sinners.[56] In this view, the object of predestination is man considered as not-yet-created and not-yet-fallen, *homo creabilis*. Virtually all the other members of the synod held the infralapsarian position—that, in predestining, God considered persons as fallen, *homo lapsus*.

It was well known that Gomarus was a supralapsarian.[57] But since he was very much in the minority, he was quite cautious about openly presenting his position on the floor of the synod.[58] So when he gave a speech on election on 18 January, Gomarus did not bring up the

---

54. Balcanqual, 2:115; *Letters from and to Sir Dudley Carleton, Knt., during his Embassy in Holland, from January 1615/16 to December 1620* (London, 1775), 342, 346.
55. Balcanqual, 2:117.
56. Beza was the first to introduce the supralapsarian perspective. See Donald Sinnema, "Beza's View of Predestination in Historical Perspective," in *Théodore de Bèze (1519–1605): Actes du Colloque de Genève, Septembre 2005*, ed. Irena Backus (Geneva: Librairie Droz, 2007), 225–29.
57. Hales, 2:57, 83, 95: "For being of the *supralapsarii*, as they term them, of those who bring the decree of God's election from before the fall, and seeing the synod not willing to move that way, but to subside in a lower sphere, [Gomarus]…"; Balcanqual, 2:124, 129, 130.
58. Hales, 2:83, 95–96; Balcanqual, 2:126.

supralapsarian issue but simply refuted four Remonstrant arguments that foreseen faith is an antecedent condition for election.[59]

When the *iudicia* of the foreign delegations were read in early March, all of them assumed that *homo lapsus* was the object of predestination. None directly disputed the supralapsarian view.[60] But when the five Dutch professors then presented their *iudicia* on Article I, on 8 and 11 March, there was little hope of full agreement. They drew up three separate *iudicia*—Polyander, Thysius, and Walaeus together presented one (signed also by Lubbertus, but not by Gomarus); Lubbertus (signed also by the three professors) and Gomarus each presented their own. The first three professors argued, using eight biblical proofs and a syllogistic argument, that God predestined persons from the human race considered as fallen in sin and lost (*prolapso ac perdito*).[61] After their statement was read, Gomarus stood up and testified verbally that he had read it and that he approved everything within it, except for the assertion that *homo lapsus* is the object of predestination. This, he said, had not yet been determined in the Dutch churches, nor in the French or English churches, nor in many others.[62]

The next *iudicium* of Lubbertus also emphasized that God predestined miserable sinners.[63] Gomarus again verbally approved his statement, but with the same exception.

In his own *iudicium*, Gomarus focused on responding to the Remonstrant viewpoint, but his own supralapsarian view is more veiled than fully developed. The closest he came to expressing his position was to state that God elected and reprobated certain people "from the whole human race [*ex universo genere humano*]."[64] When Gomarus's statement was read, Polyander testified on behalf of his colleagues that they approved everything within it, except for his view of the object of predestination, since they held the contrary view.[65]

---

59. Gomarus's speech is preserved in OSA, vol. K (7 pages).
60. *Acta*, 2:3–77; Balcanqual, 2:124, 130.
61. *Acta*, 3:4; Balcanqual, 2:124.
62. Balcanqual, 2:126.
63. *Acta*, 3:11.
64. *Acta*, 3:21, 24.
65. Balcanqual, 2:126.

In the afternoon session of 11 March, Bishop George Carleton (with approval from the whole British delegation) asked to speak and confronted Gomarus with the question: Did he indeed say that morning that the issue of whether *homo lapsus* is the subject of predestination had *not* been determined by the confession of the Church of England (that is, the Thirty-nine Articles)? Gomarus modestly answered that he did indeed say so but that it was not out of any evil intent, but only to show that, like other churches, the Church of England had left the matter undetermined. He had read in his copy of the *Syntagma Confessionum*[66] that the English confession defined no more on the matter than "some out of the human race." Bishop Carleton replied that he and his colleagues could only conclude that Gomarus's answer was touched by temerity or ignorance, for, since the British, in their *iudicium*, had identified *homo lapsus* as the subject of predestination, it was as if they presented in the synod something that was contrary to the Church of England. Then, to show the synod that this was not the case, Thomas Goad publicly read article 17 of the Thirty-nine Articles. This article included the words "deliver *from curse and damnation* those whom he hath chosen in Christ *out of the human race*," but Gomarus had left out the words "from curse and damnation." Breitinger indicates that the bishop reprimanded Gomarus severely (*reprehendit graviter*) for raising doubts about the confession of a foreign church.[67]

Gomarus replied that, if he had misunderstood the words of the confession, he would submit to the judgment of the synod. President Bogerman then roundly told Gomarus that every member of the synod was free to deliver his judgment on any question but that he ought to be very careful not to rashly meddle with the judgments of other churches.

Carleton then added that, since all the foreign theologians and all the Dutch professors, except Gomarus, had already committed to *homo lapsus* in their *iudicia*, and since he did not doubt that the other Dutch delegates would do the same, it would be very appropriate for the synod to determine the matter likewise. There was no reason for

---

66. *Corpus et Syntagma Confessionum Fidei, quae in diversis regnis et nationibus, ecclesiarum nomine fuerunt authenthice editae* (Geneva: Petrus & Iacobus Chouet, 1612), 129; mentioned by Sibelius, 81v.

67. Breitinger, 91v.

the synod to abstain from a determination of the question, for the sake of the particular opinion of one professor who dissented on this point from the judgment of all the Reformed churches.

Gomarus answered that the University of Leiden had never yet made a determination for *homo lapsus* and that both William Whitaker and William Perkins had committed to the contrary (the supralapsarian position), both of whom he took to be men who did not dissent from the Thirty-nine Articles of the Church of England. He said that the issue should first be discussed, with arguments on both sides, before anything was determined.

To this, President Bogerman answered that, after the *iudicia* of all the delegations were read, the synod would decide what should best be thought of this question. After the Canons were drafted, they would be read, and if Gomarus could show that anything contained in the Canons was contrary to God's Word, the synod would patiently hear what he had to say.[68]

Then the other Dutch *iudicia* on Article I were read. South Holland was the only other delegation that did not mention that God predestined from the *fallen* human race. They emphasized that it was not necessary to define whether the object of predestination is man considered by God as fallen or as not-yet-fallen, since, "in electing, he considered all people to be in an equal condition," so that no one was viewed as more worthy than another. Thus, they thought that the differences over the object of predestination could be reconciled.[69]

Sometime before the Canons were drafted, Gomarus prepared a thorough defense of his supralapsarian stance, but he did not submit this document for discussion at the synod. The document argued that the synod should neither define the object of predestination nor reject the supralapsarian position. It maintained that both the supralapsarian and infralapsarian positions are orthodox—the supralapsarian view is

---

68. This whole exchange is described by Balcanqual, 2:129–30. Cf. Sibelius, 81v; *Synodalia Hollandica*, 1/11 March; Tronchin, vol. 16, 114r; Heppe, "Historia," 301; Georgius Fabricius, "Synodus Dordracena, hoc est, Summaria et Compendiosissima Relatio plerorumque eorum, quae in Dordracenae Synodi Sessionibus omnibus ac singulis (publicis nimirum ac ordinariis) Proposita et Pertractata fuerunt, Anno 1618 & 1619," in HStAM, fol. 83, no. 6429, 49r.

69. *Acta*, 3:33–35; Sinnema, "Doctrine of Election," 126.

more appropriately taught in academies to counter heresies, while the infralapsarian view is more appropriately preached in the churches.[70]

In the Canons of Dordt, references to God's decree to predestine from eternity presuppose a fallen humanity. This is the infralapsarian stance that the Canons clearly assume. It is evident first of all in the order of Chapter I, which begins with the fall. When article I, 7, concerning election, was drafted, from the very first draft, written by President Bogerman, to the later drafts of the drafting committee, persons are said to be elected "out of the entire human race fallen [*ex universo genere humano...prolapso*]." Throughout the entire drafting process (with eight drafts of Chapter I), there was no change on this point.[71] Likewise, article I, 15, concerning reprobation, speaks of God's decree to leave some in the common misery (*communi miseria*) into which they had plunged themselves.

Hence the Canons are clothed in infralapsarian language, but they do not specifically define the object of predestination and do not condemn or exclude the supralapsarian position. Gomarus himself was able to sign the Canons, because the popular order and style of the Canons allowed him to interpret their infralapsarian formulations within his own supralapsarian perspective—namely, as relating to the temporal execution of God's decree—since God, actually within history, saves His chosen ones from the fallen human race.[72]

The Debate about the Extent of Christ's Redemption

The toughest difficulties arose in formulating the synod's response to Article II of the Remonstrance, concerning the extent of Christ's redemption. The issue centered on how to interpret the universal passages of Scripture that seem to teach that Christ died for all. Does

---

70. Klaas Dijk, *De Strijd over Infra- en Supralapsarisme in de Gereformeerde Kerken van Nederland* (Kampen: Kok, 1912), printed in Appendix A; analysis of the document, 177–86.

71. Sinnema, "Doctrine of Election," 128–31.

72. Sinnema, "Issue of Reprobation," 431–32; Dijk, *Strijd*, 185; J. V. Fesko, "Lapsarian Diversity at the Synod of Dort," in *Drawn into Controversie: Reformed Theological Diversity and Debates within Seventeenth-Century British Puritanism*, ed. Michael A. G. Haykin and Mark Jones (Göttingen: Vandenhoeck and Ruprecht, 2011), 120–21.

this mean He died for every particular person, or was Christ's death restricted to the elect?

Much of the discussion revolved around the familiar distinction between the sufficiency of Christ's death for all and its efficiency or efficacy only for the elect, a medieval distinction derived from Lombard.

It was well known that Bremen theologian Matthias Martinius had some sympathies with the Remonstrants regarding the extent of Christ's merit. As mentioned above, to bring him to some conformity, there was a private meeting between Martinius and certain foreign theologians in Bishop Carleton's lodging on 23 January, and he promised moderation.[73] Bishop Carleton continued to seek to change Martinius's mind on universal grace by sending him a letter expounding on John 3:16, the passage on which Martinius especially relied.[74]

On 5 February, as discussion on Article II was beginning at the synod, it became apparent that there were significant differences about this issue. Not only Martinius but also Samuel Ward differed with other delegates concerning universal grace. To settle these doubts, and to avoid a public airing of them, many private meetings were held in Bishop Carleton's lodging place. There, on 6 February, some theses were drawn up on the matter.[75]

The differences emerged not only in the synod at large but especially within the British delegation. There, the disagreement focused on the interpretation of article 31 of the Thirty-nine Articles of the Church of England, specifically the words that Christ's redemption, propitiation, and satisfaction were "for all the sins of the whole world." Are the words "whole world" to be understood as all particular people, or only as the world of the elect comprising all sorts or classes of people? John Davenant and Ward (like Martinius) thought they referred to all particular people. Bishop Carleton, Goad, and Balcanqual thought they referred to the elect of all sorts. Each side thought they were right, and neither side yielded. Meanwhile, on 9 February, Balcanqual secretly requested that Ambassador Dudley Carleton seek the advice of the Church of England's leadership on the question.[76]

---

73. Hales, 2:87, 96.
74. Hales, 2:92.
75. Hales, 2:96–97.
76. Balcanqual, 2:101.

Carleton wrote back to the British delegation, advising them either to agree among themselves or to write to England.[77]

President Bogerman also complained in a letter given to Ambassador Carleton that one of the British delegates (Ward) was a "*speculatif et demi*" who was more versed in scholastic disputes than in the practice of the church and who was threatening to breed discord amid the harmony found thus far among the foreign delegates. It is possible that, during this time, Ward was engaged in an acrimonious correspondence with Bogerman about the points in dispute.[78] Bogerman requested that Carleton seek direction from Archbishop Abbot for the British delegation. On 15 February, the ambassador informed Abbot about the growing differences and asked for his direction.[79]

Balcanqual drew up a statement that spelled out the precise state of the disagreement within the British delegation, and he sent this to Ambassador Carleton on 15 February, along with a request to forward it to Archbishop Abbot. The main issue, he stated, was whether the words "whole world," in article 31 of the Thirty-nine Articles, referred to the world of the elect or to the world of all particular people. He also wondered whether the distinction between the sufficiency and the efficiency of Christ's death should be retained. Despite the controversy within the delegation, love and amity still prevailed among them, he asserted. He hoped the archbishop would provide speedy advice to help settle the matter.[80]

On 18 February, Bishop Carleton also sent a letter to Dudley Carleton describing the dynamics of the controversy within the British delegation. As they were preparing their *iudicium* on Article II, he stated, Davenant and Ward could not agree with the three others, and they were at a standoff, which led to various conferences that only drew them further apart. Davenant and Ward held that the grace of Christ's

---

77. Milton, *British Delegation*, 200.
78. Milton, *British Delegation*, 194; Samuel Ward to Archbishop Usher, quoted in Davenant, *Exposition*, xvii.
79. Milton, *British Delegation*, 199–200.
80. Balcanqual, 2:102–3. The statement of differences is on 2:105–6; analyzed by W. Robert Godfrey, "Tensions within International Calvinism: The Debate on the Atonement at the Synod of Dort, 1618–1619" (PhD diss., Stanford University, 1974), 170–73.

redemption was general to all without exception, and they thought that this accorded with Scripture and with the Church of England. But the other three took this to be neither the truth of Scripture nor the doctrine of the Church of England. Bishop Carleton insisted that an agreement was necessary and that, if they could not agree on everything, they should identify points on which all agreed. Carleton asked them if he could be free to remove things on which they could not agree. To this the other British delegates yielded, and so they agreed on some points.

Bishop Carleton further reported that, in a private conference with Ward, he was led to admit that Scripture teaches that, where there is grace of redemption, there is also remission of sins. So, if Ward insisted that the grace of redemption is common to all, he must also admit that all have remission of sins. To avoid this conclusion, Ward devised new words to express the generality—not *redemptio*, but *redimibilitas*; not *reconciliatio*, but *reconciliabilitas* (the possibility of redemption and of reconciliation). And he was not willing to say with the Remonstrants that *impetratio* (redemption accomplished) is general, but rather that *impetrabilitas* (the possibility of obtaining redemption) is general. Such invented scholastic terms were very suspect for Bishop Carleton. Ward, however, did not keep his ideas in the private conferences; he shared them with others and publicly presented them in the synod. President Bogerman was offended by some of the things that were presented, and he asked the British to write their archbishop for his opinion. Bishop Carleton then told the other British delegates that it would be less trouble if they themselves altered some of the things that offended Bogerman rather than refer the matter to the archbishop. To this, Davenant answered that he would rather have his right hand cut off than recall or alter anything. Hence, they were driven to seek Archbishop Abbot's advice. Carleton was sure that the idea of a universal grace of redemption would not be well received in the synod.[81]

By 26 February, Bishop Carleton could report to Dudley Carleton that the "stirs" had become "well composed."[82] The bishop wrote to Archbishop Abbot on 28 February that he had cut off discussion

---

81. Milton, *British Delegation*, 200–202; Hales, 2:179–82.
82. Milton, *British Delegation*, 203–4.

of whether the grace of redemption is general to all. This he did with the consent of the whole British delegation. Yet he feared that his colleagues would not be silent if the matter should be disputed in the synod. So, he suggested that a private admonition from Abbot to his colleagues might keep them all quiet. Despite their differences of opinion, he said that the members of the delegation lived together in great love.[83]

The same day, the whole British delegation wrote to Archbishop Abbot. Noting that they had earlier requested Abbot for his advice on the authorized doctrine of the Church of England concerning the issue of universal redemption, they did not want to press him further on it now, since they had just reached a compromise among themselves on the issue. They no longer needed his advice, except for private advice.[84]

The compromise agreement of the British delegation was stated in six theses, which were then incorporated into the British *iudicium* on Article II. This *iudicium*, which was read in the synod on 12 March, was signed by all five British delegates, but it clearly reflected a compromise. In the first two theses, it affirms God's special intention to efficaciously redeem the elect, an emphasis of Bishop Carleton, Goad, and Balcanqual. But later theses relate the death of Christ to all human beings, reflecting the influence of Davenant and Ward. Thesis 3 affirms that Christ gave Himself as a ransom for the sins of the whole world, and thesis 4 affirms the universal gospel promise that whoever believes in Christ shall have eternal life. Thesis 5 implies that some fruits of Christ's death are afforded more generally than to the elect, as spiritual graces accompanying the gospel and conferred on some of the non-elect. To avoid reference to the differences within the delegation, the British *iudicium* did not mention the distinction between the sufficiency and the efficacy of Christ's death.[85]

---

83. Milton, *British Delegation*, 208; Hales, 2:182–83.
84. Milton, *British Delegation*, 209; Hales, 2:183–84.
85. *Acta*, 2:78–83; Hales, 2:186–87; British delegation to Archbishop Abbot (11/21 March), in Hales, 2:184–85; Milton, *British Delegation*, 215, 217. The British *iudicium* on Article II is analyzed by Godfrey, "Tensions," 177–79, and Michael Lynch, "John Davenant's Hypothetical Universalism: A Defense of Catholic and Reformed Orthodoxy," (PhD diss., Calvin Theological Seminary, 2019), 143–47. In a later letter to Archbishop Ussher, Samuel Ward mentions the universal benefits implied by thesis

When the Palatine delegation presented their *iudicium* on Article II the same day, they spoke "most bitterly" about some of the things that Samuel Ward had mentioned in the synod concerning Article II, according to a letter of Balcanqual to Dudley Carleton. He advised Carleton to send frequent admonitions to President Bogerman to keep the bond of peace.[86] Carleton then reported to Secretary of State Robert Naunton that Scultetus and his Palatine colleagues had spoken with much bitterness and disrespect about what Ward had said and that he complained to the agent of the Palatine Elector about it.[87]

In mid-March, the British delegation belatedly received instructions from Archbishop Abbot, after they had presented their *iudicium* on Article II to the synod. Abbot instructed them to conform to the received distinction between the sufficiency and the efficacy of Christ's redemption and to the restriction of efficacy to the elect.[88]

At about the same time, on 8 March, the British delegates received special directions from King James sent by Secretary Naunton (and forwarded by Dudley Carleton): that the British should seek to have the synod's resolution on Article II reflect the early church fathers, be agreeable to the confessions of the Church of England and of other Reformed churches, and give as little offense to the Lutherans as possible. In contrast to the archbishop's instructions, these directions pointed toward a more universal formulation.[89] In a letter to Archbishop Abbot on 19 March, Dudley Carleton noted the "diversitie of directions" in the respective instructions from Naunton and Abbot.[90]

In response to the archbishop's instructions, the British delegation, on 21 March, sent him an apologetic explanation to justify the fact that their *iudicium* on Article II contained some universal emphases. This was accompanied by a statement from Davenant containing their

---

5, a point on which he had a private debate by correspondence with Bogerman; in Davenant, *Exposition*, xvii.

86. Balcanqual, 2:135, 141.

87. Milton, *British Delegation*, 214; Carleton, *Letters*, 347.

88. Balcanqual, 2:135; Hales, 2:184; Milton, *British Delegation*, 215, 216.

89. Milton, *British Delegation*, 212, 215–17; cf. 210; Balcanqual, 2:135; Hales, 2:184–85.

90. Milton, *British Delegation*, 215.

theses, with explanations, as well as various reasons for affirming the universal emphases.⁹¹

On 13 March, it was the Bremen delegation's turn to present their *iudicium* on Article II, but the three Bremen delegates differed so much that each of them submitted a separate *iudicium*. That of Matthias Martinius inclined somewhat toward the Remonstrant position. He emphasized that Christ died for all people, since there is a common love of God for the whole human race by which He seriously wills the salvation of all, but that Christ died especially for the elect, since there is a special decree by which the saving benefits of His death are applied to the elect alone. He critiqued Remonstrant views, but also the Contra-Remonstrant idea that Christ did not in any sense die for those who perish. Henricus Isselburg, on the other hand, defended the received distinction between the sufficiency and the efficacy of Christ's death and restricted the latter to the elect. Ludwig Crocius proposed a middle way between his two colleagues.⁹²

When the Dutch *iudicia* on Article II were read, Balcanqual noted that they accepted the received distinction, but he considered the statements of Gelderland, North Holland, and Drenthe to be too rigid, and even false.⁹³

When the Canons were being drafted, the difficulties persisted, especially those pertaining to Article II. In response to the first committee draft, the majority of the synod wanted to restrict the universal statements of Scripture to the elect alone. The British delegation, on the contrary, contended that such universal statements should neither be explained nor restricted to the elect. This would lay a foundation

---

91. Milton, *British Delegation*, 216–22; Hales, 2:184–90. Milton, *British Delegation*, 218, discusses the authorship of the document. Cf. Richard A. Muller, *Calvin and the Reformed Tradition: On the Work of Christ and the Order of Salvation* (Grand Rapids: Baker Academic, 2012), 133–34.

92. *Acta*, 2:103–18; analysis by Godfrey, "Tensions," 196–202; cf. Balcanqual, 2:131; Milton, *British Delegation*, 215.

93. Balcanqual, 2:132, 134. Anthony Milton, "A Distorting Mirror: The Hales and Balcanquahall Letters and the Synod of Dordt," in *Revisiting the Synod of Dordt (1618–1619)*, ed. Aza Goudriaan and Fred van Lieburg (Leiden: Brill, 2011), 155, points out that Balcanqual's reaction was exaggerated.

for preaching the gospel to all people, and it would in large part avoid giving offense to Lutherans.[94]

In preparing the final draft of the Canons, the last remaining difficulties concerned rejections 2 and 6 of the Rejection of Errors section of Chapter II. Rejection 2 was reformulated into three rejections. The debate on the contentious rejection 6 centered on the scholastic issue of the nature of the necessity—absolute or hypothetical—of Christ's incarnation for the sufficiency of the price of human redemption. On 18 April, as the last changes were being made to the Canons, the British theologians debated the matter at length over against the rest of the synod. They thought rejection 6 was a matter of scholastic speculation, and so they argued that this rejection should be omitted from the Canons. Most other delegates of the synod wished to retain this rejection. The president proposed that it be expressed in such a way that everyone would be satisfied. On 23 April, the synod, on the recommendation of the drafting committee, finally decided to delete this rejection.[95]

The final version of Chapter II of the Canons accepted the received distinction between the sufficiency of Christ's death for all and the efficacy of His death only for the elect. But this chapter is also clothed with universal language and emphases, reflecting the influence of the British and Bremen theologians.

Conclusions

1. Despite the unanimity of all Dutch and foreign delegates at Dordt regarding the fundamentals of the Reformed faith and a desire to maintain a united front against a common threat—the Remonstrants—the Synod of Dordt was not a monolithic assembly. The Dutch delegates and leading Reformed theologians from other countries had

---

94. Balcanqual to Secretary Naunton, in *Praestantium*, 565–66.
95. Balcanqual, 2:144, 146, 148–50, 153–54; Donald Sinnema, "The Drafting of the Canons of Dordt: A Preliminary Survey of Early Drafts and Related Documents," in *Revisiting the Synod of Dordt (1618–1619)*, 304–6; Lynch, "John Davenant's Hypothetical Universalism," 169–72. On this issue, see also Lee Gatiss, "The Synod of Dort and Definite Atonement," in *From Heaven He Came and Sought Her: Definite Atonement in Historical, Biblical, Theological, and Pastoral Perspective*, ed. David Gibson and Jonathon Gibson (Wheaton: Crossway, 2013), 143–63.

Disagreements and Doctrinal Dissension 163

disagreements on many issues, concerning procedure as well as doctrine, and some of these disagreements erupted into open dissension, which sometimes became bitter and acrimonious. These differences at the synod should not be overemphasized, but they were nevertheless real.

2. The dissensions that arose among some of the delegates emerged after the expulsion of the cited Remonstrants in January 1619. While the Remonstrants were present at the synod for five weeks, open dissension on the floor of the synod was actually more intense, but this dissension was between the Remonstrants and the synod, particularly over procedural issues.[96]

3. The tensions among delegates at the synod are scarcely mentioned in the official *acta* of the Synod of Dordt, since the *acta* hardly touch on the deliberations that led to synodical decisions, and the printed *Acta* (1620), as published by the States General, were edited to portray a favorable image of the synod.[97] Therefore, information about the tensions can best be found in extant journals of some of the delegates and in contemporary letters about the synod.

4. The Hales and Balcanqual letters are the main source of information for all four issues of dissension at the synod. It is necessary to heed Anthony Milton's caution about the Hales and Balcanqual letters, namely, that they have a distorting effect on our understanding of the synod, with a tendency to highlight aspects that cast favorable light on the British delegates while criticizing certain Dutch and continental delegates.[98] Moreover, given that they are written in an engaging style, the letters sometimes exaggerate and tend to express the personal attitudes

---

96. Donald Sinnema, "Procedural Wrangling in the Remonstrant Case at the Synod of Dordt (1618–1619)," in *More than Luther: The Reformation and the Rise of Pluralism in Europe*, ed. Karla Boersma and Herman J. Selderhuis (Göttingen: Vandenhoeck and Ruprecht, 2019), 289–306. Reprinted in this volume; see chapter 2.

97. Donald Sinnema, "Introduction to the Acta Authentica, Acta Contracta and Printed Acta," in *ADSND*, 1:xliv–l.

98. Milton, "Distorting Mirror," 135–61. Cf. Godfrey, "Tensions," 173–75; C. van der Woude, *Sibrandus Lubbertus* (Kampen: Kok, 1963), 467, 469.

and emotions of the letter writers about the events. Sometimes Hales relied on reports of others, when the synod sessions were closed to spectators such as himself. While it is important to use the letters with discretion, there is no reason to doubt the veracity of the incidents that these letters describe. The Hales and Balcanqual letters provide a level of detail not found in most other journals or letters about the synod.[99] The specific details lend credibility to reports in the Hales and Balcanqual letters. Where other accounts mention the incidents, they corroborate the essential story found in the Hales-Balcanqual letters, usually without providing all the details. The biographers of Gomarus and Lubbertus, while recognizing moments of bias, also do not dispute the accounts of Hales and Balcanqual about the dissensions.[100] In using these letters, I have sought to draw only on credible details, while avoiding comments where the writers express their personal attitudes.

5. On the four doctrinal issues concerning which there was open dissension, about fifteen of the eighty-four Dutch and foreign delegates were involved. Three of the delegates—Gomarus, Martinius, and Bishop Carleton—were each at the heart of the dissension regarding three of the four issues. Scultetus and President Bogerman were each part of two issues. Martinius attracted controversy, since he pressed the limits of orthodox Reformed theology on some points. Part of the dissension was also due to the contentious personalities of certain persons, especially Gomarus, Lubbertus, and Scultetus,[101] as well as the strained relationships between certain delegates.

---

99. The Tronchin journal provides as much detail, but the handwriting of Tronchin is extremely difficult to read, so this source has not been fully utilized.

100. Van Itterzon, *Gomarus*, 230–31; Van der Woude, *Lubbertus*, 466–67; cf. J. F. Iken, "Bremen und die Synode zu Dordrecht," *Bremisches Jahrbuch* 10 (1878): 30.

101. Bernardus Dwinglo, one of the cited Remonstrants, later wrote that, "[in the closed sessions after 1 February,] the points of difference between the theologians were further discussed, in order to inform each other and give contentment. In these discussions, sometimes heavy debates and intense words were exchanged between some of the doctors, and mostly between some of the foreigners and Franciscus Gomarus, who commonly debated each one's advice and tore each one apart, so that many complained about his domineering attitude and were therefore displeased. Others also in the synod added the complaint against him that he often went too high (*hooge klom*). To cover up all of this, and to be able to more broadly boast to those who are ignorant about the mutual unity and harmony, they did not want any spectators admitted to hear

6. Because of the differences of opinion among the delegates on a wide variety of doctrinal issues, the Synod of Dordt decisions were sometimes compromises for the sake of unity in maintaining a common front against the Remonstrants. There was a need for unanimous consent in approval of the Canons. The Canons were a committee document that sought to accommodate all the delegates so that all would approve and sign them. The Canons were deliberately written in a popular, rather than a scholastic, style, so scholastic precision in defining doctrine was not necessary, leaving some flexibility for compromise. Hence, on a variety of doctrinal points, the Canons presented a compromise formulation by defining what was agreed to by all delegates while remaining silent on what was not and avoiding a rejection of the differences. Recent studies confirm that the Canons thus became a more moderate confessional statement than is often recognized.[102]

---

these conferences of the doctors except those they doubly trusted" (*Historisch Verhael*, 165r–v). While this comment exhibits a definite Remonstrant bias against Gomarus, it does corroborate other reports of his role in the contentious debates at the synod. Others also comment on the contentiousness of Gomarus and Lubbertus: Balcanqual, 2:114, 140–41; Balcanqual to Secretary Naunton, in *Praestantium*, 565; Carleton, *Letters*, 339, 340, 346; Van der Woude, *Lubbertus*, 462, 470, 566–72; Milton, "Distorting Mirror," 156.

102. Godfrey, "Tensions," 252–64, 268; Sinnema, "Issue of Reprobation," 447–50; Lynch, "Davenant," 174. Robert Letham, "Dort and its Controversies," *Mid-America Journal of Theology* 30 (2019): 5–21, offers a somewhat similar analysis of the dissension at the Synod of Dordt, but his article was not available to me when the present article was written in 2019.

Simon Episcopius, Leiden theologian and spokesman for the Remonstrants

CHAPTER 7

Church–State Entanglements at the Synod of Dordt[1]

The Synod of Dordt marked the triumph of orthodox Calvinism over Arminianism after almost two decades of religious unrest in the Netherlands. While this synod is a fascinating study in theological controversy,[2] it also affords a revealing picture of church-and-state relations at one of the critical moments in the history of the Reformed tradition.

This relationship itself was an important, but secondary, part of the Arminian controversy. The Arminians (Remonstrants) favored an Erastian subordination of religious practice and church organization to Christian civil authorities[3] and sought protection from an often

---

1. This is an expanded version of my article "Church and State Relations at the Synod of Dort (1618–1619)," published in *The Synod of Dort: Historical, Theological, and Experiential Perspectives*, ed. Joel R. Beeke and Martin I. Klauber (Göttingen: Vandenhoeck and Ruprecht, 2020), 133–48.

2. See especially Klaas Dijk, *De Strijd over Infra- en Supralapsarisme in de Gereformeerde Kerken van Nederland* (Kampen: Kok, 1912); W. Robert Godfrey, "Tensions within International Calvinism: the Debate on the Atonement at the Synod of Dort, 1618–19" (PhD diss., Stanford University, 1974); and Donald Sinnema, "The Issue of Reprobation at the Synod of Dort (1618–19) in Light of the History of this Doctrine" (PhD diss., University of St. Michael's College, Toronto, 1985).

3. This view was best articulated by Johannes Uytenbogaert, *Tractaet van t'Ampt ende Authoriteyt eener Hoogher Christelicker Overheydt in Kerckelicke Saecken* (s'Gravenhage, 1610). For Jacobus Arminius's view, see Carl Bangs, *Arminius: A Study in the Dutch Reformation* (Nashville: Abingdon, 1971), 335–36. On the Remonstrant view, see Enno Conring, *Kirche und Staat nach der Lehre der niederländischen Calvinisten in der ersten Hälfte des 17. Jahrhunderts* (Neukirchen: Neukirchener Verlag, 1965), ch. 4.

sympathetic state for their minority position. The orthodox Reformed (Contra-Remonstrants) favored the right of the church to control its own affairs, though they had come to live with a measure of state interference.[4] The focus of this chapter is not on this aspect of the Arminian controversy—namely, the views of each side on the church–state relationship, which were not openly discussed on the floor of the synod—but on the actual practice of the relationship of church and state that was evident at the synod.

This article surveys the copious evidence of the complex intertwinement of church and state at the Synod of Dordt throughout the six months of its proceedings, and it explores the nature of this relationship and its limits.

Background

Church–state relations in the Dutch Reformation have a rather distinctive history when compared to other countries in which civil authority Protestantized the church by magisterial reform and maintained its influence in church affairs. The Dutch Reformed church had developed "under the cross" and in exile, and so its first church order, adopted by the Synod of Emden (1571), allowed no role for the state in the church. However, this same synod required all ministers to sign the Belgic Confession (1561), which included an article on civil government (article 36):

> [God] has placed the sword in the hands of the government, to punish evildoers and protect and uphold good and honorable people. Its office and duty is to control and watch over [*bedwingen ende te waken over*] not only the civil state and politics but also ecclesiastical matters, in order to prevent and remove all idolatry and false worship, so that the kingdom of Antichrist may be overthrown and the kingdom of Jesus Christ promoted; and to see that the word of the gospel is

---

4. For an early Calvinist attempt to establish independent church authority in the Netherlands, see Olivier Fatio, *Nihil Pulchrius Ordine. Contribution à l'étude de l'établissement de la discipline ecclésiastique aux Pays-Bas ou Lambert Daneau aux Pays-Bas (1581–1583)* (Leiden: Brill, 1971).

everywhere preached, so that God may be honored and served by everyone, as He requires and demands in His Word.⁵

The Confession apparently had in mind here the suppression of Anabaptist and Roman Catholic forms of worship.

On the political side, the Union of Utrecht (1579), which united the northern provinces of the Netherlands, addressed the matter of religion in its article 13. Each province was guaranteed the authority to establish regulations regarding religion as they saw fit, provided that every individual was allowed personal freedom of religion, the foundation of religious toleration.⁶

As the Reformed church became more established after 1572, the Dutch state began to exert an influence in ecclesiastical affairs, although the church resisted. This resulted in a church polity tug-of-war. In 1576, a commission of the provincial States of Holland drafted an Erastian church order. The 1581 church order of the national synod at Middelburg asserted more independence for the church; while it made concessions regarding the calling of ministers, this church order was unacceptable to the States, which replied with its own draft in 1583 that was somewhat accommodating to the church. Under Leicester, the English governor-general, the church had its way and, with his support, held a national synod in 1586 at The Hague, which drew up its own church order. While this church order allowed for the first time one or two representatives of the local magistrate to attend consistory meetings and recognized a right of the approbation of ministers by the magistrate,⁷ it was provisionally approved by Leicester but was accepted only by the provinces of Holland, Zeeland, and Gelderland, after which it was soon rejected by the States of

---

5. Translation of the first Dutch edition of 1562; see F. Los, *Tekst en Toelichting van de Geloofsbelijdenis der Nederlandsche Hervormde Kerk* (Utrecht: Kemink en Zoon, 1929), 299–301. The 1566 revised edition of the Confession replaced the phrase "but also over ecclesiastical matters" with "but also to maintain (*maintenir*) the sacred ministry." The 1611 Middelburg edition of the Confession again revised this to read "but also to protect (*de handt te houden*) sacred worship." All translations are my own.

6. J. N. Bakhuizen van den Brink et al., eds., *Documenta Reformatoria* (Kampen: Kok, 1960), 1:164.

7. F. L. Rutgers, ed., *Acta van de Nederlandsche Synoden der Zestiende Eeuw* (Dordrecht: J. van den Tol, 1980), 488, 495.

Holland. They, in turn, had a commission draw up a church order in 1591, which formed a compromise between the state version of 1583 and the church version of 1586. It allowed the state a role in appointing clergy and control over who could attend the Lord's Supper, but it was not accepted by the churches. Though it was not universally adopted, the 1586 church order was used by Dutch Reformed churches in various parts of the Netherlands; the Remonstrant churches tended to follow the 1591 church order.[8]

A primary indication of growing political influence was the presence of state delegates at the annual provincial synods, where they first began to appear in 1578. No state delegates were present, however, at national synods before the 1586 Synod of The Hague, which had three representatives of the Earl of Leicester.[9] That was the last national synod to be held before the Synod of Dordt, although the 1586 church order prescribed that such national assemblies ordinarily be held every three years (art. 44). For various reasons, the States General, under the influence of the grand pensionary Johan van Oldenbarnevelt, did not allow the church to hold a national synod. Oldenbarnevelt wanted to prevent the church from hindering the state's concern for toleration and to protect the Remonstrants, with whom he sympathized, from ecclesiastical censure.[10]

By the time of the Synod of Dordt, the Reformed church in the Dutch Republic was not a state church, but rather a privileged church, the only church that was publicly recognized. Church properties that were formerly Roman Catholic were under the control of provincial or local civil authorities and were provided to Reformed churches for their use. The church also depended on these civil authorities for

---

8. For a fuller overview of this history, see Jan den Tex, *Oldenbarnevelt*, vol. 2, *1606–1619* (Cambridge: Cambridge University Press, 1973), 435–39; and J. Reitsma, *Geschiedenis van de Hervorming en de Hervormde Kerk der Nederlanden* (Utrecht: Kemink, 1933), 199–211. These church orders are printed in Rutgers, *Acta*, and C. Hooijer, ed., *Oude Kerkordeningen der Nederlandsche Hervormde Gemeenten (1563–1638)* (Zalt-Bommel: J. Noman en Zoon, 1865).

9. Rutgers, *Acta*, 538; J. Th. De Visser, *Kerk en Staat* (Leiden: A. Sijthoff, 1926), 2:485–87.

10. Den Tex, *Oldenbarnevelt*, 2:437.

financial support for their Reformed ministers. The States of Holland took charge of these matters already in 1573.[11]

Convening and Opening of the Synod

After years of theological controversy, the political climate was shifting from Oldenbarnevelt toward Prince Maurice of Orange, who controlled the military and sympathized with the Contra-Remonstrant cause. The time was ripe for a national synod to be convened by the States General.

Serious public discussion about holding a national synod to quell the unrest in the Netherlands was initiated by a letter to the States General from King James I of England in March 1617.[12] By June, four of the seven provinces in the States General were arguing for a national synod as the best means by which to resolve the unrest caused by religious controversies in the land. In October, by a majority of these four provinces, the States decided to proceed and formed a committee to prepare for the synod.[13] On 11 November, the majority of the States General approved a list of seventeen Articles to Convene a national synod, which defined the structure of the upcoming synod.[14]

These Articles to Convene declared that the States General itself would convene the synod. They determined the time—1 May

---

11. Rosemary L. Jones, "Reformed Church and Civil Authorities in the United Provinces in the Late 16th and Early 17th Centuries, as Reflected in Dutch State and Municipal Archives," *Journal of the Society of Archivists* 4, no. 2 (1970): 117, 120–23, focuses on the example of Leiden.

12. Eric Platt, *Britain and the Bestandstwisten: The Causes, Course and Consequences of British Involvement in the Dutch Religious and Political Disputes of the Early Seventeenth Century* (Göttingen: Vandenhoeck and Ruprecht, 2015), 105–12.

13. *RSG*, 3:122, 138–39, 145–46, 218–25, 228, 231–32. The provinces of Gelderland, Zeeland, Friesland, and Groningen favored a national synod; Utrecht, Overijssel, and especially Holland continued to object. Their key objection was that article 13 of the Union of Utrecht (1579) stipulated that religious matters were under provincial jurisdiction. For more details on the political debates about convening the national synod, see *ADSND*, vol. 2/1.

14. The final version of these articles is printed in the *Acta*, 1:15–18; and in *ADSND*, 2/1:740–45. An earlier draft was presented to the States General on 12 October 1617; *RSG*, 3:236–37, 261, 263–66. These articles were based in part on the majority recommendations to the *Conventus Praeparatorius* of 1607, an earlier attempt to convene the national synod; D. J. De Groot, "De Conventus Praeparatorius van Mei 1607," *Nederlandsch Archief voor Kerkgeschiedenis* 27 (1934): 129–66.

1618—and the place—Dordrecht, Utrecht, or The Hague.[15] They specified the number of delegates of various kinds: six delegates from each provincial synod—at least three ministers as well as two or three elders "or other members of the church"; professors of theology from each of the Dutch academies; representatives of the Walloon churches; three or four theologians to be invited from each of eight foreign lands, to help establish unity in religion and remove doctrinal difficulties; and two state delegates from each province. The Articles determined preparations: provincial synods must meet to prepare for the synod, and there must be a day of fasting and prayer to ask God to restore peace and unity in the church and state. They also set the basic agenda: first, the controversial Five Articles of the Remonstrance must be treated to see how the difficulties arising from them might be removed, as much as the peace of the church and purity of doctrine allowed; then, the gravamina, or overtures, referred by the provincial synods to the national synod would be considered. They determined procedure: by oath, delegates must agree to use the Word of God alone, and no human writings,[16] as the standard of truth in any dispute of doctrine; synodical decisions must be by majority vote; and adjournments would be allowed. And finally, the Articles required the synod to report to the States General regarding its decisions so that the States General might approve them.

Since the state delegates played an influential role at the synod, article 16 of the Articles to Convene is especially noteworthy:

> 16. It is also considered advisable that each province name two honorable persons, well qualified for the task, who profess the Reformed religion and are members of the Church, so that they, being fully authorized by the illustrious and mighty States [General], may regularly attend and be present in the synod and direct and regulate [*dirigant ac moderentur, de actiën ende beleyt te modereren*] all its actions, so as to prevent and remove all disorder and confusion.[17]

---

15. The time was later changed to 1 November 1618, and the location to Dordrecht; *RSG*, 3:272–75, 423.

16. Thus, the States General excluded the use of the Belgic Confession and the Heidelberg Catechism as confessional standards of orthodoxy in the synod's discussions on doctrine.

17. *Acta*, 1:18.

After months of delay, on 25 June 1618, the majority of the States General decided to reaffirm its decision to convene a national synod—on 1 November in Dordrecht—and asked the provinces to hold provincial synods in preparation for the national synod.[18] During the following months, the three holdout provinces of Overijssel, Utrecht, and Holland agreed to the synod under pressure from Prince Maurice, who had just tipped the balance of political power by arresting Oldenbarnevelt, by forcing the local city militias (*waardgelders*) in these provinces to disband, and by purging pro-Remonstrant magistrates in various towns.[19]

Eighteen state delegates were chosen by the provinces to represent the States General at the synod. They were leading civic officials, six from Holland and two from each of the other provinces.[20] At the synod, the state delegates had their own president; weekly, they took turns presiding, as was the practice in the States General. Thus, the synod formally had two presidents, though, in practice, its proceedings were conducted by the ecclesiastical president, sometimes with advice from the president of the state delegates.[21] Added to the state delegates as their secretary was Daniel Heinsius, the well-known professor of history and librarian at Leiden University.[22]

The States General drew up a set of secret instructions for the state delegates.[23] They were to open the synod and to receive and examine the credentials of all delegates. They were to assure that the synod treated no matters that were political or related to the broader

---

18. *RSG*, 3:423–24; cf. 3:231, 263–66, 276–77, 404, 418–19.

19. *RSG*, 3:445–46, 463, 470; cf. 426–28, 434, 438–42, 447–50, 452–53, 468–69.

20. Holland requested and received six state delegates because of the large number of Reformed churches in this province—about five hundred; *RSG*, 3:537, 539, 544, 548. On the role of the eighteen state delegates, see *ADSND*, 1:liii–lxi. On the personal backgrounds of the state delegates, see L. Wagenaar, *Van Strijd en Overwinning: De Groote Synode van 1618 op '19, en wat aan haar voorafging* (Utrecht: G. Ruys, 1909), 273–82.

21. H. H. Kuyper, *De Post-Acta of Nahandelingen van de Nationale Synode van Dordrecht in 1618 en 1619 gehouden* (Amsterdam: Höveker & Wormser, 1899), 103.

22. *ADSND*, 1:5. On Heinsius, see Paul R. Sellin, *Daniel Heinsius and Stuart England* (London: Oxford University Press, 1968), ch. 3.

23. These instructions, in fifteen articles, are printed in *ADSND*, 1:467–71. The instructions were initially approved on 5 and 6 November 1618, confirmed on 19 November, and then backdated 6 November; *RSG*, 3:542, 544, 548, 555, 560, 561.

church outside the Netherlands. Only the ecclesiastical matters mentioned in the Articles to Convene the synod must be treated, and then only the most necessary issues. If the synod would approve a uniform church order, the state delegates had to take care that the synod did not infringe upon or violate the rights and privileges of the provinces, especially the right of patronage.[24] Such church order matters could be discussed by the Dutch delegates alone, when the foreign theologians were no longer present. The state delegates, and the foreign theologians, were to have not only a deliberative (*deliberativum*) voice but also a decisive (*resolutivum*) voice in the synod.[25] They must see that all public synodical documents used the form: "the National Synod under the authority of the High and Mighty States General." They were to admonish the delegates not to divulge any of the proceedings until the synod ended and to take care that any recesses were short, in order to limit costs to the States. They were to arrange that all affairs of the synod be done for the well-being, peace, and unity of the Dutch churches and society and that everything be done that served to promote the Reformed Christian religion. Finally, they were to regularly correspond with the States General.

The state delegates attended the regular sessions of the synod, but they also held their own separate meetings (sixty-nine times) and kept their own acts, which were recorded by Heinsius. During the course of the synod, they sent at least twenty-seven reports, as well as thirteen personal delegations, to the States General.[26]

---

24. Most especially, the province of Groningen did not want the synod to examine whether the right of patronage was in agreement with God's Word; *RSG*, 3:560.

25. Synod delegate Gisbertus Voetius, *Politica Ecclesiastica* (Amsterdam, 1676), 4:245, later claimed that the state delegates "were not sent or seated in the synod to judge the disputed Five Articles, nor were they instructed to have any decisive vote (*suffragium decisivum*) on whatever other cases or matters that were to be treated synodically."

26. The acts of the state delegates' meetings are published in *ADSND*, 1:473–518. The reports of the state delegates to the States General were to be kept secret, and, unfortunately, they are not found in the archives of the States General. According to the States General resolutions and the state delegates' *acta*, they sent reports on 14, 19, 27, and 29 November; 9, 13, 18, and 18 December; 7, 12, 15, and 20 January; 1, 7, 13, 15, 22, 24, and 28 March; 26 and 30 April; and 2, 6, 7, 7, 15?, 16, and 18 May. A small delegation was sent by the state delegates to The Hague on 31 December, 17

Church–State Entanglements at the Synod of Dordt 175

On 5 November, the States General discussed whether the foreign theologians should have the right to vote individually or by country. It was decided to leave the decision to the synod. It was also decided unanimously to give the foreign theologians a decisive voice (*votum decisivum*) in the synod.[27]

The States General, and not the synod, issued invitations to ten foreign lands to send Reformed theologians to assist the Dutch in settling the Arminian controversy. In most of these cases, the invitations were sent to the rulers of these lands to select and send their best theologians.[28] When these theologians arrived in the Netherlands, they typically first reported to The Hague, where they presented their credentials to the States General and Prince Maurice.[29]

A prime example is the case of Great Britain, where King James I was invited to send several theologians. James selected five theologians headed by Bishop George Carleton. James sent them with special instructions to take a moderate position on controversial matters, to make decisions agreeable with Scripture and the doctrine of the Church of England, and to always consult with Dudley Carleton, the British ambassador in the Netherlands.[30] They were also to send weekly reports to the king.[31] One means of reporting was the extensive

---

January, 26 April, and 30 May; state delegate Hugo Muys van Holy reported to the States General seven times, and secretary Heinsius reported twice.

27. *RSG*, 3:547.

28. The States General sent invitations to the King of Great Britain, the Elector of the Palatinate, the Landgrave of Hesse, the Counts of Nassau-Wetteravia, and the Margrave of Brandenburg; to the republics and churches of Switzerland, Geneva, Bremen, and Emden; and to the Reformed churches of France. King Louis XIII of France prevented four Reformed theologians selected by a French synod from attending, and, due to Lutheran opposition, the Margrave of Brandenburg decided not to send his theologians; *ADSND*, 1:5–6; *RSG*, 3:278, 424, 461, 496, 501–2, 524, 527, 543, 545, 556, 590; Geeraert Brandt, *Historie der Reformatie en andere Kerkelyke Geschiedenissen in en omtrent de Nederlanden* (Rotterdam: Barent Bos, 1704), 3:9–12.

29. *RSG*, 3:548–49, 552, 588, 589; 4:15.

30. The full instructions are printed in Anthony Milton, ed., *The British Delegation and the Synod of Dort (1618–1619)* (Woodbridge, England: Boydell Press, 2005), 92–94. During one debate in the synod (session 134), the English pointed out that they were "delegated by his serene majesty the King, not by their churches"; Hales, 2:153.

31. Thomas Fuller, *The Church History of Britain* (London: Thomas Tegg and Son, 1837), 3:277.

letters of John Hales and Walter Balcanqual, which provided session-by-session accounts for Ambassador Dudley Carleton.[32] On entering the Netherlands, the English theologians were introduced by their ambassador to the States General on 6 November, and Bishop Carleton gave a speech to this body and Prince Maurice.[33]

On the other hand, the provincial synods of the Netherlands were allowed to select and send their own delegates, although the number had been determined by the States General.[34] Typically, each synod sent four ministers and two elders. Of these fifty-six Dutch delegates, nineteen were elders. Even here, there was potential state influence, since fourteen of the nineteen elders were civic officials, although they were not present in that capacity.[35]

On 12 November 1618, the Dutch delegates and the state delegates met in a preparatory meeting to discuss how to open the synod, the seating order, and the method of voting. It was decided that the state delegates should have the best seating on one side of the hall. On the other side would be the foreign theologians, seated in the order of their political importance to the Netherlands—the English first. Finally, the Dutch delegations would be seated according to the rank their provinces held in the States General. In regard to the method of voting, it was decided that each of the nineteen Dutch and foreign delegations would have one vote, as was the pattern in the States General, where each province had a vote. Also, the foreign theologians and professors would be given a decisive rather than advisory vote, although the former would have the right only on doctrinal matters.[36]

When the synod opened on 13 November, the state delegates welcomed and seated all the members. After an opening prayer, Dordrecht minister Balthasar Lydius thanked them that the States General had not despised the request for a national synod but, following in the footsteps of emperors Constantine, both Theodosiuses, Marcianus, and

---

32. These important letters are printed in Hales.
33. *RSG*, 3:548–49; Brandt, *Historie*, 3:4–9, which includes the bishop's speech.
34. In the Articles to Convene the synod (art. 3). On 13 October, the States General had determined the total number to be fifty-six; *RSG*, 3:521.
35. See the list of Dutch delegates and their titles in *ADSND*, 1:xc–civ.
36. H. Kaajan, *De Pro-Acta der Dordtsche Synode in 1618* (Rotterdam: T. De Vries, 1914), 17–20.

others, had consented to convene this eminent assembly at such great expense and that it had given the state delegates the task of presiding over the synod in the name of the States General. Then Martinus Gregorii, president of the state delegates for the first week, officially opened the synod, and at the end of his speech, he stated that deliberations and decisions on ecclesiastical matters would be left to the synod.[37]

Then the state delegates presented their commission from the States General. This included the mandate "to open the synod, and appear and be present in our name at each and every session and synodical action, and to arrange with their advice, prudence, and moderating [*moderatione*] everything subject to their care and supervision, as we have fully confided in our delegates and also specifically instructed them."[38]

The Dutch delegates then elected officers for the synod, choosing Frisian pastor Johannes Bogerman as president. After the credentials of the Dutch delegates were presented, the foreign theologians were asked if they had credentials to present. The state delegates answered that their credentials had already been presented to the States General.[39] Though such a procedure was irregular, the synod did not pursue the matter.[40]

In session 4, the state delegates instructed that the Articles to Convene the national synod be read, so that matters would be conducted according to the directions of the States General. Since article 9 required that the Five Remonstrant Articles be first on the agenda, a discussion took place regarding how the Remonstrants should be called to the synod. With the advice of the state delegates, it was decided that several leading Remonstrants should be cited to appear before the synod. How many would be summoned, and who, was left to the judgment of the state delegates.[41]

---

37. *ADSND*, 1:10–11. Gregorii's speech is printed in *ADSND*, 2/2:10–12.
38. *ADSND*, 1:11. This commission is printed in *ADSND*, 2/2:25–28. The States General approved the commission on 6 November 1618; *RSG*, 3:548. The *Acta Authentica* described the mandate of this commission as: "authority will be entrusted to the distinguished delegates, in the name of their distinguished lords [the States General], of moderating [*moderandi*] the actions of this synod and managing its good order"; *ADSND*, 1:11.
39. *ADSND*, 1:13.
40. Brandt, *Historie*, 3:30.
41. *ADSND*, 1:14, 473–74.

When the Remonstrants heard of this, they sent a petition to the state delegates requesting that they be given the freedom to send their own representatives to a conference between the two sides. The state delegates declined, saying that the Remonstrants were not a recognized body that could send its own representatives.[42]

The state delegates and the synod drew up separate citation letters that were sent to thirteen leading Remonstrants. The state delegates' letter mentioned that Remonstrant views would be "examined"; the synod's letter stated that the States General's will was that Remonstrant views be "examined and judged." Both letters summoned the Remonstrants so that they might freely state, explain, and defend, as much as they can and shall judge necessary, their Five Articles.[43] Since the state delegates' letter was the weaker statement, the Remonstrants later tended to appeal to it as that which defined their role at the synod.

Over the next three weeks, while it waited for the cited Remonstrants to appear, the synod dealt with several non-doctrinal matters referred to it by the provincial synods: a new Dutch Bible translation, catechism services and catechism instruction, the baptism of slave children, preparation for the ministry, and printing abuses.[44] On these ecclesiastical matters, there were instances in which the synod sought state support. It requested the States General to promote the proposed new Dutch translation of the Bible and to bear the necessary expenses. In order to prevent people from being distracted from attending Sunday afternoon services, magistrates were to be asked to prohibit, by strict edicts, manual labor, sports, drinking parties, and other desecrations of the Sabbath. Magistrates were also to be asked to promote the work of catechizing, to provide schoolteachers with suitable salaries, and to banish all papal catechisms from the schools. To correct the prevalent abuses in the printing trade, the synod decided to draw up a regulation to be offered as advice to the States General and to ask them to prevent all such abuses by a public edict.[45] The sources do not

---

42. Brandt, *Historie*, 3:38–41.
43. *ADSND*, 1:15–16. The two citation letters are printed in *ADSND*, 2/2:62–66.
44. On these matters, see Kaajan, *Pro-Acta*.
45. *ADSND*, 1:20, 25, 26–28, 34.

indicate that the state delegates participated in the discussion of these ecclesiastical matters.

Procedural Debates with the Remonstrants

For five weeks after the day when the Remonstrants appeared (5 December), the synod was largely entangled in procedural debates with them.[46]

The Remonstrant view of the state is evident in a written appeal for understanding that was presented to the foreign theologians on that same day. It declared that the only points of doctrinal difference between themselves and the Contra-Remonstrants were the issues of predestination, confessional revision, and the authority of the state in ecclesiastical matters. Their view of the latter was that the civil magistrate, in accord with his supreme power in ecclesiastical matters, might lawfully make resolutions conforming to God's Word and call synods—and, therefore, all ministers under such a Christian magistrate were obliged to obey and submit to their resolutions. However, they should be free to object to laws that they judged to be contrary to God's Word and their own consciences. They also pointed out that they followed the state-drafted Church Order of 1591, not that of the 1586 Synod of The Hague.[47]

The same view was expressed in a 7 December oration by Simon Episcopius, a Leiden theology professor and spokesman for the Remonstrants. He affirmed that they considered the magistrate to be the highest authority, under God and His Word, over disputable matters of faith, while the Contra-Remonstrants denied this.[48] Afterward, the state delegates required the Remonstrants to sign a copy of the speech, since it contained matters not only ecclesiastical but also political.[49] In the afternoon, they questioned Episcopius personally about

---

46. For an analysis of these procedural debates, see Donald Sinnema, "Procedural Wrangling in the Remonstrant Case at the Synod of Dordt (1618–1619)," in *More than Luther: The Reformation and the Rise of Pluralism in Europe*, ed. Karla Boersma and Herman J. Selderhuis (Göttingen: Vandenhoeck and Ruprecht, 2019), 289–306. Reprinted in this volume; see chapter 2.

47. *Acta et Scripta*, 1:12–23; and *ADSND*, 2/2:231–43.

48. *ADSND*, 1:37. Episcopius's speech is printed in *ADSND*, 2/2:267–83.

49. Hales, 2:49.

whether all he had spoken was in the written copy.[50] Shortly thereafter, a debate erupted when President Bogerman asked Episcopius for a copy of his speech, after which Episcopius replied that he had "no other copy," or "no other copy that was neatly enough written" (according to the Remonstrants). Bogerman accused Episcopius of telling a lie by denying that he had another copy of the speech. When both men were about to call upon witnesses to their versions of the story, the state delegates stepped in and ordered that the matter be dropped.[51]

As the doctrinal discussion was about to begin, all delegates were then asked to swear an oath, as prescribed by the Articles to Convene (art. 10). Each delegate swore that, in all discussion of the Remonstrants' Five Articles and any other doctrine, he would "not make use of any human writing, but only the Word of God as the sure and undoubted rule of faith."[52]

On 10 December, Bogerman asked the Remonstrants to begin explaining their Five Articles. But they wished first to read a paper that would prepare the way for the main issue. Bogerman refused, but the state delegates ordered that it be read.[53] In this paper, addressed to the state delegates, the Remonstrants asserted that they could not recognize the synod as their lawful judge and demanded that twelve conditions be met before they would accept the synod's authority. Basically, they wanted a conference between equal parties.[54] This sparked a heated debate about the lawful authority of the synod. The conditions were rejected, and the state delegates warned the Remonstrants that, if they rejected the authority of the synod, they might be considered disturbers of all civil and ecclesiastical order.[55] One of the Remonstrants, Carolus Niellius, said that they acknowledged the authority of the States and that they had due esteem for the synod; yet they challenged it to accept their conditions.[56]

---

50. *Historisch Verhael van't ghene sich toeghedraeghen heeft binnen Dordrecht, in de Jaeren 1618 en 1619* (Amsterdam, 1623), 29.

51. *Historisch Verhael*, 31.

52. *ADSND*, 1:38.

53. *ADSND*, 1:42; *Praestantium ac Eruditorum Virorum Epistolae Ecclesiasticae et Theologicae* (Amsterdam, 1684), 517.

54. Printed in *ADSND*, 2/2:308–33.

55. *Historisch Verhael*, 42.

56. *Historisch Verhael*, 43.

The state delegates responded with a resolution stating that the States General had sufficient regard for requisite conditions in their Articles to Convene, and they ordered the Remonstrants to proceed without evasion or delay and submit to the synod.[57] As the debate continued, Bogerman admonished them to obey the state delegates' orders, to which Niellius responded that the government certainly had the power to call synods and to prescribe their procedure but that it had no power over the conscience. The state delegates replied that they did not want to bind the Remonstrants' consciences but that the Remonstrants were subjects of the States General and, therefore, ought to obey its laws.[58]

As the Remonstrants persisted in their view, the state delegates repeatedly ordered them to submit to the synod. On 11 December, the Remonstrants presented a protest to the synod and a written response to the state delegates' resolution that promised obedience to political authority that is not in conflict with their consciences, and they stated that they were ready to comply with the resolution if six conditions were met—similar to the previous twelve.[59] After more heated debate, the state delegates ordered Bogerman to ask the Remonstrants individually whether they would obey.[60]

Finally, without recognizing the synod as a lawful judge, the Remonstrants yielded somewhat and agreed to "state, explain, and defend" their views of their Five Articles, as stipulated in the citation letters.[61] In short written theses, they "stated" their views on each of their Five Articles, though these *Sententiae* rejected opposing views more than they presented the Remonstrants' own position.[62]

Then Bogerman required the Remonstrants to produce their observations on the Belgic Confession and the Heidelberg Catechism. This sparked new debate, as the Remonstrants argued that the citation letters required such observations only after the Five Articles had been

---

57. *ADSND*, 1:44. Printed in *ADSND*, 2/2:333–34.
58. *ADSND*, 1:46–47.
59. *ADSND*, 2/2:350–54, 356–57.
60. *Historisch Verhael*, 54.
61. *Acta et Scripta*, 1:70.
62. *ADSND*, 1:57. The Remonstrant *Sententiae* on the Five Articles were submitted on 13 and 17 December and are printed in *Acta*, 1:113–14, 116–21.

treated. Finally, the state delegates gave them four days to present their observations individually.[63]

On 21 December, the Remonstrants submitted their *Observations* on the Confession, which were signed by all. Bogerman reprimanded them for presenting their observations jointly and for not including observations on the Catechism. At the same time, the state delegates issued a new resolution that the Remonstrants had failed to obey their command to present their observations on both the Confession and the Catechism together and to do so individually. When Episcopius asked for a copy of the resolution, he was told that it was the Remonstrants' duty to obey, not to weigh resolutions.[64] After the Christmas adjournment, the Remonstrants submitted their *Observations* on the Catechism.

Further procedural debates ensued regarding whether election or reprobation should be treated first, as well as whether the Remonstrants would have the freedom to refute opposing views, especially those concerning reprobation. With the Remonstrants still not yielding, the state delegates again told them to obey or suffer civil punishments; they also issued a resolution commanding them not to obstruct the work of the synod, to immediately proceed to the main issue, and to answer questions that would be put to them.[65]

On 28 December, Bogerman began to question the Remonstrants for a fuller explanation of their views. This sparked a new set of procedural debates regarding the validity of asking questions and the necessity of answering individually. The Remonstrants refused to answer questions without a guarantee of the freedom they sought.[66] At this point, the proceedings were locked in an impasse. Given the situation, the synod decided to soften the position that it spelled out in an earlier synodical *Decision* by providing a further *Explanation* of it. Here the synod conceded to the Remonstrants the right to refute the views of the Dutch Contra-Remonstrants.[67]

---

63. *ADSND*, 1:60–61; *Historisch Verhael*, 65.
64. *Historisch Verhael*, 77–78.
65. *ADSND*, 1:71–72; *Acta*, 1:131; *Historisch Verhael*, 101–2.
66. Hales, 2:59–62; *Historisch Verhael*, 102r–104v.
67. *ADSND*, 1:77–79; Hales, 2:64–65.

After further discussion, the state delegates ordered that each Remonstrant should be asked whether he would obey and that each should answer with a categorical yes or no. They answered that they needed time to respond in writing to the synodical *Decision* and *Explanation*, and they requested copies of these documents. President Bogerman strenuously rejected their request, but the state delegates decided to allow them to have copies and more time, a move that displeased Bogerman.[68]

On 29 December, the Remonstrants presented a written reply to the synod's *Decision* and *Explanation*, spelling out the conditions under which they would cooperate. They conceded that they were now willing to answer questions—though preferably in writing, and only after explaining and defending their own views—and that they were willing to let the state delegates (not the synod or themselves) set reasonable limits on their presentations.[69] The synod was not sensitive to these concessions and considered the Remonstrant reply a continuing refusal to submit except on their own conditions.

Again, the state delegates directed Bogerman to ask the Remonstrants to answer categorically whether they would submit to the synod. When the Remonstrants said that they would only adhere to the conditions of their written reply, the president of the state delegates put an end to the debate and declared that a delegation would be dispatched to The Hague to report the Remonstrants' obstinacy to the States General and to seek its direction in the matter.[70] The delegation included three state delegates and two officers of the synod.

On 31 December, this delegation reported to the States General, which issued a resolution on 1 January 1619. It approved the decisions of the synod and of the state delegates and commanded the Remonstrants to submit to these decisions or else face civil and ecclesiastical censures. If they continued in the same disobedience, "their opinions on religion should be investigated, examined, and, according to God's Word, be determined from their public writings," as well as from the explanations, oral and written, that they previously expressed

---

68. *ADSND*, 1:79–81; *Historisch Verhael*, 112–13.
69. *ADSND*, 1:81–82.
70. *Historisch Verhael*, 116.

both in this synod and in other provincial synods. Meanwhile, they must remain in Dordrecht and be ready to answer any questions from the synod.[71]

On 3 January 1619, the Remonstrants submitted a statement to the state delegates, which was read in the synod. They contended that their liberty to defend their view and refute the opposing view, however they deemed best, was a matter of conscience. They argued that civil authorities, even the States General, had no right to impose anything on their subjects that might burden their conscience.[72]

Also on 3 January, one of the state delegates read the States General's 1 January resolution to the synod. Since the Remonstrants continued in their refusal to answer questions except according to their 29 December conditions, Bogerman called together a committee of sixteen synodical delegates and six state delegates to discuss how to implement the government's resolution. This committee thought it advisable that the Remonstrant view be extracted from their writings and drawn up in a number of theses and that, if the Remonstrants thought that their view was not well understood, they could add a fuller explanation.[73]

After some theses were drafted, on 11 January Bogerman tried to question the Remonstrants once more and told them that they might explain their position more fully afterward. This ignited a new debate regarding whether the Remonstrants should answer the questions before or after presenting their explanation.[74] Then Episcopius made a concession and said that the Remonstrants would take the list of questions and submit written answers together with their explanations. He asked for the list of questions, but Bogerman refused to give it to him. State delegate Gregorii supported him, saying that written answers would just waste time.[75]

Then the synod decided to question the Remonstrants no longer and to examine their view from their writings. This was echoed by a resolution of the state delegates declaring that the States General

---

71. *ADSND*, 1:85–86; *RSG*, 3:598–99; 4:4.
72. *ADSND*, 2/2:644–50.
73. Hales, 2:70.
74. *ADSND*, 1:99–106.
75. *Historisch Verhael*, 135–36.

1 January resolution was to be put into effect: the Remonstrant view was to be extracted from their public writings, after which they could submit any further explanations. However, till the following Monday, they would still have the option to submit to the synod.[76]

On Saturday, 12 January, the state delegates met privately with the Remonstrants to persuade them to submit. The Remonstrants repeated that they were willing to add to their 29 December conditions that they were ready to answer questions in writing together with their explanations. The state delegates proposed a statement that they answer in writing or orally together with their explanations. This the Remonstrants were willing to sign only if their 29 December conditions were not denied to them. The state delegates mistrusted any reference to the 29 December conditions, so no agreement was reached.[77]

On Monday, 14 January, the state delegates reported on their meeting with the Remonstrants, stating that their efforts were in vain, since the Remonstrants still clung to their conditions. They advised that the Remonstrants be commanded one last time to submit. After the foreign delegates advised that they be dismissed, Bogerman called in the Remonstrants and asked them to state categorically whether they would obey the States General and the synod. They refused to say that they would submit but instead replied with a lengthy document, presenting an explanation of their views on Article I, with a preface that reaffirmed their conditions. Then Bogerman expelled the Remonstrants in a passionate speech, ending with the exclamation "Therefore, in the name of the state delegates and of the synod, you are dismissed. Get out!" The Remonstrants stalked out but were ordered by the state delegates not to leave the city.[78] Though Bogerman has often been blamed for expelling the Remonstrants, the expulsion merely implemented the States General 1 January resolution that they be judged from their writings. Implied was that this would be done outside of their presence.

---

76. *ADSND*, 1:106–7.
77. *Historisch Verhael*, 138–39; *ADSND*, 1:109–10, 485–88.
78. Hales, 2:76–77; *ADSND*, 1:109–13.

Deliberations after the Remonstrants Were Expelled

After the procedural debates and the Remonstrant expulsion, the synod's attention turned to the actual doctrinal issues. For another three months, the synod was busy examining these issues and forming its judgment on the Five Articles of the Remonstrance. Since the Remonstrants were no longer present, the synod first discussed how best to examine and judge their views from their writings. All members as well as the state delegates gave their advice on the matter; then the synod, and thereafter the state delegates, approved a decision on procedure. In the mornings, the nineteen synodical delegations would meet privately to examine and form a judgment on the Five Articles; in the afternoons, the synod would meet to hear various theologians address key Remonstrant arguments.[79]

Then the state delegates sent another delegation (two state delegates and two synodical officers) to The Hague to report to the States General on the proceedings since early January and to seek their approval of the synod's actions.[80] After hearing the report, on 18 January the States General issued a resolution that approved the synod's actions, including the Remonstrant expulsion. It ordered them to remain in Dordrecht and charged the synod to proceed in an appropriate manner according to the 1 January resolution. The delegation was asked to help shorten the synodical proceedings.[81] This new resolution was read to the synod on 21 January, and the state delegates exhorted the synod to proceed quickly to make a decision on the controversy, in order to provide some relief at last to the distressed Dutch churches.[82]

Meanwhile, the Remonstrants petitioned the state delegates for permission to send their own delegation to the States General. This request was denied, with the answer that the state delegates represented the States General, so they need go no further.[83] Soon thereafter, on 26 January, the Remonstrants sent a written defense of their cause to

---

79. *ADSND*, 1:115; Hesse: 281–82.
80. *Historisch Verhael*, 156.
81. *ADSND*, 1:117–19, 489; *RSG*, 4:18–19.
82. Hales, 2:85.
83. *Historisch Verhael*, 156; *ADSND*, 1:488–89. The request is printed in *Acta et Scripta*, 1:158–59.

the States General. There it was read but never answered.⁸⁴ Neither was a similar letter, sent to Prince Maurice.⁸⁵

The Remonstrants unexpectedly received permission to have more input in presenting their views. On 23 January, the state delegates informed them that, although the States General resolution excluded them from the synod, the state delegates, to remove all cause of complaint, had decided that they should submit briefly in writing, within fourteen days, whatever would further explain and defend their Five Articles.⁸⁶ In the following weeks, the Remonstrants exploited this opportunity to freely present their views and refute the opposing views.

After fourteen days, the Remonstrants presented to the state delegates a large document containing their *Defense* of Article I and their *Explanation* of Article II. The state delegates reprimanded them for their prolixity and for not submitting their defense of the remaining Articles, but they gave them eight more days. By the due date, the Remonstrants handed in their *Explanation* of Articles III/IV and V, and they requested more time for the *Defense*. They were allowed ten more days. When that time passed, they presented their *Defense* of Article II. The state delegates again reprimanded them for the length, accused them of delay, and told them that no more documents would be accepted. But two days later, they allowed the Remonstrants eight to ten more days to finish. Finally, on 19 March, after twenty days, the Remonstrants handed in a lengthy *Defense* of Articles IV and V, with a final appendix pleading their cause.⁸⁷ They complained that the synod prejudged their views, because various synodical delegations had handed in their judgments on the Five Articles even before the Remonstrant *Defenses* were submitted; therefore, they offered their last *Defense* not to the synod but only to the state delegates.⁸⁸

In late February, an anonymous Remonstrant pamphlet had appeared, in violation of the 22 December 1618 edict of the States General that prohibited the printing of any proceedings or documents

---

84. *Historisch Verhael*, 164. Printed in *Acta et Scripta*, 1:175–84.
85. *Acta et Scripta*, 1:184–88.
86. *ADSND*, 1:489–90; *Historisch Verhael*, 156.
87. *ADSND*, 1:492–94, 496–97; *Historisch Verhael*, 166–72, 185.
88. *Historisch Verhael*, 190–91.

of the synod without public authority.[89] Titled *Nulliteyten, Mishandelinghen ende onbillijcke Proceduren des Nationalen Synodi ghehouden binnen Dordrecht Anno 1618, 1619*, this pamphlet tried to demonstrate the illegitimacy of the synod and the injustice done to the Remonstrants by both the synod and the state delegates.[90]

Since the cited Remonstrants had been ordered by the States General to remain in Dordrecht after their expulsion from the synod, the state delegates were responsible to see that the Remonstrants observed this order. Remonstrant Henricus Hollinger requested to visit his ill wife in Grave, and Henricus Leo requested leave for the funeral of his uncle. The state delegates denied both of these requests, as well as a request from Zaltbommel that Leo be allowed to preach there over Easter. In another case, seeking to help his very pregnant wife who was about to be evicted from the parsonage in Hoorn, Dominicus Sapma left Dordrecht without permission on 1 March. After a few days in Hoorn, as he was about to leave, a riot erupted there that killed a number of persons. Returning with his wife to Dordrecht after twelve days, Sapma was called before the state delegates for two days of questioning. When he refused to answer questions except in writing, the state delegates wrote to the States General, asking for advice. The States General came to no decision, and the matter was dropped.[91]

Having finished their work, the Remonstrants, on 26 March, sent a letter to the States General requesting permission to return home to their churches, and another to Prince Maurice asking him to recommend their request. The States, however, rejected the request and ordered them to remain at Dordrecht.[92]

The process that led to the drafting of the Canons of Dordt included speeches by various theologians on the Five Remonstrant

---

89. The edict is printed in *ADSND*, 2/2:223–26. On 18 December, the state delegates wrote to the States General that they had heard that the Remonstrants planned to print some of their own documents submitted to the synod; they requested that the States General prevent both sides from publishing anything about the synod while it lasted; *RSG*, 3:594.

90. Balcanqual, 2:117–18.

91. *ADSND*, 1:490, 492–93, 494–96, 499–500; *Historisch Verhael*, 173, 176–84; *RSG*, 4:61–62, 71, 81.

92. These letters are printed in *Acta et Scripta*, 1:196–208; *Historisch Verhael*, 205; *ADSND*, 1:498–99.

Articles, as well as advice or judgments presented by all nineteen of the Dutch and foreign delegations on each of the Five Articles, each of which were read and discussed in the synod.

During the synod's discussions on Articles III and IV of the Remonstrants, concerning how God brings about conversion, a very heated exchange occurred among several synodical members, and civil authority was exerted to restore some peace to the synod.[93] Using scholastic terminology in a speech, Matthias Martinius of Bremen asserted that God is the *causa physica* of conversion. This sparked sharp rebuttals from Franeker theologian Sibrandus Lubbertus and Groningen theologian Franciscus Gomarus. When President Bogerman thanked Gomarus for his learned and accurate speech, the English Bishop George Carleton replied that synodical speeches should be for edification, not for a show of contention, and he called on the president to ensure that the knot of unity not be broken. Angrily, Gomarus replied to the bishop that the synod's business must be conducted not by authority but by reason. As the debate continued, the Bremen delegation became so offended that it was ready to head home. While the British delegation sought to reconcile the opposing parties, the Bremen theologians complained to the state delegates. The English also wanted the state delegates to take note of Gomarus's affront to Bishop Carleton. British delegate Walter Balcanqual, in his next letter to Ambassador Dudley Carleton, suggested that his counsel to the president might bring much water to this argumentative fire. The ambassador wrote to Bogerman with the desired effect. In the next session, the president entreated all members of the synod to abstain from all bitterness and personal opposition and to follow meekness and brotherly kindness. The Dutch professors moderated their language, and by the efforts of Bogerman and the state delegates, a private reconciliation of the parties was reached by 1 March.[94]

After the speeches on the Five Articles, the synod was ready, on 5 March, to begin reading the judgments (*iudicia*) the nineteen delegations had prepared on all Five Articles. From these, it was expected

---

93. On this debate, see Donald Sinnema, "Disagreements and Doctrinal Dissension among Delegates at the Synod of Dordt." Reprinted in this volume; see chapter 6.

94. Balcanqual, 2:110–12, 114–15, 117; *ADSND*, 1:493–94.

that the synod's judgment (the Canons) on the Arminian question would be formed. In a debate regarding whether the reading should take place in open or closed sessions, the British argued for open, while Bogerman argued for closed sessions. The state delegates asserted that all spectators should be excluded from the reading of the *iudicia* and entreated all members to keep synodical business as secret as possible. The synod followed their judgment.[95]

At one point in the discussion of the *iudicia*, political influence went beyond procedural matters and into doctrinal content. On the issue of Article II, regarding the extent of the atonement, the British delegation was divided, so they sought definitive advice from England.[96] After presenting their own *iudicium*, which was a compromise statement,[97] they finally received directions from England in two letters that Balcanqual promised they would heed when the time came to draft the Canons. The first letter, from Archbishop Abbot, indicated that he had consulted with King James and received his approval that the British delegation should conform to the "received distinction and restriction," that is, that Christ's death is sufficient for all but efficacious only for the elect. But directions from Secretary of State Robert Naunton, forwarded by Dudley Carleton, seemed to advise a more general view of the atonement, such that little offense would be given to Lutherans.[98] These ambiguous instructions left the English delegates with their own compromise, which was later reflected in the Canons.[99] Apart from this incident of political influence, there is no evidence that the state delegates participated in discussions of the content of the Five Articles.

After the *iudicia* from each delegation on the Five Articles were read, on 21 March President Bogerman noted that the States General expected the canons to be completed by Easter (ten days away), and

---

95. Balcanqual, 2:122–23; *ADSND*, 1:494.
96. Balcanqual, 2:101–2.
97. *Acta*, 2:78–83. On this British *iudicium*, see Godfrey, "Tensions," 177–78.
98. Here was a political concern for cooperation between the Reformed and Lutherans against the common Roman Catholic Hapsburg enemy; Godfrey, "Tensions," 235–37; Milton, *British Delegation*, 194, 212, 216–17.
99. Balcanqual, 2:135; cf. Godfrey, "Tensions," 159, 161, 254–64.

Church–State Entanglements at the Synod of Dordt 191

he proposed that they be formed from a comparison of the various *iudicia*. For that purpose, he informed the synod, he had drafted a set of canons, to which the synod might suggest amendments. Though it was supported by most Dutch delegates, this procedure immediately aroused the complaint of some foreign theologians, especially the British, that Bogerman intended to draw up the canons by himself and merely dictate them to the synod for its consent. Balcanqual wrote to Ambassador Carleton, asking that he intervene with his "good counsel" to Bogerman.[100] After a series of private meetings over the weekend, on 25 March, the state delegates, to resolve the discontent, advised that some foreign and Dutch theologians work with the president and the assessors to draft the Canons and that they should finish the project as quickly as possible, since that was the strong desire of the States General. The majority of the synod approved this advice and appointed a committee of nine that included Bishop Carleton.[101]

For about three weeks, this committee worked on preparing the Canons. After several drafts, a final version was presented to the synod, which, from 16 to 23 April, approved the Canons on all Five Articles. Then some of the foreign theologians argued for having certain hard sayings of the Contra-Remonstrants rejected in a conclusion to the Canons. The rest of the synod was in no mood to do so, and the majority approved a Conclusion that rejected only false accusations against the orthodox view.[102] Then Bogerman asked the state delegates for their advice on the Conclusion, "since this is a matter of order, not only of doctrine." The state delegates approved it and asked all delegates to be satisfied with it. They also entreated the synod to finally

---

100. *ADSND*, 1:140–41; Balcanqual, 2:139–41, 146–47. Balcanqual, in an appeal to the ambassador, wrote that "if your Lordships care do not now most of all shew it self for procuring of good counsel to be sent hither for the constitution of the Canons, we are like to make the Synod a thing to be laughed at in after ages" (p. 141). Cf. Milton, *British Delegation*, 295.

101. *ADSND*, 1:141–42, 497; Balcanqual, 2:146–47; *Epistolae Ecclesiasticae*, 565–66. Cf. Donald Sinnema, "The Drafting of the Canons of Dordt: A Preliminary Survey of Early Drafts and Related Documents," in *Revisiting the Synod of Dordt (1618–1619)*, ed. Aza Goudriaan and Fred van Lieburg (Leiden: Brill, 2011), 291–311. An abbreviated version is reprinted in this volume; see chapter 13.

102. *ADSND*, 1:143.

finish the business of the Five Articles as quickly as possible, since the States General had pressed them with repeated orders to that end.[103]

After some final changes, Bogerman noted that a good copy of the Latin Canons had been prepared for all to sign on 23 April, so that it might be sent to the States General. The state delegates indicated they had appointed a delegation to deliver the Canons, since the States General and the state of the church and the Dutch republic demanded this.[104]

The next day, the synod approved a Sentence of the cited Remonstrants, which, "supported by the authority of the High and Mighty States General," declared them guilty of error, scandal, and intolerable obstinacy against the resolutions of the States General and of the synod and deposed them from their ecclesiastical offices. The Sentence concludes with the synod thanking the States General for its necessary assistance to the church by convening a synod, for protecting faithful ministers, for conscientiously and solemnly preserving the truth of God's Word in the land, and for sparing no energy or expense to do so. The final words provide a revealing glimpse of the synod's view of the state:

> It further earnestly and humbly entreats the same most clement lords [the States General] that they may will and command that only this saving doctrine—which the synod has expressed very faithfully according to the Word of God and the consensus of the Reformed churches—may be heard publicly in their lands, that they may prevent all heresies and errors that arise, and restrain all restless and turbulent spirits, that they may continue to show themselves to be the true and kindly guardians and protectors [*nutritios ac tutores*] of the church, that they may be pleased to ratify the Sentence of the above-mentioned persons according to the right of the church established by the laws of the land, and render firm and perpetual the synodical decisions by their authority.[105]

Some Dutch delegates objected to certain phrases in the Sentence that were political—calling Remonstrants "disturbers of the Fatherland and the peace of the Republic"—matters regarding which the

---

103. Balcanqual, 2:152.
104. Balcanqual, 2:153; *ADSND*, 1:501.
105. *Acta*, 1:277.

church should not make judgments, since such crimes belonged to the domain of the civil magistrate. These phrases were dropped. When Bogerman asked the state delegates for their view of the Sentence, they replied that they would not take it upon themselves to approve it but would deliver it to the States General, from whom alone approval could be expected.[106]

On 26 April, the state delegates who delivered a signed copy of the Latin Canons to the States General reported to that body and sought further instructions on several questions. The next day, the States responded with several resolutions: It was very happy that the synod had been unanimous in its decision on the Five Articles in dispute. The state delegates must sign the Canons "*pro testimonio rerum actarum.*" The Canons ought to be publicly promulgated as quickly as possible. The Belgic Confession and the Heidelberg Catechism must be read in the full synod with the foreign theologians still present, and everyone must be asked whether anything in them was in conflict with the Word of God and the unity of the church. The time to dismiss the foreign theologians was left to the state delegates, and they should draft letters of dismissal and send them to the States General, which would then present them in its assembly. The cited Remonstrants should be told to observe the decisions and censures against them, and they should remain in Dordrecht.[107]

Honoring the wish of the States, the state delegates signed the Canons under the following statement:

> We, the delegates of the High and Mighty States General to this synod, testify by the signature of our hands that all these things included above concerning the five heads of doctrine in controversy were thus decided.[108]

Returning from The Hague, the state delegates reported on their visit and pointed out that the States General urged the synod to complete its remaining work as quickly as possible. They also noted that the States General especially wanted the Belgic Confession to be read

---

106. Balcanqual, 2:155; Heppe, 310.
107. *RSG*, 4:108–9.
108. *Acta*, 1:274.

over and examined, as was the custom in national synods,[109] and that this should be done in the presence of the foreign theologians. Every member should explain whether he noticed anything regarding doctrinal points in the Confession that did not appear to agree with God's Word or with the confessions of other Reformed churches. But, as for the manner of speaking and church order or polity, that should be further examined only by the Dutch delegates. Articles 31 and 32 of the Confession should not be examined, because both articles dealt with church polity, a matter concerning which some foreign churches (particularly the English) differed from the Dutch presbyterial system.[110]

Following this mandate from the government, the synod immediately began a review of the doctrinal content of the Belgic Confession, except for the two articles on church polity. On 30 April, all foreign and Dutch members declared that the doctrine contained in the Confession agreed with Scripture and the confessions of other Reformed churches. This approval included a more restricted version of article 36, concerning civil government, which now spoke of the government's duty "also to protect sacred worship," instead of watching over "ecclesiastical matters," which was the language found in the original version.[111] After the approval, the Dutch delegates promised to maintain and defend the Confession and asked the state delegates to intercede with the States General, that it might be pleased henceforth to protect and establish by its authority this orthodox doctrine in the Dutch churches.[112] The next day, the state delegates declared that it was also the will of the States General that the Heidelberg Catechism be reviewed and examined in the same way.[113]

---

109. Earlier Dutch national synods had reviewed the Belgic Confession, and Oldenbarnevelt had long called for a national synod to review and revise the Confession as a way to solve the religious controversy; Den Tex, *Oldenbarnevelt*, chs. 10, 12.

110. *ADSND*, 1:147–48, 501; Hales, 2:160.

111. J. N. Bakhuizen van den Brink, ed., *De Nederlandse Belijdenisgeschriften in Authentieke Teksten* (Amsterdam: Ton Bolland, 1976), 141: "maer ooc de hant te houden aen den Heyligen Kercken-dienst." This change had earlier been made in the 1611 Middelburg edition of the Confession; Los, *Tekst en Toelichting*, 311.

112. *ADSND*, 1:149.

113. *ADSND*, 1:150.

Church–State Entanglements at the Synod of Dordt   195

Following the advice of the state delegates, the synod decided to publicly promulgate the Canons on 6 May.[114] On that day, the state delegates led a solemn procession to the Grote Kerk of Dordrecht, where the Canons and the Sentence against the Remonstrants were officially read and proclaimed. Then a testimony of the state delegates was read, testifying that everything that was read had been drawn up in good faith.[115] After this ceremony, the state delegates met with the cited Remonstrants to read the Sentence to them and again ordered them to remain in Dordrecht.[116]

On 9 May, the foreign theologians were dismissed from the synod. The president of the state delegates heartily thanked them in the name of the States General for their assistance to the synod and asked them to go to The Hague to personally receive their letters of dismissal from the States General.[117] The next day, the state delegates presented each of the foreign theologians with a gold medallion as a remembrance of the synod.[118] On 13 May, while in The Hague, some of them were present to witness the beheading of Oldenbarnevelt for treason. This led someone to comment that the Canons of Dordt had shot off the head of the Lord Advocate.[119]

Post-Acta Sessions

After the foreign theologians left for home, the synod, on 13 May, turned to matters relating specifically to the Dutch churches. Since the secret instructions to the state delegates allowed treatment of church order matters by the Dutch delegates alone, as long as the rights and privileges of the provinces were not violated,[120] the state delegates agreed that the Church Order of 1586 should be reviewed

---

114. *ADSND*, 1:148.
115. *ADSND*, 1:154–55; Balcanqual, 2:166.
116. *Historisch Verhael*, 212–13.
117. *ADSND*, 1:155; *Acta*, 1:327–28.
118. *Historisch Verhael*, 215; *RSG*, 4:75, 77, 12, 109. Later, the state delegates decided to present the Dutch delegates and the Dutch professors with silver medallions; *ADSND*, 1:506; *RSG*, 4:130–31.
119. *Historisch Verhael*, 216; Johannes Uytenbogaert, *Kerckelicke Historie* (Rotterdam, 1647), 4:361.
120. *ADSND*, 1:470; arts. 12 and 13.

and examined.[121] The synod first read and approved this Church Order in substance, and it also decided to petition the States General to approve the Church Order and give it the force of public law, so that there might be a uniform church polity in all churches throughout the Netherlands.[122]

In subsequent sessions (sessions 158–62), the synod changed eight articles in the 1586 Church Order and added six new articles.[123] In its form as revised and approved, the result was the Church Order of Dordt, which was signed by the five officers of the synod on 28 May.

In the Church Order of Dordt, fifteen of its eighty-six articles made reference to the civil government. A summary of these references reveals the ongoing state influence in Dutch Reformed church polity:

4. The calling of new ministers includes their selection by the consistory and the deacons in correspondence with local Christian authorities, after which they must be approved by these authorities.

5. The calling of ministers to another church includes the same correspondence with and approval by local authorities; the right of patronage remains uncurtailed, but the government and the provincial synods should make necessary regulations regarding this right for the best interests of the churches.

---

121. *ADSND*, 1:156. The 1586 Church Order of the Synod of The Hague is printed in Rutgers, *Acta*, 487–506. Since the 1586 Church Order was first printed in the *Kercken-Ordeninghen de Ghereformeerder Nederlandtscher Kercken in de Vier Nationale Synoden ghemaeckt ende ghearresteert* (Delft: Jan Andriesz, 1612 and 1617), this was probably the edition that was read in the synod.

122. *ADSND*, 1:156–57; Kuyper, *Post-Acta*, 107–12. The 1586 Church Order had never been approved by the States General, and some provinces followed different church orders; for example, Zeeland used the Church Order of 1591, and Groningen used the Church Order of 1594 and 1595; F. L. Rutgers, *De Geldigheid van de Oude Kerkenordening der Nederlandsche Gereformeerde Kerken* (Amsterdam: Ton Bolland, 1971), 33, 86–89.

123. *ADSND*, 1:158–66; Kuyper, *Post-Acta*, 242–45.

10. A minister may not accept a call elsewhere without the consent of the authorities.

19. Students of theology are to be supported by public funds.

26. Deacons should remain in close correspondence with poorhouse directors or other alms distributors.

28. The duty of the Christian magistrate and the duties of church members to the civil authorities are defined.

37. The local magistrate shall be allowed to have one or two of its representatives, who are church members, in the consistory to listen and deliberate.[124]

49. Each provincial synod shall have deputies who carry out the synod's decisions relating to its classes and the civil government.

50. When the church that is chosen to convene a national synod consults with its classis about the time and place, it shall inform the High Government, so that the matter may be decided in the presence and with the advice of its deputies.

64. The practice of evening prayers may not be removed without the judgment of the government.

66. In difficult times, ministers shall ask the government to declare, by its authority and order, public days of fasting and prayer.

67. Ministers shall work with the authorities in places where New Year's Day and Ascension are not observed, so that they might conform with other churches in this practice.

---

[124]. This article on civil representatives in the consistory first appeared in the 1586 Church Order; Rutgers, *Acta*, 495: "Ende sal oock de Magistraet vande plaetse respectivelijcke, indient haer ghelieft, een ofte twee vanden haren wesende Litmaten der Ghemeente, by den Kercken-Raet moghen hebben, om te aenhooren ende mede vande voorvallende saecken te delibereren."

70. The High Government shall be requested to establish a general ordinance on marriage practices.

71. Christian discipline does not exempt one from civil judgment and punishment by the government.

79. Gross public sin may be punishable by the government.[125]

Of these fifteen articles, three (4, 5, and 67) were changes to the 1586 Church Order, and two (28 and 49) were newly added by Dordt; the rest remained unchanged from the 1586 version. The overall effect of these changes and additions was an increased influence of the state in church affairs.

The changes in articles 4 and 5 included a new requirement that the consistory and the deacons correspond or consult with local authorities in the selection of a minister. This change was made under pressure from the state delegates at Dordt.[126] The 1586 version of article 4 had already required subsequent approval by the authorities. In article 5, the 1586 reading that ministers must be "presented" to the local authorities was strengthened by the Synod of Dordt to "approved" by the authorities. In the same article, the statement on the right of patronage was also added. The change in article 67 on religious holidays was also a concession to the state.[127]

Of special interest is the addition of article 28, concerning the duty of the Christian magistrate:

28. Since the duty of the Christian magistrate is to promote sacred worship in every way, to recommend it to their subjects

---

125. For the Church Order of Dordt, see P. Biesterveld and H. H. Kuyper, eds., *Kerkelijk Handboekje* (Kampen: J. H. Bos, 1905), 225–50.

126. As later noted by Dutch delegate Gisbertus Voetius in his *Politica Ecclesiastica*, II.3:559–60: "Cothurnus ille correspondentiae…non est adjectus a synodo aut synodalibus, saltem non proprio eorum motu, sed a nobiliss. et ampliss. DD. delegatis Politicis, qui haec et alia quaedam episagmata suggerebant, ut ordo omnium provinciarum suprema autoritate semel tandem confirmari & muniri posset"; cited by Kuyper, *Post-Acta*, 144.

127. Kuyper, *Post-Acta*, 152. He states that the government interest in religious holidays was meant to do the people a favor and to give the civil magistrates vacation days.

by their example, and to lend a helping hand to the ministers, elders, and deacons in every occurring need, and to protect them by their good order, all ministers, elders, and deacons are duty bound to diligently and sincerely impress upon the whole congregation the obedience, love, and respect they owe to the magistrates. And all ecclesiastical persons shall set a good example to the congregation in this and, by proper respect and correspondence, seek to gain and retain the favor of the government toward the churches, to the end that, each one on each side doing his duty in the fear of the Lord, all suspicion and distrust may be prevented, and good harmony may be maintained for the welfare of the churches.[128]

The sources do not indicate how or why this article was added to the Church Order of Dordt. There was no gravamen on the agenda that gave rise to it. Kuyper suggests that the addition of this article was merely an attempt to placate the government so that it would approve the Church Order.[129]

The synod also dealt with the sensitive right of patronage, the right of local landowners to appoint ministers. Due to complaints from various churches, some synodical delegates contended that this right should be abolished. In response, the state delegates spoke about the origin of patronage and warned that this right could not be abolished, since the States General would never allow those with a valid claim to this right to be deprived of it by any church order; therefore, the synod would do well not to seek to do away with it, but rather to correct abuses of the practice if necessary.[130] Such advice was in accord with their secret instructions that the right of patronage must be preserved unviolated.[131]

The synod declared that this right was not derived from God's Word. The *Acta* of the synod, however, do not mention this decision,

---

128. *Kerkelijk Handboekje*, 233.
129. Kuyper, *Post-Acta*, 146.
130. *ADSND*, 1:157; cf. Kuyper, *Post-Acta*, 112–19.
131. *ADSND*, 1:470.

a matter that would have offended the government.[132] The synod then tried to determine the proper limits of the right of patronage in such a way that the right was retained by patrons, while its abuse would be prevented in the future. For this purpose, the synod drew up nine articles on patronage and decided to present them to the States General, with the request that it, in turn, recommend them to the provinces.[133] The main thrust of these articles was that patrons should only have the right to propose an acceptable person, that he be gifted and sound in doctrine and conduct, and that the patron not have the power to dismiss a minister without the judgment of the classis or the synod. In a later session, the synod added the statement on patronage to article 5 of the Church Order.

Several other matters treated in the Post-Acta sessions had a connection to the state. The synod decided that the way in which correspondence should be carried on with foreign churches, especially the French, should be discussed with the States General.[134] It also decided to earnestly recommend to the States General the cause of secret churches suffering persecution in the southern Netherlands.[135] A decision was also made to request the States General to prepare a marriage ordinance that might be uniformly observed throughout the Netherlands.[136] Because of an increasing abuse and desecration of the Sabbath throughout the land, the synod decided to request the States General to enact new and stricter edicts to prevent such desecration.[137] Because most violators were not church members and were not subject to its discipline, it was assumed that the state should have a primary responsibility for Sunday observance.

Since Arminianism had made great inroads in academic circles, the synod adopted ten recommendations on university reform for provinces that had academies. The synod's main concern was that those who governed the academies as well as all professors be committed to the Reformed faith and that professors of theology be approved

---

132. Kuyper, *Post-Acta*, 118.
133. These nine articles are printed in *ADSND*, 1:157–58.
134. *ADSND*, 1:163.
135. *ADSND*, 1:166.
136. *ADSND*, 1:163; cf. Kuyper, *Post-Acta*, 164–65.
137. *ADSND*, 1:166–67; cf. Kuyper *Post-Acta*, 180–83.

by and be accountable to a provincial synod.[138] A delegation of the synod presented these recommendations to the States General on 30 May, but it first made three changes that weakened the thrust of the recommendations; for example, the calling of professors of theology "by consent of" the provincial synod was altered to "with the advice of" the provincial synod.[139] Concerning elementary schools, the synod also decided to request the States General to prepare a general school ordinance, so that there might be a uniform approach to instructing youth in the land.[140]

On 25 May, three deputies sent by the States General arrived in Dordrecht to interrogate the cited Remonstrants, with the help of the state delegates. They wanted to know what the Remonstrants knew about an illegal meeting of Remonstrant ministers held in Rotterdam on 5 March, as well as whether the Remonstrants were prepared to sign a declaration that, in the future, they would be silent and would no longer act as ministers but as ordinary citizens.[141]

Before the synod concluded, it appointed Classis Dordrecht as the synodical classis to ensure that the next national synod was convened at the appointed time; at that time, the States General should be requested to invite the Dutch churches in Britain and Germany as members of the synod, as was the case in earlier synods.[142] For political reasons, such invitations were not issued for the Synod of Dordt, since these lands sent their own representatives.

In the final session, on 29 May, one of the state delegates, Hugo Muys van Holy, thanked the synod, in the name of the States General, for its faithfulness in defense of the truth of the Reformed religion against errors. He stated that the work of the synod was very pleasing to the States General and assured the churches that the States would not neglect to do anything that might serve to promote the Reformed religion. He admonished everyone to preserve the truth in brotherly love, peace, and mutual harmony. Then President Bogerman, in the name of the synod, thanked the state delegates for diligently

---

138. *ADSND*, 1:164–65.
139. Kuyper, *Post-Acta*, 175–78.
140. *ADSND*, 1:166.
141. *ADSND*, 1:505–18; *RSG*, 4:132.
142. *ADSND*, 1:183–84.

expediting the tasks of the synod and frequently helping with very beneficial advice.[143]

The Articles to Convene the synod required that it present a report of its activities to the States General for approval. Thus, two days before it ended, the synod appointed a five-member delegation, headed by President Bogerman, to go to The Hague. Besides reporting, the mandate of the delegation was to thank the States General for its protection of the churches and for convening the synod, to request that it approve the synod's decisions and put them into effect, and to request that it deal with several church matters referred to the States for action.[144]

When the synod ended, this delegation drew up a special request (*Libellus supplex*), which it presented to the States General on 30 May. This document sought approval of the synod's acts and its Church Order; requested that the States General uphold, establish, and guard the doctrine contained in the Belgic Confession, the Heidelberg Catechism, and the Canons of Dordt; and presented fourteen other requests to the States (concerning, for example, university reform, Sunday observance, a uniform marriage ordinance, and a general ordinance for elementary schools).[145] It is noteworthy that the patronage issue was not included in this document.

At the same time, this synod delegation presented to the States General several other documents: a summary report of the synod's actions since the Remonstrant expulsion; the synod's Act of Approbation of the Belgic Confession and the Heidelberg Catechism; the synod's judgment on Conrad Vorstius; and a list of recommendations for university reform.[146] They also presented eight authentic handwritten copies of the Canons—one for the States General, and one for each of the provinces. Moreover, they promised to deliver the Church Order in a day or two for the States General's approval.[147]

---

143. *ADSND*, 1:185.
144. *ADSND*, 1:177–78; cf. Kuyper, *Post-Acta*, 278.
145. The *Libellus supplex* is printed in *ADSND*, 1:177–83, and Kuyper, *Post-Acta*, 261–71.
146. Kuyper, *Post-Acta*, 475–85.
147. *RSG*, 4:142; cf. Kuyper, *Post-Acta*, 39–40, 312.

The States General thanked the delegation and promised that it would ensure that the provinces quickly approve the Canons. It also asked for fifty printed copies of the Church Order with Dordt's revisions marked in the margins. Since the synod had now ended, the States General also dismissed the state delegates, after finishing some final tasks.[148]

Aftermath

The States General authorized the printing of the Canons. After submitting one of the three originally signed copies of the Canons to the States General on 26 April, the state delegates, on 8 May, sent their secretary Heinsius to the States General to request that it authorize a known printer to publish the Canons before unauthorized copies began to appear.[149] On 14 May, the States General asked the synod secretaries to send it eight manuscript copies of the Latin Canons— one for itself, and one for each of the seven provinces. The same day, the States General decided to issue the secretaries of the synod and of the state delegates a patent for seven years to print the Canons and all other synodical acts, with the recommendation that this be done by Dordrecht printers.[150] On 16 May, the States General issued a placard forbidding anyone without a patent to publish any documents of the synod. It also instructed the synod to prepare Dutch and French translations of the Canons before it ended and gave orders that Dordrecht printers should print fifty copies (and no more) of the Dutch translation for the States General, to be distributed among the provinces.[151] In sessions held from 18 to 22 May, the synod then worked on preparing the Dutch translation.[152] When the synod delegation appeared before the States General on 30 May, they presented the eight authenticated manuscript copies of the Latin Canons. These copies were distributed

---

148. *RSG*, 4:142.
149. *ADSND*, 1:503–4. On the printing of the Canons, see Kuyper, *Post-Acta*, 306–10.
150. *RSG*, 4:124; J. J. Dodt van Flensburg, "Resolutien der Generale Staten uit de XVII Eeuw," *Archief voor Kerkelijke en Wereldsche Geschiedenissen* 7 (1848): 64.
151. *RSG*, 4:126–27; cf. 132; *ADSND*, 1:505.
152. *ADSND*, 1:169–70; Kuyper, *Post-Acta*, 204–6, 222.

to the provinces for their approval.[153] A few days later, on 3 June, the States General received the limited print run of sixty copies of the Dutch Canons. Dordrecht printer Isaac Canin was paid for printing seventy-five Dutch copies.[154] On 24 June, the States General urged the provinces of Friesland, Overijssel, and Groningen to ratify the Canons, as the other provinces had already done. Meanwhile, the Canons should be printed in Latin, Dutch, and French, but they were not to be issued before the States General gave its approbation.[155] Then, on 2 July, the States General approved an Act of Approbation of the Canons and the Sentence of the cited Remonstrants; two days later, it issued a final revised Act of Approbation. This Act was sent to the printer, Isaac Canin, so that it could be printed with the Canons. At the same time, the States General revised the 14 May patent for the Canons, such that the exclusive privilege of printing the Canons and other synodical acts for seven years was now issued in the name of Jacob Jansz Canin and his associates; this was backdated to 14 May.[156] In the last half of July, the Canons were then printed. All 1619 printings of the Canons in Latin, Dutch, and French included the patent (*Extract uyt de Privilegie*), dated 14 May, and the revised Act of Approbation, dated 2 July.

This Act of Approbation noted that the States General had convened the synod in order to remove the pernicious controversies that had arisen to the detriment of the land and the unrest of the church. It also referred to the task of the state delegates:

> Moreover, having commissioned our delegates from their respective provinces for the good management [*goede directie*] of the said assembly, in order to assist it from beginning to end, so that all things might there be conducted in the fear of the Lord, and in good order, according to the rule of God's holy Word alone, in agreement with our sincere intention.

---

153. *RSG*, 4:140, 142; Kuyper, *Post-Acta*, 303–4.
154. *RSG*, 4:147, 157. On 19 June, the Canons and the Sentence were approved by the States of Holland; Brandt, *Historie*, 3:682.
155. *RSG*, 4:158.
156. *RSG*, 4:168, 170; cf. 173, 177; Dodt van Flensburg, "Resolutien," 72–74, cf. 64. The printed versions of the patent in 1619 editions of the Canons list the name Isaac Janssen Canin instead of Jacob Jansz Canin.

The actual approval of the Canons and the Sentence reads as follows:

> Having seen, maturely understood, examined, and weighed the said judgment [Canons] and the Sentence of the synod, we have fully in all things approved, confirmed, and ratified the same and, by these presents, do approve, confirm, and ratify them, willing and enacting that no other doctrine concerning the aforesaid points of doctrine shall be taught or propagated in the churches of these lands than what is agreeable with the aforesaid judgment.[157]

On 5 July, the cited Remonstrants were summoned before the States General, and they were banished from the Dutch provinces as disturbers of peace in the land.[158]

Although the synod, in its *Libellus Supplex*, requested the States General to approve the Dordt Church Order, the States General never did honor this request for approval. On 30 May, when the synod delegation reporting to the States General promised to bring a copy of the synod's Church Order in a day or two (apparently, a copy of the 1586 Church Order with the revisions adopted by Dordt), the States General requested fifty copies of the 1586 Church Order of The Hague with the synod's revisions written in the margins, so that a general church order could be made. A few days later, on 3 June, state delegate Muys van Holy sent over forty of these copies. The States General paid Delft printer Johan (or Jan) Andriesz for printing fifty copies, as well as Daniel Watery and Loys van Berchem for reviewing and correcting forty-six copies.[159]

Gaining approval of the Church Order by the Dutch provinces was a special challenge. Since the Union of Utrecht guaranteed each province the authority to establish regulations regarding religion, the various provincial States assumed that approving a church order was part of their jurisdiction. Friesland raised the strongest objections to the Dordt Church Order, in order to preserve its provincial rights and

---

157. The Act of Approbation is printed in the *Acta*, 1:278–79, and Bakhuizen van den Brink, *Belijdenisgeschriften*, 284–87.
158. *RSG*, 4:171–73; Brandt, *Historie*, 3:686–93.
159. *RSG*, 4:142, 147, 157. It is likely that Andriesz produced a reprint of the 1586 Church Order as found in *De Kercken-Ordeninghen de Ghereformeerder Nederlandtscher Kercken in de Vier Nationale Synoden ghemaeckt ende ghearresteert* (Delft: Jan Andriesz, 1612 and 1617).

privileges. In March 1620, the States General made a special effort to gain approval of the Friesland States, but this was in vain.[160] When it became clear that the provinces would not unanimously approve the Dordt Church Order, the States General took no further action on the matter.

Gelderland, Utrecht, and Overijssel were the only provincial States that approved the Church Order of Dordt, but they did so with some minor changes or protections of provincial privileges. Uniformity was not attained, since the States of Friesland, Groningen, Drenthe, and Zeeland retained their own church orders; and Holland, after failing to introduce a number of changes, did not officially approve any church order. On the other hand, the provincial synods usually advocated for the Church Order of Dordt. In practice, however, the differences were not great. H. H. Kuyper concluded that the Dordt Church Order did not gain uniform acceptance because, from the States' perspective, Dordt did not give enough concessions to the government, and, from the church's perspective, Dordt's concessions went too far.[161]

In the aftermath of the synod, the only printings of the Dordt Church Order were those issued by the States of the three provinces where the Church Order was approved—Gelderland, Utrecht, and Overijssel.[162]

---

160. *RSG*, 4:418.
161. Kuyper, *De Post-Acta*, 310–15. On the struggle to gain provincial approval, see Rutgers, *Geldigheid*, 31–34, 75–104; A. Kuyper, *De Leidsche Professoren en de Executeurs der Dordtsche Nalatenschap* (Amsterdam: J. Kruyt, 1879), 87–97; Brandt, *Historie*, 3:683, 749–52, 959–60, 4:17–23, 284–85, 288, 317, 320, 324–30, 520–22, 765–94; and Fred van Lieburg, "Re-understanding the Dordt Church Order in its Dutch Political, Ecclesiastical and Cultural Context," in *Protestant Church Polity in Changing Contexts*, vol. 1, *Ecclesiological and Historical Contributions*, ed. Allan J. Janssen and Leo J. Koffeman (Zurich: LIT, 2014), 125–26.
162. *Kercken-Ordeninghe, ghestelt in den Nationalen Synode der Ghereformeerde Kercken...ghehouden...binnen Dordrecht, inde Jaren 1618 ende 1619. Ende (naer veranderinghe van eenighe weynighe poincten) goedt-ghevonden ende ghearresteert by de Ed. Mo. Heeren Staten des Furstendoms Ghelre und Graefschaps Zutphen* (Arnhem: Jan Jansz, 1620); *Kercken-Ordeninge, gestelt inden Nationalen Synode der Ghereformeerde Kercken...ghehouden...binnen Dordrecht, inden Jare 1618 ende 1619. Ende alsoo goetghevonden ende gearresteert by de Ed. Mog. Heeren Staten s'Landts van Utrecht, opden vi Augusti des voorsz Jaers 1619* (Utrecht: Solomon de Roy, 1620); *Kercken-Ordeninghe, ghestelt in den Nationalen Synode der Gereformeerde Kercken...ghehouden...binnen Dordrecht, inde iaren 1618 ende 1619* (Deventer: S. Wermbouts, 1625).

The States General also authorized and oversaw the publication of the *Acta* of the synod.[163] In February 1619, the state delegates had recommended that a topically organized abridgement of the synodical acts should be published and sent to foreign leaders. When this *Acta Contracta* was prepared and presented to the States General in November with a request that it be published, a committee appointed to review this work considered it defective. The States General then decided in January 1620 to appoint a new committee (including synod secretaries Festus Hommius and Daniel Heinsius) to prepare a revised version of the original *Acta Authentica* that would be amplified with appropriate documents. The States General gave some specific guidelines concerning how it was to be edited and what was to be included. Hommius wrote a historical preface describing the rise and development of the Arminian controversy, especially for the sake of the foreign churches, and, on behalf of the States General, Heinsius wrote the dedicatory letter, which was addressed to the foreign leaders who had sent their theologians to the synod.

When the *Acta* appeared in April 1620, the title page indicated that the national synod was held "by the authority of the High and Mighty States General of the Provinces of the United Netherlands."[164] The printed *Acta* omitted some parts, and altered other parts, of the original *Acta Authentica*, largely for political reasons. In general, documents by the States General and the state delegates, as well as those by the foreign theologians, were included, while many documents by the Dutch delegates (even the Post-Acta sessions) and the Remonstrants were omitted. Since the printed *Acta* was intended for an international audience, above all for the foreign leaders who sent theologians to the synod, the States General wanted to highlight the contributions of the foreign theologians and downplay or omit anything that reflected negatively on the Netherlands. Thus, as the end of the Twelve Years Truce approached, the States General used the publication of

---

163. On the process of publishing the *Acta*, see Kuyper, *Post-Acta*, 36–56; and Donald Sinnema, "Introduction to the Acta Authentica, Acta Contracta and Printed Acta," in *ADSND*, 1:xxxix–lii.

164. See Acta.

the *Acta* as a means to strengthen Dutch foreign relations with other Reformed territories.[165]

The States General paid most of the expenses of this six-month-long national synod. It appointed Jacob de Witt to serve as the treasurer and to administer the money for the synod. The expenses included the costs of the facilities in Dordrecht; all expenses (per diem stipends, lodging, and travel costs) of the foreign theologians, the Walloon delegates, and the cited Remonstrants; extra expenses of the state delegates and the synod officers; gold and silver medallions for participants; prints of the synod; and initial printing costs. In all, this amounted to almost 130,000 gulden. This amount did not include the expenses of the Dutch delegates, the Dutch professors, and the state delegates, which were to be covered by the Dutch provinces that sent these delegates.[166]

Conclusions

This overview of church–state relations over the course of the Synod of Dordt leads to the following conclusions:

1. The States General exercised primary control over the Synod of Dordt. By specific resolutions, it convened the synod, determined the number and type of participants, determined the basic agenda and procedures, invited the foreign theologians, paid most of its expenses, controlled its publications, required accountability through reports, and finally, ratified its decisions. The States General's 1 January resolution was the basis for the expulsion of the Remonstrants from the synod, and it later approved the expulsion. The States General's main concern was to use the synod as the primary means of quelling the religious and civil unrest that had arisen in the Netherlands because of

---

165. The changes have been studied by J. P. van Dooren, "De Tekst van de *Acta* van de Synode te Dordrecht 1618–1619," *Nederlands Archief voor Kerkgeschiedenis* 51, no. 2 (1971): 187–98.

166. *RSG*, 3:521–22, 524, 560, 578; 4:8, 75, 157, 244, 518; 5:136, 704; 6:117; J. J. de Geer, "Onkosten der Dordsche Synode," *Kronijk van het Historisch Genootschap gevestigd te Utrecht* 17 (1861), 340–42; H. Florijn, "Dordtse Varia," in W. van 't Spijker et al., *De Synode van Dordrecht in 1618 en 1619* (Houten: Den Hertog, 1994), 173–75; Fred van Lieburg, *Synodestad: Dordrecht 1618–1619* (Amsterdam: Prometheus, 2019), 270–74.

the Arminian controversy. Its aim in using public authority in ecclesiastical matters was to guarantee peace and order.

2. The state delegates acted on behalf of the States General to implement and enforce its resolutions on the floor of the synod.[167] They regularly corresponded with their superiors about once a week. And four times over the course of the synod, the state delegates sent a delegation to the States General to report on the synod's activities and to seek approval and direction on specific procedural questions. Afterward, they also presented a report. In the name of the States General, the state delegates officially opened the synod, advised on and sometimes determined its specific procedures. At some times, they directed the synodical president Bogerman to follow a specific procedure; at others, they overrode his procedural decisions; and, on occasion, they intervened to restore order when the proceedings became contentious. They determined which Remonstrants would be summoned before the synod, sent a letter to summon them, and repeatedly ordered them to obey when they were uncooperative. Especially during the procedural debates with the Remonstrants, the state delegates played an active role. But even after their expulsion, when the synod entered into its doctrinal discussion in the process of preparing the Canons, the state delegates made key procedural decisions (e.g., calling for a committee to draft the Canons). In the Post-Acta sessions, they again played a significant role in decisions on church order matters. However, there is no evidence that they entered into the actual doctrinal discussions.

3. At specific points, English political influence had a direct impact on Dordt. King James I initially urged that a national synod be held to deal with the unrest in the land. King James and Secretary of State Naunton weighed in on the doctrinal question of the extent of the atonement. English ambassador Dudley Carleton intervened with Bogerman to restore peace in a conflict between the Dutch and foreign theologians. The Dutch were especially receptive to such pressure because of a concern to maintain the British as their closest ally in their conflict with Spain.

---

167. Kuyper, *Post-Acta*, 102–4.

4. The Remonstrant view called for a greater level of state influence than even occurred at Dordt. They believed that the state should have supreme authority over ecclesiastical affairs, even over disputable matters of faith, and that all ministers should submit to its resolutions. But they were in an awkward position when they found this state authority directed against themselves. Then they appealed for respect of the boundary as they saw it: state authority must not violate the conscience.[168]

5. In spite of the powerful political influence at Dordt, there was a tacit recognition of a distinction between church and state. But the boundary between the respective jurisdictions of church and state overlapped somewhat. One indication of the boundary line was Bogerman's comment requesting the state delegates' advice on the Canons' Conclusion, since this was "a matter of order, not only of doctrine."[169] At Dordt, the state delegates entered into matters of order and procedure and left the church delegates to deal with matters of doctrinal content. The difficulty was that the church also had a claim on church order. The political authorities respected that claim as long as it did not impose upon their political interests, but they assumed that they had the ultimate authority in matters of church order.[170] On many matters of procedure, the synod and its officers made decisions in consultation with the state delegates. But whenever a possible conflict of jurisdiction arose in matters of church order, the synod deferred to the judgment of the state.

6. In regard to the church's jurisdiction, the synod freely deliberated on matters of doctrinal content without interference from the Dutch civil authorities, although the civil decisions on procedure in this

---

168. *ADSND*, 2/2:644–50.
169. Hales, 2:152.
170. Years later, synodical delegate Gisbertus Voetius tried to delineate the boundary line between church and state jurisdiction in matters of church order by distinguishing between *ordo internus* and *ordo externus*. The church's authority was internal order, while the state was the custodian of external order, guarding the political interests of the state against church interference in these areas; *Politica Ecclesiastica*, 4:11; cf. Kaajan, *Pro-Acta*, 47. At Dordt, however, this distinction was not operative, since the civil authorities not only guarded the political interests of the state but sometimes stepped into matters that were purely ecclesiastical in nature.

area (e.g., that the Bible alone, and not the confessions, must be the standard of truth) certainly shaped the contours of those doctrinal discussions. An exception here was the English political influence on the issue of the extent of Christ's atonement. In the area of church polity, the synod also had considerable authority. The provincial synods selected their own delegates to the national synod. The synod chose its own officers, and the ecclesiastical president Bogerman presided over the assembly and determined many specific procedures. The synod received many gravamina (overtures) that were referred to it from the provincial synods, and it freely decided on many of these questions. The synod sent out its own citation letter summoning the Remonstrants to appear. It was allowed to approve in substance and revise the 1586 Church Order that had been used in many churches, and thus the synod came up with its own Church Order of Dordt, although, on certain articles (e.g., on the appointment of ministers), the state delegates had decisive input. The synod challenged the sensitive issue of patronage, but in the end, it backed off in pursuing the matter with the state.

7. The church's own expectations of the government, as articulated in the Belgic Confession (art. 36), the Dordt Church Order (art. 28), the Sentence, and the *libellus supplex*, invited state influence in ecclesiastical affairs. The synod expected the government to be the guardian and protector of the Dutch Reformed church, to protect the church's worship and ministry, to prevent false worship, to see that the gospel was preached everywhere, to establish Reformed doctrine alone in all churches, to enforce the Church Order uniformly in all churches, and to ratify the synod's decisions.

8. The way the States General convened the synod directly contravened the 1586 Church Order. Its article 44, concerning national synods, called for such synods ordinarily every three years; they were to be convened by one church with the advice of the local classis and representatives of the government. It also specified that provincial synods were to send an equal number of ministers and elders, two of each,

to a national synod.[171] And it made no provision for state delegates at a national synod. When the States General itself convened this national synod, it required at least three ministers and two or three elders or other church members to attend, thus providing for a possible imbalance, as well as the possibility that non-office-bearers would serve as delegates. In spite of the breach of church order, the provincial synods took the opportunity to send thirty-seven ministers and nineteen elders, partly because it was difficult to find Latin-speaking elders with enough time to attend. The fact that the foreign theologians presented their credentials to the States General rather than to the synod was also a deviation from church practice. Further, the synod deviated from its own Church Order by issuing the Sentence deposing the cited Remonstrants from their ecclesiastical offices. According to articles 72 and 73, such discipline belonged to the local consistory with the help of its classis.

9. While the Canons of Dordt gained approval by the Dutch provinces in the immediate aftermath of the synod, this was not the case for the Church Order of Dordt. Although this Church Order made a number of concessions to the role of the state in ecclesiastical affairs, the individual provincial States tended to consider church polity as a legitimate aspect of their own jurisdiction, especially on matters of the calling and financial support of ministers, church property, public discipline, and patronage, and various provinces already had their own church orders in place. Although the provincial synods usually urged acceptance of the Church Order, only three provincial States approved the Dordt Church Order—but even they did so with minor changes or with the proviso that their provincial rights and privileges be respected.

10. With almost no discernible complaint, the synod accepted the increased level of state interference in its ecclesiastical affairs. The reasons are quite apparent. The synod appreciated the fact that the States General was fighting for a common cause with the church against the

---

171. Rutgers, *Acta*, 497. On these violations of church order, see K. Doornbos, *De Synode van Dordrecht 1618/19 Getoetst aan het Recht der Kerk* (Amsterdam: Buiten & Schipperheijn, 1967), chap. 2.

Remonstrants. The church bowed to the power of the civil authority and did not itself have the financial resources to hold such a national synod. Moreover, the church's own expectation was that the state should act as guardian of the church to prevent and remove false worship and to establish Reformed doctrine and church polity in all the Dutch churches.

States General, in The Hague

CHAPTER 8

The Missing Correspondence between the States General and Its State Delegates at the Synod

The Synod of Dordt was convened by the Dutch government—the States General in The Hague—which also closely oversaw the synod by way of its eighteen state delegates, whom it authorized as its representatives, especially in providing advice on matters relating to procedure.[1]

The States General provided the mandate for the Synod of Dordt and determined its parameters in its Articles to Convene the national synod (approved 11 November 1617). These Articles determined: the opening time and location of the synod; the agenda of the synod (first the Five Remonstrant Articles, then gravamina from the Dutch churches); the participants at the synod (six minister and elder delegates from each province, a Walloon delegation, professors from the Dutch universities and academies, invited theologians from various foreign lands to assist the Dutch, and two state delegates from each province); and the basic procedures (on doctrine, the Word of God was to be the only rule of faith; voting by plurality of votes). Article 16 specifically mentioned the state delegates:

> 16. It is thought advisable that two qualified persons, who profess the Reformed religion and are members of the church, shall be named by each province, and be authorized and commissioned by the States

---

[1]. On the role of the state delegates at the synod, see Johanna Roelevink, "Introduction to the Acts and the Instructions of the Delegates of the States General," in *ADSND*, 1:liii–lxi.

General to appear at and attend the meetings of the synod, to help direct and guide all its actions [*de actiën ende beleyt te modereren; actiones dirigant ac moderentur*], so as to prevent all disorder.[2]

The States General initially approved a commission for the state delegates on 6 November 1618. In the commission, which was read in the first session of the synod, the States General authorized the state delegates "to open the synod, and in our name be present and attend all the sessions and deliberations of the synod, and with their prudence, advice, and guidance arrange all matters pertaining to their consideration and care, in such a way as we have fully entrusted in our deputies and have particularly instructed them."[3]

The States General also issued secret instructions to the state delegates to guide their work at the synod. Among other points, the state delegates were instructed: to open the synod; to see that only ecclesiastical matters are treated, not political affairs; to be sure that the synod only dealt with necessary matters; to take weekly turns presiding over their delegation; to have a resolutive vote in the synod, not just a deliberative vote; to admonish the synodical delegates not to divulge the proceedings of the synod; to take care that patronage rights are not infringed, if the synod should agree on changes in church order; to see that the affairs of the synod are conducted for the peace and unity of the church and the promotion of the Reformed religion; and to keep good correspondence with the States General.[4]

On 5 November, the States General directed the state delegates, who were present and ready, to go to Dordrecht to prepare for the meetings of the synod. The others would follow immediately.[5]

Throughout the course of the synod, the States General kept in close contact with the state delegates, not only by way of letters but also by way of occasional personal reports by one or more state delegates to their principals in The Hague. Via this means, the States General also issued occasional directives to the synod at critical points.

---

2. The Articles to Convene the synod are printed in *ADSND*, 2/1:46–48, 740–45.

3. The States General commission for the state delegates is printed in *ADSND*, 2/2:25–28.

4. The States General instructions for the state delegates are printed in *ADSND*, 1:467–71.

5. *ADSND*, 2/1:227–28.

On 16 November 1618, as the synod had just begun, the States General issued a resolution to keep secret all their correspondence with the state delegates:

> It is understood and decreed that it shall be kept secret, without writing and issuing any copies of letters that shall be written by their High Mightinesses to their High Mightinesses's political commissioners in the synod at Dordrecht, nor also of those that shall be written by the aforesaid commissioners to their High Mightinesses, and also not of the papers exchanged from both sides.[6]

According to ordinary procedures, such correspondence and papers would have been preserved in the archives of the States General in a separate file (*secrete kas*) along with other secret materials. Unfortunately, at some point these important secret papers disappeared from the archives, and they are not to be found in the Nationaal Archief in The Hague, where the States General archives are housed. This correspondence is also not listed in the Index of official Synod of Dordt papers that was compiled in 1625.[7]

While the correspondence is missing, it is nevertheless possible to reconstruct a list of (almost all of) the items of correspondence, with an indication of the topics covered, primarily on the basis of two sources: (1) the States General resolutions, which quite thoroughly indicate when a letter is received from the state delegates and when the States General writes to them; and (2) the acts of meetings of the state delegates, which mention some of this correspondence. Several items have also been preserved among the archives of the synod.

The States General resolutions were usually written down by the chief clerk, or griffier, Cornelis van Aerssen. His handwriting is extremely difficult to decipher, but a fair copy of the resolutions was also made by another clerk.[8] The resolutions relating to the synod are

---

6. *ADSND*, 2/1:242.

7. This Index is found at the beginning of OSA, vol. A. It is printed in H. H. Kuyper, *Post-Acta of Nahandelingen van de Nationale Synode van Dordrecht in 1618 en 1619 gehouden* (Amsterdam: Höveker & Wormser, [1899]), 500–512.

8. The original *Minuut Resoluties* of 1618 are in the Nationaal Archief in The Hague, Archief Staten-Generaal, 1.01.02, nr. 43. The fair copy, or *Net Resoluties*, of 1618 are in the Archief Staten-Generaal, 1.01.02, nr. 3177. The *Minuut Resoluties* for

being published in the series titled *Acta et Documenta Synodi Nationalis Dordrechtanae* (*ADSND*).

Besides attending each session of the synod, the state delegates frequently met separately to discuss matters that concerned them. There are acts of sixty-nine such meetings. The acts of these meetings were composed by their secretary, Daniel Heinsius, but they are not very thorough. The original acts are preserved in the synodical archives in the Oud Synodaal Archief, vol. Q, and they have finally been published in the first volume of *ADSND*.[9]

In this article, I provide a survey of all the known correspondence between the States General and the state delegates, from the opening of the synod in November 1618 until its conclusion at the end of May 1619. The survey also includes the instances when the state delegates sent one or more of their number to personally report to the States General. The correspondence and personal reports are listed chronologically. The letters and actions of the States General are indicated in italics.

8 NOVEMBER 1618: *The States General commission for the state delegates is revised, due to some considerations from the deputies of Zeeland. When ready, the commission will be sent to the state delegates at Dordrecht.*[10]

10 NOVEMBER: *The States General reports to the state delegates that the four theologians, presented by English ambassador Dudley Carleton to their gathering on 6 November, have no special commission except this direct presentation. King James I thought this to be sufficient, and the States General agrees. Therefore, no other commission should be required of these delegates. The state delegates also receive copies of the letters submitted by the Genevan delegates from the republic and church of Geneva, in case they do not have another commission. The States General writes that the national synod may be opened the following Monday or Tuesday (12 or 13 November) with the*

1619 are missing; the *Net Resoluties* of January to June 1619 are in the Archief Staten-Generaal, 1.01.51, nr. 3178 and nr. 39.

9. *ADSND*, 1:467–518. This article is heavily indebted to Johanna Roelevink for her work in transcribing and summarizing States General resolutions and the acts of the state delegates, in *ADSND*, 2/1 and *ADSND*, 1.

10. *RSG* 3795; *ADSND*, 2/1:232. The *RSG* includes only summaries of the States General resolutions.

delegates then present, if at all possible, and the state delegates should work to see that this happens.[11]

14 NOVEMBER (received 16 Nov.): The state delegates answer the States General letter of 10 November and give a report about the opening of the synod.[12]

15 NOVEMBER: Pensionary Berck, alderman Silvius, and two other deputies of the city of Dordrecht appear before the States General and explain how the magistrate has received, welcomed, lodged, accommodated, and provided stipends for the foreign delegates to the national synod from Great Britain, the Palatinate, Hesse, Switzerland, Geneva, Bremen, and Emden, according to their status. This has been done (they hope) to the contentment of the delegates, as frugally as possible, but to the honor of both the country and the city. They will continue to do the same for the delegates who might still come. They will also please the States General in other matters concerning the national synod. They ask the States General to give orders for the further support and stipends of the foreign delegates, with their accompanying noblemen and their retinue (who behave in an orderly manner, quietly and respectfully), be it by treatment (*defroyement*) in their lodgings, by providing food, or by "*deputat*." Asked for their advice, the deputies of Dordrecht would prefer the latter, that is to say, to give everyone a sum according to their status, with the customary stipend according to the country where they come from, especially the English, the Palatines, and the Swiss.

The States General thank the deputies from Dordrecht for their care and their great efforts.

These deputies also succinctly report how the synod was opened the previous Tuesday (13 November), with prayer and an address by councillor Martinus Gregorii. Professor Daniel Heinsius was called from Leiden to become secretary of the state delegates. It was decided unanimously that the foreigners would be granted a decisive vote and that they would vote as a delegation when their views were unanimous, but in case of disagreement with one another, each might express his

---

11. *RSG* 3809; *ADSND*, 2/1:234–36.
12. *RSG* 3845; *ADSND*, 2/1:243.

opinion. The deputies also declare, without instruction, that the magistrate of Dordrecht received a letter the previous morning from the States of Holland stating that anybody who has something to propose, especially the Remonstrants, should have free access to the synod and, therefore, should be granted safe conduct to come and to go. In order to avoid discredit and slander, it seems that the city thinks it better and more authoritative that such safe conduct be granted by higher authorities and that the name "Arminians" be avoided, because it might be thought odious. The States General might like to ponder this, as well as whether a visit should be paid to the foreigners, for the honor of the country, but frugally.

The States General decides on these matters as follows: The state delegates shall decide on the stipends and further support of the foreign delegates in consultation with the city of Dordrecht. A visit to the foreigners is left to their discretion. The States General agrees that access to the synod should be free. But because the States of Holland have not been in touch with the States General regarding this safe conduct, the States General would first like to investigate the reasons for their letter and its contents. Concerning the money needed for the stipends and the support of the foreign delegations, because the provinces have consented to their quota of 100,000 guilders, and because the Council of State is authorized to dispatch the papers, the States General will send for the receiver-general Johan Doubleth or his commissioner, Volbergen, to hear how much money is available and to instruct him to send 30,000 or 40,000 guilders for the payment of the stipends for the foreign delegates, but primarily to reimburse their out-of-pocket expenses.[13]

16 NOVEMBER: *After receiving two letters from Overijssel (dated 23 Oct.) naming their state delegates for the national synod—Jonkheer Hendrik Hagen and Johan van Hemert, the burgomaster of Deventer—the States General decides to send these letters to the state delegates and asks them to accept these names and add them to their commission.*[14]

16 NOVEMBER: *The States General writes to the state delegates that the churches of the Duchy of Cleves (under the jurisdiction of Brandenburg) would like to have some delegates at the synod; some time ago, they invited*

---

13. *RSG* 3842; *ADSND*, 2/1:237–41.
14. *RSG* 3843; *ADSND*, 2/1:241.

the Elector of Brandenburg to delegate some Reformed theologians to the synod, but they are still awaiting a reply.[15]

17 NOVEMBER: *States General President Manmaker has heard from a Zeeland minister, passing through Dordrecht, that the synod is delayed for fourteen days so that it can write a status controversiarum and summon the Remonstrants who did not appear at the appointed time. If the States General does not hear from the state delegates about this before Monday, 19 November, it will write to ask whether this rumor is true and what the reasons are for the delay.*[16]

19 NOVEMBER: *The States General confirms the instruction for the state delegates and orders that it be sent to them to direct their actions.*[17]

19 NOVEMBER (received 21 Nov.): The state delegates report what has happened in the national synod up until 19 November. They attach a copy of their letter of citation for several Remonstrant ministers.[18]

23 NOVEMBER: Hugo Muys van Holy, the sheriff of Dordrecht and one of the state delegates at the synod, comes from Dordrecht to the States General and reports in more detail about the actions of the synod on behalf of the state delegates. He mentions that the treasurer of the synod, Jacob de Witt, has arrived with 30,000 guilders. Muys recommends that the States General make a decision on the stipends for the foreign delegates and on the administration and the spending of the funds designated to pay the expenses of the synod.

The States General repeats the answer it gave to the deputies from Dordrecht on 15 November, that, in writing, it will authorize the state delegates to decide, with the advice of the local government of Dordrecht, on the stipends for the foreign delegates, to the honor of the country, but frugally, either by "deputat" or by contract with their lodgings, or otherwise by whatever they find best and most appropriate. The administration and

---

15. *RSG* 3845; *ADSND*, 2/1:242.
16. *RSG* 3870; *ADSND*, 2/1:244.
17. *RSG* 3885; *ADSND*, 2/1:244–45. The instruction for the state delegates, backdated to 6 November, is printed in *ADSND*, 1:467–71.
18. *RSG* 3891; *ADSND*, 2/1:246. The letter of citation that the state delegates sent to the Remonstrants is printed in *ADSND*, 2/2:62–64.

payment of the funds will be done by the synod treasurer upon the order of the state delegates. The latter may pay a visit to the foreign delegates to make these arrangements as they see fit for the honor of the country.[19]

27 November (received 1 Dec.): The state delegates write that they, following the order of the States General, have made arrangements for stipends for the foreign delegates, according to the accompanying list, and that they are completely satisfied. The state delegates will also not neglect to visit the foreign delegates.[20]

28 November: *The trade delegation to England receives copies of the letters of the state delegates to the States General, to use them as circumstances require.*[21]

29 November (received 1 Dec.): The state delegates write, asking the States General's guidance for the stipends for all the delegates from the provinces—political, ecclesiastical, and Walloon—as well as for the cited Remonstrants, in order to avoid jealousy. They ask whether these stipends will be paid by the respective provinces or by the States General.

1 December: *The States General answers that the ministers and the state delegates will be paid by their respective provinces. Since the Walloon churches are not connected to any province, the state delegates are authorized to accord them proper stipends according to their discretion.*[22]

9 December (received 11 Dec.): The state delegates report by letter on the synod's actions up to 9 December. On 7 December, Episcopius gave a speech with great and impetuous animosity, of which they send a copy. They also send a copy of a document that the cited Remonstrants circulated among the foreign delegates on 6 December, to acquaint them with the Remonstrant perspective on the controversy.

---

19. *RSG* 3914; *ADSND*, 2/1:246–47.
20. *RSG* 3957; *ADSND*, 2/1:252–53. The list does not appear to be extant.
21. *RSG* 3937; *ADSND*, 2/1:250.
22. *RSG* 3957; *ADSND*, 2/1:252–53; *ADSND*, 1:476.

The Missing Correspondence

11 DECEMBER: *The States General commits one person each from Holland, Zeeland, and Utrecht to examine and report on Episcopius's oration and the Remonstrant document. Gelderland may add someone if it wishes.*[23]

13 DECEMBER (received 15 Dec.): The state delegates report what has happened at the national synod up to 13 December.[24]

15 DECEMBER: *The Nassau-Wetteravian delegates Johannes Bisterfeld and Johann Heinrich Alsted appear before the States General with a credential letter from the Wetteravian Association of Counts. The States General decides to send these delegates with their credential letter to the state delegates at Dordrecht, with the instruction to receive them, lodge them, accommodate them, provide them with stipends, and grant them seating in the synod.*[25]

17 DECEMBER: *Ambassador Dudley Carleton presents a British delegate from Scotland, Walter Balcanqual, to the States General, with the request that he be seated according to the rank of the Kingdom of Scotland. The States General writes to the state delegates about the presentation of Balcanqual and instructs them to receive him, lodge him, accommodate him, provide him with a stipend, and grant him seating, following the wishes of King James.*[26] In this case, the original States General letter to the state delegates has been preserved.[27] It closely follows the wording of the States General resolution of 17 December.

18 DECEMBER: The state delegates briefly write to Maurice, Prince of Orange, about all that had happened at the synod until then, especially from the time that the Remonstrants had appeared at the synod.[28]

---

23. *RSG* 4005; *ADSND*, 2/1:255. The speech of Episcopius is printed in *ADSND*, 2/2:267–83. The Remonstrant document sent to the foreign delegates is printed in *ADSND*, 2/2:231–43.

24. *RSG* 4036; *ADSND*, 2/1:258–59.

25. *RSG* 4036; *ADSND*, 2/1:258. The credential letter for the Nassau-Wetteravian delegates is printed in *ADSND*, 2/1:636–37.

26. *RSG* 4047; *ADSND*, 2/1:259–60.

27. See OSA, vol. C, 91r–92v. The letter was written by Gijsbert van den Boetselar, deputy to the States General from Gelderland, and it was signed by griffier Cornelis van Aerssen.

28. *ADSND*, 1:481.

18 December (received 22 Dec.): In a letter the state delegates report on what has happened at the synod up to 18 December. They have been told by a reliable source that the Remonstrants intend to publish writings submitted to the synod and pass them on to ordinary people in order to bring scorn to the actions of the synod or to stir up the people. The state delegates ask the States General for quick measures to forbid both parties from publishing anything about the synod for the duration of its proceedings, with such penalties as they may deem proper. By such supervision the States General may reap the fruits of this long-awaited assembly and may achieve their objective.

22 December: *The States General agrees to the request and asks the griffier to draft a placard prohibiting the publication of synod materials. This placard was issued on 22 December.*[29]

31 December: After several weeks of uncooperative behavior by the cited Remonstrants, the state delegates at the synod send a delegation to the States General, including state delegates Henrick van Essen, Hugo Muys van Holy, and Johan van Hemert, along with synod assessor Hermannus Faukelius and secretary Sebastiaan Damman. After presenting their credentials in the presence of Prince Maurice and Count Willem Lodewijk, they report on the difficulties arising from the words and behavior of the cited Remonstrants, and they come to ask how best to deal with the cited Remonstrants, since they refuse to comply with the decisions of the synod and the state delegates. For this purpose, they read all the original synodical acts and decisions, political and ecclesiastical, and the answers of the cited Remonstrants, offered orally and in writing, especially from 21 to 29 December, and also the political and ecclesiastical decisions of 27 and 28 December, along with the written Remonstrant answer of 29 December and their verbal declaration. It is evident from these acts that the foreign theologians have unanimously declared that the cited Remonstrants have not complied with the synodical decisions in their answers.

After long deliberation, and with the advice of Maurice and Willem Lodewijk, the provinces declared their opinions. Deputies Pauw, De

---

29. *RSG* 4093; *ADSND*, 2/1:264; *ADSND*, 1:480–81. The placard is printed in *ADSND*, 2/2:223–26.

Jonge, Aetsma, and Gockinga, along with griffier Van Aerssen and the synod reporters, are appointed to draft an answer and a resolution, to be approved by the whole assembly.[30]

1 JANUARY 1619: *Having heard the report of the delegation from the synod, and having read the acts and decisions of the synod and the Remonstrant answers, the States General approves a resolution on how to proceed with the cited Remonstrants. Having deliberated, with the advice of Prince Maurice and Count Willem Lodewijk, the States General declares that the political and ecclesiastical decisions and acts of the synod conform to their resolutions and instructions concerning the national synod, and therefore it approves all these acts and decisions. The cited Remonstrants should have obeyed these decrees immediately, and they must obey further decrees, or proceedings will be taken against them, not only by ecclesiastical censure but also by civil sanctions. The delegates to the synod are to continue with the principal business of the synod, which remains the same. If the cited Remonstrants continue their disobedience, the synod is to examine and judge their opinion in doctrine by the Word of God, by way of their publications and their written and verbal declarations, offered both in the national synod and in the respective provincial synods. The cited Remonstrants must stay within the city of Dordrecht unless they have the written permission of the state delegates. Also, if they are summoned, they must answer without delay and present their declarations categorically, be it verbally or in writing, on whatever may be put to them on behalf of the synod. This resolution is to be read publicly in the synod in the presence of the cited Remonstrants.*[31]

4 JANUARY: Muys van Holy appears before the States General, on behalf of the state delegates, and makes a proposal regarding stipends for the cited Remonstrants. The States General decides at its expense to give the cited Remonstrants the same stipend as other delegates at the synod.[32]

---

30. *RSG* 4119A; *ADSND*, 2/1:265–66; *ADSND*, 1:483.
31. J. G. Smit and J. Roelevink, eds., *Resolutiën der Staten-Generaal, Nieuwe Reeks 1610–1670*, Vierde Deel: 1619–1620 ('s-Gravenhage: Martinus Nijhoff, 1981), resolution 2B (1619); *ADSND*, 2/1:267–70. The States General 1 January resolution is printed in *ADSND*, 2/1:269–70; *ADSND*, 2/2:641–44.
32. *RSG* 37; *ADSND*, 2/1:271.

7 January: At the States General, Muys van Holy communicates a letter written to him by Daniel Heinsius, the secretary of the state delegates at the synod. It states what has happened since the States General 1 January resolution was read to the cited Remonstrants until Saturday 5 January. The Remonstrants are persevering in their disobedience and consider the synod to be their adversary. But the synod is continuing with its principal business.[33]

9 January: *The States General receives a letter from the cited Remonstrants, dated 3 January, along with three attached documents, which make an appeal for their innocence, and they request that they be allowed to explain and defend their cause freely and fully. After deliberating, the States General decides to send these documents to the state delegates to examine them thoroughly and advise as soon as possible about what to do, so as not to retard or prejudice the proceedings of the synod.*[34]

9 January: *Regarding the report that President Bogerman has extraordinary expenses for visits and other things, which he should not have to pay from his ordinary salary, the States General decides to write the state delegates instructing them to make a provisional payment to him of three to four hundred guilders, so that he does not have to bear the cost.*[35]

12 January: The state delegates decide to answer the 9 January letter from the States General concerning the complaints of the Remonstrants and to report on what has happened since the 1 January resolution was received. In particular, the state delegates report that they had maturely read all the documents the Remonstrants sent to the States General. Since they found nothing at all new in them, they made a resolution (on 11 January), following the order of the States General, to proceed to examine the Remonstrants from their writings, but they are giving the Remonstrants until Monday, 14 January, to consider what the president and the synod have told them.[36]

---

33. *RSG* 51; *ADSND*, 2/1:271.

34. *RSG* 63; *ADSND*, 2/1:271–72. The Remonstrant letter to the States General is printed in *ADSND*, 2/2:662–66.

35. *RSG* 63; *ADSND*, 2/1:272.

36. *ADSND*, 1:485. The state delegates' 11 January resolution is printed in *ADSND*, 2/2:666–67.

15 January: *Ambassador Dudley Carleton appears before the States General and presents Thomas Goad, sent by King James to replace British delegate Joseph Hall, who is ill and will return to England. The States General will inform the state delegates about this presentation and instruct them to receive Goad, lodge him, accommodate him, provide him a stipend, and grant him seating, like the other British delegates.*[37]

15 January: State delegate secretary Daniel Heinsius is instructed to prepare a report (*verbael*) of what has happened between the synod and the cited Remonstrants, so that the States General may understand the situation more clearly.

Secretary Heinsius should also write up credential letters to the States General for Walraven van Brederode and Hugo Muys van Holy, since they will travel to The Hague.[38]

17 January: State delegates Walraven van Brederode and Hugo Muys van Holy, along with synod assessor Hermannus Faukelius and secretary Festus Hommius, who were sent to the States General by the state delegates at the synod, report, in the presence of Prince Maurice and Count Willem Lodewijk, on the proceedings of the synod (including the expulsion of the cited Remonstrants) since the States General 1 January resolution that was issued after the report of the former delegation sent by the state delegates on 31 December. All related acts and documents are read.

Following the advice of Maurice, Willem Lodewijk, and deputies of the provinces, the States General appoints those who drafted the previous resolution to draft a new resolution responding to this report.[39]

18 January: *In response to the report of the recent delegation sent by the state delegates in Dordrecht, the States General, upon the advice of Prince Maurice and Count Willem Lodewijk, issues a resolution confirming the expulsion of the cited Remonstrants. In this resolution, it declares that it heard the report of the delegation and also heard all the original acts and decisions, both political and ecclesiastical, along with the answers of the cited*

---

37. *RSG* 91; *ADSND*, 2/1:272–73.
38. *ADSND*, 1:488. On the report concerning the conduct of the Remonstrants, see also *ADSND*, 1:498, 504.
39. *RSG* 111; *ADSND*, 2/1:274–75; *ADSND*, 1:488.

Remonstrants, from the period of 3 to 14 January, and, in particular, the answer submitted by the Remonstrants on 11 January, the advice of the foreign and Dutch delegates, and the ensuing decree of the state delegates. It especially took note of the efforts by the state delegates, on 12 January, to induce the Remonstrants to obey the 1 January resolution of the States General and the decrees of the state delegates. The States General also heard the declaration of the state delegates on 14 January, as well as how the cited persons, instead of answering fully, sincerely, and without evasion to the questioning by President Bogerman, submitted a Declaration on their First Article. This Declaration made it clear that, far from showing any obedience to the decrees, the cited Remonstrants acted as violators of the public authority with all manner of evasions, subterfuges, and fallacies, to make the national synod unfruitful. Finally, it is also evident to the States General that the foreign theologians were unanimously of the opinion that the cited persons were unworthy to be heard any longer in the synod, that there is no hope of proceeding any further with them, and that they should therefore be dismissed. Further, the synod should now proceed along the lines of the 1 January resolution—to examine and judge their teaching from their publications and their written and oral declarations in the national synod, the provincial synods, and elsewhere. President Bogerman subsequently dismissed them with words also read to the States General. Having seriously deliberated, the States General, upon the advice of Prince Maurice and Willem Lodewijk, declares, especially for the honor of God and the maintaining of true Christian religion and peace in the church, that the acts and decisions mentioned conform to the opinion of the States General. It therefore approves of these, as well as the dismissal of the Remonstrants from the synod. The Remonstrants must remain in Dordrecht unless the state delegates and the synod order otherwise. The synod is to continue its business on the basis of the States General resolution of 1 January, proceeding as it finds most appropriate. This resolution must be read publicly in the synod, together with its resolution of 1 January.

The States General also recommends that the state delegates help shorten the proceedings of the synod as much as possible, but without causing dissatisfaction or a feeling of undue haste among the foreign delegates.

The state delegates may also provide the two synod assessors and the two secretaries an extraordinary payment of 200 guilders.[40]

20 JANUARY (received 22 Jan.): The state delegates write that, on 19 January, the Nassau-Wetteravian delegate Johannes Bisterfeld died. They have buried him with honor and in an appropriate way. They leave it to the States General to invite another theologian in his place.[41]

22 JANUARY: *In a letter, the States General thanks the state delegates for the message. Since it hopes that the synod will come to an end (and since the winter is not suitable for travel), it has not invited another theologian.*[42]

25 JANUARY: Muys van Holy brings up to the States General the matter of stipends for Scottish theologian Balcanqual and for secretary of the state delegates Daniel Heinsius.

The States General decides to leave the payment of the stipend for Balcanqual up to the state delegates and to give Heinsius the same stipend as the state delegates from Holland receive.[43]

29 JANUARY: *The States General receives a letter or remonstrance (undated but sent 26 January), signed by the fifteen cited Remonstrants at the synod, appealing to the States General in defense of their cause. After deliberation, the States General decides to communicate the letter with Prince Maurice and Count Willem Lodewijk and then send it to the state delegates.*[44]

31 JANUARY: Muys van Holy reports on what has taken place at the synod from 18 to 26 January.[45]

1 MARCH (received 2 March): The state delegates write to the States General reporting that some of the cited Remonstrants have been suspended from the ministry in the Reformed church and have left

---

40. *RSG* 112; *ADSND*, 2/1:275–79; *ADSND*, 1:489. The States General 18 January resolution is printed in *ADSND*, 2/1:277–79.
41. *RSG* 132; Nationaal Archief, The Hague, Archief Staten-Generaal 3178.
42. *RSG* 132; NA, S.G. 3178.
43. *RSG* 151; NA, S.G. 3178.
44. *RSG* 173; NA, S.G. 3178. The Remonstrant letter is printed in the *Historisch Verhael van't ghene sich toeghedraeghen heeft binnen Dordrecht, in de Jaeren 1618 ende 1619* ([Amsterdam], 1623), 157–61.
45. *RSG* 180; NA, S.G. 3178.

Dordrecht. They ask what they should do in such cases; there are more who want to leave.[46]

2 MARCH: *After deliberation, the States General replies to the state delegates that they should summon cited Remonstrants Isaac Frederici, Carolus Niellius, and Dominicus Sapma to Dordrecht and give them no further permission to leave. The state delegates ought to do everything necessary to hasten the proceedings of the synod.*[47]

7 MARCH (received 9 March): The state delegates write a letter reporting on the synod.[48]

7 MARCH (received 11 March): *Since most of the state delegates have, with permission, left the synod for particular reasons, and since their presence is required as the synod is nearing its end, the States General authorizes the state delegates who are yet present to summon those who are absent, that they might assist in the synod's business.*[49]

7 MARCH (received 11 March): *The Wetteravian correspondents write, in a letter dated Büdingen 2 February, that they have chosen Georgius Fabricius, inspector at Hanau and minister at Windecken, to replace Johannes Bisterfeld as a Nassau-Wetteravian delegate at the synod. The States General decides to inform the state delegates, in order that they might receive Fabricius, accommodate him, and grant him seating in the synod to assist in its ongoing business.*[50]

12 MARCH: *The States General receives a letter (dated 10 January 1619) from the Marquis of Brandenburg, Georg Wilhelm, on behalf of his father, the Elector of Brandenburg, stating why they were not able to send theologians to the synod. It is decided to send this letter to the state delegates.*[51]

---

46. *RSG* 382; NA, S.G. 3178.
47. *RSG* 382; NA, S.G. 3178.
48. *RSG* 416c; NA, S.G. 3178.
49. *RSG* 407; NA, S.G. 3178; *ADSND*, 1:494.
50. *RSG* 407; NA, S.G. 3178; *ADSND*, 1:494.
51. *RSG* 424; NA, S.G. 3178; *ADSND*, 1:496. The letter from Brandenburg is printed in the *Acta*, 1:235–36.

13 March (received 14 March): The state delegates write that they have received complaints from the "orthodox congregation" at Kampen about gatherings of the common people there and about a Lutheran congregation that has been established there since the convening of the synod and that is siding with the Remonstrants. Since difficulties may arise from these circumstances, they ask the States General to take action against them.[52]

15 March (received 18 March): The state delegates write that Dominicus Sapma, one of the cited Remonstrants, has returned to Dordrecht from Hoorn, where his pregnant wife was being evicted from their home. Though he left without their permission, he claimed that the president of the state delegates, Jacob van Campen, had allowed him to leave. On 14 March, they examined Sapma about the incident. On certain points of questioning, especially about what happened between Sapma and Van Campen, they wanted to examine him again the next day, but Sapma refused to answer other than in writing.

Regarding the question of how the state delegates should proceed further with the matter, the States General does not decide.[53]

21 March: Since the synod has begun to conclude, the state delegates decide to send Hugo Muys van Holy to the States General to propose how the synod should proceed further, especially concerning the dismissal of the foreign theologians.[54]

22 March: Sent by the state delegates from Dordrecht, Muys van Holy reports to the States General that the business of the synod has progressed to the point that thought must be given to an honorable departure of the foreign theologians. If the States General would approve honoring the foreign theologians with a gold medallion worth between 120 and 150 guilders, the die for this medallion must be made ready as quickly as possible.[55]

---

52. *RSG* 434; NA, S.G. 3178; cf. *RSG* 476, which mentions that the magistrate of Kampen wrote that no such gathering occurred and that no Lutheran congregation was established there.
53. *RSG* 454; NA, S.G. 3178; *ADSND*, 1:495–96.
54. *ADSND*, 1:497.
55. *RSG* 477; NA, S.G. 3178.

22 March: *After deliberation, the States General decides that thank-you letters should be given to the foreign theologians for the political authorities who sent them and that the theologians should be honored with a medal with a value of 100 daalders. The state delegates are asked to propose the image and inscription and send them to the States General for its approval.*[56]

22 March: On 24 March, at the States General, Muys van Holy reports on a letter (dated 22 March) that he has received from Dordrecht. The day before, the last judgments (*iudicia*) of the synod delegations on the Fifth Article of the Remonstrants were read, and these deliberations have ended in "unbelievable harmony." On 22 March, someone from each delegation was appointed to copy and examine the canons as first drafted by President Bogerman.[57]

24 March: The state delegates advise the States General that, on one side of the gold medallion for the foreign theologians, the synod should be portrayed, with the inscription "*Restaurata Religione.*" On the other side should be Mount Zion, stormed on all sides by winds, with the inscription "*Erunt sicut Mons Sion*" from Psalm 125, highlighting the "perseverance of the saints," a doctrine that was much contested by the Remonstrants.

24 March: *After deliberation, the States General approves the medallion. The state delegates are authorized to have the die engraved.*[58]

27 March: *State delegates Henrick van Essen, Hugo Muys van Holy, and Johan van Hemert, who, with permission, are leaving for a few days to Dordrecht, are asked to inquire there and give advice about the conduct of Dominicus Sapma and the other Remonstrants. In response to a request from the cited Remonstrants (submitted 26 March) to be allowed to return home, the States General forbids the Remonstrants to leave Dordrecht without the permission of the synod.*[59]

---

56. *RSG* 477; NA, S.G. 3178.
57. *RSG* 493; NA, S.G. 3178.
58. *RSG* 493; NA, S.G. 3178.
59. *RSG* 519; NA, S.G. 3178. The Remonstrant request is printed in *Acta et Scripta*, 1:196–203.

27 March (received 5 April): *The States General writes to the state delegates that the deputies of the States of Holland brought up that, in the Dutch Republic, and for the king of Great Britain, there is great opposition to the teaching of Conrad Vorstius. The States General asks that the synod investigate his teaching as found in his books and, at an appropriate opportunity, explain what this teaching is. But the synod ought not occupy itself too long with this.*[60]

28 March: The state delegates decide to write the States General about how far the proceedings of the synod have progressed, reporting that, in the coming week, matters should proceed so far that it is possible the synod would come to pronounce its synodical decree. It is further announced, by Van Essen and Muys van Holy, that the state delegates should prepare a document on the conduct of the Remonstrants, so that the States General might thoroughly understand what has happened until now.[61]

3 April (received 6 April): *The States General writes to the state delegates, instructing them to pay Johannes Bogerman 400 guilders once again for his extraordinary work and expenses, beyond what he has already received.*[62]

5 April: *The States General receives a letter from the Landgrave of Hesse (dated 22 March), who asks that his theologians at the synod be allowed to leave, since he can no longer do without their services. It is decided to wait for the arrival of the state delegates, who will soon present a report concerning the decision of the synod on the Arminian case.*[63]

23 April: An instruction of the state delegates is read in their gathering, in which they delegated some of their members to advise the States General and solicit its opinion on certain points. On 24 April, it was revised and approved by all the state delegates, and afterward it was written out and signed by secretary Heinsius, in conformity with what was earlier drafted by Martinus Gregorii.[64]

---

60. *RSG* 519; NA, S.G. 3178; *ADSND*, 1:499.
61. *ADSND*, 1:498.
62. *RSG* 563; NA, S.G. 3178; *ADSND*, 1:499.
63. *RSG* 675; NA, S.G. 3178.
64. *ADSND*, 1:501.

26 April: A delegation of state delegates[65] appears before the States General and presents a document with ten points, which it considers in the presence of Prince Maurice:

(1) The statements and actions of the cited Remonstrants will be extracted from the synodical acts into a document and submitted to the States General.

(2) On the evening of 23 April, a unanimous judgment was made on the Five Remonstrant Articles in controversy.[66]

(3) Should the state delegates jointly sign this judgment, or should it be signed in their name by their secretary, Daniel Heinsius?

(4) What is the mind of the States General regarding the dismissal of the cited Remonstrants after the Five Points (Canons) have been promulgated?

(5) Must the Vorstius case be dealt with together with the Belgic Confession and the Heidelberg Catechism?

(6) Must this happen in the presence of the foreign theologians?

(7) Is it the States General's view that these matters must be handled by the Dutch provincial delegates after the dismissal of the foreign theologians?

(8) The States General is then asked to decide on the time of the dismissal of the foreign theologians, as well as on their letters of dismissal.

(9) Must these letters be issued by the States General in their gathering, or may they be issued by the state delegates at Dordrecht?

---

65. It appears that this delegation included Walraven van Brederode, Martinus Gregorii, Simon Schotte, and Hieronymus Isbrants; *ADSND*, 1:504.

66. On 26 April, this delegation from the synod probably submitted to the States General an original copy of the Canons of Dordt along with its ten-point document; Kuyper, *Post-Acta*, 306.

(10) The States General is asked to arrange the honoraria and the travel stipends. The status of payments after the departures needs to be considered.

After advice from Prince Maurice is heard, and after deliberation, the griffier (Cornelis van Aerssen) is instructed to draw up answers in writing.[67]

27 APRIL: *After a review and discussion of the ten points presented by the state delegates, the States General approved a resolution in response to these points:*

(1) and (2) The States General is very pleased to hear that the synod made a unanimous judgment concerning the Five Points in controversy.

(3) This judgment must be signed by the state delegates jointly and by Heinsius "pro testimonio rerum actarum."

(4) The synod's Canons ought to be promulgated publicly as quickly as possible.

(5) to (7) The state delegates ought to inquire whether the foreign theologians want to offer the States General their advice on the theology of Vorstius. If they object to doing this, the Dutch theologians ought to give a summary judgment, since it is not the intention to lose time by investigating Vorstius's writings extensively. The Belgic Confession and the Catechism must be read in the full synod, after which the theologians should be asked whether they have heard anything that is in conflict with God's Word or the unity of the church.

(8) to (10) The time for the dismissal of the foreign theologians is left to the state delegates. They will have enough time to draw up letters of dismissal and send them to the States General. The States General will then deliver the letters in their gathering. The state delegates will distribute the gold medals and the travel stipends.

---

67. *RSG* 691; NA, S.G. 3178. This document is inserted with the resolution in NA, S.G. 3178.

The decrees and censures against the cited Remonstrants shall be announced to them, with an order to abide by these. They ought to stay in Dordrecht until further notice. The state delegates ought to advise what must be done against the Remonstrants.[68]

29 APRIL: The delegation to the States General gives a report to the state delegates concerning what happened in The Hague and delivers in writing the resolution of the States General on the ten points that had been presented by the delegation.[69]

29 APRIL: Muys van Holy reports to the States General that the magistrate of Dordrecht recommends that the "*Acta synodalia*" (that is, the Canons) be printed there at Dordrecht, since this must happen accurately under the supervision of the secretaries there present.
Since the Acta are still to be examined, no resolution is taken.[70]

30 APRIL (received 1 May): The state delegates write that they have begun to carry out the decisions of the States General. They have fixed 6 May as the day on which the synodical Canons shall be promulgated at a public place yet to be determined. They also write that the Belgic Confession was read in the synod on 29 April and that they are waiting to hear if anything relating to doctrine is observed to be in conflict with God's Word or the common view of the true Reformed churches.[71]

2 MAY (received 7 May): The state delegates write that, on 30 April and 1 May, the Belgic Confession and the Heidelberg Catechism were approved by both the Dutch and foreign delegates "with a unanimity and harmony, not without great joy heard from all sincere friends of the true Reformed churches and the republic of our Fatherland." Thereafter, the synod has begun to examine the Vorstius case.[72]

---

68. *RSG* 693; NA, S.G. 3178. This resolution is found in the NA, S.G. 3178 and in S.G. 12.302, fol. 116.
69. *ADSND*, 1:501.
70. *RSG* 701; NA, S.G. 3178.
71. *RSG* 721; NA, S.G. 3178.
72. *RSG* 741; NA, S.G. 3178.

The Missing Correspondence

6 May (received 7 May): The state delegates write that the Canons were promulgated on that day. The state delegates plan to discharge the foreign theologians, and they request that 20,000 guilders be sent to the synod treasurer for this purpose.

7 May: *The States General decides to authorize the receiver-general to provide 20,000 guilders, a reduction of the requested 30,000 guilders that have been approved for the expenses of the synod beyond the previous 100,000 guilders. The Council of State may dispatch orders for this to the provinces.*[73]

7 May: The state delegates read the thank-you letters they had composed for the king of Britain and other foreign leaders who sent their theologians to the synod. It is decided to have these letters be written out and forwarded to the States General.[74]

7 May: There are various requests from a wide range of Amsterdam and Dordrecht printers to be used to print the "*acta synodalia.*" The state delegates decide to refer these printers to the States General.[75]

8 May: The state delegates decide that Secretary Heinsius should go to The Hague. Since there is fear that the Canons may be pirate-printed and thus incorrectly come into the hands of the people, they decide that he should request the States General to order that the Canons be printed by a well-known printer as soon as possible, that they might prevent such problems. The States General could decide to allow only one printer or to distribute the work among various printers, so that one is given the Latin to print and another the Dutch. It is also decided that Secretary Heinsius should take with him the letters he has drawn up for the king of Britain and other princes who sent delegates to the synod.[76]

9 May: *The drafts of the thank-you letters for the foreign leaders who sent their theologians to the synod are read and approved by the States General. The griffier is instructed to dispatch these letters so that they can be given at*

---

73. *RSG* 741; NA, S.G. 3178.
74. *ADSND*, 1:502.
75. *ADSND*, 1:503.
76. *ADSND*, 1:503.

Dordrecht to those who will not be coming to The Hague; the rest will be delivered to foreign theologians who come to The Hague.[77]

14 May: *The States General writes to the synod secretaries that it has heard that the secretaries have made eight copies of the synodical acts (that is, the Canons), for the States General and the seven provinces. The States General asks that it, not the provinces, receive the copies, since these acts will be issued in its name.*

14 May: *The States General gives the political and ecclesiastical secretaries a seven-year patent for the printing and distribution of Latin, Dutch, and French editions of the acta synodalia "in the best print and on the best paper." They may do this only after they have received orders and permission from the States General. The printers at Dordrecht ought to be considered before others.*[78]

15 May (received 16 May): *The state delegates discuss whether to again urge the States General to make an order about printing the Canons, since some think the Canons will be printed by someone else.*[79]

16 May (received 18 May): *The States General writes to the state delegates that, after receiving their letter of 15 May, it has decided to publish a placard forbidding anyone without a patent to print, have printed, or sell the acta of the synod, in whole or in part.*[80] *If there has been no decision to translate the Canons and the other synodical acts into Dutch and French, the States General would like this to be done before the conclusion of the synod and with the approval of the synod. The synod secretaries ought to have the book printers at Dordrecht print fifty copies of the Canons in Dutch (after they first take an oath that they will print no more copies without further instruction) and send them to the States General. The States General decides to divide the fifty copies of the Canons as follows: four for Gelderland, nineteen for Holland, seven for Zeeland, three for Utrecht,*

---

77. *RSG* 752; NA, S.G. 3178.
78. *RSG* 768; NA, S.G. 3178.
79. *RSG* 784; *ADSND*, 1:504.
80. *RSG* 784; NA, S.G. 3178. The placard issued by the States General is printed in the *Groot Placaet-boeck: vervattende de Placaten, Ordonnantien ende Edicten vande doorluchtige, Hoogh Mog. heeren Staten Generael der Vereenighde Nederlanden* (The Hague, 1658–1796), I k. 461.

two for Friesland, four for Overijssel, and three for Groningen; the griffier is responsible for the remaining copies. The States General is expecting the state delegates to offer advice regarding what should happen with the cited Remonstrants and how they have conducted themselves recently. The state delegates ought to come to The Hague after the conclusion of the synod to give a report on what has happened at the synod, and they should bring the acta synodalia in their final form for approval.[81]

16 MAY: The state delegates send a letter with the text of some thank-you letters the synod wants to send to King James and other foreign leaders,[82] although the States General itself had earlier written to these leaders. They also send a full report of the actions of the cited Remonstrants, and an extract of this report, so that the States General might advise.[83]

18 MAY: The state delegates send secretary Heinsius to The Hague with a written instruction to answer the 16 May letter of the States General.[84]

19 MAY: *The States General reads the memorandum of the state delegates, sent by Heinsius to Muys van Holy. Since most of the points of the memorandum have been decided earlier by the States General, it is decided to let the matter rest. In order to spare expenses, the report of the synod's deliberations will be brought by some representatives of the synod. It is proposed that, at the conclusion of the synod, medals should also be made for the Dutch participants at the synod. Since Holland first wants to consult their principals, nothing is decided.*[85]

---

81. *RSG* 784; NA, S.G. 3178; *ADSND*, 1:505.
82. These letters from the synod are found in the Oud Syndaal Archief, fol. 5:343–78.
83. *RSG* 796; NA, S.G. 3178; *ADSND*, 1:503–4. See also *ADSND* 1:488, 498. In the Oud Synodaal Archief, fol. 5:257–68, there is an extract of a report about the conduct of the cited Remonstrants. In the Bibliotheek der Remonstrantsch-Gereformeerde Gemeente Rotterdam (in the Centrale Bibliotheek Rotterdam), vol. 50, there is the "Summarisch Verhael vande Comportementen der geciteerde Remonstranten voorde Nationale Synode tot Dordrecht."
84. *ADSND*, 1:505.
85. *RSG* 814; NA, S.G. 3178.

21 May: *After reading the report of the conduct of the cited Remonstrants, the States General decides to send three of its deputies—Sweer van Appeldoorn, Nicolaes van den Bouckhorst, and Jan Nanninga—to Dordrecht, to individually interrogate, together with the state delegates, the Remonstrants on two points: (a) Whether they—by advice or by support—permitted what was proposed and begun at Rotterdam on 5 March by some ministers.*[86] *(b) Whether they will keep silence in the future and act not as preachers but as citizens, without seeking any church office. If they answer yes to the last question, the state delegates should require from each of the cited Remonstrants a written and signed declaration promising to kindly mind their own affairs in the future. The state delegates should also inquire about some letters that have been written to some persons at Leiden and then give a report. On the question of whether the States General finds it helpful that the synod is also writing to political leaders who sent their theologians to the synod, it is decided to let this matter rest, since the States General has already written to them.*[87]

22 May: *The resolution to send a deputation to Dordrecht is reviewed, but the States General decides not to change it. The deputies may expand their instructions "pro re nata" in consultation with the state delegates. On the points sent by Secretary Heinsius to Van Essen and Muys van Holy (on 18 May), the States General decides to remain with its former resolution. Provisionally, no more than fifty copies of the Canons will be printed, and the cited Remonstrants must again be ordered not to leave Dordrecht. The complaint of the Hesse theologians, that they were each charged two guilders and ten stuivers for each night of lodging at Dordrecht, will be investigated.*[88]

---

86. The March meeting of Remonstrant ministers, elders, and deacons in Rotterdam was intended to preserve the unity of Remonstrant churches and lay the foundation for separate congregations. See Geeraert Brandt, *Historie der Reformatie, en andere Kerkelyke Geschiedenissen in en omtrent de Nederlanden* (Rotterdam, 1704), 3:480–90.
87. *RSG* 823; NA, S.G. 3178.
88. *RSG* 825; NA, S.G. 3178.

25 May: *The three deputies of the States General appeared before the state delegates and interrogated the cited Remonstrants. Their individual answers are registered with the "Interrogatorien."*[89]

28 May: *The States General writes to the state delegates that, without delay, they must send the copied synodical acts (that is, the Canons) by the next morning. The provinces have postponed their work on the "landdagen" for this purpose. If the state delegates have already left, Secretary Heinsius may open this letter.*[90]

28 May: *In the presence of Prince Maurice, the three deputies—Appeldoorn, Bouckhorst, and Nanninga—report concerning their business at Dordrecht. The document with the questions and answers of the cited Remonstrants is read. The resolution about this and the summoning of some Remonstrants is postponed until the Canons are accepted by the provinces. In the meantime, the act to be declared by the Remonstrants will be drawn up.*[91]

30 May: A delegation of the synod—consisting of President Bogerman, Jacobus Rolandus, Hermannus Faukelius, Johannes Polyander, and Festus Hommius—appears before the States General. In the presence of Prince Maurice, they present a written report on the synod's deliberations, the so-called Summary Report.[92] Then they present eight authentic copies of the *Acta Synodalia* (that is, the Canons), one for each province for their principals to approve and one to set out for inspection at the office of the Generality (that is, the States General). They also deliver synodical acts concerning the synod's judgments on the Belgic Confession, the Heidelberg Catechism, and the teaching of Vorstius, as well as a copy of the revision of the Church Order of 1586.[93] The

---

89. *ADSND*, 1:505–6. The *Interrogatorien*, with the answers of the individual Remonstrants, are printed in *ADSND*, 1:507–18.

90. *RSG* 877; NA, S.G. 3178.

91. *RSG* 877; NA, S.G. 3178. The act for the Remonstrants was the "Act of Cessation (*Acte van Stilstand*)," by which they would promise to resign from the ministry and keep silent about their views. This Act is printed in Brandt, *Historie*, 3:687.

92. The Summary Report is printed in Kuyper, *Post-Acta*, 475–82.

93. The Act of Approbation of the Confession and Catechism is printed in Kuyper, *Post-Acta*, 482–84. The synod's judgment on Conrad Vorstius is printed in *ADSND*, 1:151–53. The Church Order of Dordt, which was a revision of the 1586 Church Order of The Hague, was first printed in the *Kercken-ordeninge, gestelt inden*

delegation requests the States General to make decisions on a document containing gravamina of the churches, the *Libellus Supplex*.[94]

The States General thanks the delegation. It will see that the provinces accept the Canons as soon as possible. It asks that fifty printed copies of the Church Order be delivered to it, copies in which the revisions of the synod are placed in the margin, so that it may become a general church order.[95]

30 MAY: *Since the synod has ended, the States General dismisses the state delegates at their request. They should still stay a few days, until all documents that must be ratified are delivered.*[96]

30 MAY: Muys van Holy mentions that Dudley Carleton insists that the name of King James be taken up in the *Acta Synodalia*. The issue was whether King James would be mentioned in the Preface to the Canons.

Since the Acta and the Canons have already begun to be printed, and since the names of other political leaders are not mentioned, the deputies of Holland and Zeeland are appointed to defend this decision. They will try to satisfy Carleton in another way.[97]

31 MAY: *The States General writes to the state delegates that Carleton continues to insist that the name of James be mentioned, since he has received an explicit mandate from King James about this. An insertion to this effect suggested by Carleton is forwarded. The States General wants the insertion to be taken up in print, to avoid misunderstanding.*[98]

31 MAY: Muys van Holy and Frederick van Zuylen van Nyvelt report to their fellow state delegates on the actions of the States General, and they report that the States General and Prince Maurice were content with what the synod had done.[99]

Nationalen Synode der Ghereformeerde Kercken, te samen beroepen ende gehouden…binnen Dordrecht, inden Iare 1618 ende 1619 (Utrecht: Salomon de Roy, 1620).
    94. The *Libellus Supplex* is printed in Kuyper, *Post-Acta*, 261–70.
    95. *RSG* 891; NA, S.G. 3178.
    96. *RSG* 891; NA, S.G. 3178.
    97. *RSG* 891; NA, S.G. 3178.
    98. *RSG* 891, footnote e.
    99. *ADSND*, 1:506.

3 JUNE: Muys van Holy from Dordrecht sends, along with a letter to the States General, sixty copies of the Canons and forty copies of the Church Order.[100]

Conclusion

From the available evidence, it is clear that the States General exercised close supervision over the synod by way of its state delegates. There were at least twenty-seven letters sent by the state delegates to the States General, and twenty-six letters were sent in return by the States General. One can assume that the letters of the state delegates were written by their secretary Heinsius.

In addition to the actual correspondence, the state delegates occasionally sent one or more of their number to the States General to personally report on the synod or to request direction on specific matters. Besides the initial delegation sent by the city of Dordrecht, the state delegates sent a small delegation four times to the States General, including the five synod members who presented the final report on the synod. Seven times they also sent Hugo Muys van Holy, the sheriff of Dordrecht, to personally report to the States General, and twice they sent their secretary Daniel Heinsius. The States General also sent a delegation of three to Dordrecht to interrogate the cited Remonstrants.

Early correspondence dealt with the opening of the Synod of Dordt, the status of the voting rights of the foreign theologians, access to the synod by Remonstrants, and the commission and instruction for the state delegates.

The most important function of letters sent by state delegates to the States General was to report on the deliberations of the synod. There were sixteen such reports.

A particular focus of the correspondence was the conduct of the cited Remonstrants. A decisive moment was when the States General issued the 1 January resolution stating that, if the Remonstrants did not submit to the synod, they should be examined from their writings. This was followed by the States General's confirmation of

---

100. *RSG* 914; NA, S.G. 3178. Seventy-five Dutch copies of the Canons were initially printed by Isaac Jansz Canin. The printed copies of the Church Order were actually copies of the 1586 Church Order, with the revisions of Dordt written in the margin. See *RSG* 1001.

their expulsion, as well as the prohibition to leave Dordrecht without permission. Also discussed were a personal interrogation of the Remonstrants regarding unauthorized meetings and their future intentions, their final dismissal from Dordrecht, and an Act of Cessation by which the Remonstrants were to promise not to serve as ministers and not to propagate their views.

The correspondence also dealt with the invitations the States General made to foreign lands to send some of their theologians to the synod, as well as the credentials of these theologians when they arrived. Also discussed were the lodging and treatment of the foreign theologians at Dordrecht, the time they should be dismissed to return home, gold medallions to honor their contribution, and thank-you letters to be sent to the foreign leaders who sent them.

Since the States General paid most of the costs of holding the synod, the funding and payment of the expenses of the synod—especially the stipends for the foreign theologians and their ongoing expenses—were often mentioned in the correspondence.

Since the main purpose of the Synod of Dordt was to settle the Arminian controversy, the States General had a special interest in the Canons of Dordt as the judgment on this case. Thus, it authorized a public promulgation of the Canons, gave directions and a patent for the printing of the Canons, asked for Dutch and French translations of the Canons, and requested copies of the Canons for their approval. Related to the Arminian controversy was the heterodox teaching of Conrad Vorstius, which the States General asked the synod to add to its agenda.

To ensure doctrinal and ecclesiastical unity, the States General also asked the synod to add to its agenda an examination of the Belgic Confession and the Heidelberg Catechism. It also wanted to examine revisions of the Church Order made by the synod.

Other topics covered in this correspondence were the forbidding of printing abuses, the approval of the acts of the synod, and the diplomatically sensitive issue of King James I's demand to have his name mentioned in the Preface to the Canons.

It is also important to take note of what is not found in the correspondence between the States General and the state delegates. The States General and the state delegates did not enter into the theological issues at play in the Arminian controversy or into the synod's process of drafting the Canons as its judgment on this case. Nor did they engage in the discussions of other specifically ecclesiastical topics that the synod deliberated on, such as a new Dutch Bible translation, catechism instruction, and theological training. They did, however, engage with other topics in which ecclesiastical and political interests more closely intersected, such as the printing of controversial literature and the revision of the Church Order, which touched on the right of patronage.

Besides the States General's role in setting the parameters spelled out in the Articles to Convene the synod—determining the participants, inviting foreign theologians, determining the basic agenda and procedures—the correspondence between the state delegates and the States General provides important insight into the role that the States General played in overseeing the Synod of Dordt, especially by way of its state delegates. The States General directly intervened with directives to the synod at critical points when the synod was at an impasse with the Remonstrants or when it needed direction on specific questions. However, it is clear that it was not just at critical moments that the States General was occupied with the synod; the correspondence reveals that it was regularly engaged with the synod throughout its six and a half months of deliberations. The primary concern of the States General was to have the synod settle the Arminian controversy in order to restore peace and unity in the Dutch churches, so that there would be stability in the broader Dutch society.

William Ames, theological advisor to President Bogerman

CHAPTER 9

Reformed Scholasticism and the Synod of Dordt[1]

In recent decades, a growing body of scholarly literature has focused on the emergence of Reformed scholasticism in the late sixteenth century.[2] The Synod of Dordt, probably the single most influential event in the Reformed tradition in the early seventeenth century, convened at a time when Reformed scholasticism was beginning to bloom. This naturally gives rise to the question: What influence did this scholastic trend have on the Synod of Dordt and its decisions? Some older scholarship has tended to view Dordt as a triumph of scholasticism.[3] Other

---

1. This article, somewhat revised, was first printed in "Reformed Scholasticism and the Synod of Dort (1618–19)," in *John Calvin's Institutes: His Opus Magnum*, ed. B. J. van der Walt (Potchefstroom, South Africa: Potchefstroom University for Christian Higher Education, 1986), 467–506.

2. On Reformed scholasticism, and for surveys of literature on Reformed scholasticism, see B. J. van der Walt, ed., *Our Reformational Tradition: A Rich Heritage and Lasting Vocation* (Potchefstroom, South Africa: Potchefstroom University for Christian Higher Education, 1984), 369–77; Carl R. Trueman and R. S. Clark, eds., *Protestant Scholasticism: Essays in Reassessment* (Carlisle, UK: Paternoster Press, 1999), xi–xix; Willem J. van Asselt and Eef Dekker, eds., *Reformation and Scholasticism: An Ecumenical Enterprise* (Grand Rapids: Baker Academic, 2001), 11–43; Richard A. Muller, *After Calvin: Studies in the Development of a Theological Tradition* (Oxford: Oxford University Press, 2003), 25–33, 75–78; and Willem J. van Asselt, *Introduction to Reformed Scholasticism* (Grand Rapids: Reformation Heritage Books, 2011), 1–25.

3. See, e.g., Philip Schaff, *Creeds of Christendom* (New York: Harper, 1877), 1:515: The Canons of Dort "prepared the way for a dry scholasticism which runs into subtle abstractions, and resolves the living soul of divinity into a skeleton of formulas and distinctions." Also, Basil Hall, "Calvin against the Calvinists," in *John Calvin*, ed. G. E. Duffield (Grand Rapids: Eerdmans, 1968), 28: "…the Synod of Dort in 1619 where

scholars have called this conclusion into question.[4] The issue deserves a closer investigation.

Although the Synod of Dordt met as a national synod of the Reformed churches in the Netherlands in order to settle the Arminian controversy, twenty-six leading Reformed theologians from eight foreign lands were also invited to participate. Because of its broad international character, one may expect the synod to reflect in large measure the character of contemporary Reformed theology. Dordt thus provides a good test case by which to gauge the influence of Reformed scholasticism in the early seventeenth century.[5]

Reformed scholasticism primarily refers to particular academic methods or ways of thinking, rather than to a specific set of doctrines, although a way of thinking certainly colors the results of one's thought. Several American scholars, beginning with Brian Armstrong, attempted to describe Protestant scholasticism by identifying some basic tendencies that characterize this phenomenon:[6] (1) It attempts

---

the extreme form of scholastic 'Calvinism' was achieved in the Five Articles which broke the unity of Calvin's theology and replaced his biblical dynamism by formulae." Also, Jack B. Rogers and Donald K. McKim, *The Authority and Interpretation of the Bible: An Historical Approach* (San Francisco: Harper & Row, 1979), 164: "The hyper-Calvinist majority at Dort skewed Reformed theology in a scholastic direction by their dependence on Aristotelian notions of causality, by making predestination the central doctrine to be defended in Reformed Christendom and by teaching notions, such as eternal reprobation, not specifically found in Calvin"; likewise, 188: "The Synod of Dort in the Netherlands gave confessional expression to the developing Reformed scholasticism."

4. See, e.g., W. Robert Godfrey, "Tensions within International Calvinism: The Debate on the Atonement at the Synod of Dort, 1618–1619" (PhD diss., Stanford University, 1974), 268: "If Bezan orthodoxy, arid scholasticism, and Aristotelian philosophy did triumph in seventeenth-century Calvinism, they did not win their victory at Dort."

5. On the Synod of Dordt, see Donald Sinnema, "The Issue of Reprobation at the Synod of Dort (1618–19) in Light of the History of this Doctrine" (PhD diss., University of St. Michael's College, Toronto, 1985); Aza Goudriaan and Fred van Lieburg, eds., *Revisiting the Synod of Dordt (1618–1619)* (Leiden: Brill, 2011); *ADSND*, vol. 1, *Acta of the Synod of Dordt*; vol. 2/2, *Early Sessions of the Synod of Dordt*.

6. See Brian Armstrong, *Calvinism and the Amyraut Heresy: Protestant Scholasticism and Humanism in Seventeenth-Century France* (Madison: University of Wisconsin Press, 1969), 32; J. P. Donnelly, *Calvinism and Scholasticism in Vermigli's Doctrine of Man and Grace* (Leiden: Brill, 1975), 199–201; John S. Bray, *Theodore Beza's Doctrine of Predestination* (Nieuwkoop: B. DeGraaf, 1975), 12–13; Rogers and McKim, *The Authority*

to present the Christian faith as a logically coherent and rationally defensible system of belief. (2) It is dependent upon the methodology and philosophy of Aristotle; this is reflected also in a new appreciation of medieval scholasticism. (3) It strengthens the role of reason and logic in exploring and defending religious truth. (4) It shows a strong interest in metaphysical and speculative questions, especially regarding God and His will. (5) It views Scripture in an unhistorical fashion as a self-consistent, rationally comprehensible account that can be reduced to a creedal statement, one that may then serve as a measuring stick for orthodoxy.

However, more recent scholars, led by Richard Muller, have shown that such a description of Protestant scholasticism needs to be thoroughly corrected and refined. Muller emphasizes that scholasticism refers not to particular content but to the academic method of treating a subject within the context of the university or school:

> A theological work was identified as "scholastic," when it belonged to the classroom, echoed the patterns of disputation then typical of education, and employed a refined method of argument to define the terms of debate, the *status quaestionis*, and the resolution of debate with various clearly identified opponents.[7]

The present essay seeks to gain further insight by pursuing an understanding of Protestant scholasticism within the context of its time, especially by investigating how the Synod of Dordt and its members consciously viewed this emerging scholastic trend. A keyword in such an investigation is the very term "scholastic" (Latin: *scholasticus*). How was this term used at the time of Dordt?

---

and Interpretation of the Bible, 185–86; Alister E. McGrath, *Reformation Thought: An Introduction* (Oxford: Blackwell, 1993), 129.

7. Richard A. Muller, "The Problem of Protestant Scholasticism—A Review and Definition," in Van Asselt and Dekker, *Reformation and Scholasticism*, 54; cf. Muller, *Post-Reformation Reformed Dogmatics: The Rise and Development of Reformed Orthodoxy, ca. 1520 to ca. 1725*, vol. 1, *Prolegomena to Theology* (Grand Rapids: Baker Academic, 2003), 34–37, 189–92, 197–98. Muller's *After Calvin: Studies in the Development of a Theological Tradition* (Oxford: University Press, 2003), 27, offers a description of "scholasticism" that is overly narrow. The scholastic methods used in scholastic works of the post-Reformation era often, but do not always, fit this description. Cf. Van Asselt, *Introduction to Reformed Scholasticism*, 5–9.

Contemporary Usage of the Term *Scholasticus*

In Reformed theological works of the late sixteenth and early seventeenth centuries, the term *scholasticus* (and its related forms) was used primarily in three ways.

First, the term was sometimes used in general reference to matters pertaining to schools. For instance, it relates to school prayers in Theodore Beza's *Catechismus sive Compendiaria Fidei Christianae Rudimenta; quibus adjectae sunt Preces aliquot Scholasticae* (Antwerp, 1583). Similarly, Johann H. Alsted wrote a manual on education titled *Consiliarius Academicus et Scholasticus; id est, Methodus Formandorum Studiorum* (Strasbourg, 1610).

Second, the term was sometimes used in reference to medieval scholastic theology and theologians. For example, in 1580 the Genevan theologian Lambert Daneau published a commentary on the first book of Lombard's *Sentences*. It began with an important prolegomenon in which the origin, progress, and epochs of "scholastic (*scholasticae*) theology" are shown.[8] The Heidelberg theologian Daniel Tossanus wrote a *Synopsis de Patribus, sive praecipuis et vetustioribus Ecclesiae Doctoribus, nec non de Scholasticis* (Heidelberg, 1603), in which he devoted a chapter to the medieval scholastics. Though Reformed theologians were often critical of such scholars, it was not uncommon for them to quote the "Scholastics" (usually called the "Schoolmen" in old English) with approval on certain points of doctrine. Girolamo Zanchi, in his *De Natura Dei* (Heidelberg, 1577)—just one of many examples that might be mentioned—frequently referred to the "better," "sounder," or "purer" Scholastics.[9]

Third, the term *scholasticus* was also used in reference to the teaching style and methods employed in the universities of that period. Characteristic of this style was logical rigor as distinct from rhetorical freedom of expression, as well as a precision in analysis and rebuttal that was achieved through the use of a reservoir of inherited philosophical and theological categories and distinctions. This sense of the

---

8. Lambert Daneau, *In Petri Lombardi…Librum Primum Sententiarum…Commentarius Triplex* (Geneva, 1580), *j–**iiij. All translations of Latin and Dutch are mine unless otherwise noted.

9. Girolamo Zanchi, *De Natura Dei* (Heidelberg, 1577), e.g., 628, 630, 652, 675: "meliores Scholastici," "puriores Scholastici."

term is what is meant when referring to Protestant scholasticism. Several examples may be mentioned: (1) In 1581, with Theodore Beza or Antonius Faius presiding, Raphael Eglin defended some theses on predestination at the Geneva Academy, one of which states: "Therefore we retain the scholastic distinctions [*Scholasticas distinctiones*] of necessity and compulsion, natural and voluntary necessity, absolute and hypothetical [*ex hypothesi*] necessity, necessity of the consequent and of the consequence, as true and very useful."[10] (2) One of William Ames's anti-Remonstrant writings was *De Arminii Sententia qua electionem omnem particularem fidei praevisae docet inniti, Disceptatio Scholastica inter Nicolaum Grevinchovium et Guilielmum Amesium* (Amsterdam, 1613). In a prefatory letter, Ames indicates that he wants to investigate the principles of the Remonstrants *scholastice* in order to clarify their views. (3) Ames's *Aenhangsel van de Haeghsche Conferentie* (Amsterdam, 1630) contains an appendix, "An *Explanation* of some philosophical and scholastic manners of speaking [*scholastijcke manieren van spreken*], and other unusual words or expressions." (4) In 1620 the French Reformed Synod of Alais passed an act declaring that professors who teach the theological commonplaces should explain them "solidly, and as succinctly as possible, in a scholastic manner [*d'une Maniere Scholastique*], in order that the students may be profited as much as possible and that they may be enabled to apply themselves most vigorously to disputes and metaphysical distinctions."[11]

A common expression—to treat a topic "theologically and scholastically"—should also be understood in the third sense. Some examples: Antoine de la Roche Chandieu's (also known as Sadeel) *Opera Theologica* (1593) begins with the treatise *De Verbo Dei Scripto Adversus Humanas Traditiones, Theologica & Scholastica Tractatio* (first published, Geneva, 1580). Its preface is titled "On the true method of disputing theologically and at the same time scholastically [*Theologice simul & Scholastice*]."[12] Likewise, Sibrandus Lubbertus wrote *De*

---

10. *Theses Theologicae in Schola Genevensi…sub D.D. Theod. Beza & Antonio Fayo… Propositae & Disputatae* (Geneva, 1591), 18.

11. Jean Aymon, *Tous les Synodes Nationaux des Églises Réformées de France* (The Hague, 1710), 2:210.

12. For analysis of the scholastic character of this work, see Donald Sinnema, "Antoine De Chandieu's Call for a Scholastic Reformed Theology (1580)," in *Later*

Principiis Christianorum Dogmatum Libri Septem, Scholastice & Theologice Collati cum Disputationibus Roberti Bellarmini (Franeker, 1591), and Daniel Chamier published *De Oecumenico Pontifice Disputatio Scholastica et Theologica* (Geneva, 1601).

The third sense of the term *scholasticus* again appears in the specific discipline of "scholastic theology." This concept, which is medieval in origin, was taken up in Reformed theology near the start of the seventeenth century. An early example of this is a dogmatic work by Leiden theologian Lucas Trelcatius Jr., titled *Scholastica et Methodica Locorum Communium S. Theologiae Institutio* (London, 1604) and explained "by a scholastic method." Johann H. Alsted adopted the precise term in his *Methodus Sacrosanctae Theologiae* (Frankfurt, 1614–1615); the fifth book of this work is titled *Theologia Scholastica*.

Alsted further developed this project in his *Theologia Scholastica Didactica, exhibens Locos Communes Theologicos Methodo Scholastica* (Hanover, 1618). In his preface, Alsted distinguishes between the old (that is, medieval) Scholastics and the new Scholastics. Among the latter, he includes not only the Jesuits and other "Papists" but also certain "Reformed" (*reformati*) teachers. He specifically names Antonius Sadeel (Chandieu), Girolamo Zanchi, Lambert Daneau, and Franciscus Junius and states that he follows in their footsteps. In the first chapter, titled "What Is Scholastic Theology?" Alsted defines it as "supernatural wisdom which teaches divine things in the order customary in the schools."[13] It is divided into didactic (what we might call dogmatic) theology and polemical theology. The first part teaches the truth; the second part defends the truth. "The functions of Scholastic Theology are to teach sound doctrine by an exact method, to refute those who do not hold to sound doctrine, and finally to explain theological difficulties."[14] Alsted explained his use of the term "scholastic" as follows:

> That which sets forth and explains sacred truth by a carefully worked out [*exquisita*] method is called Scholastic Theology. This method is

---

Calvinism: International Perspectives, ed. W. Fred Graham (Kirksville, Mo.: Sixteenth Century Journal Publishers, 1994), 159–90.

13. Alsted, *Theologia Scholastica Didactica* (Hanover, 1618), 4.
14. Alsted, *Theologia Scholastica Didactica*, 6.

called "scholastic" since it is the prevailing method in the schools. To this Positive Theology is relatively opposed, as its foundation and basis. Positive Theology is the Word of God itself.[15]

Franciscus Gomarus also used the distinction between positive theology and scholastic theology. In the first of his *Disputationes Theologiae* (early seventeenth century), he described the latter as "the scholastic treatment and disputation of dogmas and commonplaces against heresies."[16]

To understand the third sense of the term *scholasticus*, one must be aware of the pedagogical style and methods of the early seventeenth-century Reformed universities. Various features formed the peculiar "scholastic" manner of treating theology in the Reformed universities:

- the widespread use of the formal disputation, with its defendants and objectors;

- the introduction of metaphysics into Protestant universities at the turn of the seventeenth century and the resulting use of many metaphysical distinctions;

- the *quaestio* method of academic argumentation and of the rebuttal of objectors;

- the commonplace, or *locus*, approach;

- precision in analysis by use of inherited categories and distinctions;

- analysis by definition and division, the division proceeding according to the four Aristotelian causes, their sub-causes, effects, adjuncts, etc.;

- rational demonstration of truth and rebuttal of error, especially by means of the formal syllogism;

- teaching by the analytic and synthetic methods.

---

15. Alsted, *Theologia Scholastica Didactica*, 5. The distinction between scholastic theology and positive theology is medieval in origin; see Yves M. J. Congar, *A History of Theology* (New York: Doubleday, 1968), 170–74.

16. Franciscus Gomarus, *Opera Theologica Omnia* (Amsterdam, 1664), 2:3.

Of course, this scholastic orientation tended to spill beyond the classroom walls, especially in polemical works.[17]

The Distinction between Scholastic and Popular

Although the scholastic approach was well established by the early seventeenth century, it was nevertheless common for Reformed theologians to distinguish between the scholastic treatment of theology, especially as it was employed in the schools, and a popular treatment of theology, which was employed in preaching and in teaching the uneducated. Since this distinction has not received due recognition, it is worth listing several examples: (1) Andreas Hyperius, in his *De Formandis Concionibus Sacris* (1553), was the earliest Reformed theologian to elaborate on the distinction: "No one is unaware that two ways of interpreting the Scriptures are used in the churches, the one scholastic [*scholasticam*], the other popular [*popularem*].... The former is exercised within the narrow walls of the school; the latter takes place in spacious sanctuaries.... In the former, most things are examined by the standard of dialectical brevity and simplicity; in the latter, rhetorical abundance and copiousness garner the most favor."[18] (2) In *De Verbo Dei et eius Tractatione* (preface dated 1588), Georg Sohn states: "Interpretation is twofold, the one scholastic [*scholastica*], the other ecclesiastical or popular [*ecclesiastica seu popularis*]. And similarly, the one interpreter is scholastic, the other is ecclesiastical; the former is commonly called a professor and a doctor, the latter an ecclesiastic, a preacher, and a

---

17. The formal syllogism, for instance, appeared in ecclesiastical contexts. In *The Substance of Christian Religion* (London, 1595), the Basel theologian Amandus Polanus prescribed the following method for deliberating in ecclesiastical councils: "The order must be according to method. The positions must be definitions, distribution, short axioms. The manner of disputing must be always by syllogisms." Similarly, the chairman of the 1611 Hague Conference between several Remonstrants (Arminians) and Calvinists began the proceedings by instructing the participants to debate "briefly and syllogistically"; cited by Pieter Wijminga, *Festus Hommius* (Leiden: D. Donner, 1899), 107.

18. Andreas Hyperius, *De Formandis Concionibus Sacris, seu de Intepretatione Scripturarum Populari, Libri II* (Marburg, 1553), 4r. For analysis, see Donald Sinnema, "The Distinction between Scholastic and Popular: Andreas Hyperius and Early Reformed Orthodoxy," in *Protestant Scholasticism: Essays in Reassessment*, ed. Carl R. Trueman and R. S. Clark (Carlisle, UK: Paternoster Press, 1999), 127–43.

minister of the Word."¹⁹ (3) In a 1603 work, Matthias Martinius of Bremen distinguishes between ministers called "to teach popularly" (*ad docendam populariter*) and those called "to teach scholastically" (*ad docendam scholastice*). The former include the apostles, evangelists, and pastors; the latter include prophets and doctors.²⁰ (4) In his *Theologia Scholastica Didactica* (1618), Alsted states: "Scholastic Theology is so called, because it is accustomed to be set forth and explained by the method which is appropriate for schools and, besides, is more exact [*accuratior*] than the popular [*popularis*] method which prevails in the church among the people, since it is not the method of prudence, which is called exoteric and popular, that flourishes in the schools, but rather the method of wisdom, which is called acroamatic and scholastic [*scholastica*]."²¹ (5) Alsted's *Methodus SS. Theologiae* (Hanover, 1619) contains the following subtitle: "A System of Sacred Theology, delineated by a partly popular [*populari*] and partly scholastic [*scholastica*] method and divided into six books."²² (6) In his *Syntagma Sacrae Theologiae* (Bremen, 1636), Ludwig Crocius refers to a distinction made in didactic theology by his Bremen colleague Conrad Bergius. If a particular subject is "taught popularly [*populariter*], it is accommodated to the time, place, and capacity of the hearers, but if it is taught according to the rule of method, or scholastically [*ad artis regulam sive scholastice*], then it usually follows the laws of treating a theme logically."²³

Closely related to the distinction between scholastic and popular is the distinction between a scholastic and a rhetorical way of handling a subject. Chandieu, for example, spoke of two ways of treating a topic theologically:

> The one, abundant and composed in a copious style, teaches the uneducated and arouses the slow of comprehension to embrace the doctrine of the truth. The other, however, is exact but contracted, and, with those things set aside which are added to influence minds and with the cloak of eloquence removed, it displays to us the things

---

19. Georg Sohn, *Opera* (Herborn, 1609), 1:35.
20. Matthias Martinius, *Methodus SS. Theologiae* (Herborn, 1603), 102, 105, 516, 517, 556.
21. Alsted, *Theologia Scholastica Didactica*, preface.
22. Alsted, *Methodus SS. Theologiae* (Hanover, 1619), 29.
23. Ludwig Crocius, *Syntagma Sacrae Theologiae* (Bremen, 1636), 265.

themselves simply and plainly, and sets forth bare arguments, so that the very truth of things can almost be gazed at with our eyes and be touched with our fingers....

For just as the same hand can both be opened and, with the fingers again squeezed together, be contracted into a fist, so the same matter can be treated both copiously by continuous eloquence, and being drawn together in brief syllogisms, more precisely and concisely.[24]

Chandieu himself advocated for the scholastic treatment of theology, and he called on theologians to further develop such a method.

The distinction between scholastic and popular is extremely important in evaluating the influence of scholasticism at the Synod of Dordt. Generally speaking, the documents of the synod tend to be more popular than scholastic. On the other hand, it was common for the theologians at Dordt to employ a scholastic style in their academic writings.

Academic Writings of Dordt Theologians

A few examples may illustrate the fact that the theologians who attended the Synod of Dordt did not hesitate to use a scholastic approach in their academic teaching. First, one may point to some of the examples mentioned above. Among these, Ames, Lubbertus, Alsted, Gomarus, Martinius, and Crocius were all present at the synod.

The *Theologia Scholastica Didactica* (1618) of Alsted (a foreign delegate at Dordt from Nassau-Wetteravia) is a prime example. Besides what was said above about this work, its scholastic character is evident in its actual style and organization. It begins with the principle of knowledge (the Word of God) and then treats its divisions (God and His actions). The analysis proceeds dichotomously to the theological details of the system. Each chapter opens with a number of precepts that give the definition of the topic and its divisions. This is followed by a section of rules consisting of principles and theological conclusions. Finally, in a commentary on the precepts and rules, texts

---

24. Antoine de Chandieu, *Opera Theologica* ([Heidelberg], 1593), 11, 2. On the closed and open hand metaphor (derived from Zeno) used to illustrate the difference between dialectic and rhetoric, see Wilbur Howell, *Logic and Rhetoric in England, 1500–1700* (New York: Russell & Russell, 1956), 15, 33, 293.

of Scripture and the best opinions of the Fathers and the Scholastics are brought to bear on the topic.

In 1609, Caspar Sibelius (a ministerial delegate from Overijssel) defended a Leiden disputation, *De Dei Praedestinatione*, which was presided over by Franciscus Gomarus (a leading Dutch theological delegate at Dordt). This disputation presents a definition of God's purpose, or predestination, and then analyzes its matter (its object and subject), form, motivating cause (*causa impulsiva*), ends, and effects (both internal and external). Then it divides the genus predestination into two species: election and reprobation. Each of these in turn receives the same kind of analysis as God's purpose.

In 1615, Jacob Trigland (a prominent ministerial delegate from Amsterdam) wrote a polemical work, *Christelycke ende Nootwendighe Verclaringhe*, against a 1614 resolution of the States of Holland and West Friesland that called for mutual toleration. A typical pattern recurs in Trigland's work. He first repeats an argument (thesis) from the resolution, as well as its supporting testimonies from Scripture, the church fathers, councils, and recent theologians. Against this, he posits an antithesis that he attempts to prove by his own list of testimonies from Scripture and other authorities. Then follows a rebuttal of each proof used by the resolution. Finally, Trigland supplies additional testimonies to support the antithesis.[25]

In 1591, Sibrandus Lubbertus (a Dutch theological delegate from Franeker) published his *De Principiis Christianorum Dogmatum Libri Septem, Scholastice & Theologice Collati cum Disputationibus Roberti Bellarmini*. In countering the arguments of Bellarmine, Lubbertus described his scholastic approach in the preface in this way:

> That I may properly clear away these artifices, I have first of all carefully searched out the state of the controversy. Then I have dialectically set forth and refuted Bellarmine's arguments, having been laid bare sophistically to all. I have often borrowed refutations from others, and when the refutations of others seemed less than complete to me I have devised new ones. After this, I have pointed out the view of the orthodox church and confirmed it with arguments. I

---

25. Jacob Trigland, *Opuscula* (Amsterdam, 1640), 1:67–343.

have done all this in a scholastic style [*stylo scholastico*], without bitterness and insult.[26]

The work itself follows the *quaestio* format, with formal syllogisms (each called an *argumentum*) to prove his position and disprove Bellarmine's.

In 1616, Lubbertus presided at Franeker over a disputation, *De Aeterna Dei Praedestinatione*. It defines predestination, divides it into two parts—election and reprobation—and then analyzes each according to its definition, (motivating) cause, effects, certainty, and ends (final causes).[27]

Documents of the Synod of Dordt

Most members of the synod realized that an ecclesiastical assembly required a more popular treatment of theological issues than that found in the schools.[28] Consequently, most of the synod's documents are quite popular in character. Nevertheless, evidence of a scholastic tendency can be found, especially in some of the in-house theological investigations of the controverted Five Articles. To gauge the extent of this, the issue needs to be considered in a variety of synodical documents.

British Advice

A theme running through some of the advice given to the synod by the British delegates was that scholastic issues ought to be kept in the universities, not in the church.

---

26. Sibrandus Lubbertus, *De Principiis Christianorum Dogmatum Libri Septem, Scholastice & Theologice Collati cum Disputationibus Roberti Bellarmini* (Franeker, 1591), preface.

27. On Lubbertus's use of a scholastic method, see C. van der Woude, *Sibrandus Lubbertus* (Kampen: Kok, 1963), 372–76. On the other hand, Lubbertus's *Commentarius in Catechesin Palatino-Belgicam* (Franeker, 1618) is much less scholastic.

28. On 10 January 1619, for example, the Bremen delegates gave this advice to the synod on how to deal with the Remonstrant affair: "Just as we perceive it was formerly done in ecclesiastical synods and in preparing confessions, we should in this whole synodical handling of the affair attend especially to those things which contribute to popular [*popularem*] instruction, which can be understood by anyone, even one imbued with too little or no education, and can be devoutly recommended among the masses, and which serve to promote comfort and godliness"; *ADSND*, 2/2:755.

Before their departure for the Netherlands, the British delegation received instructions from King James I, one of which read:

> Your advice shall be to those churches, that their ministers do not deliver in the pulpit to the people those thinges for ordinary doctrines, which are the highest points of schooles, and not fitt for vulgar capacity, but disputable on both sides.[29]

Bishop George Carleton, the head of the delegation, reiterated this advice in his address to the States General of the Netherlands on 6 November 1618:

> You are seriously to take heed, that your Doctors, leaving the simplicity of holy Scriptures, divert not upon abstruse and intricate quirkes.... At least, thus much are you carefully to looke to, that those who handle the Word of Life abstaine in their sermons to the people, from those deeper speculations, which pose the Schooles themselves, and our sharpest wits, and may with probabilitie on both sides be disputed; lest the Faith of the Church, which is stable and immooveable, seeme to be ambiguous and doubtfull.[30]

The theme surfaced again in a sermon delivered before the synod on 29 November by the British delegate Joseph Hall. He explicitly distinguished between popular and scholastic, and he warned that the sons of the church should not meddle with the subtleties of the schools:

> There are, to be sure, two sorts of theology, the one scholastic [*scholastica*], the other popular [*popularis*]. The latter seems to have in view the foundation of religion; the former the form and decorations of its exterior. The latter has in view what ought to be known; the former what can be known. Knowledge of the latter makes a Christian; knowledge of the former makes a debater. Or (if you prefer), the latter usually makes a theologian; the former refines a theologian.[31]

Discussions on Catechizing and Theological Training

The manner of catechizing was an early issue on the synod's agenda. After hearing advice from the various delegations, on 30 November

---

29. Anthony Milton, ed., *The British Delegation and the Synod of Dort (1618–1619)* (Woodbridge, England: Boydell Press, 2005), 93.
30. Milton, *British Delegation*, 121.
31. *Acta*, 1:43; *ADSND*, 2/2:470.

the synod adopted a statement on this matter. Among other things, it declared that "this threefold way of catechizing ought to be diligently observed: in the home [*domestica*] by parents, in the school [*scholastica*] by school teachers, and in the church [*ecclesiastica*] by pastors, elders, readers, or visitors of the sick."[32] In this reference to a "scholastic" way of catechizing, the term is obviously used in the first aforementioned sense of that which pertains to schools.

In their advice, the Genevans urged that, in catechism preaching, ministers should "refrain from continuous oratorical explanation of the Catechism" and "avoid obscure, scholastic, inquisitive questions."[33] Similarly, the four Dutch professors advised that rural pastors especially should be directed "to use a familiar and brief style accommodated to the capacity of rural and young people, and refrain in their catechetical explanations from excessively investigating the most weighty theological questions by extended debate [*disputatione*] in the presence of the common people."[34] Following such advice, the synod decided that catechism sermons should be "rather brief and accommodated as much as possible to the capacity, not only of adults, but also of youth."[35]

When the synod discussed the topic of theological training for the ministry on 3 December, Franciscus Gomarus strongly argued, by use of four formal syllogisms, against the idea that theology students should be allowed to preach in public worship services.[36]

The Speeches of the Theologians

After the Remonstrants were expelled from the synod, many of the academic theologians at Dordt were asked to speak on various theological issues in the controversy and to answer Remonstrant arguments.[37]

Observer John Hales and delegate Walter Balcanqual remarked on the varying styles of some of these speeches. Regarding the speeches by Gomarus and Lubbertus, Hales observed: "The order of discussing these

---

32. *ADSND*, 1:26. The same formulation appeared already in the advice of Bremen, Gomarus, and Adrian Smoutius. *ADSND*, 2/2:91, 100, 111.
33. *ADSND*, 2/2:90.
34. *ADSND*, 2/2:98.
35. *ADSND*, 1:29.
36. *ADSND*, 2/2:182.
37. These speeches are found in OSA, I.17.K.

arguments is by continued discourse after the manner of Latin Sermons, or rather of Divinity Lectures, such as are read in our Schools."[38] He noted that Antonius Thysius "spoke according to the same form as Sibrandus and Gomarus had done before"[39] and that John Davenant refuted certain Remonstrant distinctions "learnedly and fully."[40] Likewise, "the point of Reprobation was Scholastically and learnedly discust by Altingius."[41]

On the other hand, Abraham Scultetus's speech was different in style: "The manner of his discourse was oratorial, the same that he uses in his Sermons, not scholastical and according to the fashion of disputation and Schools. For this cause the question was neither deeply searcht into, nor strongly proved."[42] Likewise, Balcanqual remarked that Wolfgang Mayer discussed "rather like an Orator than a Schoolman"[43] and that Jean Diodati "did very sweetly, just as he useth to preach, not as Doctours use in the Schools."[44]

The most scholastic of these speeches was that of Marburg philosopher Rudolph Goclenius (known in his day as the "Christian Aristotle"), who refuted a Remonstrant syllogism "carefully from logical principles."[45] Using complex syllogistic arguments, he arrived at the dialectical conclusion that, while, on the one hand, eternal election and the decree of election are the same, on the other, the term "election" is

---

38. Hales, appendix, 2:83. The appendix of this work contains the letters of Hales and Balcanqual about the synod.

39. Hales, 2:85.

40. Hales, 2:91. A glance at this speech reveals that Davenant refuted Remonstrant views by means of syllogistic arguments; OSA, I.17.K.1 (third document).

41. Hales, 2:90.

42. Hales, 2:92.

43. Hales, 2:113.

44. Hales, 2:125. Diodati's perspective is evident in a letter he had written on 18 January 1619 to the English ambassador Dudley Carleton, urging him to use his influence to rid the synodical debates of scholastic questions: "It is necessary to curtail all superfluous, inquisitive and scholastic questions in order to go back to the simplicity and soundness of the faith. Here, we are churchmen, to deliberate ecclesiastically, and not in the shadow and dust of the school, to exercise our minds or our curiosities." Nicolas Fornerod, ed., *Registres de la Compagnie des Pasteurs de Genève* (Geneva: Droz, 2012), 14:268.

45. From the *Acta Authentica*, the original Acts of the Synod of Dordt, published in *ADSND*, 1:120: "*accurate ex principiis Logicis.*"

used in Scripture for the execution of the decree, and so it can be said that the decree of election is distinct from election itself.[46]

The Iudicia *of the Nineteen Delegations*
In preparation for the drafting of the Canons, the various delegations submitted their written judgments (*iudicia*) on each of the Five Articles in debate. The generally popular character of these *iudicia* may partly be explained by the fact that President Bogerman had advised that, in forming their *iudicia*, the delegations should reject false Remonstrant doctrine and state orthodox Reformed doctrine "in clear words accommodated to the capacity and edification of the common people, and support everything with very solid reasons and arguments."[47]

Nevertheless, most of the *iudicia* show certain scholastic influences, some more than others.[48] Many of them present the orthodox view over against the heterodox view in the form of theses and antitheses, followed by proofs and refutations. The proofs and refutations in most *iudicia* consist of a simple appeal to Scripture, or sometimes an appeal to early church fathers (the British do this), rather than logical argumentation. However, especially the Hesse, Emden, Gelderland, Utrecht, Overijssel, and Zeeland delegations also use formal syllogisms and other rational arguments to confirm truth and refute error. For example, Gelderland's *iudicium* on Article II of the Remonstrance uses six lengthy syllogisms to disprove the Remonstrant assertion that Christ died for all.[49] The famous practical syllogism appears in the Palatine, Emden, and Gelderland *iudicia*.[50]

Many of the *iudicia* show some evidence of causal thinking. Often the "cause" of election or reprobation, for example, is examined. In such references efficient causality is meant. Sometimes the discussion focuses on subtypes of efficient causality, such as the "motivating

---

46. OSA, I.17.K.1 (fifth document).
47. Hesse: 282.
48. The *iudicia* of the Dutch and foreign delegations are printed in the *Acta*, parts 2 and 3.
49. *Acta*, 3:93–95.
50. *Acta*, 2:23, 249; 3:26, 30. The Emden version of the practical syllogism is: "He who believes in the Lord Jesus will be saved. I truly believe in the Lord Jesus. Therefore I will be saved."

[*impulsiva*] cause," the "meriting [*meritoria*] cause," or the opposite "deficient cause." Traces of causal thinking also appear in occasional references to "means" and "effects." When compared, however, to the extensive use of the four Aristotelian causes (and their sub-causes) in academic writings of the period, it must be acknowledged that the documents of Dordt make limited use of such causal categories.

Perhaps the most scholastic is the Emden *iudicium* on Article I of the Remonstrance. It begins with a definition of predestination and then analyzes it according to its efficient cause, its object or matter, its highest end, and its two species—election and reprobation. Election, in turn, is defined and analyzed according to its efficient motivating cause, its matter or object, and five intermediate means between the decree of election and its end. Likewise, reprobation is defined, and four means or (secondary) causes are spelled out by which those left in their own ruin proceed to destruction. Then both election and reprobation are examined by a long series of *quaestiones*, some of which include proofs by formal syllogisms.[51]

Remonstrant Documents

Simon Episcopius, the leader of the Remonstrants who were summoned before the synod, expressed strong criticism of the current scholastic orientation within theology in a farewell address delivered to his Leiden students just before he left for Dordt:

> I saw that the truth of many—and the greatest—things in holy Scripture itself was made complicated, obscure, and confused by phraseology [*phrasibus*] elaborated with human diligence, by clever fashioning of words, by the artificial structures of the Loci Communes, by exquisite invention of terms and formulas—so much so that an Oedipus was often necessary to solve that theological riddle....
>
> Therefore, I have always thought that the simplicity of apostolic terminology [*terminorum*], which is easy for anyone, should be restored, and that logical and philosophical speculations and speech, which the universities and schools claim for themselves as their own, should be removed....

---

51. *Acta*, 2:60–77.

This was my first concern, to recall and draw you from that vain scholastic and sophistic theology back to the simplicity of the apostles.[52]

Likewise, in his 7 December oration before the synod, Episcopius stressed that those who most safely discuss difficult points of theology that exceed our understanding are those who treat them moderately and, "as much as possible, speak with Scripture," while intentionally avoiding disputes (*disputationes*) about them.[53]

In spite of Episcopius's critical attitude, a scholastic orientation is sometimes apparent in Remonstrant documents submitted to the synod. For instance, in the preface to a lengthy *Defense* of Articles IV and V, the Remonstrants commented on the style of this work:

> We have deliberately refrained from rhetorical orations, which often contain mere words and elaborate speech, and we have confined ourselves to the circle and style of those who debate [*disputantium*] and bring forward proof [*argumentantium*], so that we might not appear to seek some support for our cause in words and phraseology rather than in the content [*rebus*] itself.[54]

This debating style is evident especially in the use of formal syllogisms. For example, in a separate section on reprobation in the Remonstrant *Defense* of Article I, the author Carolus Niellius frequently employed syllogisms to confirm truth and particularly to refute error. Usually, he supplied detailed proof of the major and minor premises.[55]

The Remonstrants more openly appealed to reason than did the members of the synod. This may be seen, for instance, in Episcopius's 7 December oration:

> Only Scripture and sound reason [*recta ratio*], which waits on her as a handmaid, shall march before us at the head of our forces.

---

52. Simon Episcopius, *Operum Theologicorum Pars Altera* (Gouda and Rotterdam, 1665), 1:170–72. Episcopius delivered the address on 13 November 1618, the day the synod convened.

53. *Acta et Scripta*, 1:32.

54. *Acta et Scripta*, 1:195. This *Defensio* was submitted to the synod on 19 March 1619.

55. *Acta et Scripta*, 2:229–78.

As long as anything other than Scripture or solid reason is opposed to them, we will not move a foot.[56]

The Remonstrants made similar explicit appeals to Scripture and sound reason in other documents and in the debates on the floor of the synod.[57] A Remonstrant document presented to the state delegates on 3 January 1619 described Scripture and reason as follows: "Sound reason is a spark of the divine image and is the silent will of the eternal God [*Nummis*]. Scripture is the other voice of God and contains a fuller expression of the divine will."[58]

The Letter of the Palatine Delegation
When the Palatine theologians went home, they left a letter (dated 12 May 1619) for the synod, containing various admonitions about how to preserve orthodoxy and peace in the church. Among other things, they advised:

> Let the manner of teaching and learning in the universities be arranged so that effort might not be exerted more in antithesis than in thesis, and that antithesis might not be treated before thesis; likewise, let scholastic theology and its thorny and useless questions be eliminated. Instead, let sound and clear [*sana et plana*] theology, taught in imitation of Melanchthon and Ursinus, prevail.[59]

Beyond the foregoing documents, two separate incidents at the Synod of Dordt relate specifically to the issue of scholasticism—the *causa physica* debate and the Maccovius case.

---

56. *Acta et Scripta*, 1:37. On the role of reason in Episcopius's thought, see G. J. Hoenderdaal, "Arminius en Episcopius," *Nederlands Archief voor Kerkgeschiedenis* 60, no. 2 (1980): 228–35.
57. See, e.g., *Acta et Scripta*, 1:145, 148, 157; Hales, 2:60; *Historisch Verhael van't ghene sich toeghedraeghen heeft binnen Dordrecht, in de Jaeren 1618 ende 1619* ([Amsterdam], 1623), 133.
58. *Acta et Scripta*, 1:144.
59. Printed in H. H. Kuyper, *De Post-Acta of Nahandelingen van de Nationale Synode van Dordrecht in 1618 en 1619 Gehouden* (Amsterdam: Höveker and Wörmser, 1899), 514.

The *Causa Physica* Debate

In the discussions that led to the drafting of the Canons of Dordt, an interesting debate flared up among various members of the synod about the use of the scholastic category *causa physica* in theology. Details are found especially in the letters of British delegate Walter Balcanqual.

On 12 February, in deliberations on Article III/IV concerning how God brings about conversion in humans, Matthias Martinius of Bremen posed the issue in this way: "Does God act physically [*physice*] in human conversion? Are the exhortations, promises, and threats of the gospel a moral action?"[60] His answer was that God is the physical cause of conversion. In the next session on 13 February, Franeker theologian Sibrandus Lubbertus responded in this way:

> In his speech, he took exceptions at some things that D. Martinius of Bremen had spoken the day before, especially that he had said, "God was *causa physica conversionis*;" he delivered some reasons against it, and desired Martinius to give satisfaction to them, and to instruct him in that which he knew not before Martinius answered for himself; but between them both there were more words than sence, for they made it a meer philosophical speculation, like to keeping a philosophie act, much against the gravity of questions to be discussed in a synod. Martinius for the truth of his assertion appealed to [the Marburg philosopher] Goclenius there present, as being *princeps philosophorum*, who were not wont to be appealed to in synodical questions, and Goclenius...told us that Themistius, Averores, Alexander Aphrodisaeus, and many more were of Martinius his opinion; and his opinion true in philosophy, but yet he would not have it to prescribe in Divinity. Sibrandus fell upon Goclenius too, so after many words lost on all sides, the president cut them off.[61]

When the synod returned to the discussion of Article III/IV on 19 February, it was Gomarus's turn to speak:

> But Sibrandus desireth the President first to give him leave to adde some few things to that he had spoken the day before; now what he added was nothing but a renewing of that strife, which was between

---

60. Breitinger, 89. These questions reveal that the debate was based on the scholastic distinction between physical and moral action.
61. Balcanqual's account is found in Hales, 2:104–5.

him and Martinius in the last session: two things he alledged, first that he had been at Goclenius his lodging, conferring with him about that proposition, whether God might be called *causa physica* of humane actions, and he delivered certain affirmations pronounced by Goclenius tending to the negative. For the truth of his relation, he appealed to Goclenius there present, who testified that it was so; next, whereas Martinius had alledged a place out of [the respected Heidelberg Reformed theologian David] Pareus for the affirmative in *opera conversionis*, Sibrandus read a great many places out of Pareus tending to the contrary; and (no question it being plotted before) he entreateth that some of the Palatines…who were Pareus his colleagues, would speak what they did know of Pareus his mind concerning the said proposition. [The Palatine theologian Abraham] Scultetus beginneth with a set speech…. The summe of it was this, that he did know upon his own knowledge, that Pareus did hold the contrary of that which had been falsely fathered upon him in the synod, that he could not endure to hear his dearest colleague so much abused, as he had been by some men in the synod; moreover that he could not now dissemble the great grief he had conceived, that some in the synod went about to trouble sound Divinity with bringing in *tricas Scholasticas*, such as was to make God *causam physicam conversionis* (that was for Martinius); such *portenta vocabulorum* as *determinare* and *determinare voluntatem*; that some men durst say that there were some doubts in the fourth Article, which Calvin himself had not throughly satisfied, nor other learned Reformed doctors; that it was to be feared that they intended to bring in Jesuites Divinity in the Reformed churches, and to corrupt the youth committed to their charge, with a strange kind of Divinity; this last speech concerned [Bremen theologian] D. Crocius.[62] Scultetus delivered his mind in exceeding bitter & disgraceful words, and

---

62. In his journal, J. J. Breitinger gave the following account of Scultetus's speech: "In the name of the Palatines, Scultetus copiously discusses Pareus' opinion and severely reproves Martinius and the other men of Bremen, without mentioning their names, but recalling their phrases and words. He says that he is grieved in his soul that the metaphysics of the Jesuits is taught in Reformed schools, under the pretext of which youth are little by little given to drink papal poison; that it is hard to believe that the present controversies cannot be defined without the new terms *voluntas determinabilis*, *determinans*, *determinative* (these were used by Crocius), since in the Scriptures there are very many very clear ways of speaking [*phrasibus*]; that he never thought it would happen that orthodox theologians would find anything lacking in Calvin, as if he had not treated fully or suitably to these present controversies the teaching of man's conversion by free choice"; Zurich, Zentralbibliothek, MS B 235, 89.

repeated his bitterest sentences twice over. He having ended, Martinius with great modesty answered, first that he would read Pareus his own words, which he did; next that for Sibrandus, he wondred that he would now in publick bring these things up, since out of his love to peace, that very day he had sent his colleague Crocius to Sibrandus, with a large explication of that sence in which he had delivered that proposition, with which explication Sibrandus himself had sent him word that he was fully satisfied, and so he made account that that business had been peaceably transacted; all this while Crocius spoke nothing.[63]

Finally, Gomarus was given his turn to speak:

I think he delivered a speech against the Bremenses, which none but a madman would have uttered.... Whereas Martinius in his answer to Scultetus had not spoken one word against him, but only this, that he was sorry that one [Martinius himself] who had now 25 years been a professor of Divinity should be thus used for using a school term. Gomarus very wisely had a fling at that too, and telleth the synod that...he himself had been a professor not only 25 but thirty five years; next he falleth upon Crocius, and biddeth the synod take heed of these men that brought in these *monstra, portenta vocabulorum* the barbarisms of the schools of the Jesuits, *determinare & non determinare voluntatem*...at last he cut off himself I think for want of breath, and the President giveth *Celeberrimo Doctori Gomaro* many thanks for that his learned, grave, and accurate speech.

Bishop George Carleton of the English delegation then took issue with President Bogerman for praising Gomarus's speech. To this, Bogerman replied that "*celeberrimus D. Gomarus* had said nothing against men's persons, but their opinions, and therefore that he had said nothing worthy of reprehension."

Next in turn to speak was the Harderwijk theologian Antonius Thysius:

---

63. This quotation and the following ones regarding the 19 February session are from Balcanqual, 2:110–14. On this stormy session, the *Acta Authentica* reports only the following: "Between the Dutch professors and the Bremen theologians there was a debate about various questions concerning the explanation of Article Three & Four, and about the use of philosophy and philosophical terms in theological controversies"; *ADSND*, 1:128.

[He] very discreetly told the synod he was sorry Martinius should be so exagitated, for a speech which according to Martinius his explication was true. Just as Thysius was thus speaking, Gomarus and Sibrandus, who sat next him, pulleth him by the sleeve, talketh to him with a confused angry noise in the hearing and seeing of all the synod, chiding him that he would say so; afterward Thysius with great modesty desired Martinius to give him satisfaction of one or two doubtful sentences he had delivered, which Martinius thanking him for his courtesie fully did. The President was certainly on this plot against Martinius, for at that same time he did read out of a paper publickly a note of all the hard speeches Martinius had used.

By 23 February, the Bremen delegates were so offended that they were ready to leave for home. Some of the foreign theologians then requested the English delegation to try to reconcile the opposing parties. Balcanqual observed that "all the *Exteri* take to heart…that strangers should be used so disgracefully, for using two school terms, which are both very common." By 1 March, a private reconciliation was reached between the Bremen theologians and Scultetus, Gomarus, and Lubbertus, and no more is heard of this debate.[64]

From this incident one may draw several conclusions: (1) At the time of the Synod of Dordt, the introduction of new scholastic terminology into Reformed theology was cause enough to give rise to intense personal hostilities. (2) Even those opposed to the use of *causa physica* (a category that would also draw objections in the Maccovius case), especially Gomarus and Lubbertus, were influenced by other scholastic traits in their academic teaching (see above). Thus, their opposition to the use of *causa physica* must not be interpreted as an opposition to the whole scholastic orientation. (3) Interestingly, those Reformed theologians most sympathetic to the Remonstrants—the Bremen and English delegations—were also most open to the use of scholastic terminology in theology. On the other hand, those most critical of the Remonstrants—Gomarus, Lubbertus, and Scultetus— were the most suspicious of the introduction of scholastic terminology.

---

64. Hales, 2:114, 117.

The Maccovius Case

One of the best barometers of the Synod of Dordt's attitude toward Protestant scholasticism is found in the synod's handling of the Maccovius case.[65] At issue was Maccovius's use of certain hard sayings (*phrases duriores*) as well as the extremely scholastic style of his teaching. This case was considered immediately after the synod approved the Canons, when the foreign delegates were still present.

Johannes Maccovius (1588–1644) was a young Polish theologian who had learned scholastic theology primarily under the teaching of the Reformed theologian and philosopher Bartholomew Keckermann. In 1615, Maccovius became a professor at the University of Franeker. He soon fell into conflict with his older colleague Sibrandus Lubbertus due to differences in personality and theological views. Maccovius was supralapsarian; Lubbertus was infralapsarian. The conflict escalated in 1617 after Maccovius presided over two disputations, titled *De Praedestinatione* and *De Traductione Hominis Peccatoris ad Vitam*.

The latter disputation—drawn up and defended by English student Thomas Parker—was a particular source of contention because of its extensive reliance on scholastic terminology. Specifically, its analysis made use of the scholastic distinction between physical and moral

---

[65] The Maccovius case was carefully studied by J. Heringa in "De Twistzaak van den Hoogleeraar Johannes Maccovius, door de Dordrechtsche Synode, ten jare 1619 beslecht," *Archief voor Kerkelijke Geschiedenis* 3 (1831): 503–664. This study must be supplemented by the later investigations of Abraham Kuyper Jr., *Johannes Maccovius* (Leiden: D. Donner, 1899), 82–100; Klaas Dijk, *De Strijd over Infra- en Supralapsarisme in de Gereformeerde Kerken van Nederland* (Kampen: Kok, 1912), 206–20; Van der Woude, *Sibrandus Lubbertus*, 338–62; Sinnema, "Issue of Reprobation," 292–95; and Willem J. van Asselt, "On the Maccovius Affair," in *Revisiting the Synod of Dordt (1618–1619)*, ed. Aza Goudriaan and Fred van Lieburg (Leiden: Brill, 2011), 217–41. These studies made use of many of the manuscript materials, but all of them, except Sinnema and Van Asselt, overlooked important original documents preserved in OSA, I.17.C.16. Regarding Maccovius's way of teaching, see also F. Postma and J. Veenhof, "Disputen omtrent de predestinatie: Het logisch denken van Johannes Maccovius (1588–1644) en de doorwerking daarvan," in *Universiteit te Franeker 1585–1811*, ed. G. Th. Jensma, F. R. H. Smit, and F. Westra (Leeuwarden: Fryske Akademy, 1985), 249–63. On Maccovius's use of scholastic distinctions, see Willem J. van Asselt, Michael D. Bell, Gert van den Brink, and Rein Ferwerda, eds., *Scholastic Discourse: Johannes Maccovius (1588–1644) on Theological and Philosophical Distinctions and Rules* (Apeldoorn: Instituut voor Reformatieonderzoek, 2009).

action (*agens physice et moraliter*), as well as the categories *moviens*, *mobile*, *motus*, and *res motu facta*.

The disputation dealt with regeneration (or conversion) and consisted of fifty-six theses. Thesis 7 describes God's gracious work in the elect as a Motion (*Motio*), which therefore requires a Mover (*Movens*), that is, God; a Movable (*Mobile*), that is, man who is moved; a Movement (*Motus*), that is, the divine action of calling; and a Thing done by the Movement (*Res Motu Facta*), that is, the effect of the divine action, faith and good works. Thesis 28 deals with the question of whether the divine action or movement is physical or moral. It concludes that "this motion of the will for the act of conversion is a true physical effect of the first Being." Moral action is not enough; it only assists by encouraging the agent to move himself. Thesis 36 states that the physical movement is the power of the Spirit; the moral movement is the power of the Word.[66]

Young Parker had sought to defend these theses at Leiden University, but they were considered too extreme. The Leiden theologian Festus Hommius, however, directed him to Maccovius at Franeker. There Maccovius agreed to preside over the disputation, but only after adding to the theses the following apology:

> Because these theses dispute against the Jesuits among others, we therefore were compelled to retain their scholastic terms [*scholasticos terminos*], lest by changing them we might appear to pervert their sense or to express it less suitably. Therefore, readers are asked to bear this manner of proceeding with a fair mind.[67]

This apology was not enough to avert Lubbertus's opposition. Maccovius was called before Classis Franeker in 1618 and was charged with fifty errors, the list of which Lubbertus probably had a hand in drawing up. Thirty-three of the alleged errors were drawn from the Parker disputation, the rest from lectures and other disputations of Maccovius. Here are some examples of the alleged errors:

---

66. A copy of the disputation may be found in OSA, I.17.N.5. Reprinted in William Ames, *Disceptatio Scholastica de Circulo Pontificio* (Leiden, 1633). It is described by A. Kuyper Jr., *Maccovius*, 90–91.

67. Johannes Maccovius, presiding, *Theses Theologicae de Traductione Hominis Peccatoris ad Vitam* (Franeker, 1617), last page.

16. He teaches that regeneration is natural.
    Disp. *De Traductione Hominis*, theses 6 & 7.
    He calls God a mover.
    He calls unregenerate man a movable.
    He calls calling a movement.
    He calls regeneration a motion of man.
    He calls the reception of Christ a thing done by the movement.
    But these ways of speaking [*phrases*] are found neither in holy Scripture, nor in our confessions.
    Besides, they are absolutely absurd and dangerous, and they appear to be used in order that that which is absolutely spiritual and supernatural may be transformed into something corporeal and natural….

30. He teaches that efficacious calling is physical….

33. He teaches that our conversion is produced by a physical influence [*influx*] of God.[68]

Classis Franeker declared Maccovius guilty of the errors, but he appealed to the provincial synod of Friesland. It referred the case to the Frisian government, which, after a fruitless investigation, referred it in turn to the Synod of Dordt.[69]

At Dordt the case was taken up on 25 April 1619, and on the following day various documents referred to the synod were read, including the list of fifty errors and two replies by Maccovius, one short and one long. In these replies, he denied some of the alleged errors and explained others. In the short reply, Maccovius pointed out that thirty-three of the errors had been gathered from the (Parker) theses, which Festus Hommius and William Ames had approved in personal letters written to him.[70] In his long reply, Maccovius complained that his accusers misunderstood the distinction between physical and moral causality:

---

68. The list of errors is found in OSA, 1.17.C.16, 297–314.
69. Heringa, "Twistzaak," 589–94.
70. OSA, I.17.C.16, 279v.

Our theologians distinguish between physical and moral cause in this matter. They call *physical* that which really produces an effect, whether that be spirit or body, God or creature, and whether it be produced by omnipotent power or by finite or limited power. They call *moral* that which is the cause of a thing by urging, warning, admonishing. Otherwise, it is usually called the motivating [*impulsiva*] cause.[71]

Maccovius asserted that, thus understood, God is the cause of conversion both morally and physically. In support of the distinction, he appealed to Ames, Pareus, and Goclenius among "our theologians" and to Bellarmine and Suárez among the Catholics.

Also read was a letter to the Frisian authorities from the theological faculty at Heidelberg. The Heidelberg theologians declared that "instead of true, sound, perspicuous, and clear doctrine we find metaphysical searchings, as if from another world, and no doubt long deliberated aerobatics and subtleties" in the theses *De Traductione* publicly disputed by Maccovius. In response to Maccovius's apology at the end of the theses, they pointed out that many others had fruitfully disputed against the Jesuits by maintaining the pattern of sound words without such subtleties, which should especially be avoided in the presently uncertain state of the church.[72]

On 26 April, Maccovius submitted a new reply to the synod, the *Responsio Posterior*. In it he again pointed out that "our theologians" used the physical–moral distinction when dealing with conversion, and he answered the accusation about the use of non-scriptural terms in theology:

> He asks whether these words [i.e., *movens, mobile*, and *res motu facta*] are found in Scripture. A pitiable matter, Mr. Critic; for it is just as if anyone would wish to remove from theology the terms cause, object, effect, and use the argument that in Scripture neither the words cause, object, effect, nor other logical terms occur. This, of course, is worthy not of refutation, but of pity. It is certain, however, that you

---

71. OSA, I.17.C.16, 288v. Balcanqual also remarked that many of the alleged errors "were based on that very accepted [*receptissima*] distinction, *agentis physice & moraliter*, badly understood by the accuser"; Balcanqual, 2:157.

72. OSA, 1.17.C.16, 267–70. The letter is dated 27 November 1617, Old Style (=7 Dec. N.S.).

act in such a way. Consult the logicians, and you will see that they often refer to cause by the term "mover," object by the term "movable," and effect by the term "thing done by the movement."[73]

When the synod discussed the case on 26 and 27 April, many members spoke in defense of Maccovius, including the British delegates Balcanqual and Goad; the Swiss delegates Breitinger, Mayer, and Koch; Alsted of Nassau; Martinius of Bremen; and the Dutch delegates Hommius, Gomarus, Thysius, Lydius, and Voetius. According to one account,

> they first and last showed that not only the material of the theses, but also the style and scholastic mode of treatment had their approval.... Goad expressed his amazement to the Doctor in the Chair that the scholastic way of treating a matter should be objected to by any. Later speakers pointed out that this way was followed by our most learned and outstanding theologians, Zanchi, Sadelis [Chandieu], Daneau, Junius, Trelcatius, and others, and that if Sibrandus Lubbertus himself had not fought with this weapon against the philosophical and scholastic madnesses of Vorstius, which were many, he would have gained little ground.[74]

On 27 April, the case was referred to a committee of six, consisting of the foreign theologians Scultetus, Stein, and Breitinger (of Heidelberg, Kassel, and Zurich, respectively) and the Dutch delegates Gomarus, Thysius, and Van Mehen. Meanwhile, Gisbertus Voetius reported to the synod that William Ames, who served as theological advisor to President Bogerman, had approved the Parker theses and was ready to defend them.[75] A written defense by Ames was submitted to the committee. Here Ames argued that Maccovius could not be blamed, because Parker accepted full responsibility. Moreover, in the two years that elapsed since the disputation, no one at Franeker had followed such a mode of treating theology, and so no new method of

---

73. OSA, I.17.N.3, point 16.
74. Report by Matthew Nethenus, based on the (now lost) journal of the ministerial delegate Gisbertus Voetius, in Nethenus, "*Praefatio Introductoria*" to William Ames, *Opera* (Amsterdam, 1658). The translation is that of Douglas Horton, trans., *William Ames by Matthew Nethenus, Hugo Visscher and Karl Reuter* (Cambridge: Harvard Divinity School, 1965), 9.
75. Hales, 2:159.

discussion was introduced by Parker's example. Ames went on to present a strong defense of the scholastic style of the theses:

> Aside from the heresies, the accusers also affirm that many other false and contradictory statements are contained in the theses, that the method is inappropriate, the thoughts obscure and ambiguous, and that philosophical, metaphysical and scholastic words are often used....
>
> Philosophical, metaphysical, scholastic—these are various adjectives meaning the same thing, in which there is no ground for any grave accusation by anyone. And this for the following reasons:
>
>> 1. Because the critics do not explain whether they wish to eliminate all plainly logical and philosophical terms from theological disputations or only those which are used in these theses. If the former, they judge not wisely, and if only the latter, not fairly.
>>
>> 2. Because on this score, the youth in question cannot be censured without a prior condemnation of treatises by Zanchi, Sadelis, Junius, and other learned men, which they have left to us, to our great benefit, on subjects of this sort written similarly against Sophists. Mr. Sibrandus himself, when he disputes with Vorstius, copiously draws from Suarez, Fonseca, and like authors whatever he thinks has to do with the matter in hand, and gives highest praise to Eglisemmius, whose writings contain nothing but lofty metaphysical and scholastic speculations. Recently indeed, he has held public disputations on the divine decree as the Being of reason and similar subjects.
>>
>> 3. Because this manner of disputing is acceptable in various universities, and these the noblest. This is especially true of England, where Parker, as a matter of fact, once studied. To condemn the method in this synod cannot but be a graceless act toward them.
>>
>> 4. Because there is almost no word in the whole disputation so philosophical or metaphysical that it cannot be cited in some approved theologian. Let those words which give the chief offense be pointed out and this will be proved.
>>
>> 5. Because the words used in these theses are so apt that it would be difficult for any of the accusers to set forth the same sentiment

> with other more perspicuous and equally brief ones. Other words, if I may say so, would be dangerous.[76]
>
> If any sin is involved here, it is a sin committed against grammar or rhetoric rather than theology; and it would seem to be beneath the dignity of this venerable synod to institute censure for such errors; nor has the synod so much leisure from graver matters that it can be concerned with these.
>
> The sum of it is that Thomas Parker—since he is a godly, learned, and modest youth, endowed with many virtues, since he is an Englishman and now has his home in England, since he has stood for the truth with all his might and combated errors even in these theses, and since he has done nothing more than to try to defeat his adversaries with their own weapons, though this is not the custom of certain others—Parker should not, I say, on the pretext of a Manlian severity in order to please his accusers, be treated with such great dishonor, that it may appear that he has deserved any synodical censure.[77]

Ames's arguments were not fully persuasive. On 30 April, the committee submitted its written judgment to the synod. It declared Maccovius free of heresy but nevertheless deserving of rebuke for his scholastic manner of teaching and for certain offensive statements:

> Doctor Maccovius has sinned in that he gave some people cause for such suspicions by having said some things obscurely or ambiguously or without enough explanation; also, in that he has supported by his presiding and by his authority that scholastic and dangerous mode of discussion and teaching about sacred matters, which is considered by some to be the ground of the misfortune in the Dutch church....
>
> Therefore, the committee judges that Dr. Maccovius should be strongly admonished: to use in his teaching a perspicuous, clear, and plain kind of language, and to speak with the Prophets, Christ and the Apostles rather than with Bellarmine, Suarez, and the like, whom he appeals to.[78]

The committee was then charged with the task of seeking a reconciliation between Maccovius and Lubbertus. In the negotiations that

---

76. Ames himself, in his *Coronis ad Collationem Hagiensem* (Leiden, 1618), 170, described the moral–physical distinction and applied it to the efficacy of God's grace.

77. This document is printed in Nethenus's preface to Ames. The translation (slightly amended) is that of Horton, *William Ames*, 10–11.

78. OSA, I.17.C.16, 261–62; printed in Dijk, *Strijd*, 212–13.

followed, it was found necessary to drop the first committee judgment and come up with a compromise formula acceptable to both parties.[79] Thus, on 4 May, the committee came to the synod with a toned-down final judgment, in which Maccovius acquiesced for the sake of peace. This judgment again declared Maccovius free of heresy, but it clearly softened the earlier warning against scholastic language:

> Maccovius should be admonished not to use ways of speaking [*phrasibus*] which cause a scandal to younger men.... In his teaching, let him use the kind of language [*genere dicendi*] which conforms to the Holy Scriptures, perspicuous, plain, the kind accepted in orthodox universities....[80]

The synod unanimously approved this judgment.

From the Maccovius case, several conclusions may be drawn: (1) A moderate scholastic style was in widespread use among orthodox Reformed theologians in the early seventeenth century, and it was generally considered acceptable, including by many leading figures at the Synod of Dordt. (2) The strong scholastic orientation of the Parker disputation, though approved by some, was generally considered excessive. (3) For the sake of achieving a reconciliation between Maccovius and Lubbertus, the synod approved only a mild warning against Maccovius's scholastic style. (4) In this particular case, the Synod of Dordt did not reject the emerging trend of Reformed scholasticism but only warned against an extreme expression of it.

The Canons of Dordt and Reformed Scholasticism

In the Canons of Dordt, the synod presented its judgment on the points in dispute in the Arminian controversy. Though theologically precise, the style of the Canons is popular in character, partly because many biblical allusions and quotations are incorporated into the text.[81] The biblical quality of the Canons is especially evident in that they usually confirm doctrinal points and refute errors by a simple appeal to

---

79. Dijk, *Strijd*, 214–16.
80. OSA, I.17.C.16, 263; printed in Dijk, *Strijd*, 216.
81. For a description and list of the biblical allusions and quotations in the Canons, see the *Acts of Synod 1985* of the Christian Reformed Church (Grand Rapids: CRC Publications, 1985), 384–87.

Scripture. Nevertheless, the Canons do not escape all scholastic influences. Several areas are worth examining.[82]

The Intended Popular Character of the Canons

On 22 March, President Bogerman dictated to the synod a draft of the Canons that he had prepared. Some members of the synod immediately complained that Bogerman wished to draw up the Canons himself and merely seek the synod's approval of them. Expressing his frustration that the foreign theologians might not have input, Balcanqual wrote: "Their Canons they would have them so full charged with Catechetical speculations, as they will be ready to burst."[83] The complaints led to a decision to appoint a nine-man drafting committee.

Before dictating his draft, Bogerman made some remarks about how the Canons should be drawn up. Attention must be paid, he said, especially to the edification of the Dutch churches, because the synod was called to restore peace in the churches. "The order and style of these Canons ought to be adapted to the instruction of these churches. Let everything be presented plainly and simply, and at the same time not too meagerly, so that the Canons may not be scholastic(?) or academic, but ecclesiastical [*scholastici(?) seu academici sed ecclesiastici*]."

In the next session, Bishop George Carleton of the English delegation presented his thoughts about the character of the Canons. Among other things, he suggested that nothing should be synodically decided concerning what can be debated *probabiliter* (e.g., the order of the divine decrees); that the style of the Canons should be popular, not scholastic (*Canonum stylus sit popularis non scholasticus*); that the Canons should not be long or prolix; and that they should begin with man's creation, followed by the fall.[84]

It is clear that the drafters of the Canons—both Bogerman and Carleton were on the drafting committee—operated with the

---

82. Andreas J. Beck, "Reformed Confessions and Scholasticism: Diversity and Harmony," *Perichoresis* 14, no. 3 (December 2016): 30–34, discusses the scholastic background of the Canons.

83. Hales, 2:141.

84. These details concerning Bogerman and Carleton are reported in the journal of the Dutch delegate Caspar Sibelius, found in the Regionaal Archief Dordrecht, MS 1113, 90r, 92r; printed in Dijk, *Strijd*, bijlage C.

popular–scholastic distinction and that they intended the Canons to be popular (or ecclesiastical) rather than scholastic in character.

The Order of Chapter I of the Canons

The popular character of the Canons is evident in the order of the first chapter. It begins not with God's decree in eternity but rather with the historical reality of the fall. The chapter moves on to the sending of God's Son, who is offered to humanity in the proclaimed Word, and then treats the response of humans in faith or unbelief. In the sixth article it finally ascends to God's eternal decree of election and reprobation in order to explain the historical fact that some receive the gift of faith, while others do not. On the level of the decree, election is treated first, then reprobation.[85]

There is a striking resemblance between the train of thought in the first chapter and that found in the Palatine *iudicium*, which added an appendix that spelled out "the manner of popularly [*populariter*] teaching the doctrine of predestination." Here also the suggested order begins with the fall; moves to the promised Son as Mediator, who is offered in the proclaimed Word; continues with faith as a gift of God; and finally rises to election from eternity, which is discussed before turning to reprobation.[86] The fact that the Palatines called this the popular manner of teaching this doctrine indicates that Chapter I of the Canons was constructed in a popular rather than scholastic manner, as Bogerman and Carleton had advised.[87]

The popular character of the Canons does not mean, however, that no scholastic thinking was involved in the formation of the Canons. In later years, Jacob Trigland, a Dutch member of the drafting committee, explained that the Canons followed the order and method of Melanchthon and Bullinger—namely, "climbing from below to above,

---

85. The Latin text of the Canons is printed in J. N. Bakhuizen van den Brink, ed., *De Nederlandse Belijdenisgeschriften in Authentieke Teksten* (Amsterdam: Ton Bolland, 1976), 225–84.

86. *Acta*, 2:22–23.

87. See W. Robert Godfrey, "Popular and Catholic: The *Modus Docendi* of the Canons of Dordt," in *Revisiting the Synod of Dordt*, 243–60, for fuller analysis of the parallels between the Palatine advice and the Canons.

from effect to causes."[88] This description of the order as ascending from effects to causes betrays the fact that behind the popularly written Canons lay, in the minds of the drafters, a somewhat scholastic understanding of their order.

By the time of the Synod of Dordt, the idea was well established in Reformed theology that predestination could be taught by either one of two methods. The synthetic method, which descends *a priori* from causes to effects (as in Ephesians), was to be used in the schools for the sake of knowledge by those who could eat solid food. The analytic method, which ascends *a posteriori* from effects to causes (as in Romans), was to be used for the common people as the best way to confirm their faith and give consolation. Johannes Polyander, another Dutch member of the Canons' drafting committee, had outlined these two methods in a disputation on predestination that he defended under Theodore Beza in 1590 as a student in Geneva.[89] For Polyander, the popularly intended Canons would obviously follow the analytic method.

The Debate about the Last Canon of Chapter II
After the drafting committee submitted its final draft of the Canons on 16 April, there was some debate in the synod about the last rejected error (canon) of Chapter II. This debate centered on the rather scholastic issue of the nature of the necessity—absolute or hypothetical—of Christ's incarnation for human redemption. The disputed canon, which was a last-minute addition, rejected the opinion of those who maintained "that likeness [*similitudinem*] to our nature in Christ was not necessary for the sufficiency of the price of our redemption." According to Balcanqual's account, the British delegation stated "that this was the first time they had seen it, and to them it

---

88. Jacob Trigland, *Kerckelycke Geschiedenissen* (Leiden, 1650), 1138–39: "namelijke van beneden opklimmende nae boven, vande effecten tot de oorsaecken."
89. *Theses Theologicae in Schola Genevensi…sub D.D. Beza & Antonio Fayo… propositae & disputatae* (Geneva, 1591), 21. The application of the analytic and synthetic methods to predestination can also be found in Georg Sohn, *Opera* (Herborn, 1609), 2:996–97; in Daniel Tossanus, *Doctrina de Praedestinatione* (Hanover, 1609), 21–22; and in Gomarus's disputation theses *De Praedestinatione Dei* (Leiden, 1604), thesis II, and *De Dei Praedestinatione* (Leiden, 1609), thesis IV.

appeared to be more a matter of scholastic speculation than of synodical inquiry," and so they desired more time to consider it.[90]

When the last canon was again discussed two days later, the British stood alone against the rest of the synod.

> The British theologians debated the matter very much. They asserted that if the canon were to be understood of an absolute necessity, that is, such as would deprive God of all power of acting otherwise, before the supposition [*ante suppositione*] of any sure decree and will, we ought not rashly to restrict God's absolute power [*absoluta potentia*]; that this is rather a matter of scholastic speculation, and therefore it should not go into the synodical Canons, especially since certain Fathers and some Reformed Doctors thought that likeness to our nature in this sense was not simply and absolutely necessary. But if the canon were to be understood of a hypothetical necessity, that is, from the supposition [*ex suppositione*] of the decree and will surely revealed to us in Scripture (in which sense they thought the word "necessity" was used in holy Scripture in this matter), they think the canon is true, but that it in no way strikes the Remonstrants, who only reject absolute necessity.... And therefore, they think it most advisable to omit this canon. Much was said about this question by many, all of which the British replied to. Most opinions, however, wished to retain that canon. The President advised that it be expressed in such a way that everyone can be satisfied.[91]

Rather than adopt an amended version, on 23 April the synod, upon the recommendation of the drafting committee, finally decided to delete the last canon.[92] Thus the final edition of the Canons avoided this scholastic issue of absolute and hypothetical necessity.

The Canons and Causal Thinking

In the early seventeenth century, there were two basic ways in which Reformed theology utilized causal thinking:

---

90. Hales, 2:148.
91. Hales, 2:149–50.
92. Hales, 2:153–54. The reason for the deletion is not stated. There was considerable pressure at this time to reach a consensus on the last unresolved points so that a synodically approved copy of the Canons could be sent to the States General.

The four causes as a heuristic tool for analysis. A theological topic, or commonplace, was often treated by way of a definition of the topic and then a division of the definition by analyzing it according to the four Aristotelian causes. The basis of this pedagogical method was that, in the Aristotelian tradition, to know something is to know its causes.[93] In the seventeenth century, the four causes were frequently subdivided into various sub-causes. For example:

Efficient cause (often called "cause" or "author")
- principal efficient or highest cause
- instrumental cause
- motivating (*impulsiva*) cause

Material cause (often simply called "matter")
- object and subject

Formal cause (often simply called "form")
- internal and external form

Final cause (often simply called "end")
- highest end and proximate or subordinate end

Such analysis often included a separate treatment of effects, adjuncts, uses, etc. Johannes Wollebius's *Compendium Theologiae Christianae* (1626) is an excellent example of this kind of pedagogical analysis.

Causality as a comprehensive framework. In this kind of causal thinking, all of reality is viewed in terms of the causal framework: from the highest cause, through secondary causes, to the ultimate end or final cause. This chain of causality encompasses the whole history of redemption. God's will, or His eternal decree, is the "highest cause." Creation and history are the "effects," or the "execution," of the eternal decree within

---

93. Aristotle, *Posterior Analytics*, I,2; II,11; *Physics*, I,1; II,3; *Metaphysics*, I,3; Thomas Aquinas, *Summa Theologiae*, II/I, Q. 55, art. 5. Likewise, the Reformed theologian Peter Martyr Vermigli, in the locus on predestination in his *Loci Communes* (London, 1583), 443, explains that he will examine the causes of predestination, "for nothing can be known which is not known through its causes." See also Girolamo Zanchi, *De Naturali Auscultatione* (Strasbourg, 1554), prefatio, e vii.

time. God's glory is the "end" of history; salvation and condemnation are "subordinate ends." To attain this end, God uses "means," or "secondary causes," or "instruments"— that is, ordained creaturely means through which the highest cause becomes executed or carried out (e.g., calling and faith). In teaching, one may approach this scheme from the top or the bottom. One method is to "descend" from cause to effects (the prerogative of theologians); the other method is to "ascend" from effects to cause (advisable in preaching and in teaching the uneducated). This decree-execution scheme is clearly expressed in Theodore Beza's more dogmatic works.[94]

Is there evidence of either of these ways of causal thinking in the Canons? First, it must be observed that the popularly intended Canons consciously seek to avoid the explicit use of both ways of causal thinking. Moreover, one must allow for the usage of the term *causa* in an innocent sense, unencumbered with the baggage of the Aristotelian causes or of the decree-execution scheme (e.g., III/IV, 7).

The Canons reveal scarcely any evident use of the four causes as a heuristic tool for analysis. They do not explicitly analyze the definitions of election and reprobation in articles I, 7 and I, 15 in terms of the four causes. Yet such analysis clearly underlies the form of the definitions. Thus, in article I, 15, for example, one could identify God as the principal efficient cause of reprobation, His good pleasure as its motivating cause, the non-elected part of fallen humanity as its matter or object, the decree to pass over (often called preterition) and the decree to condemn (often called predamnation) as its twofold form, and the displaying of God's justice as its highest end. Such analysis was common in the Reformed predestination literature of the period, and traces of it appear in the various *iudicia* submitted by the delegations to the synod on Article I (especially that of Emden).[95] A trace is

---

94. Especially Beza's *Summa Totius Christianismi* (1555) and his *De Praedestinationis Doctrina* (1582), printed in his *Tractationes Theologicae* (Geneva, 1582), 1:170–205, and 3:402–47. On this framework, see Donald Sinnema, "God's Eternal Decree and its Temporal Execution: The Role of this Distinction in Theodore Beza's Theology," in *Adaptations of Calvinism in Reformation Europe: Essays in Honour of Brian G. Armstrong*, ed., Mack P. Holt (Aldershot: Ashgate, 2007), 55–78.

95. See chapters 2 and 3 of my dissertation, "Issue of Reprobation," regarding the Reformed literature on reprobation; and see chapter 8 for an analysis of the Canons' article I, 15.

also evident in article I, 10 of the Canons, which explicitly identifies God's good pleasure as the "cause" (i.e., motivating cause) of election.

Some influence of the causality framework also shows through the popular language of the Canons at certain points. It should be remembered that the Arminian controversy arose in part as an Arminian reaction to the decree-execution theology of such Reformed theologians as Beza, Perkins, and Gomarus. The Canons, as a judgment of the Arminian position, could hardly ignore the causal problematics of the controversy.

The following evidence shows traces of such causal thinking:

(i) A member of the drafting committee (Trigland) could describe the order of Chapter I as ascending from effects to causes (see above).

(ii) The various references to God's decree (*decretum*), purpose (*propositum*), good pleasure (*beneplacitum*), plan (*consilium*), will (*voluntas*), or intention (*intentio*) sometimes clearly fit the decree-execution pattern (e.g., I, 8), although the very use of such terms does not necessarily reflect this pattern.

(iii) Article I, 5 states: "The cause [*causa*] or blame for this unbelief…is not at all in God, but in man." The early draft dictated by Bogerman simply read: "The blame for this unbelief…is in man."[96] Later, when the drafting committee added "not at all in God," it also added "cause," in order to reject more explicitly the common Remonstrant accusation against orthodox Reformed theology that it makes God the cause of unbelief.

(iv) The draft of article I, 6 dictated by Bogerman began with the words: "What God does within time, He decreed from eternity to do, 'for He knows all His works from eternity' (Acts 15:18)." This is the classic decretal principle.[97] These words were changed in the final Canons to read: "That some receive from God the gift of faith within time, and others do not, proceeds from His eternal decree."

---

96. Bogerman's dictated draft is preserved in OSA, I.5, 743–47.

97. Bogerman's dictated draft: "Quod autem Deus in tempore facit, illud ab aeterno facere decrevit; omnia enim opera sua novit ab aeterno. Act. 15:13 (*sic*, 18)." The decretal principle is found frequently in predestination literature of the period. It affirms that, whatever God by His will has decreed from eternity, He executes within the course of time; in other words, everything that happens within time is the outcome of what He has eternally decreed.

This change specified what God does within time and made the connection to the preceding article more explicit. The decretal principle still underlies the thought, although it now appears in a popularized form. The basic argument remains the same, and the same Acts 15 text is retained as proof. The popular character of the final version is also evident in the word "proceeds" (*provenit*), which is a popular way of saying "was caused," because the whole article is an answer to the question: What is the cause of the distinction between those who receive faith and those who do not?

(v) Article I, 7 presents in popularized form a definition of election that reflects the causal pattern. The definition consists of two parts. Election is God's purpose or decree first concerning the (subordinate) *end* (salvation), and then concerning the *means* to this end (effectual calling, the granting of faith, justification, sanctification, and glorification). The ultimate end of election is to demonstrate God's mercy and to give praise to his grace. Such a definition of election is evident already in many of the *iudicia* on which the Canons are based.

(vi) Article I, 9 denies the Remonstrant claim that foreseen faith or obedience is a prerequisite "cause" of election. Instead, faith, holiness, and eternal life are "fruits and effects" (*effectus*) that "flow forth" (*profluunt*) from election. The term "fruits" is a popular way of saying "effects" (cf. I, 12; I, rej. 5).

(vii) Article I, 15 denies that God is the "author" (or cause) of sin (as does the Canons' Conclusion). The Remonstrants made this accusation because they gave a logically consistent interpretation to the causal thinking of decree-execution theology: If God's decree is the cause of what happens in history, then God is the cause also of sin.[98]

(viii) Article II, 9 points out that God's plan is powerfully carried out (*impletum*), thus popularly emphasizing the effective causality of God's decree.

(ix) Article III/IV, 10 gives clear expression to the decretal principle that God decreed from eternity to do what He does within time:

---

98. It may be noted that Bogerman's earliest draft of article I, 15 (found in OSA, I.5, 750) presented reprobation as a logical consequence of election: "From this doctrine of election it necessarily follows that..." In his dictated draft, however, Bogerman changed this and based reprobation on Scripture. See chapter 8 of my dissertation for an analysis of the formation of the Canons' articles I, 6 and I, 15.

"Just as from eternity He elected His own in Christ, so within time He effectually calls them, grants them faith and repentance, and…brings them into the kingdom of His Son."

(x) Article III/IV, 14 states that faith is to be considered a gift of God "in the sense that He who works both willing and acting and, indeed, works all things in all people effects [*efficiat*] in man both the will to believe and the belief itself."

(xi) Article III/IV, 17 explicitly deals with the temporal "means" (*media*) by which God brings about His supernatural work of regeneration in the elect.

(xii) The whole of Chapter V deals with God's faithful preservation of His elect so that they persevere to the end (*ad finem*).

(xiii) Occasionally the Canons use the term "cause" in describing the Remonstrant position (I, 9; I, rej. 5; I, rej. 9; III/IV, rej. 9). The last-mentioned error even speaks of "the order of causality" (*ordine causalitatis*). In all these cases, the opposite Reformed position—that God's good pleasure or grace is the cause—may be implied.

(xiv) The Conclusion of the Canons denies the Remonstrant accusation that Reformed theology holds that, "in the same manner [*eodem modo*] in which election is the source and cause of faith and good works, reprobation is the cause of unbelief and ungodliness." Although the *eodem modo* relationship is rejected in the Conclusion, the first half of the statement, that election is the cause of faith and good works, is not.

In summary, it is clear that the Canons avoid explicit causal thinking, except perhaps for several explicit references to "cause" (understood as efficient cause), "means," and "effects." Yet traces of causal thinking are evident enough in the popular language of the Canons that it may be concluded that the decree-execution framework lies in the background of the Canons.

The Admonition in the Canons' Conclusion
The admonition in the second to last paragraph of the Conclusion mildly warns against extreme scholastic language:

> Finally, this synod urges all fellow ministers in the gospel of Christ to deal with this teaching in a godly and reverent manner, in the universities as well as in the churches; to do so, both in their speaking

and writing, with a view to the glory of God's name, holiness of life, and the comfort of anxious souls; to think and also speak with Scripture according to the analogy of faith [*cum Scriptura secundum fidei analogiam*]; and finally, to refrain from all those ways of speaking [*phrasibus*] which go beyond the bounds set for us by the genuine sense of the Holy Scriptures and which could give impertinent sophists a just occasion to scoff at the teaching of the Reformed Churches or even to bring false accusations against it.[99]

The Conclusion was approved before the Maccovius case came on the synod's agenda, so that specific issue may not have been in mind. The above exhortation was directed especially against the use of hard sayings (*phrases duriores*), such as those imprudently expressed by certain Reformed theologians.[100] Yet, since some of the hard sayings arose from scholastic ways of thinking, the Conclusion also exhorts those who use scholastic terminology and categories to stay within the limits of Scripture.

Some General Conclusions

On the basis of a wide range of evidence from Dordt, we may draw some general conclusions about Reformed scholasticism in the early seventeenth century:

1. While it is fruitful to define the nature of Reformed scholasticism by identifying its basic characteristics or methods of analysis, a full assessment should also consider contemporary awareness of this phenomenon. The Synod of Dordt demonstrates a broad spectrum of (sometimes rather strong) opinion about this scholastic orientation.

2. At the Synod of Dordt, the scholastic orientation was understood to include: a presentation of truth and error by theses and antitheses; syllogistic proofs of doctrine and refutation of error; a precise exposition of theological topics by definition and causal analysis, as well as by use of certain philosophical categories and distinctions; and speculative academic questions. In particular, a prominent use of such

---

99. Bakhuizen van den Brink, *Belijdenisgeschriften*, 278–80.
100. Dijk, *Strijd*, 187–205.

philosophical terminology in theology, along with superfluous scholastic questions, drew criticism of excessive scholastic tendencies.

3. Contemporary writings reveal that a fundamental distinction is to be made between scholastic and popular. Behind a popular style may lie a scholastic theological analysis. Thus, a theologian may be both popular and scholastic, depending on the social context. In church, for example, he may deliver sermons in a popular style, while in the university context his theological writings may be rather scholastic in character. While the documents of the Synod of Dordt, including the Canons, are generally of a popular nature, the theologians of Dordt could also be scholastic in their academic teaching, and this orientation sometimes surfaces at Dordt.

4. A moderate scholastic orientation was widespread among Reformed theologians in the early seventeenth century. The Synod of Dordt did not reject this moderate scholastic orientation, but it did warn against extreme expressions of this way of thinking.

In seeking to understand historically how scholasticism was received in Reformed circles at the time of the Synod of Dordt, this study has not addressed certain questions that are important for an appraisal of the effect of scholasticism on Reformed theology. One question concerns the relationship between popular and scholastic styles. Was the popular understanding of religious truth scholasticized by deepened reflection, or was scholastic theological analysis popularized? Another question is whether and to what extent a scholastic orientation affects theological content.[101] Was scholastic thinking detrimental to Reformed theology, was it beneficial, or was it merely a matter of style and method that left the theological content basically unaffected? More systematic reflection is needed in these areas.

---

101. On the relationship of method and content in scholasticism, see Richard A. Muller, *Calvin and the Reformed Tradition: On the Work of Christ and the Order of Salvation* (Grand Rapids: Baker Academic, 2012), 29–33.

CHAPTER 10

The Church Order of Dordt in Historical Perspective

Besides the Canons of Dordt, the most important and long-lasting contribution of the Synod of Dordt was the Church Order of Dordt. The synod dealt with church order matters in its final sessions.

The Formation of the Church Order

The Church Order of Dordt was not a new church order but a revision of the 1586 Church Order of the Synod of The Hague, the last national synod held more than thirty years earlier. However, the formation of the Church Order of Dordt has direct roots that go back further, to the national Synod of Emden (1571).[1]

Church polity in the Netherlands was also shaped by earlier church orders drawn up in the broader Reformed tradition, in countries with Reformed populations, and in Reformed refugee communities. The church orders introduced by Calvin in his reform program upon his return to Geneva—the Ecclesiastical Ordinance of 1541, which was revised in 1561[2]—laid part of the foundation for Reformed church

---

1. On the context of the formation of the Dordt Church Order, see Adriana van Harten-Tip, *De Dordtse Kerkorde 1619: Ontwikkeling, Context en Theologie* (Utrecht: KokBoekencentrum, 2018); Fred van Lieburg, "Re-Understanding the Dordt Church Order in Its Dutch Political, Ecclesiastical and Cultural Context," in *Protestant Church Polity in Changing Contexts*, vol. 1, *Ecclesiological and Historical Contributions*, ed. Allan J. Janssen and Leo J. Koffeman (Zurich: LIT, 2014), 116–36.

2. See "Ecclesiastical Ordinances, 1541," in Philip E. Hughes, *The Register of the Company of Pastors of Geneva in the Time of Calvin* (Grand Rapids: Eerdmans, 1966), 35–49; and "Ecclesiastical Ordinances, 1561," in *Paradigms in Polity: Classic Readings in*

polity. These Ordinances for the city of Geneva prescribed four ecclesiastical offices—minister, doctor, elder, and deacon—and the consistory as the body of ministers and elders overseeing the local church. The classis, or regional body of churches, was first introduced in the Synod of Lausanne of 1537.[3] Other early church orders that contributed to Reformed polity included Johannes à Lasco's *Forma ac Ratio* of 1555, which recorded the rites of the Strangers' Church of London, where he was the superintendent;[4] the French Reformed Ecclesiastical Discipline of 1559;[5] and the Palatinate Church Order of 1563.[6] The French churches closely followed the ecclesiastical structure of Geneva, although the Ecclesiastical Discipline implemented four levels of church assemblies—the local consistory, the regional colloquy (classis), the provincial synod, and the general council (national synod).[7] Also contributing were the decisions of the early Reformed synods in the southern Low Countries (especially at Antwerp) from 1563 to 1566, which followed the example of the French Reformed churches.[8]

Recent research has shown that the so-called Convent of Wesel

---

Reformed and Presbyterian Church Government, ed. David W. Hall and Joseph H. Hall (Grand Rapids: Eerdmans, 1994), 140–55.

3. C. van den Broeke, "Meerdere Vergaderingen," in *Handboek Gereformeerd Kerkrecht*, ed. Herman J. Selderhuis (Heerenveen: Uitgeverij Groen, 2019), 293.

4. Johannes à Lasco, *Forma ac Ratio tota Ecclesiastici Ministerii in peregrinorum, potissimum vero Germanorum Ecclesia, instituta Londini in Anglia* ([Emden, 1555]); Michael S. Springer, *Restoring Christ's Church: John a Lasco and the* Forma ac Ratio (Aldershot: Ashgate, 2007). A shorter version of the *Forma ac Ratio* was translated into Dutch by Marten Micron in his *De Christlicke Ordinancien der Nederlantscher Ghemeynten Christi, die van den Christelicken Prince Co. Edewaerdt den VI in 't jaer 1550 te Londen inghestelt* (1554).

5. Jean Aymon, *Tous les Synodes Nationaux des Eglises Reformées de France* (La Haye: Charles Delo, 1710), 1:1–7; "Ecclesiastical Discipline, 1559," in Hall and Hall, *Paradigms*, 134–39.

6. Emil Sehling, ed., *Die evangelischen Kirchenordnungen de XVI Jahrhunderts* (Tübingen: J. Mohr, 1969), 14:40–41, 333–408. Cf. Bard Thompson, "The Palatinate Church Order of 1563," *Church History* 23, no. 4 (Dec. 1954): 339–54.

7. Raymond Mentzer, "Calvijn en Frankrijk," in *Calvijn Handboek*, ed. Herman J. Selderhuis (Kampen: Kok, 2008), 108–9.

8. *Livre Synodal contenant les Articles résolus dans les Synodes des Eglises Wallonnes des Pays-Bas*, vol. 1, *(1563–1685)* (Den Haag: Martinus Nijhoff, 1896), 1–13; C. Hooijer, ed., *Oude Kerkordeningen der Nederlandsche Hervormde Gemeenten (1563–1638)* (Zalt-Bommel: Joh. Noman en Zoon, 1865), 1–23.

(1568) was not an actual ecclesiastical assembly, but rather just a proposal for the future organization of Dutch Reformed churches drawn up in 1568 by Petrus Dathenus.[9] A copy of this proposal ended up in London and was discovered by Symeon Ruytinck, who considered Wesel to be the first of a series of six Dutch Reformed national synods from 1568 to 1618.[10]

The first national synod of Dutch churches was actually the Synod of Emden (1571), whose church polity was modeled on the 1559 French Ecclesiastical Discipline. Though conducted in exile, the Synod of Emden laid the foundation for the polity of the Dutch Reformed churches. The first article of Emden's acts presented the anti-hierarchical basis for Reformed church polity—that no church, minister, elder, or deacon should have authority over any others. At Emden, the first regulations for church order in the Dutch churches were established, after which they were confirmed, expanded, and revised in subsequent synods. Thus, the church polity decisions of this 1571 synod were the first in a direct line of church order decisions arising from a series of synods—the provincial Synod of Dordrecht (1574), the national Synod of Dordrecht (1578), the national Synod of Middelburg (1581), the national Synod of The Hague (1586), and finally the national Synod of Dordt in 1619. While the earlier synods produced only a series of synodical decisions on church polity, the national Synod of Dordrecht (1578) produced the first formal Church Order, which was occasioned by a desire to seek government approval of the church order. This church order was followed by the 1581 Church Order of Middelburg and the 1586 Church Order of The Hague.[11] Together, these church orders formed the foundation on which the Church Order of Dordt was built.

---

9. Jesse Spohnholz, *The Convent of Wesel: The Event That Never Was and the Invention of Tradition* (Cambridge: Cambridge University Press, 2017).

10. S[ymeon] R[uytinck], *Harmonia Synodorum Belgicarum, sive Canones Regiminis Ecclesiastici in Synodis Nationalibus*, appended to Festus Hommius, *Specimen Controversiarum Belgicarum* (Leiden, 1618), 144.

11. P. Biesterveld and H. H. Kuyper, eds., *Kerkelijk Handboekje* (Kampen: J. H. Bos, 1905), xx–xxii. The acts and church orders of these synods are printed in this *Kerkelijk Handboekje*, as well as in F. L. Rutgers, ed., *Acta van de Nederlandsche Synoden der Zestiende Eeuw* (Dordrecht: J. P. van den Tol, 1980).

Since the Synod of Emden (1571) met outside the Netherlands in exile, Dutch state authorities had no influence upon this synod. In 1573, the States of Holland took charge of church property and ministers' salaries. Although, on the basis of Emden, the church wanted to maintain independence from the state, early influence of the state in church order matters played a role at the Synod of Dordrecht (1574), which requested the support and cooperation of the local magistrate in matters such as the hiring and dismissal of teachers, poor relief, the forbidding of Sunday desecration, marriage, and divorce.[12] Such state influence only increased in later years. For example, in the Middelburg Church Order of 1581 (art. 35), the States General was allowed to send representatives to the classis meeting that was preparing for the next national synod, in order to participate in the deliberations; this legitimized the influence of the States General on the calling of national synods.[13] Within a few years, the States General fully controlled the convening of national synods, which led to the situation where, in spite of calls by the churches to hold a national synod—every three years, according to the Synods of Dordrecht (1578), Middelburg (1581), and The Hague (1586)—the States General for various reasons refused to convene a national synod for thirty-two years after the 1586 Synod of The Hague.

While the church orders of the earlier national synods were operative in parts of the Netherlands, they were not politically approved by the States General or by the States of most Dutch provinces. The provinces sought more influence in church affairs, especially in the calling of ministers, where they claimed the right of patronage (*ius patronatus*). So, in the cases of Holland, Utrecht, Zeeland, and Groningen, the provinces drew up their own church orders—the Holland and Zeeland church laws of 1576, the Holland church laws of 1583 and 1591, the Utrecht church laws of 1590 and 1612, the Zeeland church order of 1591, and the two Groningen church orders of 1594 (for the city) and 1595 (for the surrounding Ommelanden).[14]

---

12. *Kerkelijk Handboekje*, 63, 69, 71, 72, 75, 85–87.

13. Adriana van Harten-Tip, "De Kerkelijke Vergaderingen in de Nederlanden in de Zestiende Eeuw," in *Handboek Gereformeerd Kerkrecht*, 138–61.

14. See Hooijer, *Oude Kerkordeningen*, for these church orders. Cf. Van Harten-Tip, *De Dordtse Kerkorde*, 64–75.

The Church Order of Dordt in Historical Perspective

In 1612, a collection of the ecclesiastical church orders—of Emden (1571), Dordrecht (1574), Dordrecht (1578), Middelburg (1581), and The Hague (1586)—as well as the political church orders of Utrecht (1590), The Hague (1591), and Zeeland (1591), was published.[15]

With the variety of church orders being observed in various parts of the Netherlands, there was a strong desire at the Synod of Dordt in 1619 to provide a single church order that would be approved by the States General, with the goal that it be uniformly observed in all churches of the country.

The Synod of Dordt's Deliberations on Church Order

In the Articles to Convene the national synod (11 November 1617), the States General specified that after the Five Articles of the Remonstrants were dealt with, the synod should treat gravamina (overtures) forwarded by the provincial synods relating to the Dutch churches.[16] The secret instructions drafted by the States General for its state delegates at the synod (6 November 1618) stated that if the whole synod agreed to devise a church order, the state delegates must take special care that the rights and privileges of the provinces were not infringed upon by decisions of the synod. These instructions also specified that such matters should be transacted only by the Dutch delegates in the absence of the foreign theologians.[17]

Hence it was that the Synod of Dordt dealt with church order matters in the Post-Acta sessions in May 1619, after the foreign delegates had departed for home. Church order issues were treated in ten sessions. The specific points that were handled arose from gravamina submitted by the provincial synods.

In the first of the Post-Acta sessions (13 May, sess. 155), it was reported that the state delegates had agreed that the regulations of the church order of the last national Synod of The Hague (1586) should

---

15. *De Kercken-ordeninghen der Ghereformeerder Nederlandtscher Kercken, in de Vier Nationalen Synoden Ghemaeckt ende Ghearresteert, mitsgaders eenighe anderen in de Provincialen Synoden van Hollandt ende Zeelandt gheconcipieert ende besloten* (Delft: Jan Andriessz, 1612; 2nd ed., Delft: Jan Andriesz, 1617). This was edited by Reynier Donteclock.

16. *Acta*, 1:15, 17, arts. 2 and 9.

17. *ADSND*, 1:470, arts. 12 and 13.

be reviewed and examined. So, in this session, the 1586 Church Order was read.[18] Which copy of this church order was read is unknown; it was probably the 1612 edition of *De Kercken-ordeninghen der Ghereformeerder Nederlandtscher Kercken*, which contained the first printing of the 1586 Church Order or the 1617 reprint.[19]

In the next session (sess. 156), the articles of the 1586 Church Order were approved *in substance* by the whole synod. Since some of the provinces had their own church orders, there was no uniform church order in the provinces. Thus, there was a desire to at least seek the unanimity of all the delegations on the basis of the 1586 Church Order. Some of the delegates explained that their provincial States had adopted special articles of church order that agreed in substance with the 1586 Church Order. It was expected that the Synod of Dordt would then update and make necessary revisions to this 1586 Church Order.

In this same session, the synod decided to petition the States General to authorize and approve these church order articles so that they might have the authority of public laws in the Dutch churches throughout the land.[20]

The first issue to be addressed was the calling of ministers, and in this connection a debate took place about whether the right of patronage (*ius patronatus*) should be done away with, or at least restricted so that the churches would not be harmed. The right of patronage was a long-standing right of nobility and landowners to appoint ministers on their lands. This right had deep historical roots, especially in the provinces of Groningen and Drenthe.[21] The South Holland delega-

---

18. *ADSND*, 1:156; the Dutch version of the Post-Acta sessions is in H. H. Kuyper, *De Post-Acta of Nahandelingen van de Nationale Synode van Dordrecht in 1618 en 1619 gehouden* (Amsterdam: Höveker & Wormser, [1899]).

19. *De Kercken-ordeninghen der Ghereformeerder Nederlandtscher Kercken, in de vier Nationalen Synoden ghemaeckt ende ghearresteert* (Delft: Jan Andriessz, 1612; 2nd ed., Delft: Jan Andriesz, 1617).

20. *ADSND*, 1:156–57; Kuyper, *Post-Acta*, 110–12.

21. On the right of patronage, see Sjaak Verwijs, "The Synod of Dordt and the *Ius Patronatus*," in *A Landmark in Turbulent Times: The Meaning and Relevance of the Synod of Dordt (1618–1619)*, ed. Henk van den Belt, Klaas-Willem de Jong, and Willem van Vlastuin (Göttingen: Vandenhoeck and Ruprecht, 2022), 277–89; and Van Harten-Tip, *De Dordtse Kerkorde*, 194–97. An example of the Groningen stance is that, on 19 November 1618, the deputies of Groningen at the States General declared that they could not condone that the twelfth article of the States General's instruction for the

The Church Order of Dordt in Historical Perspective 295

tion submitted a gravamen that complained of difficulties with the right of patronage and sought its abolition. On the other hand, the Drenthe delegation presented a gravamen requesting that the right of patronage should remain untouched.[22] The state delegates explained the origin of this right, and they informed the synod that the States General would never allow the right to be done away with and that, therefore, it should not try to abolish patronage, but only to prevent abuses of it.[23] In the secret instructions that the States General had given to the state delegates on 6 November 1618, the state delegates were explicitly instructed to ensure that, in the synod's treatment of the church order, "the right of patronage in general and in private remains preserved and unimpaired."[24]

In the next session (157), the advice of the various delegations was read, and the sentiment was expressed that the right of patronage was contrary to God's Word. However, discussion focused on the proper limits of patronage, in such a way that the synod reached a compromise—the right of patronage was left to the patrons, but its use would be restricted so that it would not prejudice the churches and abuses would be prevented. For this purpose, the synod decided to deliver a list of nine articles to the States General, with a request that it recommend them to the provinces. Among these nine articles, which were approved in session 160, the main points were: that the only right allowed to a patron was restricted to the right to present or nominate an acceptable person to serve as a minister; that patrons provide adequate support for the minister; that patrons propose only such persons who are sound in doctrine, of good behavior, and adorned with gifts for ministry; that the church has the right to reject the person; that the classis examine the proposed person and install him into ministry according to its regulations; and that the patron does not

---

state delegates at the synod allowed the synod to examine whether the *ius patronatus* and other rights conform to the Word of God. They wanted their dissent registered. See *ADSND*, 2/1:244–45.

22. Kuyper, *Post-Acta*, 112, 425, 450–51.

23. *ADSND*, 1:156–57. On the discussion concerning the right of patronage, see Kuyper, *Post-Acta*, 111–19.

24. *ADSND*, 1:470.

have the right to dismiss a minister.[25] The synod also added the right of patronage to article 5 of the Dordt Church Order, affirming that anyone's valid right of patronage will remain uncurtailed as long as it is used in an edifying way—that is, without detriment to the church and under the oversight of the civil authority and provincial synods (see below).

In session 158, six gravamina from the provincial synods, all of which related to the church order, were presented and discussed. In the following session, after each of the Dutch delegations gave their advice, the majority of the synod made the following decisions:

1. On church visitors and their office (gravamina from Gelderland and South Holland): Each classis was to appoint some experienced ministers to visit all the churches and take note whether the pastors, elders, and schoolteachers faithfully performed their duties, adhered to sound doctrine, followed the church order, and promoted the edification of the church and the youth—all so that they might admonish the slothful and give advice and help. This decision revised article 40 of the 1586 Church Order and became article 44 of the Dordt Church Order (DCO).

2. On deputies of the provincial synods (gravamina from Gelderland and South Holland): Each provincial synod was to appoint some persons to carry out all the decisions of the synod as they pertain to the government and the classes, to preside over the examinations of incoming ministers, to offer a helping hand to classes in all difficulties that arise, and to give a report to the synod. This decision became the new article 49 of the DCO. In practice, this article also enabled the provincial synods to send their synodical deputies to visit other provincial synods, in order to maintain the correspondence permitted in article 48.

3. On correspondence between particular synods of each province (gravamen from South Holland): Each provincial

---

25. *ADSND*, 1:157–58.

synod was free to maintain correspondence with neighboring synods in a form that was most edifying. This decision became the new article 48 of the DCO. This article would be of great significance in maintaining the mutual connection between the provincial synods, since there would be no national synod for two centuries.

4. On the admission of the uneducated to the ministry (gravamina from Gelderland and South Holland): No one who has not followed the regular course of studies was to be admitted to the ministry, unless they have exceptional gifts, godliness, discretion, and skill in public speaking. The classis should first examine them and then allow them to exhort privately. This decision became the new article 8 of the DCO.

5. On the voting of ministers in classes where a church has more than one minister (gravamen from South Holland): In places where there is more than one minister, all ministers should be allowed to attend classis and have the right to vote, except in matters that concern their person or church. This decision became the new article 42 of the DCO.

6. On preparing a suitable form of subscription to the Confession and the Catechism (gravamen from South Holland): The synod decided to prepare a specific form of subscription by which ministers would subscribe to the Confession, the Catechism, and the Canons, in order to certify their sound conviction and prevent wrongful evasions. This decision did not change article 47 of the 1586 Church Order regarding subscription (DCO art. 53), but it did create a new form to be used for subscription.[26]

In session 160 (15 May), the synod discussed the policy to be observed in the calling of ministers. The practice of calling ministers

---

26. *ADSND*, 1:158–60; Kuyper, *Post-Acta*, 119–34. On forms of subscription, see Donald Sinnema, "The Origin of the Form of Subscription in the Dutch Reformed Tradition," *Calvin Theological Journal* 42, no. 2 (Nov. 2007): 256–82.

varied considerably among the Dutch provinces, in part because of the influence of the state on calling. Initial drafts of the policy did not satisfy everyone, so in the next session (161) President Bogerman presented another draft, which was adopted after amendments:

> According to this policy, the lawful calling of those entering the ministry consists: (1) in the choice by the consistory and the deacons, in correspondence (consultation) with the local magistrate and with the advice of the classis; (2) in an examination into doctrine and life conducted by the classis in the presence of deputies of the provincial synod; (3) in the approbation or approval by the local magistrate, and also by the local Reformed congregation, after the person's name was announced in the church fourteen days earlier; (4) in the public installation in the presence of the congregation, with the laying on of hands by the officiating minister. This decision revised article 4 of the 1586 Church Order and became article 4 of the DCO.
>
> Concerning ministers already in the ministry who are called to another congregation, such calling should also be carried out by the consistory and the deacons, in correspondence with the magistrate and with the advice and approbation of the classis. After approval by the magistrate, and after being presented to the congregation for fourteen days, they should be installed. If someone has a valid right of presentation (patronage), this should not be curtailed, as long as it is exercised in an edifying way, without detriment to the church and good church order; in this the government and the provincial synods should maintain necessary order in the best interests of the church. This decision revised article 5 of the 1586 Church Order and became article 5 of the DCO.[27]

The stipulation about the right of patronage was an addition to article 5 in the DCO. It was also expected that the nine articles limiting the right of patronage that were adopted by the synod should form an appendix to articles 4 and 5.

---

27. *ADSND*, 1:161–62; Kuyper, *Post-Acta*, 136–46.

The changes to these two articles bolstered state influence in the calling of ministers, both through the approbation of a call by the magistrate and through required correspondence with the magistrate in the choice of a minister. The requirement of correspondence (*correspondentie*) was added due to pressure from the state delegates.[28]

In the same session, the synod added a new article on the duty of the Christian government (DCO art. 28):

> Since it is the duty of the Christian government to promote the worship services in every way, to recommend them to their subjects by their example, and to extend a helping hand to ministers, elders, and deacons in every need as it occurs and to protect them by their good order, all ministers, elders, and deacons are duty bound diligently and sincerely to impress upon the whole congregation the obedience, love, and honor which they owe the magistrates. All who hold office in the church shall set a good example to the congregation in this, and by proper respect and correspondence seek to stir up and preserve the favor of the authorities to the churches, to the end that each one on both sides, doing what he can in the fear of the Lord, may avoid all suspicion and distrust and maintain proper unity for the welfare of the churches.[29]

Such an article had not been part of any previous church order. Apparently, this article was added in an attempt to curry favor with the States General, in the hope that it would officially approve the church order.[30]

In session 162, the Dutch delegations gave their advice on six gravamina that had been presented in session 159. Two of these gravamina related to the church order.

The first gravamen—which actually consisted of several gravamina—dealt with religious holidays, the use of hymns, and the baptism of children and adults, all of which were concerned with uniformity of practice. This led to four separate decisions.[31]

---

28. Kuyper, *Post-Acta*, 142–45.
29. *ADSND*, 1:162; Kuyper, *Post-Acta*, 141–42, 146.
30. J. van den Berg, "De Synode van Dordrecht en de Dordtse Kerkorde," in Selderhuis, *Handboek Gereformeerd Kerkrecht*, 165.
31. *ADSND*, 1:162–63; Kuyper, *Post-Acta*, 134, 146–47, 151–61.

On religious holidays (gravamina from Gelderland, South Holland, and Groningen), congregations were instructed to observe Christmas, Easter, and Pentecost, along with the following day, and work toward the observance of the days of Christ's circumcision (New Year's Day) and ascension. This decision on religious holidays revised article 60 of the 1586 Church Order and became article 67 of the DCO. It was also a concession to the state, which wanted to provide a favor to the people.

On the use of hymns (gravamina from Gelderland, South Holland, and Overijssel), only the 150 Psalms were to be sung in the churches, along with a select group of hymns on the Ten Commandments, the Lord's Prayer, and the Apostles' Creed, as well as the songs of Mary, Zacharias, and Simeon. This decision revised article 62 of the 1586 Church Order and became article 69 of the DCO. The principle at issue here was that only psalms and hymns found in Scripture were to be used in public worship services.

On forms for the baptism of children and adults (gravamina from Gelderland, South Holland, North Holland, and Overijssel), ministers were instructed to use the existing forms for the administration of baptism. This decision revised article 52 of the 1586 Church Order and became article 58 of the DCO.

On adult baptism (gravamina from South Holland, North Holland, and Utrecht), it was declared that, through baptism, adults are ingrafted and accepted as members of the church and are therefore duty bound to partake of the Lord's Supper. This decision became the new article 59 of the DCO.

In response to the sixth gravamen, concerning church discipline (gravamina from North Holland, Overijssel, and the Walloon synod), the synod declared that all churches should be earnestly exhorted to see that the articles of the Church Order on the discipline of ordinary people, as well as those in ecclesiastical office, were diligently and strictly observed.[32]

In session 163 (17 May), the synod dealt with a new group of seven gravamina that had been presented to the synod the previous day. Only the second of these gravamina relates to the church order.

---

32. *ADSND*, 1:163; Kuyper, *Post-Acta*, 149, 165.

On admitting former priests to the ministry (gravamina from Gelderland and South Holland), the synod declared that newcomers, priests, monks, and those from sects should not be admitted to the ministry except with great caution, after they have first been tested for a time. This decision revised part of article 4 of the 1586 Church Order and became a separate article 9 of the DCO.[33]

Toward the end of session 175 (25 May), the changes made to the church order were read and definitively approved. At the same time, a small revision was made to article 49 of the 1586 Church Order, which became article 55 of the DCO (on the approval of books). And it was decided to insert into the church order the decision on catechizing that had earlier been made in session 17; but this was never done. It was probably in this session that the synod also appointed several members to edit the Dordt Church Order, in order to present it to the States General for approval.[34]

This is the extent of the revisions and additions that the Synod of Dordt made to the Church Order of 1586 in its Post-Acta sessions. There were eight revisions of former articles (arts. 4, 5, 9, 44, 55, 58, 67, 69) and six new articles (arts. 8, 28, 42, 48, 49, 59) added to the church order. The result was the Church Order of Dordt, with eighty-six articles in total.[35]

On 27 May, the synod appointed a delegation to go to the States General, after the synod concluded, and present a list of requests (*Libellus Supplex*) that the synod wanted the States General to address and implement. This list included the following request:

> That your High Mightinesses be pleased to approve and to order that the Church Order, as reviewed in this synod and expanded in some points for greater edification and peace, might be uniformly maintained everywhere in the churches of these lands, as much as possible.[36]

---

33. *ADSND*, 1:164; Kuyper, *Post-Acta*, 149, 165, 167, 174–75.
34. Kuyper, *Post-Acta*, 242–45.
35. The Church Order of Dordt is printed in Biesterveld and Kuyper, *Kerkelijk Handboekje*, 225–50. An English translation is in *The Doctrinal Standards, Liturgy, and Church Order of the Netherlands Reformed Congregations* (Sioux Center, Iowa: Netherlands Reformed Book & Publication Committee, 1991), 179–89.
36. *ADSND*, 1:179; Kuyper, *Post-Acta*, 263.

At least by 28 May, the committee assigned to edit the DCO completed its work. But the committee did not include in the church order the synod's earlier decisions on the right of patronage and on the manner of catechizing, as the synod had intended, perhaps due to the length of these decisions. This committee also made further revisions to two articles, including article 18 of the 1586 Church Order (DCO art. 20, on exhorting by students) and article 49 (DCO art. 55, on the approval of books).[37]

The revised Church Order received the consent of the state delegates at the synod.[38] On 28 May, the Church Order of Dordt was signed by the five officers of the synod, under the words "So done and decided in the National Synod in Dordrecht on 28 May in the year 1619."[39]

On 30 May, the synod's delegation presented the *Libellus Supplex* to the States General, and on 3 June the States General received forty printed copies of the Church Order as revised—that is, the 1586 Hague Church Order with Dordt's amendments written in the margin.[40]

As it turned out, the States General never did approve the Church Order of Dordt or order that it be maintained in all the churches throughout the country.[41]

The Structure and Character of the Church Order of Dordt

The Dordt Church Order followed the structure of the 1586 Church Order. After an introduction (art. 1), the DCO consists of four sections: (1) On Ecclesiastical Offices (arts. 2–28); (2) On Ecclesiastical Assemblies (arts. 29–52); (3) On Doctrine, Sacraments, and Other Ceremonies (arts. 53–70); and (4) On Censure and Ecclesiastical Admonition (arts. 71–83). These were followed by three concluding articles (arts. 84–86).

---

37. Kuyper, *Post-Acta*, 310–11.
38. "Summary Report to the States General (30 May 1619)," in Kuyper, *Post-Acta*, 478.
39. *Kerkelijk Handboekje*, 250. On a problem with this date, see Kuyper, *Post-Acta*, 311–12.
40. Kuyper, *Post-Acta*, 312; cf. 478–79; *RSG*, 4:142, 147, 157.
41. Kuyper, *Post-Acta*, 312–15.

The Church Order of Dordt exhibits an anti-hierarchical principle, which is explicitly evident in article 84:

> No church shall in any way lord it over another church, no minister over other ministers, no elder or deacon over other elders or deacons.[42]

This anti-hierarchical article was already found in the acts of the 1571 Synod of Emden (art. 1), which in turn was derived from the 1559 French Ecclesiastical Discipline (art. 1).[43]

The Church Order of Dordt embodies the presbyterial model of church polity. Original church authority resides in the local church in permanent consistories made up of ministers and elders, and there are occasional gatherings of classes and synods that bring local churches in connection with one another (arts. 37, 41, 47, 50).

The provision made in the DCO for correspondence between provincial synods (art. 48) allowed for a level of cooperation between these synods throughout the Netherlands. Also, the provision of synodical deputies (art. 49) provided an avenue for interaction between the provincial synods. These deputies were to take care of current church affairs until the next synod, maintain contact with the classes, and help examine new ministers. In practice, the synodical deputies also visited other provincial synods, enabling the correspondence between synods that was allowed by article 48. This was important, since no national synod would be held again in the Netherlands for two hundred years.

The DCO was the prototype of a Reformed church order, but it was not the ideal that the church wanted—there was too much state influence in internal church affairs. On the whole, the DCO gave the state a greater role in church affairs than did earlier church orders. Accommodations to the influence of the state in church affairs included an increased role of the state in the calling of ministers, and the local magistrate could influence consistories by having its representatives

---

42. *Kerkelijk Handboekje*, 249.

43. On the anti-hierarchical principle, see Klaas-Willem de Jong, "Een verkennend Onderzoek naar de Receptie van een Anti-hiërarchisch Beginsel in Nederlandse Kerkorden van het Gereformeerde Type," *In die Skriflig* 52, no. 2 (2018): a2350, https://doi.org/10.4102/ids.v52i2.2350.

present to deliberate. Especially on the matter of the right of patronage, the state delegates at Dordt played a decisive role.

The Church Order of Dordt was intended to function as a dynamic set of regulations that could be changed as the needs and circumstances of the churches changed (like the final article 53 of the acts of Emden of 1571). Article 86 specified that:

> These Articles, relating to the lawful regulations of the churches are, with common consent, so formulated and adopted, that if the benefit of the churches should require it, they may and ought to be altered, enlarged, or diminished. No particular congregation, classis, or synod, however, shall be permitted to do this, but all shall diligently observe them, until the General or National Synod shall otherwise order.[44]

However, since no national synod was held for two centuries, changes could not be formally made to the Dordt Church Order. In practice, articles of the church order that the churches disagreed with, or that ceased to be relevant, were simply not observed.[45]

Influence of the State on the Church Order of Dordt

In the Dutch republic, church and state were closely interrelated. The Dutch Reformed church was not a state church, but since 1580 it was recognized as a privileged church; thus, it enjoyed many benefits not given to churches that were only tolerated, such as the Roman Catholic

---

44. *Kerkelijk Handboekje*, 249–50.
45. Kuyper, *Post-Acta*, 315. For example, Abraham Kuyper's editions of the DCO included textual markings of political articles that no longer functioned in a neutral democratic state; A. Kuyper, ed., *Kerken-ordening gestelt in de Nationale Synode der Gereformeerde Kerken, te zamen beroepen en gehouden binnen Dordrecht in de jaren 1618 en 1619* (Amsterdam: J. H. Kruyt, 1886). In a different cultural context, the Reformed Dutch Church (Reformed Church in America) retained the original Dordt Church Order, but in 1792 it omitted all references to civil magistrates and added "Explanatory Articles" that applied to the American context. Edward T. Corwin, *A Digest of Constitutional and Synodical Legislation of the Reformed Church in America* (New York: Board of Publications of the Reformed Church in America, 1906), 160. Cf. Leon van den Broeke, "Flexibility or Fixed Idea: The Dort Church Order of 1619 as a Cultural Import in America," in *Sharing Pasts: Dutch Americans through Four Centuries*, ed. Henk Aay, Janny Venema, and Dennis Voskuil (Holland, Mich.: Van Raalte Press, 2017), 51–72.

or Mennonite churches. The Reformed churches preferred a structure where the church could manage its own affairs, but it also readily took advantage of privileges through which it benefited from government support. In some cases, the Synod of Dordt made concessions on the role of the state in church affairs, especially on the calling of ministers and the right of patronage, in the hope that the States General would approve the Dordt Church Order and implement it uniformly in all provinces.[46] Although the DCO was approved by the state delegates at Dordt, the States General never did grant its approval.

The influence of the state on the DCO is evident in fifteen of its eighty-six articles:

> Article 4: In the calling of ministers, a first-time minister is to be chosen by the consistory and the deacons, in correspondence (consultation) with the local Christian government, and after an examination, he must receive the approbation and approval of this government.

> Article 5: The calling of ministers to another church must be carried out by the consistory and the deacons, in correspondence with the local Christian government, and must also receive the approval of the magistrate before being installed. This is to be done without abridging a valid right of presentation (patronage) or any other right, insofar as it is used in an edifying way—that is, without detriment to the church. In this the States General and the provincial synods should maintain necessary order for the best interests of the church.

> Article 10: Ministers must not accept a call elsewhere without the consent of the consistory and the deacons, together with the consent of the magistrate.

> Article 19: Churches should see that there are students of theology supported by public funds.

---

46. Kuyper, *Post-Acta*, 114. On the relation of church and state at Dordt, see Van Harten-Tip, *Dordtse Kerkorde*, 191–203.

Article 26: Deacons are to consult with poor-relief directors and other alms distributors.

Article 28: This article describes the role of the Christian magistrate—to promote church services, to lend a helping hand to church leaders, and to protect them through establishing good order—and the obligation of church leaders and the congregation to obey, love, and respect the magistrates.

Article 37: The local magistrate is allowed to have one or two representatives at consistory meetings to listen and to deliberate.

Article 49: Synodical deputies are to carry out provincial synod decisions relating to the government and to the classes in its district.

Article 50: When it deliberates with its classis, the church chosen to convene the next national synod is to provide information on the time and place to the States General, which may wish to send deputies to the classis, so that the decision may be made with its advice.

Article 64: The practice of evening prayers is not to be removed without the judgment of the government.

Article 66: Ministers shall petition the government to designate public days of fasting and prayer in times of need.

Article 67: Ministers are to work with government authorities toward conformity in the observance of the day of circumcision (New Year's Day) and of ascension.

Article 70: The States General, with the advice of ministers, should make a general ordinance so that there may be uniformity in marriage practices.

Article 71: Christian discipline does not exempt anyone from civil trial and punishment.

Article 79: When church leaders commit a gross public sin that is punishable by the government, they are to be suspended or deposed.

In many of these cases, the state influence was present already in the 1586 Church Order (arts. 8, 17, 24, 34, 44, 57, 59, 63, 64, and 72), and no changes were made in the DCO on these articles. However, the DCO increased state influence, especially in regard to the calling of ministers, by adding the requirement of correspondence with the local magistrate in articles 4 and 5 and by adding the right of patronage to article 5 (cf. 1586 Church Order arts. 4 and 5). The DCO also added new articles on the office of the Christian magistrate (art. 28) and on synodical deputies carrying out decisions relating to the government (art. 49). A change was also made to article 67 (1586 Church Order art. 60), requesting the government to bring conformity to religious holidays.

The Early Reception of the Church Order of Dordt

After the Synod of Dordt, the desire for unanimity in a church order throughout the Netherlands was not achieved. The States General did not approve the Dordt Church Order, since not all provinces approved it, especially Friesland.[47] After March 1620, the issue did not again appear on the agenda of the States General.

Only three provinces approved the Dordt Church Order—Utrecht, Overijssel, and Gelderland—but they did so with reservations or minor changes.

The States of Overijssel, meeting at Zwolle on 30 July 1619, accepted the Dordt Church Order, with the proviso that its introduction not conflict with existing "privileges and regulations" of the province.[48]

---

47. For a detailed overview of the reception of the Dordt Church Order in the provinces of the Netherlands, see F. L. Rutgers, *De Geldigheid der Oude Kerkenordening der Nederlandsche Gereformeerde Kerken* (Amsterdam: Ton Bolland, 1971), Bijlage II: "Over de Politieke Approbatie van de Kerkordening, naar de Dordtsche redactie van 1619, in de onderscheidene Provincien," 75–104. See also Kuyper, *Post-Acta*, 312–15; and Van Lieburg, "Re-Understanding," 125–26.
48. Rutgers, *Geldigheid*, 76–77.

The States of Utrecht, on 6 August 1619 (Old Style = 16 Aug. N.S.) confirmed and ratified the Dordt Church Order, on the condition that, if a dispute were to arise between the local government and churches of Utrecht over the interpretation of the Church Order, the matter should be determined by the States of Utrecht, and if they could not do so, it should be left to the decision of the States General and the stadtholder.[49] The States of Utrecht also asked the provincial synod of Utrecht for clarification on articles 4 and 5 (on the calling of ministers) and article 22 (on the selection of elders). Four synodical deputies, who were delegates at the Synod of Dordt (including President Bogerman), provided an explanation of these articles, and then the DCO was approved by the provincial States.[50]

The States of Gelderland, meeting at Arnhem on 21 July 1620, approved and ratified the Dordt Church Order with small changes to three articles—articles 11, 13 (regarding support of ministers), and 41 (regarding classes).[51]

The States of Friesland most strongly objected to the Dordt Church Order, especially because they wanted to maintain the rights and privileges of local landowners and nobility in rural areas relating to the nomination and selection of ministers (the right of patronage). On 3 July 1619, the three rural districts in the States—Oostergo, Westergo, and Zevenwolden—passed a resolution to retain the previous church order (that is, the sixteenth-century church orders), modified by the rights and privileges of Friesland. When a delegation from the States General was sent to the States of Friesland in May 1620 to convince them to accept the Dordt Church Order, the majority of towns (the fourth district in the States) favored the acceptance of the Church Order, but they were outvoted by the three rural districts, which persisted in

---

49. The stadtholder was the chief executive officer of the provinces of the Dutch Republic, with responsibilities that were chiefly military in nature. The office of stadtholder was usually held by the Prince of Orange, who, at the time of the Synod of Dordt, was Prince Maurice.

50. Rutgers, *Geldigheid*, 77–81; J. Reitsma and S. van Veen, eds., *Acta der Provinciale en Particuliere Synoden, gehouden in de Noordelijke Nederlanden, gedurende de Jaren 1572–1620* (Groningen: J.B. Wolters, 1897), 6:421–24; Geeraert Brandt, *Historie der Reformatie, en andre Kerkelyke Geschiedenissen in en ontrent de Nederlanden* (Rotterdam: Barent Bos, 1704), 3:959–60, 974–76.

51. Rutgers, *Geldigheid*, 75–76; Brandt, *Historie*, 4:288. See below for the changes.

their previous resolution. President Bogerman advocated for the Dordt Church Order in a lengthy speech to the provincial Synod of Friesland, but on 17 September 1619, after seeing the States' resolution, the synod unanimously consented only to what agreed with the former Church Order of 1586, not to new practices, by which schisms could arise. However, by 1622, the majority of clergymen in Friesland were advocating for the Dordt Church Order, but the three rural districts of the States declared in July that no synodical resolution would have force before being approved by the States. They rejected the Dordt Church Order as impractical and contrary to the privileges of Friesland and forbade ministers from introducing the Dordt Church Order on threat of being deemed disturbers of the peace. The towns did not agree and supported the clergy. Later, Friesland introduced its own church order.[52]

The States of Zeeland were not initially opposed to the approval of the Dordt Church Order, but when they saw Friesland reject its approval, they decided on 5 February 1620 to retain the Zeeland Church Order of 1591, especially because of objections to articles 4, 8, 10, and 22, which concerned the calling of ministers and the selection of elders.[53]

The States of Holland, in June 1619, were initially ready to approve the Dordt Church Order, and they decided to leave it to the States General to explain obscurities in the church order—for example, what correspondence with the government meant in article 4 on the calling of ministers. But when it became clear that the Dordt Church Order would not be generally approved by all provinces, the States of Holland decided in July 1620 to revise it. The South Holland synod then petitioned the States not to resolve anything contrary to the Dordt Church Order without communication with the synod. Nevertheless, the States revised seventeen articles in the church order, most of which expanded the right of consent by the civil magistrate.[54] The majority of the clergy, however, rejected the revisions and favored the acceptance of the Dordt Church Order. In 1622, the synods of South and North Holland sent

---

52. Rutgers, *Geldigheid*, 81–86; Reitsma and Van Veen, *Acta*, 6:278–80; Brandt, *Historie*, 4:17–23, 284–85, 765–78; Kuyper, *Post-Acta*, 312.

53. Rutgers, *Geldigheid*, 89–90.

54. For a comparison of the proposed revisions with the DCO, see J. Th. De Visser, *Kerk en Staat* (Leiden: A. W. Sijthoff, 1926), 495–99.

a remonstrance to the States containing reasons for their refusal to accept the revisions. In July 1623, the South Holland synod stated that it would use the usual church order approved in former provincial synods, and a year later it said it would provisionally use the Hague Church Order of 1586. The States, however, did not approve of this, and in 1624 they declared that classes should follow what they currently practiced and respect all rights of patronage. In 1626, the South Holland synod decided that, even without authorization by the States, it would continue to follow the Church Order of Dordt, which was used in their churches. The result was that, in the province of Holland, no church order was officially authorized, and matters were left as they were.[55] The States wanted to maintain the 1591 Church Order of The Hague, while, in practice, the churches used the Dordt Church Order.

The States of Groningen did not approve the Dordt Church Order, but rather retained their own church orders. The city of Groningen had adopted a church order in 1594, and the Ommelanden (the province of Groningen except for the city of Groningen) had its own church order of 1595. These closely corresponded to the Dordt Church Order.[56]

The Landschap of Drenthe (not a regular province) also retained its own church order, which was the same as that of Groningen 1594. In 1633 a new church order was drafted, and in 1638 it was approved by the States of Drenthe.[57]

The Generality Lands, which were not part of the seven Dutch provinces and were governed directly by the States General, used the Church Order of Dordt.[58]

Since the Union of Utrecht (art. 13) specified that matters of religion were the responsibility of the provinces, the result was that most provinces did not officially authorize the DCO. The refusal by

---

55. Rutgers, *Geldigheid*, 90–104; Reitsma and Van Veen, *Acta*, 3:393–94, 414–15, 438, 454–55; Brandt, *Historie*, 3:749–52; 4:317, 320, 324–31, 520–22, 779–94. On the issue of the authorization of the Dordt Church Order by the States of Holland, see also A. Kuyper, *De Leidsche Professoren en de Executeurs der Dordtsche Nalatenschap* (Amsterdam: J. H. Kruyt, 1879), 87–97.

56. Rutgers, *Geldigheid*, 86–88.

57. Rutgers, *Geldigheid*, 88.

58. Van den Berg, "Synode," 166.

provinces to accept the church order mainly had to do with the rights of patronage, manorial rights, and governmental rights concerning the confirmation of ministers. In the view of the state, an independent church would be a danger to the unity of the nation, and the concessions to the state in the DCO did not go far enough. On the other hand, in the view of the church, the state does have a role in relation to the church—as indicated in article 36 of the Belgic Confession—but the state has no authority within the church; the concessions of the DCO had gone too far.[59]

Although most provinces did not formally approve the DCO, in practice the churches throughout the Netherlands nevertheless followed the substance of the DCO, because the various provincial church orders shared the essentials of Reformed church polity.[60] In practice, the differences were not great. The church orders of Zeeland, Friesland, Groningen, and Drenthe were largely in accord with the DCO.[61]

The model of the DCO—which contained the main lines of classical Reformed church polity, including its church offices and its ecclesiastical assemblies—formed the basis for the organization of Reformed church life in the Netherlands for the next two centuries. In practice, certain stipulations of the DCO were not observed, especially the concessions it made to the state.[62]

Early Printings of the Church Order of Dordt

There were four early printed editions of the Church Order of Dordt, which were made by authorization of the three provinces that approved of the Church Order. Each of these printings contains all eighty-six articles:[63]

(1) The Utrecht edition
Kercken-ordeninge, gestelt inden Nationalen Synode der Ghereformeerde Kercken, te samen beroepen ende gehouden by laste vande Hooghmo. Heeren

---

59. Van den Berg, "Synode," 162, 165; Kuyper, *Post-Acta*, 314–15.
60. H. Bouwman, *Gereformeerd Kerkrecht* (Kampen: Kok, 1928), 1:311–12; D. Nauta, *Verklaring van de Kerkorde van de Gereformeerde Kerken in Nederland* (Kampen: Kok, 1971), 21–22; Van Lieburg, "Re-Understanding," 128.
61. Kuyper, *Post-Acta*, 314.
62. Van den Berg, "Synode," 165, 168; Kuyper, *Post-Acta*, 315.
63. Kuyper, *Post-Acta*, 16–17.

Staten Generael van de Vereenighde Nederlanden, binnen Dordrecht, inden Iare 1618 ende 1619. Ende alsoo goetghevonden ende gearresteert by de Ed. Mog. Heeren Staten s'Landts van Utrecht, opden vi. Augusti des voorsz Iaers 1619 (Utrecht: Salomon de Roy, 1620).

The Dordt Church Order was approved and confirmed by the States of Utrecht on 6 August 1619 (Old Style = 16 Aug. N.S.). It was signed by Ant. Van Hilten on behalf of the States of Utrecht.[64] This was apparently the earliest printed edition of the DCO.

(2) The Gelderland edition

Kercken-Ordeninghe, ghestelt in den Nationalen Synode der Ghereformeerde Kercken, te samen beroepen, ende ghehouden door Order van de Hooghe Moghende Heeren Staten Generael der Vereenichde Nederlanden, binnen Dordrecht, in de Iaren 1618 ende 1619. Ende (naer veranderinghe van eenighe weynighe Poincten) goedt-ghevonden ende gearresteert by de Ed. Mog. Heeren Staten des Furstendombs Gelre und Graeffschaps Zutphen (Arnhem: Jan Janssen, 1620).

In 1620 there were three printings of this Gelderland edition of the Church Order by Jan Janssen (or Jansz) at Arnhem—one with twenty pages, one with twenty-seven pages, and one with thirty-eight pages.

This Gelderland edition of the Dordt Church Order reproduced the full church order of Dordt, but at the end it listed three changes that were made by the States of Gelderland to articles 11, 13, and 41, respectively. On 21 July 1620, the States of Gelderland, meeting in Arnhem, approved and ratified the Church Order "except for the small changes and distinct interpretation" made concerning these three articles. On behalf of the States of Gelderland, it was signed by J. Dibbets.[65]

Regarding the three changes that were made, first of all, article 11 clarifies that the consistory is obliged to ensure that the minister is provided with suitable support. Article 13 specifies that ministers who can no longer perform their duties due to age or sickness are to be honorably provided for by the churches they have served, but omitted is a requirement to provide also for the widows and orphans of such

---

64. This Utrecht edition was reprinted at Utrecht by Amelis Janssz van Paddenburch, 1640 and 1655, by Willem van Paddenburgh, 1679, and by Jacobus van Paddenburg, 1706.

65. Gelderland *Kercken-Ordeninghe*, 25–26.

ministers. In article 41, which deals with the structure and leadership of classis meetings, an addition specifies that the classes shall meet twice a year (rather than every three months) with the consent of the government and the respective Quarters of Gelderland, unless the need of the churches and the respective Quarters requires more frequent meetings.[66]

This Gelderland edition (without the three changes) is considered the most official version of the Church Order of Dordt.[67]

(3) The Overijssel edition
Kercken-Ordeninghe ghestelt in den Nationalen Synode der Gereformeerde Kercken, te samen beroepen, ende ghehouden door ordre van de Hooge Mogende Heeren Staten Generael der Vereenichde Nederlanden, binnen Dordrecht, inden Jaren 1618 ende 1619 (Deventer: S. Wermbouts, 1625).

On 30 July 1619, the States of Overijssel, meeting at Zwolle, resolved that "in the Province of Overijssel the aforesaid Church Order shall be observed, insofar as the same does not conflict with the privileges and regulations of this province in general and of its members or particulars."[68]

(4) The Walloon edition
L'Ordre Ecclesiastique des Eglises Reformees du Pays Bas, tant de l'une que de l'autre Langue, conclu au Synode National, convoque par les Haults & Puissans Seigneurs les Estats Generaulx des Provinces Unies, a Dordrecht l'An 1618 & 1619 (Middelbourgh: Symon Moulert, 1623).

This French translation of the Dordt Church Order was intended for the Walloon churches in the Netherlands. At the end, it is stated that this translation was collated with the original, which was signed

---

66. The three altered articles are printed in the *Kercken-Ordeninghe*, 25–27.

67. Biesterveld and Kuyper, *Kerkelijk Handboekje*, foreword. This Gelderland edition was reprinted in Arnhem by Jacob van Biesen, 1640, and in Harderwijk by Johan Toll, 1659. There was also an independent edition that used the Gelderland version; this edition was published in Dordrecht by De Weduwe van Jasper and Dirk Goris, 1686, and was later reprinted six times until 1758.

68. "Extract uyt het Register van de Staten van Over-Yssel," printed in *Nederlantshe Belydenisse des Geloofs, Canones des Synodi van Dordrecht, Nederlantsche Kercken-ordre, ende Houwlyckx-ordre der Kercken van Overjsel* (Swolle: Frans Jorrians and Jan Gerritsen, 1636). This Overijssel edition was reprinted in Zwolle by Jan Gerritsz and Frans Jorrijaensz, 1636, and in Deventer by Nathanaël Cost, 1647.

by Jean Polyander, Daniel de Coulogne, Arnouldt de Dannoi, and Esaie du Pré.[69]

Conclusion

The essence of Reformed church polity, which was already included in the Belgic Confession (arts. 30–32), was embodied in the acta of the Synod of Emden in 1571 and was further developed in the church orders of later national synods until the Church Order of Dordt.

Although the DCO was not officially approved uniformly throughout the provinces of the Netherlands, it remained the prototype of Reformed church polity, and, in practice, the substance of the DCO was followed in most Dutch Reformed churches for the next two centuries. Then, in 1816, it was supplanted by the "General Regulations" of the Netherlands Hervormde Kerk, which introduced a centralized bureaucratic church structure, with the church governed as a department of the state. However, the DCO was taken up again by the churches of the 1834 Afscheiding and the 1886 Doleantie.[70]

Though revised in various ways, the Church Order of Dordt has continued to provide the foundation and structure of the church orders of many Reformed denominations throughout the world—in the Netherlands, North America, South Africa, Asia, Australia, and New Zeeland.[71]

---

69. This French edition was reprinted in 1681; in A. Hulsius's *La Confession de Foy des Eglises Reformées des Païs-Bas…avec le Jugement du dit Synode sur les 5 Articles & la Discipline Ecclesiastique* (Amsterdam: Henry & la Veuve de Theodore Boom, 1687), 77–92; and in *Livre Synodal contenant les Articles résolus dans les Synodes de Eglises Wallonnes des Pays-Bas, Tome I 1563–1685* (La Haye: Martinus Nijhoff, 1896), 268–76. An Arabic translation of the Dordt Church Order was prepared in manuscript sometime after the synod. See Nabil Matar, "The Synod of Dort in Arabic: Bodleian MS Marsh 268," *The Seventeenth Century* 39 (2024), 726, who incorrectly dates the manuscript 28 May 1619, which was actually the date the Dordt Church Order was signed by the synod officers.

70. Nauta, *Verklaring*, 23–35.

71. Leon van den Broeke, "The Composition of Reformed Church Orders: A Theological, Reformed and Juridical Perspective," *In die Skriflig* 52, no. 2 (2018): a2351, https://doi.org/10.4102/ids.v52i2.2351.

CHAPTER 11

Calvin and the Canons of Dordt[1]

Discerning the influence of John Calvin on the Canons of Dordt (CD) is a much more difficult task than it may appear on the surface. The main reason is that the documents produced by the Synod of Dordt rarely refer to any theological source—let alone Calvin—of the ideas they deal with, apart from an occasional reference to Augustine or other patristic writers. The synod had a mandate from the States General of the Netherlands to base its deliberations on "the Word of God alone as the sure and undoubted rule of faith, and not any human writings."[2] All delegates were bound by oath to follow this mandate.[3] Hence the synodical documents are full of Scripture references, but they lack references to Reformation or contemporary theological writings that may have profoundly influenced the discussions and the documents of the synod. This is true not only of the CD, the main product of the synod, but also of the many judgments (*iudicia*) in which the nineteen delegations at the synod presented their views concerning the Five Remonstrant Articles that were being examined and judged by the synod. Though they were composed by a drafting

---

1. This is a revised version of the article printed in *Church History and Religious Culture* 91, no. 1–2 (Jan. 2011): 87–103.
2. *Acta*, session 4.
3. In the session of 7 December 1618, each member of the synod swore an oath in which he promised before God that, in all synodical transactions regarding doctrine, he would "not use any human writings, but the Word of God alone as the sure and undoubted rule of faith." *ADSND*, 1:38.

committee, the CD were based primarily on the sentiments expressed by the delegates in the *iudicia*.

These *iudicia* cover 540 pages in the printed *Acta* of the synod. In all of these pages, there are only 119 references to theological sources, eighty-four of which are found in the *iudicia* of the British delegation. Over half of the references (sixty-five) are to Augustine; thirty-seven are to other patristic writers (especially Prosper); and eleven are to medieval sources. There are only six references to Reformation and post-Reformation sources, all of which are found in the *iudicia* of the Bremen and Emden delegations: two references to the Heidelberg Catechism, two to Ursinus's commentary on the Heidelberg Catechism, one to the Belgic Confession, and one to Antonius Walaeus. It is noteworthy that none of the *iudicia* ever refer to Calvin.

On the other hand, some synodical documents contain citations and references to specific Remonstrant writings, since it was important to identify what were considered Remonstrant errors and to substantiate, by citation, that the errors were indeed taught by the Remonstrants.[4] For their part, some of the documents the Remonstrants submitted to the synod do contain references to a number of Reformed theologians whose teachings they rejected. These include a good number of references to Calvin.[5] So it is easier to discern the negative impact of Calvin upon the Remonstrants who were called before the synod than any direct influence of Calvin upon the synod itself and its Canons.

It is worth noting that at the time of the synod, the leaders of the Reformed movement were sometimes called "Calvinists," but the usual labels found in the synodical documents are simply "Reformed" or "Contra-Remonstrants." At the end of his speech to the synod on 29 November 1618, the British delegate Joseph Hall expressed some antipathy to the label "Calvinist" in a call for peace: "We are brothers; let us also be companions. What have we to do with those disreputable (*infami*) labels *Remonstrants, Contra-Remonstrants, Calvinists*

---

4. Such references are quite frequent in some of the *iudicia*, but especially in the "*Articuli pertinentes ad pleniorem explicationem sententiae Remonstrantium*," a compilation of Remonstrant errors, each of which is followed by references to Remonstrant sources where the errors were found; printed in *ADSND*, 2/2:781–800.

5. See chapter 12 of this volume, "Calvin as Viewed by the Remonstrants at Dordt."

(*Calvinianorum*), *Arminians*? We are Christians; let us also be of one spirit. We are one body; let us also be of one mind."[6]

Despite the lack of specific references to Calvin, it is worth examining his possible influence on the major themes in the CD. Since the CD first formulated the so-called "Five Points of Calvinism,"[7] this article offers an assessment of whether these Five Points do indeed have their source in Calvin.

While it would be feasible to examine Calvin's possible influence on each article of the CD, I will focus only on the major themes of this confessional document.

Chapter I: Election and Reprobation

The original title of the first chapter of the CD is "Divine Election and Reprobation."[8] The subtitle of the chapter indicates that this is the synod's "judgment concerning divine predestination." This identification of predestination with both election and reprobation clearly expresses double predestination.[9]

The chapter begins not with God's decree in eternity but with the fallen human condition and the gospel offer of salvation, after which it rises to the eternal decree. Since all people have sinned, God has the right to condemn them all (I, 1); but God manifested His love by sending His Son so that whoever believes in Him may have eternal life, as proclaimed in the gospel (I, 2–3). The fact that some receive the gift of faith, while others do not, stems from the eternal decree of election and reprobation (I, 6). This movement from human experience within the temporal horizon to the eternal decree exhibits an a posteriori approach to the topic of predestination.

---

6. *ADSND*, 2/2:473.
7. The full phrase did not originate with the Synod of Dordt. It appears to have originated in the early eighteenth century.
8. The only officially signed copy of the CD is preserved in OSA, vol. R.
9. A critical edition of the original Latin text of the CD is found in J. N. Bakhuizen van den Brink, ed., *De Nederlandse Belijdenisgeschriften* (Amsterdam: Ton Bolland, 1976), 225–78, there 228. The best English translation is found in *Ecumenical Creeds and Reformed Confessions* (Grand Rapids: CRC Publications, 1988), 122–45.

The CD then define election as God's eternal purpose by which, according to the good pleasure of His will, He elected in Christ to salvation a definite number of people out of the fallen human race and decreed to give them to Christ, call them, grant them faith, justify them, sanctify them, and glorify them, in order to demonstrate His mercy (I, 7). Hence the cause of election is God's good pleasure alone (I, 10), not foreseen faith; faith is the fruit or effect of election (I, 9). Reprobation, on the other hand, is God's decree, by His good pleasure, to leave those not elected or passed by in their common misery and not to grant them faith but to condemn them eternally for their unbelief and their other sins, in order to display His justice (I, 15). This formulation clearly expresses the late medieval distinction between negative reprobation (the decree to pass by in election and leave in misery) and positive reprobation (the decree to condemn for sin).[10]

As is evident from the definitions of election and reprobation, the CD are formulated in a clear infralapsarian sense (individuals are either elected from the fallen human race or left in their misery). The infralapsarian perspective is also exhibited in the fact that this first chapter begins with fallen humanity and that the decree of election and reprobation is described as merciful and just (I, 6).[11]

On the question of how Christ is related to election, the wording of article I, 7 (*ad salutem elegit in Christo*) makes it clear that not only is salvation in Christ, but it is election that is in Christ, an emphasis that reflects Ephesians 1:4. The phrase "in Christ" modifies election and not salvation, so Christ does not merely execute the decree of election by providing salvation to those who are elect. This article addresses Christ's role in salvation when it adds that Christ was *also* (*etiam*) appointed from eternity to be "the mediator and head of all those elected, and the foundation of their salvation."

---

10. Donald Sinnema, "The Issue of Reprobation at the Synod of Dort (1618–19) in Light of the History of this Doctrine" (PhD diss., University of St. Michael's College, Toronto, 1985), 410.

11. On the infralapsarian stance of the CD, see J. V. Fesko, "Lapsarian Diversity at the Synod of Dort," in *Drawn into Controversie: Reformed Theological Diversity and Debates within Seventeenth-Century British Puritanism*, ed. Michael A. G. Haykin and Mark Jones (Göttingen: Vandenhoeck and Ruprecht, 2011), 99–123.

The CD affirm three sources of the believer's assurance of election—observing the fruits of election, the internal testimony of the Spirit, and God's promises revealed in His Word (I, 12; V, 10). But the CD place the accent on seeking assurance of election from the fruits of election seen in believers themselves.

Like the CD, Calvin's approach was to address predestination by beginning from an experiential starting point rather than commencing with God's decree. In Book III of the *Institutes*, his discussion of predestination begins with the reality of the varied ways in which preaching is received. To explain this diverse response to the gospel, Calvin then turned to eternal election.[12]

Calvin's classic definition of predestination in his *Institutes* also included both election and reprobation:

> We call predestination God's eternal decree, by which he compacted with himself what he willed to become of each man. For all are not created in equal condition; rather, eternal life is foreordained for some, eternal damnation for others. Therefore, as any man has been created to one or the other of these ends, we speak of him as predestined to life or to death.[13]

While Calvin did not invent the notion of double predestination—it can be found in Augustine and Gottschalk and was revived by Bradwardine—his advocacy of it in a variety of writings certainly popularized the idea in the Reformed tradition. On double predestination, Calvin is a probable influence on the CD.

Calvin did not offer a formal definition of reprobation. He used various terms such as *reprobare, reicere, praedestinare ad mortem, destinare*

---

12. *Institutes*, 3.21.1. In his 1537 *Instruction in Faith*, Calvin likewise began with the contrasting attitudes of believers and unbelievers to the call of the gospel and then proceeded to God's counsel. See *Instruction in Faith (1537)* (Philadelphia: Westminster, 1949), 36.

13. *Institutes*, 3.21.5. Translation is from Calvin's *Institutes of the Christian Religion*, ed. John T. McNeill, trans. Ford Lewis Battles (Philadelphia: Westminster Press, 1960), 926. Calvin's view of predestination is examined by Fred H. Klooster, *Calvin's Doctrine of Predestination* (Grand Rapids: Baker, 1977); Heinz Otten, *Prädestination in Calvins Theologischer Lehre* (Neukirchen-Vluyn: Neukirchener Verlag, 1968); and A. D. R. Polman, *De Praedestinatieleer van Augustinus, Thomas van Aquino en Calvijn* (Franeker: Wever, 1936). I examine "Calvin's View of Reprobation" in *Calvin for Today*, ed. Joel R. Beeke (Grand Rapids: Reformation Heritage Books, 2009), 115–36.

exitio, praeordinare damnationem, and *praeterire,* which suggest various facets of reprobation, but he never made use of the negative–positive reprobation distinction.[14] In this respect, Calvin could not have been an influence on the CD.

For Calvin, the cause of both election and reprobation is exclusively in the good pleasure of God's will.[15] The cause of each is not divine foreknowledge of merit or sin, since all are equally unworthy.[16] The CD agree that the cause of both election and reprobation lies in God's good pleasure, but the formulation of article I, 15 also allows for the interpretation that the cause of positive reprobation is both God's will and sin,[17] a more moderate position than Calvin's. For Calvin, even though God reprobated by His sovereign will, the reprobate still deserve their own destruction.[18] Here he shifted the focus from eternal reprobation to actual temporal condemnation. It is on this temporal level alone that Calvin identified a twofold cause, based on a distinction between remote and proximate causality: though the remote cause of condemnation is in God's will, its proximate cause is sin.[19] Thus the blame for their destruction remains in the reprobate themselves. On this point, the CD identify the cause of temporal condemnation only as the unbelief and the other sins of the reprobate; no use is made of the remote–proximate distinction. By placing the cause of

---

14. Sinnema, "Issue of Reprobation," 60. Klooster, *Calvin's Doctrine*, 59, 71, 76, mistakenly sees in Calvin a distinction between preterition and condemnation as two aspects of reprobation. Calvin (and the CD) clearly distinguished between eternal reprobation (decreed before creation) and condemnation (or damnation) at the end of history.

15. *Institutes*, 3.23.10; 3.22.1; 3.23.1.

16. *Institutes*, 3.22.4.

17. Sinnema, "Issue of Reprobation," 411–12.

18. *Institutes*, 3.23.8; 3.24.14.

19. John Calvin, *Concerning the Eternal Predestination of God*, trans. J. K. S. Reid (London: James Clark, 1961), 100–101, 116 (*De aeterna Dei praedestinatione*, ed. W. Neuser [Geneva: Droz, 1998], 102, 132); *Institutes*, 3.23.3, 8, 9; John Calvin, *Selected Works: Tracts and Letters*, vol. 5, *Letters, Part 2, 1545–1553* (Grand Rapids: Baker, 1983), 366–67 (*CO* 14:380). On Calvin's distinction between proximate and remote causality, see Donald Sinnema, "Calvin and Beza: The Role of the Decree–Execution Distinction in Their Theologies," in *Calvinus Evangelii Propugnator: Calvin, Champion of the Gospel*, ed. David F. Wright, A. N. S. Lane, and Jon Balserak (Grand Rapids: Calvin Studies Society, 2006), 196–98.

condemnation in some sense also in God's will, Calvin's position is more stringent than that of the CD.

Though scholars have differed on whether Calvin was supralapsarian or infralapsarian,[20] it is incorrect to define his position as such, since this issue did not become formulated in terms of these alternatives until Theodore Beza, who was the first to present a clear supralapsarian position.[21] While Calvin could speak of God predestining a person before he was created or fallen, and while he could write that God's decree of election did not presuppose the fall of Adam,[22] in other passages he spoke in a more Augustinian fashion—that is, he wrote that God elected and reprobated from the condemned mass of perdition.[23] Calvin never presented his ideas on predestination in terms of an order of decrees, nor did he seek to identify the "object" of predestination. These are the two classic ways that the issue was formulated. Since this was not an issue for him, Calvin cannot be regarded as an influence on the CD's infralapsarian formulation.

As for the role of Christ in election, Calvin's explanation (in his commentary on Ephesians 1:4) about what it means to be elected in Christ appears to identify election with the adoption of the elect as children into the body of Christ, even though the elect do not come into possession of this benefit until they are called: "For if we are

---

20. Those who consider Calvin to be supralapsarian include Klaas Dijk, *De Strijd over Infra- en Supralapsarisme in de Gereformeerde Kerken van Nederland* (Kampen: Kok, 1912), 25; Edward A. Dowey Jr., *The Knowledge of God in Calvin's Theology* (Grand Rapids: Eerdmans, 1994), 213; and J. V. Fesko, *Diversity within the Reformed Tradition: Supra- and Infralapsarianism in Calvin, Dort, and Westminster* (Greenville, S.C.: Reformed Academic Press, 2001), 57–149. Others who consider Calvin to be infralapsarian include Henri Blocher, "Calvin infralapsaire," *La Revue Réformée* 31 (1980): 270–76; and Francis Turretin, *Institutes of Elenctic Theology* (Phillipsburg, N.J.: P&R Publishing, 1992), 1:349–50.

21. Donald Sinnema, "Beza's View of Predestination in Historical Perspective," in *Théodore de Bèze (1519–1605): Actes du Colloque de Genève, Septembre 2005*, ed. Irena Backus (Geneva: Librarie Droz, 2007), 225–29.

22. *Institutes*, 2.12.5; 3.23.7; *Predestination*, 101, 121 (*De praedestinatione*, 102, 144).

23. *Institutes*, 3.23.3; *Predestination*, 89, 101, 121, 125 (*De praedestinatione*, 82, 102, 144, 150–52); Calvin, "Congregation on Eternal Election," in Philip C. Holtrop, trans., *The Bolsec Controversy on Predestination, from 1551 to 1555* (Lewiston, N.Y.: Edwin Mellen, 1993), 2:700, 713, 715.

elected in Christ, it is outside ourselves. It is…because our heavenly Father has engrafted us, through the blessing of adoption [*adoptionis*] into the body of Christ."[24] Likewise, in the *Institutes*: "In electing His own, the Lord already has adopted them as His children."[25] This is not an interpretation that is evident in the CD.

Elsewhere, Calvin stated that, along with God the Father, the Son is the "author of election," with the right to elect, based on John 13:18: "I know whom I have chosen."[26] This interpretation of election in Christ is also found among delegates at the Synod of Dordt.[27] Both Calvin and the CD recognized that Christ is not only the foundation of salvation but also the author of election.[28] Calvin may have been an influence on the CD on this point, but because of his particular interpretation of election in Christ as adoption, his influence on the formulation of the CD concerning the role of Christ in election was likely limited.

While the CD place emphasis on finding assurance from the fruits of election in one's life, for Calvin these "latter signs" are a very secondary source of assurance; his primary emphasis was to look to Christ as the mirror of our own election.[29] On the matter of assurance of election, the CD more closely reflect the thought of Theodore Beza, whose main accent was on finding assurance by climbing from the fruits or effects of election to God's decree itself.[30]

---

24. Commentary on Ephesians 1:4.

25. *Institutes*, 3.24.1: "Suos eligendo iam in filiorum locum Dominus adoptarit." Cf. *Institutes*, 3.21.5: "Praedestinationem, qua Deus alios in spem vitae adoptat…"; 3.24.5: "Quos Deus sibi filios assumpsit, non in ipsis eos dicitur eligisse, sed in Christo suo (Ephe. 1:4)." Nevertheless, Calvin also asserted that eternal election precedes adoption in Christ (Comm. on Eph. 1:5; Comm. on Rom. 11:2), but this appears to refer to actual adoption within the course of time.

26. *Institutes*, 3.22.7; Comm. on John 13:18.

27. *Acta* (1620), 3:27.

28. W. H. Velema, "Calvijn en de Dordtse Leerregels," *In die Skriflig* 27, no. 4 (1993): 463–85, emphasizes that Christ is central to election in both Calvin and the CD and that both take an a posteriori approach to election.

29. *Institutes*, 3.14.19; 3.24.4; 3.24.5, 6; *Predestination*, 113, 126, 127, 130; Comm. on 1 John 2:3, 3:19, 4:17; "Congregation," 2:717. On Calvin's view, see A. N. S. Lane, "Calvin's Doctrine of Assurance," *Vox Evangelica* 11 (1979): 32–54.

30. Sinnema, "Beza's View," 235–38. For a more detailed analysis of Calvin's influence on Chapter I, see Donald Sinnema, "Are the Canons of Dordt a True Reflection

Chapter II: Christ's Death and Human Redemption

On the topic of Christ's death and how it accomplishes human redemption, the CD begin with the satisfaction view of the atonement—God's justice requires that sins be punished, so satisfaction must be given (*satisfiat*) to His justice (II, 1). Since sinful humans cannot give this satisfaction, God gave His Son, in our place, on the cross, in order to give satisfaction for us (II, 2). Christ's death gives entirely complete satisfaction for sins and is of infinite value and worth, more than sufficient (*abunde sufficiens*) to atone for the sins of the whole (*totius*) world (II, 3). Also, the gospel promise that whoever believes will have eternal life, as well as the command to repent and believe, ought to be declared without distinction (*promiscue*) to all (*omnibus*) nations and people (II, 5). Yet, it was God's plan and intention that the saving effectiveness (*efficacia*) of His Son's death should work itself out in all (*omnibus*) His elect, in order that He might grant justifying faith to them only (*solos*); in other words, that Christ's blood should effectively (*efficaciter*) redeem from every (*omni*) people and nation all those, and only those (*omnes et solos*), whom God elected from eternity (II, 8).

The key teaching of the CD here is that Christ effectively died only for the elect. But the formulation of this teaching is cloaked in universal language, especially upon the insistence of the British and Bremen delegations, in order to do justice to the universal passages of Scripture. This is expressed particularly in the emphasis on the universal sufficiency of Christ's death and in the obligation of a universal proclamation of the gospel. To accommodate both the particular and universal themes, the CD adopted the classic medieval distinction (first formulated by Lombard) between the sufficiency and the efficiency of Christ's death—sufficient for all, but efficient only for the elect.[31]

Calvin also taught a satisfaction view of the atonement, but his use of the term "satisfaction" has an imprecise sense that expresses various

---

of Calvin's View of Predestination?," *In die Skriflig* 52, no. 2 (2018): a2347, https://doi.org/10.4102/ids.v52i2.2347.

31. For analysis and background of the CD's view of the atonement and its extent, see W. Robert Godfrey, "Tensions Within International Calvinism: The Debate on the Atonement at the Synod of Dort, 1618–1619" (PhD diss., Stanford University, 1974).

themes of Christ's redemptive work.[32] He often spoke of Christ giving satisfaction to the Father for our sins,[33] and sometimes of Christ's death satisfying God's judgment[34] or His wrath.[35] But Calvin typically did not speak of satisfying God's justice (*iustitia*), as the CD do. That emphasis is clear in Beza,[36] who was more likely an influence on the CD concerning this point.

There is considerable debate among Calvin scholars concerning his view of the extent of Christ's redemption. Some see Calvin teaching particular or definite "atonement";[37] others think he taught universal

---

32. Robert A. Peterson, *Calvin's Doctrine of the Atonement* (Phillipsburg, N.J.: Presbyterian & Reformed, 1983), 91–93; François Wendel, *Calvin: The Origins and Development of His Religious Thought* (London: Collins, 1965), 219; G. Michael Thomas, "The Extent of the Atonement: A Dilemma for Reformed Theology from Calvin to the Consensus (1536–1675)" (PhD diss., Brunel University, 1993), 40–41. Richard A. Muller, *Calvin and the Reformed Tradition: On the Work of Christ and the Order of Salvation* (Grand Rapids: Baker Academic, 2012), 74–76, emphasizes that Calvin used the term "satisfaction" (*satisfactio*) rather than "atonement" in reference to Christ's death.

33. *Institutes*, 2.15.6; 2.16.2; 2.17.3, 4, 5; Comm. on Gal. 1:4; Comm. on Rom. 4:25.

34. *Institutes*, 2.12.3; 2.17.4.

35. *Institutes*, 2.16.1.

36. Theodore Beza, *The Christian Faith*, trans. James Clark (Lewes, UK: Focus Christian Ministries Trust, 1992), 10–11; *A Little Book of Christian Questions and Responses*, trans. Kirk M. Summers (Allison Park, Pa.: Pickwick, 1986), 10–11; (Beza, *Tractationes theologicae* [Geneva, 1582], 1:4, 657).

37. Scholars who argue that Calvin taught particular atonement include: Paul N. Archbald, *A Comparative Study of John Calvin and Theodore Beza on the Doctrine of the Extent of the Atonement* (PhD diss., Westminster Theological Seminary, 1998); Raymond A. Blacketer, "Definite Atonement in Historical Perspective," in *The Glory of the Atonement: Biblical, Historical & Practical Perspectives*, ed. Charles E. Hill and Frank A. James III (Downers Grove, Ill.: InterVarsity Press, 2004), 304–23; William Cunningham, *The Reformers and the Theology of the Reformation* (Edinburgh: Clark, 1862), 395–402; W. Robert Godfrey, "Reformed Thought on the Extent of the Atonement to 1618," *Westminster Theological Journal* 37, no. 2 (Winter 1975): 133–71; Paul Helm, *Calvin and the Calvinists* (Edinburgh: Banner of Truth Trust, 1982), 38–46; Paul Helm, "Calvin, Indefinite Language, and Definite Atonement," in *From Heaven He Came and Sought Her: Definite Atonement in Historical, Biblical, Theological, and Pastoral Perspective*, ed. David Gibson and Jonathan Gibson (Wheaton, Ill.: Crossway, 2013), 97–119; Frederick Leahy, "Calvin and the Extent of the Atonement," *Reformed Theological Journal* 8 (Nov. 1992): 54–64; Richard A. Muller, *Christ and the Decree: Christology and Predestination in Reformed Theology from Calvin to Perkins* (Grand Rapids: Baker, 1986), 33–34; John Murray, "Calvin on the Extent of the Atonement," *The*

"atonement."[38] One recent scholar makes the case that Calvin held a distinct "classical" position.[39] Still others see the evidence as inconclusive.[40] Whatever the interpretation, there is general agreement that Calvin did not write an explicit treatment on the extent of Christ's work of redemption and did not deal with this precise issue in the terms of later Reformed theology—whether Christ died for all people

---

Banner of Truth 234 (March 1983): 20–22; Roger Nicole, "John Calvin's View of the Extent of the Atonement," *Westminster Theological Journal* 47, no. 2 (Fall 1985): 197–225; Roger Nicole, "Moyse Amyraut (1596–1664) and the Controversy on Universal Grace: First Phase (1634–1637)" (PhD diss., Harvard University, 1966), 15–21; and Jonathan H. Rainbow, *The Will of God and the Cross: An Historical and Theological Study of John Calvin's Doctrine of Limited Redemption* (Allison Park, Pa.: Pickwick, 1990).

38. Scholars who argue that Calvin taught universal atonement include: David L. Allen, *The Extent of the Atonement: A Historical and Critical Review* (Nashville: B&H Academic, 2016), 48–96; Brian G. Armstrong, *Calvinism and the Amyraut Heresy: Protestant Scholasticism and Humanism in Seventeenth-Century France* (Madison: University of Wisconsin Press, 1969), 137–38; James W. Anderson, "The Grace of God and the Non-elect in Calvin's Commentaries and Sermons" (ThD diss., New Orleans Baptist Theological Seminary, 1976); M. Charles Bell, "Calvin and the Extent of the Atonement," *Evangelical Quarterly* 55, no. 2 (Aug. 1983): 115–23; Alan C. Clifford, *Calvinus: Authentic Calvinism: A Clarification* (Norwich: Charenton Reformed, 1996); Curt D. Daniel, "Hyper-Calvinism and John Gill" (PhD diss., University of Edinburgh, 1983), Appendix A: "Did John Calvin Teach Limited Atonement?," 777–828; R. T. Kendall, *Calvin and English Calvinism to 1649* (Oxford: Oxford University Press, 1981), 13–18; Kevin Dixon Kennedy, *Union with Christ and the Extent of the Atonement in Calvin* (New York: Lang, 2002); Stephen Strehle, "The Extent of the Atonement within the Theological Systems of the Sixteenth and Seventeenth Centuries" (ThD diss., Dallas Theological Seminary, 1980), 92–95; and Paul Van Buren, *Christ in Our Place: The Substitutionary Character of Calvin's Doctrine of Reconciliation* (Grand Rapids: Eerdmans, 1957).

39. Pieter L. Rouwendal, "Calvin's Forgotten Classical Position on the Extent of the Atonement: About Sufficiency, Efficiency, and Anachronism," *Westminster Theological Journal* 70, no. 2 (Fall 2008): 317–35. According to Rouwendal, the classical position—which had been common since it was formulated by Peter Lombard—held that Christ died *sufficiently* for all men but *efficiently* only for the elect. He argues that the particular and universal atonement positions arose only after Calvin's death. Rouwendal's thesis is alluring, but the textual evidence is very thin.

40. Peterson, *Calvin's Doctrine*, 91; Tony Lane, "The Quest for the Historical Calvin," *Evangelical Quarterly* 55, no. 2 (Aug. 1983): 95–113; Hans Boersma, "Calvin and the Extent of the Atonement," *Evangelical Quarterly* 64, no. 4 (Sep. 1992): 333–55; A. T. B. McGowan, *The Federal Theology of Thomas Boston* (Carlisle: Paternoster, 1997), 48–53; Thomas, "Extent," 39–55.

or only for the elect.[41] Some have drawn the conclusion that, since this issue had not yet become a matter of debate in Calvin's lifetime, the question of his view on the matter is anachronistic.[42] Others conclude that, based on the incidental statements he made, his position is ambiguous, oblique, inconsistent, imprecise, or marked by unresolved tension.[43] Beza, on the other hand, was later challenged by Lutherans on the extent of Christ's redemption, particularly at the Colloquy of Montbéliard (1586), and so he adopted a clear doctrine of particular redemption.[44]

Some of Calvin's statements seem to advocate particular redemption.[45] Others point in the direction of universal redemption. In a sermon on 2 Timothy 2:19, for example, he stated: "It is no small matter to have the souls perish which were bought by the blood of Christ."[46] He sometimes spoke of Christ suffering for the sins of the whole world[47] and of God's desire that all men be saved.[48] In certain biblical passages that speak of Christ dying for "many," he interpreted many as referring to all or the whole human race.[49] Given the abundant value of Christ's death, Calvin also stressed the universal offer or call of the gospel—"God invites all men to himself without distinction

---

41. Nicole, "Calvin's View," 197–98; Godfrey, "Reformed Thought," 137; Cunningham, *Reformers*, 396–97; Boersma, "Calvin," 335, 354; Kennedy, *Union with Christ*, 27; Blacketer, "Definite Atonement," 313; Helm, "Calvin, Indefinite Language," 98.

42. Peterson, *Calvin's Doctrine*, 90; Blacketer, "Definite Atonement," 315; Muller, *Calvin and the Reformed Tradition*, 72, 103.

43. Archbald, *Comparative Study*, 273, 364, 372, 378, 382; Boersma, "Calvin," 350, 354; Thomas, *Extent*, 54.

44. Archbald, *Comparative Study*, 357, 364; Godfrey, "Reformed Thought," 140–42; Jill Raitt, *The Colloquy of Montbéliard* (New York: Oxford University Press, 1993), 149–51.

45. John Calvin, *Theological Treatises*, ed. J. K. S. Reid (Philadelphia: Westminster, 1954), 285; Comm. on 1 John 2:2; Comm. on 1 Tim. 2:4–5; Comm. on Titus 2:11; *Predestination*, 109.

46. Sermon on 2 Tim. 2:19 (*CO* 54:165).

47. For example, his Comm. on Matt. 26:39; John 1:29; 1 Cor. 8:11; Gal. 5:12; Col. 1:14; 1 Peter 1:20; *Predestination*, 148–49.

48. Comm. on 2 Peter 3:9; *Institutes*, 3.3.21.

49. Comm. on Matt. 20:28; Mark 14:24; Heb. 9:28; Isa. 53:12; John Calvin, *Sermons on Isaiah's Prophecy of the Death and Passion of Christ*, trans. and ed. T. H. L. Parker (London: James Clark, 1956), 141.

[*promiscue*]"—with the promise to be proclaimed to all people that everyone who believes will be saved.⁵⁰

Calvin was well aware of the sufficient–efficient distinction—"that Christ suffered sufficiently for the whole world but effectively only for the elect"—though he rarely used it, and then only with qualified approval. For instance, in his comment on 1 John 2:2, he noted that this distinction commonly prevailed in the schools, and though he allowed its truth, he denied that it fit this passage.⁵¹

It is beyond the purpose of this article to determine whether Calvin favored particular or universal redemption. What may be concluded is that it is highly doubtful that Calvin could be an influence on the CD's position of particular redemption within the context of the distinction between the sufficiency and efficiency of Christ's death. Calvin's scant treatment of the issue and the ambiguity of his own position, which has caused the debate among scholars, preclude the possibility of influence. Later Reformed theologians, such as Vermigli, Zanchi, Beza, Olevianus, Perkins, Piscator, Pareus, and Ames, adopted a clear position favoring particular redemption, often relying on the distinction between the sufficiency and efficiency of Christ's death to explain the universal texts of Scripture.⁵² Before the Synod of Dordt, this developed into a rather general Reformed consensus, although there was some diversity of expression.⁵³ In the matter of particular redemption, the decisive influences on the CD almost certainly

---

50. Comm. on Rom. 10:6; also on Matt. 23:37; John 3:16; Rom. 5:18; 1 Tim. 2:4–6; and 2 Peter 3:9; *Institutes*, 3.3.21; 3.22.10; *Predestination*, 102–3, 149 (*De praedestinatione*, 106, 196); John Calvin, *Sermons on Election and Reprobation* (Audubon, N.J.: Old Path Publications, 1996), 62. See Muller, *Calvin and the Reformed Tradition*, 78–88.

51. Comm. on 1 John 2:2; see also *Predestination*, 103, 148–49 (*De praedestinatione*, 108, 196); *Sermons on Isaiah's Prophesy*, 116, 141, 144. See Muller, *Calvin and the Reformed Tradition*, 88–96.

52. Godfrey, "Reformed Thought," 138–50; Blacketer, "Definite Atonement," 315–17.

53. Godfrey, "Reformed Thought," 150, 170; Archbald, *Comparative Study*, 356. Such a general consensus is also evident in that the large majority of opinions of the delegations at the Synod of Dordt on the extent of Christ's redemption favored particular atonement within the context of the sufficiency–efficiency distinction; Godfrey, *Tensions*, 165–225. Thomas, "Extent," 250, followed by Allen, *Extent*, 161–62, deny that there was a Reformed consensus on this issue.

would have come from these later Reformed theologians rather than from Calvin.

The same can be said for the sufficient–efficient distinction found in the CD. Calvin was reticent about using this distinction, though he did not deny its truth. Later Reformed theologians readily employed the distinction to explain their position on the extent of Christ's redemption.[54] Again, the CD's use of this distinction is more likely shaped by these later theologians than by Calvin.

The one point in this chapter where Calvin may have been an influence is the emphasis of the CD on the universal call of the gospel that ought to be proclaimed indiscriminately to all people and nations.

Chapter III/IV: Human Corruption, Conversion, and the Way it Occurs

On the issue of human corruption or depravity, the CD state that man—who was created in God's image and furnished in his mind (*mente*) with true knowledge, in his will and heart (*voluntate et corde*) with righteousness, and in his emotions (*affectibus*) with purity—in the fall deprived himself of these gifts and brought upon himself blindness in his mind, hardness in his heart and will, and impurity in his emotions (III/IV, 1). This corruption spread to all his descendants by the propagation of his perverted nature, so all are conceived and born in sin, unfit for any saving good, dead in their sins, and slaves to sin (III/IV, 2, 3). Yet, a certain light of nature (*lumen aliquod naturae*) remained in humanity after the fall, by virtue of which they retained some notions (*notitias*) about God, natural things, and the difference between moral and immoral. But this light does not enable humans to come to a saving knowledge of God and conversion (III/IV, 4).

These sentiments closely reflect Calvin's views of sin.[55] In the state of integrity, he said, Adam fully possessed right understanding

---

54. Godfrey, "Reformed Thought."
55. Calvin's view of sin is explored by T. F. Torrance, *Calvin's Doctrine of Man* (London: Lutterworth, 1949), 83–115; David J. Engelsma, "Nothing but a Loathsome Stench: Calvin's Doctrine of the Spiritual Condition of Fallen Man," *Protestant Reformed Theological Journal* 35, no. 2 (April 2002): 39–60; Michael S. Horton, "A Shattered Vase: The Tragedy of Sin in Calvin's Thought," in *A Theological Guide to Calvin's Institutes: Essays and Analysis*, ed. David W. Hall and Peter A. Lillback (Phillipsburg,

(*recta intelligentia*), held his emotions (*affectus*) within the bounds of reason, kept all his senses (*sensus*) tempered in the right order, and truly referred his excellence to the exceptional gifts bestowed on him by his Maker.[56] At the fall, humans were deprived of spiritual gifts (relating to salvation), and their natural gifts were corrupted.[57] While Calvin usually spoke of two faculties of the soul, the understanding and the will,[58] in regard to humanity's fallen state he emphasized that no part of the soul remains pure, due to the inordinate impulses of the appetites (*appetituum*), the blindness of the mind (*mentem*), and the depravity of the heart (*cor*).[59] Due to original sin, which is a hereditary depravity and corruption of human nature,[60] fallen humanity is indeed utterly dead as far as the blessed life is concerned.[61]

Yet Calvin acknowledged that fallen humans have some awareness of divinity (*divinitatis sensus*), though they cannot attain a true knowledge of God.[62] Their natural gifts are corrupted, but not completely destroyed. The fall did not take away the will but made it a slave, though it was originally free.[63] Reason, by which humans distinguish good and evil, and by which they understand and judge, is a natural gift that was not completely wiped out but that was weakened and

---

N.J.: P&R Publishing, 2008), 151–67; Barbara Pitkin, "Nothing but Concupiscence: Calvin's Understanding of Sin and the *Via Augustini*," *Calvin Theological Journal* 34, no. 2 (Nov. 1999): 347–69; Luca Baschera, "Total Depravity? The Consequences of Original Sin in John Calvin and Later Reformed Theology," in *Calvinus Clarissimus Theologus*, ed. Herman J. Selderhuis (Göttingen: Vandenhoeck and Ruprecht, 2012), 37–58; Andrew T. Hancock, "The Grace of God and Faithful Christian Education: Comparing the Synod of Dort and John Calvin on Depravity and Addressing the Problem of the Corruption of the Mind," *Christian Education Journal: Research on Educational Ministry* 13, no. 2 (Nov. 2016): 315–30; Lee Gatiss, "Sin and the Synod of Dort," in *Ruined Sinners to Reclaim: Sin and Depravity in Historical, Biblical, Theological, and Pastoral Perspective*, ed. David Gibson and Jonathan Gibson (Wheaton: Crossway, 2024), 163–93.

56. *Institutes*, 1.15.3.
57. *Institutes*, 2.2.12; 2.2.16.
58. *Institutes*, 1.15.7.
59. *Institutes*, 2.1.9.
60. *Institutes*, 2.1.8.
61. *Institutes*, 2.5.19.
62. *Institutes*, 1.3.1.
63. John Calvin, "Acts of the Council of Trent, with Antidote," in *Selected Works: Tracts and Letters*, vol. 3, *Tracts, Part 3* (Grand Rapids: Baker, 1983), 109.

corrupted.⁶⁴ Something of the understanding and the will remains as a residue (*residuum*) after the fall; in humanity's perverted nature, some sparks (*scintillas*) still gleam.⁶⁵ There are some remaining traces (*notas*) of God's image that distinguish humans from other creatures.⁶⁶

While the terminology is not precisely the same, it is apparent that the CD's view of depravity reflects the ideas of Calvin. This suggests a possible influence of Calvin on the formulation of the CD, but the influence of other Reformed theologians with similar views is just as possible.

On the issue of conversion by grace and the way it occurs, the CD affirm that through the gospel God seriously (*serio*) calls people to come to Him and seriously promises eternal life for those who believe (III/IV, 8). The fact that many who are called are not brought to conversion is their own fault; but that others called by the gospel are converted is to be credited to God alone—He effectively (*efficaciter*) calls them and grants them faith and repentance (III/IV, 9–10). God works conversion in them not only by the outward proclamation of the gospel but also by the effective operation (*efficacia*) of the Spirit; He penetrates the inmost being, opens the closed heart, and infuses new qualities in the will, making the dead will alive, the unwilling one willing (III/IV, 11). The result of this entirely supernatural work is that the will, in being activated by God, is also itself active, and people themselves actually believe (III/IV, 12). This faith is a gift of God, not in the sense that it is offered by God for a person to choose whether or not to be converted but in the sense that it is actually bestowed on a person by Him who works all things in all people, producing both the will to believe and the belief itself (III/IV, 14). This divine grace of regeneration does not act on people as if they are blocks or stones; nor does it abolish the will or coerce a reluctant will by force; rather, it spiritually revives, heals, reforms, and bends (*vivificat, sanat, corrigit, flectit*) the will in a pleasing and powerful way, so that ready obedience replaces rebellion and resistance. This brings about the spiritual restoration and freedom of the will (III/IV, 16). Note that the emphasis

---

64. *Institutes*, 2.2.12.
65. *Institutes*, 2.2.17.
66. *Institutes*, 2.2.17.

of the CD is not that grace is irresistible but that grace is efficacious, overcoming human resistance.

Again, the CD here reflect Calvin's view of the manner of conversion.[67] Calvin's strong emphasis is that conversion is wholly God's doing, from beginning to end.[68] There is a general call by which God addresses both the elect and the reprobate by the outward preaching of the Word. There is also a special call that, for the most part, He gives to believers alone; by the inward illumination of the Spirit, He causes the preached Word to dwell in their hearts. Hence, He manifests His secret election by effectual (*efficaci*) calling.[69] He grants them faith as a free gift.[70] Calvin asserted that conversion is the creation of a new spirit and a new heart.[71] God removes the heart of stone and gives a new heart. He wholly transforms and renews the will. Whatever is of our own will is effaced, not insofar as it is will—for the will is not taken away by grace—but insofar as it is changed from an evil will to a good will.[72] Except through grace, the human will can neither be converted to God nor abide in Him; and whatever it can do, it is able to do only through grace.[73] Grace anticipates unwilling man, that he may will.[74] Hence, in the case of the conversion of Paul—a man who was rushing against Christ—he was called back to salvation against the intention of his own mind, forced into obedience against his will, and made a new and different man.[75] But yet, in conversion God does not move a person as if he were like a stone. Rather, Calvin explained, "God begins his good work in us, therefore, by arousing [*excitando*] love and desire and zeal for righteousness in our hearts; or, to speak

---

67. Calvin's teaching on irresistible grace has been examined by Garret Wilterdink, "Irresistible Grace and the Fatherhood of God in Calvin's Theology" (PhD diss., University of Chicago, 1974); and André -Pinard, "La doctrine de la grâce irrésistible chez Jean Calvin," (MA thesis, Laval University, 1954).

68. *Institutes*, 2.3.6.

69. *Institutes*, 3.24.8; see also John Calvin, *The True Method of Giving Peace to Christendom and of Reforming the Church*, in *Selected Works*, 3: 253–54; Comm. on John 10:27.

70. *Institutes*, 2.3.8.

71. *Institutes*, 2.3.8.

72. *Institutes*, 2.3.6; cf. 2.3.14.

73. *Institutes*, 2.3.14.

74. *Institutes*, 2.3.12.

75. Comm. on Acts 9:1, 3, 5.

more correctly, by bending, forming, and directing [*flectendo, formando, dirigendo*] our hearts to righteousness."[76] Calvin also stressed that God does not move the will in such a way that it is our choice to obey or resist, to accept or refuse, but by influencing it efficaciously (*efficaciter*). The hearts of the godly are so effectively (*efficaciter*) governed by God that they follow Him with unwavering intention.[77]

Both Calvin and the CD focus on divine grace in conversion as efficacious rather than as irresistible. Calvin tended to place a greater accent on the creation of a new heart and will, but like the CD, he also spoke of transformation and renewal by bending the heart and will to righteousness. The formulation of the CD is close enough to suggest once again a possible influence of Calvin.

Chapter V: Perseverance of the Saints

On the topic of the perseverance of the saints, the emphasis of the CD is actually on God's preservation of those whom He has regenerated until the end of life; perseverance in faith flows out of that preservation. The converted cannot remain standing in grace by their own resources; rather, God is faithful, strengthening them in the grace conferred on them and powerfully preserving them in grace to the end (V, 3). Yet those converted can, by their own fault, depart from the leading of grace and commit very serious sins, even to the point of losing awareness of grace for a time, until they return to God (V, 4, 5). But God does not let them fall so far that they forfeit the grace of adoption or become entirely forsaken by Him (V, 6). For God preserves in those saints His imperishable seed from which they have been born again (V, 7). By God's undeserved mercy, they neither forfeit faith and grace totally nor become lost (V, 8).

A similar emphasis can be found in Calvin.[78] Though he did not offer a sustained treatment of perseverance, this theme is clear here and there throughout his writings. Calvin's emphasis is that perseverance

---

76. *Institutes*, 2.3.6; see also 2.5.14 and 2.3.9–10.
77. *Institutes*, 2.3.10.
78. For Calvin's view of perseverance in historical context, see John J. Davis, "The Perseverance of the Saints: A History of the Doctrine," *Journal of the Evangelical Theological Society* 34, no. 2 (June 1991): 213–28; Jürgen Moltmann, *Prädestination und Perseveranz* (Neukirchen: Neukirchener Verlag, 1961), 31–71; and Jay T. Collier,

is a gift of God, not the merit of the person persevering.[79] It applies only to the elect, whom the Father entrusted to Christ to keep unto eternal life.[80] It is impossible that those whose faithful protector is the Son of God should fall away from salvation; because they are the sheep of His flock, no one can pluck them out of His hand.[81] God supplies those He has elected with an invincible fortitude so that they may persevere.[82] His Spirit nourishes constancy in them to persevere. God upholds and strengthens them by His power so that they may not perish.[83] He begins and completes His good work in such persons so that they persevere to the very end.[84] Hence, those rooted in God can never be pulled up from salvation; they are out of danger of falling away and shall ever remain safe because they have been made Christ's once and for all.[85] The fear and reverence of God cannot be extinguished in anyone who has been regenerated by God's Spirit.[86]

Thus Calvin asserted that the sacrifice of Christ is efficacious for believers right to the time of death, even if they repeatedly sin.[87] If someone rises again from a fall, however seriously such a person may otherwise have sinned, he is not guilty of rebellion that would lead to eternal death.[88] On the other hand, those who totally fall away from grace and completely renounce God are really apostates who have estranged themselves from the gospel of Christ that they previously embraced. Though they had a taste of God's grace, and though He illumined their minds with some glimmerings of His light, they were wholly reprobate all along and not elect; the Lord calls only the elect effectively.[89]

Debating Perseverance: The Augustinian Heritage in Post-Reformation England (Oxford: Oxford University Press, 2018).
    79. *Institutes*, 2.3.11; 2.5.3.
    80. *Institutes*, 3.24.6.
    81. Comm. on Matt. 24:24; see also Comm. on John 10:28.
    82. John Calvin, *A Defense of the Secret Providence of God*, in *Calvin's Calvinism*, ed. Henry Cole (London: Henry Atherton, 1927), 281.
    83. *Institutes*, 2.5.3.
    84. *Institutes*, 2.3.9.
    85. *Institutes*, 3.24.6.
    86. Comm. on 1 John 3:9.
    87. Comm. on Heb. 10:26.
    88. Comm. on Heb. 6:6.
    89. Comm. on Heb. 6:4–6 and 10:26.

The similarity between Calvin's position on perseverance and the CD suggests a possible influence, although the formulations are slightly different. For example, the CD emphasize the concept of God's "preservation" of the elect more than Calvin does. Here, once again, other Reformed theologians could also have directly influenced the formulation of the CD.

Conclusions

1. Calvin was not the single fountainhead of the Reformed tradition, and he was not so regarded at the time of the Synod of Dordt, either by the members of the synod or by the Remonstrants who were present. There were numerous Reformed theologians, major as well as minor figures, who may have influenced the synod and its Canons. To be sure, Calvin was a key source who shaped the tradition, but he was one of many. The influences of others on the CD may well be equal or more significant than that of Calvin.

2. Between the time of Calvin and the Synod of Dordt, there was some doctrinal development. Not only is there a large measure of continuity, but there are elements of discontinuity. Especially due to the challenge of new polemics (with Catholics, Lutherans, and Remonstrants), as well as an emerging scholastic tendency toward precision in analysis, new issues came to the fore in the course of this period that were not in focus for Calvin; or issues were formulated with greater precision and framed in different terms by the use of categories or distinctions not used or not emphasized by Calvin—for example, the supra–infralapsarian question, the distinction between negative and positive reprobation, the question of who exactly Christ died for, and the distinction between the sufficiency and efficiency of Christ's death. Since some of the issues discussed at Dordt did not become matters of debate until after Calvin's time, it is unrealistic and anachronistic to expect that Calvin would have declared his stance on them or that he would have been an influence on such formulations at Dordt.

3. Some ideas were common coin in the Reformed tradition, shared by Calvin and all other orthodox Reformed theologians—for example, the notion that God's will alone is the cause of election. In such cases, it is impossible to identify a specific influence of Calvin on the matter.

4. On points—such as double predestination—where Calvin was a major inspiration or advocate (though not the originator) of certain ideas that came to dominate later Reformed formulations, one can conclude that Calvin was a probable influence on the CD.

5. A similarity of thought and a compatibility of ideas between Calvin and the CD do not necessarily entail influence; this can only indicate possible influence. Given the lack of evidence regarding sources of influence in the documents of Dordt, one can best conclude that, on points where there is a similarity of expression—such as on human depravity, efficacious grace, and perseverance—Calvin was a possible rather than definite influence.

6. On points where Calvin was a possible or probable influence, his influence was as likely to be indirect—channeled or filtered through writings of later Reformed theologians—as it was to be direct from his own writings.

7. On balance, one is led to conclude that Calvin's influence on the CD could only have been moderate. On several points—the experiential starting point, double predestination, election in Christ, the universal call of the gospel, human depravity, efficacious grace, perseverance—his influence is possible, or perhaps probable. On other points—the infralapsarian emphasis, twofold reprobation, assurance of election, particular redemption, the sufficiency–efficiency distinction—an influence of Calvin is unlikely.

8. Calvin is not the unqualified source of the "Five Points of Calvinism" as presented in the CD. Though he was a possible or probable influence on some elements of the five points, he was an unlikely influence on others. While the CD are formulated in five points, it is historically misleading to designate these points as "Calvinism" in the sense that they all stem directly from Calvin himself. Moreover, Calvinism cannot be reduced to the five points of soteriology in dispute in the Arminian controversy.

9. When the "Five Points of Calvinism" are popularly formulated in the acronym TULIP, the result is an unnuanced oversimplification and distortion that does not well represent Calvin or even the CD. TULIP

is misleading, not only in distorting the order of the CD but also in suggesting: *total* (or absolute) rather than pervasive depravity; unconditional election with no mention of reprobation or the introductory context of the universal sinfulness of humanity and the gospel message as the remedy; *limited* atonement without the universal call of the gospel or the infinite value of Christ's death as more than sufficient to atone for the sins of the whole world; *irresistible* grace instead of efficacious grace that overcomes human resistance; and perseverance without emphasis on divine preservation.[90]

---

90. It appears that the earliest known reference to the acronym TULIP dates back only to 1905. That year Dr. Cleland Boyd McAfee, then pastor of Lafayette Avenue Presbyterian Church in Brooklyn, made use of the acronym in a popular lecture on the Five Points of Calvinism given before the Presbyterian Union of Newark, New Jersey. This is documented in an article by Dr. William Vail, "The Five Points of Calvinism Historically Considered," published in *The Outlook* (21 June 1913). I thank Kenneth Stewart of Covenant College for this reference. The Vail article is reprinted in Stewart's book *Ten Myths about Calvinism: Recovering the Breadth of the Reformed Tradition* (Downers Grove, Ill.: IVP Academic, 2011), 291–92. For a more detailed analysis of the "Five Points of Calvinism" and TULIP, see chapter 16 of this volume "Distortions of the Canons: The Tilenus Abbreviation, the Five Points of Calvinism, and TULIP."

CHAPTER 12

Calvin as Viewed by the Remonstrants at Dordt

The influence of Calvin on the Synod of Dordt is not easy to discern, since, according to the prescribed regulations of the synod, all deliberations about doctrine were to be based solely on the Word of God and not upon any human writings. Hence, documents written by delegates at the synod focused on Scripture and rarely mentioned Calvin or any other human sources.[1] However, the Remonstrants who were summoned to appear before the Synod of Dordt felt no obligation to avoid mention of human sources concerning the theological ideas that were in controversy. In fact, in their debates with the synod about their Five Articles (from their 1610 Remonstrance), they insisted on pointing out that the ideas they objected to were indeed taught by a variety of Reformed authors, among them Calvin. Hence, in the documents the Remonstrants submitted to the synod, they often presented quotations from Reformed sources they thought were objectionable.

The citation letters that summoned thirteen leading Remonstrants to appear before the Synod of Dordt required that they "state, explain, and defend" their views before the synod. Hence the Remonstrants submitted three sets of documents on the points in dispute. The *Sententia* on each of their Five Articles was supposed to state their views, the *Declaratio* or *Explicatio* was to be a further explanation, and

---

1. See Donald Sinnema, "Calvin and the Canons of Dordt (1619)," *Church History and Religious Culture* 91, no. 1–2 (Jan. 2011): 87–103. Reprinted in this volume; see chapter 11.

the *Defensio* was to be a defense of their position. In all three, the Remonstrants criticized the Contra-Remonstrant position, but it was especially in the *Declaratio*, along with its appended *Syllabus Testimoniorum*, that they presented a multitude of quotations from a variety of Reformed writers to which they objected.[2] These include a number of quotations from Calvin. There are also occasional references to Calvin in the Remonstrant *Defensiones* of their Five Articles. By examining all of these references, it is possible to discern how the Remonstrants viewed Calvin, as well as what ideas of his they found objectionable.

The *Declaratio* on Article I (On Predestination)

In the *Declaratio* on Article I, which the Remonstrants submitted to the synod on the day of their expulsion (14 January 1619), they spelled out their views and examined the opposing position in some detail.[3] The document included three parts: an explanation of election and reprobation, an overview of the order of divine decrees as conceived by both sides, and an examination of various distinctions and issues related to the topic.

One issue that the Remonstrants briefly discussed in the first part of the *Declaratio* was the object of election and reprobation. They pointed out that the Contra-Remonstrants could not agree among themselves on this issue. To support this charge, they listed six different views held by the Contra-Remonstrants.[4] This list was virtually the same as that found in a 1617 Remonstrant letter sent to foreign theologians. Though the *Declaratio* did not specifically identify the theologians who held these six views, the 1617 letter did so. It identified Calvin and Theodore Beza as rising up above the fall (*supra lapsum*) and teaching that the object of election and reprobation was humanity considered as yet-to-be-created (*condendi*)[5]—the supralapsarian position.

---

2. For the background of the *Declaratio* on Article I, see Donald Sinnema, "The Issue of Reprobation at the Synod of Dort (1618–19) in Light of the History of this Doctrine," (PhD diss., University of St. Michael's College, Toronto, 1985), 258, 305–17.

3. "Declaratio Sententiae Remonstrantium circa Primum de Praedestinationis Decreto Articulum," in *Acta et Scripta*, 2:3–46.

4. *Acta et Scripta*, 2:5.

5. *Epistola Ecclesiastarum, quos in Belgio Remonstrantes vocant, ad Exterarum Ecclesiarum Reformatos Doctores, Pastores, Theologos* (Leiden, 1617), 40–41.

Though Calvin in his various writings did not explicitly discuss the object of predestination, it is interesting that the 1617 Remonstrant letter interpreted Calvin's view as identical to Beza's well-known supralapsarian position.[6]

The second part of the *Declaratio* focused on the order of divine decrees in election and reprobation. After the Remonstrants presented their own position in an order of seven decrees, they moved on to the order of decrees found in the opposing positions of the "supralapsarians"[7] and the "sublapsarians" (i.e., infralapsarians). In this context, the *Declaratio* explicitly identified Calvin as teaching the supralapsarian view.

At the foundation of the supralapsarian position, the Remonstrants saw two principal decrees: the decree concerning the end (salvation or destruction), and the decree concerning the means by which the elect and the reprobate are led to their destined end. From various Reformed authors, the Remonstrants then constructed what they considered to be the supralapsarian order of decrees: (1) God, like a wise artisan, first decided the ultimate end of all things—the declaration of His glory—by way of His two attributes of mercy and justice, which would be revealed in two corresponding works, salvation and perdition. (2) The decree to create humans was necessary so that they might become objects of divine mercy and punishment. (3) A decree to propose the law to them was necessary, since they could not sin unless they had a free will and were subject to law. (4) A decree was necessary by which humans could not but sin and become the object of mercy or

---

6. Theodore Beza was actually the first to fully develop the supralapsarian position, both in terms of identifying the "object" of predestination as man considered as not-yet-created and not-yet-fallen and in terms of an order of divine decrees. See Donald Sinnema, "Beza's View of Predestination in Historical Perspective," in *Théodore de Bèze (1519–1605): Actes du Colloque de Genève, Septembre 2005*, ed. Irena Backus (Geneva: Librarie Droz, 2007), 225–29. It is anachronistic to label Calvin as supralapsarian or infralapsarian, since he never treated predestination either in terms of its "object" or in terms of an order of decrees.

7. *Acta et Scripta*, 2:17, 18, 20, 23; cf. 255, 257. These references in the 1619 *Declaratio* are the earliest documentary instances of the label *supralapsarii* of which I am aware. Yet even these instances assume that the term was already somewhat well known. The 1617 Remonstrant *Epistola Ecclesiastarum*, 41, refers to Calvin and Beza as rising *supra lapsum*, but this letter and other Remonstrant polemical pamphlet literature before the Synod of Dordt do not specifically mention *supralapsarii*.

justice. (5) Then followed a decree that the first man's sin should involve the whole human race so that all would be liable to eternal punishment. (6) God decreed to elect some from that miserable state by a mediator who satisfied divine justice for them alone. (7) God decreed that the reprobate might also be born of Adam in order to manifest His justice; thus, it was necessary that they be left in the fall and not be granted the grace necessary for salvation, so that they rush into all kinds of sin and, at last, give God occasion to exercise His justice in them, thereby letting His glory shine in their eternal condemnation.[8]

The Remonstrants fashioned this rationally constructed scheme of decrees from a variety of Reformed writings. As such, the scheme did not fairly represent the teaching of any particular Reformed theologian. Various aspects of the scheme did, however, reflect the thinking of some of the theologians who were cited.

The *Declaratio* then offered forty-four quotations from twelve Reformed theologians whom they accused of teaching this supralapsarian scheme. Johann Piscator is the most represented, with fourteen quotations; Calvin and Beza are in second place, each with six quotations.

The six quotations from Calvin are offered as evidence for the first, fifth, and seventh of the supralapsarian decrees. For the first decree, there are three quotations from Calvin:[9]

> *Institutes*, 3.21.5: "We call predestination God's eternal decree, by which he compacted with himself what he willed to become of each man. For all are not created in equal condition; rather, eternal life is foreordained for some, eternal damnation for others. Therefore, as any man has been created to one or the other of these ends [*finem*], we speak of him as predestined to life or to death."

> *Institutes*, 3:23.6: "Since the disposition of all things is in God's hand, since the decision of salvation or of death rests in his power, he so ordains by his plan and will that among men some are born

---

8. *Acta et Scripta*, 2:11–17.

9. *Acta et Scripta*, 2:12–13. Translations from Calvin's *Institutes of the Christian Religion* are from the Ford Lewis Battles translation (Philadelphia: Westminster, 1960). I have slightly revised this translation to provide a literal rendering of the Latin in the *Acta et Scripta*; for example, *reprobare* is more correctly rendered "to reprobate" than "to condemn."

destined for certain death from the womb, who glorify his name by their own destruction."

Institutes, 3.22.11: "If we cannot determine a reason why he vouchsafes mercy to his own, except that it so pleases him, neither shall we have any reason for reprobating others, other than his will."

(Other theologians quoted: Beza and Keckermann)

For the fifth decree, there are two quotations from Calvin:[10]

Institutes, 3.23.7: "Again I ask: whence does it happen that Adam's fall irremediably involved so many peoples, together with their infant offspring, in eternal death unless because it so pleased God? The decree is dreadful [*horribile*] indeed, I confess; yet no one can deny that God foreknew what end man was to have before he created him, and consequently foreknew because he so ordained by his decree."

Institutes, 3.23.4[?]: "We confess that it happened by God's plan and will that Adam fell and that we have all fallen into this misery of the condition in which we are now entangled."

Finally, for the seventh decree, there is one quotation from Calvin.[11]

Institutes, 3.24.12: "What of those, then, whom God created for dishonor in life and destruction in death, to become the instruments of this wrath and examples of his severity? That they may come to their end, he sometimes deprives them of the capacity to hear his word; at other times he, rather, stuns and hardens them by the preaching of it."

(Other theologians quoted: Zanchi, Piscator, Sturm, Daneau, Beza)

Since Calvin did not in fact formulate his view of predestination in terms of an order of decrees, let alone a supralapsarian order, the Remonstrants' attempt to portray Calvin as supralapsarian remains unconvincing.

---

10. *Acta et Scripta*, 2:15.
11. *Acta et Scripta*, 2:17.

The *Explicatio* on Article III/IV (On the Manner of Conversion)

The *Explicatio* on Article III/IV was submitted by the Remonstrants to the synod on 14 February. This document includes some scattered references to Calvin.

As evidence of the Contra-Remonstrant view that the sole cause for which God does not consider as many as possible worthy of the preaching of the gospel is that, by His absolute decree, they are positively reprobated from eternal life, and so, by the same absolute decree, apart from any consideration of a meriting cause, they are utterly destitute of the means of grace, the *Explicatio* quotes Calvin, Zanchi, and Piscator:

> Calvin, *Institutes*, 3.24.12: "What of those, then, whom he created for dishonor in life and destruction in death, to become the instruments of this wrath and examples of his severity? That they may come to their end, he sometimes deprives them of the capacity to hear his word; at other times he, rather, stuns and blinds them by the preaching of it."[12]

As evidence of the Contra-Remonstrant view that God does not outwardly call the reprobate with any intention to convert them but that He might render them more inexcusable—since, having been called, they do not believe—or that, through that call, He might harden and blind them so that He has cause to condemn them more severely, the *Explicatio* used quotations from Piscator and Beza, as well as the previous quotation of Calvin (from *Institutes*, 3.24.12), along with another from the *Institutes*:

> Calvin, *Institutes*, 3.24.8: "There is the general call, by which God invites all equally to himself through the outward preaching of the Word—even those to whom he holds it out as a savor of death, and as the occasion for severer condemnation."[13]

As evidence of the Contra-Remonstrant view that God wills the salvation of some by His revealed will (of the sign), and not by His secret will (of good pleasure), so that God wills and does not will this salvation, since His divine will is engaged in contrary acts of willing

---

12. *Acta et Scripta*, 3:9.
13. *Acta et Scripta*, 3:10–11.

and not willing the same thing, the *Explicatio* presents quotations from Calvin, Zanchi, and Piscator:

> Calvin, Commentary on Ezekiel 18:23: "But we must remark that God puts on a twofold character: for he here wishes to be taken at his Word. As I have already said, the Prophet does not here [18:23: 'Have I any pleasure at all that the wicked should die?'] dispute with subtlety about his incomprehensible plans, but wishes to keep our attention close to God's Word. Now, what are the contents of this Word? The law, the prophets, and the gospel. Now all are called to repentance, and the hope of salvation is promised them when they repent. This is true, since God rejects no returning sinner; he pardons all without exception. Meanwhile, this will of God which he sets forth in his Word does not prevent him from decreeing before the world was created what he would do with every individual."[14]

As evidence of the Contra-Remonstrant view that God wills and determines by His secret counsel that sins happen and that, although they happen against the precepts and the revealed will of God, yet they happen by the power of His secret good pleasure and will, the *Explicatio* presents quotations from Calvin, Daneau, Trigland, and Piscator:

> Calvin, *The Secret Providence of God*: "Nothing hinders God, by his ineffable counsel, from willing to be done for a different end something that he wills not to be done and forbids to be done."[15]

The *Syllabi Testimoniorum* on the Five Articles

In order to demonstrate that the ideas rejected in their *Sententiae* were indeed taught in the public writings of the Contra-Remonstrants and of those they considered orthodox, the Remonstrants attached to their *Declaratio* on each of the Five Articles a *Syllabus Testimoniorum* from Reformed theologians. In these *Syllabi*, the theses of the Remonstrant *Sententiae* are divided into smaller units, each of which is followed by several quotations.

The *Syllabi Testimoniorum* on Articles I, II, III/IV, and V list a total

---

14. *Acta et Scripta*, 3:12–13. Translation from Calvin, *Commentaries on the First Twenty Chapters of the Book of the Prophet Ezekiel* (Edinburgh: Calvin Translation Society, 1850), 2:248.

15. *Acta et Scripta*, 3:25–26. Translation, revised, from John Calvin, *The Secret Providence of God* (Wheaton: Crossway, 2010), 94.

of 556 quotations to which the Remonstrants objected.[16] These quotations are taken from forty-five different Reformed writers. Calvin is among them. With twenty-seven quotations, Calvin is the fifth-most represented author, after Johann Piscator (120 quotations), Sebastianus Dammannus (forty-nine quotations), the Contra-Remonstrants at the 1611 Hague Conference (thirty-nine quotations), and Girolamo Zanchi (thirty-seven quotations). Others in the top ten include Reynier Donteclock (twenty-six quotations), Jacobus Trigland (twenty-four quotations), Rippertus Sixti (twenty-three quotations), Franciscus Gomarus (twenty-two quotations), and Theodore Beza (twenty-one quotations). The results of this tabulation are not surprising. Piscator, whose extreme statements were frequently the object of Remonstrant criticism,[17] easily topped the list. With almost 5% of the quotations, Calvin is in the top five, but he is certainly not the prime object of Remonstrant objections.

A tally of the number of times each author or group of authors is quoted in the *Syllabi Testimoniorum* gives a clear indication of which authors most offended the Remonstrants:

Piscator	120	Dunganus	7	Marloratus	2
Dammannus	49	Lubbertus	7	Zepperus	2
Contra-Remonstrants		Pareus	7	Bishop of Salisbury	1
at Hague Conference	39	Revius	7	(re: Perkins)	1
Zanchi	37	Hommius	5	Bucer	1
Calvin	27	Vogelius	5	Busschoff	1
Donteclock	26	Acronius	4	Daneau	1
Trigland	24	Maccovius	4	Kimedoncius	1
Rippertus Sixti	23	Whitaker	4	Luther	1
Gomarus	22	Brouckerus	3	Rennecherus	1
Beza	21	Bucanus	3	Sohn	1
Perkins	20	Polanus	3	Szegedinus	1
Thysius	16	Sturm	3	Ursinus	1
Geselius	14	Textor	3	Classis Walcheren	1
Smoutius	13	Urbanus	3		
Mehnius	10	Gratianus			
Peter Martyr	10	Civilis	2		

---

16. *Acta et Scripta*, 2:25–46, 290–96; 3:28–54, 203–17.

17. For example, Piscator's assertion that unbelief depends on God's predestination as does an effect on a cause; see *Acta et Scripta*, 2:42.

To gain a sense of which ideas of Calvin the Remonstrants particularly objected to, I list all twenty-seven quotations from Calvin in the *Syllabi* as they appeared under a variety of theses in which the Remonstrants summarized objectionable ideas of Reformed authors.

Article I (On Predestination)
1. That God decreed to elect some to eternal life and to reprobate others from it before He decreed to create them:[18]

(Theologians quoted: Gomarus, Hommius, Beza, Perkins)

According to His good pleasure:[19]

> Calvin, *Institutes*, 3.23.1: "Therefore, those whom God passes over, he reprobates; and this he does for no other reason than that he wills to exclude them from the inheritance which he predestines for his own children."

> Calvin, *Institutes*, 3.23.1: "It is utterly inconsistent to transfer the preparation for destruction to anything but God's secret plan."

(Other theologians quoted: Gomarus, Maccovius, Hommius, Thysius, Whitaker, Beza, Piscator)

2. That God, by this plan, created in one man, Adam, all men; ordained the fall and its permission; withdrew from Adam necessary and sufficient grace; and took care that the gospel is preached, that people are externally called, and that some gifts of the Holy Spirit are granted to them, in order that these things might be the means by which He may lead some to life and deprive others of the benefit of life:[20]

> Calvin, *Institutes*, 3.2.11: "Experience shows that the reprobate are sometimes affected by almost the same feeling as the elect, so that even in their own judgment they do not in any way differ from the elect. Therefore, it is not at all absurd that the apostle should

---

18. *Acta et Scripta*, 2:15.
19. *Acta et Scripta*, 2:28.
20. *Acta et Scripta*, 2:32.

attribute to them a taste of the heavenly gifts, and that Christ should attribute to them temporary faith."

(Other theologians quoted: Bucanus, Perkins, Maccovius, Zanchi, Donteclock)

3. That creation is a common means or effect of predestination is expressed in equivalent phrases by those who teach that God created some unto life and others unto destruction:[21]

> Calvin, *Institutes*, 3.21.5: "For we are not created in equal condition; rather, eternal life is foreordained for some, eternal damnation for others. Therefore, as any man has been created to one or the other of these ends, we speak of him as predestined to life or to death."

> Calvin, *Institutes*, 3.24.12: "What of those, then, whom he created for dishonor in life and destruction in death, to become the instruments of this wrath and examples of his severity? That they may come to their end, he sometimes deprives them of the capacity to hear his word; at other times he, rather, blinds and stuns them by the preaching of it."

> Calvin, Commentary on Rom. 9:18: "Paul does not inform us that the ruin of the ungodly is foreseen by the Lord, but that it is ordained by his counsel and will. Solomon also teaches us that not only was the destruction of the ungodly foreknown, but the ungodly themselves have been created that they might perish."[22]

(Other theologians quoted: Gomarus, Maccovius, Beza, Piscator, Peter Martyr)

4. That many—namely, all the reprobate—are rejected from eternal life and from the means sufficient for it by an absolute antecedent decree, so that the merit of Christ, calling, and all the gifts of the Spirit can be of no use to them for salvation, and truly are not:[23]

---

21. *Acta et Scripta*, 2:33.
22. Translation, slightly revised, from John Calvin, *The Epistles of Paul to the Romans and Thessalonians*, trans. R. MacKenzie, Calvin's New Testament Commentaries (Grand Rapids: Eerdmans, 1973), 207–8.
23. *Acta et Scripta*, 2:38.

Calvin, *Institutes*, 3.24.13: "Observe that he directs his voice to them but in order that they may become even more deaf; he kindles a light but that they may be made even more blind; he sets forth doctrine but that they may grow even more stupid; he employs a remedy but so that they may not be healed."

Calvin, *Institutes*, 3.24.13: "We cannot gainsay the fact that, to those whom he pleases not to illumine, God transmits his doctrine wrapped in enigmas in order that they may not profit by it except to be cast into greater stupidity."

Calvin, *Institutes*, 3.24.14: "The fact that the reprobate do not obey God's Word when it is made known to them, will be justly charged against the malice and depravity of their hearts, provided it be added at the same time that they have been given over to this depravity because they have been raised up by the just but inscrutable judgment of God to show forth his glory in their condemnation."

(Other theologians quoted: Donteclock, Dammannus, Trigland, Revius, Zanchi, Polanus, Piscator, Smoutius)

Article II (On Christ's Death and Redemption and the Extent of the Atonement)

On Article II, the Remonstrants presented fifty-five quotations that they objected to from Reformed authors.[24] Of the twenty writers represented, Piscator, Zanchi, and Lubbertus head the list, with six quotations each. None of these quotations are from Calvin. Since the Remonstrants apparently had no objection to Calvin on this topic (here in the *Syllabus*, and in the broader *Declaratio* on Article II), this would suggest that they were of the opinion that Calvin did not forthrightly teach that Christ died only for the elect.

Article III/IV (On the Manner of Conversion)

1. That the efficacious grace by which anyone is converted is an irresistible force (*vim irresistibilem*):[25]

Calvin, *Institutes*, 2.3.10: "He does not move the will in such a manner as has been taught and believed for many ages—that it is

---

24. *Acta et Scripta*, 2:290–96.
25. *Acta et Scripta*, 3:30.

afterward in our choice either to obey or resist the motion—but by disposing it efficaciously. Therefore, one must deny that oft-repeated statement of Chrysostom: 'Whom he draws he draws willing.' By this he signifies that the Lord is only extending his hand to await whether we will be pleased to receive his aid."

Calvin, *Institutes*, 2.3.10: "And one may incontrovertibly conclude from John's words [John 6:44: 'No one comes to me unless my Father draws him.'] that the hearts of the pious are so effectively governed by God that they follow him with unwavering intention. 'No one begotten of God can sin,' he says, 'for God's seed abides in him' [1 John 3:9]. For the intermediate movement the Sophists dream up, which men are free either to accept or refuse, we see obviously excluded when it is asserted that constancy is efficacious for perseverance."

(Other theologians quoted: Contra-Remonstrants at the Hague Conference, Thysius, Trigland, Dunganus, Dammannus, Smoutius, Geselius, Zanchi, Donteclock, Gomarus, Perkins)

2. That God grants sufficient grace for faith and conversion only to those whom He irresistibly (*irresistibiliter*) wills to convert according to the decree of His election; but to the reprobate He neither gives nor wills to give the grace necessary for faith, conversion, and salvation.[26]

Calvin, *The True Method of Giving Peace to Christendom and of Reforming the Church*: "Seeing that God invites all indiscriminately by outward preaching, the only thing which distinguishes his elect from the reprobate is, that allowing the latter to be blind in the light, he presents the former with new eyes, by which they see, and inclines their hearts to obey his word. Hence, he manifests his secret election by effectual calling."[27]

Calvin, *The True Method of Giving Peace to Christendom and of Reforming the Church*: "For between the elect and the reprobate there is this difference, that while God addresses both by the voice of man, he specially teaches the former inwardly by his Spirit. The ministry

---

26. *Acta et Scripta*, 3:32.
27. Translation from *Selected Works*, 3:253.

of man, I say, is common to both, but the inward grace of the Spirit is peculiar to the elect."[28]

Calvin, *The Secret Providence of God*: "God gives no insincere precepts, but seriously reveals what he wills and approves. However, while in one way he wills that his elect fulfill obedience to him by efficaciously bending them to compliance, in another way he instructs the reprobate by means of an external word but does not consider them worthy to draw to himself. Stubbornness and depravity are equally natural to all men, so that none are of themselves willing and ready to take up the yoke. To some, God promises the Spirit of obedience, but others he leaves in their depravity. For whatever you might babble to the contrary, a new heart and heart of flesh is not promised to all indiscriminately, but peculiarly to the elect so that they might walk in God's precepts. What can you say to this, good judge? When God invites the whole crowd to himself, and yet the Spirit was knowingly and willingly held back from the greater part, nevertheless he draws a few by his secret provision to obedience. Is this to be condemned as a lie?"[29]

(Other theologians quoted: Contra-Remonstrants at the Hague Conference, Trigland, Geselius, Beza, Szegedinus, Piscator, Dammannus, Donteclock, Thysius, Smoutius, Peter Martyr, Zanchi, Zepperus)

3. That God calls some externally whom He does not will to call internally—that is, to be truly converted—before they have rejected the grace of His call.[30]

Calvin, *Institutes*, 3.24.12: "As God by the effectual working of his call to the elect perfects the salvation to which by his eternal plan he has destined them, so he has his judgments against the reprobate, by which he executes his plan for them. What of those, then, whom he created for dishonor in life and destruction in death, to become the instruments of this wrath and examples of his severity? That they may come to their end, he sometimes deprives them of the capacity to hear his word; at other times he, rather, blinds and stuns them by the preaching of it."

---

28. Translation from *Selected Works*, 3:254.
29. Translation, slightly revised, from *Secret Providence*, 100.
30. *Acta et Scripta*, 3:38.

> Calvin, *The Secret Providence of God*: "Nevertheless, why he willingly allows men to err, nay, even more by his secret decree he gives men over to error, men whom he commands to keep the right way, cannot be comprehended by the sober and modest. To make inquiry in the shameless way that you do shows how brazen you are!"[31]

> (Other theologians quoted: Contra-Remonstrants at the Hague Conference, Donteclock, Thysius, Trigland, Piscator, Zanchi, Peter Martyr, Beza)

4. That there is in God such a secret will that so opposes His will revealed in His Word that, according to His secret will, He does not will the conversion and salvation of the greatest part of those whom He seriously calls and invites to faith and salvation by the Word of the gospel and His revealed will, and on that account a holy pretense and a twofold character (*duplicem personam*) are to be acknowledged here in God.[32]

> Calvin, *The Secret Providence of God*: "On the contrary, this is the sum of my doctrine: that which is expressed in the law is the will of God, so that it is clearly demonstrated that he approves uprightness and hates iniquity. It is certain that, if it pleased him, he would not prevent the punishment of the wicked. However, nothing hinders God, by his ineffable counsel, from willing to be done for a different end something that he wills not to be done and forbids to be done."[33]

> Calvin, Commentary on Ezekiel 18:23: "But we must remark that God puts on a twofold character: for he here wishes to be taken at his Word. As I have already said, the Prophet does not here [18:23: 'Have I any pleasure at all that the wicked should die?'] dispute with subtlety about his incomprehensible plans, but wishes to keep our attention close to God's Word. Now, what are the contents of this Word? The law, the prophets, and the gospel. Now all are called to repentance, and the hope of salvation is promised them when they repent. This is true, since God rejects no returning sinner; he pardons all without exception. Meanwhile, this will of God which he sets

---

31. Translation, slightly revised, from *Secret Providence*, 85.
32. *Acta et Scripta*, 3:40–41.
33. Translation, revised, from *Secret Providence*, 93–94.

forth in his Word does not prevent him from decreeing before the world was created what he would do with every individual."[34]

(Other theologians quoted: Trigland, Rippertus Sixti, Zanchi, Sturm, Piscator, Thysius)

5. That God calls the reprobate to these ends, that He might harden them to a greater extent, take away all excuse, punish them more heavily, and show their lack of ability, but not that they might be converted, believe, and be saved.[35]

> Calvin, *Institutes*, 3.24.8: "There is the general call, by which God invites all equally to himself through the outward preaching of the Word—even those to whom he holds it out as a savor of death, and as the occasion for severer condemnation. The other kind of call is special, which he deigns for the most part to give to the believers alone, while by the inward illumination of his Spirit he causes the preached Word to dwell in their hearts. Yet sometimes he also causes those whom he illumines only for a time to partake of it; then he justly forsakes them on account of their ungratefulness and strikes them with even greater blindness."

> Calvin, *Institutes*, 3.24.12: "As God by the effectual working of his call to the elect perfects the salvation to which by his eternal plan he has destined them, so he has his judgments against the reprobate, by which he executes his plan for them. What of those, then, whom he created for dishonor in life and destruction in death, to become the instruments of this wrath and examples of his severity? That they may come to their end, he sometimes deprives them of the capacity to hear his word; at other times he, rather, blinds and stuns them by the preaching of it."

> Calvin, *Institutes*, 3.24.13: "Observe that he directs his voice to them but in order that they may become even more deaf; he kindles a light but that they may be made even more blind; he sets forth doctrine but that they may grow even more stupid; he employs a remedy but so that they may not be healed."

(Other theologians quoted: Gomarus, Donteclock, Perkins, Trigland, Beza, Piscator, Thysius)

---

34. Translation from *Commentaries on…the Prophet Ezekiel*, 2:248.
35. *Acta et Scripta*, 3:46.

Article V (On Perseverance)

1. That through God it happens that some do not persevere in true faith or guard themselves against sins.[36]

> Calvin, *The Secret Providence of God*: "You say that Adam fell by his free will. I reply, he would not have fallen if he had possessed the needed fortitude and perseverance that God provides for his elect when he wills to keep their integrity. This is certain, that unless virtue is provided from heaven each new moment, because we are fallen we would be ruined a thousand times over. Whomever God elects, he supports with an unconquerable fortitude for perseverance. Would this not have been provided for Adam, if he had willed him to remain unimpaired?"[37]

> (Other theologians quoted: Dammannus, Piscator)

2. That, although true believers fall into serious and horrible sins, they cannot totally or finally depart from faith (nor, indeed, drive out or extinguish the Holy Spirit absolutely or finally), and therefore they cannot perish.[38]

> Calvin, Commentary on Matthew 13:20: "As the Spirit is never extinguished in the godly, it is impossible that faith should vanish and perish when once it has been engraven in their hearts."[39]

> Calvin, *Institutes*, 3.24.6: "From this we infer that they are out of danger of falling away because the Son of God, asking that their godliness be kept constant, did not suffer a refusal. What did Christ wish to have us learn from this but to trust that we shall ever remain safe because we have been made his once for all?"

> Calvin, Commentary on Hebrews 6:5: "The elect are outside the danger of mortal lapse."[40]

---

36. *Acta et Scripta*, 3:204.
37. Translation, slightly revised, from *Secret Providence*, 76.
38. *Acta et Scripta*, 3:208.
39. Translation from John Calvin, *A Harmony of the Gospels: Matthew, Mark and Luke*, trans. T. H. L. Parker, Calvin's New Testament Commentaries (Grand Rapids: Eerdmans, 1972), 2:72.
40. Translation from John Calvin, *The Epistle of Paul the Apostle to the Hebrews and the First and Second Epistles of St. Peter*, trans. W. B. Johnston, Calvin's New Testament Commentaries (Grand Rapids: Eerdmans, 1963), 76.

Calvin, Commentary on Matthew 24:24: "For it is impossible that those whose faithful protector is the Son of God should fall away from their salvation."[41]

Calvin, *Concerning the Eternal Predestination of God*: "For we do not imagine that the elect always hold to the right course under the continual direction of the Spirit; we say that they often fall, err, suffer shipwreck, and are almost alienated from the way of salvation. But since the protection of God by which they are defended is stronger than all, they cannot fall into fatal ruin."[42]

(Other theologians quoted: Contra-Remonstrants at the Hague Conference, Donteclock, Acronius, Gomarus, Mehnius, Dammannus, Beza, Zanchi, Ursinus, Sturm, Whitaker, Piscator, Sohn)

The *Defensio* on Article I (On Predestination)

The Remonstrant *Defensio* on Article I, which the Remonstrants submitted to the synod on 7 February, also contains some scattered references to Calvin.

In an exposition of Romans 9, specifically verse 17 ("The Scripture says to Pharaoh, 'I raised you up for this very purpose, that I might display my power in you and that my name might be proclaimed in all the earth.'"), the *Defensio* argues that the term "raised up [*excitavi*]" means to "sustain," "keep," or "preserve as a witness" (not create [for destruction]), and it makes an appeal to Calvin (in his comment on the original text in Exodus), claiming that he appears to interpret the term in the same sense of "keep standing":

Calvin, Commentary on Exodus 9:16: "Others think that this sentence depends on what has gone before, and interpret it 'I have preserved thee,' or 'chosen that thou shouldest survive.' For the Hebrew verb, which is transitive in *hiphil*, is derived from עמד, *gnamod*, which means 'to stand up.' Since, therefore, God has restrained himself, he now assigns the cause of his moderation, because if Pharaoh had fallen in one trifling engagement, the glory of his victory would have been less illustrious. In fine, lest Pharaoh should flatter himself, or harden himself by vain confidence, God

---

41. Translation, slightly revised, from *Harmony of the Gospels*, 3:90.
42. Translation from John Calvin, *Concerning the Eternal Predestination of God*, trans. J. K. S. Reid (London: James Clark, 1961), 154.

affirms that he does not lack strength to destroy him immediately, but that he had delayed his ultimate punishment for another purpose, viz., that Pharaoh might slowly learn that he strove in vain against his incomparable power; and that thus remarkable history should be celebrated in all ages. But although Paul follows the Greek interpreter, there is no reason why we should not embrace this latter sense; for we know that the apostles were not so particular in quoting the words, but that they rather considered the substance. But, although we admit that by God's longsuffering Pharaoh continued to hold out, until he became a clear and notorious proof of the madness and folly of all those who resist God, yet this also has reference to the eternal prescience of God; for therefore did God spare Pharaoh to stand for a time, because, before he was born, he had been predestinated for this purpose. Wherefore, also, Paul rightly concludes that 'it is not of him that willeth, nor of him that runneth' (Rom. 9:16). For whether God raises up or upholds the reprobate, he wonderfully manifests his glory by their perverseness. Thus is their ignorance reputed, who, by this cavil, endeavor to overturn the eternal predestination of God; because it is not said, that he created Pharaoh with this intention, but that he suspended his judgment for a time. For this intermediate and progressive course of proceeding arose from this source, that Pharaoh was the organ or instrument of God's wrath."[43]

The *Defensio* mentions the interpretation of Romans 8:28–29 ("Those God foreknew He also predestined") by the "leaders and principal defenders of absolute predestination," Calvin and Beza.[44]

The *Defensio* emphasizes the dissent among the Contra-Remonstrants concerning the object of reprobation—namely, that between an older (supralapsarian) view advocated by Calvin, Beza, Whitaker, Perkins, Piscator, and others and another (infralapsarian) view introduced in the Netherlands by Donteclock and others.[45]

The *Defensio* asserts that election cannot stand without its opposite reprobation, "as the renowned Calvin rightly rebukes of childish

---

43. *Acta et Scripta*, 2:144. Translation from John Calvin, *Commentaries on the Four Last Books of Moses* (Edinburgh: Calvin Translation Society, 1852), 1:184–85.
44. *Acta et Scripta*, 2:197.
45. *Acta et Scripta*, 2:232.

ignorance those who acknowledge election in such a way that they deny reprobation."⁴⁶

On reprobation, the *Defensio* asserted:

> It is no wonder that Luther in his book, *De Servo Arbitrio*, which the Contra-Remonstrants very much esteem, Calvin in his *Institutes*, Piscator, and other very influential men, who have treated our controversies more honestly, having rejected this distinction [between preterition and predamnation], simply preferred to say, that God… condemns the undeserving [Luther]; that he predestines people by the mere will of God, apart from their own merit to eternal death [Calvin]; that God has absolutely predestined whomever he wills, by his antecedent will and good pleasure alone, to condemnation and to the causes of condemnation [Piscator], etc., as amply appears from the *Syllabus* of authors which we have adjoined to our *Declaratio*.⁴⁷

The *Defensio* argues that the teaching of an absolute decree of reprobation conflicts with God's glory and goodness. But what kind of goodness is it "first to predestine the whole human race to sin and ruin, as the renowned Calvin, Beza, Perkins, Piscator, and many of the chief leaders of the Contra-Remonstrants wish?… How cruel, to will the whole human race to be miserable, so that you may free very few from it?"⁴⁸

The *Defensio* argues that, according to the decree of absolute reprobation, God effects unbelief through the gospel to harden and blind the reprobate. Out of irreconcilable malevolence, He destines the word of the gospel to go out to the majority of humanity, provoked by none of their ungodliness or obstinacy. As proof, it quotes:

> Calvin, *Institutes*, 3.24.13: "He directs his voice to them but in order that they may become even more deaf; he kindles a light but that they may be made even more blind; he sets forth doctrine but that they may grow even more stupid; he employs a remedy but so that they may not be healed."⁴⁹

---

46. *Acta et Scripta*, 2:233.
47. *Acta et Scripta*, 2:237.
48. *Acta et Scripta*, 2:243.
49. *Acta et Scripta*, 2:261.

The *Defensio* questions whether sensing within oneself faith in Christ is a certain mark of predestination, since it can be common to the reprobate and the elect. Here appeal is made to:

> Calvin, *Institutes*, 3.2.10, 11: "The human heart has so many crannies where vanity hides, so many holes where falsehood lurks, is so decked out with deceiving hypocrisy, that it often dupes itself." "Experience shows that the reprobate are sometimes affected by almost the same feeling as the elect, so that even in their own judgment they do not in any way differ from the elect."[50]

The *Defensio* also argues that a doctrine that someone does not dare to openly propose in the churches to the people is deservedly suspect of falsehood. It notes that "Calvin himself confesses that if anyone would teach to his hearers in the church that the cause why they are not converted is because they were reprobated from eternity, he would do so very imprudently."[51]

The *Defensio* on Article IV (On the Manner of Conversion)

The *Defensio* on Article IV, submitted to the synod on 19 March, includes two references to Calvin in support of the Remonstrant position.

Here the Remonstrant *Defensio* appeals to Calvin's and Beza's interpretation of Matthew 23:37 (which describes Jesus's wish to gather the children of Jerusalem, but the scribes "were not willing"), over against the interpretation of the Contra-Remonstrants.[52]

The Remonstrants also used the following passage of Calvin, along with passages from Wolfgang Musculus and Franciscus Junius, to confirm their explanation of Isaiah 5:4, that God does not work irresistibly.

> Calvin, Commentary on Isaiah 5:4: "He first inquires what could have been expected from the best *husbandman* or householder [God], which he has not done to his vineyard? Hence, he concludes

---

50. *Acta et Scripta*, 2:269–70.
51. *Acta et Scripta*, 2:274.
52. *Acta et Scripta*, 3:70.

that they [Israel] had no excuse for having basely withheld from him the fruit of his toil."[53]

The *Defensio* on Article V (On Perseverance)

The *Defensio* on Article V, submitted to the synod on 19 March, contains several quotations of Calvin, all of which run counter to the Remonstrant view that it is possible for a person who is converted to totally fall from grace.

The *Defensio* makes reference to Calvin's commentary on Ezekiel 18:24–26. When this passage declares that a righteous man who turns away from his righteousness will die, Calvin explains that here the "righteous" refer to hypocrites, who only have temporary righteousness, not the elect who never utterly fall away.[54]

The *Defensio* quotes Calvin's *Institutes*, 3.2.12, concerning temporary faith, which can be lost: "Some are not pretending a faith, who nevertheless lack true faith; but while they are carried away with a sudden impulse of zeal, they deceive themselves in a false opinion."[55]

Finally, the *Defensio* lists ten passages from Calvin's *Institutes*, 3.2.10–12, which attribute the loss of faith to those who have only a temporary faith:[56]

> Calvin, *Institutes*, 3.2.10: "Such persons, prompted by some taste of the Word, greedily seize upon it, and begin to feel its divine power.... The assent which they offered to the Word seems sometimes to put down roots."

> Calvin, *Institutes*, 3.2.11: "God illumines their minds enough for them to recognize his grace.... God manifests to them his mercy for the time being."

> Calvin, *Institutes*, 3.2.11: "The reprobate are justly said to believe that God is merciful toward them, for they receive a gift of reconciliation, although confusedly and not distinctly enough."

---

53. *Acta et Scripta*, 3:111. Translation from John Calvin, *Commentary on the Book of the Prophet Isaiah* (Edinburgh: Calvin Translation Society, 1850), 1:167.
54. *Acta et Scripta*, 3:225. See Calvin, *Commentaries on...the Prophet Ezekiel*, 2:249–52, 256–57.
55. *Acta et Scripta*, 3:231.
56. *Acta et Scripta*, 3:234.

Calvin, *Institutes*, 3.2.12: "They are like a tree not planted deep enough to put down living roots. For some years it may put forth not only blossoms and leaves, but even fruits; nevertheless, it withers after the passage of time."

Calvin, *Institutes*, 3.2.10: "They persuade themselves that the reverence that they show to the Word of God is very piety itself."

Calvin, *Institutes*, 3.2.12: "It is evident from the teaching of Scripture and daily experience that the reprobate (who believe for a time) are sometimes touched by the awareness of divine grace, and therefore a desire to love one another must be aroused in their hearts."

Calvin, *Institutes*, 3.2.11: "There is a great likeness and affinity between God's elect and those who are given a transitory faith."

Calvin, *Institutes*, 3.2.11: "Experience shows that the reprobate (who believe for a time) are sometimes affected by almost the same feeling as the elect, so that even in their own judgement they do not in any way differ from the elect."

Finally, in a message to the state delegates at the end of the *Defensio* on Article V, the Remonstrants noted that President Bogerman and Contra-Remonstrant authors wished to persuade themselves and others, contrary to obvious truth, that there was no difference between Calvin and Melanchthon on predestination, except in method.[57]

Conclusions

The Remonstrants drew quotations from a significant variety of Calvin's writings. There are thirty-eight quotations from the *Institutes*, five from *The Secret Providence of God* (against Castellio), two from *The True Method of Giving Peace to Christendom and of Reforming the Church*, one from *Concerning the Eternal Predestination of God*, three from his commentary on Ezekiel, three from his commentary on Matthew, two from his commentary on Romans, and one each from his commentaries on Exodus, Isaiah, and Hebrews.

---

57. *Acta et Scripta*, 3:343–44.

It is noteworthy that the Remonstrants regarded Calvin, along with Beza, as supralapsarian, even though it is anachronistic to consider Calvin as holding the position first clearly espoused by Beza.

The Remonstrants also considered both Calvin and Beza as the principal defenders of "absolute predestination," the position that God predestined people to eternal life or death by the sheer act of His will, without any consideration of the faith or unbelief of those who are predestined.

It is worthwhile to provide a summary of the specific ideas in Calvin's quotations that the Remonstrants found objectionable:

1. God first decreed the ultimate end of every person—salvation or perdition.

2. There is no other cause for which God elects some and reprobates others than that He wills to do so by His secret plan, apart from any merit.

3. God created some persons for the purpose that they may live and others that they may perish; He created the reprobate for destruction to be instruments of His wrath.

4. God decreed that Adam's sin should involve the whole human race.

5. God, by His secret counsel, wills that sins be committed for a specific purpose; at the same time, He forbids these sins to be committed by the precepts of His revealed will.

6. In conversion, God does not move the will in such a way that it is our choice to accept or to resist, but He influences it efficaciously (Calvin does not use the term "irresistibly," although the Remonstrants do).

7. Though God calls all by outward preaching, only the elect receive effectual calling by the inward grace of the Spirit effectively turning them to obedience; the reprobate, however, He does not effectually draw by His Spirit.

8. God's revealed will in His Word, which calls all to repentance and promises salvation to those who repent, does not prevent Him from decreeing by His incomprehensible secret will the reprobation of some.

9. God calls the reprobate by the outward preaching of the Word not to heal them but to deprive them of the capacity to hear or to strike them with even greater blindness and more severe condemnation.

10. God sometimes gives the reprobate a taste of spiritual gifts, such as temporary faith, but this does them no good, and they will be lost.

11. God gives the elect the gift of invincible fortitude so that they persevere and are kept safe from falling away.

12. Though the elect can fall into serious sin, it is impossible for the Spirit to be extinguished from them and for them to fall away from salvation.

In sum, the key issues of Remonstrant concern were Calvin's view of God's secret and revealed will, reprobation, efficacious conversion, and the perseverance of the elect. These views of Calvin were all related to the Five Articles in controversy, and not to Calvin's broader theology. It is noteworthy that the Remonstrants had no objection to Calvin on the issues of human depravity (except on original sin) and the extent of the atonement.

The Remonstrants, in their documents submitted to the Synod of Dordt, were not critical in all their references to Calvin. In several instances, the Remonstrants appealed to Calvin in support of their own position. This is the case in their use of quotations of particular exegetical points from Calvin's commentaries on Exodus 9:16, Isaiah 5:4, and Matthew 23:37. They also appealed to Calvin when he rejected those who acknowledge election but deny reprobation; when he asserted that a sense of faith can be deceptive, since the reprobate can also share this; and when he warned that it is imprudent to teach in church that the cause for which some are not converted is because they are reprobated.

Calvin was not the single source of the Reformed tradition, and he was not so regarded at the time of the Synod of Dordt, either by the members of the synod or by the cited Remonstrants who were present. To be sure, Calvin was a key source that shaped the tradition, but he was one of many Reformed theologians, major as well as minor, whose influence was felt at the synod and by the Remonstrants.

In regard to their Five Articles—except, notably, the second and the third—the Remonstrants viewed Calvin as a significant source of objectionable ideas being propagated in the Reformed tradition, but certainly not as the only source or the most offensive source (Piscator).

The first draft of Chapter I of the Canons of Dordt

CHAPTER 13

The Drafting of the Canons of Dordt[1]

Introduction

Little is known about the three-week period in March–April 1619 when the Canons of Dordt (CD) were drafted or about the drafting process itself. The CD were drafted by a committee that kept no minutes, and the *Acta* of the Synod of Dordt are also silent on this period, since there were no public sessions.

Nevertheless, over one hundred archival documents relating to the drafting of the CD have been preserved in various archives in the Netherlands, Switzerland, Germany, and England. These materials include several drafts of the CD, amendment suggestions on some of these drafts by the various delegations at the synod, and a variety of drafting committee documents. These documents have never been gathered into a collection, few have ever been transcribed from the original Latin, and they have not been carefully studied. Since these were working documents, preliminary to the final CD, they were never considered part of the official *autographa* of the synod and were not included in the published *Acta*. The whole collection of these documents will be published for the first time in volume 3 of the series *Acta et Documenta Synodi Nationalis Dordrechtanae*.

---

1. This article is a revised and abbreviated version of my article "The Drafting of the Canons of Dordt: A Preliminary Survey of Early Drafts and Related Documents," in *Revisiting the Synod of Dordt (1618–1619)*, ed. Aza Goudriaan and Fred van Lieburg (Leiden: Brill, 2011), 291–311. That longer article provides full documentation of the many documents on which the present article is based.

As far as I am aware, there are six main repositories of archival documents relating to the drafting of the CD. These contain President Bogerman's early drafts of the CD, the drafts of the drafting committee, amendment suggestions from the various delegations, and some committee documents.

1. The *Oud Synodaal Archief*, now housed in the Utrechts Archief in Utrecht, contains the *autographa* of the synod (seventeen volumes of official documents), but it also contains volume 5, an unorganized collection of unofficial synodical papers that include many of the drafting documents.[2]

2. The journal of Caspar Sibelius, a minister delegate from Overijssel, is housed in the Regionaal Archief in Dordrecht.[3] The journal includes Sibelius's copy of the first committee draft, which became his working copy of the CD. He added later amendments into this draft as the CD developed through later drafts to its final form.

3. The Archives Tronchin, housed in the Musée Historique de la Réformation in Geneva, include papers of the Genevan delegate Théodore Tronchin. Among these are Tronchin's detailed journal of events at the synod, as well as his copies of various synodical documents.[4]

4. The Zentralbibliothek Zürich holds several manuscript volumes of materials on the Synod of Dordt, including papers of the Swiss delegate Johannes J. Breitinger and his journal on the sessions, as well as his copy of the first committee draft of the CD, which became his working copy with later amendments.[5]

---

2. H. Q. Janssen, *Catalogus van het Oud Synodaal Archief* ('s-Gravenhage: A. van Hoogstraten, 1878), 11–16; A. Fris, *Inventaris van de Archieven behorend tot het 'Oud Synodaal Archief' van de Nederlandse Hervormde Kerk, 1566–1816* ('s-Gravenhage: Stichting Archiefpublikaties, 1991), 8–17; H. H. Kuyper, *De Post-Acta of Nahandelingen van de Nationale Synode van Dordrecht in 1618 en 1619 Gehouden* (Amsterdam: Höveker & Wormser, [1899]), 500–512. Kuyper, *Post-Acta*, 3, 64–65, describes the background of OSA, vol. 5.

3. Caspar Sibelius, "Annotationes ad Synodum Dordracenam," Regionaal Archief, Dordrecht, 150, MS 1113.

4. Frédéric Gardy, ed., *Catalogue de la Partie des Archives Tronchin Acquise par la Société du Musée Historique de la Réformation* (Geneva: A. Jullien, 1946), 58. Volume 18 of the Archives Tronchin contains various documents relating to the drafting of the CD.

5. Zentralbibliothek Zürich, MSS A111, B111, B235, D237, F217, J241, S309, and Car. XV62 contain materials on the drafting of the CD.

5. The Samuel Ward Papers at Sidney Sussex College, Cambridge, contain Ward's papers from when he was a British delegate at the synod.⁶

6. The papers of the Hesse delegates kept at Marburg include the first committee draft of the CD and Hessian amendments to the first two committee drafts.⁷

Preliminary Documents

In its preparations for the drafting of the CD, the Synod of Dordt's judgment on the Five Articles of the Remonstrants (1610), the synod carefully examined the Remonstrant teachings and the Reformed position on these teachings. This resulted in the production of key preliminary documents that lay at the foundation of the CD.

For the Rejection of Errors sections of the CD, especially important is the *Articuli*, a set of theses summarizing the Remonstrant position on their Five Articles and identifying the written sources of these ideas.⁸ The *Articuli* were based on published writings of the Remonstrants as well as on documents they had submitted to the synod. The *Articuli* were dictated to the synod by President Bogerman in four sessions between 8 January and 25 February.

For the positive articles of the CD, the most significant resources were the *iudicia*, or judgments, of the nineteen Dutch and foreign delegations at the synod. Each delegation prepared separate *iudicia* on each of the Five Articles (a total of eighty-three documents), and these were read to the synod in closed session in the period from 6 to 21 March. They are all published in the synodical *Acta*.⁹

---

6. On this collection, see Margo Todd, "The Samuel Ward Papers at Sidney Sussex College, Cambridge," *Transactions of the Cambridge Bibliographical Society* 8, no. 5 (1985): 582–92. Volume L2 of Ward's papers contains several documents relating to the drafting of the CD.

7. HStAM, fol. 315a, no. 601.

8. The full title is *Articuli pertinentes ad pleniorem explicationem sententiae Remonstrantium*. The final version of the *Articuli* is published in *ADSND*, 2/2:781–800. On the context of the *Articuli*, see Donald Sinnema, "The Issue of Reprobation at the Synod of Dort (1618–19) in Light of the History of this Doctrine," (PhD diss., University of St. Michael's College, Toronto, 1985), 250–53, 338–41.

9. The *iudicia* of the foreign and Dutch delegations are published in the *Acta*, 2:1–252 and 3:1–292.

Another preliminary resource for the drafting of the CD was the speeches on various aspects of the Five Articles that twenty-two of the Dutch and foreign theologians presented to the synod from 17 January to 27 February. Concerning Article I (on predestination), eleven theologians addressed election, and one spoke on reprobation. Two theologians addressed Article II (on Christ's death and the extent of redemption). Three theologians spoke on Article IV (on conversion and how it occurs), and Article V (on perseverance) was addressed by five theologians.[10]

Since there was a lot of repetition among the many *iudicia*, the first synodical assessor (vice president), Hermannus Faukelius, drew up a *tabula*, or compendium, extracted from the *iudicia*.[11] While this document must have been very useful in preparing the CD, its influence is not possible to assess, since it is no longer extant.

The Bogerman Drafts of Chapters I and II

After the reading of the *iudicia* was finished in the afternoon of 21 March, the synod was ready to start preparing the CD, its official response to Remonstrant views. At the end of that session, President Bogerman observed that he saw great harmony in the various *iudicia*, and he noted that the States General expected a synodical judgment to be ready by Easter (31 March). For this purpose, Bogerman announced that he had already prepared a draft of the CD. He advised that each delegation should send one person the next morning to copy the Canons he would dictate. As he viewed the process, these persons would then bring the Canons to their own delegation to consult about what should be added, deleted, or changed. Their suggestions would then be forwarded to the president and the assessors, who would make any changes and refer the results back to the synod for approval.[12]

The next morning, on Friday, 22 March, Bogerman offered various recommendations concerning the format and style of the Canons. He advised that there should be a preface, a doctrinal section presenting the true view and rejecting the false, and a conclusion. The Canons

---

10. The speeches of the theologians are preserved in OSA, vol. K.

11. Sibelius, 90v; printed in Klaas Dijk, *De Strijd over Infra- en Supralapsarisme in de Gereformeerde Kerken van Nederland* (Kampen: J. H. Kok, 1912), Bijlage C, xix.

12. *ADSND*, 1:140–41; Balcanqual, 2:139.

should be set forth simply for the instruction of the churches; they should not be scholastic or academic, but ecclesiastical, and the orthodox position should be presented before the rejected errors.[13] He then dictated the draft of the Canons on Article I (positive articles) that he, in his role as president, had prepared with the advice of the assessors and secretaries.[14]

In the afternoon session, the British delegation first offered nine proposals on the character of the Canons. For example, the style of the Canons should be popular, not scholastic; nothing should be decided that can be disputed as *probabiliter*, such as the order of decrees; there should be sensitivity to the Lutheran churches; and canons should be added that reject false accusations, such as the claim that the Reformed religion teaches that God is the author of sin. The British also read some brief theses and antitheses on Article I, the tenor of which they thought should be followed in drawing up the CD.[15] Then Bogerman dictated his draft of the rejected errors of Article I and all of Article II. He indicated that he and the assessors would be available over the weekend if anyone wanted to consult them for an explanation or change in the dictated Canons.[16]

Three earlier drafts of the Bogerman Canons have been preserved in OSA, volume 5. The first is a one-page document in Bogerman's hand with only four (unnumbered) articles on Article I. Significantly, these are initial drafts of articles 1, 6, 7, and 8 of the final CD. It appears that another unidentified hand added some amendments.[17]

Bogerman's second draft is a two-page document in his hand, now with twelve articles on election and reprobation. Again, another hand added marginal amendments.[18]

Bogerman's third draft of Chapter I is a five-page document (as written before amendments were added) in the hand of an amanuensis;

---

13. Sibelius, 90r–90v; printed in Dijk, *Strijd*, Bijlage C, xviii–xix.
14. Hesse: 303.
15. Sibelius, 92r–92v; printed in Dijk, *Strijd*, xix.
16. *ADSND*, 1:141; Breitinger, 93r; Sibelius, 92v.
17. OSA, 5:723. For analysis of this first draft, see Donald Sinnema, "Johannes Bogerman's First Draft of Chapter One of the Canons of Dordt," in *Gevarieerde Oogst: Vriendenbundel voor Erik A. de Boer*, ed. Ad de Bruijne, Rob van Houwelingen, and Jan Klok (Amsterdam: Buijten & Schipperheijn Motief, 2024), 114–25.
18. OSA, 5:749–50.

Bogerman's original third draft does not appear to be extant. It contains fifteen articles and an epilogue.[19]

Bogerman himself made amendments to the same document. As amended, this is the dictated draft of Chapter I that Bogerman read to the synod on 22 March. Copies of the dictated draft of Chapters I and II have been preserved.[20]

Four early drafts by Bogerman of the rejected errors of Chapter I have also been preserved.[21] The second is a later draft of the first and consists of nine Remonstrant errors on election, seven of which are similar to errors in Bogerman's dictated draft. The other two drafts contain several errors on reprobation similar to errors in the dictated draft.

The number of Bogerman drafts on Chapter II is not evident, since the originals of such drafts are not extant. The dictated draft of Chapter II is available only in the copies.

The Call for a Drafting Committee

Bogerman's dictation of his draft of the Canons created quite a stir, especially among some of the foreign delegates, who thought Bogerman wanted to draw up canons by himself and just have the synod give its approval.[22] Over the weekend there was considerable activity in informal meetings as the British consulted with others and lobbied for a committee to draft the CD. Some Dutch delegates, including those of South Holland, agreed. The state delegates also got involved in these discussions.[23]

In the next session, on Monday, 25 March, the president of the state delegates recommended there be a drafting committee that included several foreign and Dutch theologians along with President Bogerman

---

19. OSA, 5:743–47.
20. Sibelius, 90v–92r, 92v–94r; Tronchin, 18:49r–53r; Zurich, B235, 159v–162v.
21. OSA, 5:715–17, 729–30, 563–64, and 745.
22. Balcanqual, 2:139–40; Breitinger, 93r.
23. Walter Balcanqual to Robert Naunton, 26 March/5 April 1619, in *Praestantium*, 565; cf. Anthony Milton, ed., *The British Delegation and the Synod of Dort (1618–1619)* (Woodbridge, England: Boydell Press, 2005), 295–97, published the 24 March advice of the British to the state delegates recommending a drafting committee made up of Dutch and foreign theologians.

and the assessors. He noted that the States General urged haste, and he thanked Bogerman for the preparatory work he had done.[24]

When the various delegations were asked their opinion, many, especially Dutch delegates, were displeased with this plan; they preferred to defer to the president.[25] Among the foreign delegates, Palatine theologian Abraham Scultetus offered several reasons to strongly support the actions of Bogerman. Franeker theologian Sibrandus Lubbertus passionately objected to the committee idea, especially speaking out against the British. He contended that foreign delegates had no business in this matter of the Dutch churches and that those who lobbied behind the scenes, such as the South Hollanders, deserved censure. For his intemperance, Lubbertus was admonished by both the ecclesiastical and state delegate presidents. When British theologian John Davenant wanted to respond, he was restrained by Bogerman. Elder delegate Johannes Latius of South Holland claimed that it was Lubbertus who was worthy of censure, and he argued that the CD should be drawn up by public rather than private authority.[26]

After all were heard, the majority of the delegates decided to follow the state delegates and appoint a drafting committee, with three foreign theologians and three Dutch theologians to join President Bogerman and assessors Hermannus Faukelius and Jacobus Rolandus. Bishop George Carleton was selected on behalf of the British, Genevan theologian Jean Diodati on behalf of the French-speaking, and Heidelberg theologian Abraham Scultetus on behalf of the Germans. Dutch theologians Johannes Polyander, Antonius Walaeus, and Jacobus Trigland were also assigned to the committee.[27]

The committee's task was to compose articles; send them to the individual delegations to consider any additions, deletions, or changes; and, after going back and forth in this manner, present the CD to the synod for public approval.[28]

---

24. Balcanqual, 2:146; Sibelius, 94v; *ADSND*, 1:141–42.
25. Balcanqual, 2:147; *Praestantium*, 565.
26. Balcanqual, 2:140–41, 147; *Praestantium*, 566; Sibelius, 95r.
27. Balcanqual, 2:147; *Praestantium*, 566; Sibelius, 95r; *ADSND*, 1:142.
28. Balcanqual, 2:147; *Praestantium*, 566; Breitinger, 93r.

The First Committee Draft

The nine-member drafting committee immediately began working on its own draft of the CD. Since a number of committee documents are written in the hand of Johannes Polyander, a theology professor at Leiden University, it is probable that he was the secretary of the committee.

Unfortunately, scant information is available concerning the inner workings of the drafting committee, but there are indications that the committee labored long and hard to fulfill its task. Letters of the Genevan committee member Jean Diodati mention that the committee worked more than eight hours a day for three weeks and that there were difficult negotiations with British delegates John Davenant and Samuel Ward over the wording of Chapter II:

> We are at the end of constructing of our canons, or synodical decrees. It's been fifteen days that we've been working on it 7–8 hours a day with weariness and unequalled vexation, finding ourselves in this final act with what we've never before experienced until the present; that is to say, a lot of obstinacy, scrupulousness, and capriciousness in relation to the doctrines themselves. Two English doctors, Davenantius and Wardus, are giving us this trouble. They appear to give their consent on the fundamental matters; however, they want by all means to insert or leave some dangerous points where they alone, with Bremen, disagree with others. But we no longer want to yield, and they refuse to sign otherwise.[29]
>
> The synod is lasting longer than anyone expected. The Englishmen have created so much difficulty in the preparation of the canons that they made us lose nearly three weeks of time. There are two of them who are so scrupulous and speculative that it's a pity, and we are taking great pains to find a middle point at which we must stop by necessity. I have never had such tedious work. We have been working together on it for more than 8 hours a day for the last three weeks.[30]

As the foundation for its own draft, the drafting committee used Bogerman's dictated draft of Chapters I and II. The committee also

---

29. Jean Diodati to Bénédict Turrettini, 3/13 April 1619; printed in Nicolas Fornerod, ed., *Registres de la Compagnie des Pasteurs de Genève: Tome XIV (1618–1619)* (Geneva: Droz, 2012), 348.

30. Jean Diodati to Bénédict Turrettini, 10/20 April 1619; in *Registres*, 14:351.

had available amendment suggestions on the Bogerman draft that at least several of the delegations had submitted on 25 March or later.[31] Though the committee used the Bogerman draft, it did so freely and developed its own draft of the CD.

Three days after it was appointed, on Thursday, 28 March, the committee had its first draft of Chapter I ready. That day synod secretary Sebastianus Dammannus dictated this draft to a gathering to which each delegation sent one member. It took over a week for the committee to prepare its initial draft of all five chapters. Dammannus dictated the first committee draft of Chapter II on 29 March, of Chapter III/IV on 3 and 4 April, and of Chapter V on 5 April. In the midst of this period was Easter Sunday, 31 March.[32]

The Second Committee Draft

After receiving the dictated first committee draft, each of the nineteen delegations had an opportunity to offer their observations and amendment suggestions on this draft. These were presented to the committee from 29 March until 6 April. Fourteen of these documents have been preserved.[33]

In several documents in Polyander's hand, the drafting committee then responded to these observations of the various delegations,[34]

---

31. Four of these documents with amendment suggestions—those of Overijssel, the Palatines, the Swiss, and the Genevans—have been preserved.

32. These dates are provided in Tronchin's journal (Tronchin, 16:137r–137v) and Breitinger's journal (Breitinger, 93r–93v), as well as in copies of this draft made by the Genevans (Tronchin, 18:55r, 58r, 59r, 61r, 62v). Copies of this first committee draft are preserved in Tronchin, 18:55r–64v; Ward, L2:18r–22v, 24r–24v, 33r–36v, 53r–55r (base text); HStAM, fol. 315a, no. 601; Zurich, Car. XV62:1–6, 9–26, 121–43, 149–58, 161–76 (base text); Sibelius, 95r–97v, 100r–104v (base text); and Ward, L2:18r–22v, 24r–24v, 33r–36v, 53r–55r (base text).

33. Tronchin, 18:137r; Breitinger, 93r; Balcanqual, 2:142. Amendment suggestions to the first committee draft that have been preserved include: Hesse, Swiss, and Genevan suggestions on all five chapters; British suggestions to Chapters II to V; Bremen suggestions to Chapters II and V; and Overijssel suggestions to Chapters I and II.

34. The committee observations in OSA, 5:155–56, respond to suggestions of the Dutch professors, South Hollanders, and Gelderlanders; of the British, Swiss, Hesse, and Bremen delegates; and of Palatine delegate Tossanus on Chapter I. Other committee observations in OSA, 5:160–68, respond to suggestions of the Dutch professors, South Hollanders, and Gelderlanders; of the British, Swiss, Palatine, Hesse, and Bremen delegates; and of Genevan delegate Tronchin, also on Chapter I.

and the committee made a considerable number of revisions—about 198—to the text of their first draft. The revised version is the second committee draft. This draft was not dictated in full; rather, only the amendments were dictated.

On Monday, 8 April, synodical secretary Festus Hommius dictated the amendments on Chapter I. OSA, volume 5 contains a committee document with this list of amendments on Chapter I.[35]

Due to the concerns of the British and Bremen theologians, the drafting committee scrapped its first draft of Chapter II and drafted nine all-new articles. This was dictated also on 8 April.[36]

On 9 April, Hommius dictated the second-draft amendments for the Chapter II rejection section.[37] He dictated the amendments for Chapter III/IV on 10 April, and the next day the amendments for the Chapter III/IV rejection section and for all of Chapter V.[38] That same day the committee made three observations on their new draft of Chapter III/IV and changed one article (art. 11).[39]

The Third Committee Draft

After receiving the amendments for the second committee draft, the synodical delegations again had the opportunity to offer their observations and amendment suggestions on the latest draft. On Friday, 12

---

35. "Observationes in Articulos et Canones de Electione et Reprobatione, ex totius Synodi judiciis collectae; secunda cura D. Praesidis et octo aliorum deputatorum, 8 Apr. 1619," OSA, 5:169–76.

36. Copies are preserved in Sibelius, 99r–99v; Tronchin, 18:67r–67v; and Ward, L2:29r (the base text before amendments). There was an earlier draft (not extant) of this second committee draft of Chapter II, as is evident from a committee document with a list of amendments on this earlier draft (OSA, 5:67).

37. A copy of the second draft of the Chapter II rejections is found in Sibelius, 98r–98v (the base text before amendments).

38. These dates are provided in Tronchin's journal (Tronchin, 16:137v) and in the copy of these lists of amendments, which is preserved in Tronchin, 18:65r–70v.

39. Tronchin, 16:137v; 18:68v. A copy of this second committee draft is found in Sibelius's working copy in his journal, 95r–104v (the base text with amendments written in light ink); for Chapter II, the base text is the second committee draft. Another copy is in Breitinger's working copy in Zurich, Car. XV62:9–26, 123–43, 149–58, 161–76, 237–41 (base text with some amendments).

April, the various delegations presented their suggestions. Nineteen of these documents have been preserved.[40]

In the afternoon session of the same day, the drafting committee responded to the suggestions. There are five committee documents available, with responses to British, Palatine, Gelderland, South Holland, and Zeeland suggestions.[41] It appears that, in some cases, suggestions may have been offered orally rather than in writing. That day, South Holland delegates Balthazar Lydius and Gisbertus Voetius met with the committee to discuss their suggestions.[42]

There is also evidence of private lobbying in the drafting process. The following day, the Swiss delegates Breitinger and Rutimeyer met privately with President Bogerman. They urged the acceptance of the suggestions they had made to the second committee draft, and they cautioned against allowing certain individuals (presumably the British theologians) to have slippery phrases inserted into the CD.[43]

Based on this new input, the drafting committee made amendments to their second draft; the result was the third committee draft. Once again, this draft was not dictated in full; only the amendments were dictated.[44] Hence, in the morning of Monday, 15 April, the committee amendments for the third draft on Chapter I were dictated by Eilhardus van Mehen, a minister delegate from Gelderland. In the afternoon, Van Mehen dictated the committee amendments for

---

40. Tronchin, 16:137v. Amendment suggestions to the second committee draft that have been preserved include: British suggestions on Chapters II and III/IV; Palatine and Hesse suggestions on Chapters I, II, and III/IV; Swiss suggestions on Chapters II, III/IV, and V; Genevan, Bremen, and Overijssel suggestions on Chapters I and II; and North Holland and anonymous suggestions on Chapter II.

41. Committee responses to these suggestions are in OSA, 5:135–36, 137–39, 141–42, 189–90, 197, and 199.

42. There are committee notes of this meeting with Lydius and Voetius (dated 12 April) in OSA, 5:203; cf. 189.

43. Breitinger, 245r.

44. The list of amendments for the third committee draft is preserved only in Tronchin, 18:70v–72r. A copy of the third draft is part of Sibelius's working copy in his journal. This third draft is the base text in Sibelius, 95r–104v, as amended with light and dark ink. Several minor changes in dark ink, however, were later made as amendments to the third committee draft. Another copy of the third committee draft is in Breitinger's working copy, Zurich, Car. XV62:15–26, 123–43, 149, 158, 161–76 (base text with some amendments).

Chapters II to V.[45] There were not as many amendments as for the previous draft; yet, with 129 amendments, the changes were significant.

That afternoon, there was an initial subscription of this version of the CD by all delegates except the British. The British did not want to sign before having a neatly written copy available to them.[46]

This third committee draft is very close to the final CD, except for some minor editorial changes and some amendments that would yet be made to two rejected errors of Chapter II; these were a lingering matter of debate.

The Last Changes and the Final Canons

On the same day that amendments for the third draft were dictated, the delegations again had the opportunity to offer suggestions. Apparently there were few, since the only comments preserved are those of the British and the Genevans.[47]

The following day, Tuesday, 16 April, the latest version of Chapter I was read in a regular session of the synod—the first public session in three weeks—and each delegate individually expressed his consent that these articles agreed with Scripture and the confessions of the Reformed churches.[48] The Swiss also presented a statement to Bogerman expressing approval of this third draft of the CD, but on the condition that, if any further changes were made, they would be given an opportunity to give advice on the matter before offering their full approval by formal subscription.[49]

Then Chapter II was read, but this did not receive the same level of consent. The committee had made some small changes in wording since the initial subscription of the day before. The British approved all of Chapter II except for rejection 2, which they thought could be formulated more clearly, and rejection 6, which they said they saw now for the first time (though it had been dictated the day before). The

---

45. The date is provided in Breitinger, 245v; and Tronchin, 16:137v.
46. Balcanqual, 2:148.
47. Tronchin, 18:75v, contains brief Genevan suggestions on Chapters I and II and on the first draft of the Conclusion. Ward, L2:12r–12v, contains British suggestions on all five chapters.
48. Balcanqual, 2:148; Breitinger, 93v.
49. Breitinger, 245v; cf. 93v, 163v.

British considered rejection 6 more as a matter of scholastic speculation than synodical inquiry; they requested more time to deliberate.[50]

The Hesse delegates approved Chapter II, except for article 8; they wanted the term *singulari* added in reference to God's plan but acquiesced for the sake of peace. The delegates of Bremen agreed with Hesse. The Swiss theologians said that they approved Chapter II but that they wanted to reread it due to the changes in wording that had just been made. All other delegations expressed full consent to Chapter II.[51]

In this same session, Professors Goclenius, Lubbertus, and Gomarus also suggested some grammatical changes to the CD.[52]

The morning session of 18 April was devoted to an extensive discussion of the contentious rejection 6, which rejected the notion that, for the sufficiency of redemption, a likeness of our nature in Christ is not necessary. The British were lined up against the rest of the synod. The British argued that, if this rejection were understood in regard to absolute necessity, it was scholastic speculation and that, if it were understood in regard to hypothetical necessity, it was true and not a Remonstrant error. Hence, they advised that this rejection be omitted. The majority, however, wanted to retain it. President Bogerman suggested that this rejection could be reformulated in a way that would satisfy all.[53]

In the afternoon of 18 April, Chapter III/IV was read, and everyone individually consented. Yet there were also some suggestions for editorial changes. Then Article V was read and again received the consent of all. With all of the articles read, Palatine theologian Scultetus suggested there was need for someone to put a final hand to the CD for the sake of consistency and to polish the style. Others wanted no such stylistic changes.[54]

---

50. Balcanqual, 2:144, 148; Breitinger, 93v. Ward, L2:49r, contains late British suggestions on Chapter II, rej. 2.
51. Balcanqual, 2:148–49; Breitinger, 93v.
52. Balcanqual, 2:149.
53. Balcanqual, 2:144, 149–50.
54. Balcanqual, 2:150; *ADSND*, 1:142.

In that same session, the matter of drafting a Conclusion for the CD was raised.[55] The issue was whether the Conclusion should reject certain hard sayings (*phrases duriores*) expressed by some Reformed theologians or whether it should only reject the false accusations (*calumniae*) of the Remonstrants directed against the orthodox Reformed position.[56] Thomas Goad read a list of hard sayings that the British wanted rejected.[57] The Dutch delegates wanted only a rejection of false accusations.

On Friday, 19 April, the drafting committee met to consider the suggestions for final changes to the CD and to prepare a draft of the Conclusion. A first draft was dictated to the delegations in the evening.[58] This draft only rejected false accusations. The following morning it was read in public session and was heavily debated by the foreign theologians. At noon President Bogerman and the assessors prepared a revised second draft, which recognized that some Reformed theologians had expressed hard sayings in their writings.[59] In the afternoon session the debate continued, with Dutch delegates strongly urging the synod not to reject hard sayings.[60]

The following Monday, 22 April, the state delegates indicated that they wanted to deliver a signed copy of the CD to the States General the next day, so there was pressure to complete the CD.[61] Bogerman presented a revised final draft of the Conclusion, which was closer in

---

55. Already in earlier documents, some delegations had raised the matter of how the synod should deal with hard sayings. In their advice on the Bogerman draft, the Palatine theologians offered a mild defense of hard sayings when read in context (OSA, 5:155). On the other hand, the Bremen theologians, in their suggestions on the first committee draft, wanted specific hard sayings rejected (OSA, 5:213–14, 217), and so did the Hesse theologians, in their advice on the second committee draft (OSA, 5:64).

56. On the drafting of the Conclusion, see Dijk, *Strijd*, 187–205, and Bijlage D, xxiii–xxxiv; as well as Sinnema, "Issue of Reprobation," 419–30.

57. Balcanqual, 2:150; Breitinger, 94v. This list does not appear to be extant.

58. Balcanqual, 2:150. A copy of the first draft of the Conclusion is printed in Dijk, *Strijd*, 190–91.

59. Balcanqual, 2:150–51; Breitinger, 94v–96r; cf. *Acta*, sess. 132. A copy of the second draft of the Conclusion is printed in Dijk, *Strijd*, 196–97.

60. The position of Overijssel, for example, is preserved in Sibelius, 108v, and is printed in Dijk, *Strijd*, 199–200. The most detailed account of these debates is in Tronchin, 16:138r–144v.

61. Balcanqual, 2:152–53.

The Drafting of the Canons of Dordt 377

spirit to the first draft; it only rejected a number of false accusations, and not hard sayings, but it did contain a general admonition to avoid hard sayings that go beyond the bounds of Scripture.[62] This was approved by the synod; the English, Hesse, and Bremen delegates were not satisfied, but they gave in for the sake of peace. At noon, the drafting committee met again to work on the two debated rejections of Chapter II.[63]

The next morning, on 23 April, all delegates subscribed three copies of Chapter I, one of which was intended for the States General. President Bogerman indicated that Scripture passages would be added afterward, due to the time restrictions. The drafting committee also had ready its amendments to the two rejected errors of Chapter II. They suggested that rejection 2 be reformulated into three rejections, which were then read, and they deleted the contentious rejection 6.[64] In the afternoon session, the synod approved these final changes to Chapter II. Chapters II to V were then read and subscribed by all delegates. This session lasted until 10 pm. The CD had reached their final form.[65]

Two weeks later, on 6 May, the members of the synod solemnly processed from the meeting hall to the Grote Kerk of Dordrecht. There, in the midst of a large crowd, the two synod secretaries, Hommius and Dammannus, ascended a podium and publicly promulgated the CD to the world, as they took turns reading aloud each chapter.[66]

Soon after the synod ended, President Bogerman presented a report to the States General summarizing the activities of the synod. On the drafting of the CD, the report stated:

> [The drafting committee members] for a time of about four weeks were busy with it with incredible labor and care, and they long conferred with all the Colleges [delegations] about their work until all

---

62. Dijk, *Strijd*, 202–4.
63. Balcanqual, 2:152–53; Heppe, 308.
64. A copy of these final committee amendments to Chapter II is in Tronchin, 18:73v.
65. Balcanqual, 2:153–54; Heppe, 308. The originally subscribed copy of the CD that was presented to the States General is preserved in OSA, vol. 52(R); see Kuyper, *Post-Acta*, 65–66. The final Latin text of the CD is printed in J. N. Bakhuizen van den Brink, ed., *De Nederlandse Belijdenisgeschriften in Authentieke Teksten* (Amsterdam: Ton Bolland, 1976), 225–81.
66. *ADSND*, 1:154–55; Balcanqual, 2:165–66.

members of the synod without exception acquiesced not only in the substance [*substantie*] of the matter itself but also in phraseology and all the words [*phrasiologia, ende allen de woorden*], whereupon the same Canons were read in the full synod several times and approved by each and every one, and in all articles they were subscribed with singular joy and thanksgiving to God.[67]

Conclusion

In all, I know of more than one hundred extant documents that were part of the drafting process of the CD; in some cases, there are multiple copies of the same item. Of this number, twenty-one are actual drafts of portions of the CD. Two working copies of the first committee draft have been preserved—by delegates Caspar Sibelius and Johannes J. Breitinger—on which later amendments were written. As for the breakdown of preliminary drafts of each Article, I am able to identify seven preliminary drafts of Chapter I, four drafts of Chapter II, four drafts of Chapter III/IV, and three drafts of Chapter V. Fifty-two extant documents contain the observations and amendment suggestions of the various delegations. This is a relatively small number, given the fact that there were nineteen delegations, each of which had four opportunities to offer amendments on drafts of each of the Chapters. There are also twenty-four drafting committee documents with responses to delegate suggestions or with lists of amendments for the following draft.

Why is this collection of documents on the formation of the CD significant? After all, these were mostly informal working documents and were not considered worth preserving in the official *autographa* of the synod. Let me offer two reasons why this collection is important:

1. Having available the various drafts and amendment suggestions makes it possible to trace the development of thought that went into the drafting of specific articles of the CD. It helps one understand nuances of thought and why an article is formulated

---

[67]. "Sommier van t' rapport der Gedeputeerden des Nationalen Synodj van Dordrecht, gedaen door den Praeses desseluen Synodj, ter vergaderinge vande Hooge Mogende Heeren Generale Staten der Vereenichde Nederlanden" [30 May 1619]; printed in Kuyper, *Post-Acta*, 476–77.

the way it is. In some cases, the amendment documents offer a reason for a suggested change.

2. These documents help reveal the specific contributions of individual delegations to the formation of the CD. Evident, for example, is the influence of the British delegates on the formulation of Chapter II.

When the whole collection of drafting documents is published, these many documents will finally be available to scholars so that they can conduct a closer analysis of the CD and their formation. Then a more refined understanding of the CD in their historical context will be possible.

Committee Drafts of the Canons of Dordt

	First Draft	*Second Draft*	*Third Draft*	*Final Draft*
Chapter I				
Articles	18	18 (arts. 9 & 10 combined; art. 17 new)	18	18
Rejections	10	9 (rej. 6 omitted)	9	9
Chapter II				
Articles	5	9 (all new)	9	9
Rejections	4	5 (rej. 5 new)	6 (rej. 6 new)	7 (rej. 2 becomes rejs. 2, 3, & 4; rej. 6 omitted)
Chapter III/IV				
Articles	17	17 (art. 1 new; art. 2 omitted)	17	17
Rejections	9	9	9	9
Chapter V				
Articles	14	15 (art. 9 split into arts. 9 & 10)	15	15
Rejections	9	9	9	9

Chronology of the Drafting of the Canons

		Bogerman's first draft of Chap. I (positive articles)
		Bogerman's second draft of Chap. I (positive articles)
		Bogerman's third draft of Chap. I (positive articles)
		Bogerman's early drafts of Chap. I rejections
Fri. 22 March	*AM*	Bogerman's proposals on the character of the Canons
		Bogerman's dictated draft of Chap. I (positive articles)
	PM	British proposals on the character of the Canons
		Bogerman's dictated draft of Chap. I rejections
		Bogerman's dictated draft of Chap. II
Weekend		Private meetings about the need for a drafting committee
Mon. 25 March	*AM*	Synod discusses and appoints drafting committee of nine
		Some delegations offer amendment suggestions to Bogerman draft
		Drafting committee begins its work
Thur. 28 March		First committee draft of Chap. I dictated
Fri. 29 March		First committee draft of Chap. II dictated
		Some delegations offer amendment suggestions on first committee draft of Chaps. I and II
Sun. 31 March		(Easter Sunday)
Tues. 2 April		Other delegations offer amendment suggestions on first committee draft of Chaps. I and II
Wed. 3 April		First committee draft of Chap. III/IV dictated
Thur. 4 April		First committee draft of Chap. III/IV rejections dictated
Fri. 5 April		First committee draft of Chap. V dictated
Sat. 6 April		Some delegations offer amendment suggestions on first committee draft of Chaps. III/IV and V
Mon. 8 April		Amendments for second committee draft of Chap. I dictated
		Second committee draft of Chap. II dictated (all new articles)

Tues. 9 April		Amendments for second committee draft of Chap. II rejections dictated
Wed. 10 April		Amendments for second committee draft of Chap. III/IV dictated
Thur. 11 April	*AM*	Three observations on second committee draft of Chap. III/IV dictated
		Amendments for second committee draft of Chap. III/IV rejections dictated
		Addition to Chap. III/IV, article 11
	PM	Amendments for second committee draft of Chap. V dictated
Fri. 12 April	*AM*	Delegations offer amendment suggestions on second committee draft
	PM	Committee responses to several delegate suggestions
Mon. 15 April	*AM*	Amendments for third committee draft of Chap. I dictated
	PM	Amendments for third committee draft of Chaps. II–V dictated
		Initial subscription by all delegations except British
		Some delegations offer amendment suggestions on third committee draft
		Committee makes some small changes to Chap. II
Tues. 16 April	*PM*	Synod again meets in full session; Chap. I read and approved by individual delegates
		Chap. II read and approved except for rejections 2 and 6, due to objections of British
		Goclenius, Lubbertus, and Gomarus suggest grammatical changes
Wed. 17 April		(Day of Fasting)
Thur. 18 April	*AM*	Extensive debate on Chap. II, rejection 6; British vs. others
	PM	Chaps. III/IV and V read and approved by individual delegates
		Editorial changes suggested by some, not by others
		Discussion of the character of the Conclusion

Fri. 19 April	*AM*	Drafting committee meets to consider final changes and prepare Conclusion
	PM	First draft of Conclusion dictated
Sat. 20 April	*AM*	First draft of Conclusion debated
	PM	Second draft of Conclusion dictated and debated
Mon. 22 April	*AM*	Final draft of Conclusion dictated and approved
	PM	Drafting committee meets to deal with Chap. II, rejections 2 and 6
Tues. 23 April	*AM*	Chap. I read and subscribed in three copies Amendments to rejections 2 and 6 read
	PM	Changes to rejections 2 and 6 approved (rejection 6 deleted) Chaps. II–V read and subscribed
Mon. 6 May		Canons publicly promulgated at the Grote Kerk

CHAPTER 14

The Canons of Dordt: Historical Context and Theology[1]

Historical Background

The Canons of Dordt (CD) is the popular name for the statements of doctrine adopted by the Synod of Dordt (1618–1619), which convened in the Dutch city of Dordrecht in order to settle a major controversy that arose in the Dutch Reformed churches with the advent of Arminianism.

A half century earlier, John Calvin had taught double predestination, the view (already taught by Augustine) that, from eternity, God decided to elect or choose some people to salvation and reprobate others to condemnation. While this was not a central teaching for Calvin, some of his followers—especially Theodore Beza, William Perkins, and Franciscus Gomarus—gave predestination a more prominent role and developed an extreme form of this doctrine known as supralapsarianism (the view that God, from eternity, predestined some to eternal life and others to eternal death without considering them as fallen and deserving of condemnation).

Jacobus Arminius (1560–1609), who had studied under Beza in Geneva, challenged the teachings of Calvin and his followers on several points and advocated a position that placed less emphasis on divine sovereignty and more on human responsibility in salvation.

---

1. This essay on the Canons of Dordt is part of a longer article by Lyle D. Bierma and Donald Sinnema, "The Three Forms of Unity," in *The Oxford Handbook of Reformed Theology*, ed. Michael Allen and Scott R. Swain (Oxford: Oxford University Press, 2020), 245–49.

This brought Arminius into controversy while serving as a minister of the Reformed church in Amsterdam in the 1590s. After he became a professor of theology at Leiden University in 1603, the controversy intensified as his views collided with those of his supralapsarian colleague, Gomarus. Arminius's views were most clearly expressed in his *Declaration of Sentiments* (1608).

After Arminius's death in 1609, his followers summarized the Arminian position in Five Articles in the Remonstrance of 1610 (here abbreviated):

1. God, by an eternal decree, has, in Christ, determined to save sinners in Christ who, by grace, shall believe and persevere in faith and to condemn unbelievers.

2. Christ died and merited forgiveness for all people; yet only those who believe will be saved.

3. No one has saving faith by his own free will; it is necessary to be regenerated by God in order to perform any true good.

4. All good works must be ascribed to the grace of God, but the mode of this grace is not irresistible.

5. By aid of grace, believers have abundant strength to persevere, but whether they can by negligence fall from grace must still be determined from Scripture.[2]

Later, Arminians (or Remonstrants) more explicitly based election and reprobation on human faith and unbelief foreseen by God, and they affirmed that believers can fall completely from the state of grace.

These Five Articles formed the pattern for later debates, including those at the Synod of Dordt. At a conference in The Hague between the two sides (1611), Articles III and IV were combined because both sides recognized that there was no real controversy on the third point. Thereafter, these two articles were usually treated together (as Article III/IV).

---

2. J. N. Bakhuizen van den Brink, ed., *De Nederlandse Belijdenisgeschriften in Authentieke Teksten* (Amsterdam: Ton Bolland, 1976), 288–89.

Throughout the following decade, the controversy agitated the Dutch church, university, and public square. Finally, in 1618, the Dutch government convened the Synod of Dordt in order to resolve the matter. The proceedings of the synod continued for six and a half months.

This was a national synod of the Reformed churches of the Netherlands, but it had an international character. There were fifty-eight Dutch delegates from the various provinces and the Walloon churches, including five theologians from Dutch universities and academies. But also present were twenty-six Reformed theologians from eight foreign territories (Great Britain, the Palatinate, Hesse, four Swiss cantons, Nassau-Wetteravia, Geneva, Bremen, and Emden). The Dutch government also sent eighteen state delegates to supervise the synod and advise on matters of procedure.

Thirteen leading Arminians, led by Simon Episcopius, were called before the synod not to serve as delegates but to have their views examined and adjudicated. The Arminians refused to recognize the synod as a legitimate judge of their views; they wanted a conference between the opposing parties. After five weeks of procedural wrangling, they were expelled from the synod.[3]

For the next three months, the synod debated the issues as it prepared to render its judgment on the Arminian case. On the basis of advice presented by the Dutch and foreign delegations, synod president Johannes Bogerman presented an initial draft of what would come to be called the Canons of Dordt, but the synod opted to appoint a committee of nine to draft the Canons in Latin. Over the course of three weeks, the committee prepared its own draft, received input from the various delegations, and made revisions—a process that was repeated two more times before the CD were adopted by the synod and signed by all its members.[4] In light of the diverse viewpoints of the time, the CD took a moderate Reformed stance on the disputed issues.

---

3. See *ADSND*, vol. 1, *Acts of the Synod of Dordt*. See also chapter 2 of this volume, "Procedural Wrangling in the Remonstrant Case at Dordt."

4. Donald Sinnema, "The Drafting of the Canons of Dordt: A Preliminary Survey of Early Drafts and Related Documents," in *Revisiting the Synod of Dordt (1618–1619)*, ed. Aza Goudriaan and Fred van Lieburg (Leiden: Brill, 2011), 291–311. See also chapter 13 of this volume, "The Drafting of the Canons of Dordt."

The CD have a special character because of their original purpose as a judicial decision on the doctrinal points in dispute in the Arminian controversy. Thus, the formal title is: "The Decision of the Synod of Dordt on the Five Main Points of Doctrine in Dispute in the Netherlands."

In its later sessions, the synod drew up a form of subscription by which all ministers of the Dutch Reformed churches were required to signify that all points of doctrine contained in the Belgic Confession, the Heidelberg Catechism, and the CD fully agree with the Word of God. Thus, the CD acquired a secondary purpose: they became a doctrinal standard for the Reformed churches in the Netherlands, alongside the Confession and the Catechism.[5]

The Canons, however, have a more limited character than the Confession and the Catechism. They do not encompass the whole range of doctrine but focus only on the five points in dispute—predestination and associated issues concerning the extent of the atonement, the impact of sin, the way God's grace works, and perseverance in faith. Though narrower in range, the CD elaborate more on these themes than do the other two standards. As expressed by the form of subscription, the CD are an "explanation of some points of the aforesaid doctrine" presented in the Confession and the Catechism.[6]

The CD consist of a preface, five chapters, and a conclusion. Although, in form, they have only four chapters, properly speaking there are five chapters, because the structure of the CD corresponds to the Five Articles of the 1610 Remonstrance. Following the pattern of debates after 1611, Chapters III and IV are combined.

Each of the chapters consists of a positive and a negative section, the former a presentation of the Reformed teaching on the topic, the latter a rejection of corresponding errors. Since the CD were primarily intended to provide the Synod of Dordt's judgment on the points disputed with the Arminians, this required, above all, a rejection of

---

5. Donald Sinnema, "The Canons of Dordt: From Judgment on Arminianism to Confessional Standard," in *Revisiting the Synod of Dordt*, 313–33. See also chapter 15 of this volume, "The Canons of Dordt: From Judgment on Arminianism to Confessional Standard."

6. Donald Sinnema, "The Origin of the Form of Subscription in the Dutch Reformed Tradition," *Calvin Theological Journal* 42, no. 2 (Nov. 2007): 373.

their alleged errors. The negative sections typically paraphrase, rather than directly quote, Arminian errors; then they respond to each with a brief rebuttal, usually drawn from Scripture. In order to make clear the basis for its judgment of the errors, the synod included the positive explanation of the Reformed stance on these matters. In later years, as the controversy faded, the positive sections emerged as the dominant part of the CD.[7]

Theology

Chapter I of the CD presents a moderate treatment of God's election of some people and reprobation of others. It begins not with God's decision in eternity but rather within the historical horizon, with the fallen state of humanity, which deserves condemnation. The chapter then moves to God's love in sending His Son for salvation; this work is proclaimed in the gospel message, which receives the human response of faith or unbelief. Such faith is solely a free gift of God, whereas the cause of unbelief lies in humans themselves. In the sixth article, the chapter finally ascends to God's eternal decision, or decree, of election and reprobation in order to explain the historical fact that some receive the gift of faith, while others do not. Election is explained first, then reprobation. Against the Arminian view of election and reprobation based on foreseen faith and unbelief, the CD teach that God elects some sinners to salvation solely by His good pleasure, not as a response to human belief; on the other hand, God reprobates others by the decision of His will, and yet they perish by their own fault. So, in reprobating, God does not eternally condemn innocent people. The CD treat predestination in a pastorally sensitive manner, so that this teaching might be a comfort to believers rather than a threat. The assurance of their election comes from seeing in themselves the fruits of election.

This formulation of predestination is typically infralapsarian (the view that, in predestining to life and to death, God considers those predestined as fallen and deserving of condemnation). Chapter I thus avoids—but does not condemn—the severity of the supralapsarian stance.

---

7. Sinnema, "The Canons of Dordt," 331–33.

Chapter II focuses on the nature and extent of Christ's atonement for sins. God's justice requires punishment for sin, but, on the cross, Christ completely satisfied God's justice in our place. In a universal tone, this chapter emphasizes that the infinite value of Christ's death is more than sufficient to atone for the sins of the whole world, and so the gospel message that whoever believes shall be saved ought to be proclaimed to all. Yet, contra the Arminian view that Christ died for all and obtained forgiveness for all, this chapter also teaches that the atonement is particular, in that Christ's death efficaciously redeems only those whom God has elected to salvation.

Chapter III/IV, which deals with human corruption and the way God's grace works in conversion, first stresses that, by the fall, humanity became pervasively corrupted, enslaved to sin, and utterly unable to return to God on its own. Yet humans remain human, with intellect and will; they are not mere puppets. Conversion (or regeneration) occurs not by free choice; it is a work of God by the power of the Holy Spirit through the gospel, which comes with a well-meant call to salvation. In conversion, God's grace not only works outwardly in the proclamation of the gospel but also penetrates inwardly by the efficacious operation of the Holy Spirit, softening the heart and freeing the will, thus producing faith in such a way that the person receiving grace is himself enabled to believe and repent. Faith is a gift of God, but not in the sense that God offers it to be accepted or rejected by human choice. Against the Arminian opinion that grace is resistible, this chapter asserts that God's regenerating grace works powerfully and efficaciously, not coercing a reluctant will by force, but rather spiritually reforming the will to overcome its resistance.

Chapter V focuses on the perseverance of believers in faith until the end of life. Though they are set free from slavery to sin, the converted are not free from sin in this life, and they can even be led astray into very serious sins. But God does not let them fall so far that they totally forfeit grace and faith and thus perish, a scenario the Arminians considered possible. Such persons are able to persevere not by their own inner strength but rather because God powerfully preserves them and renews them to repentance by His Word and Spirit. Though they may yet have doubts, believers can be assured of this preservation. Such assurance does not lead to false security or carelessness, as if, once saved, it does not matter how one lives; rather, it is an incentive to godliness.

The main intent of the Conclusion of the CD is to reject a number of false accusations by Arminians and others that exaggerated or misconstrued various aspects of Reformed teachings. Since some ground for several of these accusations could be found in careless statements by certain Reformed leaders of the time, the conclusion also urges ministers to refrain from ways of speaking that go beyond the limits of Scripture.[8]

The five topics of the CD are often called "the Five Points of Calvinism," even though Calvinism cannot be reduced to five points, and not all of the points stem directly from Calvin. Just as misleading is the summary of the CD by the acronym TULIP: Total depravity, Unconditional election, Limited atonement, Irresistible grace, and Perseverance of the saints. The acronym is of recent origin, dating from the first years of the twentieth century in America. Though it is helpful for memory, TULIP has had the regrettable result not only of altering the proper order of the five points but also of oversimplifying and distorting the nuanced teaching of the CD. The first point is not just about *unconditional election* but also reprobation, and it is introduced by the universal sinfulness of humanity and the gospel message. The concept *limited atonement* focuses on Christ's death as effective only for the elect, but it fails to capture the universal features of Chapter II, that His death was sufficient to cover the sins of the whole world and so should be proclaimed to all. *Total depravity* is easily misunderstood as absolute depravity, the notion that humans can do no good at all; whereas this chapter teaches pervasive depravity and the utter inability of people to save themselves, without denying that fallen humans have some sense of moral good and some desire for good outward behavior. The CD do not actually teach that grace is *irresistible*, but rather that divine grace is efficacious and overcomes human resistance. And the emphasis of the last chapter is more on God's preservation of the elect than on their own *perseverance*.[9]

---

8. "The Canons of Dort," in *Our Faith: Ecumenical Creeds, Reformed Confessions, and Other Resources* (Grand Rapids: Faith Alive Christian Resources, 2013), 119–44.

9. See also chapter 16 of this volume, "Distortions of the Canons: The Tilenus Abbreviation, the Five Points of Calvinism, and TULIP."

The CD have continued to function as a confessional standard in Reformed churches of Dutch heritage throughout the world. Although they respond to a seventeenth-century controversy, the CD remain one of the most significant confessional statements in the Reformed tradition on the recurring issue of how divine sovereignty relates to human responsibility in salvation. In a balanced and theologically precise manner, the CD affirm the central message: salvation, from beginning to end, occurs wholly by God's gracious initiative, not by human decision; and yet, this does not erode human responsibility.

CHAPTER 15

The Canons of Dordt: From Judgment on Arminianism to Confessional Standard[1]

Ever since the Synod of Dordt (1618–1619), Reformed churches of Dutch heritage have adhered to three confessional standards—the Belgic Confession (BC), the Heidelberg Catechism (HC), and the Canons of Dordt (CD). These are considered the three "forms of unity" (*formulieren van eenigheit*). It is often assumed that the Synod of Dordt drew up the Canons as a new confessional standard for the churches. But at no point did the synod ever declare the Canons to be a new confession.

It is my contention that the Synod of Dordt never intended to draw up a new confession when it drafted the Canons of Dordt; rather, it intended the Canons to be its judgment, or judicial decision, on the Five Articles of the 1610 Remonstrance that lay at the center of the Arminian controversy. However, the Canons, in effect, began to function as a confessional standard when the synod required that they be subscribed by all pastors, and this was recognized soon after the synod, when the Canons came to be regarded as one of the "forms of unity" of the Dutch Reformed churches.

This essay will carefully examine the process of confessionalization by which the CD shifted from their initial function as a judgment on Arminianism to serving as a confessional standard of orthodoxy. For this purpose, I will plot the most significant moments in the course

---

1. This article, slightly revised, was printed in Aza Goudriaan and Fred van Lieburg, eds., *Revisiting the Synod of Dordt (1618–1619)* (Leiden: Brill, 2011), 313–33.

of the formation of the CD at the Synod of Dordt. In order to gauge the perceived status of the CD, it will be necessary to take note of the following factors: all decisions of the synod pertaining to the CD; the character and basic structure of the CD; the terms used to describe the document and its major sections; how the CD actually functioned in the aftermath of the synod, especially concerning the requirement of subscription; and when they came to be called one of the "forms of unity."

Preparations for a Judgment

The Synod of Dordt was originally convened by the Dutch government for one main purpose: to seek a resolution of the Arminian controversy that had caused major unrest in the Dutch churches for about two decades. On 11 November 1617, the States General approved a list of Articles to Convene the national synod. Its ninth article spelled out the synod's basic agenda:

> IX. In the assembly, the well-known Five Articles in controversy and the difficulties that have arisen from them shall first and foremost be treated, in order earnestly to see how these may be removed from the churches with the least trouble and in the most proper manner, so that the peace of the church (but especially the purity of doctrine) may be preserved. Afterward, the remaining difficulties and gravamina—whether general or particular—relating to the churches may be presented.[2]

According to this prescribed agenda, the synod was expected to arrive at a decision that would resolve the controversy.

On 16 November, the synod sent a letter to thirteen leading Remonstrants, citing them to appear before the synod to have their views examined and judged. It cited them to come state, explain, and defend their Five Articles, as well as to present any observations they had on the BC and the HC, "in order that the said synod, after hearing and considering everything, may at the proper time be able to judge (*iudicare*) each matter in the fear of the Lord."[3]

---

2. *Acta*, sess. 4.

3. *ADSND*, 1:15. This volume publishes for the first time the *Acta Authentica*, the official Acts of the Synod of Dordt.

The day after the cited Remonstrants appeared on 6 December, the state delegates representing the States General said that they expected from the synod the "promulgation of a synodical decision" (*decreti synodici promulgationem*) on the Five Articles.[4]

This is one of the few references to the future Canons during the five weeks that the Remonstrants were present in the synod before their expulsion on 14 January. This part of the proceedings focused on examining Remonstrant views, but since the Remonstrants did not fully cooperate, these proceedings were dominated by procedural bickering. Finally, on 1 January 1619, the States General issued a resolution declaring that, if the Remonstrants would not cooperate, their opinions should be investigated and determined from their writings.[5]

On 3 January, synodical president Bogerman called together a committee of leading delegates to discuss how to implement the government resolution. This committee considered it advisable to extract Remonstrant views from the Remonstrants' own writings and draw them up in a number of theses for synodical examination. The committee also thought it necessary that a synodical writing (*scriptum Synodicum*) be prepared in which "the Orthodox view of the Five Articles would be solidly and vigorously treated at the capacity of the church, and in which it would be shown to the whole church that the synod has kept far clear of strange and blasphemous doctrines and does not approve of the hard sayings of some Doctors."[6]

The next day, the elderly Huguenot Philippe Duplessis-Mornay sent a *memoire* to his secretary Pierre Marbault with advice for the synod on how to deal with the Remonstrant issue. In it he advised that the "decision on the controverted points" be expressed in scriptural words and expressions and that, in drafting the "canons or articles" (*canons ou articles*), the synod should take care not so much to contend for victory as to confirm the truth. He also noted that, "since the canons [*canons*] that are drawn up in councils are usually brief, precise, and concise…it is especially necessary that here one seek soundness and

---

4. *ADSND*, 1:221.
5. *ADSND*, 1:267–68.
6. Breitinger, 78v.

not subtlety."[7] It is not known whether this paper was actually delivered to the synod. To my knowledge, this is the earliest documentary instance of the term "canons" in reference to the future decision of the synod.

On 8 January, President Bogerman dictated some *Theses* on Article I drawn up from Remonstrant writings, and he asked for the synod's advice regarding whether these *Theses* fairly represented the Remonstrant position. He also asked whether the examination of Article I should be finished and whether "the definitive synodical view" (*sententia synodica definitiva*) on it should be drawn up before proceeding to the other Articles.[8]

On 10 January, the various synodical delegations presented their advice on these matters. Five of the delegations had specific ideas about the form of the synod's decision. The Palatine delegation advised that the examination of the Five Articles ought to include a declaration of Remonstrant views in propositions drawn from their writings, a confirmation of these by the Remonstrants, and a judgment (*iudicium*) of their views. This judgment, they said, ought to be twofold: collegial and synodical.

> Let the former judgment be formed by the individual colleges of delegates, according to the number and order of the propositions themselves, but be brief, vigorous, and fortified with one or another testimony of Scripture. Let the latter be drawn up from the collegial judgments in the form of ecclesiastical Canons [*forma Canonum ecclesiasticorum*], just as was customarily done by all the more venerable synods till now.[9]

The Palatine delegation also suggested that a positive writing be prepared:

---

7. *Suite des Lettres et Memoires de Messire Phillipes de Mornay* (Amsterdam: Louis Elzevier, 1651), 123; reprinted in *ADSND*, 2/2:905–6.

8. Hesse: 274. In a document suggesting procedure, written between 8 and 10 January, the British delegates advised that, when fundamental theses on Article I drawn from Remonstrant writings are fully examined, and if they are found false, then "the fundamental views of the Orthodox should be opposed antithetically to them, confirmed by some solid arguments, and established by a synodical judgment [*synodali iudicio*]"; see *ADSND*, 2/2:734; and Anthony Milton, ed., *The British Delegation and the Synod of Dort (1618–1619)* (Woodbridge, England: Boydell Press, 2005), 174.

9. The advice of the Palatine delegation is printed in *ADSND*, 2/2:743.

After the heterodox doctrine has been rejected and condemned in this way, thought should be given to firmly establishing orthodox doctrine. To do this, there are certainly various means for the synod to propose and consider in its own time. In advance we would like two or three of the Dutch pastors to be assigned who, having consulted advice and writings, may draw up in the Dutch idiom some popular, moderate writing [*scriptum*], appropriate for edification and peace, concerning predestination and its associated points, and submit it to the judgment of the synod, to be published for the use of the church.[10]

Like the Palatines, the Swiss envisioned that "a sound judgment [*iudicium*] may be produced, first a collegial, then a synodical one." The Swiss also suggested a positive writing:

After the heterodox views are rejected, let the orthodox view be put in its place; let it be explained appropriately and at the capacity of the church, and let it be proved from the holy Scriptures, so that not only what the synod disapproves and what it rejects may be apparent, but also what it approves as agreeable with God's Word and judges to be believed. And let this matter similarly be entrusted to a few people, namely two or three.[11]

The Hesse delegation also considered it necessary and useful that "at the first opportunity a sound and orthodox formula [*formula*] concerning these Five Articles may publicly appear, which is opposed to the strange Remonstrance; it should be constructed as much as possible from the very words of Scripture and be firmly established with reasons from God's Word."[12]

The Zeeland delegation thought that, after Remonstrant views were examined, "finally a decisive statement [*sententia decisiva*] should be formed from God's Word."[13] It further recommended:

And since individual arguments for the orthodox view...can be expressed in synodical decrees, we think it is wholly necessary that one or two of the Dutch brothers be instructed [to draw up] some

---

10. *ADSND*, 2/2:744.
11. *ADSND*, 2/2:749–50.
12. *ADSND*, 2/2:747–48.
13. *ADSND*, 2/2:770.

sound writing [*scriptum solidum*] in which this material concerning the Five Articles is treated at the capacity of the people and for the common use of the Church, and do this not only with the received orthodox doctrine but also with a clear refutation of false doctrine.[14]

The Utrecht delegation also spoke of the "final judgment [*Iudicium finale*] concerning the view of the Remonstrants" and recommended:

> Finally, we judge it advisable and necessary that some brief writing [*scriptum*] be published that clearly embraces the view of the Reformed churches on predestination, so that the uneducated may be instructed and false accusations may be countered.[15]

Several observations may be made on the advice of these five delegations. First, they all envision the synod making a judgment on the Remonstrant views. This is variously referred to as the "synodical judgment," the "Canons," the "decisive view," or the "final judgment." It may be noted that, in the Palatine usage, the term "Canons" refers to brief negative statements expressing an ecclesiastical judgment on false doctrine. As noted by the Palatine delegates, the term was used in this sense in previous church councils. Second, they all recommend that a positive popular writing explaining the Reformed position on predestination be drawn up for the sake of firmly establishing the orthodox view in the churches. In each case, this is conceived to be a different document than the main synodical judgment on Remonstrant views. Third, neither the judgment nor the positive writing is here considered to have confessional status.

On 11 January, with the Remonstrants still not cooperating, President Bogerman asked the synod whether the time had come to examine their views only from their writings. Each delegation gave its advice, and in this context Emden proposed a somewhat different procedure, beginning with a positive statement and ending with the judgment:

> First, that the synod should first set forth a brief, clear, and sound explanation [*explicationem*] of the truth that the Reformed churches profess concerning the Five controverted Articles.

---

14. *ADSND*, 2/2:771.
15. *ADSND*, 2/2:773.

Second, that…it soundly refute those Five Articles which the cited Remonstrants presented to the synod.…

Third, that the synod…finally come down to bear a judgment [*iudicium*].[16]

On 14 January, the decision was made to implement the 1 January resolution of the States General, and so the Remonstrants were expelled from the synod. Now the synod faced the question of how best to proceed in examining and judging the Remonstrant views from their writings. On 16 January, the synod decided to follow a new procedure. In the mornings, the individual colleges or delegations would meet privately to examine and form a judgment (*iudicium*) on the Five Articles. In the afternoons, the Dutch and foreign theologians would present speeches responding to the main arguments of the Remonstrants.[17] Though the decision does not mention this, the English observer John Hales noted the synod's expectation that from the *iudicia* of the various delegations "must be gathered the Conclusion."[18] It may be noted that this procedure generally reflected the earlier Palatine and Swiss advice regarding collegial and synodical judgments.

Although the decision on procedure referred only to examining and judging the Remonstrant view, President Bogerman then orally advised the delegations "that in forming their judgments [*iudiciis*], not only the false doctrine of the Remonstrants should be rejected, but also the orthodox doctrine of the Reformed churches should be set forth, as much as possible, in the very clearest words suitable to the capacity and edification of the common people and be supported by very sound reasons and arguments."[19]

For the next two weeks, this new procedure was followed in examining Article I. On 28 January, Hales noted that, "as for any Decisive Sentence, they will give none, till they have thus gone through all the five [Articles]."[20] On the 30th, after the speeches on Article I were finished, the procedure was reviewed, and the synod decided to continue using it in dealing with the other Articles. This was also approved by

---

16. *ADSND*, 2/2:826.
17. *ADSND*, 1:115.
18. Hales, 2:84.
19. Heppe, "Historia," 282.
20. Hales, 2:91.

the state delegates, who "at the same time advised that canons [*canones*] not be produced or a decision [*arrestum*] be formed, unless everything was first properly examined and discussed publicly."[21]

Apparently in response to the 10 January advice of several delegations, President Bogerman, on 4 February, proposed that several documents be prepared as soon as possible, which would be of great use to the synod and to the churches. The synod decided in favor of this proposal. The first document was to be a "writing [*scriptum*] popularly and succinctly explaining and soundly confirming from God's Word the orthodox view of the Five Articles, with a refutation of the chief false accusations by which this doctrine is commonly defamed."[22] The second was to be a "refutative writing [*scriptum elenchticum*], in which the chief arguments of the Remonstrants are solidly refuted."[23] The English, as well as state delegate Josias Vosbergius, were opposed to the first writing because it seemed incongruous that anything should be written on the doctrine of the Articles before the synod had handed down its judgment. Nevertheless, the decision stood, and Dutch delegates Antonius Walaeus, Jacobus Trigland, and Godefridus Udemans were assigned the task of composing the didactic writing, with the advice of foreign theologians Bishop George Carleton, Abraham Scultetus, Johannes Breitinger, and Jean Diodati. Franciscus Gomarus advised that this writing should not contain unnecessary and private ideas, but only necessary points accepted by common consent.[24] These two writings were never composed;[25] instead, following the form of the collegial *iudicia*, the synod embarked on a course that would lead to one document that would combine a positive statement

---

21. *ADSND*, 1:121. The Dutch translation is "het besluyt, dat is de Canones." *Acta ofte Handelinghen des Synodi…ghehouden…tot Dordrecht, Anno 1618 ende 1619* (Dordrecht, 1621), sess. 70.

22. *ADSND*, 1:123. Hales, 2:94, called this a "scriptum didacticum" and noted that it was to appear in both Dutch and Latin.

23. *ADSND*, 1:123.

24. Hales, 2:95.

25. Later, in 1620, the South Holland provincial synod also attempted to get these two writings composed, but nothing came of it. J. Reitsma and S. Van Veen, eds., *Acta der Provinciale en Particuliere Synoden, gehouden in de Noordelijke Nederlanden gedurende de Jaren 1572–1620* (Groningen: J. B. Wolters 1892–1899), 3:439–40.

From Judgment on Arminianism to Confessional Standard 399

of the Reformed view with the expected judgment of the Remonstrant position.

It is noteworthy that, in the course of these proceedings, there was a behind-the-scenes attempt to get the synod to draw up a common confession for all Reformed churches. On 8 December, French theologian Pierre Du Moulin, who was prevented by the French king from attending the synod as a delegate, proposed in a letter that the synod should compose a confession of faith derived from the confessions of the Reformed churches of various nations—one that would contain points of doctrine on which they all agreed while avoiding issues of ecclesiastical polity and discipline—and that, after approval by the synod, this new confession should be sent to the home countries of the various delegations for approval.[26] But this matter was not on the synodical agenda, and the delegates had no mandate from their home churches to pursue such a project. Yet, after various foreign delegates expressed interest, and after King James I of England recommended having British and other selected delegates work privately on this project, President Bogerman asked Bishop Carleton and Palatine theologian Scultetus to prepare a draft of such a confession; it would be sent to James for his input and then to the synod for its public approval. By late February, however, with dissension among some delegates concerning the Remonstrant issue—especially on Article II—as well as growing time constraints, Bogerman no longer thought the project of a common confession was feasible for the synod. The matter, which was never officially discussed on the floor of the synod, was quietly dropped.[27]

From 6 to 21 March, the synod was occupied with reading the *iudicia* of the nineteen delegations on the Five Articles. Following the

---

26. Du Moulin's letter to British ambassador Dudley Carleton is printed in Milton, *British Delegation*, 152–53.

27. Milton, *British Delegation*, 148, 155, 159–60, 185, 187, 195, 197–98, 204; see also Hales, 2:58, 65–66, 85–86, 178; W. Robert Godfrey, "Tensions within International Calvinism: The Debate on the Atonement at the Synod of Dort, 1618–1619" (PhD diss., Stanford University, 1974), 244–52; and Donald Sinnema, "The French Reformed Churches, Arminianism, and the Synod of Dort (1618–1619)," in *The Theology of the French Reformed Churches: From Henri IV to the Revocation of the Edict of Nantes*, ed. Martin I. Klauber (Grand Rapids: Reformation Heritage Books, 2014), 100–102, 109–13.

earlier instructions of Bogerman, these *iudicia* all consisted of positive statements expressing the orthodox Reformed view as well as a rejection of Remonstrant errors. By this time, it was common to refer to the expected synodical judgment on the Five Articles as the "Canons." For example, the English delegate Walter Balcanqual refers to the preparation of the "Canons" in his letters of 15 and 18 February and 9, 16, and 17 March.[28]

Drafting the Canons

When all the *iudicia* had been read, President Bogerman noted that the States General "did expect that the Canons should be made" by Easter, which was ten days away.[29] He then proposed that "the synodical judgment [*iudicium synodicum*] should now be formed from all of them [the *iudicia*] compared with each other." For that purpose, he informed the synod, he had drafted "some Canons" from these *iudicia*, to which the delegations might suggest amendments.[30]

The next day, 22 March, Bogerman presented his views on the form of the proposed Canons. "The order and style of these canons ought to be directed to the instruction of these churches." They should be proposed simply, but not meagerly, "so that the Canons may not be scholastic(?) or academic, but ecclesiastical." On the question of whether the heterodox or orthodox section should be first, Bogerman thought that "the doctrine of the truth is to be placed first because it is by nature prior."[31] The English Bishop Carleton also gave advice on how the Canons should be formed. He, too, recommended that the

---

28. Balcanqual's letters are printed in Balcanqual, 2:102, 109, 121, 122, 125, 130, and 135.

29. Balcanqual, 2:139.

30. *ADSND*, 1:140. When the synod ended, Bogerman presented a summary report of the synod's actions to the States General on 30 May. In this report he noted that "it was decided that from all the advices a Synodical Judgment or Canons [*Iudicium Synodael, ofte Canones*] should be formed, in which on the one hand, the true doctrine, agreeing with God's holy Word, and on the other hand, the false, conflicting with God's holy Word, should be faithfully contained, in conformity with the received advices." Printed in H. H. Kuyper, *Post-Acta of Nahandelingen van de Nationale Synode van Dordrecht in 1618 en 1619 Gehouden* (Amsterdam: Höveker & Wormser, 1899), 476.

31. Sibelius, 90r–90v. This passage is printed in Klaas Dijk, *De Strijd over Infra- en Supralapsarisme in de Gereformeerde Kerken van Nederland* (Kampen, 1912), Bijlage C, xviii–xix.

affirmative view be placed first, then the negative, and that "the style of the Canons be popular, not scholastic."[32] The same day, Bogerman dictated to the synod the "Canons" he had drafted on Articles I and II.[33] Since these consisted of positive "articles" and a rejection of errors, it is apparent that, here, the term "Canons" referred to the whole document.[34]

This procedure immediately aroused the complaint from some foreign theologians that Bogerman intended to draw up the Canons by himself and merely dictate them to the synod for its consent.[35] To resolve the discontent, the state delegates on 25 March advised that some foreign and Dutch theologians work with the president and the assessors to draft the Canons. The synod approved this advice and appointed a drafting committee of nine.[36]

For about three weeks, the synod did not officially meet while the drafting committee was at work. Working from Bogerman's draft, the committee prepared its own draft of the Canons, which it revised twice before coming up with the final version of the CD. After receiving the Bogerman draft and each of the three committee drafts, the various delegations had an opportunity to suggest amendments.[37]

Reflecting the general structure of the *iudicia*, all of these drafts consisted of a positive section setting forth orthodox Reformed doctrine and a negative section of rejected errors. It is interesting to observe the terminology used for each section in these drafting documents. Quite consistently, the drafting committee referred to statements of the positive section as "articles" (*articuli*) and statements rejecting errors as "canons" (*canones*). For example, one of its documents (dated

---

32. Sibelius, 92r; printed in Dijk, *Strijd*, xix.
33. *ADSND*, 1:141.
34. Bogerman's dictated draft is printed in D. J. De Groot, "Stukken met Betrekking tot de Opstelling der Dordtsche Canones," *Bijdragen en Mededeelingen van het Historisch Genootschap (gevestigd te Utrecht)* 59 (1937): 163–74.
35. Balcanqual, 2:140.
36. *ADSND*, 1:141–42; Balcanqual, 2:146–47.
37. On the various drafts, amendment suggestions, and drafting committee documents, see Donald Sinnema, "The Drafting of the Canons of Dordt: A Preliminary Survey of Early Drafts and Related Documents," in *Revisiting the Synod of Dordt (1618–1619)*, ed. Aza Goudriaan and Fred van Lieburg (Leiden: Brill, 2011), 291–311. See also chapter 13 of this volume, "The Drafting of the Canons of Dordt."

8 April) is called "Observations on the Articles and Canons [*Articulos et Canones*] concerning Election and Reprobation gathered from the Judgments of the whole Synod."[38] In another document (dated 12 April), the committee noted a Gelderland suggestion that "canons" judge and "articles" declare.[39] It is apparent that the committee was attempting to be precise in its usage. The documents with amendment suggestions from the various delegations, however, are not as precise or consistent. They refer to the positive articles sometimes as "articles," sometimes as "theses,"[40] and sometimes as "canons."[41] And elsewhere they refer to the whole document as the "Canons,"[42] which was by now a fairly popular designation for the proposed document.

On 16, 18, and 23 April, the full synod, after some final changes, approved the final version of the CD.[43] Then, on the 23rd, three copies were signed by all delegates. The whole document is titled "The Judgment [*Iudicium*] of the Synod of Dordt on the Five Main Points of Doctrine in Dispute in the Netherlands."[44] This title clearly indicates that the document was officially regarded as the synod's judgment, or judicial decision, on the Arminian controversy. Each chapter begins with a section of "articles" presenting the Reformed view, followed by a "rejection of errors" (*Reiectio errorum*). The term "Canons" is not used, even though the document was popularly known as such. In the synod's documents, the CD are sometimes also referred to as the *Explanation* (*Declaratio, verclaringe*) of the synod on the Five Articles.[45]

On 22 April, the synod approved a Conclusion to the CD that refers to both its positive and negative sections:

---

38. OSA, 5:169, 174; see also 135, 137, 157, 160, 163, 168, 190.
39. "Iudicat de Canonibus reijciendis, non de Articulis veritatem asserentibus." OSA, 5:138.
40. OSA, 5:189, 211.
41. OSA, 5:195, 215.
42. OSA, 5:143, 153, 195.
43. *ADSND*, 1:142, 144.
44. The only extant originally signed copy is preserved in OSA, vol. 52(R). It is titled "Iudicium Synodi Dordracenae de Quinque Doctrinae Capitibus in Belgio Controversis."
45. *Acta*, sess. 136; Kuyper, *Post-Acta*, 124, 150, 186, 188–89, 229. This is most prominently the case in Dordt's forms of subscription (see below).

And so this is the clear, simple, and straightforward declaration [*declaratio, verclaringe*]⁴⁶ of the orthodox teaching of the Five Articles in dispute in the Netherlands, as well as the rejection of the errors [*errorum reiectio, verwerpinghe der dolinghen*] by which the Dutch churches have for some time been disturbed. This the synod judges to be derived from God's Word and in agreement with the confessions of the Reformed churches.⁴⁷

A few days later, a preface was also added to the CD.⁴⁸ It contains some pertinent comments reflecting how the synod at this point perceived the nature and purpose of the CD.

> [The States General convened the synod] so that, by the common judgment [*iudicio*] of so many theologians of the Reformed churches, those dogmas of Arminius and his followers might be carefully examined in this renowned synod and adjudicated [*diiudicarentur*] from God's Word alone; that true doctrine might be firmly established [*stabiliretur*] and the false rejected [*reiiceretur*]; and that concord, peace, and tranquility might, by divine blessing, be restored to the Dutch churches....
>
> This synod, for the glory of God, and for the integrity of saving faith, the tranquility of consciences, and the peace and well-being of the Dutch Churches, decided that the following judgment [*iudicium, oordeel*] should be promulgated [*promulgandum*], in which both the true view, agreeing with God's Word, concerning the aforesaid five main points of doctrine is explained [*exponitur*], and the false view, disagreeing with God's Word, is rejected [*reiicitur*].⁴⁹

On 24 April, the day after the CD were signed, President Bogerman asked the synod to approve a synodical censure, or Sentence (*Sententia*), of the Remonstrants who had been cited before the synod. This Sentence declared the cited Remonstrants guilty of error, scandal, and intolerable obstinacy against the decisions of the synod and the

---

46. The first draft of the Conclusion here used the term *expositione*, the second draft the term *confessio*. Printed in Dijk, *Strijd*, 190, 196.

47. *Acta*, sess. 136; J. N. Bakhuizen van den Brink, ed., *De Nederlandse Belijdenisgeschriften in Authentieke Teksten* (Amsterdam: Ton Bolland, 1976), 278–79.

48. Balcanqual, 2:160, indicates that the preface was not finally approved until 29 April, although the *acta* of session 140 (*ADSND*, 1:146) speaks of its approval already on 25 April.

49. *Acta*, sess. 140; Bakhuizen van den Brink, *Belijdenisgeschriften*, 228–29.

States General and deposed them from their ecclesiastical offices. It committed the other Remonstrants to the provincial synods, classes, and consistories and asked these assemblies to meet,

> in order that they may diligently take care that they do not admit any to the sacred ministry who refuse to subscribe to and teach the doctrine declared in these synodical decisions [*doctrinae hisce Synodicis constitutionibus declaratae subscribere eamque docere recuset*]; and retain no one whose clear disagreement can violate the doctrine approved with so much unanimity in this synod and again disturb the unity of the pastors and the tranquility of the churches.[50]

This part of the Sentence occasioned a debate among some of the Dutch delegates about whether those who would not subscribe to the CD—but who promised never to speak or teach publicly or privately against them—might be tolerated. Bogerman cut off this debate by declaring that this was a particular issue that ought to be left completely to the discretion of the provincial synods; neither did he know how much toleration the States General might allow.[51]

On the same day, the Sentence was approved by a majority of delegates, though some of the foreign theologians abstained from giving their support because they considered the discipline of Remonstrant ministers to be a Dutch matter outside their jurisdiction.[52]

The requirement that the CD be subscribed, first mentioned here in the Sentence, marks a major step toward granting the CD confessional status. Yet, even now it does not appear that the synod saw the CD as a new confessional standard or document with confessional status. Rather, subscription was required, since it was the most effective

---

50. *Acta*, sess. 138; Bakhuizen van den Brink, *Belijdenisgeschriften*, 282.
51. Balcanqual, 2:155.
52. *ADSND*, 1:144. English delegate Balcanqual was surprised that the Sentence appeared so suddenly on the agenda, and he considered it much too harsh: "This mater of the personal censure which was a thing of great consequence, we were never made acquainted with before the very instant in which it came to be read.… Between the Forenoon and the Afternoon Session, there was strange labouring with the *Exteri* for getting their consent to it; yet we meddled not with it; all I can say is, me thinketh it is hard, that every man should be deposed from his Ministry, who will not hold every particular Canon; never did any Church of old, nor any Reformed Church propose so many Articles to be held *sub poena excommunicationis*." Balcanqual, 2:145–46.

means of enforcing the doctrinal judgment made in the CD and of preventing Remonstrant error in the Dutch Reformed churches.

On 26 April, the state delegates delivered a signed copy of the CD to the States General in The Hague and reported on the actions of the synod. The next day, the States General responded with a resolution that it was very happy the synod had been unanimous in its decision on the Five Articles. It also decided that the CD ought to be publicly promulgated as quickly as possible.[53] So, on 6 May, the members of the synod marched in a solemn procession to the Grote Kerk of Dordrecht, where a crowded assembly had gathered to hear the CD be officially proclaimed to the world. There the CD and the synodical Sentence were publicly read and promulgated (*praelectum ac promulgatum*) in Latin by the two synodical secretaries, Dammanus and Hommius. They also read the names of those who signed the CD, and each member, upon hearing his name, testified his fidelity to the CD by doffing his hat.[54] This public ceremony should not be interpreted as acknowledging the confessional status of the CD; rather, it was an official public recognition of the CD as the synod's judicial decision on the Remonstrant case.

The Form of Subscription

The foreign theologians were then dismissed, and the synod turned to matters specifically of Dutch concern. One of the matters treated in these final Post-Acta sessions was the preparation of a new form of subscription, an issue brought to the synod by a gravamen from the South Holland provincial synod:

> Since the Remonstrants by their own hand sign the forms of our unity [*formulis nostrae unionis*], that is, the Confession and the Catechism, and yet interpret them wrongly, the National Synod is asked how it can counteract this mischief, and that it see fit to read the form of subscription prepared in the [South Holland] Synod of Delft and consider whether this form may protect the churches enough against the quibbling and reservations of all who are evasive.[55]

---

53. *RSG*, 4:108–9.
54. *ADSND*, 1:154–55; Balcanqual, 2:166.
55. Printed in Kuyper, *Post-Acta*, 424.

In response to this gravamen, the Synod of Dordt decided on 15 May to draft a new form of subscription that required that ministers subscribe not only to the BC and HC but also to the CD:

> It was decided that a carefully prepared form of subscription [*formulam subscriptionis*] should be drawn up, by which ministers of the churches may subscribe [*subscribant*] to the Confession, the Catechism, and the *Synodical Explanation* [*Declarationi Synodicae, sijnodale verclaringhe*] concerning the Five Articles of the Remonstrants, so that they may clearly bear witness to their orthodoxy and that the wrongful evasions of some about subscription may be prevented.[56]

On 17 May, when a draft of the new form of subscription for ministers was ready for approval, the synod again affirmed its decision:

> It was decided that to bear witness to their unanimity [*consensum*] in orthodox doctrine, each and every minister of the divine Word ought to subscribe to the Confession and Catechism of these churches and to the Canons or *Explanations* [*Canonibus seu Declarationibus*] of this Synod. And to prevent in this subscription the wrongful evasions of some, this form should be used for subscription; it was read and approved.[57]

As approved, this form of subscription read:

> We the undersigned ministers of the divine Word…do hereby sincerely and in good conscience before the Lord, declare by this our subscription that we heartily believe and are persuaded that all the articles and points of doctrine contained in the Confession and Catechism of the Reformed churches in the Netherlands, together with the explanation [*Declarationem, verclaringe*] of some points of the aforesaid doctrine made by the National Synod of Dordrecht, 1619, agree in everything with the Word of God. We promise therefore that we shall diligently teach the aforesaid doctrine and faithfully defend it.[58]

---

56. *ADSND*, 1:160; Kuyper, *Post-Acta*, 123–24. This decision was reaffirmed in similar words the following day, when a committee was appointed to draft the new form; Kuyper, *Post-Acta*, 150. Cf. Donald Sinnema, "The Origin of the Form of Subscription in the Dutch Reformed Tradition," *Calvin Theological Journal* 42, no. 2 (Nov. 2007): 256–82.

57. *ADSND*, 1:167; Kuyper, *Post-Acta*, 186.

58. Kuyper, *Post-Acta*, 186–87; *ADSND*, 1:167.

The synod also adopted forms of subscription with similar wording for schoolteachers and for theology professors.[59]

Even though the Synod of Dordt did not make a specific decision to adopt the CD as a new confession, including it in the form of subscription to be subscribed to along with the BC and the HC de facto gave the Canons a confessional status parallel to these two official forms of unity. Requiring subscription meant that the CD would function in the Dutch Reformed churches as a confessional standard by which to judge the orthodoxy of its leaders.

Nevertheless, in actual practice, it took some time before the CD were fully recognized as having confessional status on a level with the BC and the HC.

Even in the Church Order of Dordt, the CD were not accorded the same status as the other two documents. When, in its later sessions, the synod adopted its Church Order—a revision of the 1586 Church Order—articles 53 and 54 were not amended to make them consistent with the new forms of subscription. Thus, as in the 1586 Church Order, article 53 of the Church Order of Dordt required ministers and theology professors to subscribe to the BC, without adding the CD or even the HC; and article 54 only required schoolteachers to subscribe to the BC *or* the HC.[60]

After the close of the synod on 29 May, one soon begins to see how the CD actually functioned in the Dutch Reformed churches. In the summer and fall of 1619, the various provincial synods and classes met and began to implement Dordt's major decisions. All pastors were required to subscribe to the CD by use of the form of subscription prepared by Dordt. Most Remonstrant ministers refused to subscribe to the CD, and so about two hundred of them were suspended or deposed from their offices. The minutes of these provincial synods are full of disciplinary proceedings against individual Remonstrant

---

59. Kuyper, *Post-Acta*, 188–89, 229.

60. P. Biesterveld and H. H. Kuyper, eds., *Kerkelijk Handboekje* (Kampen: J. H. Bos, 1905), 240–41; compare F. L. Rutgers, ed., *Acta van de Nederlandsche Synoden der Zestiende Eeuw* (Dordrecht: J. P. van den Tol, 1980), 498–99. See also Kuyper, *Post-Acta*, 311.

ministers who refused to sign the form of subscription.[61] These ministers were issued an "Act of Cessation" (*Acte van Stilstand*), a promise not to serve in the ministry and not to propagate their views. Those who refused to keep the promise—more than eighty—were banished from the country by the States General.

Forms of Unity

As the CD were used in the Dutch Reformed churches, they soon came to be fully recognized as a confessional standard. A good indicator of when this occurred is when the CD began to be called a "form of unity" along with the BC and the HC. Already at this time this was a technical term for documents with confessional status.[62]

In the Reformed churches of the Low Countries, subscription to the BC was required as early as 1563.[63] Adherence to the HC was proposed for candidates for the ministry already in the articles of the so-called Convent of Wesel (1568), but in the next two decades, Dutch Reformed synods required subscription only to the BC and not to the HC.[64] By 1593, however, the HC was beginning to be signed as a confessional standard alongside the BC.[65] A few years after the turn

---

61. Reitsma and Van Veen, *Acta*, 2:65–66, 72–89, 99; 3:327, 335–89, 395, 406–9; 4:318–19, 321–26, 330–31; 5:172, 187–88, 315, 318, 321, 323; 6:272–73, 277–78, 280, 408–21, 428–34, 437, 439–42; 7:372; 8:240–41, 244–45. That the CD officially functioned also in Friesland is shown by Jan Hovius, "Zijn de Dordtse Leerregels van 1619 in Friesland Aangenomen en Ingevoerd?," in *Uw Knecht Hoort*, ed. W. Kremer, J. van Genderen, and B. J. Oosterhoff (Amsterdam: Ton Bolland, 1979), 11–44.

62. The term in this confessional sense likely derives from the Lutheran *Formula Concordiae* of 1580; Bakhuizen van den Brink, *Belijdenisgeschriften*, 50.

63. N. C. Kist, "De Synoden der Nederlandsche Hervormde Kerken Onder het Kruis, gedurende de Jaren 1563–1577," *Nederlandsch Archief voor Kerkelijke Geschiedenis* 9 (1849): 135.

64. Rugters, *Acta*, 15, 56, 134, 154, 155, 237, 247, 390, 498. The development of confessional writings in the Dutch Reformed churches is examined by J. Borsius, "Overzigt van het Trapswijze Toegenomen en Bekrachtigde Gezag der Geloofsbelijdenis en van den Catechismus, als Formulieren van Eenigheid in de Nederl. Herv. Kerk," *Archief voor Kerkelijke Geschiedenis* 9 (1838): 285–376; and F. S. Knipscheer, *De Invoering en de Waardeering der Gereformeerde Belijdenisschriften in Nederland voor 1618* (Leiden: Adriani, 1907).

65. Reitsma and Van Veen, *Acta*, 1:172; 3:15; A. Fanoy, "Het Onderteekeningsformulier van de Dienaren des Woords," *Gereformeerd Theologisch Tijdschrift* 28 (1928): 488; cf. Knipscheer, *Invoering*, 193–94.

of the century, both the BC and the HC began to be called "forms of unity" (*formulieren van eenicheyt, formulae consensus*),[66] and this became a familiar phrase in the Arminian controversy before and during the Synod of Dordt.[67]

That the CD only gradually came to be acknowledged as a "form of unity" is evident in the fact that, after the Synod of Dordt, one finds instances where the "forms of unity" include the BC and the HC, but not yet the CD. For example, on 3 August 1619, at the South Holland provincial synod of Leiden, Nicolaes Tijckmaekers recanted his Remonstrant views and promised "that I shall present to the congregation the pure truth following God's Word and according to the forms of unity together with the explanations [*formulieren van eenicheijt midtsgaders de verclaringhen*] of the national synod."[68] And in its dedicatory letter to the printed *Acta* of Dordt, dated 27 March 1620, the States General noted that the "Canons" were unanimously approved by all members of the synod and then stated that "we also saw to it that the very Forms of our Unity [*Unionis nostrae Formulas*], namely the Confession and Catechism used here till now, were carefully reviewed by them according to the norm of the divine Word."[69]

---

66. For example, Jacobus Arminius, *Verklaring* (1608), ed. G. J. Hoenderdaal (Lochem: De Tijdstroom, 1960), 130, 135–36; *Schriftelicke Conferentie, gehouden in s'Gravenhaghe inde Iare 1611* (s'Gravenhage, 1612), 15–17, 72; *Naerder-Bericht end Openinge vande Proceduren by den Kercken-dienaren Remonstranten ghehouden inde teghenwoordighe Verschillen* (s'Gravenhage, 1612), 57; *Copye van seker Vertooch onlanghs by eenighe Predicanten der Ghereformeerde Kercke ghedaen aende Mo. Ed. Heeren Staten van Hollandt ende West-Vrieslandt* (Delft, 1617), Biiii; *Klaer ende Grondich Teghen-Vertoogh van eenighe Kercken-Dienaren van Hollandt ende West-Vrieslandt, gestelt tegen seker Vertoogh der Remonstranten* (Amsterdam, 1617), 91–96; and Festus Hommius, *Specimen Controversiarum Belgicarum* (Leiden, 1618), praefatio.

67. For examples in the minutes of provincial synods just prior to Dordt, see Reitsma and Van Veen, *Acta*, 2:18; 3:293, 294, 297, 299, 305, 318, 319, 320; 5:147. For examples at the Synod of Dordt, see *ADSND*, 1:12, 78; 2/2:368; *Acta et Scripta*, 1:20; *Historisch Verhael van't ghene sich toeghedraeghen heeft binnen Dordrecht, in de Jaeren 1618 ende 1619* ([Amsterdam], 1623), 62v; Kuyper, *Post-Acta*, 169, 424, 485; cf. A. Th. Van Deursen, *Bavianen en Slijkgeuzen* (Assen: Van Gorcum, 1974), 407.

68. Reitsma and Van Veen, *Acta*, 3:353; Van Deursen, *Bavianen*, 409; see 415 for a similar case from November 1622.

69. *Acta*, dedicatory letter. For similar examples, see Reitsma and Van Veen, *Acta*, 3:361, 380, 421, 450; 6:442; cf. 413.

But in the months and years after the close of the synod, one also begins to find instances in which the concept of "forms of unity" includes not only the BC and the HC but also the CD. The earliest example I know of is found in a protest first presented orally to Classis Dordrecht in April 1620 by Contra-Remonstrant ministers Johannes Becius and Johannes Bocardus, who signed Dordt's form of subscription, but with reservations:

> Johannes Becius and Joh. Bocardus, being called upon to sign the forms of unity, the Catechism, the Confession and also the Canons [*formulieren van eenicheit, Catechismo, Confessie alsooc Canonibus*] of the national synod in accordance with the document prepared by the national synod, explained that they are ready and willing to do so, just as indeed they immediately signed this document, but they also explained that they understand this document in this way: first, that in regard to the refuting of errors that conflict with the aforesaid forms [*voorschreven formulieren*], each of them might do this in such a way as they in good conscience shall find most fitting for the edification of the congregation and in accord with the demands and occasion of the text they are treating.[70]

Some other examples are evident in the 1622 debate concerning whether the Leiden theology faculty should sign the form of subscription for theology professors prepared by Dordt. When pressured by the South Holland synod to sign the "Catechism, Confession, and Canons" by use of this form of subscription, the theology faculty wrote in reply that "they held the doctrine contained in the aforesaid forms [*voorsegde formulieren*] conformable in everything with God's Word" and that they had "bound the same forms [*deselve formulieren*] in the book" that they signed and kept in their archives.[71] In their report on the matter to the South Holland synod held in July 1622, delegates

---

70. Reitsma and Van Veen, *Acta*, 3:448. Likewise, at the synod of Utrecht in September 1620, the CD, the BC, and the HC are all called *formulieren* that should be bound together and thus jointly signed (6:444). There may also be an early example at the synod of Utrecht in August 1619 (6:437), but, here, *formulieren der eenicheyt* may well refer to forms of subscription; the phrase was occasionally used in this sense (6:411, 444).

71. A. Eekhof, *De Theologische Faculteit te Leiden in de 17de Eeuw* (Utrecht: G. Ruys, 1921), 26–27.

of Classis Leiden noted that they had admonished the Leiden theology professors "to sign the forms of unity in doctrine [*formulieren der eenicheyt in de leere*]"; the professors replied "that most of them had previously signed the aforesaid forms [*voorsz. formulieren*]."[72]

One more instance in which the CD are included among the "forms of unity" appears in an ordinance for the Statencollege of Leiden (1 October 1631), which prescribes that the regent of the college must sign "the Forms of unity in doctrine [*Formulieren van eenigheyt inde Leere*], namely the Confession and Catechism of the Dutch Churches, together with the further explanations or Canons [*midtsgaders de naerdere verklaringen oft Canones*] made in the recent National Synod of Dordrecht."[73]

Conclusions

From this story of the formation and early use of the CD, I draw several conclusions:

1. The original intention of the CD was that they serve not as a new confessional standard but rather as the judgment, or judicial decision, of the synod on the Five Articles of the Remonstrants. Thus, the bulk of the synod's time was spent examining Remonstrant views and rendering its judgment on these views as biblically erroneous. And so the CD were framed in five points in response to the Five Articles. As a judgment, the CD first of all needed to present a rejection of Remonstrant errors. So, the rejection of errors sections best expressed the primary intent of the CD.

2. The positive sections, expressing the orthodox Reformed view, were added as an afterthought well into the synodical proceedings. Initially it was anticipated that a separate positive document would be prepared in addition to the synodical judgment, but, following the twofold

---

72. W. Knuttel, ed., *Acta der Particuliere Synoden van Zuid-Holland 1621–1700* ('s-Gravenhage: M. Nijhoff, 1908), 1:46. On the issue of subscription by the Leiden theologians, see also N. C. Kist, "De Onderteekening der Formulieren door Hoogleeraren en Doctoren der Godgeleerdheid, sedert de Synode van Dordrecht, bijzonder aan de Hoogeschool te Leiden," in *Archief voor Kerkelijke Geschiedenis* 9 (1838): 473–500.

73. Nikolaas Wiltens, ed., *Kerkelyk Plakaat-boek, behelzende de Plakaaten, Ordonnantien, ende Resolutien, over de Kerkelyke Zaken* ('s Gravenhage: Scheltus, 1722), 1:293.

structure of the *iudicia* of the nineteen delegations, the positive section became folded into the synodical judgment. The purpose of the positive section was to make evident the orthodox biblical basis on which the negative judgment was grounded and to remove the confusion in the churches caused by the doctrinal controversy by establishing them more firmly in the truth. Because it was customary in theological discussion to present the truth before rejecting error, the positive section was placed first in the CD, even though the rejection of errors was the primary intent of the document.

3. Since they were primarily intended to be a judgment on Arminianism, the CD were originally titled a "Judgment" of the synod on the five points in dispute. This is evident not only in the title of the original manuscript but also in the titles of the first printed editions of the Canons in Latin (*Iudicium*), Dutch (*Oordeel*), French (*Iugement*), and English (*Iudgement*), all of which were published in 1619.[74]

4. The term "canons" was used in various ways at the Synod of Dordt. While the term could sometimes be used in reference to synodical decisions in general[75] and to articles of church order,[76] "Canons," even during the course of the synod, became the *popular* term to describe the synodical judgment, though it was not the official name. Different delegates variously used the term "canons" to refer to the positive articles, the rejected errors, and, most commonly, the whole document. But the drafting committee more precisely reserved the term "canons" for the negative statements in the rejection of errors section. This reflected the customary usage of other councils; for example, the Council of

---

74. *Iudicium Synodi Nationalis, Reformatarum Ecclesiarum Belgicarum, habitae Dordrechti, Anno 1618 & 1619* (Dordrecht, 1619); *Oordeel des Synodi Nationalis der Gereformeerde Kercken van de Vereenichde Nederlanden, ghehouden binnen Dordrecht, inden Jare 1618 ende 1619* (Dordrecht, 1619); *Iugement du Synode National, des Eglises Reformees du Pays-Bas, tenu à Dordrecht, l'An 1618 & 1619* (Dordrecht, 1619); *The Iudgement of the Synode holden at Dort, concerning the five Articles* (London, 1619).

75. For example, the States General's Articles to Convene the synod specified that whatever decisions were passed by majority shall be held "pro conclusione Synodali sive Canone." *Acta*, sess. 4.

76. For example, "Canones Regiminis Ecclesiastici." *ADSND*, 1:156; Kuyper, *Post-Acta*, 110.

Trent called anathematized statements "canons."⁷⁷ This should be seen as the primary meaning of the term "canons," even when the term was extended to refer popularly to the whole document.

5. In church history, a synodical judgment on a doctrinal case does not necessarily or usually become a new confessional standard. That is evident even at the Synod of Dordt, which also made doctrinal judgments on the beliefs of Conrad Vorstius and the Geysteranus brothers.⁷⁸ Because the Arminian controversy was a major threat to doctrinal orthodoxy and to the peace of the Dutch Reformed churches, the synod sought to employ strong measures to distinguish Reformed orthodoxy from Remonstrant error and to discipline proponents of the latter. In this context, the CD came to have confessional status.

6. Once the CD, as a synodical judgment, were required to be subscribed by all ministers, as prescribed by the Sentence on the cited Remonstrants and by the forms of subscription, they began to function as a doctrinal standard by which the orthodoxy of church leaders was enforced. Then it was only natural that the CD came to be regarded as having a confessional status on the same level as the BC and the HC. Yet, full recognition of the CD's confessional status was achieved only as they gradually came to be known as one of the three "forms of unity."

7. As Reformed orthodoxy became firmly established after the Remonstrant leaders were deposed, the rejection of errors section of the CD no longer had immediate relevance. Once the crisis had abated, this section had largely served its purpose. With the shift of focus from synodical judgment to confessional standard, the positive articles emerged as the primary section of the CD.

---

77. H. J. Schroeder, trans., *The Canons and Decrees of the Council of Trent* (Rockford, Ill.: Tan Books, 1978), 42, 51, 79, 101, 149, 162; Hubert Jedin, *A History of the Council of Trent*, vol. 2, *The First Sessions at Trent 1545–47*, trans. Dom Ernest Graf (London: T. Nelson, 1961), 240, 310.

78. *ADSND*, 1:144–45, 151–53.

Gold medallion, given to the foreign theologians

CHAPTER 16

Distortions of the Canons: The Tilenus Abbreviation, the Five Points of Calvinism, and TULIP

The Calvinist–Arminian controversy that centered on predestination and related issues erupted in the Netherlands in the 1590s with the teaching of Jacobus Arminius (1560–1609). After Arminius's death, his followers summarized his views in the Five Articles of the 1610 Remonstrance. These articles became the focus of the escalating debate in the following decade, until the Synod of Dordt examined and rejected Arminian (or Remonstrant) views in the Canons of Dordt (CD). The CD were structured in five chapters to respond to the Five Articles of the Remonstrants.

This article examines three efforts that have historically distorted the nuanced teaching of the CD: first, the abbreviation of the French theologian Daniel Tilenus, a strong advocate of the Arminian cause; second, the Five Points of Calvinism, which actually refer to the five topics of the CD; and third, the acronym TULIP, which has become a popular way to summarize the five chapters of the CD.

The Tilenus Abbreviation[1]

Daniel Tilenus's five-point abbreviation of the CD had a lasting influence in fostering a harsh interpretation of the document, especially in Calvinist–Arminian debates within English-language circles.

---

1. This section is largely reprinted from Donald Sinnema, "The French Reformed Churches, Arminianism, and the Synod of Dort (1618–19)," in *The Theology of the French Reformed Churches: From Henri IV to the Revocation of the Edict of Nantes*, ed. Martin I. Klauber (Grand Rapids: Reformation Heritage Books, 2014), 99–100, 127–34.

Tilenus (1563–1633) was born in Silesia but spent most of his life in France. After completing his studies, in 1590 he arrived in France, where he became a tutor in Paris. In 1599, he was called to the independent principality of Sedan to serve as a minister and professor of theology. When the national synod of the French Reformed churches reorganized the College of Sedan into the Academy of Sedan for the training of Reformed pastors in 1602, he was named professor of theology there.[2]

While at Sedan, Tilenus entered the debate against Arminius and published his *Consideratio Sententiae Jacobi Arminii de Praedestinatione, Gratia Dei et Libero Arbitrio Hominis, apud Ordines Hollandiae et Westfrisiae ab eodem declaratae* (Frankfurt, 1612). Here Tilenus attacked Arminius's views on predestination, grace, and human free will, as summarized by Arminius in his *Declaration of Sentiments* of 1608. The same year a Dutch translation of the *Consideratio* appeared. This edition included three letters, by David Pareus, Abraham Scultetus, and Tilenus himself, all very critical of the Arminians; Tilenus called them growing shoots of the Pelagian weed.[3]

The following year, Leiden minister and professor of law Johannes Arnoldi Corvinus defended Arminius in a polite but well-argued response to Tilenus, titled *Defensio Sententiae D. Iacobi Arminii de Praedestinatione, Gratia Dei, Libero hominis Arbitrio,…adversus eiusdem a D. Daniele Tileno theologo Sedanensi editam Considerationem* (Leiden, 1613).[4] Corvinus's response was so convincing to Tilenus that

---

2. For Tilenus's life, see Jean-Baptiste-Joseph Boulliot, "Notice historique et bibliographique sur Daniel Tilenus, minister du saint Evangile à Sedan, professeur à l'Académie de cette ville, et précepteur de Turenne," *Magasin Encyclopédique, ou Journal des Sciences, des Lettres et des Arts* (October 1806): 249–79; and "Tilenus, Daniel" in E. and E. Haag, *La Protestant France* (Paris, 1859), 9:383–87.

3. Daniel Tilenus, *Overlegginghe ofte Proeve van t'ghevoelen Jacobi Arminii, van de predestinatie, van de ghenade Gods, ende van de vryen wille des menschen, aen de Staten van Hollant ende West-vrieslandt van hem verclaert.… Hier achter zijn noch byghevoecht drie brieven: 1. Davidis Parei aen den autheur, 2. Des autheurs aen Pareum, 3. M. Abrahami Sculteti* (1612). Pareus was a theology professor at Heidelberg, and Scultetus a court preacher there. On this edition, see Johannes Uytenbogaert, *Kerckelicke Historie* (Rotterdam, 1647), 578–79; and Jacobus Trigland, *Kerckelycke Geschiedenissen* (Leiden, 1650), 612.

4. On this book, see Geraert Brandt, *The History of the Reformation and Other Ecclesiastical Transactions in and about the Low-Countries* (London, 1721), 2:137. Years

he changed his opinion and embraced the Arminian cause.[5] He was able to keep his post as theology professor at Sedan until the Synod of Dordt, although he had to deal with accusations from students related to teaching Arminian ideas.[6]

When the Synod of Dordt condemned Arminianism and, in its Sentence, deposed Arminian clergy who refused to subscribe to the CD, this had a direct impact on Sedan. Henri de la Tour, the duke of Bouillon and prince of Sedan, was married to a half sister of Prince Maurice of the Netherlands, and he became an ardent Calvinist. After the synod, the duke rigorously applied Dordt's Sentence in his own territory. Tilenus, whose Arminian views the duke had earlier tolerated, was deposed from his teaching post and forced to leave Sedan in the heart of the winter of 1619–1620. He told the duke that he wished to live and die an Arminian for the sake of God. He then took refuge in Paris, where he lived the rest of his life. While in Paris, Tilenus actively defended the Arminian cause and opposed the teachings of Dordt.[7] In one debate, he contended that the Calvinists offered a cruel and pitiless God who deliberately damns His creatures.[8]

On a visit to England in 1620, Tilenus met with King James I, and in a discussion about predestination, they addressed the opinion of those who made God the author of sin. Tilenus called this doctrine horrible and criticized the CD for teaching that the greatest part of the human race is condemned to hell by the mere will of God, without any regard for sin. Returning to France, he wrote his *Traité de la Cause et de l'Origine du Péché* (Paris, 1621), which criticized the teaching of Zwingli, Calvin, Vermigli, Beza, Zanchi, Du Moulin, and other

---

later, English Calvinist William Twisse responded to Corvinus in *Ad Jacobi Arminii Collationem cum Francisco Junio, et Johan. Arnoldi Corvini Defensionem sententiae Arminiae...quam adversus Danielis Tileni Considerationem edidit, Animadversiones* (Amsterdam, 1649).

5. Boulliot, "Notice," 255; Haag, *Protestant France*, 9:384; Trigland, *Geschiedenissen*, 612; Brandt, *History*, 2:137; 3:72. Brandt suggests that Tilenus became convinced by Corvinus's defense of Arminius after he had already reexamined his own views.

6. Uytenbogaert, *Historie*, 704–9.

7. Brandt, *History*, 4:73; Boulliot, "Notice," 256–58, 263; Jacques Pannier, *L'Église Réformée de Paris sous Louis XIII (1610–1621)* (Paris: Champion, 1922), 452; Haag, *Protestant France*, 9:384–85.

8. Haag, *Protestant France*, 9:384.

Reformed theologians for implying that God is the author of sin. At about this time, he told the English ambassador that his conscience would not allow him to subscribe to the CD.[9]

In 1620, the Synod of Alais, the first national synod of the Reformed churches in France to be held after Dordt, adopted the CD as a confessional standard of the French churches, alongside the French Confession of Faith (1559).[10] Along with the decision to adopt the CD, this synod also drew up an oath requiring subscription to the CD by all French Reformed ministers and elders.[11]

In 1622, Tilenus wrote a pamphlet against the decision and oath of Alais, titled *Considérations sur les Canon et Serment des Églises Réformées conclu et arresté au Synode National d'Alez.*[12] Here he tried to demonstrate that the oath of Alais was vain, false, calumnious, ungodly, imprudent, insolent, rash, and presumptuous—vain, in requiring an oath to a formulary of doctrine drawn up by humans, when it would be better to take an oath to doctrines derived directly from Scripture; false and calumnious, in charging the Arminians with reintroducing Pelagianism; ungodly, in not rejecting horrible hard sayings found in Calvinist writings; imprudent, insolent, and rash, in being so stringent as not to admit any exceptions or extenuating circumstances; and presumptuous, in insinuating that God had given possession of the truth forever to the men of Dordt and Alais and could never bestow greater light. He above all blamed the Synod of Alais for being precipitant in approving the CD after a simple reading of it, without any proper examination.[13]

The same year, Tilenus published a sharp critique of the CD in a book titled *Canones Synodi Dordracenae, cum Notis et Animadversionibus*

---

9. Brandt, *History*, 4:73–76; Boulliot, "Notice," 260, 270–71.

10. Jean Aymon, *Tous les Synodes Nationaux des Eglises Réformées de France* (The Hague, 1710), 2:182–83; John Quick, *Synodicon in Gallia Reformata* (London, 1692), 2:37–38.

11. Aymon, *Synodes*, 2:184; Quick, *Synodicon*, 2:38–39.

12. Daniel Tilenus, *Considérations sur les Canon et Serment des Églises Réformées, conclu et arresté au Synode Nat. d'Alez és Cevennes, 6 d'Oct. 1620, pour l'approbation des Canons du Synode tenu à Dordrecht en Hollande, 1618 et 1619* ([Paris], 1622).

13. Brandt, *History*, 4:195–96; Boulliot, "Notice," 275.

*Dan. Tileni.*¹⁴ His comments on the CD were learned and written in a witty style, but he was stinging in his response to the errors he sought to refute. He dedicated the work to King James I, to whom he asserted that, if the Devil had asked his angels by what lie he could render God odious to humans, he could not employ one more suitable than the dogmas of Dordrecht.¹⁵

A year later, Tilenus published a thirty-two-page pamphlet in French, again criticizing the doctrine of the CD as approved by the Synods of Dordt and Alais. This was titled *La Doctrine des Synodes de d'Ordrecht et d'Alès mise à l'espreuve de la practique* (1623).¹⁶ The same year, a Dutch translation was published by Uytenbogaert;¹⁷ this later drew a rebuttal by Gisbertus Voetius,¹⁸ a former delegate at Dordt. An English translation appeared soon thereafter.¹⁹

---

14. *Canones Synodi Dordracenae, cum Notis et Animadversionibus Dan. Tileni. Adjecta sunt ad calcem Paralipomena ad Amicam Collationem, quam cum D. Tileno, ante biennium institutam, nuper publicavit Jo. Camero* (Paris, 1622), 228 pages.

15. Brandt, *History*, 4:409; Boulliot, "Notice," 275–76.

16. Daniel Tilenus, *La Doctrine des Synodes de d'Ordrecht et d'Alès mise à l'espreuve de la practique; où, entre autres mystères, se descouvre un moyen très-aisé pour rendre l'homme immortel en ce monde* (Paris, 1623).

17. Daniel Tilenus, *De Leere der Synoden van Dordrecht ende Alez, ghestelt op de proeve van de practijcque, ofte ghebruyck, waer in onder andere verborgentheden ontdeckt wordt een seer licht middel, om den mensch onsterflijck te maecken in dese werelt* (1623); reprinted in *Verzameling der Tractaaten van P. De Fyne* (Amsterdam, 1736). H. C. Rogge, *Beschrijvende Catalogus der Pamfletten-Verzameling van de Boekerij der Remonstrantsche Kerk te Amsterdam* (Amsterdam: Scheltema, 1862), 1/1:96, identifies Uytenbogaert as the translator of this work.

18. Gisbertus Voetius, *Proeve vande Cracht der Godtsalicheyt, met goet ende christelick bescheyt op seker last-schrift, hier neffens gaende, by den Remonstranten hier te lande int nederduytsch gestroyt onder desen titul: De Leere der Synoden van Dordrecht ende Alez, ghestelt op de proeve van de practijcke ofte ghebruyck… door den vermaerden Daniel Tilenus… tot verdedinge vande leere der waerheyt ende ontdeckinge vande kracht der godtsalicheydt aende ontruste conscientien ingestelt* (Amsterdam, 1628). This volume includes a reprint of the Dutch translation of Tilenus's pamphlet, 243–59. On this work, see A. C. Duker, *Gisbertus Voetius* (Leiden: Brill, 1897), 1:381–88.

19. Its English title was *The Doctrine of the Synode of Dort and Alez reduced to practice*, according to Martin Lipenius, *Bibliotheca Realis Theologica* (Frankfurt, 1685), 1:545. This English translation does not appear to be extant. In 1659 Laurence Womock, in his *Arcana Dogmatum Anti-Remonstrantium* (London, 1659), 7–8, noted that this English translation was done by John L'Oiseau, a French minister serving in London. Womock stated that he himself had never seen a printed copy, though he was able to peruse the translation in manuscript.

In *La Doctrine*, Tilenus sought to examine the validity of the doctrine of Dordt and Alais by testing its practical use in dealing with three pastoral matters: the conversion of unbelievers, the correction of Christian wrongdoers, and the consolation of the sick and afflicted. He concluded that the doctrine of Dordt failed on all counts:

> From this test of practice, anyone can see what judgment one must make about a religion that is in conflict with the conversion of unbelievers, the correction of those who live an offensive life, and the consolation of the afflicted; that nullifies the preaching of the Word, the use of the holy sacraments, as well as the exercise of prayer; and that, to conclude in a word, overthrows and overturns from top to bottom the whole service of the church, which consists of sound doctrine and good discipline.[20]

As the basis for testing the doctrine of Dordt, Tilenus provided a five-article abbreviation of the CD at the beginning of his pamphlet. In English, his abbreviation reads as follows:

Art. 1: *Of Divine Predestination*

That God, by an absolute decree, hath elected to salvation a very small number of men, without any regard to their faith or obedience whatsoever; and secluded from saving grace all the rest of mankind, and appointed them, by the same decree, to eternal damnation, without any regard to their infidelity or impenitency.

Art. 2: *Of the Merit and Effect of Christ's Death*

That Jesus Christ hath not suffered death for any other, but for those elect only; having neither had any intent nor commandment of his Father to make satisfaction for the sins of the whole world.

Art. 3: *Of Man's Will in the State of Nature*

That by Adam's Fall, his posterity lost their free-will, being put to an unavoidable necessity to do, or not to do, whatsoever they do, or do not, whether it be good or evil; being thereunto predestinated by the eternal and effectual secret decree of God.

Art. 4: *Of the Manner of Conversion*

That God, to save his elect from the corrupt mass, doth beget faith

---

20. Tilenus, *De Leere*, 19.

in them by a power equal to that whereby he created the world, and raised up the dead; insomuch, that such unto whom he gives that grace, cannot reject it, and the rest, being reprobate, cannot accept of it.

> Art. 5: *Of the Certainty of Perseverance*
> That such as have once received that grace by faith, can never fall from it finally or totally, notwithstanding the most enormous sins they can commit.[21]

According to Tilenus, the banished Arminians had clearly proven in their writings that these five articles were in fact the doctrine of the Synods of Dordt and Alais, and they were also ready to prove that these articles were found in the writings of major Reformed theologians in the very same or even stronger terms.[22] Thus it appears that Tilenus drew up his abbreviation not simply from the CD but also from summaries of Reformed views as presented in Arminian writings.[23] As such, the five articles of Tilenus's abbreviation are not a fair representation of the actual formulations of the CD; rather, they offer an interpretation with a clear Arminian bias.

Especially in England, Tilenus's abbreviation had a profound impact, as it was often used as the basis for interpreting the CD in later Calvinist–Arminian debates. Apart from the English translation of *La Doctrine*, which apparently had very little circulation, the first appearance of the abbreviation in English seems to have been in the Arminian Laurence Womock's anonymously published *The Examination of Tilenus* (1658).[24] This satirical dialogue presents an imaginary Tilenus (based on the real Tilenus) being questioned by a board of

---

21. This English translation is from Peter Heylyn, *Historia Quinqu-Articularis* (London, 1660), 41–42, which was often the source of reference to the Tilenus abbreviation in later debates.

22. Tilenus, *De Leere*, 3.

23. Remonstrant compilations of Reformed views that Tilenus might have used include: Johannes Uytenbogaert, *Appendix Pressioris Declarationis; continens testimonia ex scriptis variorum authorum collecta* (Leiden, 1617); "Syllabus Testimoniarum," in *Acta et Scripta*, 2:25–46, 204–8, 290–96; and Simon Episcopius, *Antidotum continens pressiorem declarationem propriae et geniunae sententiae quae in Synodo Nationali Dordracena asserta est et stabilita* (Harderwyk, 1620).

24. [Laurence Womock], *The Examination of Tilenus before the Triers* (London, 1658 [i.e., 1657]), 28–29.

examiners as he seeks admission to the office of preacher.[25] Before presenting objections to the Articles (Canons) of the Synod of Dordt, he sums up this doctrine in the five articles of the Tilenus abbreviation. Since Womock mentioned in a later work of 1659 that he had never seen a printed copy of the English translation of *La Doctrine*, but only a manuscript copy of it,[26] it may be concluded that the source of the abbreviation as found in Womock's *Examination* was this manuscript copy.

The Examination of Tilenus immediately drew a rebuttal from the moderate Calvinist Richard Baxter in a work titled *The Grotian Religion Discovered* (1658). In his preface, Baxter accused the author of the *Examination* of pretending to give a concise and true sum of the doctrine of the Synod of Dordt in the five articles of the abbreviation, when in reality he "falls to falsifying and calumny."[27] Baxter then quoted the abbreviation (from the *Examination*) and tried to show how each of its five articles was a distortion of the teaching of the CD.[28] He accused this "new Tilenus" of "unworthy falsification" and making a "perverse insinuation" and "odious inferences" in words that were not in the synod's Canons.[29]

Womock immediately defended Tilenus against Baxter in a lengthy new work, *Arcana Dogmatum Anti-Remonstrantium* (1659), which was, again, published anonymously. Womock admitted that the five articles of the abbreviation were drawn up by Tilenus himself in his *La Doctrine* and not invented by the fictitious "new Tilenus" of *The Examination* (as Baxter had supposed).[30] Responding to Baxter's

---

25. Dewey Wallace Jr., *Puritans and Predestination: Grace in English Protestant Theology, 1525–1695* (Chapel Hill: University of North Carolina Press, 1982), 122–23.

26. [Laurence Womock], *Arcana Dogmatum Anti-Remonstrantium* (London, 1659), 8.

27. Richard Baxter, *The Grotian Religion Discovered, at the Invitation of Mr. Thomas Pierce in his Vindication; with a Preface, vindicating the Synod of Dort from the calumnies of the New Tilenus* (London, 1658), preface, sect. 6.

28. Baxter, *Grotian Religion*, preface, sect. 7–17.

29. Baxter, *Grotian Religion*, preface, sect. 11, 15, 17.

30. [Laurence Womock], *Arcana Dogmatum Anti-Remonstrantium, or the Calvinists Cabinet unlock'd; in an Apology for Tilenus, against a pretended Vindication of the Synod of Dort, at the provocation of Master R. Baxter, held forth in the Preface to his Grotian Religion* (London, 1659), 7–8.

accusation that the Synod of Dordt nowhere expressed many of the statements in the abbreviation, Womock asserted that Tilenus did not confine himself to the CD but took in "the doctrine of the Synod and its adherents."[31] Hence Womock sought "to make it good, that these Articles of Tilenus are consonant to the sense of the Calvinists doctrine, whether delivered in or out of the Synod."[32] In the following pages he reproduced each article of the abbreviation and offered multiple citations from thirty-three different Reformed authors to demonstrate that they indeed taught what was asserted in the abbreviation; thus he thought he cleared Tilenus from the guilt of "unworthy falsification."[33] However, none of the citations were drawn from the actual CD.

The next year, the Arminian Peter Heylyn wrote *Historia Quinqu-Articularis* (1660), a history of the Arminian controversy, especially as it was contested in England. Here he presented the Conclusions of the Synod of Dordt "as I find them abbreviated by Dan. Tilenus."[34] The margin indicates that his source for the Tilenus abbreviation was Womock's *Arcana*. Heylyn then commented: "This is the shortest, and withall the most favourable Summary, which I have hitherto met with, of the conclusions of this Synod."[35]

Heylyn became the most common source of citations of Tilenus's abbreviation in later years. As time passed, Tilenus's abbreviation often became the accepted summary of the CD in English-language circles. This can be seen, for example, in the pamphlet *The Articles of Belief, Professed by the Followers of Calvin, Luther, and Arminius; respecting those Five Points, about which there is much Dispute among Protestants* (Norwich, [1774]). Tilenus's abbreviation is printed under the heading:

---

31. *Arcana*, 5–7.
32. *Arcana*, 23.
33. *Arcana*, 23–51. The abbreviation itself is reproduced on pp. 23, 29, 33, 41, and 47.
34. Peter Heylyn, *Historia Quinqu-Articularis; or, a Declaration of the Judgement of the Western Churches, and more particularly of the Church of England, in the Five Controverted Points, reproached in these last times by the name of Arminianism* (London, 1660), 1:41–42.
35. Heylyn, *Historia*, 42.

"Five Articles, agreed to by the Synod of Dort…collected from Dan. Tilenus, see Heylyn's History of this Controversy, p. 523."[36]

By the early nineteenth century, it was sometimes simply assumed in English-language circles that the Tilenus abbreviation truly represented the teachings of the CD. A major case in point is that of Thomas Scott, in his response to George Pretyman Tomline's *A Refutation of Calvinism* (1811), which presented the abbreviation (copied from Heylyn) as the Articles of the Synod of Dordt and declared, "Such is Calvinism."[37] Scott tried to defend Calvinism by publishing *Remarks on the Refutation of Calvinism by George Tomline* (1811). In this work, Scott assumed that the articles of the abbreviation truly presented the teachings of Dordt, but he criticized each of these five articles as not representing true Calvinism.[38] "Such is not Calvinism, as contained even in Calvin's writings; and I am deeply convinced, that had Calvin been present, he would have strongly objected to the measures and conclusions of this synod."[39]

Meanwhile, in 1804 the University of Oxford published the *Sylloge Confessionum*, a collection of Reformation-era confessions, including the full CD in their original Latin.[40] From this, the distorted character of the Tilenus abbreviation was discovered and exposed.

Scott later noted that, since he had met with Tilenus's five articles in other publications favorable to Calvinism, he had no suspicion that these were not the real articles of Dordt but an abbreviation by avowed opponents of them. However, he then discovered his mistake. Seeking a copy of the real CD, he found them in the *Sylloge Confessionum* and

---

36. *The Articles of Belief* (Norwich, [Conn.], [1774]), 3. The same heading appears in later reprints of this pamphlet, New York, [ca. 1790]; Windham, [Conn.], 1796; and Middletown, [Conn.], 1817.

37. George Tomline, *A Refutation of Calvinism* (London: T. Cadell and W. Davies, 1811), 566–68. Tomline continued with his critique: "Such is Calvinism; and it is in its nature so inconsistent with the attributes of God, so contrary to the express declarations of Scripture, and so repugnant to the feelings of the human mind, that it seems only necessary to state the system simply and fully in all its parts and consequences, to ensure its rejection by every unprejudiced person."

38. Thomas Scott, *Remarks on the Refutation of Calvinism by George Tomline* (London: C. Baldwin, 1811), 2:674–86.

39. Scott, *Remarks*, 2:686.

40. *Sylloge Confessionum* (Oxford: Clarendon, 1804), 363–417.

realized that they were more discordant with the abbreviation than he could have imagined. Now, admitting that he had erroneously adopted and aided in circulating a gross misrepresentation of the synod and its Canons in his earlier *Remarks*, he wanted to make reparation in the second edition of this work (London, 1817). Along with the necessary corrections, he translated the genuine "Articles of the Synod of Dort" and inserted them into this second edition. After each chapter of the CD, which he now considered very scriptural, he included articles of the Tilenus abbreviation (from Tomline's *Refutation*) for the sake of comparison.[41] The next year, the second centennial of the Synod of Dordt, Scott published a separate edition of the CD in *The Articles of the Synod of Dort* (1818).[42] Scott's publication of a translation of the actual CD helped clear up the prevalent confusion regarding Tilenus's abbreviation.

But the use of the Tilenus abbreviation still persisted for some years. In 1821, Edward Copleston, the provost of Oriel College, Oxford, published *An Enquiry into the Doctrines of Necessity and Predestination*, in which he contrasted the teaching of the Church of England with Calvinist doctrine. He presented the Tilenus abbreviation (drawn from Heylyn) as a summary of the decrees of the Synod

---

41. Thomas Scott, *Remarks on the Refutation of Calvinism*, 2nd ed. (London: W. W. Woodward, 1817), 724–26, 732–33, 735, 741–42, 746–47, 750; reprinted in Scott, *Remarks on the Doctrine of Original Sin, Grace, Free Will, Justification by Faith, Election and Reprobation, and the final Perseverance of the Saints, to which is added a translation of the genuine Articles of the Synod of Dort*, 2nd ed. (London: A. Macintosh, 1817). Scott translated the Canons from the *Sylloge Confessionum* (Oxford, 1804). This translation includes only the positive articles of the Canons. Apparently, he was unaware that there were already four earlier English translations of the Canons: *The Iudgement of the Synode holden at Dort, concerning the Five Articles* (London, 1619); *Articles Agreed on in the Nationall Synode of the Reformed Churches of France, held at Charenton neere Paris, in the Moneth of September, 1623* (Oxford, 1623); Quick, *Synodicon* (1692), 2:126–52; and *The Constitution of the Reformed Dutch Church in the United States of America* (New York: Durell, 1793), 223–58; (repr., New York: George Forman, 1815).

42. Thomas Scott, *The Articles of the Synod of Dort* (London: A. Macintosh, 1818). In this edition, he also included the Rejection of Errors sections. On the Tilenus abbreviation, see pp. v, 2, 111–12, 120–21, 130, 142–43, 154–55. This work reappeared in several later editions: Utica, N.Y., 1831; Philadelphia, 1841; Philadelphia, 1856; Harrisonburg, Va., 1993; n.p., 2015.

of Dordt, which he considered "the most moderate and impartial account of their proceedings."[43]

In his notes to his edition of Arminius's *Works* (1825), James Nichols also mentioned the Tilenus abbreviation, but he reserved his criticism for Richard Baxter and Thomas Scott.[44]

Then, in 1831, Josiah Allport, in his "Life of Bishop Davenant," presented a brief overview of the history of the Tilenus abbreviation. He called it a garbled statement and a deliberate falsehood that was cloaked as a "favourable abridgement" of the CD.[45]

The Five Points of Calvinism

The Synod of Dordt was convened first of all to address the controversy with the Arminians, focusing on the Five Articles of their 1610 Remonstrance. The synod's response was the Canons of Dordt (1619), which answered the Five Articles in five chapters, or heads (*capita*, *hooft-stukken*), with Chapters III and IV combined. It soon became customary to say that the CD presented "Five Points," referring to the topics of the five chapters.

However, it was not until the early eighteenth century that the full phrase "The Five Points of Calvinism" appeared. This can be found, for example, in Daniel Neal's *The History of the Puritans*, vol. 2 (1733), which twice mentions "the five distinguishing Points of Calvinism,"[46] and in Daniel Waterland's *Sermons* (1742), which states that "one of the Five Points of Calvinism is, that we are justified by faith alone."[47]

---

43. Edward Copleston, *An Enquiry into the Doctrines of Necessity and Predestination* (London: John Murray, 1821), 217–18.

44. James Arminius, *The Works*, trans. James Nichols (London: Longman, Hurst, Rees, Orme, Brown & Green, 1925), 1:510–11.

45. John Davenant, *An Exposition of the Epistle of St. Paul to the Colossians*, trans. Josiah Allport (London: Hamilton, Adams & Co., 1831), 1:xviii–xx.

46. Daniel Neal, *The History of the Puritans* (London: Richard Hett, 1733), 2:148, 160. Earlier, John Edwards, *The Scripture-doctrine of the Five Points (as they are commonly called), wherein the texts in the Old and New Testament relating to those Points are, according to the Calvinian Scheme, faithfully collected, and some of them explain'd and illustrated* (London: A. Bell and W. Taylor, 1715), referred to the Five Points according to the Calvinian scheme.

47. Daniel Waterland, *Sermons on Several Important Subjects of Religion and Morality* (London: W. Innys, 1742), 1:xviii.

The five concepts that make up the so-called Five Points of Calvinism were fluid for generations after Dordt. It was not until the early nineteenth century that one begins to find the five concepts (as later formulated in the standard form) mentioned together (but still not expressed in the acronym TULIP). For example, in an address from 1832, Bishop Thomas Church Brownell of the Protestant Episcopal Church of Connecticut contrasted Episcopal teachings with the Calvinist system of beliefs:

> According to the Calvinist belief, the atonement of Christ is partial, and limited exclusively to the elect. The rest of mankind are regarded as predestinated to everlasting misery.... And upon this foundation of a limited atonement is built the theory of sovereign and unconditional election and reprobation.... The points of doctrine peculiar to the Calvinist system of theology, are the total depravity of man, unconditional election and reprobation, irresistible grace and instantaneous conversion, and the certain perseverance of the saints. These peculiarities are not set forth in the Thirty-nine Articles of our [Episcopal] Church.[48]

The Five Points of Calvinism continued to be identified in a variety of ways throughout the nineteenth century. However, toward the end of the century, Philip Schaff, professor of church history at Union Theological Seminary, identified "the five points of Dutch Calvinism" in a way that was similar to the final standard form: (1) Unconditional predestination; (2) Limited atonement; (3) and (4) Total depravity, and Irresistible grace; (5) Perseverance of the saints.[49] His list also reflected the order of the CD.

The problem with the phrase "The Five Points of Calvinism" is mainly twofold:

---

48. "Bishop Brownell's Second Charge, No. II," *Banner of the Church* 1 (11 August 1832): 197. Timothy Paul Jones, in "Proof: Who Invented the TULIP? (Part 3)," *Timothy Paul Jones* (blog), 8 August 2014, https://www.timothypauljones.com/proof-invented-tulip-part-3/, pointed out this reference. He noted a similar reference to the five concepts later in "The Seventeenth Article," *American Church Review* 25 (1873): 17–18, which was also an Episcopalian journal.

49. Philip Schaff, "The Five Points of Dort and the Five Points of Westminster," *The Independent* (27 February 1890): 2; reprinted in *The Church Eclectic* 18 (1890): 140.

1. Calvinist theology is much broader and richer than five points, and Calvinism cannot be reduced to five points. The Five Points are only the five-point response of the CD to the Remonstrant Five Articles in controversy. They only cover a specific group of doctrines centered on soteriology that were at the heart of the controversy with the Remonstrants. The CD, according to their formal title, were the "Judgment" (*Iudicium*, *Oordeel*) of the Synod of Dordt on these points of controversy. They are not a full confession, like the Belgic Confession and the Heidelberg Catechism, but only an explanation or clarification of some points in these confessional statements. These five points were never intended to be a summary of Calvinistic or Reformed theology, which comprises a much broader range of teachings than the five points, including such doctrines as the Trinity, providence, justification by faith, the covenant, the kingdom of God, the church, the sacraments, and eschatology.[50]

2. Calvin was not the unqualified source of the Five Points as presented in the CD. He was not the single fountainhead of the Reformed tradition. Other Reformed theologians influenced aspects of the CD to an equal or greater extent than Calvin. Though he was a possible or probable influence on some elements of the five points, he was an unlikely influence on others. Calvin was a probable influence on the topics of election and reprobation, especially given his emphasis on double predestination. He was a possible influence on the topics of human depravity, the universal call of the gospel, efficacious grace, and perseverance. But Calvin was an unlikely influence on the CD's infralapsarian perspective and on the themes of twofold reprobation, particular redemption, and the sufficiency–efficiency distinction. So it is historically misleading to designate the Five Points as "Calvinism" in the sense that they all stem directly from Calvin himself.[51]

---

50. Richard Muller, in "How Many Points?," *Calvin Theological Journal* 28, no. 2 (Nov. 1993): 425–33, clearly makes this case. Cf. Edwin H. Palmer, *The Five Points of Calvinism* (Grand Rapids: Baker, 1980), forward. J. I. Packer, in his "Introductory Essay" to John Owen, *The Death of Death in the Death of Christ* (London: Banner of Truth, 1959), 3–10, offers five reasons why it would not be correct to equate Calvinism with the five points. Since the Five Points are not a summary of what it means to be Reformed, identifying as a Five-Point Calvinist or a Four-Point Calvinist is reductionist.

51. For details, see Donald Sinnema, "Calvin and the Canons of Dordt (1619),"

TULIP

The acronym TULIP has become the most popular way to describe the contents of the CD, and sometimes even the heart of Reformed theology. The acronym nicely expresses the five standard concepts—**T**otal depravity, **U**nconditional election, **L**imited atonement, **I**rresistible grace, and **P**erseverance of the saints—and serves as a pedagogical tool that is helpful for memory, so it is readily used in church education classes in churches of Reformed heritage. Moreover, this flower conveniently suggests the Dutch origin of the five points of the CD.

The TULIP acronym, however, is problematic in describing the real content of the CD, for several reasons:

1. Despite the common impression of a long-standing and venerable Dutch heritage, the acronym is actually of recent origin, dating from the first years of the twentieth century in America, in a Presbyterian rather than Dutch Reformed context.

It appears that the earliest known reference to the acronym TULIP dates back only to 1905. That year, Dr. Cleland Boyd McAfee (1866–1944), then pastor of the Lafayette Avenue Presbyterian Church in Brooklyn, made use of the acronym in a popular lecture on the Five Points of Calvinism given before the Presbyterian Union of Newark, New Jersey. This is documented in a 1913 article by Dr. William Vail in the weekly New York Presbyterian newspaper *The Outlook*.[52]

While McAfee used the TULIP acronym to explain the Five Points of Calvinism, his five concepts were not yet exactly in the fixed form that would later become standard. McAfee's version had a different phrase for U:

> T: Total Depravity
> U: Universal Sovereignty
> L: Limited Atonement
> I: Irresistible Grace
> P: Perseverance of the Saints[53]

Church History and Religious Culture 91, no. 1–2 (Jan. 2011): 87–103. See chapter 11 of this volume, "Calvin and the Canons of Dordt."

52. William Vail, "The Five Points of Calvinism Historically Considered," *The Outlook* (21 June 1913): 394–95. The Vail article is reprinted in Kenneth Stewart's book *Ten Myths about Calvinism: Recovering the Breadth of the Reformed Tradition* (Downers Grove, Ill.: IVP Academic, 2011), 79, 291–92.

53. Timothy Paul Jones, in "Proof," notes that McAfee studied at Union

It is clear that the five concepts making up TULIP were at that time still somewhat fluid. After hearing McAfee's lecture in 1905, Dr. Vail checked with seven religious authorities (including seminary presidents) to see whether they agreed with McAfee in identifying the concepts that make up the Five Points of Calvinism. He found that all seven identified the concepts somewhat differently.

It was not until Loraine Boettner's popular volume *The Reformed Doctrine of Predestination*, first published in 1932, that the TULIP acronym first appeared in a printed book. This volume, which appeared in multiple printings, popularized the acronym.[54] However, the five concepts were still not in their current standard form, since Boettner labeled T as "Total Inability," and for I he preferred "Efficacious Grace."

By the 1950s, however, the TULIP acronym was quite commonly used with the five concepts in their current standard form. For example, Earle Cairns, in his *Christianity through the Centuries* (1954) wrote:

> At the risk of oversimplification, one can summarize the essence of Calvin's theology by the use of the simple mnemonic device that has been often used by students. The first letters of the main words of Calvin's theology spell the word "tulip." He believed in *t*otal depravity…*u*nconditional election…*l*imited atonement…*i*rresistible grace…*p*erseverance of the saints.[55]

Since the 1950s, it was especially Edwin Palmer's *The Five Points of Calvinism* (1954, many printings thereafter), that helped to popularize

---

Theological Seminary under Philip Schaff in the mid-1880s and that he may have gleaned the concepts for TULIP from him.

54. Loraine Boettner, *The Reformed Doctrine of Predestination* (Philadelphia: Presbyterian and Reformed, 1932), 59–60, 178. Stewart, *Ten Myths*, 75–96, surveyed eighteenth- and nineteenth-century literature and found no evidence of the acronym TULIP before McAfee. On Boettner, see Stewart, 79, 86–87, 95.

55. Earle E. Cairns, *Christianity through the Centuries* (Grand Rapids: Zondervan, 1954), 336–37. This quotation remained virtually the same in later editions (1958, 1961, 1967, 1971, 1981, 1996, 2009). In 1959, J. I. Packer, in his "Introductory Essay" to Owen, *Death of Death* (1959), 4, also mentioned the TULIP acronym with the five concepts, apparently as an established construct. Already in 1934, the *Psalter Hymnal, Doctrinal Standards and Liturgy of the Christian Reformed Church* (Grand Rapids: Publication Committee of the Christian Reformed Church, 1934; also in 1959 and 1987 eds.), "Doctrinal Standards," 44, popularized the use of the five standard concepts (in the order of the Canons) within Christian Reformed circles, but no mention was made of the acronym.

the TULIP acronym, with the five standard concepts.[56] Since then, there have been over fifty books and pamphlets published with titles that mention "The Five Points of Calvinism" or TULIP.

2. TULIP only works in an English-language context. The acronym makes no sense in the Dutch language, which spells the famous flower as *tulp*.

3. Four of the five concepts that make up TULIP are not explicitly found in the CD. "*Perseverance* of the saints" is the only concept that actually appears in the CD.

4. TULIP alters the proper order of the five points as found in the CD. If listed in the proper order, the result would be ULTIP, but that loses the connection to the famous flower.

5. TULIP exaggerates the role of T, not only by placing it first but also because Article III of the Remonstrants (that a person in a state of sin can do nothing truly good and has no saving grace of himself) was not a point of controversy in discussions from the time of the Hague Conference of 1611 until the Synod of Dordt. Thus, Article III was customarily combined with Article IV and labeled Article III/IV, which is how the two appear in the CD.

6. TULIP is often used as a tool to interpret the CD, resulting in a distortion of the full meaning of the CD.

7. TULIP is sometimes used as a summary of what it means to be Reformed.

8. In all five points, the acronym TULIP oversimplifies and distorts the nuanced teaching of the CD.[57]

---

56. Edwin H. Palmer, *The Five Points of Calvinism: A Study Manual* (Grand Rapids: Moelker Printing, 1954), 11. Lewis W. Spitz, *The Renaissance and Reformation Movements* (Chicago: Rand McNally, 1971), 417, referred to TULIP and the five concepts as "the familiar caricature of Calvin's theology."

57. Cf. Richard A. Muller, *Calvin and the Reformed Tradition: On the Work of Christ and the Order of Salvation* (Grand Rapids: Baker Academic, 2012), 58–62; Roger Nicole, "The 'Five Points' and God's Sovereignty," in *Our Sovereign God: Knowing and Serving the Lord of All*, ed. James Montgomery Boice (Grand Rapids: Baker, 1977), 29–36; Suzanne McDonald, "The Canons of Dort for the Church Today: Polemics, Pastoring, and Pulling Up TULIPS," *Calvin Theological Journal* 54, no. 2 (Nov. 2019): 415–20; Suzanne McDonald, "Pulling Up TULIPS," *The Banner* (November 2019): 35.

Unconditional Election

The CD do teach unconditional election, in that God's decision to elect is a sovereign act of His will and is not based on a preexisting condition of faith that God has foreseen in believers, as the Remonstrants asserted. However, the concept of "unconditional election" may seem to downplay the necessity of faith for conversion. Moreover, "unconditional election" fails to express the whole emphasis of Chapter I of the CD. This chapter focuses not only on election but also on reprobation. And the concept of unconditional election is placed in a broader context in which it is introduced by the universal sinfulness of humanity and the gospel message as the remedy. Likewise, it fails to mention the pastoral emphasis on the assurance of election.

The CD begin not with God's decree in eternity but rather within the historical horizon, with the fallen state of humanity, which deserves condemnation (I, 1). The first chapter then moves to God's love in sending His Son to bring salvation to the world (quoting John 3:16) (I, 2); this work is proclaimed in the gospel message (I, 3), which then receives the human response of faith or unbelief (I, 4). Such faith is solely a free gift of God, but the cause of unbelief lies in humans themselves (I, 5). In article 6, the chapter finally ascends to God's eternal decree of election and reprobation to explain the historical fact that some receive the gift of faith, while others do not receive it. Then election is explained first, along with the assurance of election, followed by reprobation.

As later chapters of the CD indicate, unconditional election does not remove human responsibility. The elect are called to repent, to believe, to persevere, to use their wills, and to do good works. They remain active, not passive. The Holy Spirit works in them to enable them to do these things.

Limited Atonement

The concept of "limited atonement" stresses the fact that Christ's death is effective only for the elect, but it fails to express the double emphasis of Chapter II of the CD—namely, the sufficiency as well as the efficiency of Christ's death on the cross: Christ's death is sufficient to save all people (II, 3), and Christ's death is efficient (effective, efficacious) only for the elect (II, 8). In other words, His death does not just

Distortions of the Canons

offer the possibility of salvation (the Remonstrant view); it is totally effective in actually achieving salvation for all whom God has chosen.

The notion of "limited atonement" neglects all the universal emphases in Chapter II of the CD: that Christ's death has infinite value—in fact, it is *more than sufficient* to atone for the sins of the whole world (II, 3, 4); that the promise of the gospel should be universally proclaimed to *all* people (II, 5); that Christ's death is effective for *all* the elect (II, 8); and that Christ's death is effective for people from *every* nation, tribe, and language (II, 8).

Moreover, "*limited* atonement" implies that Christ's redemptive work on the cross has limitations or deficiencies or that there are limits to God's mercy; whereas the CD emphasize Christ's work has infinite value and worth and is more than sufficient to redeem all. Christ's atonement itself is not limited; its application is limited to those whom God has chosen.

Instead of "limited atonement," a concept that is not found in the CD, a somewhat more appropriate label for the content of Chapter II would perhaps be particular redemption, or definite atonement, but even these terms do not capture the universal features.

Total Depravity

Total depravity—another concept that is not found in the CD—is easily misunderstood as absolute or utter depravity, the notion that humans from birth are as bad as they can be, that humans are utterly wicked all the time and can do no good whatsoever.

Chapter III/IV of the CD rather teaches pervasive depravity and the utter inability of people to save themselves. Evil spreads to all aspects of life. Every human thought and deed is tainted or affected by sin, but not every thought and deed is utterly sinful. Such depravity is pervasive, without denying that fallen humans have some sense of moral good and some desire for good outward behavior.

Moreover, the concept of "total depravity" is often misinterpreted as referring both to unbelievers and to believers after their conversion. Such depravity in fact refers only to the *fallen* state of humans, not to the regenerated state.

Regarding the fallen state, Chapter III/IV of the CD teaches that the fall of humanity brought blindness, darkness, futility, and a distortion of judgment in the mind; perversity, rebellion, and hardness of the heart and the will; and impurity in all the emotions (III/IV, 1). So, unbelievers are unfit for *any saving good*, inclined to evil, dead in sin, slaves to sin. Without grace, they are unwilling and unable to return to God, to reform their distorted nature, or to dispose themselves to reform (III/IV, 3).

Yet, a certain *light of nature remains* in fallen man. He retains some notions of God, of natural things, and of differences between the moral and the immoral. He has a certain eagerness for virtue and for *good outward behavior*. But such light does not enable conversion. Fallen man distorts and suppresses this light, even in matters of nature and society (III/IV, 4).

So, the CD do not deny that unbelievers can display good outward behavior or that they may exercise sincerely held social virtues toward others. The depravity of unbelievers does not erase their humanity but severely perverts it.

Regarding the regenerated state, however, the CD teach that believers remain sinful in this life but that they are not totally depraved.

Once renewed, the will is enabled to produce the fruits of good deeds (III/IV, 11). A person *himself*, in being regenerated by God, believes and repents (III/IV, 12), and he has a *free* will again (III/IV, 16). He is renewed, reformed, and *set free* from *slavery* to sin (V, 1).

This point is better labeled as "pervasive depravity."

Irresistible Grace
The CD, in Chapter III/IV, do not actually teach that grace is *irresistible*, but rather that divine grace is efficacious (*efficax*) in bringing about salvation.

The concept of "irresistible grace" is, like those discussed above, not found in the CD. The idea that grace is "irresistible" was actually a caricature of the CD; it was derived from Jesuits who opposed the Augustinian tradition of grace and was taken up by Remonstrants to counter the orthodox Reformed position even before the Synod of Dordt.[58]

---

58. Herman Bavinck, *Reformed Dogmatics* (Grand Rapids: Baker Academic, 2008), 4:82. Article IV of the 1610 Remonstrance stated: "with respect to the mode

Distortions of the Canons

The concept of "irresistible grace" suggests that grace is some sort of overwhelming, irresistible force that compels a person to act against his will. In reality, grace can be resisted, a fact that is explicitly mentioned in the CD (III/IV, 16). This is evident in some conversion stories—for example, Paul kicking against the pricks in his conversion experience (Acts 9:5 KJV), and Stephen bemoaning that his audience was resisting the Holy Spirit (Acts 7:51; cf. Matt. 22:3; 23:37). Sin is resistance to the will of God.[59]

Though grace can be resisted, God's grace is more powerful than human resistance. Rather than teaching that God's grace is irresistible, the CD affirm that God's *grace overcomes human resistance.*

Regarding humans in the fallen state, the CD assert that there is "rebellion" in the heart and the will (III/IV, 1); the "rebellion and *resistance* [*resistentia*] of the flesh" is completely dominant, and regenerating grace does not abolish the will or coerce a *reluctant* will by force (III/IV, 16).

Regeneration, or conversion, is totally the work of God and is not to be credited to human free choice. God efficaciously (effectively) calls His own, grants them faith, and brings them into the kingdom of His Son (III/IV, 10). Thus conversion occurs through the efficacious operation of the regenerating Spirit (III/IV, 11).

In conversion, God does not act as if people are puppets (blocks or stones); rather, God spiritually revives, heals, reforms, and bends the will in a *pleasing and powerful* manner (III/IV, 16, 12). Grace works outwardly, by seriously calling people through proclamation of the gospel and by enlightening minds by the Spirit. Grace also works inwardly, when the Holy Spirit penetrates the inmost being, opens the closed heart, softens the hard heart, infuses new qualities into the will, activates and strengthens the will, and makes the dead will alive, the

---

of [God's] grace, it is not irresistible" (G. J. Hoenderdaal, "Remonstrantie en Contraremonstrantie," *Nederlands Archief voor Kerkgeschiedenis* 51, no. 1 [1970]: 75). The Remonstrant *Sententia* on Article III/IV, presented to the Synod of Dordt, asserted that "the efficacious grace, by which anyone is converted, is not irresistible (*irresistibilis*)" (*Acta et Scripta*, 2:5), and their *Explicatio* on Article III/IV also rejected the idea that grace is an irresistible power (*Acta et Scripta*, 2:29, 32).

59. Cf. John Murray, "Irresistible Grace," in *Soli Deo Gloria: Essays in Reformed Theology: Festschrift for John H. Gerstner*, ed. R. C. Sproul (Nutley, N.J.: Presbyterian and Reformed, 1976), 56–57.

evil will good, the unwilling will willing, the stubborn will compliant (III/IV, 11).

The result of this regeneration is that a person is effectively reborn and actually believes. So a person himself, by grace, believes and repents (III/IV, 12). The Holy Spirit sets one's enslaved will free so that he can freely choose to turn to Christ (III/IV, 16). Yet, faith is totally a *gift* of God, not in the sense that it is offered by God for a person to choose; rather, faith is actively bestowed on a person, or infused in him. So God produces in man the will to believe and belief itself (III/IV, 14).

Note how the CD describe regeneration working sensitively and pleasingly, not coercively or as an irresistible force. Grace does not force anyone against his will, but it makes a person willing to be converted.

A better label for this point is efficacious (effectual, effective) grace, the actual language of the CD. God actually accomplishes what He intends to accomplish.

Perseverance of the Saints
Although the title of Chapter V of the CD is "Perseverance of the Saints," the emphasis of this last chapter is more on God's *preservation* of the elect than on their own perseverance. A focus on perseverance without preservation is misleading. It suggests that perseverance is just the human effort of the saints.

The terms "perseverance" and "preservation" (and their variant forms) both occur in Chapter V, so both concepts belong together. Believers can *persevere* not by their own strength but because God *preserves* them to the end.

Chapter V of the CD asserts that regeneration sets one free from slavery to sin, but not entirely from sin (V, 1). Believers can depart from the *leading* of grace and commit very serious sins (V, 4), so that even the exercise of faith is suspended, and a believer may lose *awareness* of grace for a time (V, 5). But God is faithful in *preserving* them to the end (V, 3); He does not let them *forfeit* grace and faith totally (V, 6, 8). God preserves through various means, such as the hearing of the gospel, the gospel's exhortations and promises, and the use of the sacraments (V, 14).

In conclusion, when the "Five Points of Calvinism" are popularly formulated in the acronym TULIP, the result is an unnuanced oversimplification and distortion that does not well represent Calvin or the CD.

Rather than reducing the teaching of the CD to five simplistic concepts—which give a misleading impression of the nuanced teaching of the CD, whether by deliberate obfuscation or for pedagogical reasons—the better course is to let the Canons speak for themselves. Read the CD themselves in context to grasp their full meaning. The articles of the CD are concise and very carefully formulated in addressing the perennial question of the relationship between God's sovereign action in the matter of salvation and humans' responsibility to respond to God's gracious initiative.

Grote Kerk of Dordrecht, used for
ceremonial opening and closing of the synod

Appendix 1

Overview of Synod of Dordt Sessions

Day	Session	Deliberations	Related Events
November 1618			
12 M		Preparatory meeting	
13 T		Sermons by Lydius & De Pours at Grote Kerk & Augustijnenkerk	
		Procession to synod hall (Kloveniersdoelen)	
	1	Welcome by state delegates	
		Opening prayer and welcome address by Lydius	
		State delegate Gregorii address to open the synod	
		Credentials of state delegates read	
		Heinsius appointed secretary of state delegates	
14 W	2	Credentials of Dutch delegates and professors submitted	
		President, assessors & secretaries chosen	
14 W	3	Dutch credentials read	
		Overijssel & Utrecht credentials questioned	
		Foreign delegates asked for credentials; already presented to States General	
		Letter from Geneva read	
15 Th	4	Utrecht Remonstrants explain credentials	State delegates meeting
		States General Articles to Convene Synod (11 Nov. 1617) read	
		Discuss how to call Remonstrants	
16 F	5	Letters of citation for Remonstrants approved	Four Remonstrant representatives arrive at Dordrecht
		Status of Episcopius discussed	
		Bogerman asks for gravamina (not re doctrine or discipline)	
		Foreign delegates asked to give Latin speeches (in order of rank)	
		Lubbertus invited from Franeker University	

Appendix 1

Day	Session	Deliberations	Related Events
17 Sa		Decide delegates to copy their gravamina & submit to officers	State delegate meeting
			Remonstrants petition state delegates re their status
18 Su			State delegate meeting
19 M	6	Opening prayers by Bogerman	
		Acta read	
		Gravamina re Bible translation	
		Discussion on need for Bible translation	
20 T	7	English delegates on methods used for King James Version	
		Advice of Dutch professors on Bible translation	
20 T	8	More advice of Dutch delegates	
		Decide on new translation from Hebrew & Greek	
		Some decisions re new translation	
21 W	9	Discuss whether to include translation of Apocrypha	
22 Th	10	Decide on Apocrypha translation; place after NT	
		Decide number and task of translators and reviewers	
23 F	11	Lubbertus arrives	Hales arrives
		Decide time of translation not to be limited	
24 Sa	12	Debate You–Thou (Ghy–Du); Decide: You (Ghy)	
		Debate "Yahweh"; Decide: "HEERE"	
		Other translation decisions	
26 M	13	Choose translators & reviewers	
		Debate re reviewer from Utrecht	
		Walloon & Drenthe delegations request to be omitted	
27 T	14	Drenthe reviewers dropped	Van Hel dies
		Acta read	
		Discuss neglect of catechism preaching	
		Decision on catechism preaching	
		Foreign delegates on their customs	
28 W	15	Bogerman speech on necessity of catechizing	Prophetess Anna Walker makes request
		Foreign & some Dutch advice on manner of catechizing	Remonstrant petition to States General presented re Grevinchoven & Goulart
			State delegate meeting
29 Th	16	Sermon on Eccl. 7:16 by Hall	Comet appears (till mid-January)
			State delegate meeting

Overview of Synod of Dordt Sessions 441

Day	Session	Deliberations	Related Events
30 F	17	Utrecht Remonstrant & other Dutch advice on catechizing	State delegate meeting
		Draft of decision re catechizing in church, school & home read	
		After some discussion, the decision was approved	
		Committee appointed to prepare two small catechisms	
		Gravamen by North Holland presented re baptism of slave children	
December 1618			
1 Sa	18	Discuss baptism of slave children - Advice of five delegations given	Duchess of Tremullio visits synod Van Hel funeral
		Begin to discuss training of theology students - Zeeland & South Holland advice read	Other delegates copy Zeeland & South Holland advice
2 Su			Remonstrants meet at Rotterdam
3 M	19	Advice of other delegations on baptizing slave children	State delegate meeting - Approve Ames as *privatus auditor*
		Advice given on training of theology students - Bogerman proposes five issues - Palatine delegates promise information on Heidelberg *Collegium Sapientiae*	
4 T	20	Discussion & decisions on theological training	
		Utrecht Remonstrants protest re decision on catechizing	
5 W	21	Homerus arrives (replaces Lolingius)	
		Brief discussion on theological training; matter tabled	
		Decision on baptism of slave children	
		Acta read	
		Bogerman wants to summon Remonstrants	
		Advice of several delegations on printing abuses	Cited Remonstrants arrive at Dordrecht
6 Th	22	Remonstrants request more time to appear	State delegate meeting
		More advice of delegations on printing abuses	Cited Remonstrants visit foreign delegates
		Remonstrants enter synod	- Give response to Walcheren letter
		Episcopius: Remonstrants ready for a "conference"	- Present paper to inform foreign delegates
		Debate re "conference," "cited," synod as "judge"	
		Remonstrants renew request re Grevinchoven & Goulart	
7 F	23	State delegates resolution re Grevinchoven & Goulart read & approved by synod	
		Discuss status of Utrecht Remonstrants	
		Episcopius oration	State delegate meeting

Appendix 1

Day	Session	Deliberations	Related Events
		Bogerman demands copy of oration	Episcopius questioned by state delegates re oration
		Synodical oath taken; not given to Utrecht Remonstrants	
8 Sa	24	Discuss status of Utrecht Remonstrants	Summary of Remonstrant views by five professors submitted to Bogerman
		Read request of South Holland synod that Rijckwaert return	
9 Su			Sermons (e.g., Diodati) against Remonstrants
10 M	25	Utrecht Remonstrant ministers join cited Remonstrants; elder sent home	State delegate meeting
		Bogerman accuses Episcopius of lie re copy of oration	
		Bogerman asks Remonstrants to present views of Five Articles	
		Remonstrant paper read re conditions for a lawful synod	
		Debate re jurisdiction of synod: Lawful? Enemies as judge?	
10 M	26	Discuss whether synod is schismatic	
		Discuss Remonstrant paper re conditions for synod; conditions rejected	
		Remonstrants reprimanded: Cited & should comply	
		State delegate resolution re Remonstrant conditions: Submit & proceed to matter at hand	
		Debate jurisdiction of synod	
11 T	27	Remonstrants asked to present views on Five Articles, Belgic Confession & Heidelberg Catechism	Remonstrant response to state delegates' resolution
		Remonstrant Protest against synod's reprimand & synod as lawful judge - Now ready to present views	
		Debate re 2 accusations of Remonstrants against Bogerman	
11 T	28	Discuss second Remonstrant accusation against Bogerman	
		Request delegations' advice on Remonstrant Protest	
12 W	29	Synod censure of Remonstrant accusations read; includes Episcopius lie	
		Foreign delegates, advice on Remonstrant Protest - Advice of Dutch delegations not read	
		State delegates, resolution re Remonstrant Protest	
12 W	30	Remonstrants asked to submit views on Five Articles	
		Episcopius paper read; against charge of lie	
		Remonstrants request copies of censures against them	
		Heated debate	

Overview of Synod of Dordt Sessions

Day	Session	Deliberations	Related Events
		Remonstrants answer state delegates & synod's censure	
		- Ready to *orally present* views on Five Articles & *defend* as far as necessary	
		Remonstrants asked to present on Art. I in *writing* the next day, without refuting	
		Debate re meaning of citation letters: Present orally or in writing?	
		Decide: May refute *after* Remonstrants defend own views	
		Remonstrants agree to present view on Art. I	
13 Th	31	Acta read	
		Remonstrant *Sententia* on Art. I read	
		Debate & decision to examine Remonstrants individually	
		Objection to negative character of *Sententia*	
		Decide: Remonstrant views to be presented only positively	PM: Each delegation to copy *Sententia*
14 F	32	Decide: To submit *Sententia* on all Five Articles before discussion	
		Bogerman: Treat election, not reprobation; positive, not negative	
		Reprobation to be treated later	
15 Sa	33	Scultetus speech exhorting to peace, from Ps. 122	
17 M	34	Nassau delegates Bisterfeld & Alsted arrive	Balcanqual presented to States General
		Remonstrants submit *Sententiae* on Arts. II–V, with reasons for negative & reprobation	
		Debate whether Contra-Remonstrants treated reprobation at Hague Conference	
		Bogerman requires Remonstrant Observations on Catechism & Confession	
		Remonstrants refuse before Five Articles treated	
		Bogerman asks individually whether Remonstrants had Observations on Catechism & Confession	
		Remonstrants to present Observations in four days	Delegations to copy *Sententiae*
18 T			Lydius sermon against Remonstrants
	35	Acta read	Arrival of Contra-Remonstrants from Kampen
		Kampen case re four Remonstrant ministers	State delegate meeting
19 W	36	Kampen case; decide to summon the Remonstrant ministers	State delegate meeting

Appendix 1

Day Session	Deliberations	Related Events
		Remonstrant & Contra-Remonstrant views of Delft articles dictated
20 Th 37	Balcanqual arrives; gives short speech	Remonstrants ask state delegates for allowances
	Bogerman asks for gravamina re doctrine besides Five Articles	
	Bogerman asks delegations for response to Remonstrant *Sententiae* on Five Articles	
	Discussion of interpretation of citation letters - Decide: Declare views as far as synod thinks necessary	
	Bogerman proposes historical account of rise of controversy	
21 F 38	Remonstrant Observations on Belgic Confession submitted; preface read	
	Hommius refutes preface	
	Resolution of state delegates re Observations	
	Bogerman reprimands Remonstrants for *joint* observations & none on Catechism	
	Bogerman individually asks whether Remonstrants agree with Observations	
22 Sa		Remonstrant Observations copied
		States General placard against printing proceedings of synod
22–26	Christmas adjournment	
27 Th 39	Remonstrant Observations on Heidelberg Catechism submitted	State delegate meeting
	Palatine delegate Scultetus wants copy	
	Debate re liberty of refuting	
	Pijnacker: Treat reprobation first of all	
	Poppius: Remonstrants do not want reprobation first	Remonstrants resolve to defend as *they* see fit
	Decide: Treat election first	
	Gomarus: Not *absolute* reprobation but predestination to sin & death	
	Decision: Treat both election & reprobation; synod to decide manner & order	
	State delegate resolution: Remonstrants must obey	
28 F 40	Remonstrant reply to synod's Decision submitted, re liberty to treat reprobation	State delegate meeting; decide to send delegation to States General
	Remonstrant books brought in	
	State delegate resolution: Contrary papers not to be read & Remonstrants must answer questions	

Overview of Synod of Dordt Sessions

Day	Session	Deliberations	Related Events
28 F	41	Bogerman begins questioning: Q 1: Do Remonstrants agree with Five Articles of Hague Conference, specifically Art. I? Remonstrants reply individually; persist in their reply to synod's Decision Debate about questioning individually (closed) Read Remonstrant reply to synod Decision Discussion re stalemate with Remonstrants Concession to Remonstrants: Explanation of synod's Decision re Remonstrant freedom	
29 Sa	42	Explanation approved & read: Remonstrants allowed to refute Dutch & freedom in answering Debate re Pijnacker's comment: Reprobation first Advice of foreign delegates on equity of synod's Decision - Most advise: Election first; treat reprobation with caution Remonstrants: Never meant reprobation first nor unlimited freedom	
29 Sa	43	Read Remonstrant reply to Explanation re liberty - Will treat election in writing, then reprobation - Will defend & refute, then answer questions Bogerman question: Who are the "orthodox"? Advice of foreign & Dutch delegates on Remonstrant conduct: - Most advise: Judge from their books; dismiss Remonstrants Remonstrants asked whether they will obey	State delegate delegation to The Hague: - To report on Remonstrant conduct
31 M	44	Polyander speech on Isa. 52:7	State delegation reports to States General
January 1619			
1 T			States General resolution re Remonstrants - Judge Remonstrants from writings if they do not obey
2 W	45	Bogerman: Look for other points besides Five Articles, esp. in Episcopius's Disputations	Committee: Copies Remonstrant Observations on Belgic Confession & Heidelberg Catechism

Day	Session	Deliberations	Related Events
		North Holland to prepare account of the controversy	Uytenbogaert letter to cited Remonstrants:
		Acts of South Holland Synod of Delft read re reform of universities	- Press issue of reprobation
		Letter from Bommel asking Leo to return; rejected	
3 Th	46	Remonstrants Frederici & Leo absent	State delegate meeting
		State delegate delegation returns; - Read 1 Jan. Resolution of States General: - Approve synod's decisions, Remonstrants to submit, otherwise judge from writings	Remonstrant paper submitted to state delegates: Issue of conscience
			Remonstrant letter to States General: They are innocent of disobedience
		Bogerman resumes questioning:	
		Q 1: Do Remonstrants accept Five Articles of the 1611 Hague Conference?	
		Remonstrant replies: Refer to their 29 Dec. statement	
		Q 2: Is the entire decree of predestination that God would save those who persevere in faith?	
		Q 3: Does God elect believers in general, or specific individuals who believe?	
		Remonstrant paper re issue of conscience read	
		Q 4: If God elects not without respect to previous obedience, what is meant by obedience?	
		Debate re extent of freedom to refute & treat reprobation - Bogerman: Not unlimited - State delegates: As far as synod thinks necessary	Private evening meeting re procedure
4 F	47	Leo summoned alone	Duplessis-Mornay advice for synod
		Leo submits paper	
		Procedure suggested by private meeting adopted	
		Bogerman proposes to extract questions from Remonstrant books	
5 Sa	48	Bogerman dictates Questions re Art. I of Remonstrance	
		Foreign clerks to copy *Status Quaestionis* by Gelderland synod	
7 M	49	Appeals of Welsingius & Rodingenus of Hoorn - Deferred to later gravamina matters	
		Bogerman continues dictating Questions re Art. I from Remonstrant writings	
7 M	50	Acta read (since 18 Dec.)	Remonstrant letter to Uytenbogaert
		Ask delegates for historical account of controversy in their provinces	
8 T	51	Bogerman dictates his *Theses* on Art. I from Remonstrant writings	
		Bogerman asks for advice on the *Theses* and on procedure	

Overview of Synod of Dordt Sessions

Day	Session	Deliberations	Related Events
9 W			Delegations study *Theses*
			English consult with Bogerman re procedure
10 Th	52	(closed): Read advice of delegations on Bogerman *Theses*	
		Bogerman four-point proposal: Whether *Theses* are true	
		Decide: *Theses* are faithful to Remonstrants	
		Advice of delegates re procedure: Most approve Bogerman	
		Some advise: Draw up fewer necessary theses	
		English, South Holland & Hommius submit examples of such theses	
10 Th	53	(closed): More advice on procedure; disagree re procedure	
		Decide: Continue *Theses* on Arts. II–V before examining Art. I	
		Bogerman dictates amendments to *Theses*; result is *Articuli* on Art. I	
		Bogerman dictates some new Questions for Remonstrants	
11 F	54	Bogerman speech to Remonstrants: Why he posed Questions	State delegate meeting
		Bogerman resumes Questions	Bogerman confers with state delegates
		Remonstrant paper in response	
		Debate re extent of freedom & whether to answer Questions before or after explanations	
		Episcopius: Remonstrants ready to answer Questions in writing	
		Bogerman refuses to provide list of Questions	
		Bogerman proposes to judge from Remonstrant books; asks advice of delegates	State delegate meeting
11 F	55	Advice of delegates:	Swiss celebrate Zurich Reformation
		- Foreign delegates think Remonstrants yielded	
		- Dutch delegates think Remonstrants did not yield; judge from their writings	
		Decide: No more examination; judge from writings	
		Resolution of state delegates: Examine from writings & get further explanations	
		Remonstrants given till Monday to submit	
12 Sa	56	Kampen case: Read two letters from Kampen magistrates	State delegate meeting
		Kampen ministers summoned	State delegate meeting

Appendix 1

Day	Session	Deliberations	Related Events
		Utrecht Remonstrants reply to Utrecht Contra-Remonstrant *Status Quaestionis*	Remonstrants summoned before state delegates: Not a matter of conscience
		Status Quaestionis dictated	Remonstrant paper: Ready to answer Questions in writing, with *Declaratio*
			State delegate proposal: Answer orally or in writing; Remonstrants refused
14 M	57	State delegates report of meeting with Remonstrants	
		State delegate proposal read	
		Foreign delegates turn against Remonstrants	
		Scultetus and others: Dismiss them	
		Remonstrant *Declaratio* on Art. I submitted; explains & refutes; preface read	
		Bogerman angry speech: Expels Remonstrants	
14 M	58	(closed) Decide to make copies of *Declaratio* on Art. I	
		Discussion re future procedure; some delegations give advice	
15 T	59	(closed) Acta read	Remonstrant table removed
		Crocius criticizes Bogerman speech	State delegate meeting
15 T	60	(closed) More advice given on method of proceeding on Five Articles	
16 W	61	(closed) Bogerman *Articuli* on Art. II dictated	
		Approve new procedure: Morning: Delegations only; Afternoon: Public speeches	
		Decide: Dutch to speak before foreign delegates Sessions to remain open for speeches	
17 Th	62	Goad arrives in place of Hall	State delegate meeting
		Hall's farewell address read	Approve delegation to States General to report
		Lubbertus speech on election	
		Kampen case, referred to committee	
18 F	63	Gomarus speech on election	State delegate meeting
		Bishop Carleton, Tossanus & others speak on election	Bisterfeld dies
			Hall leaves Dordrecht
			Delegation to States General reports
			States General resolution re Remonstrants

Overview of Synod of Dordt Sessions 449

Day	Session	Deliberations	Related Events
			Remonstrant petition to send delegation to States General
21 M	64	States General resolution read re Remonstrant dismissal	State delegate meeting
		Thysius speech on election	Remonstrants before state delegates - States General resolution read to them - Confirm dismissal; petition refused
			Committee meeting re Kampen case
			Remonstrant protest against dismissal
			Private consultations on Du Moulin union plan
22 T	65	(closed) Discussion re Christ as fundamentum & Eph. 1:4 - Gomarus–Martinius dispute: Challenge to duel	State delegate meeting Bisterfeld funeral
23 W			Carleton's "little synod": Foreign theologians meet with Martinius; agrees to moderation
			State delegate meeting
			Remonstrants before state delegates: Allowed to add to their *Declaratio* in fourteen days
24 Th	66	Polyander speech on election texts Walaeus speech on election texts	
25 F	67	Davenant speech on election (closed) Ward speech on election Goclenius speech on election; uses logic Martinius speaks on Christ as fundamentum	
26 Sa			Remonstrant paper in their defense to States General
			Remonstrant paper to Prince Maurice
28 M	68	Scultetus speech on certainty of election	Most delegations submit *iudicia* on Art. I
29 T	69	Alting speech on reprobation	State delegate meeting

Day	Session	Deliberations	Related Events
		Decide: No judgment on Art. I until all Five Articles treated	
30 W	70	(closed) Discuss method of proceeding	
		Decide: Continue with same method	
31 Th	71	(closed) Discussion of *Articuli* on Art. II	
		Bogerman dictates contracted Theses on Art. II	

February 1619

Day	Session	Deliberations	Related Events
1 F	72	Balcanqual speech on Art. II	
		Cruciger speech on Art. II	
4 M	73	(closed) Kampen case	State delegate meeting
		Three treatises proposed: Didactic, elenctic & historical writings	
		- Committees chosen for each	
		- Gomarus opposed to writing refutation	
		Propose to answer Remonstrants on Catechism	
		Propose to answer Remonstrants on Confession	
		Propose abstract of acta (*Acta Contracta*)	
5 T	74	(closed) Advice given on *Articuli* on Art. II	Balcanqual advice: Treat other Articles & consult Archbishop
		- Debate: Martinius, Ward & Davenant vs. rest of synod	
6 W	75	(open) Stein speech on Art. IV	Meeting at Carleton lodging: Draw up theses on Art. II
		(closed) Discuss Art. II	
7 Th	76	(closed) More advice on Art. II	Remonstrant *Defensio* on Art. I submitted to state delegates
		Bogerman informs synod of Remonstrant *Defensio*	
		Overijssel delegate against charity of British to Remonstrants	Remonstrant *Declaratio* on Art. II submitted to state delegates
			State delegate meeting
			Remonstrant debate with state delegates
8 F	77	(closed) Bogerman dictates *Articuli* on Art. III/IV	Bogerman asks English to refute some Remonstrant Theses on Art. II
			Martinius meets with Poppius to share views
11 M	78	Beck speech on Art. IV	State delegate meeting
		(closed) Debate on what to do with *Defensio* on Art. I	
		Decide: Read positive parts & give rest to a committee; committee chosen	
		Kampen case; referred to committee	State delegate meeting

Overview of Synod of Dordt Sessions 451

Day	Session	Deliberations	Related Events
12 T	79	Discuss Art. III/IV	Committee discusses Kampen case
		Foreign advice on *Articuli* on Art. III/IV	State delegate meeting
13 W	80	More advice on Art. III/IV	
		Lubbertus critiques Martinius on God as *causa physica* of conversion	
14 Th			State delegate meeting
			Remonstrant *Explicatio* on Arts. III–V submitted
15 F	81	Aysma replaces deceased Idzerda from Friesland	Spectators admitted till prayer in closed sessions
		Alsted speech on Art. III/IV	
		Kampen case	State delegate meeting
16 Sa			State delegate meeting
			Remonstrants before state delegates
			- Given till 25 Feb. to submit *Defensio* on Arts. II–V
18 M	82	Read from *Defensio* on Art. I & *Declaratio* on Art. II	
18 M	83	Kampen case; suspend Voscuyl & Schotlerus	State delegate meeting
		- Gomarus against Martinius (re Kampen case)	
19 T	84	Read *Explicatio* on Art. III/IV	
19 T	85	Kampen case	
		Further advice on Art. III/IV	
		- *Causa physica* debate	
		- Lubbertus against Martinius; appeals to Goclenius	
		- Scultetus defends Pareus; against Crocius	
		Gomarus advice on *Articuli* on Art. III/IV	
		- Against Martinius & Crocius	
		- Carleton critiques Bogerman	
		- Gomarus against Carleton	
		Thysius advice on *Articuli* on Art. III/IV; soft on Martinius	
		- Scolded by Gomarus & Lubbertus	
20 W	86	Read *Declaratio* on Art. V	Martinius absent for several sessions
20 W	87	Mayer speech on Art. V	
		- Ends with high praise of "holy synod"	
		Discuss Art. III/IV	
21 Th	88	Read more of *Defensio* on Art. I	
22 F	89	Read *Defensio* on Art. I on reprobation	State delegate meeting
22 F	90	Polyander speech on Art. V	

Day	Session	Deliberations	Related Events
		Gomarus, Lubbertus, Thysius, Walaeus speeches on Art. V	
23 Sa	(91)	Read more of *Defensio* on Art. I on reprobation	State delegate meeting
		Bremen delegates threaten to go home	English try to reconcile Scultetus & Bremen
			Dudley Carleton letter to Bogerman to moderate situation
25 M	91	Advice of remaining Dutch delegations on Art. III/IV	Remonstrant *Defensio* on Art. II submitted to state delegates; will accept no more writings
		Bogerman dictates *Articuli* on Art. V	
		Kampen case	
26 T	92	Read from *Defensio* on Art. II	
27 W	93	Read more of *Defensio* on Art. II	State delegate meeting
			Remonstrants meet with state delegates — Debate; allowed eight to ten days to finish *Defensio*
			Frederici & Niellius: Receive news of being deposed
27 W	94	(open) Bogerman speech: Account of public speeches so far	Remonstrant *Nulliteiten* published
		Tronchin speech on Art. V	
		Bogerman: End of public treatment of Five Articles	
28 Th	95	Finished reading *Defensio* on Art. II	
28 Th	96	Read advice on *Articuli* on Art. V (English to Swiss)	
March 1619			
1 F	97	Read more advice on *Articuli* on Art. V (up to Gelderland)	Sapma leaves Dordrecht for Hoorn
4 M	98	Kampen case	
		Letter and statement by Pareus on Five Articles submitted	
		Read final Dutch advice on Art. V	
		Read Pareus letter (31 Dec.)	
5 T	99	(open) Read Pareus statement on Arts. I & II	Stapfer funeral
5 T	100	(open) Martinius speech on Person of Christ (against Vorstius)	Rotterdam meeting of Remonstrants — Urge separate congregations — Acts & letter sent to cited Remonstrants
6 W	101	(open) Read Pareus statement on Arts. III–V	

Overview of Synod of Dordt Sessions 453

Day	Session	Deliberations	Related Events
		(closed) Begin reading British *iudicium* on Art. I	
		Davenant objection to closed session	
		Bogerman opposes public reading of *iudicia*	Noon: Bogerman tries to convince foreign delegates
6 W	102	State delegates: Read *iudicia* in closed session	State delegate meeting
		Decide: Closed sessions for reading *iudicia*	
		(closed) Read English & Palatine *iudicia* on Art. I	
7 Th	103	(closed) Read Hesse, Swiss & Nassau *iudicia* on Art. I	
7 Th	104	(closed) Read Geneva, Bremen & Emden *iudicia* on Art. I	
8 F	105	(closed) Read rest of Emden *iudicium* on Art. I	
		Read part of three Dutch professors' *iudicium* on Art. I — Critique of Gomarus's supralapsarianism	
8 F	106	(open) Diodati speech on Art. V (delay due to illness)	Cited Remonstrant reply to Rotterdam Remonstrants
			Remonstrants request more time for *Defensio*
11 M	107	(closed) Fabricius arrives in place of Bisterfeld	State delegate meeting
		Read rest of *iudicia* of three Dutch professors, Lubbertus & Gomarus on Art. I	
11 M	108	(closed) Kampen case; suspension of Voscuyl & Schotlerus confirmed	
		Carleton challenges Gomarus: Whether *object* of predestination determined in England	
		Goad reads art. 17 of Thirty-nine Articles	
		Gomarus reprimanded by Bogerman	
		Bogerman: Treat object of predestination later	
		Read *iudicia* of Gelderland, South Holland, North Holland & Zeeland on Art. I	
12 T	109	(closed) Read *iudicia* of Utrecht, Friesland, Overijssel & Groningen on Art. I	
12 T	110	(closed) Read Drenthe & Walloon *iudicia* on Art. I	
		Read British, Palatine, Hesse & Swiss *iudicia* on Art. II	
		Palatine delegates against Ward on Art. II	
13 W	111	(closed) Read *iudicia* of Nassau, Geneva, three Bremen delegates & Emden on Art. II	
13 W	112	(open) Isselburg speech on Christ's satisfaction (against Socinus, Vorstius)	Sapma returns to Dordrecht; questioned by state delegates

454 Appendix 1

Day	Session	Deliberations	Related Events
14 Th	113	(closed) Read *iudicia* of four Dutch professors, Lubbertus, Gelderland, South Holland & North Holland on Art. II	
14 Th	114	(closed) Read *iudicia* of Zeeland, Utrecht, Friesland, Overijssel & Groningen on Art. II	State delegate meeting
15 F	115	(closed) Read *iudicia* of Drenthe & Walloons on Art. II Read English & Palatine *iudicia* on Art. III/IV	State delegate meeting
15 F	116	(closed) Read *iudicia* of Hesse, Swiss, Nassau, Geneva, Bremen & Emden on Art. III/IV	
16 Sa	117	(closed) Read more of Emden *iudicium* on Art. III/IV Read *iudicia* of four Dutch professors, Lubbertus & Gelderland on Art. III/IV	
18 M	118	(closed) Letter of Marquis of Brandenburg read: Why no delegates Read *iudicia* of South Holland, North Holland, Zeeland & Utrecht on Art. III/IV	State delegate meeting
18 M	119	(closed) Read *iudicia* of Friesland, Overijssel, Groningen, Drenthe & Walloons on Art. III/IV	
19 T	120	(closed) Read *iudicia* of English & Palatinate on Art. V	State delegate meeting Some Remonstrants meet with state delegates Remonstrant *Defensio* on Arts. IV–V submitted to state delegates - Appended Remonstrant address to state delegates, re relationship to Melanchthon, etc. Debate: *Defensio* not for synod
19 T	121	(closed) Read *iudicia* of Hesse, Swiss, Nassau, Geneva & Bremen on Art. V	
20 W	122	(closed) Read *iudicia* of Emden on Art. V Read *iudicia* of four Dutch professors, Lubbertus, Gelderland & South Holland on Art. V	
20 W	123	(open) Crocius speech on justification (against Socinians, Bertius)	
21 Th	124	(closed) Read *iudicia* of North Holland, Zeeland, Utrecht & Friesland on Art. V	
21 Th	125	(closed) Read *iudicia* of Overijssel, Groningen, Drenthe & Walloons on Art. V Bogerman sees harmony of *iudicia*	State delegate meeting

Overview of Synod of Dordt Sessions

Day	Session	Deliberations	Related Events
		Bogerman draft of Canons ready	
22 F	126	Bogerman: Canons to be ecclesiastical, not scholastic	
		Bogerman dictates his draft of Canons on Art. I	
22 F	127	Bogerman dictates his draft of Canons on Art. II	
		Carleton on form of Canons: Popular, not scholastic	
		English & South Holland object to one man drafting Canons; want a drafting committee	
23 Sa			State delegate meeting
			Private meetings over weekend
25 M	128	State delegates propose committee to assist Bogerman & assessors	State delegate meeting
		Especially Lubbertus & Scultetus support Bogerman	
		Debate on who should draft Canons	
		States General wants Canons by Easter	
		Decide: Have drafting committee; members appointed	
		Some delegations submit amendments to Bogerman draft	
		Decide: No more sessions till Canons drafted	
26 T			Drafting committee works three weeks on Canons
			Remonstrant paper to States General: - Ask to return home; rejected
			Remonstrant letter to Prince Maurice
27 W			State delegate meeting
28 Th			First committee draft dictated on Art. I
			State delegate meeting
29 F			First committee draft dictated on Art. II
			State delegate meeting
31 Easter Sunday			Poppius & Dwinglo preach in private homes
April 1619			
3 W			First committee draft dictated on Art. III/IV
5 F			State delegate meeting
			First committee draft dictated on Art. V

Appendix 1

Day	Session	Deliberations	Related Events
6 Sa			State delegate meeting
			Remonstrants called before state delegates re book *Vale* just published
			Remonstrants send circular letters to Remonstrant churches
8 M			Second committee draft changes dictated on Art. I & Art. II
10 W			Second committee draft changes dictated on Art. III/IV
11 Th			Second committee draft changes dictated on Art. V
15 M			Third committee draft changes dictated on Arts. I–V
			Initial subscription of Arts. I–V
16 T	129	Bogerman comments on unity on fundamentals	
		Canons Art. I read & approved	
		Canons Art. II (after some words changed) read & approved, except rejections 2 & 6	
		British & Hesse objections; ask time to reconsider	
17 W			Public fast
18 Th	130	Debate re rejection 6 of Art. II - British against rest of synod	
18 Th	131	Canons Arts. III–V read & approved	
		British want list of hard sayings rejected	
		Others do not want hard sayings rejected	
		Discussion re changes in style of Canons	
		Bogerman: Prepare to consider Preface & Conclusion	
19 F			Drafting committee prepares first draft of Conclusion
20 Sa	132	First draft of Conclusion debated	
		British want hard sayings rejected	
		Hesse & Bremen papers on hard sayings	Officers prepare second draft of Conclusion
20 Sa	133	Bogerman reasons against rejecting hard sayings	
		Second draft of Conclusion dictated & debated	

Overview of Synod of Dordt Sessions

Day	Session	Deliberations	Related Events
		British reply to Bogerman reasons	
		British, Bremen & Hesse disapprove second draft of Conclusion	Bogerman revises second draft of Conclusion
21 Su			State delegate meeting
22 M	134	State delegates approve final draft of Conclusion	Drafting committee revises Art. II, rejs. 2 & 6
		British approve final draft with added phrase	State delegate meeting
		Synod approves Conclusion	
23 T	135	Art. I subscribed by all (three copies); - Each delegation to make copy	
		Discuss changes to Art. II; rework rej. 2, omit rej. 6	
23 T	136	Final changes to Art. II approved	State delegate meeting
		Arts. II–V subscribed by all	
		Conclusion subscribed	
24 W	137	Read draft of Sentence of Remonstrants	Death of Elder Canterus
		Foreign delegates except Geneva & Emden: It is a Dutch matter	Swiss letter re toleration
		Debate among Dutch: Whether to tolerate those who refuse to sign Canons	
24 W	138	Read revised Sentence	
		Debate about "Reformed"	
		Sentence approved, but British & Hesse abstain; Bremen does not approve	
		Subscribed only by secretaries	
		Geysteranus brothers case	
25 Th	139	Maccovius case: Maccovius petition for a hearing	
		First draft of Canons' Preface read; rejected as too long	Drafting committee draws up second draft of Preface
25 Th	140	Second draft of Preface read	
		British object to reference to pope as the Antichrist	
26 F	141	Maccovius case: Maccovius's second request	Delegation of state delegates sent to States General to report and get instructions; - Take copy of Canons
		More copies of Canons signed by all	
		Maccovius case: List of fifty errors read	
26 F	142	Maccovius case: Maccovius's two replies read - Letter from Heidelberg University read - Discuss whether to read Maccovius's larger explanation - Debate: Lubbertus against Hommius	

Appendix 1

Day	Session	Deliberations	Related Events
27 Sa	143	Report that Ames would defend Maccovius theses Maccovius case: Referred to committee Du Moulin *Confessio* on Five Articles read	States General resolutions re state delegates' requests
29 M	144	Kampen case Read letter from the Lord of Battenberg Revised Preface of Canons approved Du Moulin *Confessio* finished Report from delegation to the States General - Approve of Canons and synod's actions Discuss review of Belgic Confession (except arts. 30–32)	State delegate meeting
30 T	145	British approve Belgic Confession except equality of ministers (arts. 30–32) - Bishop Carleton critique of arts. 30–32 Maccovius case: First committee judgment read & discussed	Funeral of Elder Canterus Carleton meets some members on this issue
30 T	146	(closed) Other advice & approval of doctrinal content of Belgic Confession	
May 1619			
1 W	147	(closed) Heidelberg Catechism examined: re doctrine, not phraseology	
1 W	148	(closed) Catechism doctrine approved by all - British: Liberty to interpret descent into hell Complaint re Sunday observance in Dordrecht	
2 Th	149	Vorstius case: Vorstius letter to synod (27 April) read List of Vorstius's errors drawn up by Dutch professors read	
3 F	150	Vorstius case: Advice of all delegations read	State delegate meeting
4 Sa	151	Vorstius case: First draft of Vorstius Sentence examined	
4 Sa	152	Vorstius case: Second draft of Vorstius Sentence approved Maccovius case: Final judgment approved - Frisian elder Donia complaint	

6 M	153	Procession to Grote Kerk
		Public Promulgation of Canons
		  - Bogerman prayer
		  - Canons publicly read by secretaries
		  - Each delegate doffs his hat when his name is read
		  - Remonstrant Sentence publicly read
		  - Approval of Confession & Catechism publicly announced
		  - Bogerman asks each delegation to make copy of Canons
			State delegate meeting
			Remonstrants summoned before state delegates
			  - Sentence read
			  - Debate: Remonstrants request copy

7 T			State delegate meeting

Overview of Synod of Dordt Sessions 459

Day	Session	Deliberations	Related Events
			Remonstrants again request copy of Sentence
8 W			State delegate meeting
9 Th	154	Foreign delegates dismissed - Thanked by Gregorii & Bogerman - Final speeches of foreign delegates	Ascension Day Last report of Sibelius Banquet for delegates
10 F			State delegate meeting
12 Su			Foreign delegates given gold medallions by state delegates Palatine & Hesse delegates give Bogerman documents defending Piscator re Art. 22 of Belgic Confession
13 M			Some foreign delegates witness beheading of Oldenbarnevelt

POST-ACTA SESSIONS (closed)

Day	Session	Deliberations	Related Events
13 M	155	Church Order of 1586 read: To be examined Decide: Collate text of Latin, French & Dutch editions of Belgic Confession - Committee appointed	State delegate meeting
13 M	156	Church Order of 1586 approved in substance Decide: Petition States General to approve Church Order so that it may have authority of public law Right of patronage discussed	
14 T	157	Approve nine articles on right of patronage; - Recommended to States General	
14 T	158	Six gravamina submitted & discussed	State delegate meeting
15 W	159	Decisions on gravamina: 1) Church visitors: CO, art. 44 2) Synodical deputies: CO, art. 49 3) Correspondence between provincial synods: CO, art. 48 4) Admission of laymen to ministry: CO, art. 8 5) Voting in classes: CO, art. 42 6) Form of subscription to be drawn up Six more gravamina submitted	State delegate meeting
15 W	160	Form for calling ministers discussed, but no agreement	
16 Th	161	Second draft of form for calling ministers approved: CO, arts. 4–5 Add article on correspondence with Christian magistrates: CO, art. 28	

Day	Session	Deliberations	Related Events
16 Th	162	Decisions on gravamina: 1) Holy days & hymns: CO, arts. 67, 69 　Forms for baptism: CO, arts. 58, 59 2) Baptism by a priest or Anabaptist 3) Marriage of unbaptized 4) Correspondence with foreign churches 5) Request States General for uniform marriage ordinance 6) Discipline to be strictly followed according to Church Order Seven more gravamina submitted Committee appointed for form of subscription & form for examining adults to be baptized	
17 F	163	Decisions on gravamina: 1) Baptism of the sick outside the church 2) Admitting priests, newcomers to ministry: CO, art. 9 3) Approve articles for reformation of universities & schools 4) Marriage with non-Reformed 5) Sunday observance: Ask States General to restrain abuses 　- Debate with Zeeland re necessity of Sunday observance 6) Aid to persecuted churches	
17 F	164	Principles for Sunday observance approved for Zeeland situation Form of subscription for ministers approved Form of subscription for schoolteachers approved	
18 Sa	165	Review of Dutch translation of Canons Art. I	State delegate meeting
19 Su			Sibelius leaves due to illness
20 M	166	Review of Dutch translation of Canons Art. I	
21 T	167	Review of Dutch translation of Canons Art. II	
21 T	168	Review of Dutch translation of Canons Arts. III–V Deputies appointed to assist Utrecht provincial synod	
22 W	169	Kampen case: Voscuyl & Schotlerus deposed	State delegate meeting
22 W	170	Dutch translation of Preface and Conclusion of Canons reviewed	
23 Th	171	Revised *text* of Dutch & French Belgic Confession read 　- Give reasons for changes	
23 Th	172	Continue to give reasons for changes Read Geneva remarks on Confession Read Palatine & Hesse admonitions Bogerman suggestion to change Art. 22 opposed	
24 F	173	Addition to Art. 22 approved Dutch & French text of Belgic Confession approved	

Overview of Synod of Dordt Sessions

Day	Session	Deliberations	Related Events
24 F	174	Acta read	
		Other gravamina deferred to next national synod	State delegate meeting
		Hoorn case (appeals of Rodingenus, Wallesius & Welsingius) referred to committee	
25 Sa	175	Hoorn case	State delegate meeting
		Final text of Church Order changes read & approved	States General deputies interrogate cited Remonstrants
		Final approval of Form of subscription for ministers	
		Form of subscription for theology professors approved	
		Form of subscription for schoolteachers approved	
		Decide: Sick-visitors to subscribe in same way as schoolteachers	
		Decide: Subscription by elders left to classes & provincial synods	
		Form for Adult Baptism approved	
		Issue of private baptisms in case of necessity left to consistories & classes	
27 M	176	Hoorn case	
27 M	177	Hoorn case: Decision on Welsingius read	State delegate meeting
		Two smaller catechisms submitted	
		- *ABC Boekje* & *Kort Begrip* approved for use instead	
		Synod deputies appointed to appear before States General	
		- Instructions: To confirm synodical decisions & deal with some requests	
		[Synod's request document (*Libellus Supplex*) to States General (actually written after synod)]	
		Decide: Committee to approve abridged Acta by Dammannus when done	
28 T	178	Committee for abridged Acta (*Acta Contracta*) appointed	State delegate meeting
		Classis Dordrecht to plan next national synod	
		Decide: Request States General to invite Dutch churches of Germany and England to next national synod	
		Liturgical forms to be edited by Acta committee	
		Recommendation of Erpenius book referred to provincial synods	
		Decide: Conclude synod with public thanksgiving	
28 T	179	Acta read	
		Act of approbation of Catechism & Confession approved	
		Church Order signed by officers of synod	

Day	Session	Deliberations	Related Events
29 W	180	Procession to Grote Kerk Lydius sermon & thanksgiving Magistrates of Dordrecht thanked Return to Kloveniersdoelen State delegates thank synod Bogerman thanks state delegates & all synod delegates	State delegate committee sent to report to States General
30 Th			Synod committee reports to States General State delegates report to States General
31 F			State delegate final meeting

Appendix 2

Editions of the Canons of Dordt (1619–2019)

Donald Sinnema and Erik de Boer[1]

Latin Editions

1619a: *Synodus* (synod print). *Iudicium Synodi Nationalis Reformatarum Ecclesiarum Belgicarum, habitae Dordrechti, Anno 1618 & 1619. Cui etiam interfuerunt plurimi insignes theologi Reformatarum Ecclesiarum Magnae Britanniae, Palatinatus Electoralis, Hassiae, Helvetiae, Correspondentiae Wedderavicae, Genevensis, Bremensis, & Emdanae, de Quinque Doctrinae Capitibus in Ecclesiis Belgicis controversis, promulgatum VI May MDCXIX. Cum privilegio* (Dordrecht: Ioannes Berewout & Franciscus Bosselaer, Socios Caninii, 1619), 4º, 128 pp.

1619b: *Iudicium Synodi Nationalis Reformatarum Ecclesiarum Belgicarum, habitae Dordrechti, Anno 1618 & 1619. Cui etiam interfuerunt plurimi insignes theologi Reformatarum Ecclesiarum Magnae Britanniae, Palatinatus Electoralis, Hassiae, Helvetiae, Correspondentiae Wedderavicae, Genevensis, Bremensis, & Emdanae, de Quinque Doctrinae Capitibus in Ecclesiis Belgicis controversis, promulgatum VI May MDCXIX* (n.p.: n.p., [1619?]), 4º, 36 pp.

1619c: *Iudicium Synodi Nationalis Reformatarum Ecclesiarum Belgicarum, habitae Dordrechti, Anno 1618 & 1619. Cui etiam interfuerunt plurimi insignes theologi Reformatarum Ecclesiarum Magnae Britanniae, Palatinatus Electoralis, Hassiae, Helvetiae, Correspondentiae Wedderavicae, Genevensis, Bremensis, & Emdanae, de Quinque Doctrinae Capitibus in Ecclesiis Belgicis controversis,*

---

1. For an initial list of editions up to 1900, with analysis, see Erik A. de Boer, "The Career of the Canones. An Inventory of the Canons of Dordt during the Seventeenth to Nineteenth Centuries," in *The Doctrine of Election in Reformed Perspective: Historical and Theological Investigations of the Synod of Dort 1618–1619*, ed. Frank van der Pol (Göttingen: Vandenhoeck and Ruprecht, 2018), 235–55. We also acknowledge the help of Abram De Graaf (for Portuguese), Moh Herng Chee (for Mandarin), Sam Ha (for Korean), Jori Sharda (for Japanese), Dmytro Binsarovskyi (for Russian), and Joel Beeke, John Van Eyk, and Theodore Van Raalte (for denominational editions).

promulgatum VI May MDCXIX (n.p.: n.p., [1619?]), 4°, 36 pp. [a slightly different imprint of 1619b]

1619d: *Iudicium Synodi Nationalis Reformatarum Ecclesiarum Belgicarum, habitae Dordrechti Anno 1618 & 1619. Cui plurimi insignes theologi Reformatarum Ecclesiarum Angliae, Germaniae, Galliae, interfuerunt, de Quinque Doctrinae Capitibus in Ecclesiis Belgicis controversis, promulgatum VI Maii MDCXIX. Subiunctae sunt Sententiae, Edicta, Iudicia ab Ordin. General. Bel. & Synodo Nation. lata in publicae pacis & Ecclesiarum Reformatarum Perturbatores. Omnia ad Exemplaria Dordrechti & Hagae-Comitis impressa fideliter recusa* (Heidelberg: n.p., 1619), 4°, 72 pp. (reprint of 1619a).

1619e: *Iudicium Synodi Nationalis Reformatarum Ecclesiarum Belgicarum, habitae Dordrechti Anno 1618 & 1619. Cui plurimi insignes theologi Reformatarum Ecclesiarum Angliae, Germaniae, Galliae, interfuerunt, de Quinque Doctrinae Capitibus in Ecclesiis Belgicis controversis, promulgatum VI Maii, MDCXIX. Subiunctae sunt Sententiae, Edicta, Iudicia ab Ordin. General. Belg. & Synodo Nation. lata in Remonstrantes, D. Conradum Vorstium, & contra conventicula Arminianorum. Omnia ad Exemplaria Dordrechti & Hagae-Comitis impressa, fideliter recusa* (Cassel: n.p., 1619), 4°, 65 pp.

1620a: *Acta Synodi Nationalis, in nomine Domini nostri Iesu Christi, autoritate illustr. et praepotentum DD. Ordinum Generalium Foederati Belgii Provinciarum, Dordrechti habitae anno MDCXVIII et MDCXIX* (Leiden: Isaac Elzevir, Societatis Dordrechtanae sumptibus, 1620), fol., 1:241–75.

1620b: *Acta Synodi Nationalis, in nomine Domini nostri Iesu Christi, autoritate illustr. et praepotentum DD. Ordinum Generalium Foederati Belgii Provinciarum, Dordrechti habitae anno MDCXVIII et MDCXIX* (Dordrecht: Isaac Canin & Socii, 1620), fol., 1:249–79.

1620c: *Acta Synodi Nationalis, in nomine Domini nostri Iesu Christi, autoritate illustr. et praepotentum DD. Ordinum Generalium Foederati Belgii Provinciarum, Dordrechti habitae anno MDCXVIII et MDCXIX* (Dordrecht: Isaac Canin & Socii, 1620), 4°, 1:279–322.

1620d: *Acta Synodi Nationalis, in nomine Domini nostri Iesu Christi, autoritate illustr. et praepotentum DD. Ordinum Generalium Foederati Belgii Provinciarum, Dordrechti habitae anno MDCXVIII et MDCXIX* (Hanover: Egenolphus Emmelius, 1620), 4°, 1:340–81.

1620e: *Iudicium Synodi Nationalis Reformatarum Ecclesiarum Belgicarum habitae Dordrechti Anno 1618 & 1619…de Quinque Doctrinae Capitibus in Ecclesiis Belgicis controuersis. Cui novissime additus est Canon Synodi Nationalis*

Gallicarum Ecclesiarum, Alesti in Cebennatibus congregatae 7 Id. Octobris 1620, cum formula iuramenti ibidem praestiti super approbatione Canonum Synodi Dordracenae (Nemausus [Nîmes]: Jean Vaguenar, 1620), 4°, 70 pp.

1622: Daniel Tilenus, ed., *Canones Synodi Dordracenae. Cum notis & animadversionibus Dan. Tileni* (Paris: Nicolaus Buon, 1622).

1643: *Iudicium Synodi Nationalis, Reformatarum ecclesiarum Belgicarum, habitae Dordrechti anno 1618 & 1619, de Quinque Doctrinae Capitibus in ecclesis Belgicis controversis* (Groningen: Johannes Sas, 1643), 4°, 71 pp.

[1645?]: *Iudicium Synodi Nationalis Reformatarum Ecclesiarum Belgicarum, habitae Dordrechti anno 1618 & 1619. Cui plurimi insignes theologi Reformatarumn Ecclesiarum interfuerunt, de Quinque Doctrinae Capitibus in Ecclesiis Belgicis controversis. Ex actis eius Synodi* (n.p.: n.p., n.d.).

1654: *Corpus et Syntagma Confessionum Fidei*, 2nd ed. (Geneva: Petrus Chouët, 1654), 21–50.

1772: Gerardus Kuypers, ed., *Canones Synodi Dordrechtanae in usum juventutis academicae* (Groningen: Hajo Spandaw, 1772), 8°, 36 pp.

1804: John Randolph, ed., *Sylloge Confessionum sub tempus Reformandae Ecclesiae editarum* (Oxford: Clarendon, 1804), 363–417.
Reprint: Oxford: Clarendon, 1827.

1827: Johann Augusti, ed., *Corpus Librorum Symbolicorum, qui in Ecclesia Reformatorum Auctoritatem publicam obtinuerunt* (Elberfeld: Henricus Bueschlerus, 1827), 198–240.
Reprint: Leipzig: Friedlein & Hirsch, 1846.

1840: Hermann Niemeyer, ed., *Collectio Confessionum in Ecclesiis Reformatis publicatarum* (Leipzig: Iulius Klinkhardt, 1840), 690–724.

1846: Hendrik Egbert Vinke, ed., *Libri Symbolici Ecclesiae Reformatae Netherlandicae* (Utrecht: J. G. van Terveen, 1846), 398–457.

1877: Philip Schaff, ed., *The Creeds of Christendom* (New York: Harper and Brothers, 1877), 3:550–78.
Reprints: London: Hodder and Stoughton, 1877; New York: Harper and Brothers, 1878, 1882, 1919, [1952], 1957; Grand Rapids: Baker, 1966, 1977, 1983, 1985; Whitefish, Mont.: Kessinger Publishing, [2007]; n.p.: Forgotten Books, 2015, 2017.

1903: E. F. Karl Müller, ed., *Die Bekenntnisschriften der Reformierten Kirche* (Leipzig: A. Deichert, 1903), 843–61 [omits Conclusion].

Reprints: Zürich: Theologische Buchhandlung, 1987; Waltrop: Spenner, 1999; n.p.: Fb&c Limited, 2018.

1940: J. N. Bakhuizen van den Brink, ed., *De Nederlandsche Belijdenisgeschriften vergelijkende teksten samengesteld* (Amsterdam: Uitgeversmaatschappij Holland, 1940), 218–275.

Reprint: Amsterdam: Ton Bolland, 1976.

Dutch Editions

1619a: *Synodus* (synod print). *Oordeel des Synodi Nationalis der Gereformeerde Kercken van de Vereenichde Nederlanden, ghehouden binnen Dordrecht, inden Iare 1618 ende 1619, welcke geassisteert is ghweest met vele treflicke Theologen, uyt de Ghereformeerde Kercken van Groot Britagnien, de Cheur-Vorstelijcke Paltz, Hessen, Switserlant, de Wedderavische Correspondentie, Geneven, Bremen, ende Embden, over de bekende Vijf Hooft-stucken der Leere, daer van inde Gereformeerde Kercken deser Vereenichde Nederlanden verschil is gevallen, uytghespoken op den 6 May 1619. Uyt het Latijn ghetrouwelijck in't Nederduytsch overgheset. Met Privilegie voor seven Iaren* (Dordrecht: Isaac Ianssen Canin, ende zijne Medestanders, 1619); (Colophon: Tot Dordrecht, Gedruckt by Pieter Verhagen, Isaac Jansz. Canin, Joris Waters, Jan Leendertsz. Berewout, Francoys Bosselaer, Niclaes Vincenten, Zacharias Jochemsz., Francoys Boels, 1619), 4°, 114 pp. (p. 114 misnumbered 58); [Knuttel, 2846].[2]

1619b: *Synodus* (synod print). *Oordeel des Synodi Nationalis der Gereformeerde Kercken van de Vereenichde Nederlanden, ghehouden binnen Dordrecht, inden Iare 1618 ende 1619…over de bekende Vijf Hooft-stucken der Leere, daer van inde Gereformeerde Kercken deser Vereenichde Nederlanden verschil is gevallen, uytghespoken op den 6 May 1619. Uyt het Latijn ghetrouwelijck in't Nederduytsch overgheset. Met Privilegie voor seven Iaren* (Dordrecht: Isaac Ianssen Canin, ende zijne Medestanders, 1619); (Colophon: Tot Dordrecht, Gedruckt by Pieter Verhagen, Isaac Jansz. Canin, Joris Waters, Jan Leendertsz. Berewout, Francoys Bosselaer, Niclaes Vincenten, Zacharias Jochemsz., Francoys Boels, 1619), 4°, 114 pp. (slightly different reprint of 1619a, with correction of p. 114, but p. 95 misnumbered 39); [Knuttel, 2847].

---

2. W. P. C. Knuttel, ed., *Catalogus van de Pamfletten-Verzameling berustende in de Koninklijke Bibliotheek*, vol. 1, *1486–1620* ('sGravenhage: Algemeene Landsdrukkerij, 1889).

1619c: *Synodus* (synod print). *Oordeel des Synodi Nationalis der Gereformeerde Kercken van de Vereenichde Nederlanden, ghehouden binnen Dordrecht, inden Iare 1618 ende 1619… over de bekende Vijf Hooft-stucken der Leere, daer van inde Gereformeerde Kercken deser Vereenichde Nederlanden verschil is gevallen, uytghespoken op den 6 May 1619. Uyt het Latijn ghetrouwelijck in't Nederduytsch overgheset. Met Privilegie voor seven Iaren* (Dordrecht: Isaac Ianssen Canin, ende zijne Medestanders, 1619); (Colophon: Tot Dordrecht, Gedruckt by Pieter Verhagen, Isaac Jansz. Canin, Joris Waters, Jan Leendertsz. Berewout, Fransoys Bosselaer, Niclaes Vincenten, Zacharias Jochemsz., ende Fransoys Boels, 1619), 4°, 96 pp.

1619d: *Oordeel van het Synodus Nationael ghehouden binnen Dordrecht* (synod print). *Oordeel des Synodi Nationalis der Gereformeerde Kercken van de Vereenichde Nederlanden, ghehouden binnen Dordrecht, inden Iare 1618 ende 1619… over de bekende Vijf Hooft-stucken der Leere, daer van inde Ghereformeerde Kercken deser Vereenichde Nederlanden verschil is ghevallen, uytghespoken op den 6 May 1619. Uyt het Latijn ghetrouwelijck in't Nederlandsch overgheset. Met Privilegie* (Dordrecht: Ian Lenaertsz. Berewout, ende zijne Medestanders, 1619); (Colophon: Tot Dordrecht, Gedruckt by Pieter Verhagen, Isaac Jansz. Canin, Joris Waters, Jan Leendertsz. Berewout, Francoys Bosselaer, Niclaes Vincenten, Zacharias Jochemsz., Francoys Boels, 1619); 4°, 114 pp.

[1619?e]: *Oordeel des Synodi Nationalis der Gereformeerde Kercken van de Vereenichde Neder-landen, ghehouden binnen Dordrecht, in den Iare 1618. ende 1619… over de bekende Vijf Hooft-stucken der Leere, daer van inde Gereformeerde Kercken deser Vereenichde Nederlanden verschil is ghevallen. Uyt ghesproken op den 6 May 1619. Wt het Latijn ghetrouwelijck in't Nederduytsch overgheset* (n.p.: n.p., [1619]), 4°, 36 pp. ("Na de copye ghedruckt tot Dordrecht"); [Knuttel, 2848].

1621a: *Acta ofte Handelinghen des Nationalen Synodi inden name onses Heeren Jesu Christi, ghehouden door authoriteyt der Hoogh Mogh. Heeren Staten Generael des Vereenichden Nederlandts tot Dordrecht, anno 1618. ende 1619. Hier comen oock by de volle Oordeelen vande Vijf Artijckelen* (Dordrecht: Isaac Iansz. Canin, ende zijne geassocieerde Druckers inde selvighe Stadt, 1621); (Colophon: Gedruckt tot Dordrecht, by Isaack Jansz. Canin, Pieter Verhagen, Joris Waters, Zacharias Jochemsz., Francoys Boels, Nicolaes Centen, Francoys Borselaer, Jan Leendertsz. Berewout), fol., 1:294–321.

1621b: *Acta ofte Handelinghen des Nationalen Synodi in den name onses Heeren Jesu Christi, ghehouden door authoriteyt der Hoogh Mogh. Heeren Staten Generael des Vereenighden Nederlandts, tot Dordrecht, Anno 1618 ende 1619. Hier comen oock by de volle Oordeelen van de Vijf Artijckelen* (Dordrecht: Isaac Jansz. Canin ende sijne gheassocieerde Druckers inde selvighe Stad, 1621); (Colophon: Tot

Dordrecht ghedruckt, by Isaac Jansz. Canin, Pieter Verhagen, Joris Waters, Zacharias Jochemsz., Fransoys Boels, Niclaes Vincenten, Fransoys Bossaler ende Jan Leendertsz. Berewout, 1621), 4°, 1:335–70.

1628: *Oordeel des Synodi Nationalis der Ghereformeerde Kercken van de Vereenighde Nederlanden, gehouden binnen Dordrecht, inden Jare 1618 ende 1619; over de bekende Vijf Hooft-stucken der Leere, daer van inde Gereformeerde Kerckem deser Vereenighde Nederlanden verschil is gevallen, uyt-ghesproken op den sesten May 1619* (Amsterdam: Paulus Aertsz. van Ravesteyn, 1628), 8°, 24 pp.

1636: Everardus Shuttenius, ed., *Nederlantshe Belydenisse des Geloofs, Canones des Synodi van Dordrecht, Nederlantsche Kercken-ordre ende Houwlyckx-ordre der Kercken van Overjsel* (Swolle: Frans Jorrians and Jan Gerritsen, 1636), 45–111.

1640: *De CL Psalmen des Propheten Davids, met eenige andere Lof-sangen: uyt den Françoyschen dichte in Nederlandtschen over-geset door Petrum Dathenum. Mitsgaders de Christelicke Catechismus, de Belijdenisse des Geloofs, ende Naerder Verklaringe van eenige Hooft-stucken des selven, overgeset ende gestelt inde Synode Nationael der Nederlandtsche Gereformeerde Kercken, gehouden tot Dordrecht in de jaren 1618 ende 1619. Als oock de Liturgie der selve Kercken* [Leiden]: [Paulus Aertsz van Ravesteyn], 1640.

Reprints: Amsterdam: Jan Barentsz Smient, 1644; Dordrecht: Hendrick van Esch, 1646; Dordrecht: Abr. Andriessz., 1651.

[1643]: *Biblia, dat is: de gantsche H. Schrifture, vervattende alle de Canonycke Boecken Ouden en des Nieuwen Testaments. Nu eerst, door last der Hoogh-Mog. Heeren Staten Generael vande Vereenigde Nederl; en volgens 't Besluyt van de Synode Nationael ghehouden tot Dordrecht, inde Iaeren 1618 ende 1619…* With: *"De CL Psalmen des Propheten Davids, met eenige andere Lof-Sanghen: uyt den Françoyschen Dichte in den Nederlantschen over-gheset door Petrum Dathenum. Geheel op Musijck-Noten ghestelt, ende op een nieuw oversien en verbetert. Mitsgaders de Christelicke Catechismus, de Belijdenisse des Geloofs, ende Naerder Verklaringe van eenige Hooft-stucken des selven, overgesien ende gestelt inde Synode Nationael der Nederlandtsche Gereformeerde Kercken, gehouden tot Dordrecht in de jaren 1618 ende 1619. Als oock de Liturgie der selve Kercken.* (Leiden: Paulus Aertsz van Ravesteyn, [1643]).

1679: *Catechismus, ofte Onderwijsinge in de Christelijcke Leere, die in de Kercken ende Scholen der Nederlandtsche Gereformeerde Kercken geleert werdt; Mitsgaders de Belijdenisse des Geloofs, ende Naerder Verklaringe van eenige Hooft-stucken des selven, overgesien ende gestelt inde Synode Nationael der Nederlandtsche Gereformeerde Kercken, gehouden tot Dordrecht, inde jaren 1618 ende 1619; Als oock de Lyturgie der selver kercken* (Leyden: Felix Lopez, 1679).

Reprint: Amsterdam: Jacobus Konynenberg, n.d.

1725: *Bekentenisse of Belydenisse des Geloofs der Nederlantsche Gereformeerde Kercken, mitsgaders de Heydelbergsche Catechismus met de Schriftuur-texten, en eyndelyck het Oordeel van de Nationale Synode van Dordrecht, over de Vyf Stucken der Leere* (Dordrecht: Mattheus de Vries, 1725), 71 pp.

1747: *Canones Synodi Dordracenae of Oordeel des Synodi Nationalis gehouden binnen Dordrecht, in den Jare 1618 en 1619, over de bekende Vyf Hoofdstukken der leere, daar van, in de Gereformeerde Kerken deser Vereenigde Nederlanden, verschil is gevallen. Thans uit Synodale last nieus uitgegeven* (Groningen: Jurjen Spandaw, 1747).

1752: Wilhelmus van Irhoven, ed., *Canones Synodi Nationalis Dordracenae ofte Oordeel des Synodi Nationalis der Gereformeerde Kercken van de Vereenigde Nederlanden, ghehouden binnen Dordrecht, inden Jare 1618 ende 1619. Welcke geassisteert is gheweest met vele treflycke theologen, uyt de Gereformeerde Kercken van Groot Britagnien, de Keur-Vorstelycke Paltz, Hessen, Switserlandt, de Wedderavische Correspondentie, Geneven, Bremen, ende Embden, over de bekende Vyf Hooft-stucken der Leere, daer van inde Gereformeerde Kercken deser Vereenigde Nederlanden verschil is gevallen, uitghesproken op den 6 May 1619* (Utrecht: J. H. Vonk van Lynden, 1752), 103 pp.

Reprints: Utrecht: G. T. van Paddenburg, 1788; Utrecht: J. H. Vonk van Lynden, 1900.

1780: Jacob Amersfoordt, ed., *De Vijf Artikelen tegen de Remonstranten vastgesteld op de Synoden, gehouden binnen Dordrecht, in den Jare 1618 en 1619, opnieuw uit het Latijn vertaald* (Amsterdam: Cornelis Byl, 1780), 69 pp. [new Dutch translation].

1833: Hendrik de Cock, ed., *Besluiten van de Nationale Dordsche Synode, gehouden in den Jare 1618 en 1619 te Dordrecht, uitgegeven door en met eene voorrede van Hendrik de Cock* (Veendam: T. E. Mulder, 1833), 1–48 (omits Conclusion).

Reprint: Hendrik de Cock, *Verzamelde Geschriften* (Houten: Den Hartog, 1984), 1:1–34.

1836: Hendrik Pieter Scholte, ed., *Formulieren van Eenigheid der Christelijk Gereformeerde Kerk in Nederland* (Amsterdam: H. Höveker; 'sGravenhage: J. van Golverdinge, 1836), 65–123.

1837: [Hendrik Pieter Scholte, ed.,] *Leerregels, behelzende de Vijf Artikelen tegen the Remonstranten* (Amsterdam: H. Höveker, 1837), 63 pp.

Reprints: H. P. Scholte, ed., *Canones of Leerregels der Algemeene Synode, uit verschillende landen van Europa bijeenvergaderd te Dordrecht in de jaren 1618 en*

1619 (Amsterdam: Höveker, 1842); Amsterdam: Hoogkamer, 1842; 3rd ed., Amsterdam: Höveker, 1854.

1837: Dirk Molenaar, ed., *De Formulieren van Eenheid, bij de Hervormde Kerk in Nederland gebruikelijk* (Amsterdam: J. H. den Ouden, 1837), 271–310.
Reprint: Amsterdam: Den Ouden, 1857.

1856: *De Vijf Artikelen tegen de Remonstranten vastgesteld op de Synode gehouden binnen Dordrecht in de jaren 1618-1619* (Kampen: S. van Velzen Jr., 1856); 51 pp. [new translation from Latin by Simon van Velzen and colleagues of the Theological School of Kampen].
Reprints: Kampen: S. van Velzen Jr., 1861, 1867, 1876; *Formulieren van Eenheid der Gereformeerde kerk in Nederland* ('s-Gravenhage: S. van Velzen Jr. (W. A. Beschoor), 1884–1889.

1865: J. J. Kotzé, ed., *De Belijdenisschriften der Nederduitsch-Gereformeerde Kerk en derzelver geschiedkundige toelichting* (Kaapstad [Capetown]: Van de Sandt de Villiers, 1865).

1868: *Het Boek der Psalmen, nevens de Gezangen bij de Hervormde Kerk van Nederland in gebruik…mitsgaders de Formulieren van Eenheid, de Liturgie en de Kerken-ordening der Gereformeerde Kerken* (Kampen: S. van Velzen Jr., 1868), 2:2–32.

1869: J. J. van Toorenenbergen, ed., *De Symbolische Schriften der Nederlandsche Hervormde Kerk in zuiveren kritisch bewerkten tekst* (Utrecht: Kemink & Zoon, 1869), 121–65.
Reprints: 2nd ed., Utrecht: Kemink & Zoon, 1895; 2nd ed., Utrecht: Kemink & Zoon, 1906.

1870: *Catechismus, Geloofsbelijdenis, Kort Begrip der Christelijke Leer, Leerregelen van de Synode van Dordrecht, en de Liturgie van de Nederduitsch Gereformeerde Kerk in Zuid-Afrika* (Kaapstad [Cape Town]: n.p., 1870), 54–70 [omits Rejection of Errors].

[1880?]: *Het Boek der Psalmen, benevens eenige Gezangen…de Formulieren van Eenigheid, het Kort Begrip der Christelijke Religie, Formulieren en Gebeden, bij de Gereformeerde Kerken van Nederland in gebruik* (Leeuwarden: A. Jongbloed, n.d.).
Reprints: Leeuwarden: A. Jongbloed, [ca. 1880s], [ca. 1890s], [1900?]; Amsterdam: Van Rossum, 1906, 1911, 1913; Leeuwarden: Jongbloed, [1920?], [1930?], 1933, 1936; Grand Rapids: Eerdmans and Sevensma, n.d.

[18??]: *Het Nieuwe Testament* (Leeuwarden: A. Jongbloed, n.d.), 3:41–70.

Editions of the Canons of Dordt

1881: *Algemeene Bepalingen der Hollandsche Chr. Geref. Kerk in Amerika* (Holland, Mich.: De Wachter Drukkerij, 1881), 89–126 [reprints translation of Simon van Velzen].

1883: Abraham Kuyper, ed., *De Drie Formulieren van Eenigheid, met de Kerkorde, gelijk die voor de Gereformeerde Kerken dezer landen zijn vastgesteld in haar laatsgehouden Nationale Synode* (Amsterdam: J. H. Kruyt, 1883), 63–96.

Reprints: Amsterdam: J. H. Kruyt, 1883, 1884, 1884, 1884 (=1885); 5th ed., Amsterdam: J. A. Wormser, 1887, 1887; 6th ed., 1889; 7th ed., 1890; 8th ed., 1892; 9th ed., 1894; 10th ed., 1895, 1895; 11th ed., Kampen: Kok, 1897; [Beginning with the 11th Amsterdam edition, Kuyper collaborated with F. L. Rutgers. In subsequent editions, spelling is modernized, and the Conclusion is omitted.] 11th ed., Amsterdam: Höveker & Wormser, 1897; 12th ed., 1898; 13th ed., 1900; 14th ed., 1902; 15th ed., 1903; 16th ed., 1904; 17th ed., 1906; 18th ed., 1907; 19th ed., Kampen: Kok, 1909; 20th ed., 1910; 21st ed., 1911; 22nd ed., 1912; 23rd ed., 1913; 24th ed., 1914; 25th ed., 1916; 26th ed., 1917; 27th ed., 1918; 28th ed., 1919; 29th ed., 1921; 30th ed., 1922; 31st ed., [1924]; 32nd ed., [1924]; 33rd ed., [1928]; 34th ed., [1928]; 35th ed., [1932]; 36th ed., [1932]; 37th ed., [1945]; 38th ed., [1946]; 39th ed., [1953]; 40th ed., [1957]; 41st ed., [1962]; 42nd ed., [1972]; n.p.: Nabu Press, 2010.

1885: J. H. Donner and S. A. van den Hoorn, ed., *Acta of Handelingen der Nationale Synode, in de naam van onze Heere Jezus Christus, gehouden door autoriteit der Hoogmogende Heren Staten-Generaal der Verenigde Nederlanden te Dordrecht in de Jaren 1618 en 1619. Hier komen ook bij de volledige Beoordelingen van de Vijf Artikelen en de Post-Acta of Nahandelingen* (Leiden, D. Donner, [1885]), 1:256–83.

Reprints: facsimile reprint, Utrecht: Den Hartog, [1968]; 3rd ed., Houten: Den Hertog, 1987.

1885: *Het Nieuwe Testament of alle Boeken des Nieuwen Verbonds...benevens de Psalmen en al de Formulieren ven Eenheid en de Liturgische Schriften der Nederl. Geref. Kerken* ('s-Gravenhage: Uitgevers Maatschappij "Nederland," [1885]), 34–75 [preface by L. Lindeboom, 1885].

Reprints: 's-Gravenhage: De Erven J. L. Nierstrasz, 1892; Grand Rapids: Eerdmans and Sevensma, 1885.

1890: J. H. Donner, ed., *De Drie Formulieren van Eenigheid, alsmede het Kort Begrip, en de Belijdenissen van Nicea en van Athanasius, ten dienste van het catechetisch onderwijs* (Leiden: Donner, 1890).

Reprint: Leiden: Donner, 1900.

1895: Stefanus Jacobus du Toit, ed., *De Drie Formulieren van Eenigheid, met de Kerkorde; gelijk die voor de Gereformeerde Kerken zijn vasgesteld in haar laastgehouden Nationale Synode* (Paarl: Du Toit, 1895).
Reprint: Paarl: Du Toit, 1899.

1897: M. J. Goddefroy, ed., *De Belijdenisschriften van de Nederduitsch Hervormde Kerk, genoemd: "De drie Formulieren van Eénigheid," gevolgd door de drie oudste algemeene Symbolen en de Dordtsche Kerken-orde* (Pretoria: J. H. de Bussy, 1897), 87–131.

1897: F. L. Rutgers, with H. Bavinck and A. Kuyper, ed., *De Berijmde Psalmen; met eenige Gezangen, in gebruik bij de Gereformeerde Kerken in Nederland; alsmede hare Formulieren van Eenigheid, met de drie oude Geloofsbelijdenissen en hare Liturgie, met het Korp Begrip en den Ziekentroost* (Middelharnis: Flakkeesche Boekdrukkerij, 1897), 2:41–62 [omits Conclusion].
Reprints: Middelharnis: Flakkeesche Boekdrukkerij, 1898; Veendam: M. D. de Lange, 1906; Middelharnis: Flakkeesche Boekdrukkerij, 1913; Leeuwarden: Biblia, 1927; 3rd ed. Leeuwarden: A. Jongbloed, [1934].

1900: *De vijf artikelen tegen de Remonstranten, Canones of Leerregels, vastgesteld op de Nationale Synode, gehouden binnen Dordrecht in de jaren 1618 en 1619* (Groningen: J. Haan, 1900), 52 pp.

1904: J. D. de Lind van Wijngaarden, *De Dordtsche Leerregels of de Vijf Artikelen tegen de Remonstranten* (Utrecht: Terveen, 1904), 1–38 [text and commentary].
Reprint: Utrecht: G. J. A. Ruys, 1905.

1904: M. van Grieken, ed., *De Drie Formulieren van Eenigheid, (de Nederlandsche Geloofsbelijdenis, de Heid. Catechismus, de Vijf Leerregels van Dordt), zijnde: de drie historische Fundamentstukken onzer Nederlandsch Hervormde (Gereformeerde) Kerk* (Utrecht: Kemink, 1904).
Reprints: 2nd ed., Utrecht: Kemink, 1914; 3rd ed., Utrecht: Kemink, 1922; 4th ed., Utrecht: Kemink, 1933.

1907: F. L. Rutgers, ed., *De Formulieren van Eenigheid der Gereformeerde Kerken in Nederland, met de drie oude Geloofsbelijdenissen en haar Liturgie; benevens het Kort Begrip en de Ziekentroost* (Amsterdam: De Nederlandsche Bijbel-Compagnie, 1907).
Reprints: Amsterdam: Brandt en Zoon, [1925?]; Amsterdam: Brandt, 1937; Amsterdam: De Nederlandsche Bijbel-Compagnie, [1938]; Dordrecht: Gereformeerde Bijbelstichting, [ca. 1975].

1907: *Formulierboek der N.G. Kerk in Z. Afrika: Catechismus, Geloofs-belijdenis, Kort Begrip der Christelijke Leer, Leerregelen van de Synode van Dordrecht en*

Editions of the Canons of Dordt 473

Liturgie van de Nederduitsch Gereformeerde Kerk in Zuid-Afrika (Kaapstad [Cape Town]: Van de Sandt De Villiers Drukpers, 1907).
Reprints: Kaapstad [Cape Town]: N. G. Kerk-Uitgewers, 1962, 1969.

1909: L. Wagenaar, *Van Strijd en Overwinning: De Groote Synode van 1618 op '19, en wat aan haar voorafging* (Utrecht: G. Ruys, 1909), Bijlage I, i–xx [omits Conclusion].

1915: T. Bos, *De Dordtsche Leerregelen* (Kampen: J. H. Kok, 1915) [text and commentary].

1924: M. Meijering, *De Dordtsche Leerregels of de Vijf Artikelen tegen de Remonstranten* (Groningen: Jan Haan, 1924) [text and commentary; omits Rejection of Errors and Conclusion].

1927: F. L. Rutgers, Abraham Kuyper, Herman Bavinck, ed., *De Formulieren van Eenigheid, met de drie oude Geloofsbelijdenissen en hare Liturgie, met het Kort Begrip en den Ziekentroost* (Leeuwarden: Biblia, 1927).
Reprint: Amsterdam: J. Brandt, [1932?].

1932: *Het Boek der Psalmen nevens de Gezangen, bij de Kerken van Nederland in gebruik door last van de Hoog Moogende Heeren Staten Generaal der Vereenigde Nederlanden, uit dier Berijmingen, in het jaar 1773 gekozen* (Haarlem: Joh. Enschedé & Zonen; Amsterdam: J. Brandt & Zoon, 1932).

1933: *Psalmen: de Berijming van 1773, waaraan toegevoegd: eenige Gezangen, de drie Formulieren van Enigheid, de drie oude Geloofsbelijdenissen, de Liturgie, het Kort Begrip, de Ziekentroost* (Leeuwarden: Jongbloed, [1933]).
Reprints: [n.p.: n.p., ca. 1960]; [Apeldoorn]: De Banier, 2016; Heerenveen: Jongbloed, [2018].

1933: G. H. Kersten, ed., *De Drie Formulieren van Eenigheid* (Utrecht: De Banier, 1933), 98–136.
Reprint: Utrecht: De Banier, [1963?].

1934: *Eenige Gezangen van de Gereformeerde Kerken in Nederland, gehandhaafd en vastgesteld door de Generale Synode van Middelburg in 1933, almede haar Formulieren van Eenigheid…en haar Liturgie* (Kampen: J. H. Kok, 1934), 73–94 [omits Conclusion].

1937: J. G. Feenstra, *De Dordtse Leerregelen* (Kampen: Kok, 1937) [text and commentary].
Reprints: 2nd rev. ed., Kampen: Kok, 1950; 3rd ed., Kampen: Kok, 1968; 4th ed., Kampen: Kok, 1975; 5th ed., Kampen: Kok, 1983.

Appendix 2

1938: P. Klüsener, ed., *De Drie Formulieren van Eenigheid* ([Neerbosch]: Neerbosch' Boekhandel en Uitgeverij, [1938]).
Reprints: 2nd ed., Neerbosch: Neerbosch' Uitgeverij, 1948; 3rd ed., [1958].

1940: J. N. Bakhuizen van den Brink, ed., *De Nederlandsche Belijdenisgeschriften, vergelijkende teksten samengesteld* (Amsterdam: Uitgeversmaatschappij Holland, 1940), 218–75.
Reprint: *De Nederlandse Belijdenisgeschriften in authentieke Teksten* (Amsterdam: Ton Bolland, 1976).

[ca. 1950]: *Psalmen: de Berijming van 1949, waaraan toegevoegd: enige Gezangen, de Drie Formulieren van Enigheid, de drie oude Geloofsbelijdenissen, de Liturgie, het Kort Begrip, de Ziekentroost* (Wageningen: Zomer & Keuning, n.d.).

1957: *De Belijdenisgeschriften volgens Artikel X van de Kerkorde van de Nederlandse Hervormde Kerk* ('s-Gravenhage: Boekencentrum, 1957).
Reprints: 's-Gravenhage: Boekencentrum, 1966, 1978, 1980.

[1968]: *Kerkboek van de Kerken in Nederland* (Leeuwarden: A. Jongbloed, [1968]).
Reprints: Wageningen: Zomer & Keuning, [1968]; 's-Gravenhage: Boekencentrum, [1969]; Leeuwarden: A. Jongbloed, 1969; Leeuwarden: A. Jongbloed, [1975?].

1971: W. Dankbaar, ed., *De Nederlandse Belijdenisgeschriften* (n.p.: n.p., 1971).
Reprints: 's-Gravenhage: Boekencentrum, 1983; 3rd ed., 1986; 4th ed., 1987; 8th ed., Zoetermeer: Boekencentrum, 1998.

1973: C. den Boer, *"Om 't Eeuwig Welbehagen:" Verhandelingen over de Dordtse Leerregels* (Utrecht: Uitgeverij De Banier, 1973) [text and commentary].
Reprints: 2nd ed., Utrecht: De Banier, 1974; 3rd ed., Utrecht: De Banier, 1975; 4th ed., Utrecht: De Banier, 1980; 5th ed., Utrecht: De Banier, 1983; 7th rev. ed., Apeldoorn: De Banier, [2018].

[1975]: *Bijbel* (Leeuwarden: Jongbloed).
Reprints: Dordrecht: Gereformeerde Bijbelstichting, [1980?]; Heerenveen: Jongbloed, [1990?]; Heerenveen: Jongbloed, [2013]; Heerenveen: Jongbloed, [2016]; Heerenveen: Jongbloed, [2019]; Leerdam: Gereformeerde Bijbelstichting, [2019].

1980: E. R. Damsté, *Leer en Leven: De Artikelen van de Dordtse Leerregels en de Verwerpingen der Dwalingen in Zestig Meditaties Verklaard* (Dordrecht: J. P. van den Tol, 1980) [text and commentary].

1981: *Van Credo tot Amen: Werkboek voor der Zes Belijdenisgeschriften in Hedendaags Nederlands* (Haarlem: Vijlbrief, 1981), 93–121.

1983: E. Koop, *De Dordtse Leerregels Dichterbij Gebracht* (Kampen: Uitgeverij van den Berg, 1983) [translation and commentary].
Reprints: 2nd ed., Kampen: Van den Berg, 1985; 3rd ed. 1992.

1983: Freerk Jan Berghuis et al., trans., *De Dordtse Leerregels vertaald in gewoon Nederlands* (Groningen: Uitgeverij de Vuurbaak, 1983) [new contemporary translation].

1985: H. Lenselink, ed., *De Dordtse Leerregels* (Woerden: Jeugdbond Gereformeerde Gemeenten, 1985).

1986: *Gereformeerd Kerkboek* (Haarlem: Vijlbrief, 1986), 627–66.

1988: P. den Breeijen, ed., *De Dordtse Leerregels* (Bilthoven: Landelijk Centrum van de Hervormd-Gereformeerde Jeugdbond, 1988).

1991: L. Vroegindeweij, *De Troost der Verkiezing: Pastorale Behandeling van de Dordtse Leerregels* ([Barendrecht]: LV-fonds, 1991), deel 1–3 [text and commentary; omits Rejection of Errors and Conclusion].

1996: *De Drie Formulieren van Enigheid* (Katwijk: Het Zevende Zegel, 1996).
Reprint: 2nd ed., Katwijk: Het Zevende Zegel, 1999.

1996: C. A. van der Sluijs, *Dordt Vandaag: Actualisering van de Dordtse Leerregelen* (Leiden: J. J. Groen & Zoon, 1996) [text and commentary; omits Rejection of Errors and Conclusion].

2002: H. van Dam, trans., *Door U Alleen: De Dordtse Leerregels in Hedendaags Nederlands*, (Houten: Den Hartog, 2002), 62 pp. [new translation].

2004: K. Zwanepol, ed., *Belijdenisgeschriften voor de Protestantse Kerk in Nederland* (Zoetermeer: Boekencentrum, 2004), 195–226.
Reprint: Heerenveen: Protestantse Pers, 2009.

2009: W. Verboom, ed., *De Nederlandse Belijdenis Geschriften* (n.p.: n.p., 2009).
Reprint: Utrecht: KokBoekcentrum, [2020].

2018: *De Dordtse Leerregels: een Hertaling*, trans. W. Verboom (Zoetermeer: KokBoekcentrum, 2018) [new translation].

2019: *De Dordtse Leerregels: met Synoniemen bij Verouderde Woorden* (Leerdam: Gereformeerde Bijbelstichting, 2019).

2019: M. de Haan, ed., *De Dordtse Leerregels* (Leerdam: Gereformeerde Bijbelstichting, [2019]).

2019: *Het Boek der Psalmen* (Leerdam: Gereformeerde Bijbelstichting, [2019]).

n.d.: *De Formulieren van Eenigheid, benevens het Kort Begrip der Christelijke Religie en de Complete Liturgie bij de Gereformeerde Kerken in Nederland in gebruik* (Leeuwarden: Jongbloed, n.d.), 136 pp.

French Editions

1619a: *Synodus. Jugement du Synode National des Eglises Reformees du Pays-Bas, tenu à Dordrecht, l'An 1618 & 1619, auquel aussi se sont trouvez les Theologiens des Eglises Reformees de la Grande Bretagne, du Palatinat Electoral, de Hessen, de Suisse, de la Correspondence de Wedderau, de Geneve, de Breme, & d'Emden, touchant les Cinq Articles debatus es Eglises dudict Pays-Bas. Publié le VI de May, l'An MDCXIX. Translatè fidelement du Latijn en François. Avec Privilege* (Dordrecht: Jean Berewout & François Borsaler, Compagnons de Canin, 1619), 4°, 119 pp. (Colophon: A Dordrecht. Imprimé chez Pierre Verhaghen, Isaac Canin, Ioris Waters, Iean Berewout, François Borsaler, Nicolas Vincent, Zacharie Iochums, François Boels, 1619); [trans. from Latin]; [Knuttel, 2849].

1619b: *Synodus. Jugement du Synode National des Eglises Reformees du Pays-Bas, tenu à Dordrecht, l'An 1618 & 1619… touchant les Cinq Articles debatus es Eglises dudict Pays-Bas. Publié le VI de May, l'An MDCXIX. Avec Privilege* (Dordrecht: Jean Berewout & François Borsaler, Compagnons de Canin, 1619), 119 pp. [a slightly different imprint than 1619a; title page omits "Translatè fidelement du Latijn en François"].

1619c?: *Synodus. Jugement du Synode national des Eglises Réformées du Pays-Bas, tenu à Dordrecht, l'An 1618 & 1619… Translaté fidèlement du Latin en François* (Dordrecht: Imp. de P. Verhaghen, etc., 1619), 4°.

1619d: *Jugement du Synode National des Eglises Reformees du Pays-Bas, tenu à Dordrecht, l'An 1618 & 1619… touchant les Cinq Articles, debatus es Eglises du Pays-Bas* (n.p.: n.p., 1619), 119 pp.

1619e: *Jugement du Synode National des Eglises Réformées du Pays-Bas tenu à Dordrecht, l'An 1618 et 1619… touchant les Cinq Articles debatus es Eglises du Pays Bas. Publié le VI de May 1619* (Quevilly: J. Berthelin, 1619), 8°, 95 pp. (Colophon: Jouste la copie imprimée à Dordrecht, par P. Verhaghen, etc. 1619).

1619f: *Iugement du Synode National, des Eglises Réformées tenu à Dordrecht, l'An 1618 & 1619…touchant les Cinq Articles debatus es Eglises dudit Pays-Bas… Translaté fidelement du Latin en François. Sur la copie impr. à* Dordrecht (Geneva: Marceau, 1619), 8°, 88 pp.

1619g?: *Iugement du Synode National des Eglises Reformees, tenu à Dordrecht, l'An 1618 & 1619… touchant les Cinq Articles debatus es Eglises dudit Pays-Bas. Publié le VI de May, l'An MDCXIX. Translatè fidelement du Latin en François. Sur la copie imprimee a Dordrecht. Avec premission* (n.p.: n.p., [1619?]), 88 pp.

1619h?: *Jugement du Synode National des Eglises Réformées des Pays-Bas, tenu à Dordrecht, l'An 1618 et 1619,* touchant les 5 Articles *débatus ès Eglises dudict Pays-Bas* (Geneva: n.p., 1619), 8°.

1620a: *Iugement du Synode National des Eglises Reformees du Pays-bas, tenu à Dordrecht l'An 1618 et 1619… touchant les Cinq Articles debatus és Eglises du Pays-Bas* (Nismes: Jean Vaguenar, 1620), 79 pp.

1620b: *Jugement du Synode National des Eglises Réformées du Pays-Bas, tenu à Dordrecht l'An 1618 & 1619 … touchant les Cinq Articles debattus és Eglises du Pay-Bas. Auquel est adjousté le Canon des Egliscs Reformées de France, conclu & aresté au Synode National tenu à Alez és Cevennes, le 6 d'Octobre 1620 avec le serment d'approbation* (n.p.: n.p., 1620), 4°, 79 pp.

1621: *Jugement du Synode National des Eglises Réformées du Pays-Bas, tenu a Dordrecht l'An 1618 et 1619…touchant les Cinq Articles de doctrine, debatus ès Eglises des Pays-Bas* (Quevilly: J. Berthelin, 1621), 8°, 103 pp.

1624: *Actes du Synode National, tenu à Dordrecht l'an 1618 & 1619* (Leiden: Isaac Elsevir, 1624), 1:456–519.

1687: Antonius Hulsius, ed., *La Confession de Foy des Eglises Reformées des Païs-Bas, representée en deux colomnes, l'une portant la Confession ancienne, et l'autre la Revision qui en a esté faite au Synode National de Dordrecht, l'an 1619. Avec le Jugement du dit Synode sur les 5 Articles & la Discipline Ecclesiastique* (Amsterdam: Henry et la Veuve de Théodore Boom, 1687), 47–76 [omits Conclusion].

Reprints: Rotterdam: Jean Daniel Beman, 1726; Leiden: Elie Luzac, 1769.

1710: Jean Aymon, *Tous les Synodes Nationaux des Eglises Reformees de France* (La Haye: Charles Delo, 1710), 2:298–323.

1963: "Jugement du Synode National des Églises Réformées du Pays-Bas, tenu a Dordrecht, l'An 1618 et 1619, concernant les Cinq Articles de Doctrine" *La Revue Réformée* 14, no. 3 (1963): 1–38.

1986: Olivier Fatio, ed., *Confessions et Catéchismes de la Foi Réformée* (Geneva: Labor et Fides, 1986), 312–46.
    Reprint: 2nd ed., Geneva: Labor et Fides, 2005.

1988: *Canons de Dordrecht: le solide fondement* (Krimpen a/d Ijssel: Fondation d'Entraide Chrétienne Réformée, 1988), 112 pp.

English Editions

1619a: *The Iudgement of the Synode Holden at Dort, concerning the Five Articles* (London: John Bill, 1619), 83 pp.; (trans. from Latin); [Knuttel, 2850; STC, 7066].
    Another issue: London: John Bill, 1619, 106 pp.
    Another issue: London: John Bill, 1619, 178 pp.
    Facsimile reprint: Amsterdam: Theatrum Orbis Terrarum, 1974.

1619b: *The Judgement of the Nationall Synod of the Reformed Belgique churches, assembled at Dort, anno 1618 and 1619…Englished out of the Latine copie* (n.p.: n.p., 1619), 4°, 83 pp.

1623: *Articles Agreed on in the Nationall Synode of the Reformed Churches of France, held at Charenton neere Paris, in the Moneth of September, 1623* (Oxford: John Lichfield and James Short, 1623), 34 pp.; [STC, 11295].
    Reprint: Oxford: John Lichfield and James Short, 1624.
    Facsimile reprint: Amsterdam: Theatrum Orbis Terrarum, 1976.

1692: John Quick, *Synodicon in Gallia Reformata* (London: J. Richardson for Thomas Parkhurst, 1692), 2:126–52.

1745: *The Judgment of the Renowned Synod of Dort in Holland* (Boston: Kneeland & Green and J. Winter, 1745); [Evans 5574].

1748: *The Whole Book of Forms and the Liturgy of the Dutch Reformed Church* ([New York]: Henry De Foreest, 1748).

1793: *Constitution of the Reformed Dutch Church in the United States of America* (New York: William Durell, 1793), 223–58; [Evans, 26065]; [trans. by John Livingston from Dutch; omits Rejection of Errors].
    Reprints: New York: George Forman, 1815; New York: L. Nichols, 1834; Philadelphia: G. W. Mentz and Son, 1840; New York: Board of Publications of the Reformed Dutch Church, 1865; New York: Board of Publications of the Reformed Church in America, [1869], 1876, 1895, 1901.

1812: *Canons ratified in the National Synod of the Reformed Church, held at Dordrecht in the years 1618 & 1619* ([New York:] New York Religious Tract Society, 1812), 20 pp.
Facsimile reprint: [New York]: Early American Imprints, 1974.

1817: Thomas Scott, *Remarks on the Refutation of Calvinism by George Tomline*, 2nd ed. (London: A. Macintosh, 1817), 726–46; [trans. from Latin in *Sylloge Confessionum* (Oxford: Clarendon, 1804) omits Rejection of Errors].
Reprint: Thomas Scott, *Remarks on the Doctrine of Original Sin, Grace, Free Will, Justification by Faith, Election and Reprobation, and the final Perseverance of the Saints, to which is added a translation of the genuine Articles of the Synod of Dort*, 2nd ed. (London: A. Macintosh, 1817).

1818: Thomas Scott, *The Articles of the Synod of Dort, and its Rejection of Errors* (London: A. Macintosh, 1818); [trans. from Latin in *Sylloge Confessionum* (Oxford: Clarendon, 1804)].
Reprints: Utica, N.Y.: William Williams, 1831; Philadelphia: Presbyterian Board of Publication, 1841, 1856; London: Sovereign Grace Union, 1932; Harrisonburg, Va.: Sprinkle Publications, 1993; n.p.: Forgotten Books, 2015.

1832: *The Psalms and Hymns, with the Catechism, Confession of Faith, and Liturgy of the Reformed Dutch Church in North America… to which are added the Additional Hymns and the Canons of the Synod of Dordrecht*, ed. John Livingston (New York: William Mercein, 1832), 40–50 [omits Rejection of Errors].
Reprints: New York: William Mercein, 1835, 1836, 1837, 1838; Philadelphia: G. W. Mentz and Son, 1839, 1840, 1841; Philadelphia: Mentz & Rovoudt, 1842, 1844, 1845, 1847, 1848; Philadelphia: William Mentz, 1847, 1854; New York: Board of Publication of the Reformed Protestant Dutch Church, 1859, 1860.

1842: Peter Hall, ed., *The Harmony of Protestant Confessions* (London: John F. Shaw, 1842), 539–71.
Reprint: Edmonton: Still Waters Revival Books, 1992.

1843: *The Decision of the National Synod, of the Dutch Reformed Churches, held at Dort in the years 1618 and 1619… concerning the five heads of doctrine, which were controverted in the Dutch churches* (Norwich: A. Charlwood, [1843]); [new trans. by Owen Jones from Latin in *Sylloge Confessionum* (Oxford: Clarendon, 1827)].

[185?]: *Canons of the Synod of Dort* ([New York]: Board of Publication of the Reformed Protestant Dutch Church), 32 pp.

1853: *The Catechism, Articles of Faith, Canons of the Synod of Dordrecht, and Liturgy of the Reformed Dutch Church* (Cape Town: W. H. Marais, 1853), 71–88 [omits Rejection of Errors].

1870: *Hymns of the Church* [with the Doctrinal Standards and Liturgy of the Reformed Church in America] (New York: A. S. Barnes, 1870), 2:51–62 [omits Rejection of Errors].
  Reprints: New York: A. S. Barnes, 1873, 1874, 1897.

1876: *The Doctrinal Standards and Liturgy of the Reformed Dutch Church* (Cape Town: J. H. Rose, 1876), 87–108 [omits Rejection of Errors].

1877: Philip Schaff, ed., *The Creeds of Christendom* (New York: Harper and Brothers, 1877), 3:581–97 [reprint of 1793 ed.; omits Rejection of Errors].
  Reprints: London: Hodder and Stoughton, 1877; New York: Harper and Bros., 1878, 1882, 1919, [1952], 1957; Grand Rapids: Baker, 1966, 1977, 1983, 1985; Whitefish, Mont.: Kessinger Publishing, [2007]; n.p.: Forgotten Books, 2015, 2017.

[1897?]: *The Doctrinal Standards and Liturgy of the Reformed Church in America* ([New York]: [Maynard, Merrill, & Co.], n.d.).
  Reprint: New York: Board of Publication of the Reformed Church in America, 1907; *The Doctrinal Standards of the Reformed Church in America* (New York: Board of Publication and Bible School Work, 1924).

1903: *The Church Hymnary* (New York: Maynard, Merrill, & Co., 1903).

1907: *The Psalms and Hymns with the Doctrinal Standards and Liturgy of the Christian Reformed Church* (Paterson, N.J.: n.p., 1907).
  Reprint: Paterson, N.J.: Publication Committee of the Classis Hackensack, 1910.

1907: *Doctrinal Standards of the Christian Reformed Church* (Paterson, N.J.: Publication Committee of the Classis Hackensack, 1907).

1909: *The Psalter, with the Doctrinal Standards and Liturgy of the Christian Reformed Church* (Grand Rapids: Eerdmans-Sevensma, 1909), 2:39–56.
  Reprints: Grand Rapids: Eerdmans-Sevensma, 1914; Grand Rapids: Eerdmans-Sevensma, 1916; Grand Rapids: Eerdmans, 1927; Grand Rapids: Smitter Book Co., 1927.

1927: *The Psalter, with Doctrinal Standards, Liturgy, Church Order and added Chorale Section* (Grand Rapids: Eerdmans, 1927).
  Reprints: rev. ed., Grand Rapids: Eerdmans, 1947, 1955; 3rd rev. ed., 1960; 5th rev. ed., 1965; 6th ed., 1968; 7th ed., 1969; 8th ed., 1972; 9th ed., 1974; 10th ed., 1975; 11th ed., 1976, 1977; 12th ed., 1980, 1984, 1987, 1988, 1991; rev. ed., 1995; rev. ed., Grand Rapids: Eerdmans/Reformation Heritage Books, 1995; Grand Rapids: Eerdmans, 1998; Grand Rapids: Eerdmans/Reformation Heritage Books, 1999, 2002; rev. ed., Grand Rapids: Eerdmans, 2002, 2006;

Grand Rapids: Eerdmans/Reformation Heritage Books, 2006; Grand Rapids: Eerdmans, 2008; Grand Rapids: Eerdmans/Reformation Heritage Books, 2010; Grand Rapids: Eerdmans, 2011; rev. ed., 2012; Grand Rapids: Eerdmans/Reformation Heritage Books, 2016; Grand Rapids: Eerdmans, 2017.

1932: *The Articles of the Synod of Dort and its Rejection of Errors* (London: Sovereign Grace Union, 1932), 7–39.

1934: *Psalter Hymnal, Doctrinal Standards and Liturgy of the Christian Reformed Church* (Grand Rapids: Publication Committee of the Christian Reformed Church, 1934), 44–65 [omits Rejection of Errors].

1942: *Doctrinal Standards of the Netherlands Reformed Congregations* (Grand Rapids: n.p., 1942), 38–59.
Reprint: Grand Rapids: n.p., 1963.

1952: Leroy Nixon, ed., *Reformed Standards of Unity* (Grand Rapids: Society for Reformed Publications, 1952), 97–119 [omits Rejection of Errors sections].
Reprint: Grand Rapids: Rose Publishing, [1957].

1957: *The Articles of Faith, the Catechism, the Canons of the Synod of Dordrecht, Liturgy and Church Order of the Dutch Reformed Church of Ceylon* (Colombo, Ceylon [Sri Lanka]: Caxton Printing Works, 1957).

1958: Gordon Girod, *The Deeper Faith: An Exposition of the Canons of the Synod of Dort* (Grand Rapids: Reformed Publications, 1958), 113–35 [omits Rejection of Errors sections].
Reprint: Grand Rapids: Baker, 1978.

1959: *Psalter Hymnal, Doctrinal Standards and Liturgy of the Christian Reformed Church* (Grand Rapids: Publication Committee of the Christian Reformed Church, 1959), 44–66.
Reprint: Grand Rapids: Board of Publications of the Christian Reformed Church, 1976.

1962: *Doctrinal Standards of the Christian Reformed Church* (Grand Rapids: Publication Committee of the Christian Reformed Church, 1962), 44–66.
Reprint: Grand Rapids: Publication Committee of the Christian Reformed Church, [1975].

1965: *Book of Praise* (Hamilton: Deputies of the Can. Ref. Churches for an English Calvinistic Psalter, 1965), 71–110.
Reprint: Hamilton: Publication Committee for an English Calvinistic Psalter, 1969.

1968: Henry Petersen, *The Canons of Dort: A Study Guide* (Grand Rapids: Baker, 1968), 93–115.

1968: Peter Y. De Jong, ed., *Crisis in the Reformed Churches: Essays in Commemoration of the Great Synod of Dort, 1618–1619* (Grand Rapids: Reformed Fellowship, 1968), 229–62.
   Reprint: Grandville, Mich.: Reformed Fellowship, 2008.

1968: Gerrit T. Vander Lugt, ed., *The Liturgy of the Reformed Church in America together with the Psalter* (New York: Board of Education of the Reformed Church in America, 1968), 493–518 [translation from Dutch by Gerrit Vander Lugt; omits Rejection of Errors].

1968: Anthony Hoekema, "A New English Translation of the Canons of Dort," *Calvin Theological Journal* 3, no. 2 (Nov. 1968): 133–61 [omits Rejection of Errors and Conclusion].
   Reprint: Grand Rapids: Calvin Theological Seminary, 1968.

1970: *Doctrinal Standards of the Dutch Reformed Church, consisting of the Belgic Confession, the Heidelberg Catechism and the Canons of Dort* (Johannesburg: Andrew Murray Congregation of the Dutch Reformed Church, 1970).
   Reprint: Braamfontein: Andrew Murray Congregation of the Dutch Reformed Church, 1972.

1972: *Book of Praise: Anglo-Genevan Psalter* (Hamilton: Committee for the Publication of the Anglo-Genevan Psalter, 1972), 427–66.
   Reprints: rev. ed., Winnipeg: Premier, 1984; rev. ed., 1987, 1993 [new trans. of Canons], 1995, 1998, 2004, 2006; 9th ed., 2008, 2010, 2014, 2015.

1979: *Ecumenical Creeds and Reformed Confessions* (Grand Rapids: Board of Publications of the Christian Reformed Church, 1979), 85–109.

1980: Homer C. Hoeksema, *The Voice of Our Fathers: An Exposition of the Canons of Dordrecht* (Grand Rapids: Reformed Free Publishing Association, 1980) [text and commentary].
   Reprint: rev. ed., Jenison, Mich.: Reformed Free Publishing Association, 2013.

1983: *The Three Forms of Unity: Heidelberg Catechism, Belgic Confession, Canons of Dordrecht and the Ecumenical Creeds: The Apostles' Creed, the Nicene Creed, the Athanasian Creed, the Creed of Chalcedon* (n.p.: Mission Committee of the Protestant Reformed Churches of America, 1983).
   Reprints: n.p.: Mission Committee of the Protestant Reformed Churches of America, 1991, 1996, 1999, 2002, 2010.

1987: *Psalter Hymnal* (Grand Rapids: CRC Publications, 1987), 926–49 [new translation from original Latin].
Reprints: Grand Rapids: CRC Publications, 1988.

1987: *Ecumenical Creeds and Reformed Confessions* (Grand Rapids: CRC Publications, 1987), 121–44.
Reprints: Grand Rapids: CRC Publications, 1988; Dyer, Ind.: Mid-America Reformed Seminary, 1991, 2004, 2013.

1990: *The Doctrinal Standards and Liturgy of the Reformed Church in America* (New York: The Board of Education), 38–47.

1990: *Liturgy and Confessions* (New York: Reformed Church Press, 1990).

1991: *The Doctrinal Standards, Liturgy, and Church Order of the Netherlands Reformed Congregations* (Sioux Center, Iowa: Netherlands Reformed Book and Publication Committee, 1991), 96–117.

1991: *Book of Forms* (Geelong: Reformed Churches Pub. House, 1991).
Reprint: Geelong: Reformed Churches Pub. House, 1992.

1993: *Three Forms of Unity: The Belgic Confession, the Heidelberg Catechism, the Canons of Dort, including the Ecumenical Creeds* (Winnipeg: Premier Printing, 1993), 97–142.
Reprints: Winnipeg: Premier Printing, 1994, 1999.

1994: Cornelis P. Venema, *But for the Grace of God: An Exposition of the Canons of Dort* (Grand Rapids: Reformed Fellowship, 1994), 114–45.
Reprints: Grandville, Mich.: Reformed Fellowship, 2011; Grandville, Mich.: Reformed Fellowship, 2013.

1997: Peter G. Feenstra, *Unspeakable Comfort: A Commentary on the Canons of Dort* (Winnipeg: Premier Publishing, 1997) [text and commentary].

1999: Cornelis Pronk, *Expository Sermons on the Canons of Dort* (St. Thomas, Ontario: Free Reformed Publications, 1999) [text and commentary; omits Rejection of Errors sections and Conclusion].
Reprint: Grand Rapids: Free Reformed Publications, 2013.

1999: Joel Beeke, ed., *Doctrinal Standards, Liturgy, and Church Order* (Grand Rapids: Reformation Heritage Books, 1999).

2000: *The Three Forms of Unity: The Heidelberg Catechism, modern English version, the Belgic Confession of Faith & the Canons of Dort* (n.p.: Reformed Church in the United States, 2000).

Reprints: n.p.: Reformed Church in the United States, 2001; n.p.: Reformed Church in the United States, 2006; n.p.: Publications and Promotions Committee of the Reformed Church in the U.S., ca. 2011.

2001: *The Three Forms of Unity: The Subordinate Doctrinal Standards of the Reformed Church in the United States* (n.p.: The Reformed Church in the United States, 2001), 58–90.
Reprint: n.p.: The Reformed Church in the United States, 2006.

2003: Jaroslav Pelikan and Valerie Hotchkiss, eds., *Creeds & Confessions of Faith in the Christian Tradition* (New Haven: Yale University Press, 2003), 2:571–600.

2004: Arthur van Delden, *Lest Any Man Should Boast: The Canons of Dort Simply Explained* (n.p.: Pro Ecclesia Publishers, 2004) [text and commentary; omits Rejection of Errors].

2005: *The Confessions and the Church Order of the Protestant Reformed Churches* (Grandville, Mich.: Protestant Reformed Churches in America, 2005), 154–80.

2005: Anthony Milton, ed., *The British Delegation and the Synod of Dort (1618–1619)* (Woodbridge, England: Boydell Press, 2005), 297–321 [reprints 1619a edition; omits Conclusion].

2009: C. Vogelaar, *The Canons of Dordt Explained* (Kalamazoo: Netherlands Reformed Congregations, 2009) [text and commentary; omits Rejection of Errors and Conclusion].

[2010]: *The Psalter: with Doctrinal Standards, Liturgy, and Church Order* (Grand Rapids: Reformation Heritage Books, [2010]).

2010: Joel Beeke, ed., *The Three Forms of Unity: Heidelberg Catechism, Belgic Confession, Canons of Dort* (Birmingham: Solid Ground Christian Books, 2010).
Reprints: n.p.: Solid Ground Christian Books, 2012, 2018.

2010: *The Canons of Dort* (Pensacola: Chapel Library, 2010), 9–36.

2011: Wes Bredenhof, ed., *We Believe: The Creeds and Confessions of the Canadian Reformed Churches* (Hamilton: Providence Press, 2011), 101–41, 156–59 [includes Preface of Canons].

[2012]: Daniel Hyde, ed., *Our Faith: Ancient Christian Creeds & Reformed Confessions* (Carlsbad, Calif.: Oceanside United Reformed Church, [2012]).

2013: *Our Faith: Ecumenical Creeds, Reformed Confessions and other Resources* (Grand Rapids: Faith Alive, 2013), 118–44.

2013: Matthew Barrett, *The Grace of Godliness: An Introduction to Doctrine and Piety in the Canons of Dort* (Kitchener: Joshua Press, 2013), 159–93.

2014: James T. Dennison Jr., ed., *Reformed Confessions of the 16th and 17th Centuries in English Translation* (Grand Rapids: Reformation Heritage Books, 2014), 4:120–53.

2017: *Psalms and Doctrinal Standards, Liturgy, and Church Order* (Salford, Ontario: Gereformeerde Gemeente in Nederland, 2017), 486–507.

2018: Martyn McGeown, *Grace and Assurance: The Message of the Canons of Dordt* (Jenison, Mich.: Reformed Free Publishing Association, 2018) [text and commentary].

2018: *Trinity Psalter Hymnal* (Willow Grove, Pa.: Trinity Psalter Hymnal Joint Venture, 2018), 897–918.

2018: *Liturgical Forms and Prayers of the United Reformed Churches in North America, together with the Doctrinal Standards of the URCNA* (Wellandport: United Reformed Churches in North America, 2018), 259–86.

2019: Kevin DeYoung, *Grace Defined and Defended: What a 400-Year-Old Confession Teaches Us about Sin, Salvation, and the Sovereignty of God* (Wheaton: Crossway, 2019) [text and commentary].

2019: W. Robert Godfrey, *Saving the Reformation: The Pastoral Theology of the Canons of Dort* (Orlando: Reformation Trust, 2019), 35–77 [new translation from Latin].

2019: Daniel R. Hyde, *Grace Worth Fighting For: Recapturing the Vision of God's Grace in the Canons of Dort* (Lincoln: Davenant Press, 2019) [text and commentary].

German Editions

1619: *Urtheil des Synodi Nationalis der reformirten Kirchen in den Vereinigten Niderlanden, gehalten in Dordrecht im Jahre 1618 und 1619. Bei welchem gewesen viel treffliche Theologen aus den reformirten Kirchen aus grooß Britannien, Churfürstlicher Pfaltz, Hessen, Schweitzerland, Wedderawischen correspondentz, Genf, Bremen, und Embden, uber Die bekante fünf Haupstücke der lehre, darvon* *in reformirten Kirchen der Vereinigten Niderlanden uneinigkeit entstanden. Außgesprochen den 6 Maii 1619. Auß dem Lateinischen und Niderländischen ins Hochteutsche trewlich übersetzet* (n.p.: n.p., 1619), 4°, 60 pp.

1620: *Urtheil desz Synodi Nationalis der reformierten Kirchen in den Vereinigten Niderlanden, gehalten in Dordrecht im Jahre 1618 und 1619…uber die bekandten fünff Hauptstücke der Lehre* (n.p.: n.p., 1620), 4°.

1830: Friedrich Adolf Beck, ed., *Die Symbolischen Bücher in der evangelisch-reformirten Kirche: zum ersten Male aus dem Lateinischen vollständig übersetzt* (Neustadt a. d. Orla: Johann Karl Gottfried Wagner, 1830), 1:344–400.
  Reprint: Neustadt a. d. Orla: Johann Karl Gottfired Wagner, 1845.

1844: Friedrich Bodeman, ed., *Sammlung der wichtigsten Bekenntnisschriften der evangelisch-reformirten Kirch* (Hannover: Hahn, 1844), 35–59.
  Reprint: Göttingen: Vandenhoeck & Ruprecht, 1867.

1847: Ernst G. A. Böckel, ed., *Die Bekenntnißschriften der evangelisch-reformirten Kirche* (Leipzig: F. A. Brockhaus, 1847), 508–39.

1851: *Die Kirchenordnung, Glaubensbekenntniss und Canones der Synode zu Dortrecht; sammt Catechismen der protestantisch-reformirten niederdeutschen Kirche von Nordamerika* (New York: D. Janshaw, 1851), 128–68.
  Reprint: New York: Board of Publications der Reformirten Protestantischen Niederlandischen Kirche, 1856.

1908: *Reformirte Bekenntnisschriften und Formulare, herausgegeben in Auftrage der Klassis der altreformirten Kirchen in Bentheim und Ostfriesland* (Emden: Anton Gerhard, 1908), 95–142 [omits Conclusion].
  Reprint: [Emden]: Emder Zeitung, 1925.

2010: *Bekenntnisbuch, bestehende aus dem Heidelberger Katechismus, dem Niederländischen Glaubensbekenntnis sowie der Lehrregel von Dordrecht* (Heidelberg: Verein für Reformation in Deutschland, 2010), 213–60.

2015: Eberhard Busch, Torrance Kirby, Andreas Mühling, and Herman Selderhuis, eds., *Reformierte Bekenntnisschriften* (Neukirchen-Vluyn: Neukirchener Theologie, 2015), band 3/2:94–161.

Afrikaans Editions

1936: *Die Drie Formuliere van Enigheid en die Liturgie* (Kaapstad [Cape Town]: Nasionale Pers, 1936), 78–112.

Reprints: Kaapstad [Cape Town]: Nasionale Pers, 1937; Kaapstad [Cape Town]: S. A. Bybelvereniging, 1938.

1945: *Belydenisskrifte, Gebede en Formuliere van die Nederduitsch Hervormde Kerk van Afrika* (Pretoria: n.p., 1945), 64–99 [new translation].

1950: *Formulierboek van die Gefedereerde Nederduitse Gereformeerde Kerke in Suid-Afrika, bevattende die Belydenisskrifte, Liturgiese Formuliere en Christelike Gebede* (Kaapstad [Cape Town]: Suid-Afrikaanse Bybelvereniging, 1950), 65–88.

1951: *Die Drie Formuliere van Enigheid* (Kaapstad [Cape Town], Pretoria: Die N. G. Kerk-Uitgewers van Suid-Afrika, 1951).
Reprint: Kaapstad [Cape Town]: Suid-Afrikaanse Bybelvereniging, n.d.; 3rd ed. Kaapstad [Cape Town], Pretoria: Die N. G. Kerk-Uitgewers, 1961.

1952: *Kerkboek: waarin vervat is die Berymde Psalms, die evangeliese Gesange en die Belydenisskrifte, Gebede en Formuliere* (n.p.: S. A. Bybelvereniging, 1952).

1954: *Die Berymde Psalms in gebruik by die Gefedereerde Nederduitse Gereformeerde Kerke in Suid-Afrika, ... die Nederduits Hervormde Kerk van Afrika en die Gereformeerde Kerk, saam met die Evangeliese Gesange...(Met Belydenisskrifte, Liturgiese Formuliere en Christelike Gebede van die Gefedereerde Nederduitse Gereformeerde Kerke in Suid-Afrika.)* (Pretoria: N. G. Kerk-Uitgewers van S.A., 1954).
Reprints: Kaapstad [Cape Town]: N. G. Kerk-Boekhandel, 1955; Kaapstad [Cape Town]: N. G. Kerk-Uitgewers, 1977.

1965: *Kerkboek van die Nederduitsch Hervormde Kerk van Afrika: waarin vervat is die Berymde Psalms, die evangeliese Gesange en die Belydenisskrifte, Gebede en Formuliere van die Nederduitsch Hervormde Kerk van Afrika* (Kaapstad [Cape Town]: N. G. Kerk-Uitgewers vir die Nederduitsch Hervormde Kerk van Afrika, 1965).

1968: T. N. Hanekom, ed., *Die Dordtse Leerreëls* (Kaapstad [Cape Town]: N. G. Kerk-Uitgewers, 1968), 31 pp.

1973: *Die Dordtse Leerreëls verdor nie; die Vyf Artikels teen die Remonstrante vertaal en toegelig* (Johannesburg: Boekhandel de Jong, 1973) [trans. C. van der Waal].

[1980]: *Belydenisskrifte en Liturgie: die Die Formuliere van Enigheid...die liturgiese Formuliere...Christelike Gebede* ([Kaapstad (Cape Town)]: N. G. Kerk-Uitgewers, [1980]).

1981: *Glo en bely. Leerboek vir katkisante, opgestel in opdrag van die Algemene Sinode van die Nederduits Gereformeerde Kerk* (Bloemfontein: N. G. Sendingpers, 1981), 262–78.

1982: P. Rossouw, ed., *Ons glo… Die drie Formuliere van Eenheid en Ekumeniese Belydenisse* (n.p.: N. G. Kerk-Uitgewers, 1982), 77–117.

1983: *Diensboek* (Pretoria: Kital, 1983), 204–52.

Spanish Editions

1971: *Los Cánones de Dort: o Reglas doctrinales de Dordrecht* (Barcelona: Asociación Cultural de Estudios de la Literatura Reformada, 1971), 62 pp.
   Reprint: 3rd ed., Rijswijk: Fundación Editorial de Literatura Reformada, 1996.

1983: *Confesiones de Fe de la Iglesia: (Las tres Confesiones de la Iglesia Antigua y las tres Confesiones Reformadas)* (Rotterdam: Literatura Evangelica; Madrid: Munoz Maíllo, 1983).

2017: *Confesiones y Credos Cristianos: Las Tres Formas de Unidad y otros credos históricas* (n.p.: Editorial Clir, 2017).

2018: *Las Tres Formas de la Unidad: Catecismo de Heidelberg, Confesión Belga de Fe, Cánones de Dort* (n.p.: Iglesia Reformada en los Estatos Unidas, 2018), 76–107.

Portuguese Editions

1990: *As tres Confissoes da Igreja Reformada* (Pretoria-West: M. Taute, 1990).

2002: *Os Cânones de Dort: Os Cinco Artigos de Fé Contra os Arminianos* (Maceió: Graciliano Ramos, 2002).

2006: *As Três Formas de Unidade das Igrejas Reformadas: A Confissão de Fé Belga, O Catecismo de Heidelberg e Os Cânones de Dort* (Recife: CLIRE, 2006).
   Reprints: Recife: CLIRE, 2009; rev. ed., Recife: CLIRE, 2017.

2006: Joel Beeke, ed., *Harmonia das confissões Reformadas* (São Paulo: Cultura Cristã, 2006).

2009: *Bíblia de Estudo de Genebra*, 2nd ed. (São Paulo and Barueri: Cultura Cristã, 2009), 1774–84.

2016: A. De Graaf, ed., *Os Cânones de Dordt: Os Cinco Artigos de Fé contra os Arminianos* (Maceió: Graciliano Ramos, 2016) [new translation by Abram De Graaf].
Reprint: rev. ed., Maceió: Graciliano Ramos, 2018.

[?]: Claudio Marra, ed., *Os Cânones de Dort* (São Paulo: Cultura Cristã, n.d.).

[?]: *Bíblia de Estudo de Herança Reformada* (São Paulo and Barueri: Cultura Cristã e Sociedade bíblica do Brasil, n.d.).

Russian Editions

1997: Каноны Дортского Синода (Москва [Moscow]: ИКАР, 1997).

2003: Вера Наших Отцов (Москва [Moscow]: ИКАР, 2003) [trans. of Homer Hoeksema, *Voice of the Fathers*; text and commentary].
Reprint: Москва [Moscow]: ИКАР, 2005

Croatian Editions

2007: Jasmin Milić, *Kanoni sa Sinode u Dordrechtu 1618–1619* (Osijek: Kršćanski centar "Dobroga Pastira," 2007), 76 pp.
Reprint: Osijek: Kršćanski centar "Dobroga Pastira," 2017.

Korean Editions

1984: 개혁주의 신앙고백집 (서울 [Seoul]: 생명의 말씀사, 1984) (김의환 편역).
Reprint: 서울 [Seoul]: 생명의 말씀사, 2003.

2012: 코르넬리스 프롱크, 도르트 신조 강해 (서울 [Seoul]: 그 책의 사람들, 2012).

2012: 개혁파 교회의 고백: 3대 일치신조: 벨직 신앙고백서, 하이델베르크 요리문답, 도르트 신조. (서울 [Seoul]: 히스토리앤러브, 2012).

2013: 도르트 신조 (1619) (서울 [Seoul]: 예영커뮤니케이션, 2013).

2014: 김홍만, 52주 스터디 도르트 신조 (서울 [Seoul]: 생명의 말씀사, 2014).

2015: 개혁주의 신앙고백 (서울 [Seoul]: 부흥과개혁사, 2015).

2016: 클라렌스 바우만, 도르트 신경해설 (서울 [Seoul]: 솔로몬, 2016).

2017: 도르트 신조 노트 (수원 [Suwon-si]: 그 책의 사람들, 2017).

2018: 도르트 신조 (휴대용) (수원 [Suwon-si]: 그 책의 사람들, 2018).

2019: 마키다 요시카즈, 도르트총회, 기독교 신앙을 정의하다 (인천 [Incheon]: 아벨서원, 2019).

2019: 개혁주의 신앙고백 (수호해야 할 교회의 유산) (서울 [Seoul]: 대학생성경읽기선교회, 2019).

Mandarin Editions

1957: 湯清, 歷代基督教信條 (中國: 金陵神學院及基督教輔僑出版社, 1957).
　　Reprints: 尼科斯, 歷代基督教信條 (香港 [Hong Kong]: 基督教文藝, 1989), 202–13; 香港 [Hong Kong]: 基督教文藝出版社, 2008; 中國: 宗教文化出版社, 2010; 北京 [Beijing]: 宗教文化出版社, 2012.

1966: 任以撒, 教義信條 (台北 [Taipei]: 基督改革宗教會台灣宣教區會, 1966), 57–73.

1993: 趙中輝, 歷代教會信條精選 (台灣: 基督教改革宗翻譯社, 1993).
　　Reprint: 趙中輝, 歷代教會信條精選 (台灣: 基督教改革宗翻譯社, 2002).

1998: 信仰的根基 (Portage, Mich.: China Reformation Publishers, 1998), 131–56.

2011: 基督教六大信仰宣言 (台灣: 環球聖經公會, 2011), 39–54.

2013: 王志勇, 多特信条译注 (香港 [Hong Kong]: 雅和博圣约书院; 美国: 雅和博传道会, 2013), 85 pp.

2017: 马丁博士, 王志勇 编译, 诗篇颂扬, The Chinese Psalter (Kruiningen: "The Chinese Translators" of Biblical, Reformed Literature, 2017), 132–93.

Japanese Edition

2012: 牧田吉和、「ドルトレヒト信仰規準研究：歴史的背景と信仰規準とその神学的意義」、カルヴァンとカルヴィニズム研究所　（神戸 [Kobe]: 神戸改革派神学校、2012), 83–136.

Appendix 3

Bibliography of Sinnema Writings

Writings concerning the Synod of Dordt

"Johannes Bogerman's First Draft of Chapter One of the Canons of Dordt." In *Gevarieerde Oogst: Vriendenbundel voor Erik A. de Boer*, edited by Ad de Bruijne, Rob van Houwelingen, and Jan Klok, 114–25. Amsterdam: Buijten & Schipperheijn Motief, 2024.

De Graaf, Abram, ed. *A História de Dordt*. Vol. 1. Maceió: Graaf Editora, 2024. Collection of five articles.

General editor, with Christian Moser, Erik A. de Boer, and Herman J. Selderhuis. *Acta et Documenta Synodi Nationalis Dordrechtanae (1618–1619)*. Vol. 2/1, *The Convening of the Synod of Dordt*. Göttingen: Vandenhoeck and Ruprecht, 2023. Wrote part of "Introduction: The States General and the Convening of the Synod of Dordt," xxix–xlix.

"Doctrinal Dissension among Delegates at the Synod of Dordt (1618–1619)." In *A Landmark in Turbulent Times: The Meaning and Relevance of the Synod of Dordt (1618–1619)*, edited by Henk van den Belt, Klaas-Willem de Jong, and Willem van Vlastuin, 173–91. Göttingen: Vandenhoeck and Ruprecht, 2022.

"Snip the TULIP." *Christian Courier*, September 21, 2022, 5.

"Church and State Relations at the Synod of Dordt." In *The Synod of Dort: Historical, Theological, and Experiential Perspectives*, edited by Joel R. Beeke and Martin I. Klauber, 133–48. Göttingen: Vandenhoeck and Ruprecht, 2020.

"The Three Forms of Unity," with Lyle D. Bierma. In *Oxford Handbook of Reformed Theology*, edited by Michael Allen and Scott R. Swain, 245–49. Oxford: Oxford University Press, 2020.

Review of *De Dordtse Kerkorde 1619: Ontwikkeling, Context en Theologie*, by Adriana van Harten-Tip. *Calvin Theological Journal* 55, no. 2 (Nov. 2020): 401–4.

"Procedural Wrangling in the Remonstrant Case at the Synod of Dordt (1618–1619)." In *More than Luther: The Reformation and the Rise of Pluralism in Europe*, edited by Karla Boersma and Herman J. Selderhuis, 289–306. Göttingen: Vandenhoeck and Ruprecht, 2019.

"The Doctrine of Election at the Synod of Dordt (1618–1619)." In *The Doctrine of Election in Reformed Perspective: Historical and Theological Investigations of the Synod of Dordt 1618–1619*, edited by Frank van der Pol, 115–35. Göttingen: Vandenhoeck and Ruprecht, 2019.

Review of *Britain and the Bestandstwisten: The Causes, Course and Consequences of British Involvement in the Dutch Religious and Political Disputes of the Early Seventeenth Century*, by Eric Platt. *Calvin Theological Journal* 53, no. 2 (Nov. 2018): 490–93.

"The Documents of the Synod of Dort (1618–1619)—A New Edition." *Unio cum Christo* 4, no. 2 (Oct. 2018): 163–73.

"Are the Canons of Dordt a True Reflection of Calvin's Doctrine of Predestination?" *In die Skriflig/In Luce Verbi* 52, no. 2 (2018). doi: 10.4102/ids.v52i2.2347.

"A Virtual Tour of the Synod of Dort, 1618–1619." *Clarion*, April 20, 2018, 216–18.

"Remembering the Synod of Dordt." *Christian Courier*, February 27, 2017, 4–5.

General editor, with Christian Moser and Herman J. Selderhuis. *Acta et Documenta Synodi Nationalis Dordrechtanae (1618–1619)*. Vol. 2/2, *Early Sessions of the Synod of Dordt*. Göttingen: Vandenhoeck and Ruprecht, 2017. Wrote "Introduction," xxi–xxviii.

General editor, with Christian Moser and Herman J. Selderhuis. *Acta et Documenta Synodi Nationalis Dordrechtanae (1618–1619)*. Vol. 1, *Acta of the Synod of Dordt*. Göttingen: Vandenhoeck and Ruprecht, 2015. Wrote "Introduction to the Acta Authentica, Acta Contracta and Printed Acta," xxxix–lii; edited "Acta Authentica," "Acta Synodi Nationalis: First Printed Edition," and "Acta Contracta."

"The French Reformed Churches, Arminianism, and the Synod of Dort (1618–19)." In *The Theology of the French Reformed Churches: From Henri IV to the Revocation of the Edict of Nantes*, edited by Martin I. Klauber, 98–136. Grand Rapids: Reformation Heritage Books, 2014.

"The Attempt to Establish a Chair in Practical Theology at Leiden University (1618–1626)." In *Church and School in Early Modern Protestantism: Studies in Honor of Richard A. Muller on the Maturation of a Theological Tradition*, edited by Jordan Ballor, David Sytsma, and Jason Zuidema, 415–41. Leiden: Brill, 2013.

"Calvin and the Canons of Dordt (1619)." *Church History and Religious Culture* 91, no. 1–2 (Jan. 2011): 87–103.

"The Drafting of the Canons of Dordt: A Preliminary Survey of Early Drafts and Related Documents." In *Revisiting the Synod of Dordt (1618–1619)*, edited by Aza Goudriaan and Fred van Lieburg, 291–311. Leiden: Brill, 2011.

"The Canons of Dordt: From Judgment on Arminianism to Confessional Standard." In *Revisiting the Synod of Dordt (1618–1619)*, edited by Aza Goudriaan and Fred van Lieburg, 313–33. Leiden: Brill, 2011.

"The Origin of the Form of Subscription in the Dutch Reformed Tradition." *Calvin Theological Journal* 42 (2007): 256–82.

"TULIP Acronym Misrepresents Canons." *Christian Courier*, November 15, 1999, 5.

"The Canons of Dort." In *Psalter Hymnal Handbook*, edited by Emily R. Brink and Bert Polman, 824–27. Grand Rapids: CRC Publications, 1998.

"The Second Sunday Service in the Early Dutch Reformed Tradition." *Calvin Theological Journal* 32 (1997): 298–333.

> Spanish translation: *El Segundo Servicio Dominical en la Tradición Holandesa Temprana*. Ciudad de Guatemala [Guatemala City]: Dort Publicaciones, [2023].

"Q & A." *The Banner*, May 30, 1994, 14 [re: CD I, 17].

"Lambert Daneau," "The Remonstrants," and "The Synod of Dort." In *Encyclopedia of the Reformed Faith*, edited by Donald K. McKim, 95–96, 108–9, 317. Louisville and Edinburgh: Westminster/John Knox Press, 1992.

"The Synod of Dort." Reprinted in *The Westminster Handbook to Reformed Theology*, edited by Donald K. McKim, 62–63. Louisville, London, Leiden: Westminster/John Knox Press, 2001.

With Al Wolters. "Serpents and Commas in the Canons." *The Banner*, June 9, 1986, 8–9.

With Al Wolters. Co-translator from Latin of "The Canons of Dort." In *1985 Acts of Synod* of the Christian Reformed Church, 359–82. Grand Rapids: Christian Reformed Church in North America, 1985. Reprinted in *The Psalter Hymnal*, 926–49. Grand Rapids: CRC Publications, 1987. Reprinted in *Ecumenical Creeds and Reformed Confessions*, 122–45. Grand Rapids: CRC Publications, 1988.

"The Issue of Reprobation at the Synod of Dort (1618–19) in Light of the History of this Doctrine." PhD diss., University of St. Michael's College, Toronto, 1985.

"The Women of the Synod of Dort." *Link*, December 1981, 16.

"Preach the Catechism or Preach the Word?" *Renewal*, April 29, 1981, 4–5.

Other Writings

Review of *A Gift from England: William Ames and His Polemical Discourse against Dutch Arminianism*, by Takayuki Yagi. *Calvin Theological Journal* 59 (Nov. 2024): 448-52.

"Creative Farmers: Two Dutch-Canadian Innovations That Helped Stop Soil Drifting." *Christian Courier*, May 6, 2024, 8, 21.

"The First Edition of William Ames's *Medulla Sacrae Theologiae* (1623) as a Disputation Cycle." *Calvin Theological Journal* 58, no. 2 (Nov. 2023): 233–64.

"From Nijverdal to Nieuw Nijverdal: The Immigration of Nijverdallers as Pioneers to Southern Alberta," 2021. Available at Academia.edu.

With Heather Sinnema. "How Blue Island Got its Name," 2021. Available at Academia.edu.

With James C. Schaap. "Only Democrat Standing Has Friesland Roots." *Sioux County Capital-Democrat*, February 13, 2020, 2.

"Dryland Strip Farming and the V-Blade: Dutch Canadian Innovations that Helped Stop Soil Drifting." In *Dutch Muck—and Much More: Dutch Americans in Farming, Religion, Art and Astronomy*, edited by Earl Wm. Kennedy, Donald A. Luidens, and David Zwart, 85–108. Holland, Mich.: Van Raalte Press, 2019.

Van Nijverdal naar Nieuw Nijverdal: De Emigratie van Nijverdallers als Pioners naar Alberta in Canada. Hellendoorn: St. Noabers van 'n Oalen Griezen, 2019.

"A Lament." In Paul W. Swets, *The Coming Glory: Hope Now for Life After Death*, 139–45. Rapid City, S. Dak.: CrossLink Publishing, 2019.

"Monarch, the Home of Strip Farming" and "The Williamson-Kooy Blade." In *Nobleford Monarch History*. Vol. 2, *Sun, Wind and Soil*, 467–69. Nobleford: Nobleford Centennial Society, 2018.

"Foreword." In Joel R. Beeke, *Debated Issues in Sovereign Predestination: Early Lutheran Predestination, Calvinian Reprobation, and Variations in Geneven Lapsarianism*, 7–8. Göttingen: Vandenhoeck and Ruprecht, 2017.

With Carla Sinnema. "Sharing One Date: Halloween or Reformation Day?" *The Holland Sentinel*, October 23, 2015, A7–8.

"One Soldier's Experience of War in the Pacific: Sgt. Ernest Gerritsma's Diaries and Letters in the Second World War." In *Dutch Americans and War: United States and Abroad*, edited by Robert P. Swierenga, Nella Kennedy, and Lisa Zylstra. 201–19. Holland, Mich.: Van Raalte Press, 2014.

With Henk van den Belt. "The *Synopsis Purioris Theologicae* (1625) as a Disputation Cycle." *Church History and Religious Culture* 92, no. 4 (Jan. 2012): 501–33.

"American Influences on the First Dutch Settlement in Alberta." In *Across Borders: Dutch Migration to North America and Australia*, edited by Jacob E. Nyenhuis, Suzanne M. Sinke, and Robert P. Swierenga, 63–72. Holland, Mich.: Association for the Advancement of Dutch-American Studies, 2010.

"Calvin's View of Reprobation." In *Calvin for Today*, edited by Joel R. Beeke, 115–36. Grand Rapids: Reformation Heritage Books, 2009.

If We Begin with Christ: The Founding of Trinity Christian College, 1952–1960. Palos Heights, Ill.: Trinity Christian College, 2009.

"How to Use the Bible in Christian Scholarship." Academic Insert in IAPCHE *Contact*, June 2008.

"Beza's View of Predestination in Historical Perspective." In *Théodore de Bèze (1519–1605): Actes du Colloque de Genève, Septembre 2005*, edited by Irena Backus, 219–39. Geneva: Librairie Droz, 2007.

"God's Eternal Decree and Its Temporal Execution: The Role of This Distinction in Theodore Beza's Theology." In *Adaptations of Calvinism in Reformation Europe: Essays in Honour of Brian G. Armstrong*, edited by Mack P. Holt, 55–78. Aldershot: Ashgate, 2007.

"Johann Jungnitz on the Use of Aristotelian Logic in Theology." In *Späthumanismus und reformierte Konfession*, edited by Christoph Strohm, Joseph S. Freedman, and Herman J. Selderhuis, 127–52. Tübingen: Mohr Siebeck, 2006.

"Calvin and Beza: The Role of the Decree-Execution Distinction in Their Theologies." In *Calvinus Evangelii Propugnator: Calvin, Champion of the Gospel: Papers Presented at the International Congress on Calvin*

Research, Seoul, 1998, edited by David F. Wright, A. N. S. Lane, and Jon Balserak, 191–207. Grand Rapids: Calvin Studies Society, 2006.

"Rev. S. A. Schilstra: An Early (American) Promoter of Dutch Immigration to the Canadian Prairies, 1902–1905." In *Dutch Immigrants on the Plains*, edited by Paul Fessler, Hubert R. Krygsman, and Robert P. Swierenga, 124–38. Holland, Mich.: Association for the Advancement of Dutch American Studies, 2006.

Editor/translator. *The First Dutch Settlement in Alberta: Letters from the Pioneer Years, 1903–14*. Calgary: University of Calgary Press, 2005.

Pioneer Church Life: The Beginnings of the First Christian Reformed Church in Canada (1903–1911). Nobleford, Alberta: Rocky Coulee Press, 2005.

"History of the Granum Christian Reformed Church." In *100 Years of God's Grace: Granum Christian Reformed Church, 1905–2005*, 27–62. Lethbridge: Warwick Publishing, 2005.

"The Origin of the First Christian Reformed Church in Canada." *Christian Courier*, November 7, 2005): 10–11, 17.

"From Nijverdal to Nieuw Nijverdal: The Centennial of a Dutch Colony." *Christian Courier*, April 12, 2004, 14–15.

"Brutality in *The Passion*." *Christian Courier*, April 12, 2004, 5.

Editor, with Robert P. Swierenga and Hans Krabbendam. *The Dutch in Urban America*. Holland, Mich.: Association for the Advancement of Dutch American Studies, 2004.

"Beginnings of the First Dutch Settlement in Alberta." *Christian Courier*, July 7, 2003, 10–11.

"A History of the Park Lane Christian Reformed Church." In *God's Enduring Faithfulness: Fifty Years of the Park Lane Christian Reformed Church, 1953–2003*, edited by Donald Sinnema, 4–38. Evergreen Park, Ill.: Park Lane Fiftieth Anniversary Committee, 2003.

Review of *Reformation and Scholasticism: An Ecumenical Enterprise*, edited by Willem J. van Asselt and Eef Dekker. *Calvin Theological Journal* 37, no. 1 (Apr. 2002): 157–60.

"Beyond Integration to Holistic Christian Scholarship." In *Marginal Resistance: Essays Dedicated to John C. Vander Stelt*, edited by John H. Kok, 187–207. Sioux Center, Iowa: Dordt College Press, 2001.

"The Story of Chicago Christian College (1931–1937)." In *The Dutch Adapting in North America*, edited by Richard Harms, 9–17. Grand Rapids: Association for the Advancement of Dutch American Studies, 2001.

"Hugo Grotius." In *Biographical Dictionary of Christian Theologians*, edited by Patrick W. Carey and Joseph T. Lienhard, 229–30. Westport, Conn. and London: Greenwood Press, 2000.

"Dutch American Newspapers and the Network of Early Dutch Immigrant Communities." In *Dutch Enterprise: Alive and Well in North America*, edited by Larry J. Wagenaar and Robert P. Swierenga, 43–56. Holland, Mich.: Association for the Advancement of Dutch American Studies, 1999.

"The Distinction between Scholastic and Popular: Andreas Hyperius and Early Reformed Orthodoxy." In *Protestant Scholasticism: Essays in Reassessment*, edited by Carl R. Trueman and R. S. Clark, 127–43. Carlisle: Paternoster Press, 1999.

"Sliekers Retires from Dutch Heritage Center." *Trinity Christian College Bulletin*, Fall 1997, 17.

"In Memory of Richard Prince (1922–1996): Trinity Founder, Administrator, Professor." *Trinity Christian College Bulletin*, Fall 1996, 17.

No Rest in the Land: A Study of the Book of Judges. Toronto: Institute for Christian Studies, 1995.

"Antoine De Chandieu's Call for a Scholastic Reformed Theology (1580)." In *Later Calvinism: International Perspectives*, edited by W. Fred Graham, 159–90. Kirksville, Mo.: Sixteenth Century Journal Publishers, 1994.

"The Reformed Church Role in Trinity's Founding." *Trinity Christian College Bulletin*, Summer 1994, 13.

"The Discipline of Ethics in Early Reformed Orthodoxy." *Calvin Theological Journal* 28, no. 1 (Apr. 1993): 10–44.

"What Do We Mean by 'Reformed Perspective'?" *Trinity Christian College Bulletin*, Fall 1993, 4–7.

"Heritage Notes: Foreign Language Press Survey." *Trinity Christian College Bulletin*, Summer 1991, 18.

"Aristotle and Early Reformed Orthodoxy: Moments of Accommodation and Antithesis." In *Christianity and the Classics*, edited by Wendy E. Helleman, 119–48. Lanham, Md., New York, London: University Press of America, 1990.

Review of *Calviniana: Ideas and Influence of Jean Calvin*, edited by Robert V. Schnucker. *Sixteenth Century Journal* 20, no. 2 (Summer 1989): 365–66.

"Heritage Notes: The Chicago Messenger (1934–1937)." *Trinity Christian College Bulletin*, June/July 1989, 4.

"Heritage Notes: Chicago Christian College." *Trinity Christian College Bulletin*, April 1989, 5.

"The Year the Dutch Conquered Acadia." *Calvinist Contact*, February 17, 1989, 10–11. Reprinted in the *Fredericton Daily Gleaner*, April 1, 1989.

"The Case of the Wayward Organist." *Calvinist Contact*, May 15, 1987, 12.

"Changes in Households of Faith." *The Church Communicating*, April 1986, 3–4.

"Introducing Calvin CRC's New Assistant Minister and Family." *The Church Communicating*, October 1985, 3.

Review of *The Reformation of 1834*, edited by Peter Y. De Jong and Nelson D. Kloosterman. *Calvinist Contact*, December 21, 1984, 20.

"The New Belgic Confession Translation: Which Version?" *Calvinist Contact*, June 10, 1983, 11.

"Classis Toronto Not Entirely Without Grounds." *Calvinist Contact*, May 13, 1983, 3.

Review of *The History of the Reformation and Other Ecclesiastical Transactions in and about the Low Countries*, by Geeraert Brandt. *The Banner*, June 7, 1982, 20.

"A Seventeenth Century Call for Deaconesses." *Renewal*, May 27, 1981, 4–5.

"Luther and Calvin on Christianity and Politics." *Tydskrif vir Christelike Wetenskap* 16 (1980): 1–24. Reprinted in *Confessing Christ in Doing Politics: Essays on Christian Political Thought and Action*, edited by Bennie van der Walt, 72–103. Potchefstroom: Institute for Reformational Studies, 1995.

> Italian translation by Salvatore Loria: "Lutero e Calvino su cristianesimo e política," May 24, 2024, https://salvatoreloria.it/lutero-e-calvino-su-cristianesimo-e-politica-di-donald-sinnema-disponibile-in-pdf-in-italiano/.

"Reprobation and the Nature of Biblical Testimony." *Renewal*, May 28, 1980, 3.

Reclaiming the Land: A Study of the Book of Joshua. Toronto: Curriculum Development Centre, 1977; second printing, 1979 (Teacher edition and student edition).

"Wedding Celebration." *Vanguard*, May–June 1974, 11–14.

With Bill Kieft. "Lawing-up in Deuteronomy." *Credo*, June–July 1970, 27–28.

Name Index

Abbot, George, 157–60, 190
Acronius, Ruardus, 344, 353
Aerssen, Cornelis van, 217, 223, 225, 235
Aetsma, Rienck, 225
Allport, Josiah, 426
Alsted, Johann H., 16, 223, 250, 252, 255–56, 274, 443, 451
Alting, Heinrich, 16, 97, 101–2, 261, 449
Alting, Menso, 102
Amersfoordt, Jacob, 469
Ames, William, 112, 147, 251, 256, 272–76, 327, 441, 458
Andriesz, Johan, 205
Angelocrator, Daniel, 73
Appeldoorn, Sweer van, 240–41
Aristotle, 282
Arminius, Jacobus, 1, 2, 54–55, 57, 100, 110–11, 117, 119, 123, 383–84, 403, 415–16, 423, 426
Armstrong, Brian, 248
Augusti, Johann, 465
Augustine of Hippo, 316
Aymon, Jean, 477
Aysma, Taecke, 451

Bakhuizen van den Brink, J. N., 466, 474
Balcanqual, Walter, 16, 137, 147–48, 150, 156, 159–61, 163–64, 176, 189–91, 223, 229, 260–61, 266, 269, 273–74, 280, 400, 404, 443–44, 450
Barlaeus, Caspar, 112, 118
Barrett, Matthew, 485
Bavinck, Herman, 472–73
Baxter, Richard, 422, 426
Becius, Johannes, 410
Beck, Friedrich, 486
Beck, Sebastian, 16
Beeke, Joel, 483–84, 488
Bellarmine, Robert, 257–58, 273, 276
Berchem, Loys van, 205
Bercke, Johan, 219
Berghuis, Freerk, 475
Bergius, Conrad, 255
Bertius, Petrus, 17, 454
Beza, Theodore, 49, 110, 151, 250–51, 280, 283–84, 321–22, 324, 326–27, 338–42, 344–46, 349–51, 353–55, 359, 383, 417

Name Index

Bisterfeld, Johannes, 223, 229–30, 443, 448–49, 453
Bocardus, Johann, 410
Böckel, Ernst, 486
Bodeman, Friedrich, 486
Boer, C. den, 474
Boetselar, Gijsbert van den, 223
Boettner, Lorraine, 430
Bogerman, Johannes, passim
Boquinus, Petrus, 101–2
Borrius, Adrianus, 121
Bos, T., 473
Bouckhorst, Nicolaes van den, 240–41
Brandius, Henricus, 117–18
Brandt, Geeraert, 144
Bredenhof, Wes, 484
Brederode, Walraven van, 227, 234
Breeijen, P. den, 475
Breitinger, Johann J., 144, 148, 150, 274, 363, 373, 378, 398
Brès, Guido de, 51–52, 61–62, 69–70
Brouckerus, Fredericus, 344
Brownell, Thomas Church, 427
Bucanus, Gulielmus, 344, 346
Bucer, Martin, 344
Bullinger, Heinrich, 110, 279
Busch, Eberhard, 486
Busschoff, Bernardus, 344

Cairns, Earle, 430
Calvin, Jean, 110, 267, 289, 315–36, 337–61, 383, 417, 423, 428
Campen, Jacob van, 231
Canin, Isaac, 204, 243,
Canin, Jacob Jansz, 204
Canterus, Lambertus, 457–58
Carleton, Dudley, 137, 150–51, 156–58, 160, 175–76, 189–91, 218, 223, 227, 242, 261, 452

Carleton, George, 6, 16, 18–19, 63, 120, 126, 142, 145, 149, 153, 156–59, 164, 175–76, 189, 191, 259, 268, 278, 369, 398–400, 448–51, 453, 455, 458
Chamier, Daniel, 252
Chandieu (Sadeel), Antoine, 251–52, 255–56, 274, 276
Civilis, Gratianus, 344
Cock, Hendrik de, 469
Colonius, Daniel, 69, 72
Copleston, Edward, 425
Cornelisz, Arent, 53
Corvinus (Arnoldi), Johannes, 54, 93, 112, 118, 416
Crocius, Ludwig, 17, 148–49, 161, 255–56, 267–68, 448, 451, 454
Cruciger, Georg, 16, 73, 450

Dam, H. van, 475
Dammannus, Sebastiaan, 9, 22, 224, 344, 347–49, 353, 371, 377, 405
Damsté, E. R., 474
Daneau, Lambertus, 250, 252, 274, 341, 343–44
Dankbaar, W., 474
Dathenus, Petrus, 81–82, 291
Davenant, John, 16, 63, 121, 145, 156–60, 261, 369–70, 426, 449–50, 453
De Coulogne, Daniel, 314
De Dannoi, Arnouldt, 314
De Haan, M., 476
De Jong, P. Y., 482
De la Tour, Henri, 417
Delden, Arthur van, 484
Dennison Jr., James, 485
De Pours, Jeremias, 439
De Young, Kevin, 485
Dibbets, Johannes, 312
Diodati, Jean, 17, 19, 126, 261, 369–70, 398, 442, 453

Name Index

Donia, Keimpe, 458
Donner, J. H., 471
Donteclock, Reginaldus, 344, 346–51, 353
Doubleth, Johan, 220
Duchess of Tremullio, 441
Du Moulin, Pierre, 18, 399, 417, 449, 458
Dunganus, Cornelius, 344, 348
Du Plessis-Mornay, Philippe, 393, 446
Du Pré, Esaie, 314
Du Toit, Stefanus, 472
Dwinglo, Bernardus, 93, 164, 455

Eglisemmius, Georgius, 275,
Episcopius, Simon, 6, 12, 15, 17, 30, 34–36, 39, 45–48, 54, 93, 112, 118–19, 121, 179–80, 182, 184, 222–23, 263–64, 383, 439, 442, 445, 447
Erasmus, Desiderius, 143
Erpenius, Thomas, 461
Essen, Henrich van, 224, 233, 240

Fabricius, Georgius, 230, 453
Fatio, Olivier, 478
Faukelius, Hermannus, 9, 19, 26, 53, 69, 74, 89–90, 126, 224, 227, 241, 366, 369
Feenstra, J. G., 473
Feenstra, Peter, 483
Fonseca, Pedro da, 276
Frederici, Isaac, 93–94, 230, 446, 452
Frederick III (Palatinate), 101–3

Gabriel, Peter, 81
Georg Willem (Marquis of Brandenburg), 230
Geselius, Cornelius, 344, 348–49

Geysteranus, Johannes, 21, 31, 413, 457
Geysteranus, Petrus, 21, 31, 413, 457
Girod, Gordon, 481
Goad, Thomas, 63, 153, 156, 159, 227, 274, 376, 448, 453
Gockinga, Scato, 225
Goclenius, Rudolphus, 16, 73, 121, 145, 147, 261, 266–67, 273, 275, 381, 447, 451
Goddefroy, M. J., 472
Godfrey, W. Robert, 485
Gomarus, Franciscus, 2, 5, 16–17, 71, 89, 92, 112–13, 120–21, 125, 134, 139, 141, 143–45, 147, 149–55, 164–65, 189, 253, 256–57, 260–61, 266, 268–69, 274, 284, 344–46, 348, 351, 353, 375, 381, 383, 398, 444, 448–53
Gootjes, Nicolaas, 76
Goswinius, Thomas, 93–95
Graaf, Abram de, 489
Gregorii, Martinus, 60, 100, 177, 184, 219, 233–34, 439, 459
Grevinchoven, Nicolaas, 54, 112, 118, 440–41
Grieken, M. van, 472
Goulart Jr., Simon, 440–41

Hagen, Hendrik, 220
Hales, John, 85, 137–38, 143, 145, 163–64, 176, 260, 397, 440
Hall, Joseph, 227, 259, 316, 440, 448
Hall, Peter, 479
Hanekom, T. N., 487
Heinsius, Daniel, 7, 91, 173–74, 203, 207, 218–19, 226, 229, 233–34, 237, 239, 241, 243
Hel, Hendrick van, 440–41
Hemert, Johan van, 220, 224, 232

Heylyn, Peter, 423–25
Heyngius, Theodorus, 62, 69
Hilten, Antonie van, 312
Hoekema, Anthony, 482
Hoeksema, Homer, 482, 489
Hollinger, Henricus, 93, 188
Homerus, Wigboldus, 441
Hommius, Festus, 9, 22, 54, 62, 69, 75–76, 112, 140, 207, 227, 241, 271–72, 274, 344–45, 372, 377, 405, 447, 457
Hoorn, S. A. van den, 471
Hotchkiss, Valerie, 484
Hulsius, Antonius, 477
Hyde, Daniel, 484–85
Hyperius, Andreas, 254

Irhoven, Wilhelmus van, 469
Isbrants, Hieronymus, 234
Isselburg, Heinrich, 17, 161, 453
Itterzon, Gerrit P. van, 144

James I (England), 3, 64, 160, 171, 175, 190, 209, 218, 223, 227, 233, 239, 242, 244, 259, 399, 417, 419
Janssen, Jan, 312
Jonge de, Bonifacius, 225
Junius, Franciscus, 252, 274, 276, 356

Keckermann, Bartholomäus, 270, 341
Kersten, G. H., 473
Kimedoncius, Jacob, 344
Klüsener, P., 474
Koch, Johann, 274
Koop, E., 475
Kötze, J. J., 470
Kuyper, Abraham, 304, 471–73
Kuyper, H. H., 75, 206
Kuypers, Gerardus, 465

Lasco, Johannes a, 290
Latius, Johannes, 73, 139, 369
Laurentius, Gaspar, 54
Leicester, Earl of, 169–70
Lenselink, H., 475
Leo, Henricus, 93, 188, 446
Lind van Wijngaarden, J. D. de, 472
Lodensteyn, Johannes à, 54
Lodewijk, Willem, 224–25, 227–29
Lolingius, Johannes, 441
Lombard, Peter, 156, 250
Louis III (France), 6, 18
Lubbertus, Sibrandus, 5, 16–17, 74, 113, 120–21, 126, 139–40, 142, 147–49, 151–52, 164–65, 189, 251, 256–58, 260–61, 266–71, 274, 276–77, 344, 347, 369, 375, 381 439–40, 448, 451–55, 457
Lucas, Ritzius, 84
Luther, Martin, 344, 354, 423
Lydius, Balthasar, 27, 89, 176, 274, 373, 439, 443, 462

Maccovius, Johannes, 21–22, 31, 140, 265, 270–77, 344–46, 457–58
Manmaker, Adriaan, 221
Marbach, Johann, 102
Marbault, Pierre, 393
Marloratus, Augustin, 344
Marra, Claudio, 489
Martinius, Matthias, 17, 138–39, 143–50, 156, 161, 164, 189, 255–56, 266–69, 274, 449–52
Matthisius, Assuerus, 93–95
Maurice, Prince of Orange, 3, 4, 27, 30, 171, 173, 175–76, 187–88, 223–25, 227–29, 234–35, 241–42, 417, 449, 455
Mayer, Wolfgang, 17, 261, 274
McAfee, Cleland Boyd, 336, 429–30

Name Index

McGeown, Martyn, 485
Mehen (Mehnius), Eilardus van, 73, 274, 344, 353, 373
Meijering, M., 473
Melanchthon, Philip, 265, 279, 358, 454
Milić, Jasmin, 489
Milton, Anthony, 484
Molenaar, Dirk, 470
Montagu, Richard, 64
Müller, E. F. Karl, 465
Muller, Richard A., 249
Musculus, Wolfgang, 356
Muys van Holy, Hugo, 201, 221, 224–27, 229, 231–33, 239–40, 242–43

Nanninga, Jan, 240–41
Naunton, Robert, 160, 190, 209
Neal, Daniel, 426
Neranus, Samuel, 93
Nichols, James, 426
Niellius, Carolus, 93, 121, 180–81, 230, 264, 452
Niemeyer, Hermann, 465
Nixon, Leroy, 481

Oldenbarnevelt, Johan van, 3, 4, 23, 30, 170, 173, 195, 459
Olevianus, Caspar, 102, 327

Palmer, Edwin, 430
Pareus, David, 18, 147–48, 267–68, 273, 327, 344, 416, 451–52
Parker, Thomas, 270–71, 274–77
Pauw, Reinier, 224
Pelikan, Jaroslav, 484
Perkins, William, 151, 154, 284, 327, 344–46, 348, 351, 354, 383
Peterson, Henry, 482
Pijnacker, Philippus, 40, 93, 444–45

Piscator, Johannes, 25, 49, 65, 71, 142, 327, 340–47, 349–51, 353–54, 361, 459
Plancius, Petrus, 112
Polanus, Amandus, 454, 344, 347
Polyander, Johannes, 5, 16–17, 19, 89, 113, 120, 126, 152, 241, 280, 314, 369–71, 445, 449, 451
Poppius, Eduard, 93, 444, 450, 455
Pronk, Cornelis, 483
Prosper of Aquitaine, 316

Quick, John, 478

Randolf, John, 465
Rennecherus, Hermann, 344
Revius, Jacobus, 344, 347
Rijckewaert, Theophilus, 93, 442
Rodingenus, Johannes, 26, 446, 461
Rolandus, Jacobus, 9, 19, 126, 241, 369,
Rossouw, P., 488
Rutgers, F. L., 472–73
Rütimeyer, Markus, 373

Salvart, Jean François, 53
Sapma, Dominicus, 93, 188, 230–32, 452–53
Schaff, Philip, 427, 465, 480
Schilders, Richard, 104
Scholte, Hendrik, 469
Schotlerus, Johannes, 25, 451, 453, 459
Schotte, Simon, 434
Scott, Thomas, 424–26, 479
Scultetus, Abraham, 16–17, 19, 96, 101–2, 121, 126, 139, 148–51, 160, 164, 261, 267, 269, 274, 369, 375, 398–99, 416, 443–44, 448–49, 451–52, 455
Shuttenius, Everardus, 468
Sibelius, Caspar, 101–2, 144, 257, 364, 378, 459

Silvius, 219
Sixti, Rippertus, 344, 351
Sluijs, C. A. van der, 475
Smoutius, Adriaan, 344, 347–49
Socinus, Faustus, 103, 453
Sohn, Georg, 254, 344, 353
Stapfer, Marcus, 452
Stein, Paul, 16, 73, 274, 450
Sturm, Johannes, 341, 344, 351, 353
Suárez, Francisco, 273, 276
Szegedinus, Stephanus, 344, 349

Textor, Bernhard, 344
Thysius, Antonius, 5, 16, 53, 62–63, 69, 89, 113, 120, 141, 149, 152, 261, 268–69, 274, 344–45, 348–51, 449, 451–52
Tijckmaekers, Nicolaes, 409
Tilenus, Daniel, 415–26, 465
Tomline, George, 424–25
Toorenenbergen, J. J. van, 470
Tossanus, Daniel, 102, 250
Tossanus, Paul, 16, 101–2, 120, 448
Trelcatius, Lucas Jr., 252, 274
Trigland, Jacobus, 19, 126, 257, 279, 284, 343–44, 347–51, 369, 398
Tronchin, Théodore, 17, 132, 364, 452

Udemans, Godefridus, 69, 72, 89, 398
Urbanus, Johannes, 344
Ursinus, Zacharias, 101–2, 265, 316, 344, 353
Ussher, James, 159
Uytenbogaert, Johannes, 27, 100, 112, 419, 446

Vail, William, 429–30
Vander Lugt, Gerrit, 482
Venator, Adolf, 54
Vennema, Cornelis, 483
Verboom, W., 475

Vermigli, Peter Martyr, 327, 344, 346, 349–50, 417
Vezekius, Bernerus, 93
Vinke, Hendrik, 465
Voetius, Gisbertus, 198, 210, 274, 373, 419
Vogelaar, C. 484
Vogelius, Hieronymus, 344
Volbergen, Thyman van, 220
Vorstius, Conradus, 17, 22, 31, 202, 233–36, 244, 274, 276, 413, 452–53, 458
Vosbergius, Josias, 398
Voscuyl, Everardus, 25, 451, 453, 459
Vroegindeweij, L., 475

Wagenaar, L., 473
Walaeus, Antonius, 6, 16, 19, 113, 121, 126, 152, 316, 369, 398, 449, 452
Walker, Anna, 440
Wallesius, Johannes, 26, 461
Ward, Samuel, 16, 63, 121, 145, 156–60, 365, 370, 449–50
Waterland, Daniel, 426
Watery, Daniel, 205
Welsingius, Isaacus, 26, 54, 446, 461
Whitaker, William, 154, 344–45, 353
William of Orange, 4
Witt, Jacob de, 208, 221
Wollebius, Johannes, 282
Womock, Laurence, 421–23

Zanchi, Girolamo, 101–2, 250, 252, 274, 327, 341–44, 346–53, 417
Zepperus, Wilhelm, 344, 349
Zuylen van Nyvelt, Frederick van, 242
Zwanepol, K., 475
Zwingli, Huldrych, 417

Subject Index

Act of Cessation, 27, 408
apocryphal books, 9
Arminian controversy, 1–3, 110–12, 384–85, 392
assurance of election, 124–25, 141, 319, 322
atonement as satisfaction, 323–24

baptism, 300, 461
   of adults, 26
   of slave children, 11, 141, 441
Belgic Confession, 21, 25, 51–79, 109–10, 141–42, 168, 194, 235–36, 458, 460
   Act of Approbation, 77, 461
   art. 22 omission, 64–65, 71–74, 142
   as a confessional standard, 51–52, 67–68, 75, 79
   editions, 52–55, 61–62, 69–70
   text of, 68–78
Brandenburg, 6, 220–21, 230
Bremen delegation, 17, 148, 150–51, 161
British delegation, 63–64, 101, 153, 156–62, 175–76, 190, 223, 227, 258–59

Calvinists, 316–17, 428
Calvin's influence, 334–36, 337–61, 428
Canons of Dordt, 16, 19–22, 27, 50, 133–34, 165, 193, 203, 235, 237, 241, 244, 277–87, 383–90, 400–401, 412, 458, 460
   Act of Approbation, 27, 204–5
   as a confessional standard, 392–413
   as a judgment on Arminianism, 392–413
   Conclusion, 20, 139–40, 191, 286–87, 376–77, 402–3, 456–57
   drafting committee, 19, 126, 139, 191, 368–69, 401
   drafting of, 18–19, 126–29, 146, 363–82, 400–405, 455–56
   Dutch translation, 25
   editions, 463–490
   positive articles, 133, 135, 379, 387, 402, 411–13
   Preface, 142, 242, 403, 457
   printing of, 203–4, 236–40
   Rejection of Errors, 50, 133, 135, 379, 386–87, 402, 411–13

catechism services, 10, 81–84, 140, 260
catechizing, method of, 10–11, 26, 84–90, 259–60, 440–41
causal thinking, 281–86
causa physica debate, 146–51, 189, 266–69, 451
Christ's active obedience, controversy over, 25, 71–74
Christ's role in election, 125–26, 132–33, 143–46, 318, 321–22
church discipline, 30, 300, 307
Church Order, 195–96
    characteristics, 303–04
    Church Order of Dordt, 23–24, 27, 196–99, 205–6, 212, 289–314, 459–61
    influence of the state, 304–7
    printings of the Dordt Church Order, 311–14
    reception of the Dordt Church Order, 307–11
    structure of, 302
church-state relationship, 167–213
church visitors, 296
common confession, 397
congregational singing, 300
Convent of Wesel, 82, 290–91
conversion, manner of, 330–32, 342–43, 347–51, 356–57, 435–36

delegations of the synod, 5–6
    judgments (*iudicia*) on the Five Articles, 18, 121–26, 138, 145–46, 262–63, 315–16, 365, 397, 401, 453–54
depravity, 328–30, 388, 433–34
Dordrecht, 4, 219
duels, 143–44
Dutch Bible translation, 9–10, 26, 138, 178, 440

Dutch professors, 5–6, 113–14

election, 109–35, 317–22, 345–46, 387, 432
    definition of, 128–31, 318–19
Emden delegation, 396–97
extent of Christ's redemption, 156–62, 190, 323–28, 347, 360, 388, 432–33

Five Articles of the Remonstrants, 2, 13, 15–18, 36–37, 49, 111, 115, 120–21, 172, 338
Five Points of Calvinism, 317, 335, 389, 426–28
foreign theologians, 6, 48, 219–20
    dismissal of, 22, 195, 235, 239
forms of subscription, 25, 78–79, 104–6, 195, 297, 405–8, 460–61
French delegation, xiii, 6

Geneva delegation, 65
Geysteranus brothers case, 21
government, role of, 299, 306
Grote Kerk of Dordtrecht, 5, 22, 27

Hague Conference (1611), 3, 111–12
Heidelberg Catechism, 10, 21, 81–107, 110, 142, 235–36, 458
    Act of Approbation of, 104, 461
    as a confessional standard, 82, 106–7
    origin of, 101–3
Hesse delegation, 395
Hoorn case, 26–27, 461

infralapsarianism, 123–24, 131–33, 318, 321, 387
irresistible grace, 348, 434–36

Subject Index

Kampen case, 21, 139

liturgical forms, 26–27

Maccovius case, 21–22, 140, 270–77, 457–58
marriage ordinance, 26, 306
medallions, 22, 231–32, 239, 489
ministers, calling of, 24, 196, 297–98, 301, 304
mission to the East Indies, 11, 26

Nassau-Wetteravian delegation, 223, 230

oaths, 26

Palatinate delegation, 101–3, 126, 160, 265, 279, 394–95
   response to Remonstrant Observations on Heidelberg Catechism, 96–100
patronage system, 24, 199–200, 298
perseverance of the saints, 332–34, 352–53, 357–58, 388, 436
Post-Acta sessions, 23–27, 195–203, 293
predestination, 110, 335, 345–47, 353–56, 383
   of infants, 121, 125
preparatory meeting, 176
printing, 12, 26, 178, 224, 441
Pro-Acta sessions, 9–12, 178
provincial synods, 296–97, 303

religious holidays, 300, 306
Remonstrance of 1610, 2, 111, 384
Remonstrants, 2, 6, 263–65
   Articuli on Remonstrant views, 15, 17, 44–45, 115–18, 123, 365, 394–96, 446–47, 450, 452

defenses of the Five Articles, 18, 121, 187, 338, 353–58
explanations of the Five Articles, 17–18, 119–20, 182, 187, 337–43
expulsion from the synod, 12, 15, 47–49, 139, 185, 397, 448
letters of citation, 6, 31–32, 178, 337, 392, 439
observations on Belgic Confession, 13–14, 32, 38–39, 55–58, 182, 443–44
observations on Heidelberg Catechism, 14, 32, 38–39, 90–96, 182, 443–44
Remonstrant Brotherhood, 27
Sentence of, 140–41, 192–93, 205, 403–5
Sententiae on the Five Articles, 13, 36–37, 114–15, 443
Syllabi Testimoniorum, 120, 338, 343–53
view of Calvin, 337–61
reprobation, 13, 31, 40, 42, 141, 317–22, 345–47, 353–56, 359–60, 449
Roman Catholic priests, 26, 301

scholasticism, 348–56
scholastic-popular distinction, 254–56, 259, 278–79, 288, 400–401
scholastic terminology, 146–51, 247–88, 270–77, 375
school regulations, 26
speeches on the Five Articles, 16–17, 120, 260–62, 366, 448–52
state delegates, 6, 173–74, 177, 209, 215–16, 221, 242
   correspondence with States General, 215–45

Subject Index

state delegates (*continued*)
  delegations to the States General, 14–15, 43, 227, 234–35, 405
States General, 3–4, 14, 21, 26–27, 215
  Articles to Convene the synod, 4, 8, 171–72, 177, 202, 245
  commission for the state delegates, 218
  instructions for the state delegates, 173–74
  letters of invitation to the synod, 6, 175
  resolutions re the Remonstrants, 15, 43, 183–84, 224–25, 228, 445
sufficient-efficient distinction, 323, 327–28
Sunday observance 25–26, 142, 200
supralapsarianism, 124, 134, 151–55, 321, 338–41, 359
Swiss delegation, 395
Synod of Alais (1620), 418–21
Synod of Dordt,
  Acta, 26, 207–8
  Acta Contracta, 26–27, 207
  archives, 27–28
  closure, 22, 27, 201–22
  convening of, 3–4, 171
  debate re its jurisdiction, 13, 31–32, 34–36, 442
  delegations to the States General, 26, 202, 205, 241–42, 301–2
  disagreements among delegates, 137–65
  examination of the Belgic Confession, 58–68
  examination of the Heidelberg Catechism, 101–4

finances, 4, 208, 220–22, 225, 229, 237, 244
location, 4–5
occasion for, 1
officers, 7, 9, 177
opening, 171, 176–77, 439
participants, 5–7
phases of, 8–27, 30–31
procedural bickering, 12–16, 29–50, 112–13, 178–85, 441–48
procedures of, 7–8, 186
seating of delegations, xiii, 7
significance, ix, 1
use of Latin, 7, 23
Synod of Emden (1571), 168, 289, 291–92
Synod of Middelburg (1581), 169, 292
Synod of The Hague (1586), 83, 169–70, 289, 293–94

Three Forms of Unity, 27, 391, 408–11
Tilenus abbreviations, 415–26
training of ministers, 11, 141, 260, 297, 441
treasurer of the synod, 208, 221
TULIP, 335–36, 389, 429–37

Union of Utrecht (1579), 169
university reform, 25–26, 200–201
Utrecht delegation, 396
Utrecht Remonstrants, 5, 439, 441–42

Vorstius case, 22, 458

Walloon delegation, 5, 66, 87

Zeeland delegation, 395–96